Denis Š. Ljuljanović

Imagining Macedonia in the Age of Empire

Studien zur Geschichte, Kultur und Gesellschaft Südosteuropas

herausgegeben von

Prof. Dr. Stefan Rohdewald
(Universität Leipzig)

Band 18

LIT

Denis Š. Ljuljanović

Imagining Macedonia in the Age of Empire

State Policies, Networks and Violence
(1878 – 1912)

LIT

Cover image: Collective celebration of victory, Manastir, July 10, 1908 (1324) by Niyazi Bey and Ottoman group (*Comité Ottoman*). This significant triumph sparked the Young Turk Revolution and led to the establishment of the Ottoman constitution. Examining the attire of the individuals in this gathering reveals a remarkable moment, where the representatives from diverse ethno-religious communities were not involved in a conflict against each other, but rather they celebrated this auspicious moment together. With gratitude to the IBB Library in Istanbul for granting permission to utilise this postcard.

Denis Š. Ljuljanović
Ph.D. (2021), Marmara University/Turkey in a cooperation with Justus-Liebig University Giessen/Germany as part of the project "Regions of Conflict in Eastern Europe" (*Konfliktregionen im östlichen Europa*). His research explores social and cultural history in the Ottoman Empire, migrations, micropolitics and microhistory in Southeastern Europe, transnational and entangled history of Eastern Mediterranean. In his research, he applies a bottom-up perspective of ordinary life in order to bring the greater visibility and understanding of the actors who have been overlooked and neglected in the past.

This book is printed on acid-free paper.

Bibliographic information published by the Deutsche Nationalbibliothek
The Deutsche Nationalbibliothek lists this publication in the Deutsche Nationalbibliografie; detailed bibliographic data are available on the Internet at http://dnb.dnb.de.

ISBN 978-3-643-91446-0 (pb)
ISBN 978-3-643-96446-5 (PDF)
Zugl.: Univ., Diss., Marmara University; Project Justus-Liebig University Giessen Oktober 2021

A catalogue record for this book is available from the British Library.

© LIT VERLAG Dr. W. Hopf Berlin 2023
Contact:
Fresnostr. 2   D-48159 Münster
Tel. +49 (0) 2 51-62 03 20   Fax +49 (0) 2 51-23 19 72
e-Mail: lit@lit-verlag.de   https://www.lit-verlag.de
Distribution:
In the UK: Global Book Marketing, e-mail: mo@centralbooks.com

Falënderimi i takon Atij, i cili na urdhëroi të lexojmë.
Këtë libër ia dedikoj familjes sime, e cila më përkrahi në këtë rrugëtim
drejt leximit.

Abstract

Imagining Macedonia in the Age of Empire: State Policies, Networks and Violence (1878–1912)

The thesis is focusing on the complexity of the Macedonian Question(s) at the turn to the 20th century, which entailed multiple aspects: various local committees, the Balkan countries, the Great Powers, and the Ottomans. At that time, these actors imagined variously one part of the Ottoman territories that was becoming popular under the name of Macedonia. Many states and intellectuals developed contested strategies to include these Ottoman provinces as part of their meta–narratives and greater state projects. In this respect, the thesis aims to analyse these various actors in the time framework between the Congress of Berlin (1878) and the Balkan Wars (1912/13). By using different regional sources from the Ottoman, Bulgarian, Macedonian, Serbian and Albanian languages, and European reports in English, French, German, Italian and Russian, the scope of this work is to bring into discussion the multiplicities entailed at the international, regional and trans–regional levels. Apart from it, the thesis includes local level as well, in order to avoid the use of 'monolithic ethno–national identities' as a given, and rather to reflect the complexity of events on the ground. At that time and even today, some politicians, statesmen and intellectuals tried to implement various national narratives and worldviews according to the primordial ethnoreligious containers without reflecting that the imposed identification are ambiguous and problematic with the situation at the local level. Nevertheless, the dissertation does not aim to discard such works (and picture) of the locals that help to deconstruct the meta–narratives produced by the policies of the nation–state(s).

Acknowledgement

The present dissertation is the result of my studies at Marmara, Bologna and Justus–Liebig universities, and research visit at Central State Historical Archive in St. Petersburg, where I extended my knowledge about historical and political development of the (Eastern)Mediterranean, thanks to many extraordinary professors who inspired me for so many years. However, the final shape of the thesis was concepted at Justus–Liebig University in Gießen, where I worked for more than 4 years – since 2017. This journey between three universities and forth countries (Turkey, Italy, Germany and Russia) was a never–ending learning experience collected through my various conversations with formidable people. First of all, I express sincere gratitude to my thesis supervisors Prof. Dr. Nuray Bozbora and Prof. Dr. Stefan Rohdewald. I was lucky enough to have two independent supervisors: an academic "mother" (in German: *Doktormutter*) Prof. Bozbora and academic "father" (in German: *Doktovater*) Prof. Rohdewald. Moreover, my thesis would not be finished without the support of the thesis mentoring committee: Prof. Dr. Birsen Hekimoğlu, Prof. Dr. Nurcan Özgür–Baklacıoğlu and Prof. Dr. Nurşen Gürboğa. I am also fortunate to have remarkable institutional support by Justus–Liebig University and by LOEWE–Project *Konfliktregionen im östlichen Europa*. Here, I would like to thank all my friends and colleagues: Sophie Schmäing, Johanna Munzel, Mark Berman, Michał Turski, Ruben Biewald as well as professors Prof. Bohn and Prof. Bömelburg who were part of this amazing project. Additionally, I would like to emphasise the significant support of my friends in Istanbul, precisely my *abla* Derya Ayten, my *ağabeylerim* Emre Kurt and Sadık Müfit Bilge, my *kanka* Amer Maraqa and *vlla* Naim Gjokaj. I am also grateful to my friends in Gießen, Frankfurt am Main, Offenbach and Berlin: Mario Šain, Mustafa Aslan, Cansev Duru, Arkadiusz Blaszczyk, Danijela Majstorović, Zoran Vučkovac, Marija Spirkovska, Zerina Ćatović, Stefan Trajković–Filipović, Aleksandar Talović, Jovo Miladinović, Miloš Vojinović and Anđela Blažić. I am also thankful to my friends from Bologna: Eduart Uzeir and Besar Kolçe; my friends from Montenegro: Danira Abdović and Denisa Mahmutović; my relatives; and my family – to whom this dissertation is dedicated. I want to finish the ubiquitous list of acknowledgments with a deep appreciation for my family, particulary my mother Lirija. I am truly fortunate to have such a remarkable bond with my family, relatives, and the individuals who surround me, and it is largely due to my mother's profound influence. Her presence in my life has been instrumental in shaping the extraordinary blessings I have experienced. I also owe her the eagerness for liberty and exploration, travel and research. Unconditional support came also from my father Shaban, who is, unfortunately, not among us since last year (2022). However, he has been a pillar of support of this PhD–path and my study years. *Faleminderit babi.* My brother, *bac* Damir, and his family, Dijana and little Dario, have been a constant source of encouragement for all those years. *Ju dua shumë!*

Notes on Transliteration and Toponymies

In this study, I will employ a transliteration system that utilises Latin characters to convert texts originally written in Cyrillic and Ottoman scripts into a more accessible format. The primary focus will be on the conversion of original documentation in Bulgarian, Macedonian, and Russian languages, which are traditionally written using Cyrillic letters. To achieve this, I will follow the BGN/PCGN romanisation system(s), ensuring consistency and accuracy throughout the transliteration process. Texts, books, and documents written or translated in contemporary Macedonian language will be transliterated using the standard system based on the BGN/PCGN 2013 Agreement.[1] To address the specific requirements of Bulgarian scripts, I have decided to adopt the BGN/PCGN 1952 system.[2] Similarly, for the Russian language, the BGN/PCGN 1947 system is employed.[3] This BGN/PCGN system has been specifically designed to provide a unified approach to transliteration, making Cyrillic written texts more comprehensible and consistent when represented using Latin characters. Thus, this system enhances accessibility for individuals who may not be familiar with the Cyrillic script. By utilising the chosen transliteration system, readers who are not acquainted with the Cyrillic alphabet will find it easier to engage with the transliterated texts in the Latin alphabet.

In addition to the aforementioned languages, I have also chosen to utilise the Latin alphabet for scripts written in Serbian Cyrillic. The use of the Latin alphabet in Serbian is not a recent development, but rather a longstanding tradition. In fact, the Latin alphabet has been one of the two official alphabets of the Serbian language, and it is also employed in other

---

[1] About BGN/PCGN 2013 Agreement see:
https://geonames.nga.mil/geonames/GNSSearch/GNSDocs/romanization/ROMANIZA TION_OF_MACEDONIAN.pdf accessed 21/05/2023.
[2] See about differences between BGN/PCGN 1952 and other BGN/PCGN pre–2013 here: Lyubomir Ivanov, Dimiter Skordev and Dimiter Dobrev, "The New National Standard for the Romanization of Bulgarian," *Mathematica Balcanica* 24/1–2 (2010): 122–126.
[3] About BGN/PCGN 1947 see:
https://geonames.nga.mil/geonames/GNSSearch/GNSDocs/romanization/ROMANIZA TION_OF_RUSSIAN.pdf accessed 21/05/2023.

pluricentric languages spoken in the region, including Bosnian, Croatian, and Montenegrin.

In the case of Ottoman language, I will be using the Latin letters that are today used in modern Turkish. This transliteration system will aim to ensure consistency and accuracy in transliterating Cyrillic and Ottoman scripts into Latin for the purpose of maintaining the integrity of the original texts, while also facilitating their use and understanding in a wider audience.

In the case of Albanian scripts, I have opted to utilise the Latin alphabet that is in use today. Despite several attempts to create a standardised Albanian alphabet, it was not until the Congress of Manastir in 1908 that a modern Albanian alphabet was codified. Nonetheless, I have encountered a few texts in Albanian that incorporate some letters from the Greek alphabet, in addition to the predominantly Latin characters. Furthermore, even after the standardisation of the Albanian alphabet in Manastir, a number of Albanian intellectuals continued to write in the non-official Geg dialect, including figures such as Hasan Prishtina and Nikollë Ivanaj. In these cases, I have chosen to preserve the authenticity of the scripts and the authors' writing style, rather than "translating" them into the official Tosk dialect.

When it comes to the places and toponymies, the present dissertation has considerable technical difficulties to use one "standard" name for a village, city, region or person. Since the aim of the thesis is to use different sources, the localities and personalities can appear with various names too. As this thesis's fundamental plan is to highlight that there are different ways of interpreting events in Ottoman Macedonia (and Rumelia), depending on situation and perspectives, my aim is to demonstrate these entanglements, by adopting terminology that reflects local and regional variety in a multilinguistic context. In other words, I will utilise personal names and toponymies, to demonstrate their fluidity and to deconstruct the identity claims of contemporary historiographies. To be exact, I employ the various names of personalities interchangeably, such as: Sami Frashëri or Şemsettin Sami; Vlora Ferid Pasha or Avlonyalı Ferid Paşa; Selanik/Solun/Salonika/Thessaloniki; Üsküp/Shkup/Skopje/Skoplje etc. The names and spellings will be deployed according to the used archival source. If the (sub)chapters are based on Albanian or Turkish sources, I will spell the places or personal details in Albanian or Turkish respectively. The same rule will be applied to Slavic names, with special emphasis on names of places found in archival or newspaper materials. I will attempt to faithfully represent a name of the person or localities, when citing primary documents, as they appear in the source. The reason to do it is to recognise local and regional (rather than ethno–national) distinction among the people of the Ottoman Macedonia, who were linguistically, ethnically and religiously intermixed and interwoven. I will highlight the utility in abandoning an ethnonational labeling of the person or localities. Instead, I intend to analyze the places and personalities with multiple names deployed by local, regional and global actors in transregional context.

Table of Contents

Abstract..*vii*

Acknowledgement...*viii*

Notes on Transliteration and Toponymies......................................*x*

Table of Contents.. xiii

List of Maps...*xvi*

List of Photos ....*xvi*

Introduction *1*

1.1. Theoretical Framing...5
1.1.1. The Great Powers and the Balkans 10
1.1.2. The Great Powers and the Ottomans 19
1.1.3. Borrowed Colonialism of the Ottoman State....................21

1.2. Historiography and Methodological Design...........................29

1.3. What Do We Know About the Contentious Imaginations of Ottoman Macedonia? 49

1.4. Structural Rationale 61

Imagined Geographies and Imagined Communities: The Great Powers' Intervention in Ottoman Rumelia.....................................*65*

2.1. Imagination and Intervention...70

2.2. Great Powers' Intervention(s) in Ottoman Greece 73

2.3. Imagined Geographies and Cartography...............................80
2.3.1. Inventing the Balkans, Imagining Macedonia 83
2.3.2. Mapping Macedonia 90

2.4. The Balkan Intellectuals and Their Surrogate Hegemony ...102
2.4.1. Towards the Nation–State(s) 109
2.4.2. Russia's Forcible Intervention in Ottoman Rumelia and the Emergence of the Macedonian Questions 118

2.5. The Ottoman "Borrowed Colonialism" in Rumelia and the Civilising Mission of the Ottoman Bureaucratic Elite 122

2.6. Conclusion 131

State Policies and Mobile Intellectuals as Agents of Nationalism and Imperialism: What Has Changed Between Berlin and Ilinden (1878– 1903)? *133*

3.1. The Ottoman Consolidation of the Three Vilayets in Macedonia (1878–1903)...135

3.2. From Unitiy of Islam to Albanian Nationalism in the Three Vilayets of Macedonia 142
3.2.1. Albanianism in *Stamboll*: Against Pan–Slavism and Pan–Hellenism...144
3.2.2. Albanianism in the Diaspora: How Did Albanian Mobile Intellectuals Imagined Albania and Macedonia?.........................156

3.3. Balkan State Competitions and Agents of Nationalism and Imperialism 162
3.3.1. Greek Creation of National Space and *Megali Idea*............164
3.3.2. The Bulgarian National Revival and the Macedonian Questions 167
3.3.3. The Serbian National Movement and Ottoman Macedonia 180

3.4. Conclusion 193

Networks on the Ground: A Perspective From Below in Ottoman Macedonia (1903–1908) *195*

4.1. International Intervention(s) and Local Organisations in Ottoman Macedonia 196
4.1.1. The Great Powers and the Ottoman Administration in the Three Vilayets...200
4.1.2. The Ottoman Administration and the Local Actors in Macedonia...204

4.2. The Networks of Local Organisations in Ottoman Macedonia 207
4.2.1. Internal Macedonian–Adrianople Revolutionary Organisation (IMARO): National or Supra–National? 208
4.2.2. IMARO – Its "Left" and "Right" Wings: An Organisation of Contradictions?...215
4.2.3. Transnational Anarchists, Regional Networks: The Art of Not Being Governed 222

4.3. Greek Organisations: "Conquering the Souls" in Ottoman Macedonia 226

xiv

4.4. The Chetnik Movement **235**
4.4.1. Private Initiative: Interaction of Individuals with the State. 237
4.4.2. Organisation of Chetas on the Ground 240

4.5. Trajectories of *Toskë Kaçak*: A Micro-Historical Experience and Everyday Empire **252**

4.6. Conclusion **270**

Entangled Trajectories: From the Macedonian Reforms to the Balkan Wars ***272***

5.1. Hamidian Reforms in Ottoman Macedonia: Center in the Periphery – Periphery in the Center **273**

5.2. The Young Turks and Albanian Intellectuals in Ottoman Macedonia **281**
5.2.1. The Young Turks and Networks in Europe: From Ideology to Political Movement 285
5.2.2. Young Turks and Networks in Macedonia: From Political Movement to Revolution 291

5.3. The Young Turks and Albanian Speaking Population After the Revolution **305**

5.4. Entangled Imperialisms: The Great Powers and the Balkan States on the Road to the Balkan Wars (1912–1913) **312**
5.4.1. "Small–State Imperialism" – A Road Towards the Balkan Wars (1912–1913) 314
5.4.2. Montenegro and the Idea of a Greater State: Towards Ottoman Macedonia 330

5.5. Conclusion **342**

Conclusion ***344***

Bibliography ***362***

Archival Records **362**

Newspapers and Journals **368**

Other Printed Sources **369**

Biography ***424***

List of Maps

Map 1 Pavel Jozef Shafarik's Slovansky Zemevid 94
Map 2 Heinrich Kiepert's "Ethnographische Übersicht des Europäischen Orients" 97
Map 3 Heinrich Kiepert's "Tableau Ethnocratique des pays du sud–est de l'Europe" 99
Map 4 Slavyanskih Narodnosti 116

List of Photos

Photo 1 Greek guérillas with Ottoman captain Şerafettin 229
Photo 2 Chetnik action in Ottoman Macedonia 241
Photo 3 Toskë Kachak band in Ottoman Macedonia 262

Introduction

During one snowy day in early 2015 in Emirgān, the Sariyer district of Istanbul, a friend (of mine) and I visited Joan Miró's exhibition at Sakıp Sabancı Müzesi "Atlı Köşk," a mansion that for 30 years around the turn of the 20th century served as a royal residence and embassy of Montenegro. This latter fact aroused my interest in the presence of people from the Balkans in Istanbul, as well as in the Ottoman heritage in the Balkans, a region that at that time was known as *Rumeli*. Due to meta–narrative historiographies produced by nation–state(s), those connections between the different parts of the Balkans with Istanbul and entangled stories of people with the former capital of the Ottoman Empire and *vice versa*, were not widely part of widespread knowledge. This incongruity between historical connections and almost total absence of such entanglements from contemporary knowledge began to puzzle me. In the time that followed, I formulated my research interest in Ottoman history with regard to the Balkans as a product of these entanglements, placing a focus not only on the state perspective(s), rather encompassing the human agencies that also connected these regions. During my stay in Bologna in late 2016, I got the opportunity to work with my second supervisor Prof. Dr. Stefan Rohdewald on Southeastern European history within the sub–project "Macedonia as an International Intervention and (Dis)Integration Landspace: Global and Local Actors (1890–2015)" at the University "Justus Liebig" of Gießen (Germany). This new opportunity to work at Historical Institute in Gießen helped me to formulate the future research topic, questions, aims, and scope of the thesis. My primary goal here was to view from a local perspective, at the very least, the forgotten and overlooked entanglements of various actors who were active in the Ottoman Macedonian context. However, I did not wish to exclude the state and international perspectives that were very important for understanding the complexities of the situation that was known as the Macedonian Question, or found in the Ottoman scripts as *vilayet–i selase meselesi* ("issue/problem of three vilayets"). To better understand these complexities of Ottoman Macedonia, I aimed to use a wide range of Balkan and Ottoman, as well as European and Russian sources, focusing on four different levels (local, regional, trans–national and international or global). These levels intend to understand and interpret the escalation of the conflicts, the reasons behind the contestation of the region known as Macedonia, and the dynamics of the interlacing of actors on the ground and in the inhabitants' everyday life. Therefore, these different levels (international, transnational, national, regional, and local) help us to find out the complexity of the Macedonian Questions, which entailed multiple aspects: various local committees, the Balkan countries, the Great Powers, and the Ottomans. I intentionally employ the plural form of the term, Macedonian Questions, because I will argue that there has not been one uniform Macedonian Question as a whole, but it rather comprised many questions that lied in the eyes of the multiple beholders and actors. Each of them had a different understanding of Macedonian Question(s).

By aiming to focus on these different levels and questions, I developed several research questions: why did the Macedonian Questions become contested among the Great Powers at that time and regional Balkan states in the Age of Empire? How was Macedonia imagined? How did this imagination result in an escalation of violence, in symbolic and physical forms, among various actors (states, intellectuals, guerrillas)? What was the role and involvement of the local population in these contested imaginaries?

In order to reveal the answers to examine these questions, I start with challenging the ideas of primordial understandings of the nation and the ethnonational metanarratives made by the modern nation–states in the Balkans and Turkey (as well as in the Western Europe). This challenge to "conventional wisdom" can offer new perspectives (for example subaltern) that tell the stories not only of the larger region, but also much of modern era and its perception by "ordinary" social actors. Starting with a *moyenne duree* analysis (also *Konjunkturzyklen*) from the beginning of the XIX century[1] and covering in detail the period between 1878 and 1912, I reconsider how imagination and cartography, the competing interests of the Great Powers, Balkan states, and Ottoman Empire directly affected the

---

[1] Nikolaus Buschmann and Horst Carl, "Zugänge zur Erfahrungsgeschichte des Krieges: Forschung, Theorie, Fragestellung," in *Die Erfahrung des Krieges: Erfahrungsgeschichtliche Perspektiven von der Französischen Revolution bis zum Zweiten Weltkrieg*, eds. Nikolaus Buschmann and Horst Carl (Paderborn: Ferdinand Schöningh, 2001), p. 16.

experiences of the people living in Ottoman Macedonia or *vilayet–i selase* ("three vilayets"). Furthermore, I am driven by an initial hypothesis that the elite's imaginations and state policies cannot be explained only through their meta–narratives, which are based on national and religious fervour. In this respect, I aim to deconstruct these state–centric views, and I argue that one should pay more attention to the role played by the locals. Accordingly, my intention is to understand the Macedonian problematics, Ottoman mechanisms, the Great Powers and Balkan interventions, their inter–relations and collaborations by trying to create an entirely new approach by including the real–life situation on the ground. Although this was a period of the dissolution of the Ottoman Empire into discrete nation–state projects, the local level was far more complex than presented by the state's imaginations. More precisely, I will argue that the differences among the people living side–by–side at the local level 'were not a given' but predominantly constructed during the period of increased violence in the region (1903–1912) and later during the Balkan wars (1912–13), as well as after the Great War. The practices of the locals, the entanglements created "from the bottom up" were not (only) based on national or religious affiliations, but very often on the local, village or city, family or tribal identifications. This approach opposes the state–centric views that tried to impose a national identity on an enormous percentage of the population. In this way, this conceptualisation allows me to critically examine all state actions based on imaginations that produced imperialist policies and monoethnic greater state projects in relation to the Macedonian space. In this respect, I will analyse how those imaginations were produced, but also how they were opposed by populace or how they did not match their daily realities.[2] Moreover, I focus on the locals' subjective understandings of their contentious practices: in this dissertation, I conceptualise and examine how locals who were engaged in unconventional participation often viewed their actions as a national, non–national, or even anti–national, and I adopt the important insider perspective on how they "imagined" Macedonia.

---

[2] Peter L. Berger and Thomas Luckmann, *Die gesellschaftliche Konstruktion der Wirklichkeit: Eine Theorie der Wissenssoziologie* (Frankfurt am Main: Fischer, 2003), p. 20; Alun Munslow, *Deconstructing History* (London/New York: Routledge: Taylor and Francis Group, 2006).

This introductory section is organised in four sections. In the first part, I provide the theoretical approaches of the thesis by situating it in the broader context of transfer of knowledge from the "West" to other "peripheries"[3] such as the Balkans and Ottoman Empire. This divergence into "centre" and "periphery," I argue, was also based on the *Zeitgeist* of "civilised" versus "barbarian" discourses. Here, I intentionally use the terms "centre" and "periphery" in order to deconstruct this Eurocentric approach and to show that such distinction was in fact made by the modern colonial world model. In this respect, I hold that we need to "provincialise" the centre–periphery metaphor, to borrow Chakrabarty's famous term, and to make the agency of local actors more relevant to our understanding of political dynamics in Ottoman Macedonia. Accordingly, I also discuss the cases from below "with native principles of life"[4] which have to be worked out without the exclusive influence of Western Europe.

The second section is devoted to the historiographic discussions and methodological frameworks. The historiographic works aim to combine various approaches on this topic, while in the methodological part I show which approaches I employed by collecting various archive documents, files, newspapers, diaries, and memoirs. Furthermore, these documents will be used and elaborated on throughout fifth chapters of the thesis.

The third part shows the general knowledge about contentious imaginations of Ottoman Macedonia and it brings into discussion different

---

[3] Masood Raja suggests that the terms "Center" and "Periphery" are heavily debated in postcolonial studies, as they embody the binary geography of colonialism. However, if used without critical analysis, these terms can also reinforce the idea that European powers are the dominant center, while the colonies are viewed as inferior peripheries. See in: Masood Raja, *Center/Periphery* https://postcolonial.net/glossary/center–periphery/ accessed 21/02/2021; and Masood Raja, Jason W. Ellis and Swaralipi Nandi, *The Postnational Fantasy: Nationalism, Cosmopolitics and Science Fiction* (Jefferson: McFarland Press, 2011). In other words, I do not use this concept as static and something "given," but rather as a tool to deconstruct this dichotomy and show that "periphery" also has its' agency and it can influence its' "center." Rather, my aim is here to consolidate "global design" of European history and the silenced critical voices of "peripheral" actors (local histories) into fluidity. See: Jens Hanssen, "Practices of Integration: Center–Periphery Relations in the Ottoman Empire," in *The Empire in the City: Arab Provincial Capitals in the Late Ottoman Empire*, ed. Jens Hanssen, Thomas Philipp and Stefan Weber (Würzburg: Ergon, 2002), pp. 56–57.

[4] Gerrit W. Gong, *The Standard of 'Civilization' in International Society* (New York: Clarendon Press/ Oxford University Press, 1984), p. 106.

perspectives. Finally, I outline the dissertation structure. In this way, before I begin discussing my archival material, the reader can become familiar with the political and historical context in which this material is situated.

1.1. Theoretical Framing

In many ways, this reading has been reproduced and developed in the context of recent postcolonial studies. The current and available production under the name of "postcolonial" studies or theories emerged as a "versions of social constructivism that focus on one particular issue that influences on the intersubjective knowledge creation." [5] In the discipline of International Relations, the origins of postcolonial theory appeared with the dissatisfaction of the explanatory manner of theories such as Realism and Liberalism and their positivist approach, which focused on power politics and rivalry among states.[6] Postcolonial theory criticises these state–centric views of international relations and attempts rather to have a focus on human beings and their agency. As such, it is important to emphasise that a postcolonial researcher takes an interdisciplinary approach and critically analyses the production of knowledge forged to serve to the imperialist state policies.[7] The spread of modern European "knowledge" is no longer interpreted as a contribution to the modernisation of historical thought, but rather as an imposition of European "values" in order to provide an imperial hegemony. Thus, for many postcolonial scholars, the analytical divergences of "West" and

---

[5] Konrad Czernichowski, Dominik Kopiński and Andrzej Polus, "Polish African Studies at a Crossroads: Past, Present and Future," *Africa Spectrum* 47/3 (2012): 167–169.

[6] Steve Smith and Patricia Owens, "Alternative approaches to international theory," in *The Globalization of World Politics: An Introduction to International Relations*, eds. John Baylis, Steve Smith and Patricia Owens (New York: Oxford University Press 2006); Rita Abrahamsen, "Postcolonialism," in *International Relations Theory for Twenty–First Century*, ed. Martin Griffiths (London & New York: Routledge, 2007), pp. 111–112.

[7] Here it does not suffice to say „*Wissen ist Macht*" (knowledge is power), but rather "*Macht ist Wissen*" (power is knowledge). See also: Frederick Cooper, *Colonialism in Question: Theory, Knowledge, History* (Berkeley/Los Angeles/London: University of California Press, 2005); Michel Foucault, *Power/Knowledge: Selected Interviews and Other Writings 1972–1977*, ed. Colin Gordon (New York: Pantheon Books, 1980); Vincent Houben, "New Areas Studies, Translation and Mid–Range Concepts," in *Areas Studies at the Crossroads: Knowledge Production after the Mobility Turn*, eds. Katja Mielke and Anna–Katharina Hornidge (New York: Palgrave Macmillan, 2017), p. 201.

"East", "center" and "periphery", "civilised" and "barbarian" are products of a Western epistemology tied to imperial power, which do little but obfuscate the site of "real" politics.[8] In this respect, Postcolonial theory can help me here to understand/comprehend (*verstehen*)[9] constructed meta–narratives, the consequences of imperialistic projects, as well as issues of nation creation, nationalism, and self–perception of societies and nations created by imperialistic discourses.[10] Its arguments are that from the 16th century through the period of the Enlightenment in Western imaginations (based on prejudices and stereotypes) constructed "the East with Gramscian understanding of hegemony, and Foucault's notions about relations between power and knowledge."[11] The determination of its historical origins, the roots of contemporary empowerment of the civilisation are often traced spatially to Western Europe, temporally to the 18th century, and culturally to the Enlightenment.[12] Moreover, writers in

---

[8] This approach focuses primarily on the adverse impact of the 18th and 19th centuries on the Western European transformation relative to the rest of the world, which often employs a cultural (study) lens to destabilise the power–knowledge connection. As a critic to this focus on 18th century, Mignolo argues that "the current and available production under the name of 'postcolonial' studies leave aside the crucial and constitutive moment of modernity/coloniality that was the sixteenth century." See: Walter Mignolo, *Local Histories/Global Designs: Coloniality, Subaltern Knowledge and Border Thinking* (New Jersey: Princeton University Press, 2000), p. 37.

[9] The term understanding/comprehending (*verstehen*) was introduced by historian Johann Gustav Droysen and closely associated with the work of sociologist Max Weber. See: Wilfried Nippel, *Johann Gustav Droysen: Ein Leben zwischen Wissenschaft und Politik* (Munich: C.H. Beck, 2008); Jan Kruse, Kay Biesel, and Christian Schmieder, *Metaphernanalyse: Ein rekonstruktiver Ansatz* (Wiesbaden: VS Verlag für Sozialwissenschaften/Springer, 2011).

[10] Polus et al., *Polish African Studies*, p. 178.

[11] Sankaran Krishna, *Globalization and Postcolonialism: Hegemony and Resistance in the Twenty–first Century* (Plymouth: Rowman & Littlefield Publishers, 2009); Ania Loomba, Suvir Kaul, Bunzi Matti, Antoinette Burton and Jed Esty, "Beyon What? An Introduction," in *Postcolonial Studies and Beyond*, eds. Ania Loomba, Suvir Kaul et al. (Durham/London: Duke University Press, 2005), pp. 26–28.

[12] Postcolonialism might appear as a version of social constructivism with epistemological guidelines about the structures of knowledge and power, consisted in the works of Karl Marx's power inequalities, the Gramscian understanding of hegemony and the subaltern perspective, as well as Hannah Arendt's conceptions of power and violence, and the Saidian criticism of the Western production of the Orient. See: Gyanendra Pandey, "Voices from the Edge: The Struggle to Write Subaltern Histories," in *Mapping Subaltern Studies and the Postcolonial*, ed. Vinayak Chaturvedi (London/New York: Verso, 2000), p. 287.

the Enlightenment period started to develop an interest in the concept of "civilisation" by producing "civilised" and "uncivilised" discourses. According to Jean–Louis Carra (1742–1793) 'Enlightened Europe' was limited to England, France, Italy, and the Germanic countries, while in the eyes of the Enlightened, the South–East especially the Ottoman Empire became "uncivilised".[13] These constructed European meta–narratives legitimated the violence of imperialism upon these "impure" and "other" peoples by applying *la mission civilisatrice*. Accordingly, the historical context of the European Enlightenment privileged progress, rationality and scientific developments in order to establish and legitimate Western hegemony over the marginalised rest of the world by employing, exploiting, and intending to establish dominance over others (using the categories of race, ethnicity, tradition, and religion.).[14] In the words of Kenneth Pomeranz this "great divergence" between "East" and "West" means that the Western *Weltanschauung* is dominant – the most powerful and wealthiest world civilisation of all time.[15] In order to deconstruct these claims, it is very important to take into consideration the above mentioned term understanding (*verstehen*), especially understanding the "imperialist discourse of domination" and "imperialist incursions into local life–worlds."[16]

---

[13] Many educated Austrians shared Metternich's belief that "Asia begins where the eastern highway leaves Vienna." In this context Claude–Charles de Peyssonnel and Voltaire considered the South Slavs (including Dalmatia) as barbarians, like their ancestors who settled in VII century. See: Wojiciech Sajkowski, "From Vinko Pribojević to the French Encyclopaedia – The History of the South Slavs and the Historiography of the French Enlightenment," in *Macedonia: Land, Region, Borderland*, ed. Jolanta Sujecka (Warsaw: Wydawnictwo DiG, 2013), pp. 331–338.

[14] Fatma Müge Göcek, "Parameters of Postcolonial Sociology of the Ottoman Empire," in *Decentering Social Theory*, ed. Julian Go (Bingley: Emerald Group Publishing Limited, 2013) p. 77.

[15] Kenneth Pomeranz, *The Great Divergence: China, Europe, and the Making of the Modern World Economy* (New Jersey: Princeton University Press, 2001); Robert J. C. Young, *Postcolonialism: An Historical Introduction* (Oxford: Blackwell Publishing, 2001); Robert J. C. Young, *While Mythologies: Writing History and the West* (London/New York: Routledge, 2004); Keya Ganguly, "Temporality and Postcolonial Critique," in *The Cambridge Companion to Postcolonial Literary Studies*, ed. Neil Lazarus (Cambridge: Cambridge University Press, 2004), pp. 162–170.

[16] Sebastian Conrad, *What is Global History?* (Princeton / Oxford: Princeton University Press 2016), p. 53; Frederick Cooper, "Postcolonial Studies and the Study of History," in

Postcolonial theory helps us to understand this transformation through a fundamental claim that the modern world we inhabit is impossible to understand except in relationship to the history of imperialism and colonial rule, especially the period of "age of empire" that I highlight here in regard to the Macedonian Questions. Furthermore, I explore the production of knowledge and transfer of knowledge (*Wissenszirkulation*) in the Balkans and the Ottoman Empire during the era of imperial domination, with a particular focus on the interactions between Western powers, Ottoman and Balkan elite, and local actors on the ground.[17] To achieve this aim, I draw on concepts introduced by postcolonial theory and its subdisciplines, such as subaltern studies, which provide important analytical frameworks for understanding the power dynamics at play in these encounters.[18] This

---

Postcolonial Studies and Beyond, ed. Ania Loomba et al. (Durham/London: Duke University Press, 2005), pp. 401–402.

[17] Stefan Rohdewald, Albrecht Fuess, Florian Riedler and Stephan Conermann, "Wissenszirkulation: Perspektiven und Forschungsstand," *in Transottomanica – osteuropäisch–osmanisch–persische Mobilitätsdynamiken*, ed. Stefan Rohdewald, Stephan Conermann and Albrecht Fuess (Göttingen: University Press, 2019), pp. 83–84; Detlef Haberland, *Buch– und Wissenstransfer in Ostmittel– und Südosteuropa in der frühen Neuzeit* (Munich: Hamadeh–Shirine, 2004); Achim Landwehr, "Das Sichtbare sichtbar machen: Annäherungen an ,Wissen' als Kategorie historischer Forschung," in *Geschichte(n) der Wirklichkeit: Beiträge zur Sozial– und Kulturgeschichte des Wissens,* ed. Achim Landwehr (Augsburg: Wißner Verlag, 2002), pp. 61–69. Furthermore, in "Southern Theory" Raewyn Connell showed how social theory from the world periphery has power and relevance for understanding the changing world. See: Raewyn Connell, *Southern Theory: The Global Dynamics of Knowledge in Social Science* (London: Allen & Unwin, 2007).

[18] In this sense, it is developed in the context of the method and theory of Interpretation (*Deutungwissen*) and hermeneutics through the work of Friedrich Schleiermacher, Wilhelm Dilthey, and Martin Heidegger. Therefore, this work will try to understand/comprehend the historical context (starting from the Enlightenment period) of the problems, in order to interpret or arrive at an exegesis of the Macedonian Question as a 'crisis zone,' the Great Powers and Balkan states intervention, as well as the Ottoman colonial mechanisms. The works that helped me to frame these understandings in theoretical approach are listed in: Christopher A. Bayly, *The Birth of the Modern World, 1780–1914: Global Connections and Comparisons* (Malden MA: Blackwell Publishers, 2004); Sven Beckert, *Empire of Cotton: A Global History* (New York: Alfred A. Knopf, 2014); Dipesh Chakrabarty, *Provincializing Europe: Postcolonial Thought and Historical Difference* (Princeton: Princeton University Press, 2000); Leon Fink, *Workers Across the Americas: The Transnational Turn in Labor History* (Oxford: Oxford University Press, 2011); Leela Gandhi, *Postcolonial Theory: A Critical Introduction* (Oxford: Oxford University Press, 2008); Paul Gilroy, *The Black Atlantic: Modernity and Double Consciousness* (London: Verso, 1993); Eliga H. Gould, "Entangled Histories,

incredulous stance emerged as a criticism to the Eurocentric teleologies and tries to open up a space for new stories in other parts of the world. Based on these critical approaches to Western domination and ethnocentric worldview, I aim to contribute to the development of concepts on trans–cultural interaction, circulation, exchange, and flow of knowledge, ideas, institutions, people and practices on the ground as well. More important, these interchanges between "West" and "East", "center" and "periphery", "civilised" and "barbarian", were not uniform; the variation in experiences at all levels were much more complex and intersectional. The prevailing Eurocentric worldview is based on the notion that the progress of the "West" has taken place in isolation from the rest of the world. However, my research takes a trans-cultural perspective and examines how entities and discourses such as "West" and "East," "civilised" and "barbarian" were constructed in the context of global circulation between various regions, and how they influenced the Macedonian context. This approach challenges the conventional Eurocentric understanding of history and contributes to the field of Entangled History, which aims to comprehend

---

Entangled Worlds: The English–Speaking Atlantic as a Spanish Periphery," *The American Historical Review,* 112/3 (2007): 764–786; Steven van der Walt and Lucien Hirsch, *Anarchism and Syndicalism in the Colonial and Postcolonial World, 1870–1940* (Leiden: Brill, 2010); Klaus Hock and Gesa Mackenthun, *Entangled Knowledge: Scientific Discourses and Cultural Difference* (Münster: Waxmann, 2012); Patrick Manning, *Navigating World History: Historians Create a Global Past* (New York: Palgrave Mcmillan. 2003); Matthias Midell and Katja Naumann, "Global History and the Spatial Turn: From the Impact of Area Studies to the Study of Critical Junctures of Globalization," in *Journal of Global History* 5/1 (2010): 149–170; Walter Mignolo, *The Darker Side of Western Modernity: Global Futures, Decolonial Options* (Durham: Duke University Press, 2011); Sidney W. Mintz, *Sweetness and Power: The Place of Sugar in Modern History* (New York: Penguin Books, 1986); Jürgen Osterhammel, *Geschichtswissenschaft jenseits des Nationalstaats: Studien zu Beziehungsgeschichte und Zivilisationsvergleich* (Göttingen: Vandenhoeck & Ruprecht, 2011); Jürgen Osterhammel, *Die Verwandlung der Welt: Eine Geschichte des 19. Jahrhunderts* (Munich: Beck, 2009); Stefan Rinke and Delia González de Reufels, *Expert Knowledge in Latin American History: Local, Transnational, and Global Perspectives* (Stuttgart: Heinz, 2014); Daniel T. Rodgers, *Atlantic Crossings: Social Politics in a Progressive Age* (London: Belknap Press of Harvard University Press, 1998); Immanuel Wallerstein, *The Modern World–System I: Capitalist Agriculture and the Origins of the European World–Economy in the Sixteenth Century* (New York: Academic Press, 1974); Michael Werner, Benedicte Zimmermann, "Vergleich, Transfer, Verflechtung: Der Ansatz der Histoire croisée und die Herausforderung des Transnationalen," *Geschichte und Gesellschaft* 28/4 (2002): 607–636. in 609–611.

the interconnectedness of the past and overcome the narrow perspectives. By adopting a trans–cultural perspective, this study not only explores the influences and interactions between different regions and cultures but also recognises the complexity and diversity of these interactions. The Entangled History framework allows for a more nuanced analysis of the past and provides a more comprehensive understanding of the multiple ways in which individuals, ideas, and practices circulated and interacted across different contexts. Their basic assumptions are that neither empires, nor nations are developed in a vacuum and that the history of humankind is based on the interconnectedness of societies, interdependencies of human beings, and the multidirectional character of transfers. Sanjay Subrahmanyam defined these entanglements with the term "connected history,"[19] while Sebastian Conrad and Shalini Randeria have elaborated a similar perspective to *Histoire Croisée* within a postcolonial articulation.[20] Before we enter into analysis, one should emphasise that exist distinctions between postcolonial studies and entangled (and global) history, but there are much more commonalities and areas of overlap. They are by no means hermetically distinct, and, in fact, influence one another in many ways. Both of disciplines made major contributions to an understanding of the interactions across cultural borders and transnational context, what is also the scope of this thesis.

1.1.1. The Great Powers and the Balkans

The Europe's commercial and scientific as well as political revolution affected significantly the Ottoman Empire and the Balkans as one of its parts. These transformations of "western civlisation" were actually, as Leften Stavros Stavrianos states, "acceptable, and even desirable (…) for

---

[19] Sanjay Subrahmanyam, "Connected Histories: Notes towards a Reconfiguration of Early Modern Eurasia," *Modern Asian Studies,* 31/3 (1997): 740–742; Cooper, *Postcolonial Studies and the Study of History*, p. 412.

[20] Sebastian Conrad and Shalini Randeria, *Jenseits des Eurozentrismus: Postkoloniale Perspektiven in den Geschichts– und Kulturwissenschaften* (Frankfurt am Main: Campus, 2002); Shalini Randeria, "Geteilte Geschichte und verwobene Moderne," in *Zukunftsentwürfe: Ideen für eine Kultur der Veränderung*, ed. Jörn Rüsen, Hanna Leitgeb and Norbert Jegelka (Frankfurt am Main: Campus, 1999), pp. 87–89.

Orthodox peoples in the Balkans."[21] On the other hand, the French political revolution became a symbol of a dramatic turning point spreading the ideas of nationalism, national independence, nation–state building, and unification that were accepted by the local intellectuals in the Balkans. To a significant degree, the intellectual stratum of the Balkan population turned to the "West" for ideas, institutions, and technology.[22] In the Balkans those ideas did not appear immediately, but passed through several phases, transformations, and different foreign influences. For example, this process of transformations last almost the whole century that resulted in state–independency of the Balkans: the Greek independence (1830), continued with the Serbian, Montenegrin, Romanian (1878), and Bulgarian (1908) independence, and completed by the Balkan wars with Albania (1912). Therefore, it can be concluded that the commercial, scientific, and political revolutions that transformed Western Europe transformed the Ottoman Empire and Balkans too.[23] These changes made possible the replacement of multinational empire with the nation–state ideas and projections. Together with idea of the independent nation–state, as Leften S. Stavrianos argues, the concept of greater state was also developed with the new type of imperialism that originated in Europe.[24] In the Macedonian context, the Balkan states adopted strategies and policies to construct this region as an integral and imagined territory of

---

[21] Leften Stavros Stavrianos, "The influence of the West on the Balkans," in *The Balkans in Transition,* eds. Charles and Barbara Jelavich (Berkeley/Los Angeles: University of California Press, 1963), p. 188; Zdravko M. Deletić, *Zanat istoričara: Metodologija istoriopisanja* (Kosovska Mitrovica: Filozofski fakultet u Prištini s privremenim sedištem u Kosovskoj Mitrovici/Istorijski arhiv Kraljevo, 2019); Božidar Jezernik, *Wild Europe: The Balkans in the Gaze of Western Travellers* (London: Saqi Books and the Bosnian Institute, 2004).

[22] Cyril E. Black, "Russia and the Modernization of the Balkans," in *The Balkans in Transition,* eds. Charles and Barbara Jelavich (Berkeley/Los Angeles: University of California Press, 1963), p. 147.

[23] Stavrianos, *The influence of the West*, p. 195.

[24] Ibid., p. 197; Slavenko Terzić, *Islam, Balkan i velike sile XIV–XX vek* (Beograd: Istorijski institut SANU, 1997), pp. 273– 312; Christian Marchetti, "'Frontier Ethnography': Zur *colonial situation* der österreichischen Volkskunde auf dem Balkan im Ersten Weltkrieg," in *Wechselwirkungen: Austria Hungary, Bosnia–Herzegovina, and the Western Balkans, 1878–1918*, ed. Clemens Ruthner et al. (New York: Peter Lang, 2015), pp. 363–366; Edin Hajdarpašić, *Whose Bosnia? Nationalism and Political Imagination in the Balkans, 1840–1914* (Ithaca/New York: Cornell University Press, 2015).

greater state projects among the Balkan elites. According to Kemal Karpat, these ideas effectively dismantled the pluralist (Ottoman) order and led to the adoption of the concept of a single ethnic and linguistic nation based on European models by the newly independent Balkan states. [25] The transformations that occurred in the Balkans thus serve as a microcosm and localised manifestation of a broader, global phenomenon. This phenomenon is the result of a multifaceted process of knowledge transfer, interconnectedness, and interactions between elites in the Western and Southeastern European regions. In this context, Vesna Goldsworthy's *"Inventing Ruritania: The Imperialism of the Imagination"* suggests that expanding the parameters of imperialism, despite the absence of a "conventional" European colonial presence in the Balkans, is nevertheless applicable to this region. [26] Accordingly, the Balkans underwent the process of "colonisation of the mind,"[27] and their intellectuals constructed imperialist narratives and ideological formulations in Macedonia, as a part of the "small state imperialism" projects. [28] Such "colonisation of the mind," according to Maria Todorova, "was imposed as the hegemonic paradigm in Europe, as the gold standard of 'civilised' political organisation."[29] The uncertain Balkan elites tried to imitate this European

---

[25] Kemal Karpat, "The Social and Political Foundations of Nationalism in South East Europe after 1878: A Reinterpretation," in *Studies on Ottoman Social and Political History: Selected Essays and Articles*, ed. Kemal Karpat (Leiden: Brill, 2002), p. 357.

[26] Vesna Goldsworthy, *Inventing Ruritania: The Imperialism of the Imagination* (Oxford: Oxford University Press, 2012), p. 15.

[27] Artemis Leontis, *Topographies of Hellenism: Mapping the Homeland* (Ithaca/New York: Cornell University Press, 1995), p. 68; Charles Stewart, *Colonizing the Greek Mind? The Reception of Western Psychotherapeutics in Greece* (Athens: DEREE – The American College of Greece, 2014); Sally Matthews, "Colonised minds? Post–development theory and the desirability of development in Africa," *Third World Quarterly* 38/12 (2017): 4–6.

[28] These various influences were a trigger to the Macedonia's own imagination as a socio–spatial consciousness and political/ideological agenda of the Balkan nations. See: Marharyta Fabrykant and Renee Buhr, "Small State Imperialism: The Place of Empire in Contemporary Nationalist Discourse," *Nations and Nationalism* 22/1 (2015): 116–118.

[29] Maria Todorova, *Imagining the Balkans* (Oxford: Oxford University Press, 2009), p. 167; Maria Todorova, "The Ottoman Legacy in the Balkans," in *Imperial Legacy: The Ottoman Imprint on the Balkans and the Middle East*, ed. L. Carl Brown (NewYork: Columbia University Press ,1996), pp. 45–47; Maria Todorova, "Introduction: Learning Memory, Remembering Identity," in *Balkan Identities: Nation and Memory*, ed. Maria Todorova (London: Hurst & Company, 2004), pp. 22–24.

model of civilised West.[30] Therefore, the relationship between the Balkans and Western Europe can be grasped as substitution of an "colonisation of mind"; accepting ideas of the West in order to define and create one's own space of expansion that became Macedonia.[31] The Balkan case is unique in that it did not undergo administrative colonialisation by the West, but rather an imaginative colonisation. This process involved a dual perception: on the one hand, the Balkans were seen as part of Europe, while on the other hand, they were considered the "darker side" of Europe, embodying an Oriental difference. This ambivalent oscillation between "Europeanness" and "oriental difference" allowed the Balkan states to imagine themselves as part of the civilised West and to construct their own "Orient." This perpetual process was defined by Milica Bakić-Hayden as "Nesting Orientalism."[32] This concept explains a tendency of each region to view the cultures and religions to its South and East as more conservative and primitive.[33] It explains how a group that creates the 'orientalised other' can also be the subject of 'orientalisation' by another group. According to the concept of nasting orientalism, the Ottoman space was more "east" or "other" than Greece, Bulgaria or Serbia, and the 'asiatic Ottomans' needed to abandon Macedonia, which had been "the heart of Slavic empires for centuries."[34] It is in the context of these interactions and

---

[30] Katherine E. Fleming, "Orientalism, the Balkans, and Balkan Historiography," *The American Historical Review* 105/4 (2000): 1221.

[31] According to Katherine Elizabeth Fleming's observation "there is a big difference between 'metaphoric colonialism,' 'surrogate colonialism,' 'colonialism of the mind,' and colonialism of the sort with which Said is concerned." Fleming, *Orientalism,* p. 1223.

[32] Milica Bakić–Hayden, "Nesting Orientalisms: The Case of Former Yugoslavia," *Slavic Review*, 54/2 (1995): 917–918; Tanja Petrović, "Understanding Southeastern Europe and the Former Yugoslavia (De)Colonising Socialist Experience," in *From the Highlands to Hollywood: Multidisciplinary Perspectives on Southeastern Europe Festschrift for Karl Kaser and SEEHA*, ed. Siegfried Gruber, Dominik Gutmeyr, Sabine Jesner, Elife Krasniqi, Robert Pichler and Christian Promitzer (Münster/Vienna: LIT Verlag, 2020), pp. 95–99.

[33] Ibid.

[34] The second influence can be traced in the concept of the "invention of tradition." This concept was coined in the book "The Invention of Tradition" in 1983 that was edited by Eric Hobsbawm and Terence Ranger. Hobsbawm's introduction argues that many "traditions" which "appear or claim to be old are often quite recent in origin and sometimes invented." See in: Eric Hobsbawm and Terence Ranger, *The Invention of Tradition* (Cambridge: Cambridge University Press, 1983). This invented tradition was promoted among the Balkan elite and its promoters of nationalism who were influenced by European ideas of the nation–state and imperialism through the process of knowledge

influences of the political and ideological projects that the Great Powers and Balkan states discursive formulations in the framework of the Macedonian crisis can be analysed. Additionally, an important role played the religious context of "anti–Islamic/anti–Turkish discourses"[35] and "sacralisation of the heroes," which also belonged to part of the invented medieval tradition(s). The use of religious difference in the form of anti–Islamic and anti–Turkish discourses reflected the formulation of political ideologies and goals of the statesmen and political actors, and their implementation in the context of Ottoman Macedonia. The sacralisation of heroes, on the other hand, reflected the desire to create a nationalistic narrative that could unite people behind a common cause. The policy of sacralisation of the heroes in the 19th century helped the promotion of a sacred "chosen" nation in the context of *Svetoslavlje* or Prince Nikola's myth of "Montenegrins as the best/purest Serbs," that was to be a motive for liberation from the Ottomans, who were often portrayed by the leading figures of the competing Balkan states as 'Asiatic barbarians.' According to Stefan Rohdewald, "especially in the territorial rivalry between Bulgaria and Serbia over Macedonia, one may observe a competition over the national identity of local groups, in which religious figures of memory played a decisive role."[36] Macedonia became a struggle area of veneration of saints such as Saint Sava, Cyril and Methodius. The foundation of the Saint Sava Association in Belgrade, which was active in Macedonia, aimed particularly at the "direct competition with the national projects of neighbours"[37] and generally "praised (Saint Sava) as the 'Sun of Serbian

---

transfer. In the Bulgarian case, Ohrid, Skopje, and Bitola had for a while been capitals of the Bulgarian First Empire, while Prizren and Skopje were capitals of the Serbian Empire.
[35] The Balkan states interventions in Macedonia during the Balkan wars were described as: "Holy war to free our brethren" (Montenegrin context), "a war of the Cross against the Crescent" (Bulgarian context), a struggle against a "medieval system of feudal exploitation" (Serbian context), and a "crusade of progress, civilization, and liberty against Asian conquerors" (Greek context). See: Fikret Adanır, Ethnonationalism, Irredentism and Empire, in *The Balkan Wars from Contemporary Perception to Historic Memory,* eds. Katrin Boeckh and Sabine Rutar (London: Palgrave Macmillian, 2016), p. 13; Andreas Hemberger, *Illustrierte Geschichte des Balkan Krieges 1912/13* (Vienna/Leipzig: Hartleben, 1914), pp. 42–48.
[36] Stefan Rohdewald, *Sacralizing the Nation through Remembrance of Medieval Religious Figures in Serbia, Bulgaria and Macedonia* (Leiden: Brill, 2022).
[37] Ibid.

heaven' (…) representing and reproducing powerful images of the national golden age, national reconciliation and unification and martyrdom for the Church and the nation."[38] In its engagements, the Orthodox Church hurried to stress the crusade character of the struggle "for the realisation of God's justice' by 'the sword brought by Christ the Savior' against 'the infidels' crescent of oppression and blood,' in the name of 'the triumph of justice, peace and the life–giving cross' and 'raising the cross in the place of the crescent.'"[39] As Fikret Adanır points out, "the Balkan War thus was conceived and propagated as a crusade both in the sense of a Christian remedial enterprise and of an effort to demonstrate the superiority of European civilisation."[40] As part of the broader interactions and connectivities, the role of Russia should not be neglected either, because some members of the Balkan intellectuals were often in cooperation with imperial Russian statesmen in order to keep connections with "spiritual brothers" and to realise these "greater state projects."[41] As meter of these cooperations, the Pan–Slavist ideas were developed[42] – a movement in which nationalist elements were mingled with supra–national and often

---

[38] Bojan Aleksov, "Nationalism in Construction: The Memorial Church of St. Sava on Vračar Hill in Belgrade," *Balkanologie Revue d' etudes pluridisciplinaries* 7/2 (2013): 47; Andrej Mitrović, *Prodor na Balkan i Srbija, 1908–1918* (Beograd: Zavod za udžbenike, 2011).

[39] Yura Konstantinova, "Political Propaganda in Bulgaria during the Balkan Wars," *Études balkaniques* 2/3 (2011): 79–116, here in 83–84.

[40] Adanır, *Ethnonationalism*, p. 14; Dariusz Kołodziejczyk, "The 'Turkish Yoke' Revisited: The Ottoman Non–Muslim Subjects between Loyalty, Alienation, and Riot," *Acta Poloniae Historica* 93 (2006): 177–180; Laurence Cole and Daniel L. Unowsky, "Introduction: Imperial Loyalty and Popular Allegiances in the Late Habsburg Monarchy," in *The Limits of Loyalty: Imperial Symbolism, Popular Allegiences, and State Patriotism in the Late Habsburg Monarchy*, eds. Laurence Cole and Daniel L. Unowsky (New York – Oxford: Berghahn Books, 2009), pp. 1–10.

[41] Cyril E. Black, "Russia and the Modernization of the Balkans," in *Balkans in Transition: Essays on the Development of Balkan Life and Politics Since the Eighteenth Century,* ed. Charles and Barbara Jelavich (Berkeley/Los Angeles: University of California Press, 1963), p. 147.

[42] Supporters of Pan–Slavism: Jozef Dobrowsky (1753–1829), Jan Kollar (1793–1852), Pavel Jozef Šafarik (1795–1861), Ludovik Štur (1815–1856), František Palacky (1798–1876), Stanko Vraz (1810–51), Taras Shevchenko (1814–61), Adam Mickiewicz (1789–1855), Zygmunt Krasiński (1812–1859), Juliusz Slowacki, Adam Czartoryski, Jernej Kopitar (1780–1844), Vuk Karadžić (1787–1864), Petar II Petrović Njegoš etc.

imperialist trends.[43] The word was first used in 1826 by Slovak writer Jan Herkelin in a Latin treatise on Slav philology. It should be emphasised here that 'Slavs (ethnical) self–awareness' and their memory space (*lieux de mémoire)* was to some extent present among the intellectuals, even before the French Revolution.[44] These memory spaces were also featured among the early modern Dalmatian humanists who in the 16th century had invented the classical name of 'Illyrian' for the Slav–speaking inhabitants of these provinces and called for the unification of the all Slavs in one Tsardom. It may be that the first germs of these thoughts emerged as a result of the influence of the Italian philosopher Machiavelli, who called for Italian unity. Since the Dubrovnik merchants were linked to the Italian city–states, it might be that these intellectuals from early–modern period were inspired by those scripts, thus, wrote about the unity of the Slavs in the same period. One of them was Ivan Gundulić, who wrote the poem *"Osman"* (1626), in which he calls for Slav unity under the Polish king after the siege of Hotin (1621). Furthermore, priest Juraj Križanić (1616–1683) put forward the idea of unification and liberation under the leadership of the Russian emperor and the Catholic Church. According to professor Ortaylı, both Turkish and Balkan historiography tend to overestimate Russia's role in the national resurgence of the Balkan Slavs.[45] However, the Russian role grew in importance after Küçük Kaynarca (1774) and especially after the Congress of Paris (1856), but we should not consider Russia as the only determining factor in the national

---

[43] Hans Kohn, *Pan–Slavism, its History and Ideology* (Indiana: University of Notre Dame Press, 1953), p. 1; Alexei Miller, *The Ukrainian Question: The Russian Empire and Nationalism in the 19th Century* (Budapest/New York: Central European University Press, 2003); Alexei Miller and Stefan Berger, *Nationalizing Empires* (Budapest/New York: Central European University Press, 2014); Jane Burbank, "Paul W. Werth, The Tsar's Foreign Faiths, Toleration and the Fate of Religious Freedom in Imperial Russia," *Cahiers du monde russe* 56/4 (2015): 1–5.

[44] Pierre Nora, *The Realms of Memory: Rethinking the French Past (*New York: Columbia University Press, 1997); Ulf Brunnbauer and Robert Pichler, "Mountains as 'lieux de mémoire': Highland Values and Nation–Building in the Balkans," *Balkanologie: Revue d'études pluridisciplinaires* 6/1–2 (2002):77–100, here in 81–83; Vangelis Kechriotis, "Postcolonial Criticism Encounters late Ottoman Studies," *Historein: A Review of the Past and other Stories* 13 (2013): 39–46.

[45] İlber Ortaylı, *Najduži vek imperije* (Beograd: Srpska književna zadruga, 2004), p. 60. See also original: İlber Ortaylı, *İmparatorluğun En Uzun Yüzyılı* (Istanbul: Kronik Kitap, 2018).

consciousness of the Balkan Slavs. [46] The agency of the Balkan intellectuals should be taken also into consideration as determining factor and equal contributors to the Pan–Slavist formulations. According to Hans Kohn, the national awakening did not emanate from Moscow or St. Petersburg, but from the French Revolution, romantic poetry, and German idealist philosophy, spreading primarily through Vienna, where the Balkan Slav intellectuals and merchants met with nationalism as an ideology and orientalism as a new construction against the Ottomans.[47] By means of this knowledge transfer the Balkan elite accepted the ideas of the West and adopted their political and ideological agenda against the Ottoman Empire. Therefore, it is indeed highly important to ascertain that Pan–Slavism did not originate only as an imperialist movement with the Russians, but with the interaction of non–Russian Slav world in the Balkans, as it felt the need of closer cooperation in order to succeed in the liberation from the 'backward Asiatic Turks.' Indeed, this was the message that prince–bishop ('*vladika*') Petar I Petrović Njegoš conveyed in his letter to Tsar Alexander (8/20 May 1817):

"My Highness Lord! Think about our relationship which binds us (Montenegrins) to your Tsardom, and because of this common love, we need a better rapprochement of relations; therefore, do not support what is against the Slavism (*Slovenstvo*)."[48]

---

[46] As can be seen from Križanić's example, the Balkan Slavs went ahead of Russia. This idea spread in Russia thanks to the Greeks and South Slavs who translated documents from Greek and Church Slavonic. The liturgy of the Russian Orthodox Church was merged with the Byzantine in the mid–seventeenth century. The Russian Church benefited greatly from the Balkan priests and manuscripts from Balkan monasteries. Thus/This demonstrates that the relationship between Russia and the Balkan Slavs was established through the church, not as a trade through the West.

[47] Kohn, *Panslavism*, p. 4; Miller, *The Ukranian Question*.

[48] Vladan Đorđević, *Crna Gora i Austrija 1814–1894* (Begrad: Štamparija Rodoljub, 1924), p. 9; This book was written as a part of Montenegrin–Austro–Hungarian Relations. See about similar works on Austro–Hungary and regions of the Balkans such as Sanjak and Montenegrin–Serbia Borderland: Tamara Scheer, "A Micro–Historical Experience in the Late Ottoman Balkans: The Case of Austria–Hungary in Sanjak Novi Pazar (1879–1908)," in *War and Nationalism: The Balkan Wars (1912–13) and Socio–Political Implications*, eds. M. Hakan Yavuz and Isa Blumi (Salt Lake City: University of Utah Press, 2013), pp. 197–229.

In 1838, Ljudevit Gaj too sent a memorandum to the Russian Tsar stating it necessary that the Russian mission unify the Slavs of the three cities of Villach, Varna, and Skutari (including the Bulgarians), and to liberate the Slavs from the Habsburg and Ottoman Empires.[49] We can thus conclude that, in the first half of the 19th century, Pan–Slavism was a movement of the Southern and Western Slavs, while in the second half was transformed and negotiated that it became a predominantly Russian movement, rooted in a feeling of spirituality and grandeur, and in a consciousness of a historical destiny.[50] Religion played a crucial role in this ideology, as the acceptance of Orthodoxy was seen as a crucial aspect of Slavic identity among the Russian Pan–slavists.[51] The religious and cultural aspects of Slavic identity were deeply intertwined with political goals and aspirations. The *"Letter from Moscow to the Serbs"* by Khomyakov stated that a Slav cannot be truly Slav outside of Orthodoxy, emphasising the importance of religion in Slavic identity.[52] Imperialistic projects against the Ottoman Empire were driven by the desire to gain control of territories, especially in the contested region of Macedonia. This desire was shared by various Balkan nations and Great Powers, leading to conflicts and tensions in the region. The ideology of Slav unity presented at the second Pan–Slav Congress had significant political and cultural implications, influencing imperialistic projects and contributing to tensions in the Balkans.[53] The

---

[49] Kohn, *Panslavism*; Pieter Troch, *Nationalism and Yugoslavia: Education, Yugoslavism and the Balkans before World War II* (London/New York: I. B. Tauris, 2015).

[50] Ibid., p. 99.

[51] The Moscow Pan–Slav Congress was not initiated by the government. It was organised by the Slav Committee of Slavophiles (Pogodin, Aksakov, Khomyakov, Tyutchev). Therefore, the movement was not immediately supported by the government, while later Danilevsky had none of the religious interests of these Slavophiles. For him the idea of Slavdom (*slavyanstvo*) was the highest idea of uniting the Russians, Czech, Serb, Croat, Slovene, Slovak, Bulgar, and Pole. His Pan–Slavism was an answer to the powerful centralised German state. This idea spread widely in Russia after the unification of Germany. Thereafter, Russian Emperor Alexander III and his mentor Konstantin Pobedonostsev wished to subject the Russian Empire to an integral Russian nationalism based upon the Orthodox Church, as was promoted by Sergey Uvarov and Tsar Nicholas I few decades earlier. See on Serbian and Yugoslavian case: Danilo Šarenac, "Remembering Victory: The Case of Serbia/Yugoslavia," *Südosteuropa-Jahrbuch* 42 (2018): 225–245; See: Kohn, *Panslavism*, pp. 172–173. Miller, *The Ukranian Question*. Miller et. al., *Nationalizing Empires*.

[52] Ibid., p. 138.

[53] Ibid., p. 139.

Congress emphasised the importance of a shared identity and common goals among the Slavic nations. However, this ideology excluded non–Slavic groups and laid the foundation for imperialistic projects among the intellectuals from the Balkan. The role of religion in this ideology highlights the complex relationship between politics and culture, and the ways in which cultural factors can shape political aspirations. Overall, these ideas of Panslavism had a lasting impact on the Balkans, shaping political ideologies and contributing to conflicts in the region.

1.1.2. The Great Powers and the Ottomans

The impact of Western European penetration on the Ottoman Empire and the Balkans has been the subject of much scholarly debate.[54] Isa Blumi, a historian and scholar of the Ottoman Empire, argues that the Western perception of the "East" as unchangeable and ahistorical created two distinct Western oriental factions: one advocating for occupying the Ottoman Empire or empowering ethnic and religious minorities, and another championing stronger relations with "noble savages" through the system of Capitulations.[55] Blumi contends that the system of Capitulations, which granted European powers a degree of extraterritoriality and special privileges within the Ottoman Empire, ultimately empowered European imperialist policies that emphasised religious and ethnic affinities. In this regard, the Ottoman Empire became a place of expansionist European imperialism and the Balkans became a

---

[54] The European "civilisation" formulated by the Enlightenment writers and reflected in the international system and international law of the 19th century (through legitimation of humanitarian intervention, will be discussed in further chapters), was founded on a dialectical opposition in the historical developments of the "East" and the "West," or European and non–European based on the superiority of the European civilization. See: Huri İslamoğlu–İnan, Oriental Despotism in World–System Perspective, in *The Ottoman Empire and World–Economy*, ed. Huri İslamoğlu–İnan (Cambridge: Cambridge University Press, 1987), p. 1. and 13; Benjamin C. Fortna, *Education for the Empire: Ottoman State Secondary Schools during the Reign of Sultan Abdulhamid II, 1876–1909* (Chicago: University of Chicago, 1997).
The Ottomans were not members of the club of civilised nations; at best, theirs was a half–civilised state whose sovereignty the Europeans neither recognised nor respected. See: David Rodogno, *Against Massacre – Humanitarian Interventions in the Ottoman Empire (1815–1914)* (Princeton: Princeton University Press, 2012), p. 24.
[55] Isa Blumi, "Reorientating European Imperialism: How Ottomanism Went Global," *Die Welt des Islams* 56 (2016): 295–302, here in 299.

mechanism for greater state projects. The weakening of the Ottoman Empire in the international power balance led to structural changes in the region that reinforced economic underdevelopment and political marginalisation. [56] By analyzing the historical context of the region, scholars can gain a deeper understanding of the complexities of imperialism and the lasting impact of colonialism on developing nations. The Ottoman Empire and the Balkans provide a useful case study for examining the dynamics of imperialism and their effects on the developing world. Blumi's argument highlights the need to consider historical perceptions of the East, as well as the role of Western European penetration in shaping the region's political and economic landscape. By examining the historical context of the region, scholars can gain a deeper understanding of the dynamics of imperialism and the lasting impact of colonialism. With a focus on the Ottoman state's position within the global order, Maurus Reinkowski emphasises that, as the Ottoman Empire faced expansionist Europe from the 18th century onward, its history must be studied in the context of the wider European power system. For the last 150 years of its existence, the Empire cannot be fully understood without taking into account both its manifold attempts to emulate Europe and, at the same time, its struggle against the West.[57] As the Ottoman Empire faced the expansionist powers of Europe, it is essential to study Ottoman history in the context of this wider European power system. In order to preserve its territorial integrity, the Ottoman Empire implemented its own form of colonial policy, [58] which has been defined as "borrowed

---

[56] Ibid; Ryan Gingeras, *Sorrowful Shores: Violence, Ethnicity, and the End of the Ottoman Empire, 1912–1923* (Oxford: Oxford University Press, 2009), pp. 31–35; Tolga U. Esmer, "Economies of Violence, Banditry and Governance in the Ottoman Empire Around 1800," *Past & Present* 224/1 (2014): 163–166.

[57] Maurus Reinkowski, Hapless Imperialists and Resentful Natioalists: Trajectories of Radicalization in the Late Ottoman Empire, in *Helpless Imperialists: Imperial Failure, Fear and Radicalization*, ed. by Maurus Reinkowski and Gregor Thum (Göttingen: Vandenhoeck & Ruprecht), p. 50.

[58] Terminologically, (the term) "colonialism" is often conflated with "imperialism," yet many scholars have argued that each have their own distinct definition. Therefore, due attention should be paid to terminology in order to distinguish the Western imperialism and Ottoman "borrowed colonialism." Furthermore, "Imperialism and colonialism have been used with similar meanings in order to describe state's superiority (in this case European), domination, and influence upon a person or group of people." Robert Young writes that while "imperialism operates from the center, is a state policy and is developed

colonialism."[59] In this context, the Macedonian case provides an example of how the Ottoman state implemented "borrowed colonialism" in an Ottoman periphery, namely Macedonia, through governmental attempts to "civilise" the population in the *vilayet–i selase*, or "three vilayets." These vilayets, including Selanik, Manastir, and Kosovo, were Ottoman administrative divisions of the Macedonian territory. However, before delving into the case, I will present several approaches which could be useful for further analysis.

1.1.3. Borrowed Colonialism of the Ottoman State

The term "borrowed colonialism," often used as "internal colonialism" as well, defines the relations between 'metropole' and 'colony' to describe the "blurred" lines between geographically close locations that are clearly different in terms of culture, language, religion, physical appearance, uneven development etc. According to a handful of postmodernist authors (Thomas Nicholas, Michel Foucault, Jean–François Lyotard etc.) the whole of modernity can be understood as a colonialist project, which is as

---

for ideological as well as financial reasons (…), colonialism is simply the development for settlement by individual communities or for commercial purposes by a trading company." See in: Robert Young, *Postcolonialism: An Historical Introduction* (New Jersey: Blackwell Publishers, 2001), p. 16; According to the Russian leader Lenin, "imperialism was the highest form of capitalism." Moreover, "imperialism developed after colonialism, and was distinguished from colonialism by monopoly capitalism." See: Mary Gilmartin, *Colonialism/Imperialism, Key Concepts in Political Geography* (London: Sage Publications Ltd, 2009), p. 116; Furthermore, Edward Said highlights the difference between imperialism and colonialism by stating that imperialism involved "the practice, the theory and the attitudes of a dominating metropolitan center ruling a distant territory", while colonialism refers to the "implanting of settlements on a distant territory." See: Edward Said, *Orientalism* (New York: Pantheon, 1978).

[59] Selim Deringil, *The Well–Protected Domains: Ideology and the Legitimation of Power in the Ottoman Empire, 1876–1909* (London/New York: I. B. Tauris & Co Ltd, 1999); Accordingly, imperialism includes some form of colonialism, but colonialism itself does not automatically imply imperialism, as it lacks a political focus. Therefore, in order to probe the Ottoman case, it might be useful to gain an insight into the "internal colonialism" model, defined by Michael Hechter, who analyses the relationships between England as the 'national center,' and its 'periphery,' the Celtic fringe. See: Michael Hechter, *Internal Colonialism: The Celtic Fringe in British National Development* (New Jersey: Transaction Publishers, 1999); A similar study has been done by Nicola Zitara where he states that after the Unification of Italy, the regions which belonged to the Kingdom of the Two Sicilies were transformed into an internal colony of Piedmont. See: Nicola Zitara, *L'unità d'Italia: Nascita di una colonia* (Milan: Jaca Book, 1971).

much a cultural, as it is an economic and political process.[60] More specifically, in the era of modernisation the Ottoman Empire passed through a transition from Tanzimat to Abdulhamid II and the Young Turks, viewed as "representing the transformation, respectively, from Ottomanism (understood as a civic nationalism based on common Ottoman identity), to Islamism (often glossed as Unity of Islam) to Turkism (sometimes framed as Pan–Turkism)."[61] These mechanisms of state centralisation were the Ottoman response to the imperialism in the form of counter–colonialism. Therefore, the Ottoman Empire tried to define itself as a player on a equal footing, especially after the Treaty of Paris (1856) which afforded it entry into the Concert of Europe. The Ottoman administrative elite gradually adopted the Western ideas of modernity and colonialism in order to implement, in the 'periphery,' its policy known as "borrowed colonialism."[62] However, taking on board the

---

[60] Thomas Nicholas, *Colonialism's Culture: Anthropology, Travel and Government* (Cambridge: Cambridge University Press,1994).

[61] Howard Eissenstat, "Modernization, Imperial Nationalism, and the Ethnicization of Confessional Identity in the Late Ottoman Empire," in *Nationalizing empires* eds. Stefan Berger and Alexei Miller (Budapest/New York: Central European University Press, 2015), p. 430.

[62] Apart from "borrowed colonialism" several authors of the Ottoman studies used the terms such as "Orientalism allaturca," "Ottoman civilising mission," "Ottoman Orientalism," "Ottoman man's burden," and "modern Ottoman imperialism." Makdisi's term "Ottoman imperialism" can prove instrumental for an analysis of the concepts of "unity of Islam" (*İttihad–ı İslam*) as 'transnational' which was not only present in the area of Arabic and Balkan peninsula, but also among the Ottoman Syrian diaspora in South America, and among Russian and Indian Muslims. During World War I, Ottoman subjects served as an important window of opportunity for the unity of Islam to extend beyond the spiritual battleground of the Indian Ocean and to the Atlantic world. See: Christoph Herzog, Raoul Motika, "Orientalism 'allaturca': Late 19th / Early 20th Century Ottoman Voyages into the Muslim 'Outback'", *Die Welt des Islams* 40/2 (2000): 139–195; Christoph Herzog, "Nineteenth–century Baghdad through Ottoman Eyes," in *The Empire in the City: Arab Provincial Capitals in the Late Ottoman Empire*, eds. Jens Hanssen, Thomas Philipp and Stefan Weber (Bayreuth: Ergon Verlag, 2002), pp. 311–328; Ussama Makdisi, "Ottoman Orientalism," *American Historical Review* 107/3 (2002): 768–796, here in 771–772; Ussama Makdisi, "Rethinking Ottoman Imperialism: Modernity, Violence, and the Cultural Logic of Ottoman Reform," in *The Empire in the City: Arab Provincial Cities in the Ottoman Empire*, eds. Jens Hanssen and Thomas Philipp (Bayreuth: Ergon Verlag, 2002), pp. 300–303; When it comes to Ottomanism, the most active supporters of Ottomanism were the Christian brothers Miguel and Naguib Samra who published the al–Zamān out of Buenos Aires. See: Blumi, *Reorientating European Imperialism,* p. 313.

aforementioned definitions of imperialism and colonialism, for the Ottoman case and the framework of the Macedonian Questions, I will use the term "borrowed colonialism" as an Ottoman strategy to keep Macedonia closer to its' 'center.'[63] Accordingly, the Ottoman 'borrowed colonialism' was a "survival tactic" and, was therefore very different from "the aggressive industrial empires of the West."[64] In the context of the Macedonian Questions, the Ottoman "colonial" relations with the locals were much more nuanced in comparison to the relations of its Western European counterparts with their imperial subjects. However, there are few points in common, such as the Ottoman attempt of rationalising the use of lands and extracting the taxes which were misused by 'backward nomads,' implementing the 'civilising mission' in order to discipline the locals,[65] and establishing the regulations to reorganise the state, with the aim of being accepted among the Great Powers. Therefore the tax extraction, 'civilising mission,' and regulations of order were parallel steps taken by the Ottoman state art to maintain its imperial status and to define its efforts of extending power, the aim of which was to convince its subjects and the Great Powers to its right of existence. This imperial idea implies the importance of the quest for legitimacy, or in Weberian terms, the *Gewaltmonopol des Staates,*[66] which means "the monopoly on legitimated

---

[63] See also terms: "internal colonialism," "colonialism without colonies," "Ottoman civilising mission," "colonial Ottomanism," „colonisation oft he countryside." Özgür Türesay, "The Ottoman Empire seen through the lens of Postcolonial Studies: A Recent Historiographical Turn," *Revue d'histoire moderne et contemporaine* 60/2 (2013): 141–145; For a critique of the theoretical construction of "colonialism without colonies," and its derivative "internal colonialism," see Jürgen Osterhammel, "'Colonialisme' et 'Empires coloniaux,'" *Labyrinthe* 35 (2010): 61; Thomas Kühn, "Shaping and Reshaping Colonial Ottomanism: Contesting Boundaries of Difference and Integration in Ottoman Yemen, 1872–1919," *Comparative Studies of South Asia, Africa and the Middle East* 27/2 (2007): 315–323.

[64] Ibid., p. 39.

[65] Furthermore, in this Ottoman instance, the locals retained their agency and negotiated relations with the Ottoman capital, Western Europe, and their local counterparts.

[66] "Monopoly on violence" is the tradition which argues that the state has legitimate monopoly over the control of the means of violence across a territory, performed by means of a military, courts, laws, police force, and tax bureaucracy. The tradition is associated with scholars like Max Weber, Otto Hintze, Anthony Giddens, Charles Tilly, Michael Mann and others.

use of physical force."[67] In order to be able to use physical force, states introduced military reforms too.

In the view of Bob Jessop, the state can be regarded as an apparatus primarily concerned with the making of war and the repression of its citizens. It is tasked with defending its territorial integrity against external forces and maintaining social cohesion within its borders, even if this necessitates resorting to coercion.[68] In fact, the state has historically focused on promoting territorial consolidation, modernisation, centralisation, differentiation of the instruments of government, and the monopolisation of its means of coercion – all fundamental state-making processes.[69] Due to the impared state power of the Ottoman Empire in the 19th century, its state displayed a greater 'obsession' with centralisation and legitimation. As a result, the state created legitimation devices such as coats of arms, the Friday prayer, the caliphate, education, propaganda wars against foreign missionaries, proselytisation among its own subjects/citizens, and world fairs.[70] Furthermore, during this period the Ottoman administration was trying to develop state–centralist terminology as *tanzimat* (measures for regulating order), *vergi* (taxation), *vatan* (fatherland), *asayış* (public order/tranquillity), *mülkün mamurluğu* (prosperity), *emniyet* (security), *adalet* (justice), even *vahşı* (wild), and *cahiliyyet* (ignorant), adressed to the people living at periphery. A reciprocal relationship between the state and its subjects emerged, wherein

---

[67] See: Max Weber in *Politics as a Vocation* published in original as: Max Weber, *Politik als Beruf* (Munich: Gesammelte Politische Schriften, 1921), pp. 396–450.

[68] Bob Jessop, *State Power: A Strategic–Relational Approach* (Cambridge: Polity Press, 2007), p. 63.

[69] Ibid.

[70] Deringil, *The Well–Protected Domains.* See also: Fehmi Özatalay, *Türk Silahlı Kuvvetleri tarihi: Balkan Harbi, Garp Ordusu, Karadağ Cephesi*, III. cilt / 3. Kısım (Ankara: Genelkurmay Başkanlığı, 1993), p. 20; Erik Jan Zürcher, "Teoride ve Pratikte Osmanlı Zorunlu Askerlik Sistemi (1844–1918)," in *Devletin Silâhlanması: Ortadoğu'da ve Orta Asya'da Zorunlu Askerlik (1775–1925)*, ed. Erik Jan Zürcher (Istanbul: Istanbul Bilgi Üniversitesi Yayınları, 2003), pp. 87–104, here in 92; Gültekin Yıldız, *Neferin adı yok: Zorunlu Askerliğe Geçiş sürecinde Osmanlı Devleti'nde Siyaset, Ordu ve Toplum, 1826–1839* (Istanbul: Çağaloğlu Kitabevi, 2009); Fatih Yeşil, *İhtilâller Çağında Osmanlı Ordusu: Osmanlı İmparatorluğu'nda sosyoekonomik ve sosyopolitik Değişim üzerine bir İnceleme (1793–1826)* (Istanbul: Tarih Vakfı Yurt Yayınları, 2016); Tobias Heinzelmann, *Cihaddan Vatan Savunmasına: Osmanlı İmparatorluğu'nda Genel Askerlik Yükümlüğü, 1826–1856* (Istanbul: Kitap Yayınevi, 2009).

the former provided security, prosperity, and justice to the latter, who were, in turn, expected to offer complete obedience to the state. Thus, the state was regarded as a symbol of guardian/protector (*himayet*), while subjects were expected to demonstrate obedience (*itaat, mutabaat, inqiyad*). The payment of taxes was a critical demonstration of obedience and recognition of the state's legitimacy. [71] In order to convince the subjects to pay their taxes, to be obedient, and to participate in the mechanisms against Western penetration, the state first borrowed ideas and practices from the Europe, which it then tried to implement by colonisation in the form of *mission civilisatrice*. This "borrowed colonialism," defined by Selim Deringil, led Ottoman officials to depict the provincial subjects as living in "a state of nomadism and savagery."[72] Maurus Reinkowski offers an example related to the Mirdita tribes in northern Albania, highlighting the Ottoman Empire's need to secure rule in the region. To achieve this, the Empire embarked on a more ambitious project of civilising the peripheries by providing a higher standard of education and living.[73]

---

[71] Maurus Reinkowski, The State's Security and the Subjects' Prosperity: Notions of Order in Ottoman Bureaucratic Correspondence (19th Century), in *Legitimizing the Order: The Ottoman Rhetoric of State Power* eds. Hakan Karateke and Maurus Reinkowski (Leiden and Boston: Brill, 2005), p. 200.

[72] Deringil, *The Well–Protected Domains*. pp. 39–42; and See: Selim Deringil, "'They Live in a State of Nomadism and Savagery': The Late Ottoman Empire and the Post–Colonial Debate," *Comparative Studies in Society and History* 45/2 (2003): 311–342; Some Balkan peoples, living in the Ottoman periphery, were considered by Ottoman statesmen as "noble savages at best and corrupt slaves at worst" ; or as "pig herding" for the Montenegrin, "pig farmers" for the Serbian, and "wild and ignorant" or "wild and brave" for the Albanian people. See: Ebru Boyar, *Ottomans, Turks and the Balkans: Empire Lost, Relations Altered* (London/New York: IB Tauris, 2007), p. 74;

[73] The status of the Mirdita region and their loyaty was not defined as mutavaat (submission) but as husn–i hizmet ve sadakat (good services and loyalty) oteden beri (from the olden times). This is how the state applied the principle of istimalet (strategy of reconciliation in newly conquered territories) and imtiyazat (privileges); See: Reinkowski, *The State's Security,* p. 207; Brunnbauer et. al., *Mountains as 'lieux de mémoire.'*; Robert Elsie, *The Tribes of Albania: History, Society and Culture* (London/New York: I.B. Tauris, 2015); See also: Maurus Reinkowski, "Double Struggle, No Income: Ottoman Borderlands in Northern Albania," *International Journal of Turkish Studies* 9/1 (2003): 239–253; Isa Blumi, "The Commodification of Otherness and the Ethnic Unit in the Balkans: How to Think about Albanians," *East European Politics and Societies: and Cultures* 12/3 (1998): 527–569; Nathalie Clayer, "Kosova: The Building Process of a Territory from the Nineteenth to the Twenty–First Century," in *Ottoman Legacies in the*

Additionally, in the regions of Rumelia, the Ottoman Empire introduced a concept that can be recognised as Foucauldian 'governmentality'[74] since the 1860s. This concept emphasises the methods by which a state builds infrastructural power and implements governmentality through the establishment of a bureaucracy. This approach allows for greater efficiency in the distribution of authority and spreads bureaucrats to ensure rule in each field, taking full advantage of their expertise. Exactly with this introduction of bureaucratisation, the autonomous status of the Mirdita and other autonomous regions in the Balkans was no longer accepted. Due to the latter, the Ottoman state introduced the Committee for the Mountains of Shkodra (*Işkodra Cibali Komisyonu*) considering the Malisors/Mirditas and even Gega tribal grouping in Kosovo and Debre as *vahşı* (wild) and *cahiliyyet* (ignorant). These tribes (*asabiyet*) lived in mountainous regions and governed themselves according to the Law of Lek Dukagjini. In order for the Ottoman Empire to establish control over them, punishment and castigation were introduced under such terms as *tedbi* (punishing for a fault) and *terbiye* (correcting, educating), whose goal was to make the tribes submit to *inzibat* (discipline).[75] The 'backward' regions on the periphery of the Empire, such as the Balkans, were particularly targeted by this enforced modernisation, in the course of which the civilised imperial state apparatus was pitted against savage, tribal local populations. The Ottoman principles of civilising and disciplining were introduced as a process of 'borrowed colonisation' in order to prevent the influence from

---

Contemporary Mediterranean: the Balkans and the Middle East Compared, eds. Ginio Eyal and Karl Kaser (Jerusalem: The European Forum at the Hebrew University, 2013), pp. 79–92; Eva Anne Frantz, "Kosovo," in *Das Südosteuropa der Regionen*, eds. Oliver Jens Schmitt and Michael Metzeltin (Vienna: Verlag der Österreichischen Akademie der Wissenschaften, 2015), pp. 201–275; Karl Kaser, "Pastoral Economy and Family in the Dinaric and Pindus Mountain (14th–early 20th Centuries)," in *Household and Family in the Balkans: Two Decades of Historical Family Research at University of Graz*, ed. Karl Kaser (Berlin: LIT Verlag, 2012), pp. 289–303; On Mountain regions of North Albania, Kosovo and Montenegro see: Franz Baron Nopcsa, *Aus Šala und Klementi: Albanische Wanderungen* (Sarajevo: Druck und Verlag und Daniel A. Kajon, 1910); Mirko Barjaktarović, "Rugova," in *Naselja srpskih zemalja (knj. 36): Srpski etnografski zbornik (knj. LXXIV)* (Beograd: Srpska akademija nauka i umetnosti, 1960), pp. 165–241.

[74] For similar terms, see also: Michael Mann, "The autonomous power of the state: its origins, mechanisms and results," *European Journal of Sociology* 25/2 (1984): 185–213.
[75] Reinkowski, *The State's Security*, p. 208.

outside and to bring economic income to the state apparatus.[76] Within the Ottoman *Tanzimat* reforms (1839–1876), there was a concerted effort to change the nature of the state subjects, legitimacy, and order by developing a sense of membership in the form of an Ottoman political identity or nationalism known as "Ottomanism." A group of intellectuals known as Young Ottomans developed this "Ottomanism" named also in the Ottoman scripts as "Unity of the Elements" (*İttihad–ı Anasır*). This ideology was envisaged by Tanzimat bureaucrats and intellectuals of that time in order to protect the unity of the Ottoman empire and maintaining the loyalty of ethnic religious groups toward the imperial center.[77] The essence of this "Unity of the Elements" was the idea that all subjects of the sultan were brought together in a "brotherly union," which became a matter of state policy in the period of the reforms. To the contrary, the decisions from the Congress of Berlin where Serbia, Romania and Montenegro got independence, intensified nationalist and imperialist projects among the Balkan intellectuals. This new Ottoman map, without the large portion of the Christian inhabitants, was one of the reasons to turn Islam first into a more colloquial, rather than formal component of Ottoman state. According to Behlul Özkan, "Unity of Islam became the dominant ideology of the state after the 1877–1878 war with Russia, when the Ottoman Empire lost almost one–third of its territory and its Christian population decreased from 40 percent to 20 percent."[78]

Consequently, Abdulhamid's ideological mechanisms were incorporated into Unity of Islam (*İttihad–ı İslam)* both internally and externally.[79] In the Macedonian context, it resulted often with exclusion and dissatisfaction of Christians, since the Hamidian policy was primarily dealing with recruitment of the Muslim population (but not exclusively), in fact, Albanian speaking locals into the Ottoman administration, who constituted the stronghold of the Ottoman presence in the Balkans or "the pillar of

---

[76] Ibid., p. 212.

[77] Behlül Özkan, *From the Abode of Islam to the Turkish Vatan – The: The Making of a National Homeland in Turkey* (New Haven/London: Yale University Press, 2012), p. 42.

[78] Ibid., p. 42.

[79] Donald Quataert, *The Ottoman Empire, 1700–1922* (Cambridge, UK: Cambridge University Press, 2005), p. 198.

support in Rumeli."[80] The aim was to promote an Albanianism closely linked to strong common "Islamic" values, which would respond to Hellenism and Pan–Slavic regional threats. Şemsettin Sami Frashëri viewed those two concepts (Albanianism and unity of Islam) as "different sides of the same coin." [81] Therefore, Abdulhamid II supported the 'Albanianism' and organised resistance force of the Prizren League (1878) against the invading states and tried to imbue an Islamic spirit into the resistance an Islamic overtone. [82] Nevertheless, Abdulhamid wanted to identify himself as 'father (*baba*) of the Albanians' in order to "establish an enlightened rule in his domains."[83] The Ottoman Empire's recruitment of Albanians was aimed at binding them not to an independent national movement, but to religious feelings. External threats and the internal civilising mission formed the basis of these recruitments, which had the effect of strengthening Ottoman authority over Albanian territories. The Debre meeting on October 14, 1878, as has Governor of Kosovo Hafiz Pasha pointed out, served as a catalyst for this policy and it was deemed "unwise to leave a vast territory in the hands of uneducated and uncivilised people, as this would invite foreign interference in the region." [84] In Kosovo vilayet more than in other administrative units of Macedonia, local officials requested to deploy troops to assist the fulfilment of government functions and to bring 'civilisation' (*medeniyet*) and 'humanity' (*insaniyet*) to the wild regions.[85] One such bureaucrat was Mehmed Esad Safvet Pasha, who submitted a memorandum on 12 April 1880, advocating to formulate a separate policy for those Albanian speaking Muslims (but often their Christians' compatriots as well) who were the 'essence of support' (*maya–ul–istinadi*) of the Ottoman state and could fight against enemies of the state.[86] Additionally, it is worth noting that Dervish Pasha's call for recruitment extended specifically to Albanian-speaking

---

[80] George Gawrych, *The Crescent and the Eagle: Ottoman Rule, Islam and the Albanians, 1874–1913* (New York: I.B.Tauris, 2006), p. 55.

[81] Ibid., p. 37.

[82] Nuray Bozbora, "The Policy of Abdulhamid II Regarding the Prizren League," *Turkish Review of Balkan Studies* 11 (2006): 47.

[83] Gawrych, *The Crescent,* p. 107.

[84] Ibid., p. 53.

[85] Ibid., p. 117.

[86] Ibid., p. 73.

populations in the Balkans who possessed military experience. This recruitment strategy can be seen as part of a broader effort by the Ottoman Empire to build a more cohesive and effective military force.[87] By focusing on the recruitment of Albanian-speaking soldiers, the Ottoman Empire was able to create a more effective fighting force that was better suited to defending its territory against external threats. In order to prevent the spread of the dangerous European imperialism,[88] the Ottomans claimed to be conducting a *mission civilisatrice* in its own peripheries, in this case to civilise and recruit Albanian speaking population, who would serve as defensive barriers against future foreign threats. On the other hand, Balkan states attempted to penetrate and to cooperate with the Christian subjects of the sultan, with the goal of advancing their own imperialistic projects. This situation of competition and conflict created instability over the Balkans especially in Ottoman parts of three vilayets.

1.2. Historiography and Methodological Design

The history of 19th and partly of 20th century was shaped by national ideologies produced from the top layers of the hierarchy for 'the people.' According to Georg Iggers this was the period of "increasing ideologisation of historical writing. Historians went into the archives to find evidence that would support their nationalistic and class preconceptions and thus give them the aura of scientific authority."[89] Balkan historiographies passed through a similar phase (some of them still are). During the nation– and state–building processes of the Balkan countries, the aim was to use name references that would signal, for the Montenegrins or Serbs, a linear historical continuity of the medieval Duklja and Nemanjić dynasties; in the Bulgarian case of the First

---

[87] Ibid., p. 75.
[88] Reinkowski, *The State's Security*, p. 212; Oliver Jens Schmitt, *Der Balkan im 20. Jahrhundert: Eine postimperiale Geschichte* (Stuttgart: Kohlhammer Verlag, 2019); Oliver Jens Schmitt, *Kosovo: Kurze Geschichte einer Zentralbalkanischen Landschaft* (Vienna: Böhlau Verlag, 2008); Oliver Jens Schmitt and Michael Metzeltin, "Das Südosteuropa der Regionen: Einleitung," in *Das Südosteuropa Der Regionen*, eds. Oliver Jens Schmitt and Michael Metzeltin, (Vienna: Verlag der Österreichischen Akademie der Wissenschaften, 2015), pp. 7–12.
[89] Georg G. Iggers, *Historiography in the Twentieth Century: From Scientific Objectivity to the Postmodern Challenge* (Hannover and London: Wesleyan University Press, 1997), p. 28.

Bulgarian Empire in the medieval period; while in the Greek and Albanian cases the line of this linear historical continuity was drawn from the ancient Hellenes and Illyrians. These regionalist perspectives of the 19th and 20th centuries were attempts to describe the events which took place in ancient and medieval times as primordial ethno–national foundations. In the Macedonian context, in order for the Greeks and Albanians to legitimise their actions, they claimed direct links to the Hellen and Illyrian inhabitants of the Balkans as predecessors to the Slavic invasion of the VI century, while Montenegrins, Serbs and Bulgarians presented an imaginary of their medieval empires. The constructions of these meta–narratives were based on the European understandings of "civilisation" and "progress" versus the "Orient," and thus, followed the assumption that the Ottoman conquest created "primitive and barbarian" [90] socioeconomic relations in the Balkans.[91] These Balkan "regionalist" perspectives assert that Ottomans "were usurpers of a primordial Christian order or agents who suppressed the nationalist yearnings of intact national peoples"[92] and that they were responsible for "discontinuity of the progress," "devastation," "backwardness," "social lag of the Balkan peoples,"[93] and "unenlightened slavery."[94] It is clear today that in many cases the modes of representation

---

[90] This problematic interpretation has been studied by Branislav Đurđev, "Osnovni problem srpske istorije u period turske vlasti nad našim narodima," *Istoriski glasnik* 3/4 (1950): 108; The historiographies of the Balkan state were in effect neglecting the pre–Ottoman Byzantine *Lebenswelt* and avoiding writing about the Byzantine institutional heritage of the Ottoman Empire.

[91] On the contrary, the Turkish historians such as Fuad Köprülü and Halil İnalcık maintain that the Ottomans rather intermingled with no animosity towards the Byzantine and Slavic institutions, and that "the Ottoman heritage is actually, to an extent, the Byzantine heritage."; See: Fuad Köprülü, *Bizans müesseselerinin Osmanlı müesseselerine tesiri hakkında, Türk Hukuk ve İktisat tarihi mecmuası, I* (Istanbul: Evkaf Matbaası, 1931), pp. 165–331; Halil Inaldžik, "Od Stefana Dušana do Osmanskog carstva," *Prilozi Orijentalni Institut u Sarajevu* 3/4 (1953): 23–55; Wayne S. Vucinich, "Some Aspects of the Ottoman Legacy," in *The Balkans in Transition*, eds. Charles and Barbara Jelavich (Berkeley/Los Angeles: University of California Press, 1963), p. 80.

[92] Isa Blumi, *Reinstating the Ottomans – Alternative Balkan Modernities (1800–1912)* (London: Palgrave Macmillan, 2011), p. 31.

[93] Vucinich, "Some Aspects of the Ottoman Legacy," p. 82.

[94] Petr N. Tretiakov, *Istoriia Bolgarii* (Moscow: Akademiia nauk SSSR, 1954); Robert J. Crampton, *A Concise History of Bulgaria* (Cambridge: Cambridge University Press, 2005); Venelin I. Ganev, *Bulgaria: The Uneven Transition* (London: Routledge, 2003); Roumen Daskalov, *Bulgarian Historical Review: Special Issue on Bulgaria in the*

have not changed significantly. Namely, in the views of Maurus Reinkowski, the history writing of "the South East Europe, is still limited in its scope to the framework of the respective nation states,"[95] while by contrast Istanbul's "centralist perspective is seen from the viewpoint of the centre (…) owed to ideological attitudes (and) also to the nature of archival material to be found in Istanbul's imperial archives insofar as it reflects the viewpoint of the centre."[96]

Similarly, Gül Tokay and Mehmed Hacısalihoğlu point out that "in studying Ottoman historiography related to the Balkans of the 19th century, one faces two major drawbacks. First, there is still a major gap in historical writing on the late 19th century Ottoman Balkans, and second, Ottoman bilateral relations have been largely neglected by historians to

---

Twentieth Century (Sofia: Bulgarian Academy of Sciences Press, 2005); Tsvetlin Stepanov, *The Bulgars and the Steppe Empire in the Early Middle Ages: The Problem of the Origin of the Bulgars* (Leiden: Brill, 2010); Marshall Lee Miller, *Bulgaria During the Second World War* (Stanford: Stanford University Press, 1975); Mercia MacDermott, *A History of Bulgaria: 1393–1885* (London: George Allen & Unwin, 1962); Mark Mazower, *The Balkans: A Short History* (New York: Modern Library, 2000).

[95] Maurus Reinkowski, "The Ottoman Empire and South Eastern Europe from a Turkish Perspective," in *Images of Imperial Legacy: Modern Discourses on the Social and Cultural Impact of Ottoman and Habsburg Rule in Southeast Europe*, eds. Tea Sindbaek and Maximilian Hartmuth (Berlin: LIT Verlag, 2011), p. 21.

[96] Ibid., pp. 26–30; According to Maurus Reinkowski there are three reasons why the non-Turkish parts of the Ottoman Empire are poorly represented: Major parts of South East Europe were relatively inaccessible to Turkish researchers, Turkish historiography concentrates on those provinces of the Ottoman Empire that form part of today's Turkey and Turkish historical writing – like Ottoman Studies in general – suffers from the difficulty of handling a multitude of languages when studying the history of South East Europe; See further: Halil Berktay and Suraiya Faroqhi, *New Approaches to State and Peasant in Ottoman History* (London/New York: Routledge, 2016), p. 36; Hans Georg Majer, *Die Staaten Südosteuropas und die Osmanen* (Munich: Südosteuropa Gesellschaft, 1989); Sylvie Gangloff, *La perception de l'héritage Ottoman dans les Balkans/The Perception of the Ottoman Legacy in the Balkans* (Paris: L'Harmattan, 2005); Maximilian Hartmuth, *Centres and Peripheries in Ottoman Architecture: Rediscovering a Balkan Heritage* (Sarajevo: Cultural Heritage Without Borders, 2011); Tea Sindbaek and Maximilian Hartmuth, *Images of Imperial Legacy: Modern Dis-courses on the Social and Cultural Impact of Ottoman and Habsburg Rule in Southeast Europe* (Berlin: LIT Verlag 2011); Hans Georg Majer, "Herkunft und Volkszugehörigkeit muslimischer Amtsträger als historisches Problem in der Osmanistik," in *Ethnogenese und Staatsbildung in Südosteuropa*, ed. Klaus–Detlev Grothusen (Göttingen: Vandenhoeck & Ruprecht, 1974), pp. 40–51; Oliver Jens Schmitt, "Südosteuropa im Spätmittelalter: Akkulturierung – Integration – Inkorporation?" in *Akkulturation im Mittelalter*, ed. Werner Rösener (Berlin: De Gruyter, 2014), p. 81.

date."[97] According to Suraiya Faroqhi and Fikret Adanır "by dint of this 'centralising' scholarly tradition, Turkish historians of the republican period, once the initial distaste for Ottoman history had faded away, 'appropriated' the Ottoman center. From the perspective of Turkish scholars, the wish to 'rehabilitate' the Ottoman Empire undoubtedly was strong, especially after Ottoman victories and cultural florescence had come to be regarded as a source of national pride."[98] As it might be concluded from these statements, in the Ottoman–Balkan relations the "centralist" and the "regionalist" views have not yet been combined in a productive scholarly manner and multiple parts of the Ottoman Balkans were in fact depicted as 'periphery' in the Turkish historiography, and the Ottomans perceived as the 'barbarian' among the Balkan nation–states.

In the context of the Macedonian questions, many contemporary historians (and historians from the 20th century) from the neighbouring Balkan countries have considered these events as a struggle of the Balkan nations against the "Ottoman/Turkish yoke" by relying solely on the sources of their own state and national archives. In these researches, Greek historiography tended to represent the Slavophone population of the Orthodox Christian as belonging to a wider Greek nation,[99] opposing the

---

[97] Gül Tokay and Mehmed Hacısalihoğlu, "Turkish Historiography on the Balkans during the Late Ottoman Period (1878–1914)," *Balkanistica* 22, 2009: 181.

[98] Suraiya Faroqhi and Fikret Adanır, *The Ottomans and the Balkans – A Discussion on Historiography* (Leiden/Boston/Cologne: Brill, 2002), p. 24; On (the topic of) Balkan historiographies see: John R. Lampe and Constantin Iordachi, *Battling over the Balkans: Historiographical Questions and Controversies* (Budapest/New York: Central European University Press, 2020); Fikret Adanır, *Balkans: History and Historiography* (Istanbul: Eren Yayınları, 2014).

[99] Aristotle Tziampiris, "Greek Historiography and Slav–Macedonian National Identity," *The Historical Review/ La Revue Historique* 8 (2011): 220; John S. Koliopoulos and Thanos M. Veremis, *Greece – The Modern Sequel: From 1831 to the Present* (London: Hurst and Company, 2002); Paschalis M. Kitromilides, "'Balkan Mentality': History, Legend, Imagination," *Nations and Nationalism* 2/2 (1996): 177. See also Paschalis M. Kitromilides, *An Orthodox Commonwealth: Symbolic Legacies and Cultural Encounters in Southeastern Europe* (Aldershot: Ashgate Press, 2007); Paschalis M. Kitromilides, *The Enlightenment as Social Criticism: Iosipos Moisiodax and Greek Culture in the Eighteenth Century* (Princeton: Princeton University Press, 1992); Anastasia N. Karakasidou, *Fields of Wheat, Hills of Blood: Passages to Nationhood in Greek Macedonia, 1870–1990* (Chicago: Chicago University Press, 1997); Anastasia N. Karakasidou, "Politicizing Culture: Negating Ethnic Identity in Greek Macedonia," *Journal of Modern Greek Studies* 11 (1993): 1–28.

Bulgarian policy in Ottoman Macedonia. On the other hand, Bulgarian historiography have tried to represent Bulgaria as claiming a "historical right" to the former Ottoman territories that are recognised as Macedonia,[100] and numerous Bulgarian historians have been publishing on these Macedonian issues in numerous collections.[101] On the contrary, Serbian, as well Yugoslav and Macedonian historiographies have often represented this subject from opposite points of view. Thus, Macedonian as well as Bulgarian historiography portrayed several organisations like IMARO and its members (i.e. Delchev, Gruev) as fighters for the national cause.[102] Referring to these disputes, Stefan Troebst summarised that

---

[100] Ruzha Bozhilova, "Srbia i Bŭlgarskoto natsionalnoosvoboditelno dvizhenie v Makedonia v nachaloto na XX veke," *Izsledvania po Bŭlgarska Istoria* 8 (1986); Svetlozar Eldarov, "Nachalo na Srbskata vaorazhena propaganda v Makedonia," *Voennoistoricheski sbornik* 1 (1984); Svetlozar Eldarov, "Srbskata vaorazhena propaganda i bŭlgarskoto natsionalnoosvoboditelno dvizhenie v Makedonia sled Ilindensko–Preobrazhenskoto vastanie (1903–1904)," *Voennoistoricheski sbornik* 3 (1984); Svetlozar Eldarov, "Bŭlgarskoto pravitelstvo i VMORO v borba sreshu srbskata vaorazhena propaganda v Makedonia (1903–1908)," *Izvestia na voennoistoricheskoto nauchno druzhestvo* 44 (1987); Svetlozar Eldarov, *Srbskata vaorazhena propaganda v Makedonia 1901–1912* (Sofia: Voennoizdatelski kompleks 'Sv. Georgi Pobedonosets', 1993); Elena Grozdanova, "Bŭlgarskata osmanistika na granitsata mezhdu dve stoletia – priemstvenost i obnovlenie," *Istoricheski pregled* 1/2 (1998): 98–157; Elena Grozdanova, "Bulgarian Ottoman Studies at the Turn of Two Centuries: Continuity and Change," *Études balkaniques* 3 (2005): 93–114; Rossitsa Gradeva, *Rumeli under the Ottomans 15th–18th Centuries: Institutions and Communities* (New Jersey: Gorgias Press, 2010); Olga Todorova, "Drugiat hadzilŭk: kŭm istoriata na myusulmanskia hadz ot bŭlgarskite zemi prez XV–XVII vek," *Istorichesko bŭdeshte* 1/2 (2006): 220 –277.
[101] The following collections are but a few among a host of published historical sources, documents, and memoirs on the subject: Velichko Georgiev Stajko Trifonov, *Istorija na Bŭlgarite (1878–1944) v Dokumenti (1878–1912)* (Sofia: Prosveta, 1994); Velichko Georgiev and Stajko Trifonov, *Grchkata i srbskata propagandi v Makedonia/Krayat na XIX–nachaloto na XX vek: Novi dokumenti* (Sofia: Prosveta 1995); Hristo Siljanov, *Osvoboditelnite Borbi na Makedonia* (Sofia: Darzhavna Pechatnia, 1983); Tushe Vlahov, "Bŭlgaria i Mladoturskata Revolutsia," *Godishnik na Sofiskia Universitet Filosofski–Istoricheski Fakultet* 3 (1965): 3–77; Pejo Javorov, *Gotse Delchev* (Sofia: Prosveta, 1992).
[102] Gligor Todorovski, "Srpskata četnička organizacija i nejzinata aktivnost vo Makedonija," *Glasnik na institutot za nacionalna Istorija* 1 (1968): 181–204; Mihailo Apostolski, *Istorija na makedonskiot narod II: od početokot na XIX vek do krajot na Prvata svetska vojna* (Skopje: Institut za Nacionalna Istorija, 1969); Manol Pandevski, *Nacionalnoto prašanje vo makedonskoto osloboditelnoto dviženje (1893–1903)* (Skopje: Kultura, 1974); Gligor Todorovski, *Srbija i reformite vo Makedonija: sredinata na XIX vek do Mladoturskata revolucija 1908* (Skopje: Institut za nacionalna istorija, 1987); Manol Pandevski, "Makedonskoto Osloboditelno Delo vo XIX i XX vek," in *Političkite*

Bulgaria considered Macedonian nationalism as a Serbian instrument (!); while the Greek viewed it as a short–lived will–o'–the–wisp of Moscow provenance; the Serbian intellectuals believed in the reversibility of the new Macedonians into 'Southern Serbs.'[103] These disputes between the Balkan states over Macedonia and over the question to which state or nation its national heroes belong, complicate the research, because they reduce the national heroes only to their "national" belonging, rather than regarding them as multifaceted historical agents. In addition, it prevents a broader view on these actors, and disables the usage of the Ottoman sources or other international rapports, as Dritan Ergo's work confirms.[104] In his work, Fernand Braudel highlighted the importance of exploring lesser-known perspectives in order to gain a deeper understanding of historical events. He argues that it is necessary to go beyond familiar narratives and seek out "unknown voices" that can be uncovered through

---

partii i organizacii vo Makedonija (1908–1912), ed. Manol Pandevski (Skopje: Misla, 1987); Manol Pandevski, *Vnatreshnata makedonska revolucionerna Organizacija i Neovrhovizmot 1904–1908* (Skopje: Misla, 1983); Manol Pandevski, "Jane Sandanski and the Macedonian Liberation Movement," in: *Macédoine (Articles d'Histoire),* eds. Aleksandar Matkovski and Krste Bitoski (Skopje: Institut d'histoire nationale, 1981), pp. 243–264; Manol Pandevski, *Mladoturskata Revolucija i Makedonija* (Skopje: 1968); Manol Pandevski, "Razvitokot na politichkiot život vo evropska Turcija vo periodot na mladoturskoto Upravuvanie 1908–1912," in *Istorija* 15/2 (1979): 105–116. For the accounts of the Serbian historiographies over Macedonian see: Vladimir Ilić, *Srpska četnička akcija 1903–1912* (Beograd: Ecolibri 2006); Biljana Vučetić, "Srpska revolucionarna organizacija u Osmanskom carstvu na početku 20. veka," *Istorijski časopis* 53 (2006): 359–374; Miloš Jagodić, *Srpsko albanski odnosi u kosovskom vilajetu, 1878–1912* (Beograd: Zavod za udžbenike, 2009); Uroš Šešum, "Srpska četnička organizacija u Staroj Srbiji 1903–1908. Terenska organizacija," *Srpske Studije/Serbian Studies* 2 (2011): 239–258; Miloš Jagodić, "Srpske čete u Makedoniji 1897–1901 godine," *Zbornik radova sa naučnog skupa Ustanci i pobune Srba u Turskoj u XIX veku (povodom 170. godina od izbijanja Niške bune)* 1 (2012): 111–130; Uroš Šešum, "Društvo protiv Srba 1897–1902," *Srpske Studije/Serbian Studies* 4 (2013): 73–103; Uroš Šešum, "Četnička organizacija u Skopskoj Crnoj Gori 1903–1908, godine." *Zbornik Matice srpske za istoriju* 93 (2016): 55–70.
[103] Stefan Troebst, "IMRO + 100 = FYROM? The politics of Macedonian historiography," in *The New Macedonian Question,* ed. James Pettifer (London: Palgrave Macmillan, 2001), pp. 60–78.
[104] Dritan Egro, *Historia dhe ideologjia: Një qasje kritike studimeve osmane në historiografinë shqiptare (nga gjysma e dytë e shekullit XIX deri më sot)* (Tiranë: Instituti i Historisë, 2007).

thorough research.[105] It is with this approach that the present dissertation aims to shed light on the complex history of the Balkans. Therefore, the aim of this dissertation is not to investigate the Balkans only from an imperial point of view, or more importantly, to turn a blind eye to the rich sources of Istanbul archives in order to keep an approach from a peripheral standpoint, but to combine and bring the "centralist" and "regionalist" perspectives into a coherent dialogue by using comparative sources. In addition, the Western perspectives study the events of the 19th century in the Balkans within the framework of the Eastern Question, rarely adopting a comparative approach that analyses the region within the Ottoman context. Moreover, the treatment of the imperial competition over the Balkans neglects the local perspective, considering the Balkans and Ottoman Empire as Europe's peripheries.

Beside these historiographic gaps and histories written for the purpose of state ideology, there are a few monographies about the Macedonian Questions worthy of mention for understanding the complexity of Macedonia and the relations among the Great Powers, Balkan states, and Ottomans. One of the first studies on this topic is Fikret Adanır's "*Die makedonische Frage: Ihre Entstehung und Entwicklung bis 1908*,"[106] which incisive represented the construction of Macedonian nation(s)–building (*den Konstruktionscharakter der makedonischen Nationsbildung zu zeigen*). In this respect, he used several European and south–Slavic sources in order to show the socio–economic structure and complexities on the ground, together with the influences of the Great Powers on the *Orientpolitik*. However, in these findings, he omitted the rich sources of Istanbul archives that could contributed to better understanding of multilayered relations on the local and regional levels. Nevertheless, this is an important work that paved attention on 'top–down,' but also 'bottom–up' approaches. A part from nationalist movements in Ottoman Macedonia, Adanır integrates the rural Ottoman life and peasantries into

---

[105] Fernan Brodel, *Mediteran – prostor i istorija* (Beograd: Centar za Geopoetiku, 1995), p. 18; in original see: Fernand Braudel, *La Méditerranée et le monde méditerranéen à l'époque de Philippe II* (Paris: Armand Colin, 1949). Here Fernand Braudel has stated that "we do not need to listen to voices that we know, but to try to find out other unknown voices produced by a keyboard that always requires using both hands."

[106] Fikret Adanır, *Die makedonische Frage: Ihre Entstehung und Entwicklung bis 1908* (Wiesbaden: Franz Steiner Verlag, 1979).

broader regional analysis. Another important work is the doctoral dissertation of Gül Tokay entitled *"The Macedonian Question and the Origins of the Young Turk Revolution, 1903–1908,"*[107] focusing on the Ottoman military and the influence of the Macedonian Question into the Young Turk Revolution. Additionally, Mehmet Hacısalihoğlu's book *"Die Jungturken und die Mazedonische Frage (1890–1918)"*[108] centres on the Young Turk policy and even on the period after the Revolution (1908), as well as on how the Macedonian Question shaped and transformed this movement. In comparison to Adanır's work, he integrated relevant documents from the Istanbul archive and materials based on Young Turk movement. I would like to emphasise this work contains with a significant number of British, German, Austrian, Ottoman, Bulgarian, and Macedonian archival resources, which helps to undertake comparative approaches. These studies also focus on Ottoman Macedonia as a whole, accepting the existence of a unified Macedonian Question, and do not base their discussions on several different problematics that created Macedonian questions (in plural). Three other important studies on this topic written in German are: one by Stefan Troebst, entitled *"Das makedonische Jahrhundert: von den Anfängen der nationalrevolutionären Bewegung zum Abkommen von Ohrid 1893–2001,"*[109] another by Stefan Rohdewald, *"Götter der Nationen: Religiöse Erinnerungsfiguren in Serbien, Bulgarien und Makedonien bis 1944,"* and Benjamin Langer's *"Fremde, ferne Welt: Mazedonienimaginationen in der deutschsprachigen Literatur seit dem 19. Jahrhundert."*[110] All these works discuss the Macedonian Question through a *longue durée* analysis based on various German, French, English, but also South–Slavic sources. Works originating from Serbian scholarship, such as Biljana Vučetić's *"Naša*

---

[107] Gül Tokay, "The Macedonian Question and the Origins of the Young Turk Revolution, 1903–1908" (PhD diss., University of London, 1994).

[108] Mehmet Hacısalihoğlu, *Die Jungtürken und die Mazedonische Frage, 1890–1918* (Munich: R. Oldenbourg Verlag, 2003).

[109] Stefan Rohdewald, *Götter der Nationen: Religiöse Erinnerungsfiguren in Serbien, Bulgarien und Makedonien bis 1944* (Cologne/Weimar/Vienna: Böhlau Verlag, 2014).

[110] Benjamin Langer, *Fremde, ferne Welt: Mazedonienimaginationen in der deutschsprachigen Literatur seit dem 19. Jahrhundert* (Bielefeld: Transcript Verlag, 2019).

stvar u Osmanskom carstvu" [111] and Aleksandar Rastović's *"Velika Britanija i Makedonsko pitanje"* [112] constitute important Serbian and British sources, while the works of Jordan Ivanov *"Bǔlgarski starini iz Makedonia"* [113] and *"Makedonia – Sbornik ot dokumenti i materiali"* [114] demonstrate the Bulgarian presence in Macedonia from the medieval to the modern period on the basis of important diplomatic documents, newspapers, parts from the book sections etc. Ivanov views was actually introduced to present prevalently Bulgarian 'element' and importance as a part of Bulgarian meta–narratives. In opposition to the aforementioned books, Krste Misirkov's seminal work *"Za makedontskite raboti"* [115] explores the complexities of the "Macedonian matters, " with a particular focus on the question of national identity and the struggle for recognition of Macedonians as a distinct people. By using Bulgarian and Austrian sources, Teodora Toleva in her two works: *"Vlianieto na Avstro – Ungaria za sǔzdavaneto na albanskata natsia (1896–1908)"* [116] and *"Vanshnata politika na Dyula Andrashi i vaznikvaneto na Makedonskia vǔpros"* [117] approaches to Macedonian and Albanian questions by reiterating the most important findings in Austro–Hungarian archives and points out the facts that Austro–Hungarian policy shaped the unique development of the Albanian nation. By analysing the Albanian national development and Macedonian question, she took into consideration the basic characteristics of the Albanian population, especially its religious, tribal and linguistic division. Furthermore, the monograph of Douglas Dakin, *"The Greek*

---

[111] Biljana Vućetić, *Naša stvar u osmanskom carstvu* (Beograd: Istorijski Institut, 2012).

[112] Aleksandar Rastović, *Velika Britanija i makedonsko pitanje 1903–1908* (Beograd: Istorijski Institut, 2011)

[113] Jordan Ivanov, *Bǔlgarski starini iz Makedonia* (Sofia: Izvestiia na Instituta za arkheologiia, 1970); first published in 1931.

[114] Dimitar Kosev, Hristo Hristov, Nikolay Todorov and Valentin Stankov, *Makedonia – Sbornik ot dokumenti i materiali* (Sofia, Izdatelstvo na Bǔlgarskata Akademia Naukite, 1978).

[115] First published: Krste Misirkov, *Za makedontskite raboti* (Sofia: Pechatnitsa na Liberalnii klub, 1903); Here used in the manuscript: Krste P. Misirkov, "Za makedonskite raboti," in *Krste P. Misirkov, Sobrani dela 1– tekstovi na makedonski jazik (1900–1905)* eds. Blaže Ristovski and Biljana Ristovska–Josifovska (Skopje: MANU, 2005).

[116] Teodora Toleva, *Vlianieto na Avstro–Ungarija za saǔzdavaneto na albanskata nacija: 1896–1908* (Sofia: Siela Norma AD, 2012).

[117] Teodora Toleva, *Vanshnata politika na Dyula Andrashi i vaznikvaneto na Makedonskia vǔpros* (Sofia: Tsiela, 2013).

Struggle in Macedonia (1897–1913)," [118] and the doctoral thesis of Georgios Michalopoulos, *"Political Parties, Irredentism and the Foreign Ministry of Greece and Macedonia: 1878–1910*"[119] focus more strongly on the Macedonian Question from a Greek perspective but using American and British sources too. A broader perspective based on a Greek point of view, but challenging its historiography, is taken in *"Fields of Whet, Hills of Blood: Passages to Nationhood in Greek Macedonia, 1870–1990,*"[120] written by Anastasia N. Karakasidou and in *"Steam over Macedonia, 1870–1912: Socio–Economic Change and the Railway Factor,*"[121] written by Basil C. Gounaris. In his book *"Kosova dhe reformat ne Turqi,*"[122] Emin Pllana analyses the Ottoman reforms and Kosovo in the period of 1839–1912 by using Austrian, Bulgarian, Macedonian, Albanian, and Serbian sources. A connection to the Macedonian Questions and the importance of the Albanian element therein can be traced also in the work of Nuray Bozbora *"Osmanlı yönetiminde Arnavutluk ve Arnavut ulusçuluğu'nun gelişimi.*"[123]

From the West European perspective one can mention Nadine Lange–Akhund's *"The Macedonian Question (1893–1908) from Western Sources,*"[124] which engages with diplomatic archives of France and Austria, complemented by recent foreign publications from Germany, Austria, Britain, and the US. A study of the changes of British foreign policy towards the Macedonian Question is Julian Brook's *"Managing Macedonia: British Statecraft, Intervention, and 'Proto–peacekeeping' in*

---

[118] Douglas Dakin, *The Greek struggle in Macedona 1897–1913* (Thessaloniki: Institute for Balkan Studies, 1966).

[119] Georgios Michalopoulos, "Political Parties, Irredentism and the Foreign Ministry Greece and Macedonia: 1878–1910" (PhD diss., University of Oxford, 2013).

[120] Anastasia N. Karakasidou, *Fields of Whet, Hills of Blood: Passages to Nationhood in Greek Macedonia, 1870–1990* (Chicago: University of Chicago Press, 1997).

[121] Basil C. Gounaris, *Steam over Macedonia, 1870–1912: Socio–Economic Change and the Railway Factor* (New York: Columbia University Press, 1993).

[122] Emin Pllana, *Kosova dhe reformat ne Turqi* (Prishtinë: Rilindja, 1978).

[123] Nuray Bozbora, *Osmanlı yönetiminde Arnavutluk ve Arnavut ulusçuluğu'nun gelişimi* (Istanbul: Boyut Kitapları, 1997).

[124] Nadine Lange–Akhund, *The Macedonian Question (1893–1908) from Western Sources, East European Monographs* (New York: Columbia University, 1998).

Ottoman Macedonia, 1902–1905."[125] Duncan Perry's *"The Politics of Terror: Macedonian Revolutionary Movements, 1893–1903*"[126] intends to remain unswayed by any sort of bias as regards the Macedonian Question. He sets a goal "to present a balanced rendering of the history of the Macedonian movements based on the available evidence, without regard to contemporary political or nationalistic considerations."[127] It might be asserted that he has reached his goal by and large throughout the book. A combination of European and local sources in Greek and Ottoman Turkish is traceable in the work of İpek Yosmaoğlu, *"Blood Ties: Religion, Violence and the Politics of Nationhood in Ottoman Macedonia, 1878– 1908,*"[128] which explains the origins of the shift from sporadic to systemic and pervasive violence through a social history of the Macedonian Question. However, Yosmaoğlu also analyses the Macedonian question as a whole. Moreover, she focuses predominantly on the Salonika vilayet (district of Serres) and the dynamics that influenced that specific region, without interconnecting it in a broader trans–regional context. When referring to one specific region or administrative unit, such as the Selanik vilayeti, one can talk about the Macedonian question as a unified one. The structure, societies and dynamics in the Selanik vilayeti were often different from the Kosovo or Manastir vilayeti, but still interconnected and entangled on many levels. Furthermore, in many of these studies the Kosovo vilayet is omitted from the closer analysis. In this thesis, I highlight that the Kosovo vilayet and its administrative centre Skopje was an important administrative unit of the Ottoman Empire and integrative part of the three vilayets that comprised Macedonia – at least the region that the Great Powers and the Balkan states imagined when using this name. As such, I believe that the Kosovo vilayet should not be analysed separately and should not remain outside the analysis of Macedonia. My opinion is that these three vilayets were interconnected at many levels and

---

[125] Julian Brooks, "Managing Macedonia: British Statecraft, Intervention, and 'Proto–Peacekeeping' in Ottoman Macedonia, 1902–1905" (PhD diss., Simon Fraser University, 2014)

[126] Duncan Perry, *The Politics of Terror: Macedonian Revolutionary Movements, 1893–1903* (Durham: Duke University Press, 1988).

[127] Ibid., p. xiii.

[128] İpek Yosmaoğlu, *Blood Ties: Religion, Violence and the Politics of Nationhood in Ottoman Macedonia, 1878–1908* (New York: Cornell University Press, 2014).

thus should be analysed in the broader context with other parts of the Empire and regional dynamics as well. In this regard, this study differs from other works, because it tries to include perspectives and parts of Ottoman Macedonia that were often neglected or less researched inside the Macedonian Questions. In this sense, the present dissertation draws upon research representing various traditions and worldviews, and thus tries to integrate them in a global perspective that combines multi–layered relations. Although the works of all the aforementioned authors agree that in the late 19th century four states laid claims to Macedonia: Bulgaria, Greece, Serbia, and Romania, I highlight here that other actors were at play, whose roles were very important. By looking closely at this period of time, one can discern that Montenegro played a very important role at the border with the Kosovo vilayet. Nevertheless, Montenegro was also the first Balkan country that declared war to the Ottoman Empire in 1912 and initiated the beginning of the Balkan Wars – a war that initiated the partition of Ottoman Macedonia. It is also worthy of mention that other studies neglect the Montenegrin involvement in the Macedonian Questions and its role in the Balkan Wars. Therefore, in the last chapter I will contribute the Montenegrin point of view in the framework of the Macedonian Questions, as a lesser known and insufficiently researched part of this topic. In addition, the 'Albanian element' in the Macedonian Question(s) is also omitted among the researchers of this topic. By the 'Albanian element,' I do not mean a uniform and monolith ethno–national group, but rather Albanian–speaking individuals, intellectuals, or notables, as well as local population who played very important roles in organising the masses that could change policy decisions. These notables, with individual or group "agency," were undoubtedly neglected in past studies about the Macedonian Question(s). To the contrary, the armed conflict that escalated in nowadays North Macedonia between Macedonians and ethnic Albanians in 2001, showed that the 'Albanian element' should not be ignored regarding the Macedonian case. This recent escalation of violence began to puzzle me and awoke a desire to (re)search for a more detailed overlook of the historical account of the transnational origins of the conflict. Digging through several archives, dictionaries, and files helped me to understand better that the Albanian–speaking population also played a very important role in the Macedonian Questions during the Age of

Empire. Bringing new sources and a deep understanding to bear on the 'Albanian element,' this dissertation ultimately shows that many Albanian–speaking notables (Ahmed Niyazi Bey, Ohrili Eyub Sabri, but also locals at the Ferizaj/Ferizovik meeting) played important parts in triggering the Young Turk Revolution in 1908. Apart from this event, the 'Albanian element' had a significant presence during the Albanian uprisings (1909–1912), to the result of which was autonomous Albania, promised by the Ottoman government in August 1912. In this study, I will show that this potential autonomous Albania was not desirable for the Balkan states, which drove them to declare war on the Ottoman Empire and thus initiate the First Balkan War. Since these events are of great relevance for an understanding of the situation in Ottoman Macedonia, my hypothesis here is that without this 'Albanian element' one cannot have a clear picture of the multi–layered interactions and situations at play that triggered many political decisions of the Great Powers, Balkan states, and Ottoman Empire. In this vein, my study differs from the above–mentioned works, because it includes two important hitherto neglected actors: Montenegro and the Albanian–speaking players who were not bereft of agency. As has been already mentioned, Montenegro had developed various policies towards these territories and had many political involvements with the local Albanian– and Slavic–speaking population in the three vilayets, particularly in the Kosovo vilayet. In this regard, the study aims to present their entanglements, political engagements, and complexities on the ground that often influenced the decisions of policy–makers. In my research, to a [certain] point I argue in this study that Montenegro, the 'Albanian element,' and the local population warrant a closer look regarding the Macedonian Questions at the turn to 20th century. Therefore, the exclusion of these (Montenegrin and Albanian) perspectives in the scholarships presents an opportunity here to reassess the region's relationships within a broader, trans-regional context. Apart from it, the aforementioned authors also analysed Macedonian Question as a whole, while I will argue that there were multiple Macedonian Question(s) during the Age of Empire. An acclaimed historian, Eric Hobsbawm describes the period between 1875–1914 as the "Age of

Empire,"[129] linking it with the development of European imperialism that resulted in the World War I. Based on Holly Case's approach that this period is simultaneously "the age of questions,"[130] I will highlight that one cannot talk about the Macedonian Question as a unified problem, but rather consider the existence of many questions dependent also on the real–life dynamics and the perspectives of multiple actors who were at play. In this regard, this study is the first attempt to connect the Macedonian Questions to post–colonial theory and its discussions of the subaltern studies. As a result of these deliberations, this thesis endeavors to scrutinise the perspectives of state actors and intellectuals, while also incorporating the viewpoints of the local population by recognising the significance of multi-layered interactions and entanglements. In fact, these Macedonian Questions were entengled across various regions and spheres of daily life. A number of life trajectories are encountered in the study that allow a scholar to better gauge agencies and experiences at the local level. This thesis seeks to comprehend the lifeworlds of individuals 'from below,' who are considered part of the subaltern as introduced by post-colonial theory authors.[131] It is commonly asserted that these lifeworlds are a product of 'communicative action' among various components.[132] It is essential to underscore that this world is not solitary but instead an intersubjective realm that is shared among various state and non-state

---

[129] *The Age of Empire: 1875–1914* is a book by the British historian Eric Hobsbawm, published in 1987. It is the third in a trilogy of books about "the long 19th century" (coined by Hobsbawm), preceded by *The Age of Revolution: Europe 1789–1848* and *The Age of Capital: 1848–1875*. A fourth book, *The Age of Extremes: The Short Twentieth Century, 1914–1991*, acts as a sequel to the trilogy. See: Eric Hobsbawm, *The Age of Empire, 1875–1914* (London: George Weidenfeld and Nicolson, 1987).

[130] Holly Case, *The Age of Questions: Or, A First Attempt at an Aggregate History of the Eastern, Social, Woman, American, Jewish, Polish, Bullion, Tuberculosis, and Many Other Questions over the Nineteenth Century, and Beyond* (Princeton: Princeton University Press, 2018).

[131] Gayatri Chakravorty Spivak, *Can the Subaltern Speak? Postkolonialität und subalterne Artikulation* (Vienna/Berlin: Turia + Kant Verlag, 2020).

[132] Alfred Schütz, Thomas, Luckmann, *The Structures of the Life–World vol. 2* (Evanston: Northwestern University Press, 1989), pp. 53–56; Jürgen Habermas, *The Theory of Communivative Action, vol. 2: Lifeworld and System: A Critique of Functionalist Reason* (Boston: Beacon Press, 1987).

actors.[133] However, by trying to give a voice to subalterns (or locals), one challenges the mapped spaces and imagination of the ruling elites, statemen, and state–centred policies. We should also keep in mind that the actions of the locals and their life trajectories were far from linear. In fact, they often clashed with state projections and elitist imaginations, but also sometimes joined the state policies depending on many factors and contexts. Thus, these dynamics were not developing in a vacuum, but rather in the space of "multiple arenas of domination and opposition."[134] Since the scope of the dissertation is to understand the complexities of the 'arena' known as Ottoman Macedonia, I will use various documents and a mixture of sources in different languages. I preponderouly focused on two vilayets of Macedonia: Kosovo and Manastir. The third, Selanik vilayeti receives lesser coverage in this dissertation, due to my limited command of the Greek language. However, several British, Ottoman, Albanian and Serbian sources (i.e. consular reports) from Thessaloniki have been incorporated. In addition to these sources, this study also includes documents in the Macedonian, Bulgarian, Russian, German, French, and Italian languages, and therefore takes a trans–cultural perspective in order to contribute to postcolonial studies and entangled (and global) history by including various (local, regional, and international) approaches to the notions of 'periphery' and 'centre.'

Still, the main collection of sources stems from: the Prime Minister Ottoman Archive (BOA) in Istanbul; State Archives of North Macedonia (DARSM) in Skopje; Historical Archive of Macedonia in Thessaloniki (IAM); State Archives of Serbia (DAS) in Belgrade; National Library of Bulgaria "St. Cyril and Methodius" in Sofia; State Archive of Montenegro (DACG) in Cetinje; Central State Archive of Albania (AQSH) in Tirana;

---

[133] David F. Crew, "Alltagsgeschichte: A New Social History 'From Below'?," *Central European History* 22/3–4 (1989): 394–407, in pages 395–397; Jim Sharpe, History from Below, in *New Perspectives on Historical Writing,* ed. Peter Burke (Pennsylvania: Pennsylvania State Universtity Press, 1991), pp. 36–37; Selim Karahasanoğlu, "Introduction," in *History from below: A Tribute in Memory of Donald Quataert,* eds. Selim Karahasanoğlu and Deniz Cenk Demir (Istanbul: Istanbul Bilgi University Press, 2016), pp. 1–23; Georg Simmel, *Soziologie: Untersuchungen über die Formen der Vergesellschaftung* (Berlin: Dunckler & Humblot, 2013).

[134] Joel Samuel Migdal, Atul Kohli and Vivienne Shue (eds.) *State Power and Social Forces: Domination and Transformation in the Third World* (Cambridge: Cambridge University Press, 1994), p. 9.

the State Archive of Austria in Vienna (HHStA) collected in five volumes in *"Politik und Gesellschaft im Vilayet Kosovo und im serbisch beherrschten Kosovo 1870–1914,"[135]* edited by Oliver Jens Schmitt and Eva Anne Frantz; *"Austro–Ugarska i Srbija 1903–1918 – Dokumenta iz Bečkih Arhiva/Österreich–Ungarn und Serbien 1903–1918 – Dokumente aus Wiener Archiven,"[136]* edited by Andrija Radenić; *"Istorija srpske Diplomatije Dokumenta: Generalni konzulat Kraljevine Srbije u Solunu (1887–1902),"* and *"Istorija srpske Diplomatije Dokumenta: Generalni konzulat Kraljevine Srbije u Serezu (1897–1900)"[137]* edited by Aleksej Timofejev; and *"Shqipëria në Dokumentet Austro–Hungareze (1912),"[138]* edited by Marenglen Verli; Central State Historical Archive in St. Petersburg (TsGIA SPb); Archiginnasio Library in Bologna; Bibliotheque nationale de France in Paris; Staatsbibliothek in Berlin; Deutsche Bank Berlin Orientbüro (OR) in Berlin; Ottoman diplomatic documents based on the Origins of World War I, *"The Macedonian Issue (1879–1912),"[139]* edited by Sinan Kuneralp and Gül Tokay; documents based on Young Turk correspondence *"Osmanlı Terakki ve İttihat Cemiyeti: Paris Merkezi Yazışmaları Kopya Defterleri (1906–1908),"[140]* edited by Çiğdem Önal Emiroğlu and Kudret Emiroğlu; and ISAM (*Türkiye Diyanet Vakfı ve İslam Araştırmaları Merkezi*), where one can find *"Hüseyin Hilmi Paşa Evrakı Kataloğu."[141]* The last source is particularly important due to

---

[135] Oliver Jens Schmitt and Eva Anne Frantz, *Politik und Gesellschaft im Vilayet Kosovo und im serbisch beherrschten Kosovo 1870–1914* (Vienna: VÖAW, 2020).

[136] Andrija Radenić, *Dokumenta iz Bečkih Arhiva/Österreich–Ungarn und Serbien 1903–1918 – Dokumente aus Wiener Archiven* (Beograd: Istorijski institut, 1973).

[137] Aleksej Timofejev, *Istorija srpske Diplomatije Dokumenta: Generalni konzulat Kraljevine Srbije u Solunu (1887–1902)* (Beograd: Arhiv Srbije, 2016); and also edited by Aleksej Timofejev, *Istorija srpske Diplomatije Dokumenta: Generalni konzulat Kraljevine Srbije u Serezu (1897–1900)* (Beograd: Arhiv Srbije, 2016).

[138] Marenglen Verli, *Shqipëria në dokumentet Austro–Hungareze (1912)* (Tiranë: Qendra e Studimeve Albanologjike Instituti i Historisë, 2012).

[139] Sinan Kuneralp and Gül Tokay, *Ottoman Diplomatic Documents Based on the Origins of World War I, the Macedonian Issue (1879–1912)* (Istanbul: ISIS Press, 2011).

[140] Ciğdem Onal Emiroğlu and Kudret Emiroğlu, *Osmanlı Terakki ve İttihat Cemiyeti: Paris Merkezi Yazışmaları Kopya Defterleri (1906–1908)* (Istanbul: Tarih Vakfı Yurt Yayınları, 2017).

[141] Mustafa Birol Ülker, Ömer Faruk Bahadur, Asiye Kakırman Yıldız, Müslüm İstekli and Kenan Yıldız (eds.), *Hüseyin Hilmi Paşa Evrakı Kataloğu* (Istanbul: İSAM Yayınları, 2006).

Hüseyin Hilmi Pasha's position as an Ottoman statesman and imperial administrator in the three vilayets known as Ottoman Macedonia. In the most crucial period, between 1902 and 1908, he was the Ottoman Inspector–General of these provinces. In addition, several published archival collections that cover Ottoman, Serbian, Bulgarian, and Albanian sources have been included in this study.[142]

Apart from these archival collections and documents, I used several memoirs and diaries. In the former, the research deals with two important Turkish sources *"Osmanlı Devleti'nin Makedonya Meselesi"* [143] by Süleyman Kani Irtem and Tahsin Uzer's memoirs *"Makedonya Eşkiyalık Tarihi ve Son Osmanlı Yönetimi."* [144] Both books employ a critical approach to the Hamidian regime and are an important account of authors' views on the Ottoman Empire and the society in Ottoman Macedonia. Next, Tahsin Uzer was even a member of the Young Turk movement, along with Ahmet Riza, Enver Pasha, Talat Pasha, Kazim Karabekir, and Mithat Şükrü Bleda, who wrote memoirs and diaries: *"Ahmet Riza Bey'in Anıları,"* [145] *"Enver Paşa'nin Anıları,"* [146] Talat Paşa's *"Hatıralarım ve Müdafaam,"* [147] Kazim Karabekir's *"İttihat ve Terakki Cemiyeti,"* [148] and

---

[142] The edition titled Documents on Foreign Affairs of the Kingdom of Serbia, 1903–1914 that was being published between 1980 and 2015 in 42 volumes. It has been digitised: http://diplprepiska.mi.sanu.ac.rs/ accessed 28/03/2021. See also other published editions Milić F. Petrović, *Dokumenti o raškoj oblasti, 1900–1912* (Beograd: Arhiv Srbije, 1995); Živko Avramovski, *Britanci u Kraljevini Jugoslaviji: Godišnji izveštaji Britanskog poslanstva u Beogradu 1921–1938, vol. I (1921–1930)* (Beograd/Zagreb: Arhiv Jugoslavije – Globus, 1986); Ljubodrag Dimić and Đorđe Borozan, *Jugoslovenska država i Albanci, vol. 1–2* (Beograd: JP Službeni list SRJ/Arhiv Jugoslavije/Vojno–istorijski institut, 1998/99); Biblioteka Kombëtare e Shqipërise: https://www.bksh.al/ accessed 28/03/2021; Sinan Kuneralp and Gül Tokay, *Ottoman Diplomatic Documents on the Origins of World War One IV the Macedonian Issue 1879–1912* (Istanbul: ISIS, 2011); Atatürk Kitaplığı: https://ataturkkitapligi.ibb.gov.tr/tr/Anasayfa accessed 28/03/2021; See also Bulgarian National Library: https://www.nationallibrary.bg/ accessed 28/03/2021.

[143] Süleyman Kâni İrtem, *Osmanlı Devleti'nin Makedonya meselesi* (Istanbul: Temel Yayınları, 1998).

[144] Tahsin Üzer, *Makedonya eşkiyalık tarihi ve son Osmanlı yönetimi* (Ankara: Türk Tarih Kurumu, 1999).

[145] Ahmed Riza, *Ahmet Riza Bey'in anıları* (Istanbul: Dizgi Yayınları, 2001).

[146] Enver Paşa, *Enver Paşa'nın anıları, 1881–1908* (Istanbul: İş Bankası Kültür Yayınları, 2018).

[147] Talat Paşa, *Hatıralarım ve Müdafaam* (Istanbul: Kaynak Yayınları, 2006).

[148] Kazim Karabekir, *İttihat ve Terakki cemiyeti* (Istanbul: Yapı Kredi Yayınları, 2009).

Mithat Şükrü Bleda's "*İmparatorluğun Çöküşü.*"[149] These books help us to understand their entanglements with Albanian–speaking Young Turks who were originally from Ottoman Macedonia and played important roles in the Ottoman Empire. In this respect, this research will analyse the memoirs of Albanian speaking personalities such as Ibrahim Temo "*İttihat ve Terakki Anılarım,*" [150] Ismail Qemali's "*Memoirs*" [151] (written in English) and those of his cousin, Sureyya Bey Avlonyalı, "*Osmanlı Sonrası Arnavutluk.*"[152] Sureyya Bey's son, Ekrem Bey Vlora, wrote his memoirs in German, known as "*Lebenserinnerungen.*"[153] At that time, it was common to write memoirs in different languages, since these personalities lived in different parts of the world, sometimes as fugitives, but also voluntarily. These writings are helpful in depicting people, ideas, places and social interactions from the perspectives of the local Albanian–speaking population. Of no lesser importance are also Ahmed Niyazi Bey's "*Hatırat–i,*"[154] Bekir Fikri's "*Balkanlarda Tedhiş ve Gerilla,*"[155] and Hasan Prishtina's "*Nji shkurtim kujtimesh mbi kryengritjen shqiptare të vjetit 1912,*"[156] all of whom were born in different parts of the Ottoman Macedonian vilayets. Hasan Prishtina was born and raised in Kosovo, while Ahmed Niyazi and Bekir Fikri were born in the Manastir vilayet. Their memoirs also verify links with the broader region and detail such events as the meetings and personal contacts with different personalities that established interactions with the locals as well. These autobiographical texts make it possible to afford an insight into the ways in which individuals established connections and cooperations with each other and to understand the real–life entanglements at the local level.

---

[149] Mithat Şükrü Bleda, *İmparatorluğun çöküşü* (Istanbul: Destek Yayınları, 2010).

[150] Ibrahim Temo, *İttihat ve Terakki anılarım* (Istanbul: Alfa Yayınları, 2013).

[151] Ismail Qemali, *The Memoirs of Ismail Kemal Bey* (London: Constable and Company LTB, 1921).

[152] Sureyya Bey Avlonyalı, *Osmanlı sonrası Arnavutluk (1912–1920)* (Istanbul: Klasik Yayınları, 2018).

[153] Ekrem Bey Vlora, *Lebenserinnerungen* (Berlin/Munich: De Gruyter Oldenbourg, 1973).

[154] Ahmed Niyazi Bey, *Hatırat–i yahut tarihçe–i inkilab–i kebir–i Osmani'den bir sahife* (Istanbul: Sabah Matbaası, 1326 [1910]).

[155] Bekir Fikri, *Balkanlarda tedhiş ve gerilla* (Istanbul: Vakfi Yayınları, 2008).

[156] Hasan Prishtina, *Nji shkurtim kujtimesh mbi kryengritjen shqiptare të vjetit 1912* (Tiranë: Eurorilindja, 1995).

From the South–Slavic perspective(s), one should mention the memoirs and diaries of gang activists and members of various organisations, either nationalist or anarchist and socialist. Their plans, projects, and interactions with locals can be traced in the memoirs of Milan Matov, *"Nai komitata raskazva, zhivot za Makedonia;"*[157] Hristo Tatarchev, *"Spomeni na Hristo Tatarchev: Prviat Komitet na VMRO;"*[158] *"Makedonia i Odrinsko 1893– 1903, s dve karti,"* published in 1904 as a memoir of the International Organisation (*Vatreshnata Organizatsia*);[159] Hristo Matov, *"Osnovi na vatreshnata revolutsionna organizatsia"*[160] and *"Shto byahme – shto sme;"*[161] Angel Tomov and Georgi Bazhdarov, *"Revolutsionnata borba v Makedonia;"*[162] Dimitri Vlahov, *"Memoari;"*[163] Mihail Gerdzikov, *"V Makedonia i Odrinsko Spomeni,"*[164] Petar Mandzukov, *"Predvestnitsi na buryata Spomeni,"*[165] and Pavel Shatev, *"Solunskiat attentat i zatochenitsitie v 'Fezan.'"*[166] The memoirs important for their records of the events before the Balkan Wars were edited in nine volumes by Lyubomir Miletich, *"Materiali za istoryata na makedonskoto osvoboditelno dvizhenie;"*[167] the tenth was edited by Stefan Avramov, and the eleventh by Bojan Mirchev. Here I focus mostly on the discussions inside the IMARO members and I try to deconstruct their 'primordial' ethno–national positions 'given' by Bulgarian and Macedonian historiographies as monolith and constant. Rather, I will highlight their

---

[157] Milan Matov, *Nai komitata raskazva, zhivot za Makedonia* (Sofia: Kulturno–blagotvoritelna fondacia ‚Bratya Miladinovi', 2002).

[158] Materiali za Istoriata na makedonskoto osvoboditelno dvizhenie, kniga IX (Sofia: Pechatnitsa P. Gluskov, 1928).

[159] Memoari na Vatreshnata Organizatsia, Makedonia i Odrinsko (1893–1903) (Sofia: N.P., 1904).

[160] Hristo Matov, *Osnovi na vatreshnata revolyutsionna organizatsia* (Sofia: N.P., 1904).

[161] Hristo Matov, *Shto byahme – shto sme* (Plovdiv: N.P., 1905).

[162] Angel Tomov and Georgi Bazhdarov, *Revolutsionnata borba v Makedonia* (Sofia: Paskalev, 1917).

[163] Dimitri Vlahov, *Memoari* (Skopje: Nova Makedonija, 1970).

[164] Mihail Gerdzikov, *V Makedonia i Odrinsko Spomeni* (Sofia: Glusov, 1928).

[165] Petar Mandzukov, *Predvestnitsi na buriata Spomeni* (Sofia: Federatsiata na anarhistite v Bulgaria, 2013).

[166] Pavel Shatev, *Solunskiat attentat i zatochenitsitie v 'Fezan'* (Sofia: Makedonski nauchen institut, 2015).

[167] Lyubomir Miletich, *Materiali za istoriata na makedonskoto osvoboditelno dvizhenie, knyiga IX* (Sofia, 1925–28).

views as part of changable dynamics that were developed in the trans–regional context. However, my aim here is not to focus only on IMARO members, since this topic has been quite researched. Thus, apart from these memoirs and materials written in Bulgarian and Macedonian, I will also draw on the memoirs written by members of the Serbian gang organisation known as *Četnička akcija*. In the works of some of their members, such as Vasilije Trbić's "*Memoari*,"[168] or their raports closely analysed by Biljana Vučetić and Uroš Šešum, where they published important information about the contacts between various groups and their actions in Ottoman Macedonia. Apart from the archival documents, books, memoirs, and diaries, there are several maps, cartography, and photos, which I analyse through the lens of imagination.[169] Important sources are also gazettes, journals, and newspapers written in Ottoman Turkish, like *Tanin, Ibret, Tercuman–ı Şark, Balkan,* which are available online. The newspapers have been digitised as a part of the Ottoman newspaper collection (*Osmanlıca Gazeteler*).[170] Relevant newspapers and journals, such as *Kanun–i Esasi, Şuiurâ–yi Ümmet, Içtihad, Anadolu,* and *Osmanlı* are stored in the IBB Atatürk Library in Istanbul. Further Ottoman Turkish books from the period are also in the same library, while several of them are also available online on the library's website.[171] The newspapers published in Albanian, such as *Kalendari Kombiar, Besa, Drita, Shpnesa e Shqypnis, Shqiptari (Arnavut)*, are stored in the General Directorate of Archives in Tirana. The newspapers in Serbian, such as *Politika, Carigradski Vestnik,* one can find online in a digital library.[172] This also applies to the Montenegrin newspaper *Glas Crnogorca*[173] and the

---

[168] Vasilije Trbić, *Memoari* (Beograd: Kultura, 1996).

[169] Dimitar Rizov, *Bulgarite v tehnite istoricheski, etnograficheski i politicheski granitsi 679–1917* (Berlin: Königliche Hoflithographie/ Hof–Buch–und Steindruckere Wilhelm Greve, 1917); Henry Robert Wilkinson, *Maps and Politics – A review of the Ethnographic Cartography of Macedonia* (Liverpool: Liverpool University Press, 1951);

[170] Osmanlıca Gazeteler: https://www.Osmanlıcagazeteler.org accessed: 11/11/2019.

[171] Atatürk Kitaplığı İstanbul: http://ataturkkitapligi.ibb.gov.tr/ataturkkitapligi/index.php accessed 11/11/2019.

[172] Digitalna biblioteka matice Srpske: http://digital.bms.rs/ebiblioteka/ accessed 11/11/2019.

[173] Digitalna biblioteka Crne Gore: http://dlib.me/ accessed 11/11/2019.

Bulgarian newspapers *Makedonia, Yugozapadna Bŭlgaria, Svoboda,* and *Gayda*.[174]

1.3. What Do We Know About the Contentious Imaginations of Ottoman Macedonia?

If we take into consideration that the spatial territories are in fact often constructed by power of imaginations, one simoultaneously acknowledges that within one polity many different borderlands exist depending on one's imagination. Thus, these notions of spatiality and territoriality should be analysed as imagined, made, moulded, percieved, constructed, but not given as natural entities.[175] Nowadays, by using different archival sources, it is a commonly accepted view that is not such a consensus for the geographical borders of Macedonia. Instead of discussing them as something given, rather they "can be interpreted as manifestation of socio–spatial consciousness and imaginations."[176] Nevertheless, the formation of nation–states and nation–building during the *age of empire* marked a crucial period in the development of socio–spatial consciousness. [177] During this era, there was a strong emphasis on meta–geography and a spatial imaginary, which played a significant role in organising and shaping people's understanding of the world. The spatial imaginary is a term used to describe the way in which people imagine and perceive space

---

[174] Natsionalna Biblioteka "Sv. Sv. Kiril i Metodii": http://nationallibrary.bg/wp/?page_id=1337 accessed 11/11/2019.

[175] Maurus Reinkowski, "Double Struggle, No Income: Ottoman Borderlands in Northern Albania," *International Journal of Turkish Studies* 9/1 (2003): 239–253, here p. 241; James Anderson and Liam O'Dowd, "Borders, Border Regions and Territoriality: Contradictory Meanings, Changing Significance," *Regional Studies* 33 (1999): 594. On the center–periphery paradigm see Şerif Mardin, "Center–Periphery Relations: A Key to Turkish Politics?," *Daedalus* 102/1 (1973): 169–190; Şerif Mardin, "Turkish Islamic Exceptionalism Yesterday and Today: Continuity, Rupture and Reconstruction in Operational Codes," *Turkish Studies* 6/2 (2005): 145–165. Metin Heper, "Center and Periphery in the Ottoman Empire: With Special Reference to the Nineteenth Century," *International Political Science Review* 1/1 (1980); See also: Kemal H. Karpat, "Comments on Contributions and the Borderlands," in *Ottoman Borderlands: Issues, Personalities and Political Changes*, eds. Kemal H. Karpat and Robert W. Zens (Madison: The University of Wisconsin, 2003), pp. 1–14.

[176] Anssi Paasi, "Constructing Territories, Boundaries and Regional Identities," in *Contested Territory: Border Disputes at the Edge of the Former Soviet Empire*, ed. Tuomas Forsberg (Aldershot: Edward Elgar, 1995), p. 43.

[177] Ibid., p. 43.

and specific geographic region or their notion of nation–state. The formation of nation–states and nation–building during the "Age of Empire"[178] marked a crucial period in the development of socio–spatial consciousness, characterised by a strong emphasis on meta–geography and a spatial imaginary. The example of Balkan nationalists in the 1990s illustrates how socio–spatial consciousness can influence political ideologies and actions and thus, produce violence and imagine national borders much wider. These nationalists interpreted boundaries beyond their nation–state borders, reflecting a belief in the importance of a broader geographic region beyond their immediate territory. This era is particularly marked by meta–geography and a spatial imaginary that played a powerful role in organising and shaping understandings of the world, and by extension, influenced actions.[179] According to Peter Haslinger's analysis, in the same way that the collective history and tradition has to be 'imagined' or 'invented,' space too undergoes a similar process in the form of 'invented territory' or 'imagined territory.'[180] Therefore, claims to a imagined territory are very important for the propagation of nationhood as imagined community. What is more, national–territorial arguments can make each side shy away from compromise and perceive any compromise over territory as a defeat. This applies to the Macedonian case, where every party claimed that it had a historical mission in Ottoman Macedonia. Liberating these provinces from the Ottoman yoke was the objective pursued by different protagonists – Greece, Bulgaria, Serbia, Romania.[181] However, many works about Macedonia fail to report on the Montenegrin mission towards these territories. Therefore, in this thesis I will present and interpret the additional issue of Prince Nikola's attempts to conquer parts of the territory of the three vilayets. An important remark at this point is that the borders of present–day Northern Macedonia should not be

---

[178] Hobsbawm, *The Invention.*

[179] Andreas Faludi, "Multi–level (territorial) governance: Three criticisms," *Planning Theory and Practice* 13 (2012): 197–211, here in 204.

[180] Peter Haslinger, *Nation und Territorium im tschechischen politischen Diskurs 1880–1938* (Munich: Oldenbourg, 2010), p. 30; In this vein, Pierre Nora's concept of *lieux de mémoire* (memory places) can be comprehended as an attempt to disclose the way in which imagined territorial space is filled with identity sites that reinforce its claims to be a historically legitimate national and political entity.

[181] Lange–Akhund, *The Macedonian Question*, p. 7.

mixed with those of the territories of *vilayet–i selase*, which were broader and encompassed parts of present–day Serbian, Bulgarian, Greek, Albanian, and Montenegrin territories too. After the Congress of Berlin (1878), Macedonia was divided into three vilayets (administrative districts): Salonica, Manastir, and Kosovo, headed by a governor (*vali*) who was appointed by the sultan. For each of the Balkan states, Macedonia occupied a special place in their concept of boundaries, background, and affiliation of its population. Consequently, after 1890, Macedonia became the playground of several nationalist movements: Serbian, Greek, Bulgarian, Albanian, Turkish etc. Each party involved in the conflict surrounding Macedonia and the Macedonians incorporated them into their own regional and local identity narratives. These narratives encompassed a wide range of elements, including ideas about nature, landscape, cultural heritage, ethnicity, dialects, economic success or recession, relationships between periphery and center, marginalisation, stereotyped images of both the people and the community, historical accounts that may have been invented or distorted, as well as divergent arguments regarding the identification of the people.[182] These elements are used contextually in practices, rituals, and discourses to construct narratives of more or less closed, imagined communities and territories. This social construction of territories and regions means that boundaries are shaped by the collective perception of identities and meanings.[183] Because the territories/regions are constructed, their names and meanings in the historical context are different. It means that the meaning of the term 'Macedonia' was not the same in the past as it is today, and that it was frequently modified. In line with the latter, Arabian geographer Muhamed Al–Idrisi termed the Balkans of today as the "Macedonian mountains" (*gebel al–Maqedoni*)[184] including even the Danube region west of Belgrade. Many lands of the Balkan Peninsula were called "Macedonia, such as Stara Srbija, Zeta,

---

[182] Anssi Paasi, "Region and Place: Regional Identity in Question," *Progress in Human Geography* 27/4 (2003): 478.

[183] Raimo Vayrynen, "Regionalism: Old and New," *International Studies Review* 5 (2003): 37.

[184] Đoko Slijepčević, *The Macedonian Question: The Struggle for Southern Serbia* (Chicago: The American Institute for Balkan Affairs, 1958), p. 10.

Albania, and Bosnia and Herzegovina."[185] Moreover, Božidar Vuković Podgoričanin too used to say that he came from "the Diocletian lands, in Macedonia, from the town of Podgorica."[186] In the same way, in one of his letters to the Pope Urban VIII, bishop Mardarije from Montenegro introduced himself as:

> "Marderius, by the grace of God bishop of Macedonia, the fatherland of Alexander the Great, in the Montenegrin Monastery of Jovan Crnojević in Cetinje on the border with Kotor. (*Marderius, Dei gratia episcopus Macedoniae patriae Magni Alexandri, Montisnigri in Monasterio ducis Ioannis Cernovichii in campo Cetinae ad confinum Cathari*)."[187]

Similarly, on 28 January 1712 Montenegrin bishop Danilo Petrović (founder of dynasty Petrović–Njegoš) signed off his letter to the Russian Tsar Peter the Great with the words: "from Montenegro in Macedonia."[188] In addition, the famous Austro–Hungarian and Czech historian Konstantin Jireček (1854–1918) pointed out that "in the Middle Ages the whole of present–day Rumelia was often called Macedonia." [189] Following the Ottoman conquest of Macedonia it became part of Rumeli and was divided into sanjaks, which brought about major changes in the toponymy and demographics. This led to a complete disappearance of the use of the name 'Macedonia' in the Ottoman administration, but for the texts of authors

---

[185] Jovan Cvijić, *Osnove za geografiju i geologiju Makedonije i Stare Srbije knjiga I* (Beograd: Državna štamparija kraljevine Srbije, 1906), pp. 38–42.

[186] Ljubomir Stanojević, *Stari srpski zapisi i natpisi* 494 (1924): 161.

[187] Vuk Uskoković, "Identitet Crne Gore u prvoj polovini 18. vijeka," in *O Identitetu*, ed. Dragan Vukčević (Podgorica: CANU, 2015), p. 16.

[188] Stanojević, *Stari srpski*, p. 161; In the case of *Stara Srbija* see: Bogdan Trifunović, "Memory of Old Serbia and the Shaping of Serbian Identity," *Balcanica Posnaniensia: Acta et Studia* 24 (2015): 252; Miloš Jagodić, *Srbija i Stara Srbija (1839–1868): Nasleđe na jugu* (Beograd: Evoluta, 2016); and Srđan Atanasovski, *Mapiranje Stare Srbije: Stopama putopisaca, tragom narodne pesme* (Beograd: Biblioteka XX vek, 2017).

[189] Konstantin Jireček, *Geschichte der Bulgaren* (Prague: N.P., 1876), p. 157; Roumen Daskalov, *Bulgarian Historical Review: Special Issue on Bulgaria in the Twentieth Century* (Sofia: Bulgarian Academy of Sciences Press, 2005); Tsvetlin Stepanov, *The Bulgars and the Steppe Empire in the Early Middle Ages: The Problem of the Origin of the Bulgars* (Leiden: Brill, 2010); Marshall Lee Miller, *Bulgaria During the Second World War* (Stanford: Stanford University Press, 1975).

such as Idris Bitlisi, Hoca Sadeddin, Aşık Mehmed, Evliya Çelebi etc,[190] where Macedonia was present and identified with the *Rumeli* (the Balkans) and Istanbul as ancient Macedonia. Since the beginning of 19th century Macedonia got not just geographical, but also a political meaning imagined variously by different actors. One description was given by Hugo Grothe (1869–1954), who states that "only three vilayets (Salonica, Bitola, Kosovo) may today be regarded as constituting Ottoman Macedonia."[191] According to Irena Stefoska, in the 19th century "the term Macedonia refers to geographical region of Macedonia in a supra–national sense (…) including the territory of today's Republic of Macedonia, territories in south–western Bulgaria, northern Greece and small portions of southern Serbia, southern Kosovo and south–eastern Albania."[192] In general, there was no accepted definition of Macedonia. In this regard, the issue of defining Macedonia is a complex one that lacks a universally accepted definition. In modern times, Macedonia has never formed a cohesive unit in terms of language, ethnicity or politics, and it is not even a clearly defined geographical term.[193] Therefore, to understand the concept of Macedonia, a multi–perspective approach is necessary, treating it as a part of broader Macedonian questions. It is important to recognise that there is not a single, monolithic Macedonian question, but rather a set of questions that depend on the point of view of the actor(s) involved. Each party involved in the question of Macedonia has its own interests, motivations, and agendas, which can lead to different interpretations of what Macedonia represents. As such, any discussion of Macedonia should take into account

---

[190] Dragi G'orgiev, "The Name Macedonia in the Ottoman Period (14th–19th Century)," in *Macedonia: Land, Region, Borderland,* ed. Jolanta Sujecka (Warsaw: University of Warsaw, 2013), pp. 109–111; Evliya Çelebi, *Günümüz Türkçesiyle Evliyâ Çelebi Seyahatnâmesi – 2. Cilt 1. Kitap* (Istanbul: YKY, 2008), p. 77. Quote here: *"Bu dünyaya dört İskender gelmiştir, Yunanlıların sözüne göre. Ama bu İzmit'te dünyaya gelen İskender ünlü büyük bir padişah olup İzmit'i öyle mamur edip sağlam bir kale yapmıştı ki Istanbul'a denk bir kale idi. Hâlâ yapılarının kalıntıları, burçları ve bedenleri açık seçik bellidir. Onun için İzmit'e Yunan tarihlerinde Makedonlu İskender derler. Temmuz ayında Istanbul karşısında İskender Çamlıca dağında yaylalanırdı. Hâlâ Üsküdar, İskenderî'den bozulmadır."*
[191] Hugo Grothe, *Auf turkisher Erde* (Berlin: N.P., 1903), p. 358.
[192] Irena Stefoska, "Fragments from the Medieval History of Macedonia," in *Macedonia: Land, Region, Borderland,* ed. Jolanta Sujecka (Warsaw: University of Warsaw, 2013), p. 69.
[193] Dakin, *The Greek*, p. 3.

the diverse perspectives and interests of the various actors involved. This approach can provide a more nuanced understanding of the issues at hand and can help to understand layers of state politics and networks on the ground. In the Greek state formulations of the socio–spatial consciousness inside the *Megali Idea* project, as Macedonia were considered the territories of the Manastir and Salonika Vilayet. Thus, viewed from a "Greek" lens, [194] the Macedonian Question has been nothing but the compulsory struggle for the spread of Hellenism. Textbooks from 1892 stated that "the whole ancient Macedonia, the homeland of the philosopher Aristotle, of Philip and of Alexander the Great, is and has stayed 100% Greek."[195] In this period the reinterpretation of Alexander of Macedonia changed too, as he became a symbol of the 'Macedonian province and Greek ethnicity' in order to maintain a continuity of the Greekness of the Macedonian territory. As for "Bulgarians,"[196] their main aspiration was to re–gain the territories lost as a result of the Treaty of San Stefano. According to these arguments, the imagined territories of Macedonia contain the areas of the mountains Shar and Skopska Crna Gora in the north, through the Skopje Sanjak to the Manastir and Salonika Vilayets in the southeast and south. Furthermore, in Bulgarian sources the term

---

[194] Here is rather meant Greek intellectuals and statesmen who defined Greek policies toward Ottoman territories. In order to avoid generalisations and essentialisations with the total Greek speaking population, I used quotation marks.

[195] Demetrius Kiminas, *The Ecumenical Patriarchate: A History of Its Metropolitanates with Annotated Hierarch Catalogs* (Cabin John: Wildside Press LLC., 2009); Olimpia Dragouni, "Macedonia in Greek Textbooks (19th–20th Century)," in *Macedonia: Land, Region, Borderland,* ed. Jolanta Sujecka (Warsaw: University of Warsaw, 2013), p. 420; Basil C. Gounaris, "Social cleavages and national 'awakening' in Ottoman Macedonia," *East European Quarterly* 29 (1995): 409–426; Basil C. Gounaris, "Preachers of God and martyrs of the Nation: The politics of murder in ottoman Macedonia in the early 20th century," *Balkanologie* 9/1–2 (2005); Basil C. Gounaris, "IX. National Claims, Conflicts and Developments in Macedonia, 1870–1912," in *The History of Macedonia* ed. Ioannis Koliopoulos (Thessaloniki: Museum of the Macedonian Struggle, 2007). pp. 183–213; Douglas Dakin. *The Greek*, p. 538; Dimitris Livanios, "'Conquering the souls': nationalism and Greek guerrilla warfare in Ottoman Macedonia, 1904–1908," *BMGS* 23 (1999): 195–221; Lora Gerd, *Russian Policy in the Orthodox East: The Patriarchate of Constantinople, 1878–1914* (Berlin: De Gruyter Open, 2014). p. 10.

[196] As in Greek case, by Bulgarians here is rather meant Bulgarian intellectuals and statesmen who defined Bulgarian policies toward Ottoman territories. In order to avoid generalisations and essentialisations with the total Bulgarian speaking population, I used quotation marks.

'Macedonia' sometimes refers to 'southwestern Bulgaria.'[197] An article published in the newspaper *"Yugozapadna Bŭlgaria"* (Southwestern Bulgaria) on 11 September 1893 highlights the significance of the region that was called Southwestern Bulgaria or Macedonia within the words: "we will fight for this land which is called South-Western Bulgaria or, as history knows it, under the name of Macedonia."[198] The (unknown) author of this text advocates for the restoration of this land, which was "separated from the free Principality after the Berlin Congress." The article illustrates how different historical and political contexts shape the understanding and usage of geographical terms. Similarly, "The Sun" newspaper on 16 June 1903 reports that "the Turks do not accept the mention of the name Macedonia in any form or manner in the translation of the New Testament of Bible." The report indicates that "the term vilayet of Salonika and Monastir" was preferred instead of "the ancient geographical term Macedonia, which appeared in the Epistle of Paul the Apostle to the Thessalonians."[199] The Ottoman Empire, as a ruling power, sought to control the narrative by regulating the usage of geographical terms in official documents, religious texts, and political speeches. Even a delegate from Thessaloniki, Hristo Delchev, was interrupted and warned to use the term *'vilayet–i selase'*[200] instead of Macedonia when he mentioned the name in Parliament in January 1909. These examples illustrate the complexity of naming and defining geographical regions, which is not only influenced by historical and cultural factors but also by political interests and power dynamics.

During the Serbian–Ottoman Wars (1876–1878), the invented territory of 'Old Serbia' was expanded almost across the entire territory of the Macedonian region. Even some years later, following the establishment of the St. Sava Society (1886), "Macedonia was an integral part of 'Old Serbia', (…) its Slavic inhabitants were Serbs, and (…) their dialect was a

---

[197] Quote: "The image of Macedonia and the categories rod–narod–natsia in literature from Macedonia in the 19th and first half of the 20th century," written by Jolanta Sujecka in *Macedonia: Land, Region, Borderland*, ed. Jolanta Sujecka (Warsaw: University of Warsaw, 2013), p. 138.

[198] Yugozapadna Bŭlgaria, No. 1, Sofia, 11. September,1893.

[199] Dragi Gjorgiev, *Makedonsko prašanjevo Osmanliski v parlament 1909* (Skopje: MANU, 2010), pp. 25–27.

[200] Ibid., p. 124.

southern dialect of Serbian."[201] The renowned Serbian geographer of the time, Jovan Cvijić, points out that "many of our writers consider the region of 'Old Serbia' to lie within King Milutin's country's borders, and some of them add Thessaly, Epirus, and Thrace to it; only Thessaloniki and its surroundings are considered to be truly Macedonia."[202] In later works Jovan Cvijić locates the borders between Old Serbia and Macedonia south of the towns of Prilep and Veleš.[203] At the beginning of the 20th century, its territorial definition also entailed the northern part of the Albanian region. However, one can notice that throughout the given historical time the term 'Old Serbia', whose territorial scope kept changing especially with regard to the south, had one territorial constant – the Kosovo area and Sanjak region,[204] which belonged to the Ottoman administrative unites of *vilayet–i selase*. According to Albanian historiographic works, two vilayets of *vilayet–i selse* (Kosovo and Manastir) were inhabited by a majority of Albanians who "had been living there during the whole of their history."[205] This meta–narrative appears in the work of an Ottoman–Albanian intellectual named Şemsettin Sami (Frashëri), who described the territories of Macedonia that since antiquity had been inhabited by the Pelasgians, ancestors of the Albanians.[206] According to him, "[T]his people [Albanians/Pelasgians] have resided in the Balkan Peninsula since earlier times than history has record of."[207] In the chapter about Macedonia in the encyclopaedia "*Kamus al–alam*," Şemsettin Sami (Frashëri) states further that "there is no doubt that the ancient Macedonians were originally

---

[201] Sujecka, *Macedonia*, p. 160.

[202] Jovan Cvijić, *Promatranja o etnografiji makedonskih Slovena* (Beograd: G. Kon, 1906), pp. 38–42; In the case of *Stara Srbija* see: Trifunović, "Memory of Old Serbia."; Jagodić, *Srbija i Stara Srbija*; and Atanasovski, *Mapiranje Stare Srbije*.

[203] Jovan Cvijić, *Govori i članci (drugo izdanje), Sabrana dela, knjiga 3* (Beograd: SANU, 1991), p. 153.

[204] Makedonka Mitrova, "The Kingdom of Serbia and Mursteg reforms in Ottoman Macedonia," in *Journal of History* 1 (2015/2016): 181–182.

[205] Stefanaq Pollo, Aleks Buda, Kristaq Prifti and Kristo Frashëri, *Historia e Shqipërisë (vitet 30 te shek. XIX–1912) vëllimi i dytë* (Tiranë: Akademia e shkencave e RPS te Shqipërisë – Instituti i Historisë, 1984), pp. 35–37.

[206] According to one version that Sami Frashëri represented, the name Pelasgian derives from the Albanian word "*plak*" (Turkish *ihtiyar* or *kadım*) that was given to the old people as Albanians. According to him they were widespread on all sides of the Balkan Peninsula and western parts of Anatolia.

[207] Sami Bey Frashëri, *Kamus al–alam I* (Istanbul: Mihran Matbaası, 1306 [1889]), p. 86.

Albanians (*eski Makedonyalıların sırf ve halis Arnavut bulunmuş olduklarında şüphe kalmaz*)."[208] These Albanian national intellectuals have seen the Macedonian Question often as an Albanian Question.[209] In similar way, Nuray Bozbora argues that "for the Albanians the Macedonian issue would continue to be the most dangerous threat."[210] Albanian nationalist intellectuals of the late Ottoman period aimed to establish an autonomous province for Albanians within the Ottoman Empire. For many of them, autonomy did not necessarily imply secession from the empire, but rather the preservation of their commitment to the Caliph Sultan.[211] However, while Abdulhamid II did not explicitly endorse the idea of an autonomous Albania submitted directly to the Sultan, his imperial policy was seen as indirectly responsible for the forging and formation of Albanian national identity.[212] One example of this indirect contribution can be seen in the introduction of *Kamus al-alam* (1889-1898) by Şemsettin Sami (Frashëri), who praised Abdulhamid II for allowing the Albanian people (*kavim*) to establish a school in the Albanian language. This initiative aimed to create an Albanian national literature (*edebiyat-i milliye*) in order to counter Greek and Slavic territorial claims to the regions, including Macedonia. [213] This demonstrates how Abdulhamid II's policies were aimed at creating a sense of national identity among the Albanian people in order to solidify Ottoman control over the Balkans. This can be seen in the formation of the League of İpek, where some members advocated for the unification of the four Ottoman vilayets with an Albanian-speaking majority (Janina, Kosova, Shkodra, and Manastir), while others aimed to include the vilayet of Selanik (Salonika) in this entity. The inclusion of the vilayet of Selanik in the proposed autonomous Albanian entity was seen by some as a means to establish a stronger and

---

[208] Ibid., p. 117.

[209] Sami Frashëri, *Shqipëria çka qenë, çështë e çdo të bëhet* (Tiranë: Mesonjëtorja e parë, 1999).

[210] Nuray Bozbora, "Failures and Achievements of Albanian Nationalism in the era of Nationalism," *Balkan Araştırma Enstitüsü Dergisi–Trakya Üniversitesi* 1 (2012), p. 5.

[211] Ibid., p. 14.

[212] Nathalie Clayer, The Young Turks and the Albanians or Young Turkism and Albanianism? in *Penser, agir et vivre dans l'Empireottoman et en Turquie,* eds. Nathalie Clayer and Erdal Kaynar (Paris: Collection Turcica, 2013), p. 71.

[213] Ibid., p. 72.

more direct connection with the Ottoman capital of Istanbul and the Sultan.[214]

The ideas of an "imagined territory" and an "imagined community" have been an implicit part of geography and history for a long time. Traditional approaches to territory, region, and ethno–nation often emphasise their primordial nature, highlighting their distinct "personality" and the unity and harmony between a region and its inhabitants.[215] In the case of Macedonia, both the region and the people have multiple imaginaries and even different names. In reality, there has never been a precise unified definition of what is meant by the terms "Macedonia" and "the Macedonian people."[216] The lack of a clear definition highlights the complex and multifaceted nature of the concepts, which can vary depending on the perspective of the individual or group in question. Therefore, it is important to approach the concepts of Macedonia and the Macedonian people with a nuanced and multi–perspective approach. Such an approach can help to uncover the various imaginaries that exist within the region and among its inhabitants, leading to a more comprehensive understanding of the issues at hand. This lack of clarity may stem from the fact that the situation on the ground was different from the above imaginations and representations. Did the locals have national awareness and socio–spatial consciousness of that time? Can we talk about monolithic national communities? How people at the local level understood their world priory to the Balkan Wars (1912/13)? How we understand the ambiguous matrix on the ground or its local level in the late Ottoman Macedonia? In this regard, Spiridon Gopcević noted that "there were people here [in Macedonia] who felt no enthusiasm for Serbia,

---

[214] Though it was well known that there was no significantly Albanian population living in the Salonika vilayet, the following tripartite conclusion can be drawn from here: (1) Albanian landlords wanted to incorporate Salonika because it occupied a large part of the land in this vilayet, (2) the Albanian religious group wanted to prevent potential annexation of this territory by the neighbouring states or Great Powers, as it was/provided for an important connection to Istanbul and the Caliph, and (3) Albanian national revivalists (*rilindasit shqiptar*) wanted to create a socio–spatial consciousness of Macedonia as a territory of Ottoman Albania and of old Macedonians as Albanians.

[215] Paasi, *Region and Place*, p. 476.

[216] Slijepčević, *The Macedonian*, p. 9.

Bulgaria or Greece."[217] Aligned with these were the statements of Krste Misirkov that all people in Macedonia share the same "fate" and "if we crossed the border of Macedonia (...) to Bulgaria, Greece or Serbia, we would immediately feel a different wind blowing: we would feel that we were uninvited guests and if they wanted to make it seem that we are brothers they would do so in order to rob and exploit us."[218] Therefore, it is very important to take into consideration the entire complexity of Macedonia (including the locals, too) in order to deconstruct the heavy emphasis on meta–narratives that attempted to champion uncritical acceptance of claims, such as that people living in such a vast geographic area shared more in common with unknown people living hundreds of miles away because they were categorically of the same 'ethnicity' than with neighbors who were often of a different faith and thus a different 'ethnic group.'[219] On the local level, being a 'Serb,' 'Greek,' 'Turk,' 'Montenegrin,' 'Macedonian,' 'Albanian,' or 'Bulgarian' had an entirely different meaning prior to the Balkan Wars, because "they had no firm ethno–national consciousness that superseded their immediate local needs," and thus, they rather "associated and collaborated with people who would today be considered their 'ancient enemies.'"[220] In this respect, the   events on the ground (upon the Balkan wars) were much more complexed and not driven by national affiliations as represented by national historiographies.[221] People on the local level gave often more

---

[217] Spiridon Gopčević, *Makedonija i Stara Srbija* (Beograd: Sazvežđe, 2016), First published in 1890, pp. 311.

[218] Krste P. Misirkov, "Za makedonskite raboti*,*" in *Krste P. Misirkov, Sobrani dela 1 – tekstovi na makedonski jazik (1900–1905)* eds. Blaže Ristovski and Biljana Ristovska – Josifovska (Skopje: MANU, 2005), p. 134. See also here about Macedonian Question (*Makedonskoto prašanje*).

[219] Blumi, *Reinstating the Ottomans*, p. 5.

[220] Ibid., p. 9.

[221] If we take into consideration Miroslav Hroch's chronological stages of nation–building processes of small nations, the following three phases can be identified:
Phase A) Groups in the ethnic community start to discuss their own ethnicity and conceive of it as a nation–to–be: scholarly enquiry into and dissemination of an awareness of the linguistic, cultural, social, and historical attributes of the nation–to–be; Phase B) A new range of activists try to "awaken" national consciousness and to persuade as many members as possible of the ethnic group: (1) development of a national culture based on the local language and its use in education, administration and economy, (2) civil rights and self–administration, (3) creation of a complete social structure – beginning of a

importance to tribe, family, neigbours or religion as presented by the British journalist Henry Noel Brailsford who wrote:

> "I questioned some boys from a remote mountain village near Ohrida which had neither teacher nor resident priest, and where not a single inhabitant was able to read, in order to discover what amount of traditional knowledge they possessed (...) I took them up to the ruins of the Bulgarian Tsar's fortress which dominates the lake and the plain from the summit of an abrupt and curiously rounded hill. 'Who built this place?' I asked them. The answer was significant – 'The Free Men.' 'And who were they?' 'Our grandfathers.' 'Yes, but were they Serbs or Bulgarians or Greeks or Turks?' 'They were not Turks, they were Christians.' And this seemed to be about the measure of their knowledge."[222]

Brailsford's detailed raport of local life in parts of the Manastir vilayeti, nevertheless, highlights how the situation on the ground contradicted the ambitions of local actors as forerunners of the nation (i.e. Serbs, Bulgarian, Greeks or Turks), the terms, associated today with concepts of modernity that were imposed by "Western" understandings. According to Isa Blumi, "the ethno–national subjects living under Ottoman rule" thus, should not be analyzed in "fixed, essentialist terms,"[223] because this situation in the administrative unity of Manastir vilayet was not exception, but rather a wide–spreaded phenomenon inside the "three vilayets." A similar illustration was presented in the work of Leon Sciaky who described Salonika and his childhood. In one of his statements, he describes the city as a place where people of diverse backgrounds and ethnicities lived in close proximity and portrayed his school years, friends and neighbours with the following words:

---

national movement; Phase C) A mass movement is formed which pursues these aims: a fully–fledged social structure of the would–be nation comes into being.
See: Miroslav Hroch, "From National Movement to the Fully–formed Nation: The Nation–Building Process in Europe," in *Mapping the Nation* ed. Gopal Balakrishnan (New York and London: Verso, 1996). pp. 78–97. See also the following publisher in *Becoming National* eds. Geoff Eley and Ronald Grigor Suny (Oxford: Oxford University Press, 1996), pp. 60–77.

[222] Mark Mazower, *Kratka povijest Balkana* (Zagreb: Srednja Europa, 2007), p. 59; Henry N. Brailsford, *Macedonia – Its Races and Their Future* (London: Methuen & Co.,1906), pp. 99–100.

[223] Ibid., p. 3.

"Le Petit Lycee Francais opened its doors early in the year 1904 (...) The lower group, in which I was placed, was made up of three French boys, one Greek, four Spanish Jews, a Serb, a Mamin, an Armenian, a Turk, and a Montenegrin boy who had come from Cetinje expressly to join us (...) Soon Mehmed, the Turkish boy, was volunteering explanations of the rites of Kurban Bairam, the holiday following Ramadan; Yovanovich, a relative of King Nicholas of Montenegro, spoke freely of his people and his mountains; and we found with Papopoulos that the Greeks had many customs in common with the Serbs, when Ivan, the son of the consul, told us of his home celebration of Easter. As we talked freely together and played together, as we made warm friendships, visited one another's homes, and shared our confidences, we came to know more intimately of those things about one another's ways which, viewed from the outside, might have appeared strange and meaningless."[224]

By using such sources, the aim of this work is to take into consideration these multiplicities entailed at the local level, in order to avoid the use of 'monolithic ethno–national identities' as a given, and rather to reflect the complexity of events on the ground. At that time and even today, some politicians, statesmen and intellectuals tried to implement various national narratives and worldviews according to the primodial ethnoreligious containers without reflecting that the imposed identification are ambiguous and problematic with the situation at the local level. Nevertheless, the dissertation does not aim to discard such works (and picture) of the locals that help to deconstruct the meta–narratives produced by the policies of the nation–state(s).

1.4. Structural Rationale
In this introduction, I have provided the theoretical approaches, together with methodological and historically interpretative discussions by placing them into a historical and socio–political context of Ottoman Macedonia. Furthermore, the chapters progress chronologically and thematically, in order to fit in a theoretical framework and contextualisation of events from the point of view of the actors that lived in that time and to avoid

---

[224] Leon Sciaky, *Farewell to Salonika – City at the Crossroads* (Sansom: Paul Dry Books, 2003), pp. 152–154.

anachronistic conclusions. I have structured the remaining chapters of the dissertation as follows:

• Chapter II presents the emergence of the Macedonian Question and contentious politics between the Great Powers, the Ottoman state, and Balkan elite. Here I chronologically trace the ways in which Macedonia became popularised among the Great Powers during the period of the Enlightenment and Romanticism and in which it was imagined by the European elite. By using British, French, and German sources, I show (thematically) that the Great Powers regarded this territory (along with Greece) as the the wellspring of "European civilisation" since ancient Hellenic times. For most Hellenophiles in Europe, these Ottoman territories were the "cradle of European civilisation." Thus, this dissertation begins with a careful analytical overview of relevant developments in Western Europe and their imaginations of Macedonia. This source of knowledge was circulating (*Wissenszirkulation*) among the Balkan elite too, who produced the narratives against the Ottomans, and labels such as "Turkish yoke" and "Asiatic Mongols" or "barbarians." By illuminating a spotlight on this 'top–down' approach, I argue that the European elite, together with Balkan intellectuals developed prejudice against the "Oriental other" Ottomans and imagined Macedonia into their future nation–state projects.

• Chapter III covers contentious projects of the Balkan states and Ottoman consolidation during the period from 1878 to 1903, that is, after the Congress of Berlin and up to the Ilinden Uprising. Here I demonstrate how the Ottoman state, especially the Hamidian regime tried to keep its remaining territories in Rumelia (Serbia, Montenegro, and Romania gained independence in 1878). In order to respond to the "small state imperialism" of the Balkan states and their nationalist projects in Ottoman Macedonia, I argue that the Ottoman state introduced a counter–colonialist strategy known as "borrowed colonialism." This strategy entailed a centralisation policy and was influenced by European ideas of the time, constructing narratives of the "civilised centre" (Istanbul) and a need to bring civilisation (*mission civilisatrice*) to the Ottoman peripheries. By using Ottoman and Albanian sources, I highlight that the Albanian element in three vilayets played a very important role during the rule of Sultan Abdulhamid II in keeping the three vilayets close to its centre – Istanbul.

From a different perspective, I show how the Serbian, Bulgarian, and Greek sides formulated policies in Macedonia, often by narrowing spiritual associations and reinforcing education by indoctrinating members of societies.

• Chapter IV studies the period between the Ilinden Uprising (1903) and the Young Turk Revolution (1908) and introduces various organisations and movements (that were active) on the ground (i.e. IMARO, Chetnik, Young Turks etc.), which cooperated with the local population or often originated from the local regions of Ottoman Macedonia. Here I introduce a 'bottom–up' perspective and argue that the situation on the ground was far more complex than represented by nationalist promoters and the state elite. By deploying various local examples from Bulgarian, Macedonian, Serbian, Ottoman Turkish, and Albanian sources, I argue that the organisations were not 'purely' national, but consisted of members with different religious and ethnical backgrounds. This argument largely aims to deconstruct meta–narratives and narratives of the superiority of "civilised Europe" that were produced by nation–states during the short 20th century.

• Chapter V delves into contentious practices of the local and state agents during the period from the Young Turk Revolution (1908) to the First Balkan War (1912). Here too I adopt a 'bottom–up' perspective and show how the locals were influential in changing the state strategies and projects. In this regard, I draw on the examples of Albanian– and Turkish–speaking locals (e.g. Ahmet Niyazi Bey, Enver Bey, Ohrili Eyüp Sabri) in the three vilayets and the importance of the Ferzovik meeting (Kosovo vilayet) in triggering the Young Turk Revolution. These events reflect the significance of the 'periphery' and its influence on 'centre' by changing the government in 1908 and dethroning Sultan Abdulhamid II in 1909. Here, I aim also to show that 'periphery' can be active and its peripheral populations were not bereft of agency. Apart from it, other uprisings of the local Albanian population in 1912 triggered the decisions of the Balkan states to declare war to the Ottoman state and opened up the room for implementing 'small state imperialism' in Macedonia.

The conclusion takes findings from all chapters into account and provides a diachronic perspective for discussing how each macro– and micro– process affected contentious practices and vice versa. This dissertation offers insights into the complex ways in which Macedonian societies were transformed from different regional viewpoints, focusing on the interplay between Great Power politics, Ottoman state reforms, Balkan state nationalist projects, and social dynamics on the ground. All of these developments were in correlation with each other, and it is therefore important to situate events in a broader Ottoman and transnational context. Moreover, my research demonstrates the conceptual bearings of this case study on debates in Ottoman Studies, Postcolonial Theory, History of Eastern Mediterranean and (South)Eastern Europe, Entangled History, and Social History.

Imagined Geographies and Imagined Communities:
The Great Powers' Intervention in Ottoman Rumelia

Since Edward Said's seminal study *Orientalism,*[1] scholars have been aware that the post–Ottoman space – the Balkans and the Near East as well – was referred to multiple meanings by politics, and that it was imagined variously dependent on the interests of a certain ideology. In this sense, Macedonia became contested terrain and a place to be imagined, invented, and variously constructed by the Great Powers and Balkan intellectuals. Next, it also became a space for several interventions by European states and Imperial Russia. In order to understand these processes of imagination and intervention, the present chapter analyses them through the lenses of geographical imagination[2] and the emergence of international law, which gave legitimacy to the Great Powers to interfere in Ottoman affairs and to formulate political programs according to their interests. The aim of this chapter is to scrutinise these various imaginations and policies, complex relations and interventions through the entanglements and circulation of knowledge between the Great Powers, the Ottoman Empire, and the Balkan population in the Macedonian context. In this sense, these relations will be exempflied through discursive, spatial, and political dimensions, by contextualising the Macedonian Question within a larger historical perspective. Inspired by the *Annales* School,[3] I analyse the situation in

---

[1] Edward W. Said, *Orientalism* (New York: Vintage Books, 1979).

[2] Ibid., p. 106; Gregory Derek, *The Colonial Present* (New Jersey: Blackwell, 2004); Mohnike Thomas, *Imaginierte Geographien* (Würzburg: Ergon–Verlag, 2007); Joanne P. Sharp, *Geographies of Postcolonialism* (London: Sage Publications, 2011); Ó' Tuathail Gearoid, *Critical Geopolitcs: The Writing of Global Space* (London: Routledge, 1996); For example, sociologist Wright Mills and geographer David Harvey developed the idea of the "sociological imagination" (1961) and "geographical imagination" (1973), relating these terms to the metaphorical ways in which people conceptualised spaces. Their analysis shows that imagination is the tool for reaching greater understanding of the 'self' as civilised/developed and the 'other' as uncivilised/undeveloped. Edward Said (1979) thus demonstrates how the Western society posits an imaginary "Orient" through travelogues, art, literature, and scholarly work in order to justify and advance its colonial ambitions and practices. These fundamental colonial ambitions brought about the image of superiority of the 'European Western–white–Christian–male.'

[3] Fernand Braudel, "History and the Social Sciences: The Longue Durée," in *On History*, ed. Fernand Braudel (Chicago: University of Chicago Press, 1980), pp. 25–54. Originally published as "Histoire et sciences sociales: La longue durée," *Annales ESC* 13/4 (1958): 725–753; Fernand Braudel, *The Mediterranean and the Mediterranean World in the Age of Phillip II, translated by Sian Reynolds* (Berkeley: University of California Press, 1995),

Macedonia through a middle–term approach (*moyenne duree*), encompassing the time framework between the late 18th century and the Congress of Berlin (1878). I argue that by analysing this long–term historical dynamic, one can better understand the changing processes within a larger transregional setting of South–Eastern Europe, and follow more with greater ease the mobility dynamics and circulation of knowledge (*Wissenszirkulation*)[4] between various actors such as the Great Powers, the Ottoman Empire, and the Balkan intellectuals. Thus, I first highlight the imaginaries and production of knowledge about Macedonia by European intellectuals and the Great Powers, and secondly, I analyse the circulation of this knowledge and the entanglements of imaginaries about Macedonia, especially among the Balkan intellectuals and the Ottoman Empire. In this regard, the analysis will follow: European political interventions in Ottoman Rumelia and their imagination of a geographical region of "Turkey in Europe" including Macedonia of that time, which had been a virtual *terra incognita* for many Europeans; historical changes of the Balkan's intellectuals that accepted "colonisation

---

pp. 1–20. Originally published as *La Méditerranée et le monde méditerranéen à l'époque de Philippe II* (Paris: Armand Colin, 1949); Siniša Malešević, "Empires and Nation–States: Beyond the Dichotomy," *Thesis Eleven* 139/1 (2017): 3–10; Siniša Malešević, "The Foundations of Statehood: Empires and Nation–States in the Longue Durée." *Thesis Eleven* 139/1 (2017):145–161, here in 152.

[4] See, for example Stefan Rohdewald et al. "Wissenszirkulation: Perspektiven und Forschungsstand," pp. 87–89; Ulrich Johannes Schneider, "'Wissensgeschichte, nicht Wissenschafsgeschichte'," in *Michel Foucault: Zwischenbilanz einer Rezeption* eds. Axel Honneth and Martin Saar (Frankfurt am Main: Suhrkamp, 2003); Jakob Vogel, "Von der Wissenschafts– zur Wissensgeschichte: Für eine Historisierung der 'Wissensgesellschaf'," *Geschichte und Gesellschaft* 30 (2004); Philipp Sarasin, "Was ist Wissensgeschichte?," *Internationales Archiv für Sozialgeschichte der deutschen Literatur* 36 (2011); Daniel Speich Chassé and David Gugerli, "Wissensgeschichte: Eine Standortbestimmung," *Zeitschrif für Geschichte* 1 (2012); Jürgen Renn, "From the History of Science to the History of Knowledge and Back," *International Journal of the History of Science & Its Cultural Aspects* 57 (2015); Pierre Bourdieu, "Les conditions sociales de la circulation internationaldes idées," *Actes de la recherche en sciences sociales* 145/1 (2002); Johanna Sumiala, "Circulation," in *Keywords in Religion, Media, and Culture* ed. David Morgan (London: Routledge, 2008), pp. 44–55; Wiebke Keim, "Conceptualizing Circulation of Knowledge in the Social Sciences," in *Global Knowledge in the Social Sciences: Made in Circulation* eds. Wiebke Keim, Ercüment Çelik, Christian Ersche and Veronika Wöhrer (Farnham: Ashgate, 2014), pp. 87–113; Katja Valaskivi and Johanna Sumiala, "Circulating Social Imaginaries: Theoretical and Methodological Reflections," *European Journal of Cultural Studies* 17/3 (2014): 229–43.

of the mind," discourses of Orientalism, interventions, building of nation–states, and imperial projects; and Ottoman imperial enforcement toward its peripheries defined also as "borrowed colonialism" or "colonisation of the countryside". In fact, these politics and imaginaries are closely connected with what has been termed "the discovery of the future." In his famous work *Die "Entdeckung der Zukunft*,"[5] Lucian Hölscher, researched "the historical visions of the future" (*Zukunftvorstellungen*) in the European modern period during the late 18th and beginning of 19th century. According to Hölscher, the crucial driving force for the change from premodern to modern visions of the future was the progressive historicisation of the world through modern historical science that led to imperialism. Due to this development, the change of the world was no longer considered to be the result of Christian determination and eschatological expectation, but a consequence of historical events that for their parts were now increasingly interpreted as "progress."[6] However, even after the implementation of the modern concept of the future, older ideas about the past still continued to exist. Following Peter Burke, "many historians referred to the rationality of the modern period and the ability of many people in this period to anticipate and plan future developments long–term."[7] In fact, this "long–term planning," also known as "the vision of the future," was often glorified on behalf of "progress" be use of elements of the ancient past, especially through the imagination of the Greek, Hellen (Macedonian), and Roman heritage. In this regard, the Bloch's notion of *die Ungleichzeitigkeit des Gleichzeitigen*[8] can be applied to provide an explanation for ethnic and territorial imagination, state–

---

[5] Lucian Hölscher, *Die Entdeckung der Zukunft* (Göttingen: Wallstein Verlag, 1999).
[6] Ibid.
[7] Peter Burke, *History and Social Theory* (New York: Cornell University Press, 2005).
[8] Ernest Bloch coined the term "the non–contemporary of the contemporary" (*die Ungleichzeitigkeit des Gleichzeitigen*) as a way of understanding the complexity of historical time. Bloch argues that different social, economic, and cultural phenomena can coexist in the same historical moment, but they may have different historical trajectories and levels of development. This non–synchronicity creates tensions and contradictions within society, which can lead to social change and transformation. See: Ernst Bloch, *Das Prinzip Hoffnung* (Frankfurt am Main: Suhrkamp Verlag, 1959); Falko Schmieder, "Gleichzeitigkeit des Ungleichzeitigen: Zur Kritik und Aktualität einer Denkfigur," *Zeitschrift für kritische Sozialtheorie und Philosophie* 4/1–2 (2017): 325–363, here in 334.

building, and nation–building processes constructed in the contemporary as "the vision of the future" with non–contemporary elements of the past. More specifically, the modern colonial empires, their rulers and elite were revealed as imagining "contemporary" Europe as a continuity of the "non–contemporary" ancient Greek civilisation. These ideas were disseminated during the period of the Enlightenment and the French Revolution, transforming all spheres of European life: from intellectual to social, industrial, and technological. These historical events have been analysed by the German historian Reinhart Koselleck as the emergence of a new reality aimed to assimilate the previous understanding of the present as a "space of experience" (*Erfahrungsraum*), and to create a new understanding of modern historical consciousness as a "horizon of expectation" (*Erwartungshorizont*).[9] By using elements of the past (i.e. of the Greek civilisation), the latter focused on "the vision of the future," on upcoming or expected events. This relocation happened with the promise of modernity for infinite human improvement, progress, freedom, civilisation, mission, etc. To bring these ideas to fruition, each present era was once based on an imagined future and a belief of a better tomorrow. Since that time, "the infinite geographical surface of our globe shrunk into a finite and interdependent space of action."[10] The acceleration of this kind of understandings was associated with the possibility of humanity to make history, to create change with the power of imagination. These imaginations are aimed to construct geographic, political, or cultural borders defined by maps in order to enforce their control over territories. The construction/invention of territories and the employment of territorial strategies are bound together to maintain and to impose the power of a dominant group.[11] These "imagined geographies" are charted in maps in order to serve the power which creates its own field of exercise through knowledge. According to Koselleck, these imaginations conjoined questions that emerged squarely in the period 1750–1850. He regarded it

---

[9] Reinhart Koselleck, *Vergangene Zukunft: Zur Semantik geschichtlicher Zeiten* (Frankfurt am Main: Suhrkamp Verlag, 1979), in English see: Reinhart Koselleck, *Futures Past: On the Semantics of Historical Time* (New York: Columbia University Press, 2004).

[10] Ibid. p. 56.

[11] David Storey, *Territories: The Claiming of Space* (London: Routledge, 2012).

as a "saddle–period" (*Sattelzeit*), or period of transition, wherein concepts emerged that were abstract as well as future oriented. This future was often constructed according to the maps that had the aim to involve a practice of violating others' frontiers. In the Macedonian context it included a "humanitarian intervention" of the Great Powers against the Ottoman Empire. From the perspective of the history of Ottoman Macedonia, which was very important for the Great Powers at that time, the following questions arise: when and under what circumstances did happen a transition from eschatological expectation to the modern (more secular) vision of the future in Western Europe and Ottoman Macedonia? What were their driving forces during this change? Why was Macedonia important for the Great Powers and European elite? How was it imagined by them? Why did the Great Powers interfere in Ottoman affairs and initiate interventions in Ottoman Rumelia (defined also as "Turkey in Europe")? What was the relation between the Great Powers and Balkan intellectuals regarding the imagination of Macedonia? How did the circulation of knowledge take place[12] between these actors? Can one find entanglements between Western Europe and South–Eastern Europe, specifically, and between the Great Powers' statesmen and elite, the Balkan intellectuals or Ottoman modernists?

---

[12] Circulation has become a popular term among historians of postcolonial studies, such as Claude Markovits, Jacques Pouchepadass, and Sanjay Subrahmanyam. Jacques Pouchepadass and Sanjay Subrahmanyam emphasised that "Circulation is different from simple mobility, inasmuch as it implies a double movement of going back and forth and coming back, which can be repeated indefinitely. In circulating, things, men and notions often transform themselves. Circulation is therefore a value–loaded term which implies an incremental aspect and not the simple reproduction across space of already formed structures and notions." See in: Claude Markovits, Jacques Pouchepadass and Sanjay Subrahmanyam (eds.), *Society and Circulation: Mobile People and Itinerant Cultures in South Asia, 1750–1950* (London: Anthem, 2006), pp. 2–3; On this topic see also: Arjun Appadurai, *Modernity at Large: Cultural Dimensions of Globalization* (Minneapolis: University of Minnesota Press, 1996), p. 22; Walter D. Mignolo, *Local Histories/Global Designs: Coloniality, Subaltern Knowledges, and Border Thinking* (Princeton, NJ: Princeton University Press, 2012), p. 56; Carolyn Steedman, *Dust: The Archive and Cultural History* (New Brunswick, NJ: Rutgers University Press, 2001), p. 87; Anna Lowenhaupt Tsing, *Friction: An Ethnography of Global Connection* (Princeton, NJ: Princeton University Press, 2005), p. 104; Steven Vertovec and Robin Cohen (eds.), *Conceiving Cosmopolitanism: Theory, Context, and Practice* (Oxford: Oxford University Press, 2002), p. 12.

2.1. Imagination and Intervention

The study of imagination and "the vision of the future" may seem an exotic pursuit, but there is a vast literature devoted to this topic, which includes various studies of images of the Orient in Edward Said's context of "Orientalism," Larry Wolff's famous *Inventing Eastern Europe*,[13] Vesna Goldsworthy's masterpiece, *Inventing Ruritania*,[14] and Maria Todorova's *Imagining the Balkans*.[15] All of them are concerned with European views of the region that emerged during the period of the Enlightenment. The philosophy of the Enlightenment presented emancipation from the medieval worldview and move towards the victorious modernity and imagination, which changed the perception of geography, space, regions, territories and people.[16] This epoch forged spatial imagination among the European elite that contributed to the development of geography as a scientific discipline. At the same time, geography became a discipline that stimulated "dreams and fantasies, poetry and painting, philosophy, fiction, and music."[17] This geographic knowledge was not developed in a vacuum, but rather circulated around and influenced the Ottoman space, especially parts that later became known as Macedonia. One should not only

---

[13] Larry Wolff, *Inventing Eastern Europe: The Map of Civilization n the Mind of the Enlightenment* (Redwood City: Stanford University Press, 1996).

[14] Vesna Goldsworthy, *Inventing Ruritania: The Imperialism of the Imagination* (New Haven: Yale University Press, 1998).

[15] Maria Todorova, *Imagining the Balkans* (Oxford: Oxford University Press, 1997).

[16] The years between 1790 and 1830 announced the "arrival of a whole new age, a new world of social and individual traumas and possibilities (…) within the historical map of modern imperialism and modern capitalism." The upcoming Romanticism was not merely a response to this transformation brought about by the Enlightenment. More precisely, these two movements overlapped in the sense that "the idea of the imagination forms a hinge connection of the Enlightenment and Romanticism" and "it becomes the resolving and unifying force of all antithesis and contradictions (between Enlightenment and Romanticism)." Imagination changed numerous areas of thoughts and generated other ideas that were developed in the Enlightenment and triumphed in Romanticism. See in: Saree Makdisi, *Romantic Imperialism: Universal Empire and the Culture of Modernity* (Cambridge: Cambridge University Press, 1998), p. xi; James Engell, *The Creative Imagination: Enlightenment to Romanticism* (Cambridge: Harvard University Press, 1981), p. 6.

[17] Simon Schama, *Landscape and Memory* (New York: Vintage 1995), p. 30; Edward Said, "Invention, Memory, and Place," *Critical Inquiry* 26/2 (2000): 181; For philosophy would be Heidegger's *Holzwege*, about fiction one should think of Walter Scott's Highland novels, and music is present in Sibelius's Finlandia or Copland's Appalachian Spring.

understand this construction of Macedonia and the Orient as a geographical space and ethnographical description, but rather as a political one, based "on the mapping, conquest, and annexation of territory."[18] İpek Yosmaoğlu points out that this rather subtle discourse in the form of a political program was used explicitly to "chase the Turks out of Europe once and for all."[19] Furthermore, she stressed that "inextricable link between geographical knowledge and imperial ambition became even more pronounced in the 19th century as European colonial projects not only charted and measured their overseas acquisitions but also created and named entire regions according to their interests." Thus, it is useful to take into consideration the political programs of the Great Powers, Balkan intellectuals, and the Ottoman Empire regarding Macedonia, which became a battleground of spatial and geographical imaginations for all parties involved and as a result intersecting it on different levels (international, regional, local).

Aforementioned excerpt is an early reminder of a specific rhetoric among the European elite that helped develop geography as a discipline, as well as of the political programs based on a "Western civilisation" that found its source in Greek philosophy and Hellen culture during the period of Enlightenment and Romanticism. Maria Todorova also noticed that an interest in classical antiquity, discovery, and imagination of "the ancient world through the lives of the contemporary inhabitants" emerged during this era, which generated "an awareness of the present Greeks and their problems,"[20] which soon extended to "the Slavs and other ethnic groups inhabiting the peninsula who became the live figures of what came

---

[18] Said, "Invention, Memory," p. 181; Hans–Dietrich Schultz, "'Natürliche Grenzen' als politisches Programm," in *Grenzenlose Gesellschaft?*, ed. Claudia Honegger, Stefan Hradil and Franz Traxler (Oplande: Leske + Budrich, 1999), pp. 328–343; Tara Zahra, "Looking East: East Central European 'Borderlands' in German History and Historiography," *History Compass* 3/1 (2005): 1–23.

[19] Yosmaoğlu, *Blood Ties*.

[20] Todorova, *Imagining,* p. 62; Eric J. Hobsbawm, "Introduction: Inventing Traditions," in *The Invention of Tradition*, eds. Eric J. Hobsbawm and Terence Ranger (Cambridge: Cambridge University Press, 1992), pp. 1–14. See also: Eric J. Hobsbawm, "Mass–Producing Traditions: Europe, 1870–1914," in *The Invention of Tradition*, eds. Eric J. Hobsbawm and Terence Ranger (Cambridge: Cambridge University Press, 2012), pp. 263–307.

increasingly to be seen as the Volksmuseum of Europe."[21] Moreover, the centrality of the classic world during the Enlightenment produced a Greco-–Roman lineage that "not only branded the peoples that fell outside the confines of that intellectual heritage as inferior but also created a foil for the submission of the same peoples to European colonial power."[22] Additionally, during the early 19th century, in the period of the Enlightenment and Romanticism, a colourful and motley Orient that imagined "the Greeks a little too magnificent and the Turks a little too Tatar" was invented.[23] These ideas of a uniform superior world divided between the Occident and the Orient, Europe and the Ottoman Empire, encouraged the European elite to construct a discourse based on the notions of "civilised" versus "barbarian" worlds. In the fulfilment of this objective, they constructed geographical spaces of ancient Greece and Macedonia as a "cradle of the European civilisation" and accordingly, no place for the "Turks," who did not belong to Europe. In order to "chase the Turks out of Europe once and for all," one part of the European "enlightened" elite produced the knowledge about Macedonia and Orient by using the power of imagination. Thus, they contributed to the development of geography as a discipline, drew maps and cartographies, and politically called upon an intervention in Ottoman Macedonia in order to restore the "cradle of the European civilisation."[24]

---

[21] Yosmaoğlu, *Blood Ties*, pp. 62–63; Marc Schalenberg, *Kulturtransfer im 19. Jahrhundert* (Berlin: Centre Marc Bloch, 1998); Steffen Bruendel, "Negativer Kulturtransfer. Die 'Ideen von 1914' als Aufhebung der 'Ideen von 1789'," in *Kulturtransfer im 19. Jahrhundert*, ed. Marc Schalenberg (Berlin: Centre Marc Bloch, 1998), pp. 153–169; Marc Schalenberg, "Einleitung: Historische Fluchtlinien von Kultur," in *Kulturtransfer im 19. Jahrhundert*, ed. Marc Schalenberg (Berlin: Centre Marc Bloch, 1998), pp. 12–15.

[22] Yosmaoğlu, *Blood Ties,* p. 87; Vedran Duančić, *Geography and Nationalist Visions of Interwar Yugoslavia* (London: Palgrave Macmillan, 2020).

[23] Gaston Deschamps, *La Grece d'aujourd'hui* (Paris: N.P., 1901): first published 1892, p. 390; Eleni Bastea, "Nineteenth–century travellers in Greek lands: politics, prejudice and poetry in Arcadia," *Dialogos – Hellenic Studies Review* 41/ 2 (2014): 23–36, here in 26–28.

[24] Alexis Heraclides, *The Macedonian Question and the Macedonians: A History* (London: Routledge Histories of Central and Eastern Europe, 2021), p. 216.

2.2. Great Powers' Intervention(s) in Ottoman Greece

In recent decades historians of international law have started to research the imperial context of their discipline and studied how international law was fashioned in such a way as to serve the interests of the Great Powers. According to James Tully, "European constitutional states, as state empires, developed within a global system of imperial and colonial law from the beginning."[25] The global 18th and 19th centuries presented the colonial domination in the form of a "global liberal constitutional moment."[26] In the view of Achille Mbembe, "in modern philosophical thought and European political practice and imaginary, the colony represents the site where sovereignty consists fundamentally in the exercise of a power outside the law."[27] The Great Powers undoubtedly served as a vehicle for the imposition of "liberal" ideas in order to project colonial domination. Years later Slavoj Žižek defined Western policy as a form of "cultural imperialism." Žižek and postcolonial theorists see human rights and European law issues as feeble excuses for imperialist intervention.[28] Furthermore, Gustavo Gozzi emphasises that the European powers constructed the conceptual paradigm of the 19th century, revealing the character of hegemonic technique that hides partisan interests in the form of universal concepts, such as 'humanity' (*umanita*), 'human rights' (*diritti umani*), and 'responsibility to protect' (*responsabilità di proteggere*).[29] These developments appeared in Hugo Grotius's work *De Jure Belli ac Pacis*, making the argument that legitimised the Western colonial expansion program (*legittimavano l'espansione coloniale occidentale*) through the denied/negated rights (*ius denegatum*) of 'others' who were not Europeans. Hugo Grotius's concept of denied/negated right was in opposition to the right of a humanitarian society (*ius humane*

---

[25] James Tully, *Public Philosophy in a New Key: Imperialism and Civic Freedom* (Cambridge: Cambridge University Press, 2008), p. 200.

[26] Christopher Alan Bayly, "Rammohan Roy and the Advent of Constitutional Liberalism in India, 1800–30," *Modern Intellectual History* 4 (2007): 25–41; Nasser Hussain, *The Jurisprudence of Emergency: Colonialism and the Rule of Law* (Ann Arbor: University of Michigan Press, 2003).

[27] Achille Mbembe, "'Necropolitics'," *Public Culture* 15/1 (2003): 23.

[28] Ian Almond, "Anti Capitalist Objections to the Postcolonial on Žižek and History," *Ariel: A Review of International English Literature* 43/1 (2012): p. 4.

[29] Gustavo Gozzi, *Umano, non Umano: Interventoumanitario, Colonialismo, 'Primavera arabe'* (Bologna: Il Mulino, 2015).

societatis) to be involved in the affairs of another state.[30] In this respect, the Westphalian order was nothing else than an "imperial system of hegemonic and subaltern states."[31] The Ottoman Empire was part of the subaltern states, situated outside the European civilisation, whereby it became a topic for cartographic, geographic, and spatial research. On the other hand, Paschalis Kitromilides argues that a superior European civilisation was constructed in order to grant legitimacy to interventions.[32] The idea of grant legitimacy also represents one of John Stuart Mill's arguments in the essay "A Few Words on Non–Intervention" (1859) to justify the intervention and imperialism towards the barbarian people of Algeria and India, declaring that "a civilised government cannot help having barbarous neighbours" and that "the intervention recommended would really give them freedom."[33] Possibly, the first historical example of such an intervention in the internal affairs of another state/country on the grounds of humanitarian concern, took place during the Greek War of Independence in the early 19th century, when Great Powers such as Imperial Russia, Great Britain and France intervened in Navarino (1827) to secure independence from the Ottoman Empire on behalf of the Greeks.[34] The legitimating action of this humanitarian intervention was manifestly justified through 'international' law that ensured the rights of civilised people, like Christians and Westerns (*il diritto dei popoli civili, cristiani, occidental*), to intervene. Especially at the beginning of the 19th century these "humanitarian practices" were associated with religious and political programs. David Rodogno's initial assumptions are that the coercive interventions "on grounds of humanity" took place on behalf of

---

[30] Gustavo Gozzi, *Diritti e Civilta: Storia e filosofia del diritto internazionale* (Bologna: Il Mulino, 2010), p. 2.

[31] Tully, *Public Philosophy*, p. 140.

[32] Paschalis M. Kitromilides, *Enlightenment and Revolution* (Cambridge: Harvard University Press, 2013), p. 16; In his words "for the first time in the history of European civilization, a sharply self–conscious and committed intellectuals, with an intense awareness of its social and intellectual role, developed across cultures and state boundaries acting as the evangelists of a cosmopolitan outlook of shared human values."

[33] John S. Mill, "A Few Words On Non–Intervention, Foreign Policy Perspectives," *Fraser's Magazine 25* (August 1836): 214–221. This essay is also included in Mill's collected works, which were published as "Essays on Politics and Society" in *Collected Works of John Stuart Mill, Volume XVIII* (Toronto: University of Toronto Press, 1977).

[34] Gozzi, *Diritti e Civilta.*

Ottoman Christian populations.[35] Europeans intervened militarily when the "barbarous" Ottomans used the same "savage" methods to repress insurrections of the Christians that the Europeans were systematically using in their own colonies. These humanitarian interventions undertaken by European governments can be considered "on the same basic assumptions of imperialism."[36] In Gustavo Gozzi's views, in the second half of 19th century, the Western powers tried to form an international law as the expression of a "global society" (*società globale*), in order to force the Ottoman Empire, China, and Japan to accept the regional legal system, that was implemented in Europe. The established system of Western domination and superiority has been in place ever since.[37] According to David Rodogno, "it was the presumption of superiority of the European civilisation that, throughout the 19th century, shaped interventions against massacre in the Ottoman Empire" where the "theories of progress became more triumphalist, less tolerant of cultural differences and more specifically national."[38] Therefore, I argue that, as the beliefs of superiority and progress as the promises of modernity emerged from the new understanding of the 'horizon of expectation,' they also evoked a "civilisational confidence" that was manifested in the form of intervention – to liberate Ottoman Christians and give them freedom – and civilising mission – to expel the savage Ottomans from the cradle of European civilisation situated in Greece, Macedonia, Epirus, and Illyria. It is not a coincidence that during the Enlightenment period the understanding that ancient Greece was source of "Western Civilisation" was established, and to the contrary, the "Ottoman civilisation was fatalistic and stagnant, voiceless, feminine, irrational, despotic, backward, and lacking in European moral character or a fully developed concept of the state."[39]

---

[35] Davide Rodogno, *Against Massacre: Humanitarian Interventions in the Ottoman Empire* (Princeton: Princeton University Press, 2011), p. 15.

[36] Ibid, p. 17.

[37] Gozzi, *Diritti e Civilta,* pp. 33–36.

[38] Rodogno, *Against Massacre,* p. 12.

[39] Ibid., p. 37; M. Christian Ortner, "Erfahrungen einer westeuropäischen Armee auf dem Balkan: Die militärische Durchsetzung österreichisch–ungarischer Interessen während der Interventionen von 1869, 1878 und 1881/82," in *Am Rande Europas? Der Balkan–Raum und Bevölkerung als Wirkungsfelder militärischer Gewalt*, eds. Bernhard Chiari and Gerhard P. Groß (Munich: R. Oldenbourg Verlag, 2009), pp. 67–87.

Especially since the Congress of Vienna (1815), European political leaders' supported these discourses against the Ottoman Empire, and started to define them as the Eastern Question. In European history of diplomacy, the Eastern Question was related to the strategic competitions and interventions of the Great Powers in the Ottoman Empire. These interventions were developed according to the "universal values" that Europeans can interfere in the politics of "barbarous/barbarian" Ottomans. By interfering and intervening on behalf of the Christian population in the Ottoman Empire, the enlightened European intellectuals started to also imagine this area as a source of the European civilisation or better–known at that time as the "cradle of Civilisation."

There were widespread calls among some Europeans to make an intervention into their cradle of Civilisation, in order to halt Ottoman atrocities. Some, such as the British poet Byron, volunteered to fight on the side of Greece. The imagination of ancient Greece as a cradle of European civilisation aroused an interest in Greece, but also in geography as a discipline, which became a curricular requirement for the educated classes.[40] Due to this engagement, the Greeks were the 'chosen ones' by

---

[40] Jeremy Black, *Maps and History* (New Haven: Yale University Press, 2000), p. 30; These processes of domination and imagination began by the late 18th and early 19th century, when there was a gradual shift of travellers', adventurers', and geographers' interests in imagination and exploration. In John Kirkland Wright's words, "what distinguishes the true geographer from the true chemist or the true dentist would seem to be the possession of an imagination." Daniel Gade concludes that "geography is curiosity about places," but according to John Wright "curiosity is a product of the imagination." Therefore, Immanuel Kant, in his work '*Antropology*' (1798) emphasised that "to start talking of the latest news from Turkey" we need to consider "the power of the imagination (*Einbildungskraft*)." The following thinkers: Johann Gottfried von Herder, Wolfgang Goethe, Johann Gottlieb Fichte, and Wilhelm von Humboldt advocated in a romantic spirit that human understanding (*Verstand*) is more than reason (*Vernunft*). On the one hand, the Enlightenment contributed to the construction of an imagined superior Europe flourishing in progress, cosmopolitanism, prosperity of reason (*Vernunft*), while on the other, the romantic sensibility helped to develop the new understanding/meaning (*Verstand*) of geography, regions and borders, defining them according to their/Europe's own interests represented through the power of the imagination (*Einbildungskraft*). See: John K. Wright, "Terrae Incognitae: The Place of Imagination," *Geography Annals of the Association of American Geographers* 37 (1947): 4–6; See also these discussions in: Daniel W. Gade, *Curiosity, Inquiry, and the Geographical Imagination* (New York: Peter Lang, 2011), p. 66; Ian Almond, *History of Islam in German Thought From Leibniz to Nietzsche* (London: Routledge Studies in Cultural History, 2009), p. 29.

Europeans, who as a result had a duty to help the Greeks through the interventions. The first intervention began on 6 March 1821, when a Russian general of Greek origin and the leader of the Society of Friends (*Filiki Eteria*), Alexander Ypsilantis, crossed the Pruth River and "invited the Christians in the Ottoman Empire to throw off the sultan's yoke."[41] In addition, he addressed a request to the Russian Tsar Alexander I to help Orthodox coreligionists in the fight against the Ottomans.

After Easter Sunday 1821, when the Sublime Porte publicly hanged Patriarch Gregory V, which symbolised the Ottoman suppression of Orthodox Christians, the Russian minister of foreign affairs (*minister inostrannih del*) Ioannis Kapodistrias of Greek origin, became increasingly active in support of Greek independence. However, he could not convince the Tsar to grant him the requested support, since Alexander I's project of Holy Alliance restricted ideas of liberalism and nationalism, in order to prevent the potential riots that could threaten its conservative monarchy regimes. Despite this obstacle, the religious affiliation, the cooperation between Russia and the Ottoman Greek leading elite in Moldova and Wallachia, the presence of Greek merchants in Odessa, Russian Empress Catharina's Greek project (1774) of conquest of Constantinople etc. strengthened the ties between Russia and the Greeks, which led to closer personal relations and creation of family ties through marriages among them. The British Foreign Secretary Castlereagh sympathised with the Greek cause too, but still regarded the Greeks in the same way as Russia, as insurrectionists against a political order that was associated with the Concert of Europe.[42] It seems that at the beginning the Greek War of Independence did not receive much support from the Great Powers. More precisely, solely philhellenes were directly involved in keeping the Greek Question alive in Europe. They were a diverse group consisting of travellers, adventurers, and a handful of policy–makers. In 1823 they established the London Philhellenic Committee, supported by John

---

[41] Miroslav Šedivy, *Metternich, the Great Powers and the Eastern Question* (Pilsen, University of West Bohemia, 2013), p. 59; David Brewer, *The Greek War of Independence: The Struggle for Freedom from Ottoman Oppression and the Birth of the Modern Greek Nation* (New York: Woodstock, 2003), p. 53.

[42] Theophilus C. Prousis, "British Embassy Reports on the Greek Uprising in 1821–1822: War of Independence or War of Religion?," *History Faculty Publications* 21 (2011): 182.

Bowring, Lord Byron, Shelley, George Canning, David Urquhart, Robert Walsh and others. These philhellenes became "the locus for opposition to the politics of the Holy Alliance in support of liberty."[43] Similarly, French philhellenes such as Chateaubriand, La Fayette, Sebastiani, de Broglie, Laffitte, founded the Societe Philanthropique en Faveur des Grecs (1825). One of their supporters, painter Eugene Delacroix, painted in 1826 "*La Grèce sur les ruines de Missolonghi.*" which portrayed the Greece awaiting the fate in resignation or despair. His aim was to awake and influence the Europeans to protect their 'cradle of Civilisation.'[44]

Philhellenism has been defined as "an international movement of protest in which nationalism, religion, radicalism and commercial greed all played a part, as well as romantic sentiment and pure heroism."[45] The movement was trying to convince state elites to take action for the benefit of the Greeks. David Rodogno demonstrated how "this tiny group of people proved to be so influential" that they "put forward the question of Ottoman sovereignty over Greek lands."[46] One of these philhellenes, François–René de Chateaubriand, wrote about "civilised" Christian Greeks who were under the yoke of "barbarity and Mahometanism" and needed European help. In his book *Note sur la Grece* (1825), he justified intervention by arguing that the Greeks, as Christians (*comme les peoples chretiens*), were usurped by the Turks, who did not acknowledge European laws (*ne reconnoit point le droit politique de l'Europe*), but were adhered to their Asiatic customs of government (*se gouverned'apres le code des peoples de l'Asie*).[47] Since Turks ruled according to Asiatic customs, which were not part of Europe and Christianity, the Ottoman Empire's sovereignty was not applicable to its Christian provinces. Another prominent figure was Edward Blaquiere, who wrote "*Greece and Its Claims*" (1826) and "*Letters from Greece: With Remarks on the Treaty of Intervention*" (1828). He argued that Europe should advocate for "the fate of our Christian brethren of the East" against "the fiery zeal and bigoted

---

[43] Rodogno, *Against Massacre*, p. 72.

[44] Nina M. Athanassoglou–Kallmyer, *French Images from the Greek War of Independence (1821–1830): Art and Politics under the Restoration* (New Haven: Yale University Press, 1989), p. 73.

[45] Todorova, *Imagining*, p. 70.

[46] Rodogno, *Against Massacre*, pp. 72–73.

[47] François–René de Chateaubriand, *Note sur la Grece* (Paris, 1825), p. 20.

enthusiasm of the followers of Islam."[48] These arguments were based on his *"Report on the Present State of the Greek Confederation and on Its Claims to the Support of the Christian World"* (1823), which emphasised the "illegitimacy of Ottoman rule over Greece."[49] According to Blaquiere, it was necessary "to make another appeal to the British public (…) addressed to the religious communities generally. These are bound by every tie, both as Christians and as man, to succour the Greeks and contribute towards their speedy restoration to the bosom of the European family, as well as to the blessings of an extended civilisation."[50] It was necessary to contribute to the intervention for "the cause of civilisation and Christianity" against the Ottomans as a symbol of "barbarism, vice and ignorance."[51] Therefore, in Theophilus C. Prousis' words, "the Greek struggle represented a strange mix of traditional and modern elements: religious ardor and confessional identity interacted with secular notions of liberty and nationality."[52] The books from this period demonstrate how Europe as "civilised" should undertake a modern crusade (intervention) against "barbarians," in order to rescue their cradle (Greece). However, this intervention could not happen without Russian involvement since it was the protector of Ottoman Orthodox subjects.

After years of negotiation, the Great Powers finally decided to intervene in the war on the side of the Greeks. The battle of Navarino (20 October 1827) became the turning point and symbolic triumph of "civilisation" against "barbarity." As the result of the events in Greece, David Urquhart's return to England was postponed.[53] He travelled to Greece in 1827 in order to champion the Greek cause in the war of independence there, which would (later) be one of the reasons for his appointment to Sir Stratford Canning's mission to Constantinople. In his book *"The Spirit of the East"* (1838), he wrote: "[I]t is only necessary to cast a glance on the map of Greece, to appreciate the value of this arm of the sea (…) inspired her (Greece) with fresh hopes, and called forth the renewed energy of her

---

[48] Edward Blaquière, *Greece and Her Claims* (London: G.B. Whittaker, 1826), p. iii.
[49] Rodogno, *Against Massacre,* p. 74.
[50] Edward Blaquière, *'Report on the Present State of the Greek Confederation, and on Its Claims to the Support of the Christian World* (London: G.B. Whittaker, 1823), p. 18.
[51] Ibid., p. 20.
[52] Theophilus C. Prousis, "British Embassy Reports," 173.
[53] David Urquhart, *The Spirit of the East* (London: H. Colburn, 1838), p. 4.

sons."[54] An Irish historian and writer, Robert Walsh, analysing the situation from Istanbul, reported that "Constantinople was immersed in darkness and ferocity", while the "destiny of Greece [was] fixed." According to him, the destiny of the Ottoman Empire "remain[ed] in the womb of time – whether, enlightened by literature and civilisation which ha[d] dawned on it, it [would] finally adopt the religion and free institutions of the West, and so became a member of the great European family; or, falling under the power of a neighbor, it [would] merge into a province of a state half Asiatic, add other millions to the slaves already in bondage, and improvement end in engrafting European vices on Oriental ignorance."[55]

2.3. Imagined Geographies and Cartography

The previously mentioned European interventions popularised the Ottoman space among educated Europeans. By intervening in Ottoman Greece, aroused an interest among many travellers and adventurers to explore other parts of the Ottoman Empire (i.e. Macedonia), as this region was for them an uncharted territory – *terrae incognitae*. In the opinion of Viscountess Emily Anne Beaufort Smythe Strangford, who visited Ottoman Rumelia, "the geography of the country, for one thing, [was] very little known, as regard[ed] much of European Turkey."[56] She even compared some regions in Ottoman Albania with "the Hoti and the Clementi, to Shalla and Pouka, and the subjects of Prince Bib – tribes of good Catholics who [were] more unknown to [them] than the Waganda and the Wagogo of Equatorial Africa."[57] The similar opinion was shared by Vuk Karadžić while criticising the French colonel, Vialla de Sommieres, who visited Montenegro in 1813 and stated that "the Montenegrin language [was] the dialect of the Greek."[58] According to Vuk Karadžić "surely they were of that opinion since some French diplomats

---

[54] Ibid., pp. 21–22.
[55] Robert Walsh, *A Residence at Constantinople: During a Period Including the Greek and Turkish Revolution* (London: Westley & Davis, 1836), p. 486.
[56] Viscountess Emily Anne Beaufort Smythe Strangford, *The Eastern Shores of the Adriatic in 1863: With a Visit to Montenegro* (New York: Palala Press, 2015), p. 305.
[57] Ibid., p. 202.
[58] Vialla de Sommieres, *Voyage Historique et Politique au Montenegro* (Paris: Alexis Eymery Libraire, 1820).

(as Dominique Dufour de Pradt), were dividing the Ottoman Empire and Greek border to the Danube. They could not have held these ideas if they had already known that between Greece and the Danube live[d] a people more numerous than the Greeks, and which from them obviously differ[ed] not only in language, origin, and character, but also in ethnic hatred and contempt."[59] Also, this was one of the reasons for Leon Hugonnet to publish a book on the "unknown Turkey," which among other regions described Macedonia, and was titled *La Turquie inconnue: Roumanie, Bulgarie, Macedoine, Albanie* (1886). It seems that during the 19th century the Ottoman space was subject to the discovery and imagination of the Europeans. As Jeremy Black concludes, "in European eyes, non–European lands could appear empty, non–European societies unsophisticated" and thus, there was a necessity for "inventing territories according to their interests."[60]

In order to understand these parts of "non–European lands", geography was recognised as a discrete academic discipline, and became part of a typical curriculum at European universities (especially Paris and Berlin). In Edward Said's understanding, this discipline became important for making "projections – imaginative, cartographic, military, economic, historical, or in a general sense cultural. It also [made] possible the construction of various kinds of knowledge, all of them in one way or another dependent upon the perceived character and destiny of a particular geography." [61] With this aim, multiple geographical societies were established around Europe, such as: the *Société de Géographie* in 1821, *Die Gesellschaft für Erdkunde* in 1828 and the *Royal Geographical Society* in 1830. At the same time there were established the *Russian Geographical Society* in 1845, *American Geographical Society* in 1851, and the *National Geographic Society* in 1888.[62] This European "science"

---

[59] Vuk Karadžić, *Montenegro und die Montenegriner: Ein Beitrag zur Kenntniss der europäischen Türkei und des serbischen Volkes* (Stuttgart: Verlag der J. G. Cotta'schen Buchhandlung, 1837), translation: *Crnogorci* (Beograd: Nolit, 1972).
[60] Black, *Maps and History*, p. 134.
[61] Edward Said, *Culture and Imperialism* – Lecture held in Toronto at York University, February 10, 1993. See this lecture and collection of his essays in Edward Said, *Culture and Imperialism* (New York: Vintage Books, 1994), p. 78.
[62] Susan Schulten, *The Geographical Imagination in America, 1880–1950* (Chicago: University of Chicago Press, 2001), p. 5.

and "universalism" based on the power of imagination and "law of intervention" produced knowledge, maps, and museums in order to serve the politics of imperialism.[63] By default, the Ottoman space was turned into "an imaginary waiting room of history."[64] According to Zygmunt Bauman, "whoever travelled faster could claim more territory – and, having done that, could control it, map it and supervise it." [65] In constructing itself as superior, the imperial force or colonising agent was able to justify its actions in the form of interventions against the "Other."[66] This construction of a space and a discursive "Other" occurred through an array of images, myths, texts, maps etc. Foucault asserts that knowledge is always related to power, thus, these imagined geographies constructed by "knowledge" could be seen as a tool of European power to subordinate the Ottomans. In this sense, I take on board Count Hermann Keyserling's claim that "if Macedonia (the Balkans) had not existed, they would have been invented",[67] since this part of the Ottoman Empire served as a canvas onto which to project European preoccupations. In what follow, I will further delineate how the geographic appellation known as Macedonia was

---

[63] Ibid, p. 174.

[64] Dipesh Chakrabarty, *Provincializing Europe: Postcolonial Thought and Historical Difference* (Princeton: Princeton University Press, 2000), p. 8.

[65] Zygmund Bauman, *Liquid Modernity* (Cambridge: Cambridge University Press, 2000), pp. 110–112.

[66] Joanne Sharp, *Geographies of Postcolonialism: Imagining the World* (London: SAGE Publications Ltd, 2009); Frederick Cooper, *Colonialism in Question: Theory, Knowledge, History* (Berkley: University of California Press, 2005), p. 4; See also: Derek Gregory, *Geographical Imaginations* (New Jersey: Blackwell, 1994); Derek Gregory, *Violent Geographies: Fear, Terror, and Political Violence* (London: Routledge, 2006). In this respect Gregory develops an argument that the "War on Terror" represents a continuum of imagined geographies that Edward Said already discussed. Accordingly, the Islamic community and its followers have been unfairly portrayed as uncivilised, barbaric, backward, and unsuccessful. This biased perception is often linked to military interventions in Afghanistan and Iraq in recent years. Moreover, it highlights the persistence of Orientalism and colonialism in mainstream media and political discourses.

[67] Hermann Keyserling, *Europe* (London: George Allen & Unwin, 1928), p. 22–23; Burnett Bolloten, *The Spanish Revolution: The Left and the Struggle for Power during the Civil War* (Chapel Hill: University of North Carolina Press, 1979), p. 35; Geoffrey Cocks, *The State of the Novel: Britain and Beyond* (Chichester, UK: Wiley–Blackwell, 2008), p. 88; Ruth Sonderegger, *Hermann Keyserling: Eine Biographie* (Würzburg, Germany: Königshausen & Neumann, 2014), p. 102; Hans Speier, *Europe: A History of an Idea* (New York: Harper & Row, 1970), p. 63.

transformed into a widespread pejorative "Macedonian salad" – a symbol of inter–ethnical conflict.

2.3.1. Inventing the Balkans, Imagining Macedonia

It is indisputable that the Balkans were created by the European imagination. This is exemplified by the concept of the Balkan Peninsula, which lacks a geographical foundation since the Balkan Mountain range does not cover the entire peninsula. Firstly, German naturalist Johann August Zeune coined this term in his work *"Gea: Versuch ein erwissenschaftlichen Erdbeschreibung"* (1808) using the term "Balkan Halbeiland" ("Balkan Peninsula").[68] By referring to the relief of this part of Europe, Zeune imagined and wrongly concluded that the "Balkan mountains (*Stara Planina*) or the former Albanus, Scardus, Haemus, which, to the northwest, joins the Alps in the small Istrian peninsula" and are stretched from the Adriatic to the Black Sea and is the central mountain range that divides the European mainland from its sub–continent.[69] Thus, it was due to the mistake of a geographer that the name "Balkan" was circulated throughout the whole of South–Eastern Europe.[70] However, the term "Balkan Peninsula" was soon challenged by Austrian geographer and geologist Ami Boue.[71] In 1864 the Austrian Consul in Ottoman Janina, who was one of the founders of Albanian studies, Johann Georg von Hahn, used the term "South Eastern European peninsula" (*Süd–ostereuropäische Peninsula*) for the same region, while he was defining the European territories under Ottoman rule (south of the Sava and Danube rivers). The European interest in classical antiquity and the intensification of the activities of Ottoman Christians for their political sovereignty, contributed to the attempts of the European imagination to define this region according

---

[68] August Zeune, *Gea: Versuch einer wissenschaftlichen Erdbeschreibung, Blindenanstalt, Doct. der Weltweisheit, Mitglied der Jenaischen mineralogischen Gesellschaft – Nebst zwey Karten* (Berlin: bey Wittich, 1808). p. 8.

[69] Velimir Veljko Rogić, *Regionalna geografija Jugoslavije: prirodna osnova i historijska geografija* (Zagreb: Školska knjiga, 1982), p. 284.

[70] Mirela Slukan Altić, "Hrvatska kao zapadni Balkan – geografska stvarnost ili nametnuti identitet?," *Društvena istraživanja Zagreb* 20 (2011): 401–413.

[71] Ami Boue, *La Turquie d'Europe ou observations sur la ge'ographie, la geologie, l'histoire naturelle, la statistique, les moeurs, les coutumes, l'archeeologie, l'agriculture, l'industrie, le commerce, les gouvernements divers, le clerge, l'histoire et l'etat politique de cet empire* (Paris: Arthus Bartrand, 1840).

to respective European interests and to view the Balkans as an ambiguous region, potentially civilised but still under barbarous Ottoman influence. Thus, the geographical discovery in Europe went hand in hand with the invention of the Balkans, which until the Congress of Berlin (1878), was called by different names: "Hellenic peninsula," "Greek peninsula," "Illyrian peninsula," even "Macedonia," "Rumelia," "European Turkey," "Turkey–in–Europe," "European Levant," "South Eastern European peninsula," etc. Therefore, the Balkans' geographical position in Europe did not allow for it to be regarded as (part of) the Orient. However, a French geographer André Blanc has correctly noted that the term "Balkan" rather denotes a problem (especially after 1913), than a region.

As I have argued before, the Balkans were not physically colonised, but were influenced by European colonial ideas defining this process as "colonisation of the mind." In this respect, Maria Todorova considers that the Balkan as a place where "its Christianity (Civilisation) opposed it to Islam (Barbarism) and fed the crusading potential of western Christendom."[72] In this respect, due to its majority of Christian elements, the Balkans had the potential to "join" Civilisation. Especially after the Congress of Berlin (1878), some countries (Montenegro, Serbia, and Romania) liberated them (the Balkan region) from the "barbarous" Ottoman yoke, which gave them more space to define themselves as part of Civilisation. Hence, influenced by the European imagination, power–knowledge relations and their ability to construct, map, and name, the Balkan states automatically questioned existence of such names as "Turkey in Europe" or "European Turkey." It was necessary for them to find a new geographical determinant, that would cover the same part of Europe. A prominent role in this process played the famous Serbian geographer Jovan Cvijić (1865 – 1927), who published *La Peninsula Balcanique* (1918) in Paris, in the same year when the creation of the Kingdom of Serbs, Croats, and Slovenes (Yugoslavia) was decided on. The revitalisation of the name "Balkan Peninsula" was important for the demonstration of a homogeneous geographical region of South Slavic unity. What is more, Cvijić even shifted the borders of the Balkans towards

---

[72] Maria Todorova, "Balkans: From Discovery to Invention," *Slavic Review* 53 (Summer, 1994): 455.

the Alps to include Slovenia too. [73] Thus, the notion of the Balkan Peninsula became solidified with the creation of the Kingdom of Yugoslavia, whereby it had more of a political than geographical connotation. In this manner the Balkans were invented, that is, using its name and borders to best serve the states' interests. With this, Macedonia became a region inside the not–well–defined and wrongly depicted Balkan Peninsula. The increase of interest in Macedonia arrived with the Greek war of independence, since "the resurrection of Greece [was] considered the original front of Western culture," which was "connected with new spiritual, political or cultural revival."[74] The Greek war of Independence provided an opportunity to explore and imagine new areas of Turkey in Europe or the Balkan Peninsula. The French explorer, diplomat, and historian, Francois Pouqeville, who published his *Travels in Epirus, Albania, Macedonia, and Thessaly* (1820) just one year before the Greek events, "" emphasised that "before us, and to the right, lay several villages, inhabited by Christian and Mahometan Bardariotes, noted for being the mildest and the most hospitable of all the country–people of Macedonia."[75] In his imagination religious distinction was more important surpassed ethnical. Even the advice of his friend, who was his dragoman, contained more religious than ethnical connotations. Thus, Pouqeville's dragoman recommended: "[M]ake the best use you can, and quickly too, of this indulgence: but remember; be on your guard against the Turks (Muslims)," stressing that "the Turks [had] no conception of your sciences and knowledge."[76] The notion of Western knowledge against the barbarous Ottomans gained importance during the Greek war of independence. Many travellers started to explore their "cradle" of civilisation – Greece. With this eruption of exploratory travel, Pouqeville became one of the most prominent philhellenes, informing Europe about events in Greece through his five–volume *"Voyage en Grèce"* (Paris, 1820–1822), which reached 20 editions by 1826–1827. Another prominent French figure was G. A. Mano,

---

[73] Jovan Cvijić, *La Péninsule balkanique: géographie humaine* (Paris: Librairie Armand Colin, 1918).

[74] David Roessel, *Byron's Shadow: Modern Greece in the English and American Imagination* (Oxford: Oxford University Press, 2002), p. 5.

[75] Francois Pouqeville, *Travels in Epirus, Albania, Macedonia, and Thessaly* (London: Printed for Sir Richard Phillips and Co, 1820), p. 81.

[76] Ibid., p. 84.

who became inspired by French naturalist Jean–Baptiste Bory de Saint–Vincentand and his well–known research *"Resume de la géographie de la Peninsule Iberique"* (1826), and (similarly) decided to carry out a detailed analysis of these historic events in Greece and other parts of Turkey in Europe in his book *"Résumé géographique de la Grèce et de la Turquie d'Europe"* (1826). Beside Greece, he described Macedonia as one of most fertile provinces of Turkey in Europe and as the second province of Rumelia (first was Thrace), divided in three parts. Accordingly, the first part included Peonie and Dardania (Kosovo), or Illyrian Macedonia (*Macedoine illyrienne*), bordered to the north by Servia and a part of Bosnia; while the second part bordered Bulgaria and Thrace to the east; and the third part spread to the Archipelago and Thessaly, and to the west to Albania.[77] He included the following sanjaks as parts of Macedonia: Pristina, Uscup, Qustendil, Seres, Thessaloniki, Monastir, and Ochrida.[78] Moreover, he emphasised that the "Kingdom of Macedonia originated as a Greek colony" and that its territory belonged to Hellenes since the time of Alexander the Great.[79] According to Esprit Marie Cousinéry, "view of Alexander as divine [was] widespread among the Greeks (*repanduparmi les Grecs*),"[80] but unfortunately this "glorious Macedonia" became "humiliated by the Bulgarians and debased under Ottoman reign."[81] The image of Macedonia as humiliated and debased, evoked among the Europeans to reformulate their interest and to establish *mission civilisatrice* against Ottoman barbarity. As an illustration of the latter, Cousinery wrote: "I did not let escape this opportunity to revisit some of the provinces (of Macedonia) that I had already explored, and I thought I should try a description that has always seemed to inspire great interest."[82]

---

[77] Gaston A. Mano, *Résumé géographique de la Grèce et de la Turquie d'Europe* (Paris: N.P.,1826), pp. 515–516; See quote: *"estl'une de plus fertile provinces de la Turquie d'Europe."*

[78] Ibid., pp. 515–551.

[79] Ibid., pp. 238–244.

[80] Esprit Marie Cousinéry, Pierre Langlumé, *Voyage dans la Macédoine: contenant des recherché sur l'histoire la géographie et les antiquités de ce pays* (Paris: N.P., 1831), p. 257; See quote: *"La royaume de macedoine avaiteu pour origine un ecolonie grecque."*

[81] Ibid., p. 11; In original quote: *"si humiliee sous les Bulgares, et enfinsiavilie sous le fer ottoman."*

[82] Ibid., p. 5; *"paru propre a inspirer un grand interet."*

Many travellers, adventurers, and diplomats started to imagine and define Macedonia in different ways, mostly in alignment with their sympathies and governments' interests. As already discussed in G.A. Mano's examples, in the territory of Macedonia he included the territories of today's Kosovo and Serbia as part of *Macedoine illyrienne*. These geographical parts he then joined with northern Albania, "which leads to the bank of the Drino, a little above Alessio (Lezha)." The French traveller, Francois Pouqueville, named it "Macedonian Illyricum."[83] For Edmund Spencer, a prolific British traveller and writer of the mid–19th century, the city of Prizren or "the ancient Priscopera, [which was] supposed to have been founded by Philip of Macedonia."[84] Still, it was placed in today's territory of Kosovo, which Spencer named "Upper Albania," while the first city in Macedonia he termed Kalkandelen.[85] The continuous ascent and descent of the mountain ridges, with their impenetrable forests, jutting rocks, and deep defiles form a natural boundary between Macedonia and Albania as "the most execrable and dangerous for the traveller in European Turkey."[86] On the other hand, August Griesebach, a German botanist and geographer, asserts that "Macedonia and Albania were on the border," but he recognises that sometimes they comprised "one overlapped Prefecture, while at others they had an "opposite dividing line from the West to the East."[87] Jean–Henri–Abdolonyme Ubicini, who was a French historian, journalist, and honorary member of the Romanian Academy, described "the eyelets of Yania (Epirus) and of Selanik (Salonica)" that "compromise[d] the ancient Epirus and Macedonia," while "the eyelets of Uskup and Roumelia [were] formed from Albania."[88]

---

[83] Pouqeville, *Travels in Epirus*, p. 29.
[84] Edmund Spencer, *Travels in European Turkey, in 1850 Through Bosnia, Servia, Bulgaria, Macedonia, Thrace, Albania, And Epirus; with a Visit to Greece and the Ionian Isles. A Homeward Tour Through Hungary and the Slavonian Provinces of Austria on the Lower Danube* (London: Colburn and Co., Publisher, 1851), p. 11.
[85] Spencer, *Travels in European Turkey*, p. 20.
[86] Ibid., p. 65.
[87] August Griesebach, *Reise durch Rumelien und nach Brussa im Jahre 1839* (Göttingen: Vandenhoeck und Ruprecht, 1841), p. 369; Quote: "*Macedonien und Albanien in der Umgrenzung (...) der neue gebildeten Präfecturen zusammen übereintreffen (...) der bisherigen entgegengesetzten Teilungslinie von Westen nach Osten.*"
[88] Abdolonyme Ubicini, *Letters on Turkey: An Account of the Religious, Political, Social and Commercial Conditions of the Ottoman Empire* (London: John Murray, 1856), p. 15.

One of the first significant examples of not only defining the Macedonian borders, but also of including an ethnographic map of imagined Macedonia, was the research of the Austrian geologist Ami Boué, who was educated in Paris and Geneva (1840). His book, *La Turquie d'Europe ou observations sur la géographie, la géologie* (1840), along with its map (which will be analysed later) changed the perception of the region as "Greek." For the first time, Bulgarians were said to constitute a major ethnical population in Macedonia.[89] He mapped Bulgarian residents in almost the whole of Macedonia until Ochrida (*leur Bulgarians residence a Ochri*).[90] His other work, written in German, *Beiträge zur Geographie Serbiens* (1856) for the first time exposes Serbia's ambitions towards Old Serbia (Kosovo) and Macedonia: "[N]ew rough maps related to Serbia should imagine Old Serbia and Macedonia inside (its territories)."[91] This is coterminous with the period when Edmund Spencer's "Upper Albania" became imagined as "Old Serbia" (*Stara Srbija*) and "Macedonia" as "South Serbia" (*Južna Srbija*) among Serbian intellectuals. In his book *Considérations sur l'état social de la Turquie d'Europe* (1842), Louis Auguste Blanqui favours the role of Serbia in liberation from the "Ottoman yoke." According to him, "in Europe Turkey offers a serious obstacle to the fulfilment of their (the Christians') new destinies."[92] Therefore, the role of "emancipated Servia (*la Servie emancipee*)" was to "light the first fires of eastern liberty." This is the place where "Christianity claimed its first victory, after which were "today's population of Bulgaria, Thrace, and Macedonia was born."[93] Viewed from this perspective, "the European policy should focus on inhabitants who are part of the Greek religion (*la*

---

[89] Yosmaoğlu, *Blood Ties,* p. 91.

[90] Ami Boué, *La Turquie d'Europe ou observations sur la géographie, la géologie* (Paris: Bertrand, 1840), p. 76.

[91] Ami Boue, *Beiträge zur Geographie Serbiens* (Vienna: K.K. Hof–und Staatsdruckerei in Commission bei Karl Gerold's Sohn, 1856), p. 3; Quote: *"Diese grobe Skizze sollte nicht nur das jetzige Serbien, sondern auch das alte bis Macedonien vorstellen."*

[92] Louis Auguste Blanqui, *Considérations sur l'état social de la Turquie d'Europe* (Paris: W. Coquebert, 1842), p. 35; Quote: *"la Turquie d'Europe offer un serieux obstacle a l'accomplissement de leurs/ chretiens nouvel les destinees."*

[93] Ibid., p. 39; Quote: *"s'allumeront les premiers feux de la liberte orientale (...) le christianisme a remportesa premiere victoire (...) soupirent aujourd'hui les populationes de la Bulgarie, de la Thrace et de la Macedoine."*

religion grecque)." [94] In his book *Travels in European Turkey* (1851), Edmund Spencer declared that the "consolidation of these provinces (Bosnia, Servia, Bulgaria, Macedonia, Thrace, Albania, and Epirus), (…) would call into existence several new Christian States with their energetic inhabitants, and at the same time increase the wealth and commercial prosperity of civilised Europe." Indeed, the mission of Europe was to liberate these Christian provinces and to leave "Osmanli… to their Asiatic possessions," which "would still leave Turkey a respectable power, and [while they became] more concentrated and united in the bonds of one common faith and nationality," The latter would have left behind "the Turks, [and] their ignorance and self–sufficiency." [95] This idea of the Balkans without Turks was common among most travellers and geographers in the mid– and second half of the 19th century. For example, the renowned French poet, diplomat, and politician Alphonse–Marie–Louis de Lamartine, who travelled to the Ottoman Empire and passed through the Balkans in the early 1830s, in his study *"Souvenirs, Impressions, Pensées et Paysages Pendant un Voyage en Orient"* (1835) wrote: "if this people (in the Balkans), establish a new Slavic empire (*d'un nouvel empire slave*) by reunion of Bosnia, parts of Bulgaria, warrior hordes of Montenegrins (and Serbia) as they desire to, a new state will appear in Europe risen from the ruins/ashes of Turkey." This new state should have a "European protectorate and assistance towards the disappearance of the Ottoman Empire for leaving Europe and Asia." [96] In order to materialise this romantic fantasy, he advocated against the Ottomans with the words: "do not help barbarity and Islamism against civilisation." [97] In a similar way, in the work *"La Serbie: Son Passé et Son Avenir"* (1862), Henri Thieres recognises that the "Bosniaks and Bulgarians are of the same race (*sont de meme race*) as the Montenegrins

---

[94] Ibid., p. 42.

[95] Spencer, *Travels in European Turkey*, p. 453.

[96] Alphonse–Marie–Louis de Lamartine, *Souvenirs, Impressions, Pensées et Paysages Pendant un voyage en Orient* (Paris, 1835), pp. 8–9; Citation: *"l'Europe verra un nouvel Etat surgir des ruines de la Turquie (...) la disparation de l'empire ottoman va laisser en Europe comme en Asie."*

[97] Ibid., p. 289; Citation: *"ne vous faites pas les auxiliaires de la barbarie et de l'islamisme contre la civilization."*

and Serbs" and that they "will form a Slavic empire that Europe will allow to exist."[98]

2.3.2. Mapping Macedonia

As I have argued above, the regions are socially constructed and imagined territories. The social construction of territories/regions, their mapping and imagination means that boundaries are shaped by the collective perception of identities and meanings.[99] Since it is considered that territories and regions are constructed and invented, their names and meanings are different too, according to historical context. Therefore, the meaning of the term "Macedonia" varied, and it was frequently modified by changeable dynamics. As we have already seen, during the medieval period Macedonia appeared as another name for the whole Balkans without, reference to a precise territory. However, the Enlightenment triggered the transition from a medieval understanding to modern, where maps, cartography, and regions gave meanings to "imagined territories" and politicised the regions. The process was often conducted by "scientific" attempts to define certain regions according to the interests of politics.[100] In fact, there is a close connection between map–making and imperial conquest and rule, since "maps are used both to assert territorial claims and to settle them."[101] These politics are central to the production and understanding of maps, because "the maps are a medium" which "is multifaceted and, as with individual maps, it is possible to offer several analyses of its purpose and means of operation."[102] In this way, the language of maps and cartography – as a mean of production of knowledge – was constructed in order to shape "spheres of contest" and "ideologies

---

[98] Henri Thiers, *La Serbie: son passé et son avenir* (Paris: Dramard–Baudry, 1862), p. viii; *"formeront un empire slave le jour oul'Europe leur permettr a d'exister."*

[99] Raimo Vayrynen, "Regionalism: Old and New," *International Studies Review* 5 (2003): 37.

[100] Ibid., p. 9.

[101] Ibid., p. 9.

[102] Ibid., p. 168; Also, a British geographer, Brian Harley analysed maps as essentially documents that contribute to the discourse of power, and that should be seen in that light. In his understanding maps and cartography are a form of language which should be deconstructed as Roland Barthes and Jacques Derrida did. See: Brian Harley, "Deconstructing the Map," *Cartographica* 26/2 (Spring, 1989): 1–20.

of colonised terrains." [103] In the Macedonian context, the medieval understanding of multiple identities –where many Montenegrins or Albanians considered themselves also as Macedonians – was no longer acceptable. The naming and mapping of the regions and defining their people and races, as well as the legitimacy and the right of belonging, was shrunk to only one nation with a monolithic identity. The construction of "imagined geographies" was accompanied by a construction of "imagined communities." Among these communities, the concepts of races, ethnicities, religions, and languages started to be discussed and applied as if they were primordial. Thus, Jeremy Black considers that these "races are constructed as much as described, and mapping plays a role in such construction."[104] Therefore, mapping and cartography played an important role during the nation–building and state–building processes as well.

In this chapter, I discuss how the nations were imagined and how their boundaries were drawn across the land. In the Macedonian case, various European intellectuals, together with the Balkan intellectuals, variously perceived, imagined, and mapped these territories and its population. According to Irena Stefoska, during the 19th century, "the term Macedonia referred to the geographical region of Macedonia in a supra–national sense (...) including the territory of today's Republic of Macedonia, territories in south–western Bulgaria, northern Greece and small portions of southern Serbia, southern Kosovo and south–eastern Albania."[105] In general, there was no accepted definition of Macedonia. As already have been mentioned, Macedonia did not form neither a racial, linguistic or political

---

[103]Black, *Maps and History*, pp. 18–19; Jeremy Black ponders the relationship between power and space, noting that spaces are created through the exertion of power. This perspective led Harley to view cartography and mapping traditions as a product or construction of imperialist powers. Harley believed that the colonised people's sense of place and naming conventions had been appropriated, and that their understanding of territory and boundaries had been ignored. This suggests that non–Western societies are not entitled to their own cartographic knowledge, and that this knowledge and power is exclusive to Western map–makers. Such a hierarchical view positions non–Western cartography as primitive and uncivilised, serving a harmful agenda.

[104] Ibid., p. 48.

[105] Irena Stefoska, "Fragments from the Medieval History of Macedonia," in *Macedonia: Land, Region, Borderland,* ed. Jolanta Sujecka (Warsaw: University of Warsaw, 2013), p. 69.

unit, nor was Macedonia a definite geographical term.[106] Almost every state has had its own imagined geographical boundaries and maps of Macedonia. However, an ethnic classification in the Ottoman context was introduced in 1821 by member of the Prussian Army, F. A. O'Etzel, who was interested in ethnographic cartography depicting the Greeks as the predominant ethnic group in the Balkans.[107] It is note–worthy one of the maps he created, appeared at the beginning of Greek War of Independence. Therefore, its importance lies in its political support of the Greek national movement, the revival of Ancient Greece, and the rise of philhellenism.[108] As we have seen, this interest in neo–classicism and philhellenism became a hallmark of the *Zeitgeist* of Europe. For the Bavarian King Ludwig I and his son, Otto, who later inherited the Greek throne, Greek revolt against Ottoman rule represented the return of antique Hellenic virtue.[109] This process, together with the national independence movements in Serbia (1801–1830) and Montenegro (1689–1858), increased the interest of German cartographers in South–Eastern Europe.

In the wake of geopolitical changes, the Geographical Institute of Weimar published a new map of European Turkey, made by Carl Ferdinand Weiland, depicting the the new, fixed borders with Greece and Serbia.[110] In the same period, Tyrolean traveller and historian Jakob Philipp Fallmerayer challenged the knowledge about this region in his "*Geschichte der Halbinsel Morea während des Mittelalters*" (1830), and stated that the then Greeks had no relations with the ancient Hellenic population. In his second volume from 1836, he added that the Greek War of Independence was a "purely Shqiptarian (Albanian), and not a Hellenic Revolution (*rein*

---

[106] Dakin, *The Greek Struggle*, p. 3.

[107] Wilkinson, *Maps and Politics*, p. 11.

[108] Ibid., pp. 16–20.

[109] Damian Valdez, *German Philhellenism: The Pathos of the Historical Imagination from Winckelmann to Goethe* (London: Palgrave Macmillan, 2014).

[110] Mirela Slukan Altić, "German Contribution to the 19th Century Cartography of European Turkey – With Special Regard on the Map of Heinrich Kiepert," in *Joint Commission Seminar on Historical Maps, Atlases and Toponymy, International Cartographic Assotiation*, ed. Jana Moser (Leipzig: Leibniz–Institut für Länderkunde e.V, 2016), pp. 6–7; Quote: "*Das osmanische Europa oder die europaeische Türkey nebst dem Königreiche Griechenland und den Jonischen Inseln/entworfen und gezeichnet von C. F. Weiland. 1:3,000,000. Weimar, Geographisches Institut, 1832.*"

schkypitarische, nicht eine hellenische Revolution)."[111] In similar ways, in 1842 W. Müller designed a map where he resurrected Pelasgians in southern Macedonia, emphasising that "these peoples were not the descendants of ancient Greeks," while "Albanians comprised the majority of the inhabitants of the Greek archipelago (…) and western Macedonia."[112]

Moreover, in his 1951 book on maps of Macedonia, Henry R. Wilkinson notes that Müller had used the term "Pelasgian," and the notion that he "had distinguished so many Albanians, Zinzares, and Zigeuner, where O'Etzel had marked only Greeks, was further proof of a trend for ideas to veer away from the conception of a Hellenistic Balkans."[113] Evidently, by the mid–19th century the fashion of depicting a Greek majority in the Balkan Peninsula was in decline, while the Slav interpretation gained momentum. The development of Slavic nationalism by South–Slav–speaking intellectuals affected in increased number of new explorers in the Peninsula. In this regard, it is important to state that Pavel Jozef Shafarik was the first author who depicted ethnographic maps based on linguistic affinity (1842).[114] This Slovakian philologist, historian, and ethnographer, became one of the most influential Slavists in his time. He wrote the well–known *Slovansky narodopis* (1842), translated into English as *Slavic Ethnology*, where he gave a detailed account of Slavic nations and their ethnic borders. This study was combined with the ethnographic map *Slovansky Zemevid*, which presented all Slavs as one nation, divided into a number of units (tribes). In the Macedonian context there were two units of Slavs, Serbo–Croats and Bulgarians, and non–Slavs as Turks, Greeks, Albanians, and Romanians. In this map (see the next page), the majority of Ottoman Macedonia's population consisted of Slavs of the Bulgarian unit.

---

[111] Jakob Phillip Fallmerayer, *Geschichte der Halbinsel Morea während des Mittelalters* (Stutgart: Cotta'sche Verlagsbuchhandlung, 1836), p. 74.

[112] Wilkinson, *Maps and Politics,* pp. 21–22; Joseph Müller, *Albanien, Rumelien und die österreichisch–montenegrische Grenze – Nebst einer Karte von Albanien: Mit einer Vorrede von Dr. P. J. Šafarik* (Prague, 1844).

[113] Ibid., p. 22.

[114] Ibid., p. 33.

Map 1 Pavel Jozef Shafarik's Slovansky Zemevid[115]

A similar portrayal was provided by Ami Boue, the above–mentioned Austrian geologist, traveller and author of "*La Turquie d'Europe*," (1840), which depicted different races in Macedonia and was published in the form of a map in Berghaus's atlas of 1847.[116] He was the first European traveller who presented a major Slavic population (Bulgarians) living in Macedonia. Boue's map displays (striking) similarities with Shafarik's version, yet my archival research did not yield records that would evidence an exchange of ideas between them. However, there is an extant, detailed analysis of Boue's conclusions, done by French traveller Albert Montemont in the "*Bulletin de la Société de géographie,*" from 1844, the Bulletin of the world's oldest geographical society. Montemont concludes there that "Bulgarians occupied (…) the majority in Macedonia,"[117] while "Albanians were spread towards the Bulgarians along the Macedonian

---

[115] Dimitri Rizoff, *Bŭlgarite v tehnite istoricheski, etnograficheski i politicheski granitsi 679–1917* (Berlin: Königliche Hoflithographie, Hof–Buch–und Steindruckere Wilhelm Greve, 1917), p. 24.
[116] Ibid., p. 36.
[117] Albert Montemont, *Bulletin de la Société de géographie Société de géographie* (Paris, 1844), p. 74; Quote: *"Bulgares occupent… le noyau principal de la population de la Macedoine."*

frontiers/borders."[118] He points out that "all of the Orientals (referring to people living in Eastern Europe) have a more or less vivid imagination."[119] Accordingly, this "vivid imagination" among Balkan populations appeared when they had already accepted the "colonisation of the mind," and the implementation of "surrogate hegemony." Furthermore, these European travellers and scientists increased their exploration of the Turkish regions/territories in Europe so as to further their interests in subordinating the region and establishing hegemony. As an example, the French ethnographer and geographer Guillaume Lejean travelled twice to European Turkey (1857–1858 and 1867–1869), of which the second time in the capacity of the French Vice–Consul. He was appointed to prepare a detailed analysis of Turkey in Europe on behalf of the French imperial government. Consequently, he wrote *Ethnographie de la Turquie d'Europe*" (1861), published in the German and French languages by the then famous German publisher Justus Perthes. According to Lejean, nearly all of Macedonia (with the exception of Salonica and a part of the borderlands in south–east Macedonia), the whole district of Nish, the coastal district of Dobrudja, and a part of Russian Bessarabia were chiefly Bulgarian territories. In his depiction, Albanians comprised the majority in Kosovo and northern Macedonia.[120]

This demarcation was partly due to the influence of Johann Georg von Hahn, who regarded the region between Drin and the Vardar as Albanian, and not as Serb or Bulgarian, as was otherwise thought. Hahn was an Austrian diplomat and specialist in Albanian language and history, known for his work *"Albanesische Studien*" (1854). Furthermore, his other volume, *"Reise von Belgrad nach Saloniki*" (1861), featured an ethnographic map as an appendix that depicted Albanians in the Western part of Macedonia, as well as in Kosovo.[121] Worthy of mention are also works of British female–travellers Muir–Mackenzie and Irby, who travelled through a large part of the Balkan Peninsula in the years 1862

---

[118] Ibid., p. 75; Quote:*"les Albanais s'associent encore aux Bulgares, vers la frontiere macedonienne."*

[119] Ibid., p. 82; See the quote: *"tous les Orientaux ont une imagination plus ou moins vive."*

[120] Guillaume Lejean, *Ethnographie de la Turquie d'Europe* (Gotha: Justus Perthes, 1861).

[121] Rizoff, *Bŭlgarite v tekhnite istoricheski*, p. 34. See also Johann Georg von Hahn's *"Croquis des westlichen Gebietes der Bulgarischen Morava."*

and 1863, and then published their research in a book titled "*The Turks, the Greeks and the Slavons: Travels in the Slavonic Provinces of Turkey–in–Europe*" (1867). Therein they presented a map where nearly all Macedonia was shown as inhabited by "the Bulgarian race."[122] This work was positively accepted by William Gladstone, who wrote the preface to its second edition (1877), asserting that "with the possession of such knowledge, we have obtained a great advantage."[123]

This production of knowledge about the Balkans appeared in Elisée Reclus' wide–ranging study "*Nouvelle Géographie Universelle*" (1875–1894) published in 18 volumes in Paris. Reclus' work underlines the basis of nationalism, supporting the self–determination of the Balkan peoples and the eviction of Turkey from Europe.[124] His views were reflecting the political and nationalistic interests of the time, especially wide-spread in Europe. While the study undoubtedly contributed to knowledge about the region, it also served as a means of advancing political agendas.[125]

One may argue that these maps were put in the service of politics and the interests of the states. One of the geographers who decided to serve the political interests of Europe and Greece was Heinrich Kiepert. Along with Alexander von Humboldt and Carl Ritter, Kiepert is considered one of the founders of modern German geography. His numerous maps have great scientific value for the advancement of geography, confirmed by receiving the prestigious "Grand Prix" at the Paris International Exhibition (1867). Three of his maps are of particular significance to the Macedonian context of my study. The first map is from 1853, which represents European Turkey and is considered "the best scientific synthesis of German cartography of the 19th century."[126] Its scientific value notwithstanding, this map had an additional political background, as it was created in the climate of the Russo–Ottoman War (1853–1856).

The second (see the next page) is the map titled "*Ethnographische Übersicht des Europäischen Orients*" (1876), for which he did scientific

---

[122] Muir Mackenzie and Irby, *Travels in the Slavonic provinces of Turkey–in–Europe* (London: Daldy, Isbister and Company, 1877).

[123] Ibid., p. vii.

[124] Michel Sivignon, "Le politique dans la géographie des Balkans: Reclus et ses successeurs, d'une Géographie universelle à l'autre," *Hérodote* 117/2 (2005): 153–182.

[125] Ibid.

[126] Altić, *German Contribution*, p. 3.

explorations by visiting parts of European Turkey and territories of Macedonia. This ethnographic map had historical impact when it was instrumental to Bismarck at the Congress of Berlin for demarcating the frontiers/borders of the Bulgarian provinces during the Great Eastern Crisis (1875–1878). According to this map, the west of Ottoman Macedonia was inhabited by an Albanian–speaking population, the south was inhabited by Greeks, while the Ottoman districts of Nish and other major parts of nowadays Northern Macedonia were inhabited by a Bulgarian–speaking population.[127]

Kiepert's *Ethnographische Übersicht des Europäischen Orients* is a testament to the importance of ethnographic research in cartography and the impact that accurate maps can have on historical events. Kiepert's map was not only influential during the Congress of Berlin but also became a significant reference for future research and ethnographic mapping of the Balkans. The accuracy of his ethnographic observations and cartographic skills helped establish him as one of the leading scholars of his time in the field of geography and cartography.

Map 2 Heinrich Kiepert's "Ethnographische Übersicht des Europäischen Orients"[128]

---

[127] Rizoff, *Bŭlgarite v tehnite istoricheski*.
[128] Ibid., p. 44.

The third and final map is from 1878, titled *"Tableau Ethnocratique des pays du sud–est de l'Europe,"* and presents diametrically opposed vision compared to the previous map (1876). According to İpek Yosmaoğlu, "the simple replacement of the term ethnographic with ethnocratique" from the title of the map "suggests that the author does not even pretend to be presenting a purely 'scientific' assessment of data but draws a direct link between the representation of ethnic groups on a map and political claims over the region."[129] In fact, this map is a testament to the extent to which science was put to the service of the state interests and imperialist projects. On the one hand, the growing pan–Slavic ideas and Russian threats to the European interests in Ottoman Rumelia, and on the other, the efforts of the Greek elites to change the present perception of Macedonia as a Bulgarian land, demonstrate how geography and cartography as disciplines became instruments of "Civilisation." For instance, Constantine Paparrigopoulos was the founder of Greek historiography and repeatedly in the service of Greek state projects whose goal was to lay the foundation for the formation of the national Greek identity in modern times. He offered a unified image of the Greeks from the ancient through the Byzantine to the modern era with the purpose to serve the greater state projects (*Megali Idea*). In this sense, Macedonia was represented as part of Greece, since it was the homeland of Phillip II and Alexander the Great. Therefore, he utilised an opportune time (when the threat of Russia emerged) to undertake correspondence with Heinrich Kiepart in order to persuade him to create a new map sponsored by Syllogos (Society for the Dissemination of Greek Letters). It seems that during Paparrigopoulos's stay in Berlin (1877), he convinced Kiepert to "draw a new map of the region comprising roughly the Peloponnese, Thessaly, Epirus, Macedonia, Thrace, and Eastern Rumelia."[130]

The new map "Tableau Ethnocratique" (see the next page) that Kiepert ultimately created reflected a significant departure from his earlier depictions of the region. Kiepert's earlier maps had emphasised the complex ethnic and linguistic makeup of Ottoman Macedonia, prevalently

---

[129] İpek Yosmaoğlu, "Constructing National Identity in Ottoman Macedonia," in *Understanding Life in the Borderlands: Boundaries in Depth and in Motion* ed. William Zartman (Athens: The University of Georgia Press, 2009), p. 167.
[130] Yosmaoğlu, *Blood Ties,* p. 122.

presents by Slavic speaking population, while the new map drew clear and distinct borders around regions that were seen as historically and culturally Greek.

Map 3 Heinrich Kiepert's "Tableau Ethnocratique des pays du sud–est de l'Europe"[131]

The fact that Kiepert made such a significant change to his earlier depictions of the region suggests that Paparrigopoulos was successful in persuading him to adopt a more Greek-centric view of the Balkans. This reflects the larger geopolitical context of the time, in which nationalist movements were emerging and seeking to assert their dominance over their respective territories. Nonetheless, the creation of the new map highlights the complex relationship between cartography and politics, and the ways in which maps can be used to advance political interests and agendas, like in case of the German cartographer who "change[d] his

---

[131] Rizoff, *Bŭlgarite v tekhnite istoricheski*, p. 46; Goran Sekulovski, "Le géographe Kiepert et les Balkans à Berlin (1878): les archives diplomatiques mises en perspective – cartes & géomatique," *Cartographie et traités de paix (XVe–XXe siècle)* 228/6 (2016): 73–81. on page 76.

earlier depiction of the region almost entirely, in line with Greek claims."[132]

In a similar vein, maps in favour of Greece emerged in other parts of Europe, too. Two significant examples published in 1877 favoured Greek claims over Macedonia. One was the Stanford Map, while the other was the map drafted by F. Bianconi, a French engineer and geographer.[133] In the same year, a pro–Greek map was published by A. Synvet, a French philhellene and a teacher of geography at Galatasaray Lisesi that "received considerable publicity in Europe." [134] For him, Macedonia consisted mostly of "Greeks of Bulgarian tongue" (*Vulgarophoni Hellini*). It seems that his work did not directly dispute the earlier maps showing sizeable Bulgarian populations, but it merely showed "that the Greek population of the Ottoman Empire had been grossly underestimated" [135] or even misinterpreted. The French, British, and Greeks were not the only ones who "aimed at destroying the idea of Slav supremacy in the Balkans. Austria had always a vital interest in Balkan affairs."[136] This presented an opportunity for Carl von Sax, who was a long–time Austro–Hungarian Consul at Sarajevo, at Rustschuk, and at Adrianople. He maintained that Europe misunderstood the region since they were placing more importance to linguistics and race, while in the Balkans religion was a more important tool, shaping "group consciousness" or in his terms, "*das eigene nationale Bewusstsein.*"[137] In his opinion, linguistic criteria could only mislead the understanding of the region, an example of which were the Muslims, Orthodox, and Catholic Slavs in Bosnia, who spoke the same language, but were affiliated with different communities.[138] Therefore, he listed nine groups of Slavs in the region, while Greeks consisted the majority unit. This division would consequently constitute a reason for Salisbury to

---

[132] Ibid., p. 122; K. Paparrigopoulos, note in Heinrich Kiepert. See: Yosmaoğlu, *Constructing National,* p. 167.

[133] Ibid.

[134] Rizoff, *Bŭlgarite v tehnite istoricheski.*

[135] Yosmaoğlu, *Blood Ties,* p. 94.

[136] Wilkinson, *Maps and Politics,* pp. 75–76.

[137] Ibid, p. 77.

[138] Ibid, p. 78; Carl von Sax, *Geschichte des Machtverfalls der Türkei bis Ende des 19. Jahrhunderts und die Phasen der 'orientalischen Frage' bis auf die Gegenwart* (Mainz/ Vienna, 1913); Quote: "*Die bosnischen Mohammedaner, deren Muttersprache die serbische ist, haben sich niemals Serben nennen lassen, sondern 'Türken.*"

declare, at the Congress of Berlin, that "Turkey should be freed from Russia's domination (…) driving back the Slav State to the Balkans and substituting it with a Greek Province." [139] According to the Bulgarian politician and diplomat, who served in Montenegro, Skopje, Belgrade, Rome, and Berlin, Dimitar Rizov (or Dimitri Rizoff), "one has to keep in mind that the map was designed in 1878" and that at that time "the official diplomats of Austria were afraid of Russia's expansive policy, and fought openly for a separation of Macedonia from the newly created Principality of Bulgaria." [140] He also published a book "Bulgarians within their Historical, Ethnographic, and Political Boundaries" [141] to provide a comprehensive analysis of the Bulgarian people, their culture, and their history within the context of the Balkans. The book was published in 1917, during a tumultuous period in Bulgarian history, when the country was part of the Central Powers fighting against its neighbours, aiming to include Macedonia inside the Bulgarian state borders. His book was published in four languages (Bulgarian, French, German, and English) with the aim of presenting Bulgaria's perspective and legitimacy over Macedonia to the international community.

One can hence conclude that all parties involved imagined, perceived, and mapped the Macedonian territories as well as its imagined communities in different ways. Patrick H. Liotta and Cindy R. Jebb rightly conclude that "it is not that symbolic geography creates politics, but rather the reverse."[142] The politics produced knowledge about certain regions (i.e. Macedonia) expressed in the form of maps. Furthermore, these maps depicted imagined communities according to state interests. [143] In this regard, mapmakers produced a "vision of the future" according to their imaginations and political interests, rather than what was actually in front of them on the ground. It may not be erroneous to conclude that, in one way or another, all the maps presented entailed domination, objectification, interventions, and thus, ultimately, constructions of the

---

[139] Ibid, pp. 88–89.
[140] Rizoff, *Bŭlgarite v tehnite istoricheski.*
[141] Ibid.
[142] Patrick H. Liotta and Cindy R. Jebb, *Mapping Macedonia: Idea and Identity* (Santa Barbara: Greenwood Pub Group, 2004), p. 93.
[143] Black, *Maps and History*, p. 112.

"barbarian Others."[144] However, this imagination did not only typify the Western Europeans, but also circulated as (a) knowledge among the Balkan intellectuals, who also imagined Macedonia, developed their own state policies, and mapped this region according to their interests.

2.4. The Balkan Intellectuals and Their Surrogate Hegemony

The century following the Peace of Carlowitz in 1699 saw many changes in the relations among the European powers, the Ottomans, and people living in the Balkans. While the European powers were moving towards the process of centralisation, the Ottoman Empire was passing through a more decentralised system where some regions became semi–independent and autonomous. These changes had an indirect bearing on the destiny of the South Slav population who lived under Ottoman rule, which started to establish ties with its "Orthodox brothers" in Imperial Russia. Tsar Peter the Great and the Empress Catherine began to play a major part in these affairs of Europe and the Ottoman Empire.[145] Thus, the ideas of state–centralisation, special imagination, and interventions did not remain confined within Western Europe, but this knowledge circulated and expanded in the direction of "Europe's peripheries" towards Russia, the Balkans, and Ottomans.[146] In fact, I will highlight here an entangled

---

[144] Matthew H. Edney, "Mapping Empires, Mapping Bodies: Reflections on the Use and Abuse of Cartography," *Treballs de la SCG* 63 (2007): 93.

[145] Peter the Great has a special place in Imperial Russian policy, since his was the initiative to open Russia up to new western ideas in the form of modernisation and centralisation; See: Fred Singleton, *A short history of the Yugoslav Peoples* (Cambridge: Cambridge University Press, 1985), p. 73; Andrew Rossos, *Russia and the Balkans: Inter–Balkan Rivalries and Russian Foreign Policy, 1908–1914* (Toronto: University of Toronto Press, 1981); Alexei Miller, *The Ukrainian Question: The Russian Empire and Nationalism in the 19th Century* (Budapest/New York: Central European University Press, 2003); Allexei Miller and Stefan Berger, *Nationalizing Empires* (Budapest/New York: Central European University Press, 2014); Jane Burbank, "Paul W. Werth, The Tsar's Foreign Faiths, Toleration and the Fate of Religious Freedom in Imperial Russia," *Cahiers du monde russe* 56/4 (2015): 1–5.

[146] In Vissarion Belinsky's opinion, Russia would probably still have accepted European civilisation and modernisation even without Peter the Great, but it would have done so in the same way in which India adopted the English ones. Belinsky saw Russia's Westernisation as a response to the anxiety of being colonised by the West, though of course this anxiety was also the result of European influence. See: Alexander Etkind, *Internal Colonization – Russia's Imperial Experience* (Cambridge: Polity Press, 2011), pp. 15–16.

history (*histoire croisee*) based on the interconnectedness of societies, from the West to the South–East and East of Europe. I will argue that the circulation of knowledge enabled various connections between large geographic areas and triggered multiple trajectories of cooperation over imperial borders. In this respect, these transfers of knowledge and relations between various layers of societies did not interact in a vacuum, but rather circulated, were accepted, imagined, and perceived in the form of a "colonisation of mind" or "surrogate hegemony." During the 18th and 19th centuries, the imaginary of "Orthodox and Slavic unity" was strengthened and negotiated between Imperial Russia and Ottoman Orthodox subjects. The first such attempt happened in the Russo–Ottoman War (1710–1711), when Peter the Great sent the first delegation to Montenegro (1711). The head of this delegation was a Russian general, a South Slav from Herzegovina, Mihailo Miloradović, who along with his brothers, Gabriel and Aleksandar, entered the imperial service of Tsar Peter the Great, and stood against the Ottomans. Miloradović carried an imperial decree (*gramata*), in which the Tsar called on the Montenegrins for "a crusade war against the Turks, who tried to occupy their 'fertile' (*blagorodne*) lands, and to enslave (Montenegrin) 'persons' (*osobe*) together with all who worshipped the crucified Christ – our God (*svi narodi koji obožavaju razapetog Hrista – Boga našega*)." Therefore, the duty of the believers in the "Greek and Roman religion" (*grčke i rimske vjere*) was to put up a hard fight against the Ottomans "as in the ancient times, on the side of Alexander of Macedon."[147] During the 18th century, it was a common

---

[147] Aleksej Jelačić, *Istorija Rusije* (Beograd: Romanov, 2000); The early 18th century brought many South Slavs from this part of "Macedonia" into the Russian administration in order to strengthen ties with them by translating different books displaying a proto–Pan–Slavic character, such as Mavro Orbin's *"Il regno degli Slavi"* (The Realm of the Slavs). One of those mediators and translators was Sava Vladislavić, who became a famous Russian diplomat from Ragusa (Dubrovnik). He played a multidimensional role, from a person responsible for the cooperation between Russia and the South Slavs, to that between Russia and the Ottomans, where, together with Peter Tolstoy, he was appointed head of the Russian mission to Istanbul. Similar examples of such interconnections, transfers, and entanglements will be present during the whole 18th and 19th century, especially after the Russian advances and victories against the Ottomans (1739, 1774, 1792), when the Russians began to play a significant role alongside the major European powers in the determination of the affairs in this undefined land of Macedonia. The Orthodox Christian inhabitants of this region turned to St. Petersburg for diplomatic and military support by raising questions on their behalf.

belief that the army of Alexander of Macedon consisted of Illyrians who were then considered the ancestors of the Slavs. Even in the aforementioned decree, Tsar Peter the Great referred to Montenegrins as "the good fighters since the time of Alexander the Great (Macedonian) and the wars of Skanderbeg against the Ottomans."[148] Beliefs that South Slavs were descendants and companions of Alexander the Great and ancient Macedonians, living in this ancient land of Macedonia, were present during the entirety of the early modern period. [149] In this regard, Miloradović reported that he visited "Doklea, Zeta, Montenegro, the provinces of Macedonia."[150] The Imperial Russian administration kept its connections with the Montenegrins, as they represented a so–called Russian mirror in the Ottoman Empire.[151] Osman Karatay remarked that "although this (Montenegrin) community was small in membership, one could consider that it became the first Balkan independent community."[152] This in turn enabled frequent communication between St. Petersburg and Cetinje. Thus, during July 1789, when Bastilla was on fire in Paris, Montenegrin *guvernadur* Radonjić addressed a letter to Catherine the Great, pleading with her to help the South–Slav population to "regain (possession of) all glorious Serb lands (*slavnu srpsku zemlju*)" which were "under Barbarian yoke (*varvarskim igom*)." Furthermore, he stressed that they had enlisted the help of "other Serb brothers, which want to attack the Turks from all sides. All we, Serbs, from Montenegro, Herzegovina, Banjani, Drobnjak, Piper, Bjelopavlović, Zeta, Kliment, Vasojević, Bratonozić, Peć, Kosovo, Prizren, Arbanija, and Maćedonija, belong to your majesty (*vašemu veličanstvu*) and we beseech help from you as we

---

[148] Ibid.

[149] Oliver Jens Schmitt, *Shqiptarët* (Tiranë: K&B, 2012), p. 28; In original: Oliver Schmitt, *Die Albaner: Eine Geschichte zwischen Orient und Okzident* (Munich: C.H. Beck, 2012). An Albanologist, Oliver Schmitt gives the example of the Albanian priest Frang Bardhi, who introduced himself with the words: "I am from the land of Macedonia, from Shkodra'' (*Jam dheut ce Matsedoniese, i shkodernjane*), p. 96.

[150] Jelačić, *Istorija Rusije*, p. 27.

[151] Ibid.

[152] Osman Karatay, "Osmanlı Hakimiyetinde Karadağ," in *Balkanlar el Kitabi cilt 1*, eds. Bilgehan A. Gökdağ and Osman Karatay (Ankara: Akçağ Basım Yayım Pazarlama, 2013), p. 358.

would from our merciful mother (*milostiva naša majka*)."[153] This notion of the "liberation of Serb lands" from "Barbarian yoke" was in effect a result of the influence of the European ideas of the time, according to which the rest of the world was considered barbaric. In the view of Larry Wolff, "the Eastern Europe was located not at the antipode of civilisation, not down in the depths of barbarism, but rather on the developmental scale (…) which was essentially in between (…) in short, the Slav peoples, are a link between Europe and Asia, between civilisation and barbarism."[154] Therefore, as I have already stated, the idea of Eastern Europe never attained a status of consummate "otherness" like that of the Orient, but rather the status of a space that had the potential to "belong to civilisation."[155] In this respect, the Balkan population could be integrated "into common historical destiny of the continent."[156] In order to develop (along) the same pathways as civilised Europe, the Balkan intellectuals constructed discourses of itself as "the guardian(s) of European values rather than the barbarian at Europe's gate."[157] In Alexander Kiossev's point of view this is a metaphorical "self–colonisation" which "can be used for cultures having succumbed to the cultural power of Europe and the west without having been invaded and turned into colonies in actual fact (…) but, affected either by important colonial conflicts or by the techniques of colonial rule."[158] In similar ways, Ewa Thompson defines this process as "surrogate hegemony," in the sense that "members of the colonised elite" display "a view that Western countries are a model to

---

[153] Gligor Stanojević, *Crna Gora pred stvaranje države 1773–1796* (Beograd: Istorijski Institut, 1962), p. 289.

[154] Wolff, *Inventing Eastern Europe,* p. 13.

[155] Ibid., p. 358.

[156] Paschalis Kitromilides, "The Enlightenment East and West: a comparative perspective on the ideological origins of the Balkan political traditions," *Canadian Review of Studies in Nationalism* 10/1 (1983): 55.

[157] Goldsworthy, *Inventing Ruritania,* p. ix.

[158] Alexandar Kiossev, *The End of Self–Colonization: Contemporary Bulgarian Literature and Its Global Condition* (Sofia: Bulgarian Literature as World Literature, 2020). p. 1; Alexander Kiossev and Daniela Koleva (eds), *Trudniat razkaz: Modeli na avtobiografichnoto razkazvane na sotzializma mezhdu ustnoto i pismenoto* (Sofia: Tsiela, 2017); For Ranajit Guha this is process of 'hegemony without domination' that consists foreign cultural supremacy and voluntary absorption of their basic values and categories of colonial Europe. See: Ranajit Guha, *Dominance without Hegemony: History and Power in Colonial India* (Cambridge: Harvard University Press, 1998).

follow in every way, that one travels westward to enjoy liberty and well–being, and to learn how to interpret history and the present."[159] However, this "self–colonisation" or "surrogate hegemony" aimed to turn the local elites and their imagined geographies into civilised members of Europe, since they believed that they had a new duty, that is "to spread progress and modernity, freedom from Asiatic tyranny, self–determination, and human rights among the backward ones."[160] This self–imagination has constructed the West in opposition to East Europe, but also the "civilised Balkans" in opposition to the "Asiatic Turks," by defining concluding "Easts" in the world, and none of them is without signification.[161] This represents a process that Milica Bakić–Hayden calls "nesting Orientalism", that is the tendency towards (constructing) the essentialised Self as superior, progressed/advanced, or developed, while constructing the oriental "Other."[162] In this respect, the Balkan elite accepted the knowledge of a Europe as superior and dreamt of a replacement of this "Asiatic" Ottoman Empire by a new "European" republic of the Balkans. In 1797, the revolutionary vision of Rigas Velestinlis imagined a Jacobin–inspired "Hellenic Republic," which would unite "all Balkan ethnic, cultural and religious communities under the rule of law."[163] Next, Velestinlis introduced the idea of the "liberty to assault tyranny, break the (Ottoman) yoke of despotism, and establish justice and freedom throughout the land that extended from Bosnia and Montenegro through Roumeli and Mani to Crete and Asia Minor, to Syria and Egypt."[164] Similar aspirations were expressed by Velestinlis' friend, Adamantios Korais in his famous *"Report on the present state of civilisation in Greece"* (1803). He wrote about the circulation of knowledge from "the (French) *Encyclopédie* (…) to Greece." Accordingly, he emphasised: "We are the

---

[159] Ewa Thompson, *The Surrogate Hegemon in Polish Postcolonial Discourse* (Houston: Rice University, 2007), p. 4.

[160] Kiossev, *Trudniat raskaz.*

[161] Ibid., p. 15.

[162] Bakić–Hayden, *Nesting Orientalisms,* p. 918.

[163] Kitromilides, *An Orthodox Commonwealth*, p. 46.

[164] Paschalis Kitromilides, *Enlightenment and Revolution: The Making of Modern Greece* (Cambridge: Harvard University Press, 2013), p. 228.

descendants of Greeks (…) we must either try to become again worthy of this name, or we must not bear it."[165]

In the Greek case, this circulation of knowledge led to the imagination of the ancient Hellenic origins, while the Serbs and the Bulgarians sought their distinct historical personality by turning to their medieval imperial past. Firstly, they started with the historiographical projects of Jovan Rajić and Paisij Hilendarski in the second half of 18th century. After Montenegrin tribes defeated the Ottoman army in 1796 (in the battles of Krusi and Martinići), vladika Petar I Petrović established the state apparatus and its first Law (*Zakon opšči crnogorski i brdski*), established the tribes' independent status, and opened up the possibility of imagining the new state in the Balkans, which would play a significant role in the subsequent anti–Ottoman movements. The following Serbian Uprisings (1804 and 1815) raised awareness among South Slavs of the need of change.[166] In 1806, the leader of the Serbian Uprising Petar Karađorđe wrote to Montenegrin vladika Petar I Petrović: "[W]e are always, in our hearts and minds, united (*svagda, i u srcu i u mislima*)" and "you will be great and powerful support to the liberation of the Serbs/Serbian people (*srpskom narodu u oslobođenju, velika i moćna potpora biti*)." [167] Therefore, at the beginning of the Russo–Ottoman war (1806–1812), in 1807, vladika Petar I Petrović of Montenegro wrote a letter to Russian Tsar Alexander I, envisioning a new state of Slav–Serb Tsardom (*Slaveno– serbsko carstvo*), consisting of Bosnia, Herzegovina, Dalmatia, and Montenegro with its centre and seat in Dubrovnik. On the other hand, vladika wrote to the egumen of the Dečani Monastery that "in this year, we Montenegrins, along with our brethren, the Serbs from Belgrade, wish

---

[165] Adamantios Korais, "Report on the Present State of Civilization in Greece," in *Late Enlightenment – Emergence of the Modern 'National Idea'*, eds. by Balazs Trencsenyi and Michal Kopecek (Budapest/New York: Central European University Press, 2006), p. 144.

[166] Almost a hundred years after Montenegro, Serbia established ties with Russia, by sending, in 1804, one of the leaders of the rebels, Prota (Archpriest) Mateja Nenadović to Russia. Nenadović left a detailed account of his journey to Russia in his memoirs. See: Mateja Nenadović, *Memoari* (Beograd: Portalibris, 2017).

[167] Ibid.

to attack our enemies, the Turks, and if we can, banish all of them (*ako možemo vsje da izbavimo*)."[168]

This desired and imagined alliance of all Serbs was praised as a sacred, political, and spiritual duty, which was to be presented before the whole of Europe.[169] In this sense, the wealthiest Serb in Hungary, Sava Tekelija, submitted a Memorandum first to Napoleon (in 1804), then to the Habsburg Emperor Francis II (in 1805). Ultimately he printed the Geographic Map of Serbia, Bosnia, Dubrovnik, Montenegro, and other neighbours (in 1805) in order to define the potential national claims of the Serbs and to find allies for the re–establishment of their medieval empire.[170] Commenting on the latter, Larry Wolff notes that "Napoleon's creation of Adriatic provinces of Illyria in 1809" was not to be the "last time that armies of Western Europe sought to establish an empire in (south)Eastern Europe." [171] These programmes, coupled with their European tutors and predecessors, can be considered as the first instances of the imagination of national liberation and the attempt for "resurrection of the Serbian state" (*vaskrs države srpske*). It is worth noting that the intellectual influence of the European Enlightenment among one part of the "awakened Serbs" imagined this state as protected by Russia (e.g. Stevan Stratimirović, vladika Petar I). On the other hand, another part (e.g. Dositej Obradović, Sava Tekelija) advocated for a departure from the hegemony of the church and the creation of a new state based on European models. This desire to put Serbs in contact with contemporary European culture was reinforced by the influence of German Romanticism and "the trends of folklorism that became priority of South–eastern European thought in the 19th century."[172] The aim of the latter Serbian intellectuals was in fact to construct a national Serbian identity based on the Serbian medieval empire narrative, supported by the Serbian Church.

---

[168] Ibid.

[169] Dušan T. Bataković, "A Balkan–Style French Revolution? The 1804 Serbian Uprising in European perspective," *Balcanica* 36 (2005): 116; Radoslav Perović, *Prvi srpski ustanak* (Beograd: Narodna knjiga, 1977), pp. 175–177.

[170] Ibid., p. 118. See also: Vladislav Sotirović, *Serbia, Montenegro and Albanian Question 1878–1912* (Saarbrücken: Lambert Academic Publishing, 2015). p. 69.

[171] Wolff, *Inventing Eastern Europe.*

[172] Kitromilides, *The Enlightenment East and West*, p. 59.

2.4.1. Towards the Nation–State(s)

The role of the intellectuals in promoting national agendas has been recognised in the works of Benedict Anderson,[173] Anthony D. Smith,[174] Ernest Gellner,[175] Eric Hobsbawm,[176] to name a few. This European invention, closely bound with the emergence of the modern state, constructed new "imagined communities" and "invented traditions." However, as I have already stated, these processes should not be analysed in a vacuum, as nationalist historiographies would argue, but rather as interconnected processes that influenced different entities in creating the states. It is conceivable that during the first half of 19th century, the histories of the Balkan Christian communities were entangled. The Balkan intellectuals were relatively united in their attempts at liberation from the Ottoman Empire. For example, Alexander Ypsilanti did not invite the Greeks, but "the Christians in the Ottoman Empire to throw off the sultan's yoke."[177] Many prominent figures from different parts of the Balkans adopted this duty. Thus, the veteran of the Serbian Uprising, vojvoda Hadži Prodan accepted the service of the Greek Revolution to liberated "Orthodox brothers" from "Turkish cruelty" (*turski zulum*). Another important figure was the Montenegrin general Vaso Brajović (Vasos Mavrovunotis), who, together with his "spiritual brother" (*kum, vlami*) Nikolaos Kriezotis, played a significant role against the Ottomans.[178] Among these soldiers were famous Orthodox Arvanites and Albanian Souliotes (e.g. Marko Boçari, Kiço Xhavella), renowned as Greek national heroes and fighting against their "brothers in nation," the (Muslim) Ottoman Albanians. More specifically, the concept of "entangled history" helps us to avoid the replacement of these personalities with one nationalist discourse, and to accept their interconnectedness in one common

---

[173] Benedict Anderson, *Imagined Communities: Reflections on the Origin and Spread of Nationalism* (London: Verso, 1983)

[174] Anthony D. Smith, *The Ethnic Origins of Nations* (Oxford: Basil Blackwell, 1986).

[175] Ernest Gellner, *Nations and Nationalism* (Oxford: Basil Blackwell, 1983).

[176] Hobsbawm, *The Invention of Tradition*.

[177] David Brewer, *The Greek War of Independence: The Struggle for Freedom from Ottoman Oppression and the Birth of the Modern Greek Nation* (New York: Woodstock, 2003), p. 53.

[178] Stefanos P. Papageorgiou, "Vasos Mavrovunotis (Vaso Brajović) – Crnogorac U Grčkoj Revoluciji," *Matica Crnogorska* 62 (2015): 45.

imagination of belonging to (Orthodox) Christianity and European "Civilisation." Influenced by European ideas, their historical mission at the beginning of 19th century was to liberate their imagined "holy land" from the "barbarous" Ottomans, and to (re)establish their own states. The imagination of the new states occurred went hand in hand with the imagination of community. All Balkan nations were under the influence of the great European powers, including Imperial Russia.[179] It is worth noting that "imported" ideas from Europe did not contend with their Balkan nations' religious and Slavic ties with Russia. In a certain manner, these two processes complemented one (an)other, especially after the Crimean War of 1856. In fact, most of the educated South Slavs imagined united states or empire divided into tribes (Serbs, Bulgarians, Illyrians/Croats, etc.). Thus, in a letter sent to Georgi Zolotovich in November 1843, Bulgarian philosopher Ivan Seliminski wrote the following:

> "The closer our relationship becomes to other peoples and especially to those of Slavic origin, the stronger will be our ties, the greater and more sincere our help and compassion, the sounder the foundations of our national welfare. The more our people studies history and the advanced literature of other nations, especially the Slavs, the sooner it will advance its own to reach the glory of its ancestors and of modern civilised peoples."[180]

Hence, the combination of "civilised Europe" with the peoples' "Slavic origin" composed the preponderant *Weltanschauung* of the Balkan "surrogate hegemony." Applied through a "colonisation of the mind," this policy influenced many members of the Serbian intellectuals based in Vienna and prompted them to prepare strategies for the implementation of "surrogate hegemony." One of these strategies appeared in Dimitrije Davidović's work *Djejanija k Istoriji Srpskoga naroda* translated as

---

[179] See the works of Yuri Venelin about Bulgarians and their political, ethnographic, historical and religious relations to the Russians in: Roumen Daskalov, *Bulgarian Historical Review: Special Issue on Bulgaria in the Twentieth Century* (Sofia: Bulgarian Academy of Sciences Press, 2005); Marshall Lee Miller, *Bulgaria During the Second World War* (Stanford: Stanford University Press, 1975).

[180] Ivan Seliminski, "Letter to Georgi Zolotovich," in *Late Enlightenment – Emergence of the Modern 'National Idea'*, eds. Balazs Trencsenyi and Michal Kopecek (Budapest/New York: Central European University Press, 2006), p. 186.

History of the Servian People, It was accompanied by the map "Territories inhabited by Servians," which represented Serbia as the centre of liberation from the "barbarous" Ottomans. Still, in this map, Serbia was depicted without Kosovo/Old Serbia and Macedonia. However, the major reformer of the Serbian language, Vuk Karadžić, in his famous pamphlet *Serbs All and Everywhere* (1836/1849), developed a wider conception of Serbian territories, emphasising: "[I]t is known that Serbs now live in present–day Serbia (between the Drina and Timok, and between the Danube and the Stara Planina Mountain), in Metohija (from Kosovo over the mountains, where King Dušan's capital Prizren, the Serbian Patriarchate of Peć, and Dečani Monastery were), in Bosnia, Herzegovina, Zeta, Montenegro, Banat, Bačka, in Srijem, the western Danube region from Osijek to Sentandrija, in Slavonia, Croatia (Turkish and Austrian parts), Dalmatia, and the Adriatic region from Trieste to Bojana (Montenegro)." He points out that it was known with certainty that a Serbian population inhabited, while "it [was] still not known how many Serbs [were] living in Albania and in Macedonia. When I was in Cetinje (Montenegro), I talked with two men from Dibra, who told me that there were many Serbian (*serpskijeh*) villages, in which Serbian was spoken, as well as such where a language between Serbian and Bulgarian was spoken, closer to Serbian than Bulgarian." [181] These imaginations, that Macedonia was populated by Serbs or a people who speak "a language (…) closer to Serbian than Bulgarian" defined the main Serbian policy after the Congress of Berlin. However, one should notice that in the mid–19th century this differentiation of Serbs and Bulgarians was not highly important, since they were just (separate) tribes of the more widely imagined "South–Slav nation." Apart from its significance for the Macedonian case, Vuk Karadžić's work is also famous for the establishment of the myth about "the battle of Kosovo" as the key theme of the Serbian instance of "invented tradition." According to Aleksandar Pavlović and Srđan Atanasovski, "the myth served not only as a literary achievement, but also as a veritable battle cry and a trump card of Serbian expansionistic

---

[181] Vuk Stefanović Karadžić, *Srbi svi i svuda – Kovčežić za istoriju, jezik i običaje Srba sva tri zakona* (Beč: N.P., 1849). The book was written in 1836, but it was published in 1849 in Vienna.

politics."[182] This myth is important due to its being an integral part of a broader context of Macedonia, via three dimensions: the myth was constructed in the territory of Kosovo, which according to the above–mentioned authors, was part of what was imagined as the "Macedonian Illyricum," and which after the Congress of Berlin composed one of the three vilayets (*Vilayet–i selase*/Macedonia); the myth revives the heroes who fought against the Ottomans in 1389; and in this Kosovo battle the Serbian Empire of Tsar Dušan was obliterated, along with its legacy that placed its core in Macedonia (capitals of the empire were Skopje and Prizren). This Kosovo myth evoked such folk heroes as Kraljević Marko, son of King Vukašin Mrnjavčević, who ruled in Prilep (Macedonia) until his death in 1371.[183] The legendary Marko is the embodiment of all that "the Serbs wanted to believe of themselves — his heroism, his gentleness, his respect for the religious and social customs of his people, his 'machismo', even his cruelty, but above all their fierce opposition to the Turks and his intense national pride."[184] In similar ways, the brothers Miladinov (Dimitar and Konstantin) collected Bullgarian epic poems (*pesne*) from Macedonia, published them in Zagreb in 1861as "*Bŭlgarski narodni pesni*" (Bulgarian Folk Songs), sponsored by the eminent supporter of the Southern Slav idea, the Croat Catholic Bishop Strossmayer. A similar work was published in Belgrade by Stefan Verković, *Folk songs of the Macedonian Bulgarians* (1860), supported by Serbia. It seems that during the mid–19th century the South Slavs were moving towards a common project that found its grounds and support in Russian Pan–Slavism. The prominent figure who wanted to contribute to the Russian involvements and liberation from the "yoke of the Asiatic tribe (*unerträgliche asiatische Joch*)" was Mihailo Polit Desančić. In his work "*Die Orientalische Frage und ihre Organische Lösung*"[185] (1862), he presented his views on the Eastern Question (*die orientalische Frage*) by stating that Europe did not assist in the liberation of the Balkan peoples

---

[182] Aleksandar Pavlović and Srđan Atanasovski, "From Myth to Territory: Vuk Karadžić, Kosovo Epics and the Role of Nineteenth–Century Intellectuals in Establishing National Narratives," *Hungarian Historical Review* 5/2 (2016): 371.

[183] Singleton, *A short History,* p. 45.

[184] Ibid., p. 45.

[185] Mihailo Polith, *Die Orientalische Frage und ihre Organische Lösung* (Vienna: Franz Leo's Verlag 1862).

against the Turks. In his opinion, "of all European states, only Russia was the protector of the Christians against the wild Asiatic tyranny of the Turks."[186] With this aim in mind, he believed that the "final solution" for the liberation from the "Asiatic tribe" and their "Asiatic tyranny" was the help of Russia. To this end, he suggested an "organic solution (*organische Lösung*)" by "dividing Turkey (*die Teilung der Türkei*) among the Balkan peoples (and uniting them) into a confederation of the nations."[187] For this reason, Desančić believed that "the fight against the Asiatic barbarians was a sacred commitment for the Balkan peoples."[188] His friend, Svetozar Miletić, president of the Society for Serbian Unification and Liberation (*Družina za ujedinjenje i oslobođenje srpsko*) also supported this "organic solution" against the Ottomans and, for the solution of the Eastern (Macedonian) Question, he suggested a political unity of all Slavs.[189] In a similar vein, Montenegrin vladika Petar II Petrović Njegoš supported the "pan–South Slavic" unity and its "anti–Turkish" elements. His heroic folk poem *The Mountain Wreath* (*Gorski Vijenac*), published in Vienna in 1847, is considered the crucial anti–Turkish work in the literature(s) of the Balkan nations, dedicated "to the ashes of the Father of Serbia," Karađorđe, the leader of the First Serbian Uprising (1804–13) against the Turks. In the poem, Njegoš represents Montenegro as the only free region surrounded by the "big Asiatic Mongol" (*azijatski veliki mongol*).[190] In his poem *The False Tsar Stephen the Little* (*Lažni car Šćepan Mali*), published in 1845, he wonders:

"What East did with the West/ what kind of disasters did/ what kind of force changed the time (…) what Osman broke/ in order to eat the world!/ Only pain Kur'an brought to Slavs/ among brothers blood was shed/ Despite this, who would believe/ just one small people (Montenegrins)/

---

[186] Ibid., p. 21; Quote: *"…dass von allen europäischen Staaten Rußland die größte und in manchen Fällen die einzige Schußwehr der Christen gegen die wilde asiatische Tyrannei der Türken war."*
[187] Ibid., p. 40.
[188] Ibid., p. 1; Quote: *"…dass ihre Befreiung vom assiatischen Joche zugleich einen Sieg des sittlichen Principes involvire. Ihr Kampf gegen die asiatischen Barbaren erscheint ihnen daher al sein heiliger."*
[189] Svetozar Miletitsch, *Die Orientfrage* (Neusatz: Serbish–Nationale Vereins–Buchdruckerei, 1877).
[190] Petar Petrović Njegoš, *Lažni car Šćepan Mali* (Titograd: Grafički zavod, 1965).

can stand up against/ wild force, combined by all evils/ to the Stambol's disaster rulers (*stambolskijeh grubijeh hakanah*)/ and to their poisoned faith/ I salute you, Slavic sanctity (*Pozdravljam te, svetinjo slavenska.*)"[191]

Njegoš's poems contain a criticism of European Christians, as he accuses them of merely "scoffing and spitting" at the Turks, who had caused destruction to Christianity wherever they ruled. In *The Mountain Wreath*, he highlights that those who refused to be enslaved by the Turks and did not betray their faith sought refuge in the mountains of Montenegro. Njegoš emphasises the importance of shedding blood, heroically keeping sacred oaths, and preserving freedom to maintain a name of honor.[192] This led Montenegro to assume the role of Europe and fight the "big Asiatic Mongol" in the name of civilisation. While Njegoš was a devout Orthodox, Stedimlija maintains that he remained a pure Westerner, but with retained Orthodox elements.[193] These ideas had a strong influence on Montenegro (and other Balkan countries) and its implementation of "surrogate hegemony" as the triumphant victory spirit of Western culture and civilisation. Vuk Karadžić, who was considered the greatest intellectual of his time, and Petar II Petrović Njegoš, who was regarded as the greatest poet of the Serbian language,[194] both played significant political roles. Karadžić invented the Kosovo myth and depicted Serbian territories, while Njegoš praised these territories and aimed to restore "European civilisation to its roots."[195] Njegoš attributed a significant role to Montenegro in the liberation from Ottoman rule and the formation of a larger state or empire. This stance was instrumental in fostering anti-Ottoman sentiments.

---

[191] Ibid.

[192] Petar Petrović Njegoš, *Gorski Vijenac* (Beograd: Branko Dinović, 1963).

[193] Savo M. Stedimlija, *The Foundation of Montenegrin Nationalism* (Zagreb, 1937), p. 127. Among the literary works which were announced for publishing in the manuscript, the following title is found at the beginning of this brochure: "Croatia and Montenegro, articles and essays," in p. 48.

[194] Armando Pitassio, "The Building of Nations in South–Eastern Europe. The Cases of Slovenia and Montenegro: a Comparative Approach," in *The Balkans: National Identities in a Historical Perspective*, ed. Stefano Bianchini and Marco Dogo (Ravenna: Longo Editore, 1998) p. 49.

[195] Aleksandar Pavlović, "Naming/Taming the Enemy: Balkan Oral Tradition and formation of 'the Turk' as the Political Enemy," in *Us and Them Symbolic Divisions in Western Balkan Societies*, ed. Ivana Spasić and Predrag Cvetičanin (Beograd: Institut za filozofiju i društvenu teoriju Univerziteta u Beogradu, 2013).

However, this view was contested by two other significant works that also advocated for anti-Ottoman programs. These two works appeared in the same year (1844) and were known as Ilija Garašanin's Greater Serbia project, defined in *Načertanije*; and Ioannis Kolettis' Greater Greece project, defined in *Megali Idea*. The former, Serbian statesman Ilija Garašanin, belongs to the group of Serbs who had a vision of "South Slavic" liberation combined with Serbian expansion. In his opinion, "Serbia should take part among other European states (*u red ostalih evropejskih država postaviti*)" by becoming a greater [something] through the policy of "uniting all Serb peoples that it is surrounded by (*priljubiti sve narode srpske koji je okružavaju*)."[196] In this attempt, he finds a basis and a harking back to the old Serbian medieval empire of Tsar Dušan, which had its centre in Skopje (Macedonia) and Prizren (Old Serbia).[197] According to Garašanin, "if the (new) reborn Serbian Tsardom appear[ed], then the other South Slavs [would] understand and happily accept this idea, because nowhere in the European land (*evropejskoj zemlji*) as among the Turkish Slavs (*Slovena turskih*) is a historical remembrance of the past presented (*spomen istoričeske prošlosti*)." [198] According to Stefan Rohdewald, the memory based on medieval empires influenced "the imagination of geographical spaces (*geographische Räume imaginierten*)."[199] This memory, based on a common history during the medieval empire, triggered the Serbian state to cooperate with the Bulgarian Committee during 1866. Serbia was pivotal to Bulgaria in these years as a source of hopes of military aid, asylum, or assistance in the liberation from the Ottomans.[200] Having joined forces with the Bulgarian Committee, Montenegro, Greece, and Romania, Serbia formed the first Balkan Alliance (1867) in order to wage a common struggle against the Ottomans. In the same year, Rusian Slavenophiles staged the Slavic Exhibition, which showcased an ethnological map (see map 4) of all the Slavic races as liberated and united. M. F. Mirkowitch, a Russian

---

[196] Ilija Garašanin, *Načertanije* (Beograd: Ethos, 2016), pp. 23–24.
[197] Singleton, *A short History*, p. 93.
[198] Garašanin, *Načertanije*, p. 28.
[199] Rohdewald, *Götter der Nation*, p. 763.
[200] Mark Pinson, "Ottoman Bulgaria in the First Tanzimat Period — The Revolts in Nish (1841) and Vidin (1850)," *Middle Eastern Studies*, 11/2 (May, 1975): 122–124.

geographer and ethnographer, drew this map and titled it "*Ethnological Map of the Slavic peoples*," as it strove to demonstrate the strong Slavic unity around the Continent (in green: see the map).[201]

Map 4 *Slavyanskih Narodnosti*[202]

The similarities among the Slavs were presented in August Petermann's collections of maps, books, and notes. He drew a map of the Balkans in 1869, marking Serbs and Bulgarians with the same colour. Rather than differences, his map underscored similarities which could indicate a common political future. Before the 1870s the question whether the inhabitants of Macedonia were Serbs or Bulgarians did not carry a lot of weight, since they both were parts of a broader South–Slavic family or, in the words of Muir–Mackenzie and Irby, "Yugo–Slavi." Similarly, in "*Die Slaven in der Turkei*,"[203] Croatian professor Franjo Bradaska claimed that the "Slav inhabitants in Turkey [were] spread from the rivers Dau and Donau to the Aegean Sea, and from the Adriatic to the Black Sea, (…) constituting one unity of different tribes (*Stamme*)."[204] Arguing along similar lines, Vladimir Jovanović, a Serbian politician and the most significant liberal ideologue, considered that these Slavic tribes belong to

---

[201] Wilkinson, *Maps and politics,* p. 53.
[202] Rizoff, *Bŭlgarite v tekhnite istoricheski*, p. 36.
[203] Franz Bradaska, "Die Slaven in der Turkei," *Mitteilungen aus Justus Pethers' Geographischer Anstalt* 15 (1869): 458.
[204] Ibid., pp. 441–446.

the same nation.[205] In this regard, in his essay "Serbian Nation and the Eastern Question" (1863) he pointed out that Serbia should have a leading role in the unification of these tribes and the solving of the Eastern Question. Furthermore, he presented his views on the future map of the Balkans in his two other studies: *"Serbes et la Mission de la Serbie dans l' Europe d' Orient,"*[206] and *"The Emancipation and Unity of the Serbian Nation or the Regeneration of the Eastern Europe."*[207] Jovanović believed that liberated Serbia should become the champion of liberal and progressive ideas in South–Eastern Europe.[208] There is no evidence if these books and maps have any relation with the establishment of the Balkan Alliance in 1867. However, it is evident that in this period the Slavs, together with other Christian subjects of the Ottoman Empire, were united in the idea of implementing "surrogate hegemony" and liberating from the Ottomans. These established entanglements among various strata of population and regions were much more interconnected than what contemporary national historiographies tend to present. Yet, the idea of Slavic unification was soon challenged by French geographer C. Delamarre, who in 1868 introduced an ethnographical map indicated that "Pan–Slavism from a linguistic and literary point of view was a myth."[209] Notably, only a few years later, a schism divided the Balkan intellectuals as well. Firstly, the Bulgarian–Greek conflict escalated inside the Orthodox Church. The Patriarch accused the Exarchate for spreading Bulgarian ethno–nationalist propaganda in Macedonia. In the Bulgarian newspaper "Macedonia," published in Istanbul, was demonstrated as "infinitive senseless of the Greek words (*beskrajni grchki palavri*)."[210] In Fikret Adanır's opinion, this conflict became one of the main reasons for the Macedonian conflicts.[211] This contestation was soon joined by Serbia,

---

[205] Vladimir Yovanovics, *Les Serbes et la Mission de la Serbie dans l' Europe d' Orient* (Paris: A. Lacroix, Verboeckhoven et Cie Éditeurs 1870), p. 9.
[206] Ibid.
[207] Vladimir Yovanovitch, *The Emancipation and Unity of the Serbian Nation or the Regeneration of the Eastern Europe* (Geneva: H. Georg 10, Corraterie 1871).
[208] Yovanovics, *Les Serbes et la Mission de la Serbie,* pp. 5–6.
[209] Wilkinson, *Maps and politics.*
[210] Makedonia, Istanbul, 8. Januar, 1871.
[211] Adanır, *Die makedonische Frage*, p. 134. See quote: *"(...) Aus diesem Grunde entstanden zahlreiche Konflikte zwischen den Gemeinden und den Behörden des Exarchats. Bei solchen Auseinandersetzungen ergriffen die makedonischen Lehrer*

and a separate policy was supported by the Serbian historian Miloš Milojević. He published the *"Odlomci istorije Srba i srpskih – jugoslavenskih – zemalja u Turskoj i Austriji"* (1872), where he declared that the "Serbian language and culture extended much further in the south (in the territories of Macedonia)."[212] This break of relations among the different members of the former Balkan Alliance in the 1870s only intensified their competition towards Macedonia during the "Age of Empire." The policy of liberation from the "big Asiatic Mongol" and inclusion of Macedonia in one common Balkan or South–Slavic state was to transform the competition politics between the former "Orthodox brothers." To the contrary, the intellectuals involved constructed different narratives about Macedonia, joined various state policies, and reflected contested imperialist projects, as will be seen in further chapters.

2.4.2. Russia's Forcible Intervention in Ottoman Rumelia and the Emergence of the Macedonian Questions

Barbara Jelavich asserts that, between 1806 and 1914, Russia was involved in six wars, five of which were due to its deep involvement in Balkan affairs.[213] The emergence of the Eastern Question at the end of the 18th and its development during the 19th century was one of Tsar Nicholas I's reasons to define the Ottoman disintegration at the beginning of the Crimean War (1853–1856) as a "sick man" who "has fallen into a state of decrepitude (*u nas na rukah bolnoy chelovek, ochen bolnoy chelovek*)."[214] Inside this Eastern Question, the Orient (Ottoman Empire) became a space of European colonial dominance in which Russia had its own share.[215] The borrowing of Western orientalist idioms legitimised Russia's aggressive policy towards the Ottoman Empire within the idea of Russia's own

---

gewöhnlich die Partei der Gemeinden, weil die Einbeziehung der Schulen in das Schulsystem des Exarchats bedeutete, daß die Lehrer künftig von der Schulkuratel beim Exarchat ernannt werden würden."

[212] Miloš Milojević, *Odlomci istorije Srba i srpskih – jugoslavenskih – zemalja u Turskoj i Austriji* (Beograd: 1872).

[213] Barbara Jelavich, *Russia's Balkan Entanglements*, p. ix.

[214] Viktor Taki, *Tsar i Sultan – Osmanskaya imperiya glazami Rossiyan* (Moscow: Novoe literaturnoe obozrenie, 2017), p. 168.

[215] Viktor Taki, "Orientalism on the Margins – The Ottoman Empire under Russian Eyes," *Slavica Publishers* 12/12 (2011): 323.

integration into the "Occident" as a "part of Civilisation."[216] This process of Russian orientalising was simultaneously a manifestation of Russian Occidentalism in the first half of the 19th century.[217] Articulated by means of borrowed idioms, the Russian views of the Ottoman Empire, can be also analysed as an example of "nesting Orientalism."[218]

This understanding of the Orient as "barbaric" increased the Russian "mission" to solve the Eastern Question and to liberate its Orthodox brethren from Ottoman rule. According to Barbara Jelavich, "the Orthodoxy was of particular importance for the Russian relationship with the Balkan people," considering that "the Christian nations together represented a moral unity and that they should cooperate (as in the Greek War of Independence)."[219] Therefore, Russia tried to strengthen its ties with the Balkan Orthodox elite by sending numerous travellers to map this region and undertake activities in the form of: protection of Ottoman Orthodox subjects, and intervention in Serbia, Greece, Montenegro, and the Danubian Principalities. With the Crimean disaster and the Treaty of Paris (1856), Russia lost its rights and obligations to protect the Ottoman Orthodox subjects, which had a major influence on its foreign policy, reflected in its increase of emphasis on the Slavic people. The "surrogate hegemony" of the Balkans, their aim of liberating from the Ottomans, coupled with the new expansionist Russian policy based on common roots with their South Slavic brothers, strengthened the already existing ties and established new trans–regional entanglements. In the second half of the 19th century, Russia reinforced its ties with the 'South–Slav brothers,' especially with the Bulgarian intellectuals, whose national movement had not proceeded as fast as the corresponding Serbian, Greek, and Romanian movements. Barbara Jelavich notes that the "Bulgarians also sought a foreign patron, and they had only one possible choice. They could not expect the assistance from France, the Habsburg Empire, or Britain, largely because of their geographic location and the lack of historic involvement in the area by Western powers. Russia was, therefore, the only

---

[216] Ibid., p. 337.

[217] Ibid, p. 324.

[218] The phenomenon was first explored in the Balkan context. See: Bakić–Hayden, *Nesting Orientalisms*, p. 917.

[219] Barbara Jelavich, *Russia's Balkan Entanglements*, p. 92.

state to which they could turn."[220] Bulgarian nationalism was to a great extent imported from Russia, where Slavophile/Slavenophile romanticism spread in the mid 19th century, but was built upon European national models. Therefore, this "late Bulgarian awakening" was expressed by Konstantin Fotinov, the creator of the first Bulgarian magazine *Lyuboslovie* (1842) with the words:

> "Where are their daily newspapers and magazines, or the weekly and monthly ones (...) Where is their history, written in detail and widely spread among people, such as the other nations have and which would help us to stand side by side with the others and make the others aware of the fact that we are as verbal as the rest of God's creatures?''[221]

The question implied by the above list is: where is the complete Bulgarian culture, built up according to the European model? Hence, as I have stated above, this European model was not in contrast with Russian expansionist policy, but rather compatible with its strategy towards the Balkans. In fact, Russian politicians were aware that the Bulgarians could fall under European influence (as Greece, Serbia, and partly Montenegro had) and attract the respective powers for their own interests. To prevent this, Imperial Russia intensified its activities with the Bulgarian intellectuals. In this regard, Istanbul became one of the centres of their cooperation, especially when Nikolay Pavlovich Ignatyev was appointed Russian minister to the Porte (1864–1877). He supported the Pan–Slavic ideas among the South Slavs, particularly among Bulgarians, and he helped in promoting recognition of the Bulgarian church by the Patriarchate.[222] In this attempt, Russia's policy firstly tacitly supported the Bulgarian

---

[220] Ibid., p. 159; On Russian policy towards the Balkans see also few documents at: Central State Historical Archive in St. Petersburg (TsGIA SPb), f. 408, op. 3, d. 383, l.4; See also: Aleksandar Trajanovski, *Ruski dokumenti za Makedonija i makedonskoto prašanje, 1859–1918* (Skopje: Državen arhiv na Republika Makedonija, 2004), pp. 67–82.

[221] Kiossev, *The End of Self–Colonization.*

[222] Victor Roudometof, *Collective Memory, National Identity, and Ethnic Conflict: Greece, Bulgaria and the Macedonian Question* (New York: Praeger Publisher, 2002), p. 88; Thomas A Meininger, *Ignatiev and the Establishment of the Bulgarian Exarchate, 1864–1872* (Madison: State Historical Society of Wisconsin for the Department of History – University of Wisconsin, 1970), p. 17.

Exarchate (in the early 1870s), and secondly, supported the Bulgarians during the Eastern Crisis (1875–1878) and the Russo–Ottoman war (1877–1878).[223] This support was realised in the form of the Russian intervention into the Patriarchate and Ottoman Rumelia. The group of Bulgarians who published the newspaper *"Makedonia"* in Istanbul defined the Bulgarian Question as a "Pan Slavic Question (*Panslavistskiyi vŭpros)"* [224] that needed support from Imperial Russia. This support was actually achieved during the Russian intervention into Ottoman affairs in 1877 and 1878, which I analyse as a "forcible Russian intervention." This was in fact the second intervention in Ottoman Rumelia (the first took place in Greece) undertaken by one of the Great Powers. As in the Greek case, when Philhellenists played a crucial role in the European intervention, in this case Pan–Slavists became very active in helping their "Slavic brothers" in the Ottoman Empire. The members of the *Slavic Benevolent Societies* (I. S. Aksakov, A. A. Kraevski, and General Mikhail Cherniyaev) became active supporters that collected funds and recruited medical personnel to send to the Balkans. During this period, Count Ignatiev defined the Russian vision related to the South Slavs. In his letters, he writes:

> "I undertook negotiations with all the Slavic peoples, preparing them for independence. The work of undermining the Treaty of Paris and of countering Western and all foreign influences on the Bosporus, especially those of Turkey itself and of Austria–Hungary, had to be continued until the development of Russia's strength and until propitious events in Europe would permit us to effect an independent solution of the Eastern Question in the Russian sense, that is, by forming territories (*oblastii*) of coracialists and coreligionists bound to Russia by indissoluble bonds, while leaving the Straits to our disposition."[225]

---

[223] Roudometof, *Collective Memory,* p. 89.

[224] Makedonia, Istanbul, 1. Januar, 1872.

[225] Nikolay P. Ignatiev, "Zapiski Grafa N. P. Ignatieva 1875–1877," *Istoricheskiivestnik I* (1914), p. 56; Michael Boro Petrovich, *The Emergence of Russian Panslavism* (New York: Columbia University Press, 1958), p. 262; Miller, *Nationalizing Empires*; Burbank, "Paul W. Werth, The Tsar's Foreign Faiths," pp. 1–5; On Pan–Slavism few documents in Central State Historical Archive in: St. Petersburg (TsGIA SPb), f. 109, op. 38, 1863, item 23, p. 175. See also: Trajanovski, *Ruski dokumenti za Makedonija i makedonskoto prašanje.*

These efforts were made in April 1877, when Imperial Russia declared war to the Ottoman Empire. The Russian troops intervened in Ottoman Rumelia and advanced to Yeşilköy (a district in Istanbul). According to Count Ignatiev, "it was necessary to bring the war to an end, fulfilling the historic task of Russia and ensuring long–term peace (*ispolni v istoricheskuyu zadachu Rossii i obespechiveyi prodolzhitelniyi mir*)."[226] Precisely Count Ignatyev was appointed to sign the Treaty of San Stefano (3 March 1878) in order to "fulfil Russia's historic task" by creating a new map of the Balkans. As stipulated by this Treaty a "Great Bulgaria" was established, which included major imagined Macedonian territories. This state was actually an instance of the long arm of Russia in the Balkans, which was opposed by many Great Powers. Subsequently, the Treaty of San Stefano was abolished and the Great Powers decided to negotiate the future of the Balkan states in Berlin.

2.5. The Ottoman "Borrowed Colonialism" in Rumelia and the Civilising Mission of the Ottoman Bureaucratic Elite

The ideas of the Enlightenment (the concept of reason, *mission civilisatrice*, and its superiority), Romanticism (the formation of national movements and activities of intellectuals), and modernism (the efforts to create a strong state apparatus) were not only influential in the rule over the Ottoman Christian subjects in Rumelia, but also influenced the Ottoman centre – Istanbul. As we saw above, the concepts of modernity, civilisation, imagination, and imperialism started with the Enlightenment in Europe, and spread more widely through circulation of knowledge.[227] In Imperial Russia this knowledge was accepted in the early 18th century when Peter the Great accepted discourses of European "Civilisation" and started to threaten its "Orient", the Ottomans. In Japan and the Ottoman Empire, these initial programmes were developed in the form of

---

[226] Ignatiev, "Zapiski Grafa."

[227] Ibid., pp. 5–6; If this idea was born in "the West," however, modernisation was a process developed in "the periphery," as a product of a reaction to technological modernity. According to Dankwart Rustow and Robert Wardone, the reasons for the emergence of modernisation included "the threat of European invasion or conquest in countries (such as Russia, China, Japan, Turkey, Iran, and Thailand)." See: Dankwart Rustow and Robert E. Ward, *Political Modernization in Japan and Turkey* (Princeton, NJ: Princeton University Press, 2015), p. 8.

"defensive modernisation"[228] in the mid 19th century. The adoption of "defensive modernisation" in the Ottoman Empire was driven by both external and internal factors. Externally, the development of the Eastern Question among the Great Powers created a need for the Ottoman Empire to modernise to maintain its territorial integrity and international standing. Internally, the emergence of semi-autonomous provincial forces, such as the ayans, [229] and religious factions, further weakened the empire, necessitating modernisation efforts. The Eastern Question posed a critical inquiry, specifically, the question of who would assume the authority left by the progressive fragmentation of the Ottoman Empire in Europe.[230] It seemed at that time that Russia, as an already "modernised" state, could "impose even more severe terms than those which it dictated in 1774."[231] As a reflection of the latter, the Russian novelist Fyodor Dostoevsky wrote in his *Diary* (1876) that "in connection with the Eastern question, there has run into Europe some small beast (*piccola bestia*) which does not give to all good, peace–loving people a chance to calm down – people who love mankind and wish to see it flourishing."[232] In his opinion, this *piccola bestia* did not belong to "civilised" Europe, and therefore, "it [did] seem that with the final solution of the Eastern question, all other political strife in Europe [would] be terminated." [233] During the 19th century, contemplating "final solutions" was a prevalent trend, which culminated in imperialism after the Congress of Berlin. However, for many individuals considered "civilised," the Eastern Question was initially perceived as a Balkan Question until 1878, when it shifted to a Macedonian Question until the Balkan wars in 1912. Richard Coudenhove-Kalergi, a pioneer of European integration, noted in his book *Pan-Europa* (1926), that at the time, the significance of the European

---

[228] Ibid, p. 8.

[229] Matthew Smith Anderson, *Peter the Great (Profiles in Power)* (Harlow, UK: Pearson Education Limited, 1995), p. xix; Daniel S. Hamilton and Stefan Meister, eds., *The Eastern Question: Russia, the West, and Europe's Grey Zone* (Washington, DC: Center for Transatlantic Relations, 2016).

[230] Singleton, *A short History*, p. 100.

[231] Anderson, *Peter the Great*, p. xii.

[232] Fyodor Dostoyevski, *A Writer's Diary* (Evanston: Northwestern University Press, 2009), p. 428.

[233] Ibid., p. 428.

Question for the world was akin to what the Balkan Question was for Europe throughout the 19th century: a source of internal insecurity and upheaval. [234] This "insecurity" and "disturbance" appeared with the emergence of semi–autonomous provincial notables (*ayans*) and religious forces (*vladika* in Montenegro, *vožd* and *prota* in Serbia, *archontes* and *kocabaşı* in Greece, etc.) in Ottoman Rumelia, who started to challenge the central authority in Istanbul. The Ottoman policy for the centuries was based on "policy of accommodation" (*istimalet*) in an attempt "to win the subjected peoples over to their side" by granting partial autonomy and self-–governing bodies (in Moldavia and Wallachia, Dubrovnik, the mountainous areas of Montenegro, the northern Albanian region of Malësia, Bosnia, Mani in the Peloponnese, Souli and Himara in Epirus, etc.). [235] In fact, these were the "large areas which had never been administered directly from Constantinople." [236] This emboldened the ascendancy of provincial authorities striving to bring some parts of the empire under their control. At the end of the 18th and beginning of the 19th centuries, such provincial power–holders were Kara Mahmud Pasha Bushatli in Shkodër, Osman Pazvanoğlu in Vidin, the Janissarie troops known as the "four leaders" (*dayi/dahije*) in Serbia, Ali Pasha of Tepelen in Janina, Husein–kapetan Gradaščević, also known as the Dragon of Bosnia (*Zmaj od Bosne*), and other landowners outside Ottoman Rumelia. The internationalisation of this problem among the Great Powers related to the power struggles in Rumelia, and simultaneously influenced Sultan Selim III to undertake military reforms in the form of a "New Order" (*Nizam–i Cedid*) based on "enlightened ideas."[237] This state making was

---

[234] Richard Coudenhove–Kalergi, *Pan–Europa* (Vienna: Paneuropa–Union Österreich, 1979) first published in 1926, p. 24; "*die europäische Frage bedeutet heute für die Welt ungefähr das, was durch ein Jahrhundert die Balkanfrage für Europa bedeutet hat: eine Quelle ewiger Unsicherheit und Beunruhigung.*"

[235] Fikret Adanır, "Semi–autonomous provincial forces in the Balkans and Anatolia, in Cambridge History of Turkey," in *The Later Ottoman Empire, 1603–1839,* ed. Suraiya Faroqhi (Cambridge: Cambridge University Press, 2006), pp.158–160.

[236] Anderson, *Peter the Great*, p. xv.

[237] Fikret Adanır, "Semi–autonomous provincial," p. 185; Charles Tilly, "War Making and State Making as Organized Crime," in *Bringing the State Back In,* ed. Peter Evans (Cambridge: Cambridge University Press, 1985), p. 183; According to Charles Tilly, "the building up of war making capacity likewise increased the capacity to extract. The very

connected with notions of centralisation and modernisation introduced by the Enlightenment and its understanding of central government as "superior" in comparison to its "peripheries."[238]

The first attempt toward Ottoman recentralisation[239] came to coincide with the beginnings of military and administrative modernisation. In other words, its success depended on a new kind of rule characterised by the deployment of greater state strength based on an infrastructure of governance. If successful, this modernisation would bring the Ottoman entity closer to the centralised, territorial state model of Europe.[240]

These introduced reforms, on the one hand appeared as a necessity to avoid military defeats, territorial losses, and the traumatic notion of the Eastern Question, while on the other the ideas of modernity brought a new understanding of control of the empire's periphery.[241] The development of nationalism and the rise of rebels in the periphery followed the process of centralisation of the Empire's centre, in order to bring its subjects closer, even though the 'centre' had traditionally enjoyed autonomy and experienced low levels of infiltration, infrastructural power and extraction of the core state. In this regard, Michel Foucault's work enables us to analyse a historical transition in social forms from the disciplinary society

---

activity of extraction (...) created organization in the form of tax–collection agencies, police forces, courts, exchequers, account keepers, thus it again led to state making."

[238] Gökhan Bacık, "Turkey and Russia: Whither Modernization?," *Journal of Economic and Social Research* 3/2 (2001): 55; According to Gökhan Bacık, modernity is typically associated with the center, while the periphery is linked to the ancient and outdated. Throughout history, both Russia and Turkey (Ottoman Empire) have chosen modernisation as a central goal, rather than the periphery. As a result, the periphery has often felt responsible for preserving the *status quo* in this division of labor.

[239] It is used the word recentralisation because in the 16th century the Ottoman Empire was centralised, but during the 17th and 18th began with more decentralised formation. See: Gabor Agoston, "Military Transformation in the Ottoman Empire and Russia, 1500–1800," *Kritika: Explorations in Russian and Eurasian History* 12/2 (2011): 288.

[240] Metin Heper, "Political Modernization as Reflected in Bureaucratic Change: The Turkish Bureaucracy and a 'Historical Bureaucratic Empire' Tradition," *International Journal of Middle East Studies* 7 (1976): 510; According to Metin Heper, this process of modernisation in the Ottoman case was in fact a "selective Westernization." The state in order to compete with a technologically advanced Europe, the Ottoman Empire especially during the time of Sultans Mahmud II (1808–1839) and Abdül Mecid (1939–1861), introduced (re)centralisation process.

[241] Kıvanç Karaman and Şevket Pamuk, "Ottoman State Finances in Comparative European Perspective, 1500–1914," *The Journal of Economic History* 70/3 (2010): 621.

to the society of control. In his analysis, the concept of biopolitics is a political rationale which takes administration as a project "to ensure, sustain, and multiply life, to put this life in order."[242] He stresses different forms of power and governmentalities and their distinctive aims and technologies of control of societie in the form of biopolitics.[243] These conceptions of control of societies and biopolitics describe central aspects of the modern state that were adopted by Ottomans too. In this sense, the Ottoman drive to achieve modernity like their "Western rivals" resulted in a "whole grab bag of concepts, methods and tools of statecrafts, prejudices, and practices," termed by Selim Deringil a "borrowed colonialism."[244] In his opinion, the Ottomans adopted a colonial stance toward the peoples of the periphery of their empire.[245] I argue that the appearance of the traumatic Eastern Question, along with the semi–autonomous empire's periphery, were the reasons for state centralisation, bureaucratisation, defensive or reluctant modernisation, selective Westernisation, borrowed colonialism, governmentality, and biopolitics in order to facilitate "bringing the state back in."[246]

This process of centralisation also generated an "Ottoman orientalism," which was reflected in the forms of suppression of insurrection (*isyan*) or repression of all forms of disobedience by punishing misbehaviour (*te'dib*), and by trying to correct, educate, and civilise rebels *terbiye*) in order to discipline 'people of the peripheries' (*inzibat*).[247] In this context,

---

[242] Michel Foucault, *The History of Sexuality Volume 1* (New York: Pantheon Books, 1978), p. 138.

[243] Ibid., p. 141.

[244] Deringil, *The Well–Protected Domains*, p. 312; He adopted Dietrich Geyer's "borrowed imperialism," which he uses for late imperial Russia. See Dietrich Geyer, *Russian Imperialism: The Interaction of Domestic and Foreign Policy 1860–1914* (Hamburg/New York: Leamington Spa, 1987), p. 124.

[245] Ibid., p. 313.

[246] Theda Skocpol, "Bringing the State Back In: Strategies of Analysis in Current Research," in *Bringing the State Back In* ed. Peter B. Evans (Cambridge: Cambridge University Press, 1985).

[247] Reinkowski, *The State's Security*, pp. 203–208; On the other hand, according to Şerif Mardin, "the forces of the periphery, such as locally powerful families, saw the central officials as persons with whom they had many points of contact, and also as rivals who tried to get the greatest possible share of the agricultural surplus and other values for the center, which meant less for themselves." See: Mardin, *Center–Periphery Relations*, p. 174.

the Ottoman Empire implemented "borrowed colonialism" towards its "Orient" (domestic Orientalism) in many different ways in order to spread civilisation. This *mission civilisatrice* had the aim of bringing closer its peripheral subjects (Christian and Muslim) and was stipulated in the Imperial Reform Edict (*Hatt–ı Hümayun*) as a granting of "equality of all peoples of the empire – Muslims, Christians and Jews." [248] The enforcement of this edict culminated with the Ottoman formal recognition as a legitimate member of the Concert of Europe (1856), where in Article 9 of the Treaty of Paris, the Great Powers "recognised the high value of Hatt–i Hümayun," which gave "no right of intervention in the internal affairs of the empire."[249] However, this non–intervention was valid for a short time, but still was important for the Ottoman government to consider its "centre" as "part of civilisation." Thus, the government administration was reorganised, the judiciary and executive councils were established, legislation and laws were regulated, technological developments in the form of roads, telegraphs, and railways were built, all in order to bring its provinces closer than ever before.

Since the Macedonian Question was not yet in existence or was known as the Balkan Question and Eastern Question, the Ottoman government was focused on bringing the whole of Ottoman Rumelia under control. One of the most prominent figures of this initiative was Ottoman scholar, Tanzimat bureaucrat and historian, Ahmed Cevdet Pasha, who wrote the famous history of the Ottoman Empire known as *"Tarih–i Cevdet"* (1854– 57). He emphasised that the obligation of "civilised humankind [was] to bring solidarity to different communities" that were "living in the villages far away from civilisation."[250] According to him, the Ottoman Empire belonged to the traditionally much greater Islamic civilisation, which was not part of Europe, since "it was for centuries divided and far away from

---

[248] Roderic H. Davison, *Reform in the Ottoman Empire 1856–1876* (Princeton: Princeton University Press, 1963), p. 3.

[249] Ibid., p. 4.

[250] Ahmet Cevdet Paşa, *Osmanlı İmperatorluğu Tarihi* (Istanbul: İlgi Kültur Sanat Yayınları, 2008), p. 37; Quote: *"(...) insane yaratılışından medeni olduğundan, dayanışma için yer yer topluluklar meydana getirir (...) köy halkı şehir halkına nispetle medeniyet nimetlerinden uzak oldukları gibi."*

civilisation." [251] Between 1855 and 1865 Ahmed Cevdet Pasha was appointed to different administrative positions to analyse parts of the Ottoman Empire. In another collection of the notes he authored, *Tezakir*", one can notice the notions of "orientalism" and applied governmentality towards the mountainous people in Rumelia, especially the Montenegrins (*Karadağlular*).[252] Ottoman colonialism and its mission were active in other parts of the Empire, where another prominent figure, Ahmed Mithad Pasha, was appointed. He was chosen by the Ottoman administration for the significant mission of introducing the Tanzimat and discipline to its periphery (in Nish in 1861–1864 and in the Danube region in 1864–1868, as well as in Anatolia and the Arab Peninsula).[253] As Nadir Özbek asserts, the aim of these bureaucrats was "to extend their authority into the provinces, which at that time could be described as only marginally under Ottoman sovereignty according to contemporary definitions of the term."[254] In Mithad Pasha's memoirs, "*Hayatım İbret Olsun*," he points out that he was appointed in the Balkans (*Rumeli*) in May 1855 (Nisan 1271) "to fulfil the government's aim of security and order (*devletçe asıl maksadın hasıl olduğu emniyet ve asayiş*)" and to suppress "bandits and robbers (*eşkiyalik ve haydutluk belasının ortadan kaldırılması*)." [255] Therefore, by the regulations of the provinces (*Vilâyet Nizamnâmesi*) in

---

[251] Ibid., pp. 236; Quote: *"Avrupa halkı kendi problemleri içine dalmış ve medeniyetten uzak durumdaydılar."*

[252] Ahmet Cevdet Paşa, *Tezakir* (Ankara: Türk Tarih Kurumu Basımevi, 1953), p. 15; According to Cevdet Paşa, the Montenegrins "were attacking parts of the Empire (*nevahiye tecavüze başladıklarından*)" that "forced the Exalted State to bring up/educate/civilise them (*Devlet-i aliyye dahi anların terbiyesine mecbur oldu*)." Elsewhere he also described them as wild and barbarous (*âmelât-i vahsiyâne*). Thus, Ahmed Cevdet Pasha's recommendations were that northern Albanians have sufficient capacity to defeat the Montenegrins, while the Ottomans should integrate this part in order to discipline (*inzibat*) the Montenegrins. With this purpose, the Ottoman government created a Committee for the Mountains of Shkodra/Skadar in 1856 (*İşkodra Cibali Komisyonu*). See also: Maurus Reinkowski, "Double Struggle, No Income: Ottoman Borderlands in Northern Albania," *International Journal of Turkish Studies* 9/1 (2003): 239–253.

[253] See the Vilayet Nizamnamesi, Düstûr 1. Tertip (Istanbul, 1289), pp. 608–624; Hüdai Şentürk, *Osmanlı Devleti'nde Bulgar Meselesi, 1850–1875* (Ankara: Türk Tarih Kurumu, 1992), pp. 253–271.

[254] Nadir Özbek, "Policing the Countryside: Gendarmes of the Late 19th–Century Ottoman Empire (1876–1908)," *International Journal Middle East Studies* 40 (2008): 47.

[255] Mithat Paşa, *Hayatım İbret Olsun* (Istanbul: Temel Yayınları, 1997), p. 23.

1864 and 1871 a radical administrative reorganisation in the provincial administration was conducted. Before and after these changes, Macedonia did not exist administratively in the Ottoman Empire, but with these reorganisations its imagined territories were divided into three Ottoman vilayets (Manastir, Selanik, and Kosovo). In the words of Mithad Pasha, "the real aim (*asıl maksat*) of such reorganisation was to develop the homeland (*memleketin kalkınması*), to increase fortune/wealth (*tezayid–i servet*), and to live in happiness (*saadet içinde yaşamasıdır*)." [256] Therefore, in the period of Tanzimat, Macedonia enjoyed greater development, fortune, and happiness, since its entanglements had not been yet transformed into a question, and the Ottoman Empire was more preoccupied with bringing under control its wider peripheries (Serbia, Montenegro, Romania, etc.). In order for this governmentality policy to succeed, "in the vilayets were introduced new forces of soldiers and gendarmeries (*vilayetin asker ve zaptiyesi*)," which aimed "to discipline and to suppress the bandits (*disiplinli bir şekle... eşkiyaların yok edilmesine önem verilerek*)."[257]

In Nadir Özbek's opinion, the "gendarmerie thus emerged in both Europe and in the Ottoman Empire as integral to modern state formation and its technologies of government."[258] Özbek is also aware that this "extension of central government administrative apparatuses into provinces" can be conceptualised "as a kind of 'colonisation of the countryside'."[259] This "colonisation of the countryside" that I referred as "borrowed colonialism" emerged with Tanzimat, developed with the establishment of the gendarmerie (*asakir–i zabtiye*) in 1840 and of irregular units of armed men

---

[256] Ibid., p. 47.

[257] Ibid., p. 49.

[258] Özbek, "Policing the Countryside," p. 47; Erik Jan Zürcher, "Teoride ve Pratikte Osmanlı Zorunlu Askerlik Sistemi (1844–1918)," in *Devletin silâhlanması: Ortadoğu'da ve Orta Asya'da zorunlu askerlik (1775–1925)*, ed. Erik Jan Zürcher (Istanbul: Istanbul Bilgi Üniversitesi Yayınları, 2003), pp. 87–104; Gültekin Yıldız, *Neferin adı yok: Zorunlu askerliğe geçiş sürecinde Osmanlı Devleti'nde Siyaset, Ordu ve Toplum, 1826–1839* (Istanbul: Çağaloğlu Kitabevi, 2009).

[259] Özbek, "Policing the Countryside," p. 49; Fatih Yeşil, *İhtilâller çağında Osmanlı ordusu: Osmanlı İmparatorluğu'nda sosyoekonomik ve sosyopolitik değişim üzerine bir İnceleme, 1793–1826* (Istanbul: Tarih Vakfı Yurt Yayınları, 2016); Tobias Heinzelmann, *Cihaddan vatan savunmasına: Osmanlı İmparatorluğu'nda genel askerlik yükümlüğü 1826–1856* (Istanbul: Kitap Yayınevi, 2009).

(*başıbozuk*), incorporated in the forms of annual registers (*salnameler*), law regulations, and regulations of the provinces for a uniform provincial administrative system that retained its military character.[260] Thus, one of the goals of the reorganisation was to show that the Ottoman Empire had the capacity to be treated as part of "civilisation." Authors such as Şemsettin Sami Frashëri went as far as to blame "Christianity for the decline of the Greek civilisation. It was, however, Islam which had brought back the Greek civilisation, which meant that Europe received the Greek civilisation, which the Europeans claimed to be the root of European civilisation, from the Islamic civilisation."[261] Another prominent figure, Namik Kemal, argued in the July 22, 1872 issue of the newspaper *İbret* that "Europe [did not] know the East (*Avrupa şarkı bilmez*)."[262] In another article, titled "*Vatan*", published on March 22, 1873, apart from defending the Ottoman civilisation, Kemal developed the concept of "homeland" (*vatan*), explaining that "in every civilisation the love of homeland (*vatan*) is the most important virtue and the most sacred duty."[263] The concepts of "Civilisation" and "homeland" were employed with the such an aim that, in the age of questions and imperialism, a unity of the Ottoman nation (*Millet–i Osmaniyye*) would be achieved, composed by various ethnical and religious backgrounds. In the comments of Mithad Pasha, the most important aim of the Ottoman government should be to bring exactly these "different races, religions and sects" under the "territorial integrity" and the rule of "basic law."[264] The implementation of this idea, as I have argued, was conceptualised on the basis of "borrowed colonialism," implemented by the *mission civilisatrice* towards its periphery/countryside, which was challenged by the nationalism of the

---

[260] Ibid., p. 52; Ortner, "Erfahrungen einer westeuropäischen Armee auf dem Balkan," pp. 82–87.

[261] Boyar, *Ottomans, Turks and the Balkans*, p. 86; Şemsettin Sami (Sami Frashëri), *Kamus ül–Alam: Tarihve Cografya Lügatı Vol. VI* (Istanbul: Mihran Matbaası, 1306 [1889]).

[262] Ibid., pp. 85; Namık Kemal, "Avrupa Şarkı Bilmez," *Ibret,* 7 (22. July 1872); See also: Mustafa Nihat Özön, *Namık Kemal ve İbret gazetesi* (Istanbul: Remzi Kitabevi, 1938), pp. 54–59.

[263] Özkan, *Vatan,* p. 40.

[264] Mithat Paşa, *Yıldız mahkemesi ve taif zindanı (Mirat–ı Hayret)* (Istanbul: Temel Yayınları, 1997), pp. 23–25; Quote: *"ırk, din ve mezhep olarak farklı ve ayrı olmalarıyla beraber (...) tamamiyet–i mülkiyesi (...) Kanun–u Esasi."*

Balkan peoples and threatened by the Russian mission of solving the Eastern Question. The years of the Eastern Crisis (*Şark Buhranı*) were key moments in the changing of policies and strategies among the Ottomans, Great Powers, and Balkan states. The Ottoman statesman and politician Eğinli Said Pasha, in his memoires written between 1876 and 1880, observed that "these days were very dangerous for the Exalted State" since on the one hand the "Russian nation, due to religious agitations, [was] aiming to conquer," and on the other, the "Austrian state, in order to protect its territories, [would] be obliged to send soldiers in Bosnia."[265] These predictions came true at the Congress of Berlin (1878) in the form of establishments of the new independent Balkan states, which would be the stepping stone for policies and practices that further defined their "living space" (*Lebensraum*) towards the rest of Ottoman Rumelia, known as Macedonia (*Vilayet–i Selase*). On the other hand, during the reign of Sultan Abdulhamid II the Ottoman Empire transformed its conception of unity of the Ottoman nation (*Millet–i Osmaniyye*) into a unity of Islam (*İttihad–ı İslam*) as an ideology that incorporated Muslim Albanians as "guardians" of the three vilayets.

2.6. Conclusion

Here I presented the emergence of the Macedonian Question and contentious politics between the Great Powers, the Ottoman state, and Balkan elite. All this is to say that the imaginations, maps, and cartography, together with media and newspapers popularised Macedonia as a geographic region, especially among the Great Powers. By using several European sources (British, French, and German), I thematically traced the Great Powers' imagination of Macedonia, which regarded this territory (along with Greece) as the wellspring of "European civilisation" since ancient Hellenic times. I illustrated the latter through a few examples of Hellenophiles across Europe, who through the media popularised these Ottoman territories as "cradle of European civilisation." Furthermore, I

---

[265] Said Paşa, *II Abdülhamid'in İlk Mabeyn Feriki Eğenli Said Paşa'nin Hatiratı, I–II (1876–1880)* (Istanbul: Bengi Yayınları, 2011), p. 104; Quote: *"Devlet–i aliyye bugünkü gün gayet tehlikeli bir halde bulunuyor (...) Rusya millet efkar–i diniyesinin galeyaniyle devleti sürüp götürmekte oldugundan ahaliyi zabt etmek (...) Avusturya devleti kendisini muhafaza içün Bosna'ya asker şevk etmeye mecbur olacaktır."*

argued that this understanding of Macedonia as a geographical region did not stop with Europe, but was circulating in the form of knowledge (*Wissenszirkulation*) throughout the Ottoman Empire, especially among the Balkan elite. Such knowledge about Macedonia spilled over into regional politics of the Ottoman Empire, where the Balkan intellectuals produced narratives against the Ottomans and labels such as "Turkish yoke" and "Asiatic Mongols," or "barbarians." By taking into consideration several examples from the European and Balkan literature and media, I argued that the European elite, together with the Balkan intellectuals developed prejudice against the "Oriental other," the Ottomans, and imagined Macedonia into their future nation–state projects. It also opened up windows of opportunity for cooperation (especially with Russia) and build up various entanglements across the regions. Actually, this small "civilised" group of Balkan people needed the assistance of the Great Powers against "the fiery zeal and bigoted enthusiasm of the followers of Islam." This delivery of "civilised" ideas – for the Slavs, Catholics, Jews, Serbs, Bulgarians, and Greeks – transformed the Macedonian Questions into European ones. In this respect, I showed that the Macedonian Questions did not concern the Balkans and Ottomans only, but also the whole of the West of Europe. Thus, I openly argued that the Macedonian Questions should also be studied as a globalised "problem" by including various local, regional, and international perspectives.

State Policies and Mobile Intellectuals as Agents of Nationalism and Imperialism: What Has Changed Between Berlin and Ilinden (1878–1903)?

The Congress of Berlin, held between 13th June and 13th July, brought different representatives of the six great powers (Imperial Russia, Great Britain, France, Dual Monarchy, Italy, and Germany) to the table, the Ottoman Empire, and Balkan statesmen of Greece, Serbia, Romania, and Montenegro. This Treaty terminated the Russo–Ottoman war of 1877–78, replaced the preliminary Treaty of San Stefano, which had granted a "Greater Bulgaria" under Imperial Russian influence and came at the end with decisions to establish new independent Balkan states (Serbia, Montenegro, and Romania; and semi–independent Bulgaria). [1] In the southern parts of Ottoman Macedonia, Eastern Rumelia was established under a special administration, and the region of Macedonia was returned to the control of the Ottomans, with the condition, arranged by the Great Powers, that the Ottoman administration should introduce reforms. According to Article 23, these reforms were to be "implemented under European guidance, which was bound to lead to a conflict of authority and encourage the Christians." [2] According to Gül Tokay, "European intervention under the guise of 'reforms' brought complications by not only further weakening the Ottoman administration but also by encouraging the communities involved to take advantage of the fortuitous circumstances to express their national aspirations." [3] Along these lines, in the last fifty years scholars have paid attention to how late–19th century

---

[1] The Treaty of Berlin guaranteed semi–independent principality of Bulgaria within the Ottoman Empire, with much smaller borders than "Greater Bulgaria" foreseen by the Treaty of San Stefano. See: Christian Stachelbeck, "Lernen aus Imperialkriegen: Einführung," in *Imperialkriege von 1500 bis heute: Strukturen – Akteure – Lernprozesse*, eds. Tanja Bührer, Christian Stachelbeck and Dierk Walter (Paderborn/Munich/Vienna/Zürich: Ferdinand Schöningh, 2011), pp. 418–424; Lothar Höbelt, "Der Berliner Kongress als Prototyp internationaler Konfliktregelung," in *Am Rande Europas? Der Balkan – Raum und Bevölkerung als Wirkungsfelder militärischer Gewalt*, eds. Bernhard Chiari und Gerhard P. Groß (Munich: R. Oldenbourg Verlag, 2009), pp. 47–53.

[2] Gül Tokay, "A Reassessment of the Macedonian Question between 1878–1908," in *War and Diplomacy, The Russo–Turkish War of 1877–1878 and the Treaty of Berlin*, eds. Hakan Yavuz with Peter Sluglett (Salt Lake City: Utah University Press, 2011), p. 4.

[3] Ibid., p. 1.

reforms and education affected the development of modern national identifications. Few historians of the Ottoman Empire and Balkan states have recently documented that the same patterns influenced not only Western Europe, but also its south–eastern parts – the Balkans and the Ottoman Empire. Due to factors that I will highlight below, the scheduled reforms in Ottoman Macedonia, introduced at the Congress of Berlin and promised by the Ottoman Empire, opened a space for the interference of the Balkan states into Ottoman affairs, especially regarding the education that predictably should have influenced the ethno–national affiliations of the local population.

Nevertheless, the reforms were foreseen for the Ottoman provinces of Selanik, Monastir, and Kosovo and two independent sanjaks, namely Drama and Serres. Even in the Protocols of the Congress of Berlin, the Representatives of Great Britain, Austria–Hungary, France, Germany, Italy, Russia, and Turkey did not define precisely if these three provinces should be named "Macedonia". Lord Salisbury in general proposes to substitute the words "Greek Provinces" for "the border provinces with the Kingdom of Greece" that included even imaginary spaces of Macedonia, Thrace, and Crete.[4] The questions that one might hence pose would be: what was then Macedonia? Which parts of the Ottoman Empire did it include? How did it become popularised by the Great Powers and regional states? How did these local and regional questions become globalised? What kind of policies were introduced by the Ottoman Empire on the local and regional levels? What was the reaction of the Albanian intellectuals? Can one trace cooperation and clashes between the Ottoman government and Albanian–speaking bureaucrats? What was the reaction of the Bulgarian, Serbian, and Greek states? What kind of policies did they develop? What was their strategy in influencing the locals and rural

---

[4] Protocols of Congress of the Representatives of Great Britain, Austria–Hungary, France, Germany, Italy, Russia, and Turkey for the Settlement of Affairs in the East (Berlin: June/July, 1878), pp. 904–908; Quote: "*seront remplaces par ceux de 'provinces Grecques (...) e'est–a–dire, sur la question de savuir si les mots 'provinces limitrophes.*" See also: Nathalie Clayer, "The Dimension of Confessionalisation in the Ottoman Balkans at the Time of Nationalisms," in *Conflicting Loyalties in the Balkans: The Great Powers, the Ottoman Empire and Nation–Building*, eds. Hannes Grandits, Nathalie Clayer and Robert Pichler (London/New York: I. B. Tauris, 2011), pp. 89–109.

population? In order to answer these questions, I will use various sources (Ottoman, Albanian, Bulgarian, Serbian, and English, French, and German) and use the "top–down" approach that can help us to understand the formulations of the state policies and mobile intellectuals who tried to install the national affiliations to the locals on the ground. Thus, following chapter aims to represent the emergence of the Macedonian Question(s), which started with competing state policies and contested strategies between the Ottoman Empire and Balkan states over the Macedonian population. These political competitions will be analyzed in the time frame from the Congress of Berlin (1878) to the Ilinden Uprising (1903) by taking into consideration the role of mobile intellectuals and their instrumentalisation of education for nationalist purposes.

3.1. The Ottoman Consolidation of the Three Vilayets in Macedonia (1878–1903)

If one analyses the Treaty of Berlin, one would find no mention whatsoever of the term "Macedonia." Even in Article 23, which referred to the Ottoman territories of the "three vilayets," Macedonia by was not stated under its name. It was rather compared to the reforms "in the Island of Crete by the Organic Law of 1868" and the Treaty expressed the necessity that reforms "be introduced into the other parts of Turkey in Europe for which no special arrangement has been provided by the present Treaty." [5] The Ottoman administration did not employ the term "Macedonia" for the "parts of Turkey in Europe" and referred to these provinces as *vilayet–i selase*, as the "three provinces," or sometimes only as Rumelia.[6] The meaning of Rumelia was in fact the land of the Romans (decedents of the Roman Empire). It did not include Anatolia, but rather the territories on the western side of the Bosphorus. Likewise, the Ottoman administration insisted on the term "Rumelia," a term that defined the European Provinces of the Ottoman Empire. However, since Rumelia did not have clearly demarcated boundaries, during the 1880s, the Ottoman

---

[5] Deutsches Reichsgesetzblatt Band, No. 31 (Berlin: N.P., 1878), pp. 307–345.

[6] Tokay, *A Reassessment,* p. 4; Erik Jan Zürcher, "Macedonians in Anatolia: The Importance of the Macedonian Roots of the Unionist for Their Policies in Anatolia after 1914." *Middle Eastern Studies* 50/6 (2014): 960–975; Burcu Akan Ellis, *Shadow Genealogies: Memory and Identity among Urban Muslims in Macedonia* (New York: Columbia University Press, 2003).

administration decided to limit the reforms only to the three vilayets (the Selanik, Manastir, and Kosovo provinces) in order to avoid interference of the Great Powers in the whole Rumelia region. Thus, the Ottoman statemen together with Rumelia, started to use the term "*vilayeti–i selase*" or simply "three provinces" more frequently. According to Article 23 of the Treaty of Berlin, the three provinces should have been an autonomous region under the control of the European Commission, instituted for Eastern Roumelia.[7] In order to prevent this autonomy, on 23 August 1880 the Ottoman state introduced a reform project in the form of draft law named "The Law of the Rumeli Provinces" (*Rumeli Vilayeti Kanunu/Layiha*). These Rumeli provinces included Kosovo, Manastir, and Selanik, by then known officially as the "three provinces" (*vilayeti selase*). On the other hand, the name "Macedonia" was promoted in European media and among the European diplomats. This term was later also accepted by the regional Balkan states who often had internal synonyms for it such as "Southern Serbia" (*Južna Srbija*) or "South–western Bulgaria" (*Yugozapadna Bŭlgaria*).

However, the Ottoman administration predominantly referred to it as the "three vilayets." In order to exert direct control over these vilayets from Istanbul, the Ottoman administration also introduced a gendarmerie to apply security measures that provided it with the advantage to constitute the region as a kind of semi–colonial province based on "borrowed colonialism." In seeking greater control of its territories, the Ottoman Empire pursued a programme of state centralisation in Ottoman Macedonia. In Article 151, the draft law stipulated that the Ottoman state and its central administration (*idare–i merkeziyesi*) would appoint governors (*mutasarrif ve kaymakam*) in the provinces in order to provide

---

[7] Deutsches Reichsgesetzblatt Band 1878; See also: İpek K. Yosmaoğlu, "Counting Bodies, Shaping Souls: The 1903 Census and National Identity in Ottoman Macedonia," *International Journal of Middle East Studies* 38/1 (2006): 55–77, here in 68; Mehmet Hacısalihoğlu, "Borders, Maps, and Censuses: The Politicization of Geography and Statistics in the Multi–Ethnic Ottoman Empire," in *Comparing Empires: Encounters and Transfers in the Long Nineteenth Century*, eds. Jörn Leonhard and Ulrike von Hirschhausen (Göttingen: Vandenhoeck & Ruprecht, 2011), pp. 171–210, hear in page 182.

general security (*canibinden asayiş–i umumiye*).[8] According to Article 258, the gandarmerie (*jandarma*) was accountable to the Ministry of Justice (*Adliye Nazareti*)[9] in order to provide the central administration with direct control.[10] This institutionalisation developed into one of the key bureaucratic agencies of the modernising Ottoman Empire, arranging long–distance surveillance of the local situation. [11] The policy of appointing gandarmerie in the three vilayets can also be analysed in the broader context of the Ottoman counter–colonialist response to European imperialism and Balkan small–state imperialism. [12] Furthermore, in pursuing this policy, the Ottoman administration in the Macedonian context was appointing prevalently Muslim bureaucrats for applying this centralisation policy.

Article 308 of the draft law clearly proclaimed that "the non–Muslim population [was] exempt (as before) from its service,"[13] implying that the distinction between Muslim and Christian elements was still (strongly) emphasised. In this regard, the Ottoman administration "in every vilayet appoints a colonel or gendermerie" (see Article 315) that belong to the Muslim community.[14] This gandarmerie force was in fact often recruiting Albanian–speaking locals.[15] This recruitment could be also studied as an

---

[8] Gábor Demeter and Krisztián Csaplár–Degovics, "Social Conflicts: Changing Identities and Everyday Strategies of Survival in Macedonia on the Eve of the Collapse of Ottoman Central Power (1903–1912)," *The Hungarian Historical Review* 3/3 (2014): 18; Rumeli Vilayeti Kanunu Layiha, Ahali–i Vilayetin Hukuku Umumiyesi (Istanbul: Matbaa–i Amire, 1296/1880), p. 38.

[9] Ibid, p. 57; See also: Başbakanlık Osmanlı Arşivi or BOA/Istanbul, Y.PRK.MYD, 8/57, 26 L 1306 [25/06/1889]

[10] Ibid., p. 64; Quote: *"şehir ve karyelerde emniyet–i umumiyenin muhafazası evvela jandarma saniyen şehir ve köylerdeki zaptiye neferatı vasıtasıyla temin kılınmıştır."*

[11] BOA, Y.EE. No. 101/54, Hicri, 4 Zilhicce 1297, (7 November 1880).

[12] Isa Blumi, "Ottomanism Then and Now: Historical and Contemporary Meanings," *Die Welt des Islams* 56 (2016): 290–317, in the pages 301–306.

[13] Rumeli Vilayeti Kanunu Layiha, p. 65; Quote: *"gayrimuslim jandarmalar hizmetlerinin imtidadı müddetce bizzat askeriyeden muaftırlar."*

[14] Ibid., p. 66; Quote: *"her vilayette bir miralay/alay beyi veyahud bir kaymakamın kumandası tahtında olarak bir jandarma fırkası bulunacaktır (...) her kazada bir yuz basının veya mulazimi evvelin kumandası altında olarak bir jandarma bölüğü bulunur."*

[15] In order to respect the Treaty of Berlin and its article 23, the European Commission needed to approve this draft of law that can be seen from its last part (*fasil–i Mahsus*) on the date 11 and 23 August 1880 (*11 ve 23 Auğustos sene 80 Darussaadet*) by Asim Paşa (*Hariciye Nazarı*), Sahak Abro Efendi (*Şurayı Devlet Azası*), Austrian (Mosyo Kusan),

Ottoman attempt to "civilise" its "periphery" in order to bring the locals closer to the "centre." One of the mechanisms of this *mission civilisatrice* aimed to bound local Muslims under the direct supervision of the Sultan as the Caliph of all Muslims. This strategy also sought to bind Ottoman Rumelia to religious notions of the "Unity of Islam" (*İttihad–ı İslam*).[16] Abdulhamid II's support of "Albanianism"[17] was thus an attempt to bind Albanian–speaking Muslims to Unity of Islam instead of an independent national movement.[18] The main supporter of such ideas was Mehmed E. Safvet Pasha, a former Grand Vizier, who on 12 April 1880 submitted a memorandum advocating a separate policy for the people living in the periphery, especially the Albanian–speaking groups who offered "essence of support" (*maya–ul–istinadı*) to the Ottoman bureaucracy in combatting its enemies.[19] Not only the recruitment of the Albanian–speaking population by the Ottoman Empire, but also the threats of the Great Powers (together with the Balkan states) affected inter–community relations between Muslims and Christians.[20] As a response to this threat, Haxhi Mulla Zeka (1832–1902), a notable Albanian–speaking Muslim, met in Peja with other 450 Albanian–speaking Muslims in order to reach an agreement (*kararname*). On 29 January 1899 this event was known as the

---

German (Bronesoyan), French (Obara), English (Fiyc Moris), Italian (Vernoni) and Russian (Hitrov) representatives. *"Babiali 13 Temmuz sene 78 tarihinde Berlinde akdolunan muahedenamenin yirmi üçüncü bendi ahkamını icraen muahedename–i mezkurede kendileri için teşkilat–i mahsusa tasrih kılınan Rumelideki vilayeti sahaneye idhal kılınacak nizamat hakkında Rumeli Şarki Avrupa komisyonunun rey ve mutalaasini istifsar etmiş."* See: Rumeli Vilayeti Kanunu Layiha, Ahali–ı Vilayetin Hukuku Umumiyesi, Istanbul, Matbaa–i Amire, 1296 (1880), p. 67; See also State Archives of North Macedonia (DARSM) in Skopje, N 135, 12.08.1880.

[16] Celal Nuri İleri, *İttihad–ı İslam ve Almanya* (Istanbul: Yeni Osmanlı Matbaa ve Kütüphanesi, 1333/1914).

[17] Nathalie Clayer, "The Albanian Students of the Mektebi–i Mülkiye: Social Networks and Trends of Thought," in *Late Ottoman Society: The Intellectual Legacy*, ed. Elisabeth Özdalga (London/New York: Routledge Curzon, 2005).

[18] Nuray Bozbora, "The Policy of Abdulhamid II regarding the Prizren League," *Turkish Review of Balkan Studies* 11 (2006): 47; Sultan Abdulhamid II tried to give an Islamic character to the organised resistance of Albanian notables in the Prizren League (1878) in order to oppose preparations for the Congress of Berlin and eventual consequences of the Treaty.

[19] Gawrych, *The Crescent*, p. 73.

[20] Zef Jubani, *Historia e popullit shqiptar: për shkollat e mesme* (Prishtinë: Libri Shkollor, 2002), pp. 182–185.

creation of the League of İpek, whose aim was to protect the Ottoman territories in Rumelia against the foreign invasion of the Great Powers or regional Balkan states, and to discuss a potential autonomous Albanian Vilayet. It is worth noting that two fractions at this League were represented: the first major, conservative group demanded that the five vilayets (including all three vilayets of Macedonia) be united into one semi–autonomous "Albanian vilayet;" and the second group, that of more radical members, wanted full administrative autonomy for the four vilayets (Thessaloniki was excluded).[21] For the first, the more conservative group, the vilayet of Thessaloniki was a buffer–zone of the "Albanian–Turkish division of powers," which would preserve a connection with Sultan Abdulhamid II, who was the *Halife–i Müslüminzillullah–i firaz* ("the shadow of God on earth").[22] Therefore, for this conservative group of Albanian–speaking notables in the Kosovo vilayet, the connection with the Sultan–Caliph expanded more of a platform that was rather religious than national.[23] As has been presented, these notables were often offered important posts in the local administration and gendarmerie, or as guards at the Palace in Istanbul. As a result, large numbers of male Albanian–speaking Muslims (and few Christian Albanians) accepted their position in the Ottoman administration, joining the Ottoman bureaucracy and often playing an active role on its borders with Serbia, Greece, or Bulgaria.[24]

---

[21] Charles Jelavich and Barbara Jelavich, *The Establishment of the Balkan National States, 1804–1920* (Washington: University of Washington Press, 1986), p. 86.

[22] Nathalie Clayer, *Në fillimet e nacionalizmit shqiptar: Lindja e një kombit me shumicë mysliman në Evrope* (Tiranë: Perpjekja, 2012); in original Nathalie Clayer, *Aux origines du nationalism albanais: la naissance d'une nation majoritairement musulmane on Europe* (Paris: Karthala, 2007), p. 546; According to Nathalie Clayer, in return to this loyalty, "he (Abdulhamid II) pursued a policy of reconciliation towards Albanians, by giving decorations and always appearing as Sultan–Caliph, protector of Albanian Muslims."

[23] Gawrych, *The Crescent*, p. 125.

[24] The key figure in the Ottoman modernist movement was Namik Kemal, who considered the Western democratic institutions as invention of Islam. Similar ideas will be represented by Abdülhamid's Pan–Islamism policy. For the genesis of this understanding see: Şerif Mardin, *The Genesis of Young Ottoman Thought: A Study in the Modernization of Turkish Political Ideas* (Syracuse: Syracuse University Press, 2000). Linda Darling (1998) challenged this conception of the Ottoman Empire as "stagnant and declining," revealing that became "promoted during the age of imperialism with the spread of Western hegemony development of capitalism through political violence and economic exploitation of the rest of the world."; See: Linda T. Darling, "Rethinking

These local, Albanian–speaking Muslims constituted a powerful group in helping to bring both religious unity and security to borderland areas. Their engagements aimed to preserve Sultan Abdulhamid's four pillars of the state (*dört rüknlu devlet*) by being active subjects along the Empire's western border (the pillar of support in Ottoman Rumelia). [25] This Albanian–speaking group recognised the Hamidian regime as their protector, if for no other reason than that it had provided opportunities for their long–term survival. In return, they were expected to re–establish and preserve stability in the Ottoman peripheries (i.e. Macedonia), or to be incorporated in the Sultan's private guard.

Apart from the role of religion and the gendarmerie in recruiting locals to work for the state, another tool applied to bringing this population closer to the state was (that of) education. Articles 18[26] and 63[27] of "The Law on the Rumeli Provinces" (*Rumeli Vilayeti Kanunu/Layiha*) recognised freedom of education under the supervision of the Ottoman government. The schools built by the Ottoman government in Rumelia, much like their European and American counterparts, were meant to impose a level of homogeneity over otherwise culturally diverse populations. [28] In this respect, in several Ottoman reports from the 1880s, the role of the Albanian mobile intellectuals was underscored, predominantly of those from the south (the Tosk region), who were lobbying at the Palace for opening Ottoman and Albanian schools in order to resist the educational hegemony

---

Europe and the Islamic World in the Age of Exploration," *Journal of Early Modern History* 2/3 (1998): 221–246, in the page 233; Fatma Müge Göçek, "Parameters of a Postcolonial Sociology of the Ottoman Empire," in *Decentering Social Theory* ed. Julian Go (Bingley: Emerald Group Publishing Limited, 2013), p. 86.

[25] Gawrych, *The Crescent*, 55.

[26] Rumeli Vilayeti Kanunu Layiha, Quote: *"Umur–u talim ve tedris serbesttir ve hukumetin nezareti tahtında çari olacaktır. Bu nezaret bilaistisna bilctimle mekaniye şamil olacaktır."*

[27] Ibid., Quote: *"Mabet ve mekatib ve mirata merbut bulunan ve meşrut lehi (?) munderc olan evkaf hasilati umur–u maarife sarf olunmak ifin bulunduklari vilayete terk edilmiştir. Bu varidat vakfiyeden her cemaat evkafi varidatı o cemaat mekatibine mahsus olacaktır. Varidat–i vakfiye–i mezkure her cemaatin cemaat meclisi marifetiyle ve maarif mudürunün nezaretiyle idare ve sarf olunacaktır."*

[28] Isa Blumi, "Teaching Loyalty in the Late Ottoman Balkans: Educational Reform in the Vilayets of Manastir and Yanya, 1878–1912," *Comparative Studies of South Asia, Africa and the Middle East*, 21/1–2 (2001): 15.

of the Patriarchate Church and the "Greeks." [29] At this point one should note that the audience of these reports were exclusively southern, Albanian–speaking intellectuals who often lobbied for schools to be opened in their home areas such as the Manastir, Yanina, or Salonika Vilayets.[30] With this interest, the Albanian intellectuals from the south, who were part of Istanbul's intellectual power circle, received approval from the Ottoman government on 7 March 1887 for the foundation of a private school with instruction in Albanian, known as *Mësonjëtorja*, in Korça (then part of the Manastir vilayet). Contrary to claims of Albanian historians, the activities of the local Albanian–speaking population did not aim at resisting the Ottoman institutions; rather, Albanian speakers actively lobbied in Istanbul for the construction of these Ottoman or Albanian schools in their communities in order to oppose the Balkan regional states and their claims. Such lobbying for the schools and education aimed in fact to complete the task of the Albanian intellectuals in Istanbul and Ottoman bureaucrats of indoctrinating the population and bringing them close to the state.

Such engagements were favoured by the Hamidian regime as they added to the opposition to Pan–Slavism and Hellenism in Ottoman Macedonia, as well as to European imperialism globally, with a "unified politico–religious entity vis–à–vis the colonial West with its ties to Christendom."[31] These reforms in education and an elaborate military bureaucracy accompanied by "borrowed colonialism" had the aim of building a protective stronghold in Rumelia by the Albanian–speaking locals.[32] The

---

[29] Ibid.

[30] In this regard, I argue that there was still not present a "pan–Albanianism" among the intellectuals, but rather local initiatives. A fact, that in Kosovo vilayeti were only seven Ottoman state–founded primary schools show that the southern Albanian intellectuals in Istanbul supported rather their regions of origin that was often Manastir or Yanya vilayet.

[31] Kamal Soleimani, "Modern Islamic Political Thought, "Islamism" and Nationalism," *Journal of Humanities and Cultural Studies* 2/1 (2017): 11.

[32] Examples of this policy were: Pashko Vasa – governor of Lebanon, Bajram Curri – captain in Pristine's gendarmerie, Shemsi Pasha – the commander of the 18th division in Mitrovica, Gjakovali Riza Bey – the mayor of Halepo, Isa Boletini served rank in the palace guard (*tüfekçi*), and many others *Malisors* were given entry into the Sultan's palace guard. Other personalities, such as Sami Frashëri, helped the reforms in education. In addition, Vlora Mehmed Ferid Pasha became a Grand Vezier during the Macedonian crisis between 1903 and 1908 helping in management of the local crisis. According to Nuray Bozbora, "the appointed Albanian high–ranking bureaucrats's loyalty to

First secretary (*Mabeyn–i Hümayun Başkâtibi*) of the Ottoman Empire, Tahsin Pasha, between 1894 and 1908 wrote that "Abdulhamid II's guards in the top ranks were Albanians" (*Padişahın muhafazası olarak Arnavutlar birinci safı işgal ederlerdi*).[33] Albanians enjoyed a special status in the Sultan's palace *(Sultan Hamidin Arnavutlara karşi bu itimadı onun için bir siyastin temelini teşkil ediyordu)* because they were an Ottoman fortress in Rumelia *(Rumelide Arnavutlar, Abdülhamid siyasetinin kalesi gibi görülürdü).*[34] At the turn of the century, it was common to find in Ottoman palaces Albanian–speaking individuals from Ottoman Macedonia who were recruited on the grounds of the 'Unity of Islam.'

3.2. From Unitiy of Islam to Albanian Nationalism in the Three Vilayets of Macedonia

Although Albanianism emerged as part of Abdulhamid II's support of the local Albanians in the framework of the Unity of Islam, one should also bear in mind that, at the turn of the century, Albanian nationalism was under major influence of different studies as well, done by European travellers interested in Albanian communities throughout the Eastern Mediterranean. Specifically, in the context of Central Eastern Europe, it has been observed that intellectuals strived to establish "national history" as a scientific discipline, thus blurring the boundaries between science and the national imagination.[35] Influenced by Romantic nationalism and processes of inventing different national traditions around the Balkans, the Austrian linguist Johann Georg von Hahn, in his work "*Albanesische Studien*" (1854), developed a "scientific claim" that "the Pelasgians were

---

Abdulhamid II cannot be neglected (…) even during the Macedonian crisis developed by Serb, Bulgarian and Greek activities." See: Nuray Bozbora, *Osmanlı Yönetiminde Arnavutluk*, p. 216; See also: Osman Köksal, "Osmanlı Devletinde Sıkı Yönetim ile İlgili Mevzuat Üzerine bir Deneme," *AÜ Osmanlı Tarihi Araştırma ve Uygulama Merkezi Dergisi* 1/2 (2001): 157–171; Ragip Sarıca, *Fransa'da ve Türkiye'de Örfi İdare Rejimi* (Istanbul: Baro Macmuasi, 1941); Naci Şensoy, "Osmanlı İmparatorluğunun Sıkı Yönetime Müteallik Mevzuatı Üzerinde Sentetik bir Deneme," *İÜHFM* 13/1 (1947): 95–114.

[33] Tahsin Paşa, *Sultan Abdülhamid'in Sirdaşı* (Istanbul: Yakın Plan Yayınları, 2000), pp. 33–36.

[34] Ibid., 33.

[35] See: Monika Baár, *Historians and Nationalism: East–Central Europe in the Nineteenth Century* (Oxford: Oxford University Press, 2010), p. 50.

the original proto–Albanians and the language spoken by the Pelasgians, Illyrians, Epirotes, and ancient Macedonians was closely related to the Albanian spoken at the time."[36] Furthermore, he emphasised that "[Albanians and] Macedonians [had in fact originated] from a Pelasgo–Illyrian tribe (*Makedonern sind pelasgisch–illyrische Volksstamm*)."[37] In this context, this narrative established an approach that suggested that the ancient Greek civiliation and its achievements also had a Pelasgian, that is "Albanian origin". The most important feature of this "scientific claim" was the transfer of knowledge of an emerging nationalism. Hence, there is no doubt that this narrative influenced many Albanian intellectual personalities that saw this development as "the greatest expansion of the Hellenic civilisation and rule [that] occurred thanks to an 'Albanian' and not a Hellen."[38] Figures originating from the ancient period, such as Alexander the Great and Pyrrhus of Epirus were enveloped in a national narrative and claimed by the intellectuals as Albanian men of antiquity. Thus, the late nineteenth–century Albanian intellectuals had a pivotal role in establishing the Pelasgian–Macedonian–Albanian heritage as the crucial subject of Albanian literature, culture, and politics. In particular, this understanding was transformed into a national narrative during the struggle in the three vilayets (*vilayeti selase*). Commenting on this, Nathalie Clayer developed a question in the form: "Where did the borders of 'Albania' lie, in particular with Macedonia?"[39] On the basis of this

---

[36] Johann Georg von Hahn, *Albanesische Studien* (Jena: F. Mauko, 1854), pp. 222–226; Karl Kaser, "Ahnenkult und Patriarchalismus auf dem Balkan," *Historische Anthropologie* 1/1 (1993): 93–122.

[37] Hahn, *Albanesische Studien*, p. 228; According to Hahn "the Macedonians were represented by the Greeks as an alien tribe (*Makedoner ofters als Barbaren und fremden Stammes (von Griechen gezeichnet)*" belonging to Barbarians. See the quote: "*Wenn nun aber sämmtliche Epiroten und Makedoner entweder Pelasger oder Abkömmlinge der Pelasger heissen, wie geht es zu, dass sie auch Barbaren gennant werden? – Wir antworten einfach, weil eben die Pelasger keine Hellenen, sondern nach hellenischer Ausdrucksweise Barbaren waren.*" According to this theory, Macedonians were not ancient Greeks but rather Pelasgian/Illyrian whose descendants – in opinion of many Albanian intellectuals of that time – are Albanians.

[38] Noel Malcolm, "Myths of Albanian national identity: Some key elements," in *Albanian Identities: Myth and History* eds. Stephanie Schwanders–Sievers and Bernd J. Fischer (Bloomington: Indiana University Press, 2002), p. 77.

[39] Nathalie Clayer, "The Young Turks and the Albanians or Young Turkism and Albanianism?" in *Penser, agir et vivre dans l'Empire ottoman et en Turquie*, eds. Nathalie

question, this sub–chapter aims to analyse how the Eastern Question (i.e. Macedonian Question) influenced the Albanian national movement(s) and developed understandings related to Unity of Islam or nationalist program(s) that intervened into entangled trajectories. The study will trace the transformation of the late nineteenth–century and early twentieth–century points of view of the Albanian mobile intellectuals that differs from in space and time from their activism. In this regard, one cannot analyse the Albanian national movement as a unified project developed in a vacuum, but rather as processual constructs of multilayered understandings of national narratives and historical intersectionalities, all of which had something in common: to influence the locals' national affiliations on the ground.

3.2.1. Albanianism in *Stamboll*: Against Pan–Slavism and Pan–Hellenism

We shall now take a look at a memorandum of 1877, in which the Austrian consul in Shkodër, F. Lippich, portrayed Albanians as inhabitants of many parts of what will later be known as Macedonia. Excerpts of it follow:

> "The [Albanian] northern linguistic frontier runs from west to east,…somewhat below Antivari, above the mountain ridge and the northwestern corner of the Shkoder lake, following the Sem upstream above Fundina through Kuči to Vasojević and Kolašin; the latter two districts, although Serbian–speaking in the majority, still seem to be in part of Albanian origin–perhaps the only instance of slavisation of Albanians…
>
> In its further course, the linguistic frontier moves from Kolasin to Gusinje and Plava, upstream the Ibar river to Rožaj, then from Suhodol and Gulgovik to Duga Poljana, on the Rogosna plateau, west and southwest of Novi Pazar, where it climbs the districts of Vucitern, Kurcunli and Prokoplje up to the Serbian border and descends again to the Toplica, reaching its junction with the Bulgarian Morava… on the course of this river [Morava] and the Moravica… bending westward and running along the southern slope of Karadağ through the Lepenc pass. It then crosses the

---

layer and Erdal Kaynar (Paris/Louvain/Walpole: Peters – Collection Turcica Vol XIX, 2013), p. 69; Kurt Gostentschnigg, *Wissenschaft im Spannungsfeld von Politik und Militär: Die österreichisch–ungarische Albanologie 1867–1918* (Wiesbaden: Springer Fachmedien Wiesbaden, 2018).

Vardar valley near the junction of the Treska with the Vardar, and pursuing the Treska through the sandjak of Monastir, it runs along its boundary with Dibra as far as the northern shore of the Lake Ohrid."[40]

There is evidence to suggest that Albanian intellectuals were influenced by this spatial imagination to create their own perception of Macedonia as a territory that is belonging to their national heritage. In the midst of the Great Eastern Crisis (1875-1878), a group of Albanian intellectuals residing in Istanbul founded the Central Committee for Defending Albanian Rights (*Komiteti Qendror për Mbrojtjen e të Drejtave të Kombësisë Shqiptare*), also known as the Istanbul Committee, on December 18, 1877. Their goal was to assert their claims over certain territories that they imagined as part of their national heritage, a sentiment shared by the Austrian consul at the time. The initial political programs of Albanians were formulated in collaboration with Ottoman authorities and led by intellectuals from both Muslim and Christian communities, such as Abdul Frashëri and Vaso Pasha. These programs were published in the Ottoman newspaper, *Tercüman–ı Şark*,[41] which advocated for the creation of a single Albanian vilayet consisting of Kosovo, Manastir, Janina, Scutari, and sometimes Salonica Vilayet.[42] The League of Prizren, which was formed as a result of this effort, initially considered parts of

---

[40] Skendi cites the relevance of this memorandum as "It [the memorandum] may be held sufficiently reliable on account of the special interest of Austria–Hungary in this portion of Albania and Lippich's personal knowledge of it." See: Stavro Skendi, *The Albanian National Awakening* (Princeton, NJ: Princeton University Press, 1967), p. 32; Engelbert Deusch, *Das K. (U.) K. Kultusprotektorat im Albanischen Siedlungsgebiet in seinem kulturellen, politischen und wirtschaftlichen Umfeld* (Vienna/Cologne/Weimar: Böhlau Verlag, 2009); Otto von Gerstner, *Albanien* (Wien und Leipzig: Wilhelm Braumüller, 1913); Franz Baron Nopcsa, *Aus Šala und Klementi: Albanische Wanderungen* (Sarajevo: Druck und Verlag und Daniel A. Kajon, 1910); Lovro Mihačević, *Durch Albanien: Reise–Eindrücke* (Prag: Druck und Verlag des Bonifatius–Buchdruckerei, 1913); Robert Elsie, *The Tribes of Albania: History, Society and Culture* (London/New York: I. B. Tauris, 2015); Isa Blumi, "The Commodification of Otherness and the Ethnic Unit in the Balkans: How to Think about Albanians," *East European Politics and Societies: and Cultures* 12/3 (1998): 527–569.
[41] Tercüman–ı Şark was issued by Şemsettin Sami Frashëri. The first number appeared on 29 March 1878; Şemsettin Sami, *Kamus'ül–a'lam: Tarih ve Coğrafya Lugatı ve Tabir–i Esahha Kaffe–yi Esma–yı Hassayı Camidir, vol. I* (Istanbul: Mihran Matbaası, 1306 [1889]), about "*Arnavudluk*," on pages: 149–153.
[42] Clayer, *Aux origines du nationalism albanais*, p. 463.

Macedonia, or vilayeti selase, as part of Albania. The Istanbul Committee drafted a program in 1878 to protect Albanian lands from any external invasions and to support the unification of the Albanian vilayet, including those in Macedonia. This programme emerged during the Eastern Crisis and Russo–Turkish War (1877–1878), when the Russian Empire simultaneously supported Pan–Slavism. Under such circumstances, the leader of the League of Prizren and member of the Istanbul Committee, Abdul Frashëri, wrote in *Messager de Vienne* that the "Albanians serve the cause of humanity and civilisation better than any other people of the East," and that they "[would] always be the best vanguard against Russian pan Slavism."[43] According to this article, the chief aim of Albanian intellectuals was to construct a national narrative that would oppose the Pan–Slavism influence in Ottoman Macedonia (considered Albanian heritage).[44] In this regard, Nathalie Clayer posits that the emergence of "Albanianism" is directly connected to the anti–Slav reactions of Ottoman society, respectively, after Russia expanded its influence in the Balkans. As a result, partly anti–Slavic and partly Islamic in nature, an important sense of belonging emerged among Ottoman Albanians.[45]

The emergence of Albanianism during the Eastern Crisis can be observed through the shift from Ottoman imperial ideology to the concept of Unity of Islam.[46] While some regarded the League of Prizren as a Muslim organisation, others emphasised its distinct Albanian national program.[47] In my view, it is essential to note that both elements coexisted during this period, as the development of Albanianism and Unity of Islam were not

---

[43] See: Abdyl Frashëri in newspaper Messager de Vienne, No. 22, Vienna, 31. May, 1878, p. 5; See also archive documents in Tirana: AQSH, GF6, Fondet personale, FO 1, No. AP 1, Dosje, 1 (12.04.1881), quote: *"Telegram i zëvendësprefektit të Elbasanit Naim, dërguar dikujt, mbi marrjen e masave për të kapur Abdyl Bej Frashërin."*

[44] Ljubodrag Dimić and Đorđe Borozan, *Jugoslovenska država i Albanci, vol. II* (Beograd: JP Službeni list SRJ/Arhiv Jugoslavije/Vojno–istorijski institut, 1999); Clayer, *Aux origines du nationalism albanais*.

[45] Ibid.

[46] Dimitris Stamatopoulos, *The Eastern Question or Balkan Nationalisms: Balkan History Reconsidered* (Vienna: Vienna University Press, 2018), pp. 43–44.

[47] Isa Blumi, *Reinstating the Ottomans: Alternative Balkan Modernities, 1800–1912* (New York: Palgrave Macmillan, 2011); Nathalie Clayer, "The Albanian Students of the Mekteb-i Mülkiye: Social Networks and Trends of Thought," in *Late Ottoman Society: The Intellectual Legacy*, ed. Elisabeth Özdalga (London/New York: Routledge: Taylor and Francis Group, 2010), pp. 291–311.

mutually exclusive. To the contrary of the Serbian and Greek nationalisms, the Albanian one, thus, did not emerge from an anti–Ottoman struggle and at its early stage was not based on separation from the Ottoman empire.[48] Albanian intellectuals played a significant role in the Eastern Crisis and the formation of Albanianism, as demonstrated by their involvement in the League of Prizren (1878). The League submitted a memorandum to the British representative at the Congress of Berlin on 13 June 1878, declaring their opposition to being turned into Turks, Slavs, Austrians, or Greeks, and asserting their desire to be Albanians. Although the League separated Albanianism from the notion of the "Turk," it still placed a significant emphasis on religion. The Ottoman state and Sultan Abdulhamid II contributed to the Islamic connotation of the League and Albanianism. The Ottoman authorities initially showed great sympathy for the League of Prizren and offered no hindrance to its formation. Albanian intellectuals supported this policy, as stated in the first article of the *Kararname*[49] of the League proclaimed that "our [Prizren] league has come together to oppose any government other than that of the Sublime Porte and to defend our territorial integrity by all possible means."[50] Accordingly, Albanians did not gather in Prizren to oppose the Ottoman Empire, but rather to protect its border especially on the lines inhabited by Albanians. Furthermore, Article 16 of *kararname* described the importance of the League, respectively with meanings for Islam: "whoever abandons it (the League) will be treated as if he had abandoned our Islamic faith and will be the object of our curses and scorn."[51] In addition, the Islamic notion was further emphasised in the *kararname* of the meeting at Marash Tekkesi in Prizren in 1879, where it was declared that "God make it to be forbidden (*mazallah*) to all Albanian people (*bütün Arnavud kavmi*) to become part

---

[48] Clayer, *The Young Turks and the Albanians*, pp. 71–72.
[49] On 18 June 1878, see: http://www.albanianhistory.net/1878_League–of–Prizren/index.html (access. 26.06.2019.); Additionally: HHStA, Vienna, Consulate of Shkodra, Note 64, AIH, A–VI–10, pp. 73–77. Appendix to a report by Austro–Hungarian consul Jelinek of Prizren, to Consul Lippich in Shkodra, 13 July 1878; in *Aktetë Rilindjes Kombëtare Shqiptare, 1878–1912,* eds. Stefanaq Pollo and Selami Pulaha (Tiranë: Instituti i Historisë 1978), pp. 40–48; and *La Ligue albanaise de Prizren, 1878–1881* eds. Stefanaq Pollo and Selami Pulaha (Tiranë: Institut d'Histoire 1978), pp. 55–65. Translated from the German, Albanian and French by Robert Elsie.
[50] Ibid.
[51] Ibid.

of another state and to separate from the general Islamic order."[52] In this regard, Noel Malcolm also describes the League of Prizren as a purely Muslim, conservative movement for the preservation of the old order of the Ottoman state combined with "new Pan–Islamic ideology."[53] This policy was also admitted by the highest Ottoman official, Dervish Pasha, who thought that "the League of Albania would be useful to the Empire (*quela Ligue de l'Albanieserait utile à l'Empire*)."[54] In line with this politicisation of Albanianism, Pashko Vasa demanded the formation of a single Albanian province (composed of the provinces of Janina, Kosovo and Shkodër) emphasising that "the division of Albania into three vilayets was already sufficient to completely destroy the beneficent [*sic*] action of administrative unity without aggravating it by a heterogeneous medley."[55] As an Ottoman bureaucrat of Albanian origin, Pashko Vasa developed this programme in his book "*Études Sur L'Albanie Et Les Albanais.*" This work was first published in Istanbul in 1879, printed in the press of the newspaper *La Turquie*. According to Kristaq Prifti, this work was not published by the author or the Albanian Committee in Istanbul, but by "the Turkish (i.e. Ottoman) Embassy through a direct order from the government of Istanbul."[56] Being interested in securing its borders in the Balkans, particularly in Macedonia, the Ottoman government accepted for the embassies to be engaged in the dissemination of Pashko Vasa's work

---

[52] See: Vali Kabashi, "Lidhja e Prizrenit – Organizata më e madhe politiko–ushtarake" *Gazeta Koha Ditore*, 9. June, 2018; BOA, HR.SYS. 214, 25, 1879; Hugo Kerchnawe, "Die Militärverwaltung in Montenegro und Albanien," in *Die Militärverwaltung in den von den Österreichisch–Ungarischen Truppen Besetzten Gebieten*, eds. Hugo Kerchnawe et al. (Vienna: Hölder–Pichler–Tempsky A.G., 1928), pp. 270–304.

[53] Noel Malcolm, *Kosovo a short history* (New York: New York University Press, 1998), p. 222; see a quote: "I think it's clear that the Sublime Porte and the League had the same opinion and were working to realise a common purpose – protecting the province."

[54] Kristaq Prifti, "Certains aspects des rapports de la Ligue albanaise de Prizren avec la Sublime Porte selon les documents ottomans (1878–1881)," *Studia Albanica* 1 (2012): 50. In the Document: *Ahmet Moukhtar Pacha, le 20 mars 1295/1 avril 1880. Le maréchal Dervish Pacha, chargé par la Sublime Porte dans les années 1880–1881 pour réprimer la Ligue albanaise*; BOA, Fon: Yildiz Esas Evraki. Doc. N° 14 88/16 88/12, in the Document: *Rapport envoyé au Conseil des Ministres par Dervish Pacha, Shkodra, le 15décembre 1296/27 décembre 1880. en Istanbul.*

[55] Pashko Vasa, *The Truth on Albania and the Albanians: Historical and Critical* (London: Centre for Albanian Studies, 1999). p. 42.

[56] Kristaq Prifti, *Botimi dhe perhapja në Evrope e vepres se Pashko Vases: E verteta per Shqiperinë dhe Shqipëtaret* (Tiranë: Studime Historike, 2002), p. 59.

in Europe, publishing it in German and English. The central idea of this work of Pashko Vasa was the recognition of the Albanian nation by the Great Powers and the European public opinion as a nation quite separate from its neighbours, the Greeks and Slavs. Therefore, it should exist as "united Albania into one *solo vilayet*" and "inaugurated under the aegis of His Majesty the Sultan [in] an era of unity, of concord, and of fraternity for all faiths and all religions."[57] Considering this attempt to incorporate the future Albania into the Ottoman Empire, he dedicated himself to the struggle for recognition of his nation and Ottoman Empire and the following attempt to help his country make the leap towards the rest of the "civilised nations."[58] With a "progressive" *Weltanschauung*, he as an ardent nationalist of the 19th century evidently believed in progress, emphasising that "with a little more civilisation and better conditions, Albania not only would have nothing to envy Switzerland, but surpass it in beauty, in poetry, and in force."[59] Furthermore, Pashko Vasa was a member of the Istanbul Society of the Albanian Letters (*Shoqëri e të Shtypuri Shkronja Shqip*),[60] a society close to the Ottoman government and Abdulhamid II's policies.[61] In 1880, the society translated Vasa's work *Études Sur L'Albanie Et Les Albanais* into Turkish,[62] and its members made a significant contribution to education in the Albanian language during that period. In addition to Vasa, other members of the society emphasised the importance of literacy and the alphabet in relation to "progress and civilisation." They stated in the Statute of the society the following:

> "All enlightened and civilised nations, are enlightened and civilised due to the writings of/in their own languages. And every nation which does not write in its own language, and does not have writings of its own language, stays in darkness and barbarian. Even Albanians, while not writing in their

---

[57] Balázs Trencsényi, Ahmet Ersoy, Michal Kopeček, Maciej Górny and Vangelis Kechriotis, *Late Enlightenment: Emergence of Modern National Idea* (Budapest/New York: Central European University Press, 2006), p. 124.

[58] Isa Blumi, *Foundations of Modernity: Human Agency and the Imperial State* (New York: Routledge, 2011).

[59] Vasa, *The Truth on Albania*, p. 33.

[60] Prifti, *Botimi dhe perhapja në Evrope*, p. 57.

[61] Ibid.

[62] Translated title: Pashko Vasa Efendi, *Arnavutluk ve Arnavutlar* (Istanbul: 1287/1880).

own language and not having an alphabet of their own languages, remain so, and the presupposition and hope from three thousand years ago (as far as history is known) to be enlightened and civilised by using the languages and writings of their neighbours, proved to be useless...Without having, nor wanting, anyone better than the others between us, who will come after us, we pray to the God of Life, to bless the existence of this/us, the Society for the Publication of Albanian Writings."[63]

This statement in the statute of the Society played a crucial role in the national revival of Albanian literature and the development of the Albanian national identity. The statement emphasised the importance of writing and publishing in the Albanian language, which was necessary for the advancement and enlightenment of the Albanian people and their civilisation. In this line, Şemsettin Sami Frashëri in his book "*Medeniyet–i Islamiye*"[64] (1879), elaborated that the roots of "civilisation" lies in Islamic tradition. He claimed that European civilisation has Islamic roots that need to be returned to their source.[65] According to him, civilisation is a result of Islam,[66] and any nation that accepted Islam was already part of civilisation.[67] In "*Medeniyet–i cedidenin ümem–i islamiyeye naklî*"[68] (1833), he further stated that "saving the Muslim peoples from ignorance

---

[63] See: Kanonizmë e shoqërisë të shtypuri shkronja shqip (Konstandinopojë: Ndëshkronjës shtypëtoret të A. Zelicit, 1879), pp. 1–2; in original see: "*Gjithë sa kombe janë të ndrituarë dhe të qytetëruarë prej shkronjas ndë gjuhët të veta. Edhe çdo komb që nuk ka shkruar gjuhën e vet, edhe s'ka shkronja ndë gjuhët të vet është ndë t'errëtë dhe barbar. Edhe shqiptarët tue mos shkruarë gjuhën e tyre dhe tu me mos pasur shkronja ndë gjuhët të tyre, kështu gjenden edhe pa ndihma e shpresa këtu e tri mijë vjet përpara (saqë mund të njihet historia) që të ndriçoheshin dhe të qytetëroheshinë me gjuhët të fëqinjët e të huajët u dëftue e kotë, edhe trimëria e të miratë, që kanë duart tona në prej shokësh, që duke mishkruarë në fund secili me dorët të vet. Edhe nuk e kena, as duamë, ndonjë prej ma tepër se shokët e tjerë, që kanë me u ba pas nesh, por i lutemi Zotit të jetesë, te vejë mbarë shoqëria jone, Shoqëria e të shtypurit shkronjash.*"
[64] Şemsettin Sâmi, *İslâm Medeniyeti* (Istanbul: Mihran, 1879/1296; edition from 1980).
[65] Ibid., pp. 28–29; In original: "*Avrupalıyı cehâletten kurtaran şey, İslâm medeniyetidir. Vahşi Avrupalının zihnini nurlandıran öğretmenler genellikle Müslüman hocalardır.*"
[66] Ibid; In original: "*Medeniyeti sâdece İslâm dininin semeresi ve mahsûlüdür deriz.*"
[67] Ibid. pp. 25–26; In original: "*Her hangi bir kavim İslâm dinini Kabul ettiyse, bu medeniyet dairesine dahil oldu. Bu medeniyet İslâm dininin semeresi (ürünü) dir.*"
[68] Şemsettin Sami Frashëri, "Medeniyet–i cedideninümem–i islamiyeye naklî," in *Güneş* 1/4 (1883–1884): 179–184. Translation from Turkish and Introduction by M. Şükrü Hanioğlu.

and once again bringing them to civilisation are among the most important priorities of any zealous person who loves his religious community and fatherland since the survival and glory of Islam are contingent upon this alone."[69] Therefore, every nation that is part of Islam has the aim to "transfer contemporary civilisation to the Islamic nations."[70] To achieve this, they used various means such as newspapers, books, pamphlets, sermons, etc., to spread the view that European civilisation was borrowed from the Muslims and that Islam is not an obstacle to true civilisation. They also emphasised that most of the science and technology seen in the hands of Europeans today is made up of Muslim discoveries. Albanians, in this context, had an obligation to write in their own language and promote their national ideas and civlisational line rooted in Islam. Furthermore, Şemsettin Sami Frashëri praised Abdulhamid II for allowing the Albanian people (*kavim*) to establish schools in the Albanian language in order to create Albanian national literature (*edebiyat–i milliye*), aiming "to counter Greek and Slavic territorial claims on these regions (including Macedonia)."[71] During its early stages, the Albanian national programme did not contradict the Unity of Islam (*İttihad–ı İslam*), as it was perceived as being in line with the Ottoman unity that accommodated ethnic diversity.[72] According to Şemsettin Sami Frashëri, Albanianism and Unity of Islam were complementary concepts. He also emphasised the longstanding presence of Albanians in the Balkan Peninsula "since very early times that history cannot score."[73] In his chapter on Macedonia in the *Kamus al–alam* encyclopedia, he claimed that the original Macedonians were Albanians (*eski Makedonyalıların sırf ve halis Arnavut bulunmuş olduklarında şüphe kalmaz*)."[74] For many Albanians, the core of their national identity was rooted in Rumelia, comprising Albania and Macedonia. Thus, the establishment of an autonomous Albania was viewed as a means to preserve the commitment of the Caliph Sultan to

---

[69] Ibid; See also: Charles Kurzman, *Modernist Islam, 1840–1940* (Oxford: Oxford University Press, 2002).

[70] Ibid.

[71] Clayer, *Aux origines du nationalism albanais*, p. 72.

[72] Ibid.

[73] Şemsettin Sami Frashëri (Samy–Bey Fraschery), *Kamus al–alam I* (Istanbul: Mihran Matbaası, 1306 [1889]), p. 86.

[74] Ibid., p. 117.

conservative Muslim Albanians.[75] Although Abdulhamid II did not support the idea of autonomy, he was indirectly responsible for the development of Albanianness.[76] After the Oriental Crisis (1876–1878), Abdulhamid II and his advisors began to regard the 'lbanians' as the backbone of the Ottoman presence in Europe, particularly the Albanian Muslims residing in the border regions with Montenegro, Serbia, and Greece. This was aimed at strengthening their allegiance to Ottoman rule and to Islam, as pointed out by George Gawrych.[77] Sultan Abdulhamid II also wanted to bind this emergence of Albanianism to religious notions of the Unity of Islam and simultaneously undermine the development of national–separatist tendencies. Therefore, Abdulhamid II's support of the Albanianism and the organised resistance of the Prizren League (1878), which tried to give an Islamic spirit to its resistance,[78] was an attempt to bind Albanians not to an independent national movement but to religious feelings. In this regard, Sultan Abdulhamid II wanted to identify himself as the "father (*baba*) of Albanians" in order to "establish an enlightened rule in his domains, and he had some definite ideas about Albania and Albanians."[79] In Kosovo in particular, local officials requested to employ troops to assist the government functions and to bring "civilisation" (*medeniyet*) and "humanity" (*insaniyet*) to the wild regions of Macedonia and Albania.[80] As mentioned above, the main supporter of such ideas was former Grand Vizier Mehmed Esad Safvet Pasha, who on 12 April 1880 submitted a memorandum advocating for forming a separate policy for people living in the periphery, especially Albanians.[81] This policy was also supported by the highest Ottoman official, Dervish Pasha. [82] This promotion of Albanianism closely linked to strong common "Islamic" values was important as a response to Hellenism and Pan–Slavic regional

---

[75] Ibid. p. 14.
[76] Clayer, *The Young Turks and the Albanians*, p. 71.
[77] Ibid. 68.
[78] Bozbora, *The Policy of Abdulhamid II*, p. 47.
[79] Gawrych, *The Crescent*, p. 107.
[80] Deringil, *They Live in a State of Nomadism*.
[81] Ibid., p. 73.
[82] Prifti, *Botimi dhe perhapja në Evrope*, p. 50.

threats.[83] The aim was of course to counter Greek and Slavic territorial claims to these regions. In order to strengthen the Albanian narratives in Ottoman Macedonia, between 1889 and 1896 official Ottoman salnames of the European provinces drew on the descriptions of Şemsettin Sami Bey in his *Kamus al–alâm*, and depicted some Balkan regions, such as Epirus and Macedonia, as having been inhabited since remote antiquity by the Pelasgians, the ancestors of the Albanians, on whom further information was provided.[84] The assertion that certain territories were attributed with an Albanian narrative line by the Ottoman authorities disappeared after 1896. However, the growing involvement of the Great Powers in Macedonia from 1897, and particularly from 1903 onwards, led to a renewed interest in this idea. This period also saw some Albanian intellectuals opposing Ottoman policies towards Albania and Macedonia. One such individual was Sami Frashëri, who initially supported Albanianism as part of the Unity of Islam, but later switched his allegiance. This shift suggests that intellectuals could espouse multiple ideologies and nationalist visions over their lifetime. Sami Frashëri subsequently formulated a more independent programme, as outlined in his book "*Shqipëria – Ç'ka qënë, ç'është e ç'do të bëhetë? Mendime për shpëtimt të mëmë–dheut nga reziket që e kanë rethuarë*," published in Bucharest in 1899.[85] Indeed, this book has always represented the main work by Frashëri, used in the construction of his mythologised image in Albania,

---

[83] Some of them worked as gunman (*tüfekçi*), part of gendarme (*hadim jandarma*) or commandants in different parts of Ottoman Empire as Iskodrali Tahir Pasha, Kranyali Tahir Pasha, Küçük Tahir Bey, Halil Bey Skeja and Osman Pasha – the general of brigades and commandant of battalions of guardians (*zuaveve shqiptare*). See: Denis Ljuljanović, ""Turkonegrins" between Montenegro and the Ottoman Empire: Brothers or Others?," in *Etnické komunity – Neviditelní, přehlížení, zapomenutí*, eds. Dana Bittnerová and Mirjam Moravcová (Praha: Fakulta humanitních studií Univerzity Karlovy 2019), pp. 35–57; Clayer, *Aux origines du nationalism albanais*; Theodor Ippen, *Skutari und die Nordalbanische Kuestenebene* (Sarajevo: Daniel A. Kajon, 1907), pp. 41–42.

[84] Şemsettin Sami Frashëri (Samy–Bey Fraschery), *Kamus al–alam.*

[85] Bülent Bilmez, "Shemseddin Sami Frashëri (1850–1904): Contributing to the Construction of Albanian and Turkish Identities," in *We, the People: Politics of National Peculiarity in Southeastern Europe,* ed. Diana Mishkova (Budapest: Central European University Press, 2009), pp. 341–371; See also: Sami Frashëri, *Shqipëria ç'ka qënë, çështë e çdo të bëhët?* (in translation: Albania – What It Was, What It Is and What Will Become of It? Reflections on Saving the Motherland from Perils which Beset It) (Tiranë: Mesonjëtorja e parë, 1999).

because it has always been seen as (one of) the first "manifesto(s)" of Albanian political nationalism anticipating an Albanian state. This work is indicative as a main book for formulation of Albanian national identity at the turn to the century. Actually, its aim was to promote full Albanian autonomy within the Ottoman Empire, as a first step to Albanian state independence. With regard to Sami's book, its first section, titled "Pelasgians", claims that the "Albanians are the oldest people of Europe and direct descendants of the Pelasgians."[86] He emphasises that the Albanians are Pelasgians and the tribes (*fise*) their branches – Illyrians, Epiriots, Macedonians, and Thracians. He underlines the benefits of the Albanians' centuries-long isolated life, which kept them remote from civilisation during what he refers to as "barbarian times." Frashëri argues that the preservation of the Albanian language and nationality was not due to their possession of letters, knowledge, or civilisation, but rather their freedom and isolation from other people, as well as their refusal to allow foreigners to live among them. This savage mountain life allowed the Albanians to maintain their language and nationality despite their lack of exposure to the world, knowledge, civilisation, and trade."[87] This romanticist image of isolated "barbarian" life might remind us of Rousseau's idea of the "noble savage," which is also displayed, though implicitly, when Frashëri admires Albanians for being brave warriors. Nevertheless, Frashëri's main goal is the modernisation of Albania, which is compatible with that of the Ottoman government, which had actually been attempting modernisation of the empire, including Albania. However, he distinguishes Albanians and Turks as totally different entities. Sami Frashëri points out that the Turks:

> "Do not have any more right to live like this than these other savage peoples, yet even today they continue to live as freeloaders. They no longer have such rights. Up to now, they have created neither a state nor a government, as other countries have. They prefer to live in savagery. They will fall and must perish so that humankind can survive. But what have we done to them that, in their fall, they want to take us down with them? What do we have in common with them? Did we arrive with them? No, not at

---

[86] Ibid., pp. 3–6.
[87] Ibid., pp. 17–18.

all. We are not Turks, nor did we arrive from the wilds of Asia. We are the oldest people of Europe. We have more rights to live in Europe than any others."[88]

His argument that the Albanians are the "oldest people of Europe" and the view of the Turks as a "savage people" belonged to a *Zeitgeist* of politically formulated "national superiority" and of nation–state projects, not just among the Albanian intellectuals, but also among the political elites of the new emerging nations in the Balkans.[89] In the Albanian case generally, and in Frashëri's example particularly, there were broadly two types of claims in the formulation of these projects. First, the claim that the nation had existed in the same territory "from time immemorial." Second, that the ancestors of the nation settled permanently in their current location, establishing a decisive presence and adding an important contribution to "civilisation." Sami Frashëri emphasised that Albanians had achieved their accomplishments during the time of Alexander the Great. He recounted Alexander's story and expressed a desire to bring about a "Greater Albania," with the ultimate objective of preserving the Albanian language and national identity, preventing division by foreign powers, and thwarting the spread of Greek and Serbian influences that undermine the foundations of Albania and threaten its people. Frashëri called on all true Albanians and the Albanian league to fiercely combat

---

[88] Ibid.

[89] Holm Sundhaussen, "Eliten, Bürgertum, politische Klasse? Anmerkungen zu den Oberschichten in den Balkanländern des 19. und 20. Jahrhunderts," in *Eliten in Südosteuropa: Rolle, Kontinuitäten, Brüche in Geschichte und Gegenwart*, eds. Wolfgang Höpken and Holm Sundhaussen (Munich: Südosteuropa–Gesellschaft, 1998); Antōnēs Anastasopulos, "Introduction," in *Provincial Elites in the Ottoman Empire*, ed. Antōnēs Anastasopulos (Rethymno: Crete University Press, 2005); Gudrun Krämer, "Der Reiz des Gesellschaftsvergleichs: Kategorien sozialer Ordnung im islamisch geprägten Vorderen Orient," in *Europa in der Welt des Mittelalters: Ein Colloquium für und mit Michael Borgolte*, eds. Tillmann Lohne and Benjamin Scheller (Berlin/Boston: De Gruyter, 2014), pp. 101–118; Johann Büssow and Astrid Meier, "Ottoman Corporatism, Eighteenth to Twentieth Centuries: Beyond the State–Society Paradigm in Middle Eastern History," in *Ways of Knowing Muslim Cultures and Societies: Studies in Honour of Gudrun Krämer*, eds. Bettina Gräf, Birgit Krawietz and Schirin Amir–Moazami (Leiden: Brill, 2019), pp. 81–110.

anything that hinders this goal and to wholeheartedly embrace and support anything that advances it.[90]

3.2.2. Albanianism in the Diaspora: How Did Albanian Mobile Intellectuals Imagined Albania and Macedonia?

Although the Frashëri family (Abdyl, Naim, and Sami) have been accepted as three of the founders of Albanian nationalism, historians often downplay the role of Mithat Frashëri, who was an Ottoman bureaucrat in Palestine and one of the leading figures of Albanian nationalism. He was the son of Abdyl and the nephew of the aforementioned Ottoman scholar and Albanian nationalist(s) Sami Frashëri (and Naim Frashëri). While his activist career began in the years leading up to the Committee for Union and Progress (CUP) takeover of power, he abandoned the ideals of the Ottoman Empire after 1908, similar to his uncle Sami Frashëri who had done so in 1898.[91]

It seems that Mithat Frashëri supported integrationist ideas for Albania within the Ottoman Empire before the Young Turk Revolution. During his time in the vilayet of Salonika from 1905 to 1910, he published the weekly newspaper *Lirija* and edited a monthly magazine entitled *Diturija*, in which he praised Albanian Istanbul society established by his uncle Sami Frashëri and promoted cultural, literary, and scholarly interests in Albanian history.[92] He was against the threats posed by the Slavic side and the Greek side, and declared Albanian dominance over those nations.[93]

---

[90] Frashëri, *Shqipëria ç'ka qënë.*

[91] Isa Blumi, "Publishers, Hitmen, Diplomats, and Dreamers: Switzerland's Ottoman–Albanian Diaspora,1899–1920," *Schweizerische Zeitschrift für Geschichte* 52 (2002): 318; Nathalie Clayer, "The Dimension of Confessionalisation in the Ottoman Balkans at the Time of Nationalisms" in *Conflicting Loyalties in the Balkans: The Great Powers, the Ottoman Empire and Nation–Building*, eds. Hannes Grandits, Nathalie Clayer and Robert Pichler (London/New York: I. B. Tauris, 2011), pp. 89–109.

[92] Diturija, No.1, Selanik (Thessaloniki), 1. Januar,1909, p. 5; in original: *"N' është pra se sot sqipes' i degohete zeri, kete ja kemi hua asaj shoqëris' s' Stambolit që ka qen'e para punë kombiare. "* See also about Mithat Frashëri: AQSH, Fondet personale, GF 6, FO 24, No. AP 5/1: *"Proklamata që bëjnë fjalë për të drejtat e shqiptarëve për pavarësinë e Shqipërisë, për një luftë të organizuar, shkruar nga Lidhja e Shqiptarëve të Shkodrës, Mehmet bej Frashërit etj. "*

[93] Diturija, No. 1, Selanik, 1. Januar. 1909, pp. 4–5; in original: *"Pas luftes'se Rusisë, pas tratatit te Shent Stefanojt dhe te Berlinit ne rezik i madh u tregua per vendin tene ng' an'*

Mithat Frashëri believed that among all the nations living in the Ottoman empire, Albanians played the most important role. He claimed that Albania "became part of Turkey" not as a conquered place but "as a friendly and equal nation." [94] He suggested that "Albania was ruled by the local government, and Turkey only had a symbolical authority over the country."[95] Furthermore, he appreciated the excellent role of Albanians occupying a crucial position in "Turkish history" and he underlined that "Albanians were also always the first in the whole Empire, looking at Turkey as their own place, not just for work and profit, but also for ruling the Empire."[96] He suggests that Albanians should rule over a vast territory spanning from the Shar mountains to Basra and from the Black Sea to the Red Sea.[97] However, he believed that this kind of dominance could only be achieved if Albanians had a strong foundation in written literature. He followed in the footsteps of his uncle Sami and saw the creation of an Albanian alphabet as a means of civilising and enlightening his people. Frashëri believed that this invention would enable Albanians to learn both dialects and bring them to the spoken level.[98] As an editor of the *Kalendari Kombiar*, an annual almanac known as "Albanian Encyclopedia" – published in Sofia since 1897, he promoted moderate positions that

---

e Slavevet. Ger m' ahere Shqiperija kish rezik te madh ng' an e grekeret qe perpiqeshin te na humbasine guhene dhe te na prishine kombësinë. "

[94] Diturija, No. 3, Selanik, 1. Mars, 1909, p. 33; in original: *"Nga kaqe kombe qe jan' ne Tyrqi Shqipetaret jan' ata qe kane lojture me te madh rol!. Pas njezet e pes vjet lufte nene flamur te ndricim te Skenderbeut, dhe pas nje kundreqendrimi te ndercim. Shqiperija hyri nene sunim te Tyrqise, jo si nje vent i mundure, po si nje komp shok dhe baras. "*

[95] Ibid; in original: *"Tyrqija vec emrin kish mi vendin tene, se qeveri e vendit ka mbeture kurdohere ne duar te shqipetarevet, te femijevet te vendit, qe kane mbajture ger fort afre mevethesin' e tyre, aqe sa qeveri e Tyrqise s' kish asnje fuqi ne Shqiperi. "*

[96] Ibid; in original: *"Një veshtrim i cpejte n' istori te Tyrqise na tregon fort bukure radhen e shkelqyere qe kane mbajture Shqipetaret. Shqiperija jo vetsm ka qen' e zonja te mbane vethen' e saj te lire dhe te pa poshteruare, po dhe ka diture qe te jet' i par' i kombevet ne te tere mbreterit, duke shikuare gjithe Tyrqine si nje vent te hapure per te, ku jo vetem ka punuare, ka fituare, po ka urdheruare dhe mbreteruare. "*

[97] Ibid., p. 36; in original: *"Tani Tyrqija e ter' eshte hapure per Shqipetare: qe nga mal' i Sharit e ger ne menge te Basres, qe nga det' i Zi e ger ne det i Kuq, i tere ky shesh eshte i celure: Ie te jet'i zoti dhe te refehet i pare te mbreteroje dhe te urdheroj. "*

[98] Diturija, No. 11 and 12, Selanik, 1. Dhjetor 1909, p. 146; in original: *"Duhete pra qe te dime te dy djalektet dhe per këtë pune Geget lipset qe te kEndojne librat toskerisht dhe Toskete librate gegerisht, me nje menyre qe te dy ke foljet t' i dukene si te tijate dhe jo vetem t'i kupetojë, po dhe te mundin ti flas njeriu. "*

supported Albanian unity, education in Albanian, and opposed foreign power intervention in Macedonian affairs. Additionally, the almanac advanced the notion that the ancient Macedonians were the ancestors of the Albanians. In 1898, an article from the "Albanian Encyclopedia" claimed that "the Albanians had a significant historical figure in Alexander the Great, who had conquered the world, and the most celebrated hero among them was Skenderbeg, who fought valiantly against the Turks."[99] This "invention of tradition" was a familiar tactic used to assert ancient lineage for the purpous of nation-building. The press was one way that national and imperialistic ambitions could forge this sense of identity. The Albanian elite aimed to create a narrative that would foster national consciousness among the masses at the local level. They often explicitly claimed the legacy to the heritage of "Alexander the Great of Macedonia, who conquered the whole Balkans that became inhabited by the Pelasgians, the forefathers of the Albanians. Then, yes, Alexander the Great was Albanian."[100] In addition to claiming this heritage, there were also assertions of territorial legitimacy, with proclamations that "half of the Albanian territories contain Macedonia together with the vilayet of Thessaloniki."[101]

The construction of national and ethnic identities, along with their meta-narratives that aim to establish political legitimacy by claiming an

---

[99] See about Kalendari Kombiar: AQSH, GF 9, FO 96, Koleksioni i Shoqërive Shqiptare në Bullgari, No. AP. 27. Dosje, 504 (1899–1904); Kalendari Kombiar, No. 2, Sofje, 1898, p. 66; in original: *"shqipetarët kanë ndritur në kohet t' Aleksandit te Madh kane mundure te tëre boten e që dihesa here: ne kohet te Iliros u dane dermen Romanevet, deme pastaj Filipi, Perseja, Genço ja kane Ieftuare trimerist kunder ushterisë, qe dergonte Roma; pom' i madhinjeri qe ka nxjere Shqiperia është Skenderbegu. Qe Ieftoj me trimërite çudiçme kondra Tyrqvet. Po keto punerat t embeda, qe kanë bere Shqipetaret janë si vetem, de skaneduruare. Ne e dençiner te mentcim, njeris'munttedote se ka kombmë te Zguare se Shqipetaret Ali Pashe Tepelena mundi kaqe vjet Porten (Babialine) vetem me fjalë."*

[100] Kalendari Kombiar, Sofje, 1900, p. 15; in original: *"323 Para Kristit vdiq Aleksandr' i madh, mbret' i Maqedonise, n' ato kohe ni jo vetem Maqedonia po e tere Sinisi e Badhkaneve tis mbuluare nga Pellazgete, nipet e te cilet jemi ne Sqipetarete, pra de Aleksandr' i madh is Shqipetar."*

[101] Ibid., p. 17; in original: *"Bullgaret kerkojne otonomine e Maqedonise. Fjala Maqedoni mer de Yskyb, Dibre, Korçe etj., dmth. gjysmen e Shqiperise; pra komitete bulgare kerkojne qe Maqeuouia dmth. gjysma e Shqiperise e tere vilajet i Selanikut te behete gjysme me vethe, de kestu qe dite te baskohet elehtazime Bulgarine. Ahere Shqiperija do te mbetete qe pip i nguste si breze vgiti – ane detit."*

exclusive and continuous past, can be influenced by promotion. This promotion of national meta-narrative can come in various forms, including newspapers, textbooks, and national literature that shape political ideologies. In Albania, the Illyrian past was merged with the ancient history of Macedonia to create a narrative where Albanians were portrayed as the descendants of the Macedonians who lived under Philip II, Alexander the Great, and the Romans. This narrative was used to legitimise political objectives, such as the creation of a greater Albania based on its "ancient borders" and the claim of being the "oldest people of Europe." One of the special promoters of this national narrative was the uncle of Mithat, brother of Sami Frashëri, named Naim.[102] With this purpose, Naim Frashëri wrote text books for Albanian schools and about the history of Albania and Skenderbeg. His writings were very important in the Albanian national movement that aimed to "educate" the local population regarding the consciousness and awareness of Albanianism. Furthermore, his writings were influential in the wider Albanian national movement and played a significant role in the development of a shared Albanian national consciousness. In addition to Naim, there were other influential figures who promoted Albanian identity and culture. One such individual was Faik Bey Konica (1875–1942).[103] He was one of the leading Albanian intellectuals during the early 20th century and was one of the first Albanians who promoted Albanian independence from the Ottoman Empire. Visar Dodani described him as "the first Muslim Albanian who became brave enough to say: 'Muslim brothers, leave the Turks! We are Albanians and not Turks, while the Sultan is a deceiver."[104] Konica, openly supported the idea of independent Albania and he published a periodical *Albania* in Brussel. In one of its issues, he emphasises that "our motherland needs us in order to continue our progress

---

[102] Naim Frashëri wrote also textbooks as *"Histori e Pergjithshme per Mesonjetoret e Para"* (In English: General History for the First Schools) published in 1886 and used until 1914, *"Mesimet"* (Lessons); *"Shqipëria"* (Albania); *"Istoria e Skenderbegut"* (History of Skenderbeg); *"Istori e Shqipërisë"* (History of Albania).

[103] AQSH, GF 6, Fondet personale, FO 13, No. AP 1, Dosje 1: *" 'Vajtim përmbi robëri të shqiptarëve' vjershë e Faik Konicës."*

[104] Visar Dodani, *Memoriet e mija* (Constanza: Albania, 1930); quote in original: *"i pari musulmane që kuxoj të bërtase: vellezër musulmane, hiqni dore nga turku! Ne jemi shqipetare musulmane, nuk jemi turq. Sulltani është kursar."*

down the civilisational path." [105] Konica believed that being part of civilisation was important for Albania's progress and independence. He stresses the importance of opening schools in Albanian to give children education in their mother tongue, as he fears that "outsiders could come and teach them another language, leading to the loss of their homeland." He argues that all "civilised nations have learnt their own language" and "worked towards a holy mission," implying that the Albanian people must do the same "to preserve their culture and identity."[106] In his *Memoirs* from 1899, Konica observed that where there is a school, it becomes "a nucleus for propaganda," and people naturally start collaborating to distribute publications. He gave the example of Korça, where *Albania* newspapers were read in cafes, which became possible only after the establishment of Albanian schools, despite attempts by the Turkish government "to prevent the spread of Albanian language and literature."[107] It can be inferred that Faik Konica believed that the promotion of education and literature in Albanian was crucial for the advancement and prosperity of the Albanian people. He saw this as a civilisational mission that would help the Albanians distance themselves from the perceived barbarity of the East. Similar ideas were presented by Giuseppe Schiro, who was an Italian subject born in Sicily. In his book, "*Gli Albanesi e la Questione Balkanica*," written in 1904, he supported the idea of Italian involvement in Albania. For him, there should not be any Albanian–Ottoman "cooperation to safeguard Albanian interests as for him it was counterproductive to achieving Albanian independence."[108] Contrary to him, Girolamo de Rada – a prominent Albanian from Calabria –was opposed to the (idea of) Italian involvement in Albania. He was a supporter of Albanian nationalism, and simultaneously a defender of federal and

---

[105] Albania, Brussel, 25. April, 1897, p. 18; in original: *"memedheu ka nevoj te madhe prej nesh (...) te vazhojme perparime ttona ne kete kaqe te bukur rruge qyteterie."*
[106] Ibid., p. 19; in original: *"shqiperia do drite; te hapim shkolha shqipne per tere Shqiperine, qe veghelia te mesojne ne ghuhet e tyre; te mospresim tevijne te huaj te te na mesojne dhelperit' e tyre per dem, e per humbjen e memedhut tone. Keshtu kane bere dhe bejne ghithe kombet e qyteteruara. Është detyre e ghithë Shqipëtareve të perpiqen per këtë te shenteruare pune."*
[107] AQSH, GF 6, Fondet personale, FO 13, No. AP 1, Dosje 1: *"'Vajtim përmbi robëri të shqiptarëve' vjershë e Faik Konicës."*
[108] Gueseppe Schiro, *Gli Albanesi e la Questione Balkanica* (Napoli: A spese dell'editore Ferd. Bideri, 1904).

multicultural Italy and Ottoman Empire.[109] His popularity has been fostered through various adaptations of Italian federalism and ideas of Carlo Cattaneo that Italy should rather preserve its multicultural society. However, after the Italian unification in 1861, he became disappointed in the Italian statist threat to Italo–Albanian cultural and religious specificities. He concluded that the Italian nation–state has not been friendly to Albanians.[110] Therefore, he advocated for Albanian autonomy inside the Ottoman Empire by strengthening of this brotherhood, according to the English–Scottish or Austro–Hungarian examples. According to him, "it [could not] be denied that tearing Albania from Turkey would open a wound (*non puo negarsi che, per la Turchia tutta, lo sbranamento dell'Albania fu una ferita*)." In this regard, the Albanians in the Ottoman Empire "want[ed] peace in Europe and Albania, entailing that Albanians should not abandon their position under the Sultan's rule (*noi volevamo, e il dicemmo, per la pace d'Europa e il bene della Skjiperia, che questa non ci staccasso dal Sultano.*)."[111] This comes as no surprise, since Girolamo de Rada generally relied heavily on the Italo–Albanian experience in post–Risorgimento years, disappointed in the nation–state project. Perhaps this experience influenced him to support the autonomous status of Albania inside the Ottoman Empire, but not its independence.[112] In this regard, one can conclude that the Albanian national movement was not unified, but rather a product of discussions, negotiations, and disputes. Often, Albanian intellectuals cooperated with Ottoman authorities, while

---

[109] Artan Puto and Maurizio Isabella, "From Southern Italy to Istanbul: Trajectories of Albanian Nationalism in the Writings of Girolamo de Rada and Shemseddin Sami Frashëri ca. 1848–1903," in *Mediterranean Diasporas: Politics and Ideas in the Long 19th Century* eds. Maurizio Isabella and Konstantina Zanou (London: Bloomsbury Academic, 2015), pp. 176–178.

[110] Ibid.

[111] Newspaper: Fiamuri Arberit/La Bandiera dell'Albania, No. 2, Corigliano Calabro, 30. September, 1883, pp. 1–2.

[112] Fiamuri Arberit/La Bandiera dell'Albania, No. 6, Corigliano Calabro, 30. March, 1884, p. 4; See in original:
"O Sultano, non dare il tuo assenso
Ti serberemo noi stessi la Skjiperia
Noi non andremo col Montenero,
Ne con Serbo, necon Austria,
Non con Turco, non con la Grecia,
Vogliamo di noi stessi l'autonomia."

at other times they challenged and resisted the central policy. This indicates that national movements did not arise in isolation, but were influenced by transnational and transregional factors that varied according to the situation and context. Thus, it is crucial to understand the decision-making processes of mobile intellectuals by placing events in their historical context. The stakeholders involved were not limited to the Ottomans and Albanians, but also included Bulgaria, Greece, and Serbia, who vied for the loyalty of the majority Christian Orthodox population in the struggle for Macedonia.

3.3. Balkan State Competitions and Agents of Nationalism and Imperialism

In contrast to the Ottoman and Albanian discussions in the three vilayets, who were focused mostly on majority Muslim population in these regions, the conflict among the Orthodox Christian population initially began through educational and religious issues. This discussion among the Orthodox Christian population in the Ottoman Empire began between supporters of the Ecumenical Patriarchate of Constantinople – who were Greek–speaking (and also Slavic–speaking or bilingual) communities that identified themselves as Greek; and supporters of the Bulgarian Exarchate, who promoted a Bulgarian national consciousness. This competition was soon joined by Serbia in the 1870s, where some members of the Serbian intellectuals declared that the Serb language and culture extended much further into the south (Macedonia) and that Serbia should formulate its own policy.[113] These claims over Macedonia also triggered Serbia to join the competition. The break of relations among the different parts of the former Balkan Alliance (established in 1867, as showed in the previous chapter) in the 1870s, just intensified their competition towards Macedonia during the Age of Empire. The policy of liberation from the "big Asiatic Mongol" and inclusion of the idea of Macedonia in one common Balkan or South–Slavic state was changed by the rivalry of the "civilisational agents of Europe" and fights of the "Orthodox brothers." Their imitation of the Great Powers, acceptance of "colonisation of the mind" and implementation of "surrogate hegemony" towards the Ottoman Empire

---

[113] Miloš Milojević, *Odlomci istorije Srba i srpskih – jugoslavenskih – zemalja u Turskoj i Austriji* (Beograd: 1872).

produced the "Macedonian Question(s)" as a part of the wider "Eastern Question." This period of the "Age of Empire," the American historian of modern Europe, Holly Case, also named "the age of questions."[114] Indeed, the Age of Empire was simultaneously the age of questions. It seems that between the Congress of Berlin (1878) and the Balkan Wars (1912–13), the Balkan states were involved in "solving" these questions titled "Macedonian". Thus, they developed colonial policies and imperialist projects, like their "European tutors." While the Great Powers competed over Africa, Asia, or parts of South America, the Balkan states clashed around competing nationalist policies, each of which imagined Macedonia as an integral part of its future "greater state" and "nation." In this regard, in the 1870s, the Macedonian Question(s) became a central issue in Balkan politics. In mapping this region as part of their greater nation–state(s), its intellectuals used education and gangs as tools in order to influence the local population on the ground. Between the state and locals there were intermediating political actors who have been defined by Charles Tilly as "political entrepreneurs" and "specialists in violence."[115] According to him, the political entrepreneurs were in fact connectors and organisers of collective violence whose specialty consisted of organising, linking, or dividing a distinct group or networks, or they helped to integrate locals or groups into larger nationalist coalitions.[116] They were often mediators between the state (regional level) and rural population (local level) in a trans–regional context. Such examples include members of intellectuals, priests, teachers, or other promoters of education who were employed at the village schools across Ottoman Macedonia. Their "mission" was to install "national pride" in the hearts of pupils and to campaign for the locals to join the political committees or the nation–states they served. In the following sub–chapters I will show the role of the mobile intellectuals and intellectuals, the priests and teachers respectively as "political

---

[114] Holly Case, *The Age of Questions: Or, A First Attempt at an Aggregate History of the Eastern, Social, Woman, American, Jewish, Polish, Bullion, Tuberculosis, and Many Other Questions over the Nineteenth Century, and Beyond* (Princeton, NJ: Princeton University Press, 2018).

[115] Charles Tilly, *The Politics of Collective Violence* (Cambridge: Cambridge University Press, 2003), p. 40.

[116] Ibid.

entrepreneurs" in influencing the local population for their political and nationalist interests.

3.3.1. Greek Creation of National Space and *Megali Idea*

In the Greek case, its intellectuals tried to construct a myth of their ancient Hellen descent, even among the Orthodox Slavic speakers in the Macedonian villages. The idea of "Ancient Macedonian nationhood" was also included in the national mythology of the Greek education platform and its school system.[117] In particular, it was developed as a reaction to the Bulgarian Exarchists who insisted on usage of the Bulgarian language and education. These rivalries between the Greek and Bulgarian intellectuals and priests, which sometimes were members of the same community or served the same church, initially took the form of educational and ecclesiastical competition. As a result, it furnished the conflicting Greek–and Bulgarian–oriented parties, also known as the Patriarchists and the Exarchists, with a clearly defined cause to shape the local population according to the state interests. One of the tools was undoubtedly education, which enabled the spread of nationalism as "imagined community" and sense of belonging to common space as "imagined geography."

If we take into consideration Miroslav Hroch's chronological stages of nation building processes of small nations developed through three phases like "scholarly inquiry," "patriotic agitation," and "mass movement,"[118] then one might conclude that this process fits in the Macedonian case. According to Julian Brooks, "intellectuals were the ones doing the 'scholarly inquiry,' often as students in neighbouring 'free' countries or in Western Europe or Russia. Upon their return, they embarked as teachers on programs of 'patriotic agitation' through the forum of community

---

[117] Anastas Vangeli, "Nation–building ancient Macedonian style: the Origins and the Effects of the so–called Antiquization in Macedonia," *Nationalities Papers* 39/1 (2001): 22.

[118] See: Hroch, "From National Movement."; Mark Mazower, *Kratka povijest Balkana* (Zagreb: Srednja Europa, 2007).

schools."[119] The millet system of the Ottoman Empire[120] enabled intellectuals and teachers to develop their "patriotic agitation" and to bring the local population into a "mass movement." In other words, the nationalist teachers or political entrepreneurs could now pursue their imaginations and were willing to 'enlighten' the locals. In general, during the 1880s, despite the Bulgarian advance in Macedonia, the Greek state was opposing military action until the mid–1890s. Instead, Greek intellectuals decided to strengthen the Greek educational institutions and the Patriarchist churches in Macedonia, and in this way to influence the consciousness of the locals.[121] Education was an instrument to raise in these communities a national consciousness in the form of bounded "imagined community." According to these intellectuals, "Macedonia was part of Hellenic civilisation, the birthplace of Alexander the Great, and for centuries an integral part of the Byzantine Empire."[122] In fact, the Greek nationalists imagined Macedonia as an integral part of "Greater Greece", based on the *Megali Idea*. In this respect, the Greek government provided several books espousing the glory of Ancient Macedonia and Alexander the Great, such as *The Prophecies of Alexander.*[123]

The distribution of such books was often provided by the assistance of the political entrepreneurs who worked in manifold schools in Ottoman Macedonia. According to Greek statistics, "between 1878 and 1885 the number of Greek schools in Macedonia increased by 7 percent and from 1878 to 1905 by 81 percent."[124] Only after the establishment of the Internal Macedonian (Adrianople) Revolutionary Organisation (IMARO), did the Greek nationalists respond by military action, that is, by establishing the secret Greek nationalistic organisation *Ethniki Etaireia* in 1894. It was founded by a number of nationalist officers who advocated for the

---

[119] Julian Brooks, "Education Race for Macedonia, 1878–1903," *The Journal of Modern Hellenism* 31 (2015): 24–25.

[120] Millet system enabled actually to nations and religious communities to established the schools in their languages. See: Karen Barkey and George Gavrils, "The Ottoman Millet System: Non–Territorial Autonomy and its Contemporary Legacy," *Ethnopolitics* 15/1 (2015): 24–42. and Aylin Koçunyan, "The Millet System and the Challenge of Other Confessional Models, 1856–1865," *Ab Imperio* 1 (2017): 59–85.

[121] Gounaris, *Steam over Macedonia*, p. 8.

[122] Ibid. p. 36.

[123] Karakasidou, *Fields of Whet*, p. 96.

[124] Gounaris, *Steam over Macedonia*, p. 285.

realisation of the *Megali idea*. As in the case of the Bulgarian and IMARO bands, a large number of Greek bandsmen were refugees from the three vilayets. However, one should not think that these Greek parties (*Ethniki Etaireia*, the Greek government, and Patriarchate) had a uniformed national programme. On the ground, these institutions, based in Ottoman territories (in Istanbul or Macedonia), often rivalled those based in Athens. According to historian Evangelos Kofos, Greek government consuls and the Patriarchate's bishops were "more frequently than not, at loggerheads." [125] On 14 April 1898, the newspaper *The Times* also reported:

> "They [the Bulgarians] enjoy the advantage of simple organisation, for the Exarchate alone directs the propaganda, while in the case of their rivals' disputes between the Consulates and the spiritual authorities over the application of funds often exercise a paralyzing effect. The Greeks in general have committed the error of assuming a combative and repressive attitude towards the other nationalities instead of devoting all their attention to the organisation and the development of their own movement."[126]

As in the Albanian case, highlighted above, the Greek case in Ottoman Macedonia was also multi–layered, contested, and often leading to clashing of rivalries inside the same communities. Competition between rising nationalisms, but also within nationalist movements was often shaped according to the current needs and interests of various members of the organisations and institutions. Thus, the controversies between the ecclesiastical and educational parts, also between the state and brigandage, often resulted in clashes and support of various interests.

---

[125] Evangelos Kofos, "Dilemmas and Orientations of Greek Policy in Macedonia: 1878–1886," in *Macedonia Past and Present,* ed. Evangelos Kofos (Thessaloniki: Institute for Balkan Studies, 1992), p. 143.

[126] Brooks, *Managing Macedonia*, p. 38; See in: "The Situation in Macedonia," *The Times*, 14. April, 1898; James Walter Frusetta, "Bulgaria's Bulgaria's Macedonia: Nation–Building and State–Building, Centralization and Autonomy in Pirin Macedonia, 1903–1952" (PhD diss., University of Maryland, 2006).

3.3.2. The Bulgarian National Revival and the Macedonian Questions

The beginning of the Bulgarian national revival is considered to be marked by the work of Saint Paisius of Hilendar, who opposed Greek domination into Bulgarian cultural life and religious practices, in his well–known work *"Slavic–Bulgarian History"* (*Istoria Slavyanobŭlgarskaya*), which appeared in 1762. This is considered as the first work of Bulgarian historiography, where Paisius focused on Bulgarian medieval past with an aim of reviving the spirit of the Bulgarian community. Based on this book, which gave importance to education in Bulgarian, many Bulgarian intellectuals started publishing textbooks in Bulgarian.[127] These books were often based on Bulgarian songs, mostly the epic poems of mediaeval Bulgarian empires. The collecting was assessed by intellectuals such as Kuzman Shapkarev, Lyuben Karavelov, Ivan Bogorov, Rayko Zhinzifov (considered also as Macedonian writers in North Macedonian historiography), Nesho Bonchev and others. Additionally, these works were also supported by priests who established a Bulgarian Exarchate in 1870 and reinforced the "invented tradition" based on the Bulgarian mediaeval empires.[128] The Exarchate, in other words, is considered a direct product of the culmination of the Bulgarian nation building process on the memory of mediaeval Tsardom.[129] The struggle for an independent church proved vital for the formation of a new "imagined community" that was to establish a new Bulgarian Tsardom.[130] The centre of the Exarchate was in Istanbul, and the Bulgarian intellectuals were also active in the Ottoman

---

[127] Leo Wiener, "America's share in the regeneration of Bulgaria (1840–1859)," *Modern Language Notes* 13/2 (1898): 33.

[128] The Bulgarian Exarchate was set up by the Sultan's order, and the first Bulgarian Exarch, Antim I, became the natural leader of the emerging nation. The imperial *ferman* issued on March 12, 1870, recognised the establishment of a semi–autonomous Bulgarian Church in Constantinople, with an Exarch who ranked between Archbishop and Patriarch. This recognition came after a long struggle that started in the late 18th century, led by influential Bulgarian lay members in Istanbul and clergy who were unhappy with what they saw as a Greek bias and dominance in the church hierarchy.

[129] Yosmaoğlu, *Blood Ties*, p. 55; Stefan Rohdewald points out that this was not only the case with Bulgaria, but also with other nations in the region. See: Rohdewald. *Götter der Nationen*, p. 20. See the quote: *"Die überregionalen Heiligenkulte der Südslaven des Mittelalters und der frühen Neuzeit waren oft nicht auf ein Volksgruppe ode rein Staatswesen begrenzt."*

[130] Boyko Penchev, "Tsarigrad/Istanbul and the Spatial Construction of Bulgarian National Identity in the Nineteenth Century," *Nexus* (2002 – 2003): 1.

imperial capital, rather than areas with large Bulgarian–speaking populations in the Balkans. Just as Istanbul was a hub for Albanian intellectuals, it also served as a focal point for Bulgarian scholars who advocated for ecclesiastic independence and worked towards advancing Bulgarian scholarly research and patriotic activism. While in Istanbul, these Bulgarian intellectuals developed a national program based on the medieval concept of Bulgarians, with influential figures such as Ivan Bogorov and Petko Slaveikov. At that time, Bogorov published newspaper *Tsarigradski Vestnik* (1860) in Istanbul and highlighted the work of brothers Miladinov, who collected Bulgarian folk songs in Ottoman Macedonia. Slaveikov, on the other hand, published newspapers like *Gayda* (1863–1867)[131] and *Makedonia* (1866-1872) to promote a sense of national consciousness among Bulgarians, linking it to the continuity of Samuil's empire. Although it was one of the centres of the Bulgarian national movement, Istanbul was often represented in a negative way.

In the book "*Pisma na edno desetgodishno dete, koeto sega pruv put e doshlo v Tsarigrad*,"[132] written by Peter Slaveikov in 1864, Istanbul was depicted as the centre of the Bulgarian–Greek dispute.[133] Furthermore, Slaveikov took part in the struggle for an autonomous Bulgarian church and later became a teacher in the newly established Bulgarian Exarchate. He was also the first author who coined the term "Macedonian Question" (*Makedonskiat vŭpros*) in an article written in the newspaper *Makedonia*. He published this article on 18 January 1871 defining the irredentist policy:

> "The whole humanity moves toward the self–rule, and not toward the oppression, but the point is that the self–rule will be achieved only through union in one body. Today all nations recognise this need and are in a hurry to achieve it; are we going to be the only ones to go in the opposite

---

[131] The first published poem by Bulgarian poet and national revolutionary Hristo Botev "*Majtze si*" (To My Mother) was printed in the *Gayda* newspaper, where he emphasised a strong desire for the imagined motherland.

[132] Ibid., pp. 2–3. Translation: "Letters of a Ten–Year–Old Boy, Who Travels to Tsarigrad for the First Time."

[133] Ibid. Translation: "The story is about a young boy asking his father if there were any Bulgarians who owned houses in Istanbul/Tsarigrad. The answer is "Yes!" Then, "But where are their wives?," insists the boy. The father answers with the words: "Most of them are married to Greek women, that's why no Bulgarian women can be seen there."

direction? Others unify, although they have been separated for ages, like Pruss and Bavarians, Piemontians and Napolitanians, and we want to separate now, to separate although we are from uniform element and we have been united until now. Isn't that wise and commendable?"[134]

Drawing inspiration from the prevailing European ideas of the time, he envisioned an independent Bulgarian state that encompassed Macedonia. To him, Macedonia was the heart of the medieval Bulgarian empire in Ohrid, a constructed tradition that could serve the present-day of imagined community. According to his views, the region of Macedonia has undergone significant population changes over time, with new settlers mingling with the local population. Eventually, the Bulgarians emerged as the dominant power in the region, establishing a "kingdom in Ohrid, which is considered the birthplace of many fervent Macedonians." Having lived in the area for a considerable amount of time, "the Bulgarians assimilated the entire population into their own." He questioned whether it is possible to determine the ethnic origins of the Macedonian people, asking "who can say for sure whether they are of Bulgarian descent or the descendants of the ancient Macedonians?" He believed that it is impossible to answer this question without "becoming funny and shallow."[135] Therefore, Slaveikov was not only criticising Ottoman policies towards Bulgarians but also the Greek and Serbian policies that disputed Bulgarian nationhood and Macedonian heritage, making it difficult for the formulation of a Bulgarian nationalist program.[136] In this regard, he wrote the article *"Dvete kasti i vlasti,"*[137] published in the *Makedonia* newspaper,[138] which led to his arrest by the Ottoman authorities due to his relations with the Bulgarian Revolutionary Central Committee (*Bŭlgarski revolutsionen tsentralen komitet*) in Bucharest. He often had assistance from another prominent figure, Kuzman A. Shapkarev (1834–1909) who was born in Ohrid in

---

[134] Peter Slaveikov, *Makedonskiat vŭpros*, Makedonia, Istanbul, 18. January, 1871.

[135] Ibid.

[136] Ibid.

[137] The newspaper was banned because of the *"Dvete kasti i vlasti"* text published on 25. July 1872, No. 18, p. 1.

[138] In the 1860s was promoted pan–Slavic ideas. See the following articles in Makedonia newspaper: 'Bŭlgari i Srbi' from 13. April 1968; 'Juzhnit Slavjani, Panslavizm i Rusizmit' from 22. June 1868.

Ottoman Macedonia and was a folklorist, ethnographer, author of textbooks and ethnographic studies, and a significant "regenerator" of the Bulgarian (or Macedonian) "invented tradition" based on mediaeval Bulgarian empires. In the Macedonian historiography, he is quite properly hailed among the greatest and most diligent collectors of Macedonian folk art based on mediaeval stories. However, he wrote the following textbooks that consisted 'Bulgarian' prefixes such as: *A Bulgarian Primer* (1866), *A Big Bulgarian Reader* (1868), *Mother Tongue* (1874), *Short Book of Religion* (1868), *Short Land Description* in other words *Geography* (1868), all published in Istanbul.[139] He once emphasised also that his books were written "comprehensibly for the Bulgarian Macedonians (*po–vrazumitelno makedonskit Bŭlgarin*)."[140] In this respect, he insisted in using the term Bulgar next to Macedonian. According to him, the ancient ethnonym "Macedonians was imposed on the local Slavs and began to replace the traditional one Bulgarians."[141] In a letter addressed to Marin Drinov in 1888, Kuzman Shapkarev questions the name "Macedonians" that was imposed on them by "outsiders only a decade or two ago," not by their own intellectuals. He finds it strange that people in Macedonia are "unaware of this ancient name," which has been reintroduced with both "a cunning and stupid agenda." Instead, they know for themselves only the older word "*Bugari.*"[142] Shapkarev, along with Peter Slaveikov, was a member of the Bulgarian Revolutionary Central Committee (BRCC), which was founded in 1869 among Bulgarian patriots living in Romania. While Shapkarev and Slaveikov were based in Istanbul, other members such as Vasil Levski, Lyuben Karavelov, Georgi Rakovski, Subi S. Popovich, and Hristo Botev were based in Bucharest. The decisive

---

[139] Desislava Lilova, "Barbarians, Civilized People and Bulgarians: Definition of Identity in Textbooks and the Press (1830–1878)," in *We the People: Politics of National Peculiarity in Southeastern Europe* ed. Diana Mishkova (Budapest/New York: Central European University Press, 2009), pp. 179–206; Kuzman Shapkarev was a contributor of many Bulgarian newspapers and magazines such as Tsarigradski vestnik, Gayda, Makedonia, Pravo, Savetnik, Bŭlgarska pchela and others. The son of Kuzman Shapkarev – Kliment Shapkarev was one of the leaders of IMRO.
[140] Kuzman Shapkarev, *Bŭlgarska Chitanka* (Istanbul: 1868); Tasos Kastopoulos, "'Land to the Tiller: On the Neglected Agrarian Component of the Macedonian Revolutionary Movement, 1893–1912," *Turkish Historical Review* 7/ 2 (2016): 134–166.
[141] Ibid.
[142] Makedonski pregled, IX, 2, 1934, p. 55.

influence for the establishment of the Committee was exerted by the *Svoboda* newspaper, which Lyuben Karavelov began to publish in Bucharest between 1869 and 1873. He was elected as chairman of the BRCC in the spring of 1870. Karavelov also prepared the first programme of the organisation, which imagined the liberation of Bulgaria based on French revolution ideals and democratic principles circulated around the European intellectuals at that time. In parallel to it, an important role also played the Internal Revolutionary Organisation (*Vtreshna revolutsionna organizatsia*) or IRO, which was a Bulgarian revolutionary organisation founded by the Bulgarian revolutionary Vasil Levski around 1870s. This association is an example of networks of revolutionary committees that was built up in the town of Lovech. Its founding aimed at shifting Bulgarian revolutionary activities from Romania to what were considered 'Bulgarian lands.' [143] The successful creation of an "imagined community" through institutions, organisations, and education that relied on an "imagined geography" necessitated "patriotic agitation" to motivate a mass movement. The church and BRCC members, serving as political entrepreneurs, played a pivotal role in propelling the Bulgarian mass movement of medieval revival forward.

Next to *Svoboda*, patriots like Karavelov and Botev started to publish a second newspaper in 1873, *Nezavisimost* (Independence), where they were influenced by Orientalist discourses circulating around Europe at the time. In this newspaper they stated that the "Turks [were] incapable of any development" and that there was "great Asiatic opulence."[144] The reason for their backwardness was the "Turkish religion, which [was] against any development and this kind of religion [had] deep roots among the Turkish population."[145] In this respect, Karavelov and Botev wanted to represent

---

[143] In 1871, Levski drafted a document known as the Charter, which reflected his political beliefs. His goal was to achieve Bulgaria's freedom from Ottoman rule by means of a nationwide uprising. Furthermore, the Charter called for the establishment of a democratic republic that would offer all of its citizens – regardless of their ethnicity or religion – the same rights and privileges.

[144] Nezavisimost, No. 24, Bukurest, 3. Mart, 1873, p. 185; In original quote: *"turskoto tupoumie i turskata nesposobnost za razvitie i za napredok (...) mnogochislenite aziatski roskoshi/mnogobroyna aziatska raskosh."*

[145] Nezavisimost, No. 25, Bukurest, 9 .Mart, 1873, p. 193; In original: *"turskata religia e protivna na siki edin napredok, a taya religia e pusnala dulbok korin mezhdu turskoto naselenie."*

Bulgaria as part of the broader European civilisation against the "barbaric Turks." One of the tools used for this purpose were definitely newspapers and books, and education and schools, as has been seen in the Greek and Albanian cases. Accordingly, the core of the education and preserver of Bulgarian national consciousness was in the notion that "Bulgariana had independence of their church since 10th century (*bŭlgarite si imale cherkovna nezavisimost oshe v X. vek*)."[146] They also clearly emphasised that this church was always "present in Thrace and Macedonia as well (*namirat v Trakia i Makedonia*)."[147] In this sense, Lyuben Karavelov wrote an article on the national and church struggle of the Bulgarian people against the Phanariots and certain Serb patriots who in the 1870s started propaganda against their Bulgarian "brothers." Karavelov wrote:

> "The justified unrest and the severe persecution and hatred against the Greek clergy which arose in the Danubian parts of Bulgaria some years ago, are also being repeated in the Western Bulgarian areas, which are called Macedonia, in accordance with the wish of the Greek learned men. Numerous facts show that the struggle in these parts is crueller, and more energetic, and more fierce. Naturally fierce oppression and violent tempests call for fierce and violent resistance. And, in point of fact, we know of no other Bulgarian or other Eastern Orthodox land that has suffered as much from the blessed Phanariots and the Hellenistic Klephti (propagandists) as Western Bulgaria."[148]

Karavelov here breaks out directly with "Hellenistic" policy in Macedonia and accusing the "Greeks" for violence. Along with the "Greeks," he accused several "Serbs" for "Serbian propaganda." Interestingly, in this attempt, he does not accuse the Serbian state, but rather Miloš Milivojević, as a Serbian nationalist. In this regard, the societies from Istanbul *Bratstvo* (Brotherhood) and *Makedonskata Drouzhina* (The Macedonian Company) [149] published an open letter in the newspaper *Pravo*

---

[146] Nezavisimost, No. 26, Bukurest, 16. Mart, 1873, p. 205.
[147] Ibid., p. 207.
[148] Nezavisimost, No. 19, Bukurest, 23. Februar, 1874.
[149] Both are Bulgarian societies in Constantinople.

(Justice/Law) addressed to Mr. Marinović,[150] regarding Miloš Milivojević that he founded Serbian societies with the purpose of "spreading Serbianism" not only "in Macedonia and Thrace" but also "along the shores of the Mediterranean in Spain and Africa."[151] Hristo Botev also wrote an article against Milojević's article "Bulgarian Espionage and Inquisition."[152] Botev, in comparison to Karavelov, accused the Serbian

---

[150] Jovan Marinović (1821–1893) was a prominent Serbian politician and diplomat, known for his efforts to introduce enlightened reforms into the Serbian political system. Marinović worked closely with the influential Minister Ilija Garašanin and quickly rose through the ranks, eventually becoming the leader of the Serbian Conservatives and later the Prime Minister of the Principality of Serbia. Educated in Paris, Marinović was a cultured gentleman who believed that European culture and reforms could enlighten the Serbian peasant society. From 1861 to 1867, Marinović served as the first aide to Prime Minister Ilija Garašanin and Prince Mihailo Obrenović, during their ambitious policy of forming a wider Balkan alliance and encouraging a general Christian uprising against the Ottomans. Marinović became the Prime Minister on November 3, 1873, under a Liberal–Conservative coalition and held the additional position of Foreign Minister from November 3, 1873, to December 7, 1874.

[151] Nezavisimost, No. 21, Bukurest, 9. Mart, 1874; Hristo Botev also respondend to Milojević: "You adduce facts with which you accuse the Bulgarians and their Exarchate of using espionage and inquisition to Bulgarise the poor, unfortunate Serbians in Turkey, and you say we do not answer your facts but swear instead. Well, how are we to answer facts which you yourselves base on the philological madness of Miloš Milojević, i.e. that Serbians have lived in the Balkan Peninsula since time immemorial, that only a handful of 200,000 Bulgarian–Tartars came here and, in a short time, Bulgarised all these Serbians? How are we to answer these facts when their philological madness is clad in political tendencies, i.e. when you and your government are striving to ensure that there will really be only 200,000 Bulgarians, or, to use your words, Tartars, while the rest are Serbianised, i.e. Slavicised?" See: Hristo Botev, *Sŭchinenia, Avtentichno izdanie* (Sofia, 1960), pp. 219–222.

[152] Istok, Beograd, 20. Jun, 1875. Botev also directed some pointed inquiries towards Serbian nationalists, asking whether there was a group of so–called patriots in Belgrade, headed by Miloš Milojević, that sent money, books, and teachers to "purely Bulgarian villages and towns in Macedonia" and some parts of northwestern Bulgaria. Botev further questioned the motives behind these actions, asking whether the goal was to enlighten their Bulgarian brothers or to promote proselytism. Botev also suggested that the society was established by the Tempter and morally and materially supported by the Serbian government. He asked whether the society's purpose was to demonstrate that only Serbians lived on the Balkan Peninsula. Botev challenged the Serbian nationalists to answer these crucial questions, promising to provide evidence in the next edition of the Bulgarian newspaper 'Zname' to support their criticisms of "Serbia, Russia, and everything that the people themselves desire." Botev argued that the people no longer listened to those who cheated them in the past. See: Hristo Botev, *Sŭchinenia, Avtentichno izdanie*. These ideas were supported as well by important personalities of Bulgarain

state policy for attempting "to deceive us [Bulgarians] with the good intentions of 'the South–Slavonic Piedmont.'" According to Botev, this South–Slavonic (Slavic) Piedmont, which is Serbia, considered "the Bulgarian people as Tartars, who, in order to be liberated from the Turks, should first be Serbianised."[153] Here one can also trace the "nesting Orientalism" of the Balkan states, where Serbian intellectuals considered that the "Bulgarians," together with the "Turks," were part of the Orient. Thus, in Botev's view, the Serbian state tried to "civilise Bulgarians" through "Serbisation." However, not all Bulgarian intellectuals shared Botev's views. During the April Uprisings of 1876,[154]some advocated for cooperation with the "south-Slav brothers," including Serbians. As such, Bulgarian intellectuals engaged in discussions and debates about their ideas, contested decisions, strategies, and policies. While Botev was against Serbian policy, there were other Bulgarians who supported the Serbian government and its aid in their attempts to resist Ottoman rule. Along these lines, the events that took place during April were reported on in a newspaper titled *Bulgarian voice* (*Bŭlgarski Glas*) (1876–77), published in Bolgrad in Romania. In its first issue from 17 April 1876, it is stated that the aim of Bulgarians should be "the liberated state that can help us to express our free aspirations towards the political life of our brothers/brethren on this side of the Danube."[155] This was a brotherhood advocated for a unity of all Slavs, which would overlook the Macedonian issue. Their plan was to achieve this by providing support to Bosniaks, Herzegovians, Serbs, and Montenegrins in order to "overthrow the

---

National Revival (*Bŭlgarsko natsionalno vazrazhdane*) in Macedonia were Nako Stanishev and Ilyo Markov. See also: Hacısalihoğlu, *Die Jungtürken und die Mazedonische Frage*, pp. 89–94.

[153] Ibid.

[154] During the Batak massacre in 1876, the Ottoman irreGülar troops or bashibazouk mainly Pomaks (Slavic Muslims), were sent to Bulgarian Christian villages. The massacres, or known also as the "Bulgarian horrors," named by William Gladstone in a pamphlet. Gladstone also gave voice to what would remain the liberal European public opinion of Ottoman Turks, who were, in his memorable words, "upon the whole, from the black day when they first entered Europe, the one anti–human specimen of humanity." Yosmaoğlu, *Blood Ties*, p. 22; See about the April Uprising: Adanır, *Die makedonische Frage*, p. 78.

[155] Bŭlgarski Glas, No. 1, Bolgrad, 17. April, 1876, p. 1; in original: *"svobodna drzhava da mozhem svobodno da iskazvame nasheto narodno stremlenie kam politicheskiat zhivot za nashite otvut Dunava bratya."*

Ottoman Empire."[156] An analytical approach to these events could be through the perspective of post-colonial theory, which viewed the idea of "Pan-Slavic unity" as a division between "civilised Europe" and the "barbaric Asiatic Turks," who should be removed from Europe. One source further highlighted that the only way for "barbarian Asiatic Turks" to change their nature was by accepting European civilisation and integrating with other European nations while abandoning their "wild Quran and superstitious laws."[157] The same discourse we find in another newspaper of that time, *New Bulgaria* (*Nova Bŭlgaria*), whose publication started in 1876. Its first issue maintains that the aim of Bulgarians should be "to throw out the Turks from Europe by giving liberty to all Slavs (*izgonat Turtsite iz Evropa, i togava, namstvo da dadat svoboda na Slavyanete*)."[158] Another article stated that "the Turks brought the Tatars and Cherkes to Bulgaria to humiliate the Bulgarian homes and Christian churches."[159] Thus, the only solution to expel them was by a call to "fight, Bulgarian brothers! God [was] helping the Christians (*na boi bratia Bulgari! Bog veche chudesno pomaga na hristianite*)."[160] It can be inferred that the colonial discourse was prevalent in Bulgarian media and was influenced by the prevailing *Zeitgeist* that brought imperialist policies to small nations. This policy viewed the Slavs as a unified body, highlighting that "all Montenegrins took the weapon yatagan; all the Serbs [had] guns; the Herzegovians and Bosniaks organised their gangs; and the Bulgarians [were] joining them to fight the Turks. The Russian cannon [would] be heard at the end of the world as well. Russia [was] strong and great [was]

---

[156] Bŭlgarski Glas, No. 4, Bolgrad, 8. Maj, 1876; in original: *"neka podadem bratska ruka na boshnyakit i hercegovcit, srbinit i chernogorcit i po skoro da otidem nie pri protsesit na pogrebenieto na Turtsia."*

[157] Bŭlgarski Glas, No. 5, Bolgrad, 18. Maj, 1876; in original: *"aziatetsit (turtsi) samo togova mozhe da promeni svoiat harakter i da prieme evropeiskata tsivilizatsija, kogato toi sa pritopi mezhdu drugite narodi, t.e. kogato se izbavi ot diviat muhamedov Koran i negovite suevrni zakoni."*

[158] Nova Bŭlgaria, No. 1, Bukurest, 5 .Maj, 1876, p. 1.

[159] Ibid.

[160] Ibid., p. 2; in original: *"Turtsite dovedoh goli tatari da im pravit Bulgarite kushi (...) turtsite dovedoh haiduti cherkezi da im napravat kushi Bulgarite (...) Turcite hulyat, psuvat hristovata charkova; narichat hristianite bezvrni gavuri."*

the Slavic family."[161] But paradoxically, this policy also led the Slavs (in this case, the Serbs and Bulgarians) to compete against each other over Macedonia. Indeed, the imperialist policies of the Balkan states were shaped by various factors, including political, economic, and ideological considerations, and were not developed in isolation. The competition between the Slavic states over Macedonia is a prime example of this complex dynamic. Despite the rhetoric of Pan-Slavic unity, the imperialist policies of the Balkan states often resulted in competition and conflict between them. It is also important to note that intellectuals played a crucial role in shaping these policies and promoting national consciousness among the local population. They often acted as mediators between the local and global levels, working to globalise the problems among the Great Powers and to advance the interests of their respective nations. In doing so, they operated in a trans-regional context, navigating complex political, social, and economic factors to promote their goals. For example, among the best–known Bulgarian intellectuals, who promoted the April Uprising in Europe, and cooperated strongly with the locals, were Marko Balabanov and Dragan Tsankov.[162] They sent a joint memorandum to all Great Powers to inform them about the situation in the Ottoman Empire, looking for their understanding in the realisation of Pan–Slavic brotherhood. Their backgrounds were typical of Western–educated Bulgarian nationalists, and their careers were made by championing the Bulgarian national cause. To

---

[161] Nova Bŭlgaria, No. 44, Bukurest, 17. November, 1876, p. 171; in original: *"Skoro pak she izvadi Chernogoretsa yatagana si; skoro she grabni Sirbina pushkata si; skoro she sya stekit i pak hercegovski i boshnashki cheti, skoro she zape bŭlgarina pod liskata znamya… drago mi e na polto s turchin da se bia. Skoro she pripne kazashkia vihrohod kony, she zagrmi Ruskiat top i she e chue do kraja na sveta; Silna e Rossia, velika e slavyanskata familia."*

[162] Tsankov (1828–1911) graduated from the first Bulgarian–language school in Gabrovo and later studied at the Odessa seminary, a high school in Kiev, and philology in Vienna. In 1856, he founded the Community of Bulgarian Literature in Constantinople, which was a precursor to the Bulgarian Literary Society in Brăila. He also established the influential magazine "Bulgarian Booklets" (*Bŭlgarski knizhitsi*) in 1858 and the journal "Bŭlgaria" in 1859, and worked on and off in the Ottoman administration and as a teacher. Balabanov (1837–1921) studied in Athens, Heidelberg, and Paris before becoming a lawyer and editor of the Constantinople newspaper "Century" (Vek) in 1870. There, he wrote in support of the creation of the Bulgarian Exarchate (Bulgarian Orthodox Church) and autocephaly from the Greek Orthodox Church, which was achieved in 1872.See also: Mehmet Hacısalihoğlu, *Die Jungtürken und die Mazedonische Frage*.

carry out this project, they also supported the role of Russia,[163] because they believed that only "Russia [could] seal the Eastern Question (*Russkata pechat vrhu vistochnit raboti*)."[164] Balabanov also edited the newspaper *XIX Vek* published in Istanbul until May 1876. Like his colleagues, he also used Orientalist discourses and claimed that "the Christian population in the Turkish Empire [were] without doubt by civilisation stronger than the East."[165]

Nevertheless, the Congress of Berlin marked a turning point in the representation of Macedonia by Bulgarian intellectuals, who increasingly viewed it as a misfortune. They expressed concern that, of all the Christian peoples in the East, only "the Macedonian Bulgarians had been unlucky" and were now "receiving a fatal blow." Some intellectuals believed that "no war had been fought for Macedonia, and there was no Russian aid available to help them." They argued that Macedonia, "the birthplace of Cyril and Methodius" and "the cradle of Slavdom," was in danger of falling under even worse oppression than before."[166] This perception of Macedonia as a pivotal place in the history of Slavdom was reflected in the views of many intellectuals during the Kresna-Razlog events, the April Uprisings, the San-Stefano Treaty, and the Congress of Berlin. Hence, after the ideas of "south–Slav unity" failed, some of the Bulgarian intellectuals shifted positions and imagined Macedonia exclusively as Bulgarian. Bulgarian intellectuals who had previously advocated for a pan-Slavic approach now sought to emphasise the Bulgarian character of Macedonia and promote the idea of a separate Bulgarian national identity. This shift can also be seen as an attempt to consolidate Bulgarian national identity in the face of competition from other Balkan states, particularly Serbia, which also claimed a historical and cultural connection to Macedonia. The idea of Macedonia as "the cradle of Slavdom" was now used to support Bulgarian claims to the region and to justify Bulgarian efforts to gain control over it. In the newspaper *Bulgarin*, a report stated

---

[163] "Rossia i Slavianet" in *XIX vek*, No. 17, Istanbul, 24. April, 1876.

[164] XIX vek, No. 18, Istanbul, 1. May, 1876.

[165] XIX vek, No. 17, Istanbul, 24. April, 1876. In original: *"Hristianskit narodnonaselenia v turskata drzhava, shiha bez vsako sumnie da su po moschni za tsivilizatsiata na Vistok."*

[166] Maritsa, No. 9, Plovdiv, 25. August, 1878.

that "the events in Macedonia are Bulgarian uprisings (*Makedonia – bŭlgarskto vostanie*)" and "our movement will not be a brotherly connection of hearts with the living population in Macedonia, but also the connection of our Macedonian brothers with this part of the population (living in Bulgaria)."[167] In this respect, the uprisings in Macedonia were represented by these political entrepreneurs as an "uprising in Bulgaria (*vstanyata v Bŭlgaria*)," because the rebels were part of the same "folk living in Macedonia (*vistaneto na nashite ednorodtsi v Makedonia*)."[168] Regarding promoting this idea of complete unity, another important newspaper, *Tselokupna Bŭlgaria* (in translation "the whole/completed Bulgaria"), was edited in June 1879, which emphasised that "the first aim [was] to support and educate the people regarding our efforts towards a union (*nashi vestnik e da podrzha i da odgoiava tezhneniata na naroda ni kim obiedinenie*)." [169] This was one of the turns for the Bulgarian intellectuals, because they did not give importance only to military actions, but also to education. In schools, Bulgarian intellectuals tried to define imagined map of Bulgaria. Books and newspapers often taught that Bulgaria consisted of "Northern Bulgaria, Southern Bulgaria as Eastern Rumelia, and Western Bulgaria or Macedonia (*Severna Bŭlgaria, Yuzhna Bŭlgaria ili Istochna Rumelia i Zapadna Bŭlgaria ili Makedonia*)."[170]

One of the promoters of such ideas in schools and education was Vasil Kanchov, who was an important political entrepreneur in Ottoman Macedonia. He played various roles in the Bulgarian education system in the region, including teaching at the Bulgarian Men's High School in Thessaloniki from 1888 to 1891, serving as a school director in Serres, and becoming the chief school inspector of Bulgarian schools in Ottoman

---

[167] Bŭlgarin, No. 105, Gyurgevo, 9 November, 1878, p. 2; in original: *"nashi dvizhenie ne samo che she se postigne s bratsko srtse ot vsichkiti zhivushi v Makedonia, no dazhe she se podkrni ot dvut, zashoto e dvizhenie obsho na stranata (...) s nashiti bratya makedontsi."*

[168] Bŭlgarin, No. 107, Gyurgevo, 16. November,1878, p. 2.

[169] Tselokupna Bŭlgaria, No. 1, Tarnovo, 20. June, 1879; This newspaper was edited by the above mentioned Petko Slaveykov. He issued also the newspapers *Osten* (1879), *Tselokupna Bŭlgaria* (1879), *Nezavisimost* (1880–1883), *Tarnovska konstitutsia* (1884), *Istina* (1886), *Sofiski dnevnik* (1886) and *Pravda* (1888).

[170] Ibid., p. 4.

Macedonia from 1894 to 1897.[171] Kanchov wrote two influential books on the region, *"Makedonia: Etnografia i statistika"* (1900) and *"Orokhidrografia na Makedonia"* (1911). In the latter he states:

> "It is impossible to mark the precise borders of the area of Macedonia, since it is not limited with strict geographic features, nor is it administratively separated from the other areas. Only in the ethnographic sense does Macedonia have somewhat defined borders, since the Bulgarian tribe is settled in the entire country, and rarely exits its limits."[172]

Kanchov believed that the imagined geography of Macedonia and the imagined community of Bulgarians had no clear borders or limits. Instead, he suggested that the general perception of the population, which he considered to be the local Bulgarian population, should guide the determination of Macedonia's borders. [173] However, this kind of imagination of living space can lead to violence by creating and reinforcing boundaries and stories that promote destructive campaigns against non-Bulgarian locals. The Saint Cyril and Methodius School, also known as the Bulgarian Men's High School in Thessaloniki, was an institution that produced similar knowledge. It was established in 1880 with the support of the local Bulgarian community and the Bulgarian Exarchate. [174] Among the the teachers and initiators of this high school were noted various Bulgarian (and Macedonian) political entrepreneurs such as Vasil Kanchov, Kuzman Shapkarev, Konstantin Velichkov and Grigor Prlichev. Furthermore, these political entrepreneurs and the new schools directly contributed to the emergence of a political movement demanding independence of Macedonia from the Ottomans by training the leadership cadres of IMARO, an outcome not necessarily foreseen by the Bulgarian upper classes who pioneered the scholastic leap forward.

---

[171] See Vasil Kanchov, *Orokhidrografia na Makedonia* (Sofia: Bŭlgarskoto knizhovno druzhestvo, 1911).

[172] Ibid., p. 18.

[173] Ibid; Bernard Lory, "Schools for the Destruction of Society: School Propaganda in Bitola 1860–1912" in *Conflicting Loyalties in the Balkans: The Great Powers, the Ottoman Empire and Nation–Building*, eds. Hannes Grandits, Nathalie Clayer and Robert Pichler (London–New York: I. B. Tauris, 2011), pp. 46–63.

[174] Yosmaoğlu, *Blood Ties,* p. 73; Rohdewald, *Götter der Nationen.*

IMARO would become one of the principal political forces leading the insurgency against the Ottoman Empire and would maintain its influence (and retain its violent tactics) during the interwar years. Nearly all the founders of IMARO – Damian Gruev, Anton Dimitrov, Ivan Hadzi Nikolov, Hristo Batandzhiev, and Petar Poparsov – were school teachers, trained either in Bulgaria or Macedonia.[175] Although on the one hand the IMARO's members were educated intellectuals, on the other hand the movement also blended bandits from this region. Some of the local dissidents from Ottoman Macedonia were convinced they could obtain their goals only through armed struggle, and not only education. In this regard, political entrepreneurs often overlap with this significant type of political actors, whom Charles Tilly terms "specialists in violence."[176] The inclusion of these violent actors within IMARO would give the organisation a significant edge in the struggle against the Ottomans, allowing it to pursue both political and violent means to achieve its objectives. This also created tensions within the movement, as the more moderate members sought to distance themselves from the violent tactics employed by the bandits. By the late 1890s, these "Bulgarian" bands had proliferated and were causing divisions within the organisation, as well as conflicts with the Bulgarian government and Exarchate. Like the nationalist movements in Greece and Albania, the IMARO was not a unified or purely nationalist movement, and it spawned discussions about the idea of imagined Macedonia as part of Bulgaria, an independent state of Macedonia, or a supra-national Balkan unity. The consequences of these divisions and discussions would continue to shape the region well into the 20th century.

3.3.3. The Serbian National Movement and Ottoman Macedonia

In the 19th century, the Serbian policy towards the Ottoman territories was based on a mediaeval narrative that emerged into the imagination of Ottoman Macedonia as a territory that was the "heart" of the mediaeval

---

[175] Studied or being teachers Gotse Delchev, Dame Gruev, Todor Aleksandrov, Andrey Lyapchev, Ivan Mihaylov, Petar Darvingov, Anton Ketskarov and others; See: Hacısalihoğlu, *Die Jungtürken und die Mazedonische Frage;* Tokay, *The Macedonian Question.*
[176] Tilly, *The Politics*, p. 40.

Serbian Empire. The two Serbian Uprisings (in 1804 and 1815) facilitated the construction of this narrative among the Serbian intellectuals. In this sense, Ilija Garašanin, a statesman and inventor of Greater Serbia (*Velika Srbija*), wanted to achieve this revival of the Serbian state and Serbdom in such a manner that it could not be said that the Serbs demanded something they had never had. Accordingly, the mediaeval Serbian state was the mould on which its modern counterpart was to be built. Hence, this building of "a new Serbian empire," Garašanin said, "must now be completely cleared of ruins and raised above ground; then, on this firm and stable historical basis, we must begin upon and extend the new building." [177] Serbian intellectuals gave to these uprisings a national element, although it was in fact rather local than national, [178] and constructed a narrative about Serbdom in Ottoman Macedonia. Furthermore, a series of internal rebellions in the Ottoman Empire followed by the territorial loss of some of the Empire's provinces like Greece (independent as of 1830) or Serbia (autonomous as of 1835), enabled many Serbs to develop cultural and national activities in the Habsburg and Ottoman provinces, more precisely in Macedonia. Thus, Serbian intellectuals had already established a National Foundation (*Matica Srpska*), founded in Pest in 1826, and later moved to Novi Sad in the Habsburg Empire. In this regard, cities like Vienna, Budapest, or Novi Sad had become shelter places for the promotion of Serbian national culture and Serbian nationalism, but these ideas did not remain only on the side of the Danube in the Habsburg Empire.

The ideas of belonging to one and the same nation would spread also in the other Ottoman provinces where the local population spoke (a) south–Slavic language(s). After obtaining its independence at the Congress of Berlin (1878), Serbia clashed with the Bulgarian national developments in

---

[177] Slijepčević, *The Macedonian*, p. 146; Ferdo Šišić, *Jugoslovenska misao* (Beograd: Balkanski Institut, 1937), pp. 91–92; Bogdan Trifunović, "Memory of Old Serbia."
[178] About the Serbian Uprisings and the Serbian history see: Holm Zundhausen, *Istorija Srbije od 19. Do 21. veka* (Beograd: Clio, 2008); in original: Holm Sundhaussen, *Geschichte Serbiens. 19. – 21. Jahrhundert* (Vienna: Böhlau Verlag, 2007). Holm Sundhaussen argues that "it is more appropriate to speak of peasant uprisings than of a revolution." See: Zundhausen, *Istorija Srbije,* p. 76; Phillip Longworth does not share the same thought that nationalism played a significant role in these events: Philip Longworth, *Making of Eastern Europe* (London: Palgrave Macmillan, 1997), pp. 176–177.

Ottoman Macedonia. After 1878, the independent Serbian state tried to achieve territorial expansion in the territories that they called "Old Serbia (*Stara Srbija*)"[179] and "South Serbia (*Južna Srbija*)."[180] Between the Congress of Berlin and the Balkan Wars, the Serbian state and its intellectuals tried in various ways to oppose the Bulgarian policy in Ottoman Macedonia or as their intellectuals termed it, "Southern Serbia." Hence, the annexation of Eastern Rumelia by Bulgarian Principality in 1885 disturbed the balance of power in the Balkans, especially between Serbia and Bulgaria. In this regard, Jovan Ristić published an article in the newspaper *Nova Ustavnost*, explaining that "Bulgaria annexed a large and rich province with a population of eight hundred thousand, the balance of power in the Balkans is immediately destroyed. If the Balkan states [did] not rise in protest against Bulgarian aggrandisement, they had to think of means of restoring the equilibrium in their favour. Serbia [would] seek compensation in Old Serbia and northern Macedonia:

> "We need not do anything rash, but we must keep this danger [of increased Bulgarian activity in Macedonia] before our eyes and be prepared to remove it. We must not allow anything that we—still more, anything that our forefathers— have acquired to be lost."[181]

Jovan Ristić was one of the leaders of Serbian diplomacy, specialised in Macedonian issues. After he was appointed in Istanbul in 1861, he became Prince Mihailo's close advisor in many issues related to Serbian foreign policy. As a member of the Society of Serbian Slavdom (*Društvo Srpske Slovenosti*), he was involved in the promotion of the Serbian language in the Ottoman Empire. During his time, quite active was the Department for

---

[179] Stara Srbija was a term used mostly for Kosovo vilayet (latterly Kosovo); See: Jovan Hadži–Vasiljević *Južna stara Srbija: istorijska, etnografska i politička istraživanja* (Beograd: Nova štamparija Davidović. 1913); Miloš Jagodić, *Srbija i Stara Srbija (1839–1868): Nasleđe na jugu* (Beograd: Evoluta, 2016); Miloš Jagodić, *Srpsko–albanski odnosi u Kosovskom vilajetu (1878–1912)* (Beograd: Zavod za udžbenike i nastavna sredstva, 2009).

[180] Južna Srbija was a term used mostly for Manastir and Selanik Vilayet (latterly Macedonia), See: Jovan Hadži–Vasiljević, *Prilep i njegova okolina* (Beograd: Nova Električna Štamparija Petra Jockovića, 1902); Srđan Atanasovski, *Mapiranje Stare Srbije: Stopama putopisaca, tragom narodne pesme* (Beograd: Biblioteka XX vek, 2017).

[181] Đoko Slijepčević, *The Macedonian*, p. 159.

Churches and Schools in Old Serbia (*Odbor za crkve i škole u Staroj Srbiji*),[182] established in 1868 to promote education in Serbian and to preserve "the Orthodox faith in Old Serbia (*sačuvanje pravoslavlja u Staroj Srbiji.*)"[183] One of its founding members was Jovan Ristić.[184] After Bulgaria annexed Eastern Rumelia, Serbia declared war to the Bulgarian state, which was decisively lost by Serbia. [185] Following this disappointment, the Serbian policy towards Macedonia acquired a new momentum in 1886, with the establishment of another Society named Saint Sava[186] (*Društvo Sveti Sava*), whose goal to protect the Serb people (*srpski narod*) in Ottoman Macedonia (*Old and Southern Serbia*) and to suppress Bulgarian politics and the Bulgarian Exarchate church's influence. [187] Svetomir Nikolajević was elected its first president, who was known for his moderate views of the Greek claims in Macedonia, but held harsh views against the Bulgarian developments in Ottoman Macedonia. [188]

---

[182] Slaviša Nedeljković, "Delovanje Odbora za škole i učitelje u srpskim oblastima u Makedoniji od 1868. do 1876. godine," *Vardarski zbornik* 8 (2011): 283–305, here in 288.

[183] Ibid; Jagodić, *Srbija i Stara Srbija*; Jagodić, *Srpsko–albanski odnosi u Kosovskom vilajetu.*

[184] Ibid.

[185] Ibid; Atanasovski, *Mapiranje Stare Srbije*; Cvijić, *Osnove za geografiju i geologiju*, pp. 38–41.

[186] Saint Sava was a prominent historical figure in Serbia who held many roles, including as a prince, monk, diplomat, and the first Archbishop of the autocephalous Serbian Church. He was born as Rastko, the youngest son of Serbian Grand Prince Stefan Nemanja, and briefly ruled the appanage of Hum in 1190–92 before becoming a monk on Mount Athos with the name Sava. He is revered as the founder of Serbian law and is widely considered one of the most important figures in Serbian history. The Serbian Orthodox Church honors him as its founder on January 27, and he is also the patron saint of Serbia, Serbs, and Serbian education. Many works of art throughout history have depicted his life and accomplishments. See: Rohdewald, *Götter der Nationen,* pp. 512–522.

[187] Stanoje Stanojević, *Narodna enciklopedija srpsko–hrvatsko–slovenačka* (Novi Sad: Izdavačka knjižarnica Zorana Stojanovića, 1929), p. 575; Adanır, *Die makedonische Frage*; Heiner Grunert, *Glauben im Hinterland: Die Serbisch–Orthodoxen in der habsburgischen Herzegowina, 1878–1918* (Göttingen: Vandenhoeck & Ruprecht, 2016).

[188] Svetomir Nikolajević was one of the founders of the Radical Party, the Society of Saint Sava, and the Belgrade Masonic Lodge 'Pobratim.' He was also the Rector of the Great School between 1888–1890.

Other founding members were such individuals as Ljubomir Kovačević, Miloš Milojević, Milojko Veselinović, and Jovan Hadžić–Vasiljević.[189] These members, who can also be considered as political entrepreneurs, established a journal titled *Brotherhood* (*Bratstvo*). Its first issue contains many texts about "Southern Serbia," especially about cities such as Veles, Prilep, Ohrid, and Thessaloniki (*Solun*). This issue maintained that "Macedonia was conquered by the Bulgarians in the 9th century, when Serb brothers began a clash among themselves."[190] Furthermore, the city of Prilep was glorified: "[A]ll Serbs heard of the capital of the Marko Kraljević (*nema valjda Srbina, koji nije čuo za Prilep, prestonicu Marka Kraljevića, sina Vukašinova*)."[191] Moreover, the issue also mentioned the southern borders of the Serbian Tsardom during the time of Tsar Dušan (*južne granice Dušanova carstva*)[192] and that "Macedonia belong[ed] to an old Serb glory of the Serbian state."[193] Hence, a text written as a "geographic and ethnologic survey in Macedonia and Old Serbia (*geografsko–etnografski pregled Maćedonije i Stare Srbije*)" was promoted. [194] A map was also added to it, where Macedonia was presented as an old Serbian territory. [195] The aim was to emphasise that "Macedonians [did] not have anything to do with the Greeks. Macedonians

---

[189] Mihailo Vojvodić, Milorad M. Radević, *Društvo Svetog Save: dokumenta 1886–1891* (Beograd: Arhiv Srbije, 1999); Bojan Aleksov, "The Serbian Orthodox Church," in *Orthodox Christianity and Nationalism in Nineteenth–Century Southeastern Europe*, ed. Lucian N. Leustean (New York: Fordham University Press, 2014), pp. 65–100.

[190] Bratstvo (Beograd: Kraljevska državna štamparija, 1887), p. 21; in original: "*koristeći se srpskom neslogom i pocepanošću, (Bugari) osvojiše Maćedoniju i držaše je do propasti bugarske države 971 godine.*"

[191] Ibid. p. 36.

[192] Ibid. p. 109.

[193] Ibid., p. 111; in original: "*Maćedonija je deo stare slavne srpske države i narod njen.*"

[194] Ibid., p. 187.

[195] Ibid; Petar Kostić, *Crkveni život pravoslavnih Srba u Prizrenu i njegovoj okolini u XIX veku (sa uspomenama pisca)* (Beograd: Grafički institut Narodna misao A. D., 1928), pp. 88–96; Nedeljko Radosavljević, "Episkop, mirski sveštenik, monah: obeležja svakodnevnog života," in *Privatni život kod Srba u devetnaestom veku: od kraja XVIII veka do početka Prvog svetskog rata*, eds. Ana Stolić and Nenad Makuljević (Beograd: Clio, 2006).

are not of Greek origin. Macedonians speak the Serbian language and celebrate Serbian heroes, kings, and tsars."[196]

In this issue of the journal *Bratstvo*, a poem, also known as 'Serbian folk poem,' was also dedicated to Saint Sava.[197] The editor of this journal was Jovan Hadži–Vasiljević, who was a prominent Serbian historian and ethnographer of that time. As an official of the Ministry of Foreign Affairs of the Serbian state, he served from 1898 to 1904 in Ottoman Macedonia, in the cities of Bitola and Skopje. He was also a secretary of the Society of Saint Sava and worked for the "national enlightenment of Serbs in the Ottoman Empire."[198] The high value of his work is due to it being based on field research, especially in the regions of Old Serbia and Macedonia (South Serbia). To these works belong books as *"Prilep i njegova okolina"* (1902); *"Južna Stara Srbija, istorijska, etnografska i politička istraživanja"* (published in two parts in 1909 and 1913); *"Četnička akcija u Staroj Srbiji i Maćedoniji"* (1928) and *"Skoplje i njegova okolina"* (1930). In the book about Prilep, he points out that "among the cities and centres in our southern parts that are under the rule of the Turks, Prilep is the most important one. (…) Prilep is a very important political and cultural centre and great city." [199] Also the book emphasised that "Bulgarians used our indolence and incapability, started to count our

---

[196] Ibid. p. 189; in original: *"sadanji Maćedonci nemaju ničeg srodnog sa Grcima. Maćedonci nisu porekla grčkog. Maćedonci, naročito zapadni, zbore srspski, slave, pevaju srpske junake, kraljeve i careve."*

[197] Bratstvo, p. 105.
"Zbor zborila gospoda rišćanska
Kod bijele crkve Gračanice:
Bože mili, čuda velikoga!
Kud se đede car–Nemanje blago,
Sedam kula groša i dukata?
Tu se desi Nemanjiću Savo,
Pa govori gospodi rišćanskoj:
Oj Boga vam, gospodo rišćanska!"

[198] Jovan Hadži–Vasiljević, *Južna stara Srbija: istorijska, etnografska i politička istraživanja* (Beograd: Nova štamparija Davidović. 1913).

[199] Jovan Hadži–Vasiljević, *Prilep i njegova okolina* (Beograd: Nova Električna Štamparija Petra Jockovića, 1902), p. 1; in original: *"između gradova i centara u južnim predelima našim pod Turcima, Prilep se ističe kao prvi po važnosti svojoj. (...) Prilep je sa svojim predelima bio vrlo važan politički i kulturni centar. U ono vreme Prilep nalazimo kao velikoslavni grad."*

regions as their own."[200] Thus, the mission of the Serbian state should be "suppression of the Bulgarisation in the glorious city of Prilep (*da se bugarština i u veliko–slavnom gradu Prilepu suzbije*)."[201]

In the book about "Southern Serbia" titled "*Južna Stara Srbija, istorijska, etnografska i politička istraživanja I–II*", Jovan Hadži–Vasiljević clearly states that "Southern Old Serbia is the nucleus of Serbian state life in medival ages."[202] There is no doubt that the mediaeval Serbian kingdom was a "nucleus" for the further imagination of Ottoman Macedonia as part of Serbian state. The most prominent historian of that time, Ljubomir Kovačević was appointed to promote this idea in the Serbian educational system and among the population in Ottoman Macedonia. In this regard, together with Ljubomir Jovanović, he wrote the well–known two–volume edition of *History of the Serbian People for the Secondary Schools* (in original: *Istorija srpskog naroda za srednje škole*).[203]

Kovačević also wrote on "monumental history" for Serbian schools, glorifying Serbian rulers from Kosovo and Macedonia[204] such as Despot

---

[200] Ibid., pp. 3–4; in original: *"jer je Bugarima, koristeći se prilikama i našim nehatom, pa i neumenjem, već u narav preslo, da naše krajeve u onim stranama onamu u svoju sferu računaju kao svoje opisuju."*

[201] Ibid., p. 212.

[202] Hadži–Vasiljević, *Južna stara Srbija*, p. 7; in original: *"ovaj, s razmerno dosta prostran, teren ispitivanja nazvali smo Južnom Starom Srbijom; tako smo ga nazvali s toga što su oblasti na tom terenu, koje u ovim knjigama opisujemo, za vreme srpskog državnickog života u Srednjim Vekovima sačinjavale sa okolnim oblastima jezgro Kraljevine Srbije…"*; See also: Vladan Jovanović, *Jugoslovenska Država i Južna Srbija 1918–1929: Makedonija, Sandžak, Kosovo i Metohija u Kraljevini SHS* (Beograd: Institut za noviju istoriju Srbije, 2002).

[203] Ljubomir Kovačević and Ljubomir Jovanović, *Istorija srpskog naroda za srednje škole* (Beograd: Štamparija Kraljevine Srbije, 1893–94); Aleksandra Ilić, *Udžbenici i Nacionalno Vaspitanje U Srbiji 1878–1918* (Beograd: Univerzitet u Beogradu Filozofski Fakultet, 2010).

[204] See on Serbian policy towards Kosovo (and Macedonia): Ivan Čolović, *Smrt na Kosovu polju: Istorija kosovskoj mita* (Beograd: Biblioteka XX veka, 2017); Olga Zirojević, "Kosovo in the Collective Memory," in *The Road to War in Serbia: Trauma and Catharsis*, ed. Nebojša Popov (New York: Central European University Press, 2000), pp. 189–211; Dušan Lj. Kašić, "Koreni kosovke misli, " in *Sveti Knez Lazar: Spomenica o šestoj stogodišnjici Kosovskog boja, 1389–1989*, eds. Episkop raško–prizrenski Pavle et al. (Beograd: Sveti arhijerejski sinod SPC, 1989), pp. 11–24; Sima M. Ćirković, "Kosovska bitka kao istorijski problem," in *Kosovska bitka u istoriografiji (okrugli sto)*, ed. Sima Ćirković (Beograd: Istorijski institu, 1990), pp. 109–118.

Stefan Lazarević,[205] King Vukašin, Tsar Uroš,[206] Vuk Branković,[207] Stefan Nemanja,[208] Stefan Prvovenčani.[209] Accordingly, using monumental history, he aimed to (mis)use and (ab)use[210] the past in order to inspire the local people to attempt "great things." Popular histories of the Kosovo Battle (1389), personalities such as Despot Stefan Lazarević or Vuk Branković, for instance, usually belong to the monumental histories. The great men of the past are held up for admiration among the masses and locals, and to inspire them in participating in their struggles, doubts, and triumphs for the "nation" and the "land." "We take heart," Friedrich Nietzsche said, from "the knowledge that the great which once existed, was at least possible once, and may well again be possible some time."[211] In this context, when Ljubomir Kovačević's son died during the Balkan Wars in Ottoman Macedonia (Kumanovo), Kovačević added:

"My son, depart in peace. You have done your duty. My son, I do not weep: I am proud of you. You have joined the heroes whose sufferings and death of old saved by millions the lives and souls of our nation. Tell the heroes of Kosovo, Dušan and Lazar and all the martyrs of former days, that today Kosovo is avenged."[212]

Furthermore, one of the most important personalities during this period (1878–1903) was Vladimir Karić. He was a prominent geographer of that time, who mostly inspired Jovan Cvijić – his pupil that became the most

---

[205] Ljubomir Kovačević, *Despot Stefan Lazarević za vreme turskih međusobica (1402—1413)* (Beograd: N.P., 1880).
[206] Ljubomir Kovačević, *I opet kralj Vukašin nije ubio cara Uroša* (Beograd: N.P., 1884).
[207] Ljubomir Kovačević, *Vuk Branković* (Beograd: N.P., 1888).
[208] Ljubomir Kovačević, *Nekoliko pitanja o Stefanu Nemanji* (Beograd: N.P., 1891).
[209] Ljubomir Kovačević, *Žene i deca Stefana Prvovenčanog* (Beograd: N.P., 1901).
[210] About this concept of "monumental history" see: Friedrich Nietzsche, *Vom Nutzen und Nachteil der Historie für das Leben* (Leipzig: Verlag Panitzsch, 1874); Nada Boškovska, *Das jugoslawische Makedonien 1918–1941: Eine Randregion zwischen Repression und Integration* (Vienna/Cologne/Weimar: Böhlau, 2009).
[211] Ibid.
[212] Jovan Pejčić, "Jedna potresna sahrana u Beogradu 1912, zbog koje je plakala cela Srbija, gde god je ima," *Nacionalna Revija* 41 (2018); Jovan Pejčić, *Slova, slike, simboli: srpski pesnici druge polovine XX veka: govori, predgovori, pogovori* (Niš: Niški kulturni centar, 2021).

famous geographer in the Balkans.[213] Vladimir Karić wrote several geographical books for the Serbian schools.[214] During the 1880s, he also wrote the books *Serbian Lands* (Srpska zemlja) in 1882[215] and *Serbia: Landscape, People, and State* (*Srbija: opis zemlje, naroda i države*) in 1887, intended to influence the consciousness of the rural population through the school system.[216] In these books, he emphasised the contours of the Serbian claims in Ottoman Macedonia. According to him, due to the fact that Serbia had no widespread propaganda network there, the local population started to identify themselves with the Bulgarians or Greeks.[217] In this sense, the Serbian people were behind the Greek and Bulgarian states, which promoted their identities in the region through education and ecclesiastic churches. In order to promote the Serbian identity in Ottoman Macedonia, Karić was appointed Serbian Consul in Skopje in 1889 and worked to strengthen the Serbian nationalist policy in Ottoman Macedonia. For this purpose, he was promoting the opening of Serbian schools and churches in the region and to "strengthen Serbian national consciousness in the Ottoman Empire (*jačati srpsku nacionalnu svest u Osmanskom carstvu.*)[218] In Vladimir Karić's opinion, Serbia also needed an ally that could provide a common policy regarding the local population in Macedonia.[219] For this reason, the Serbian military attaché in Istanbul, Jevrem Velimirović, contacted Greek representatives in 1882. In his report, he noted that the Serbs could benefit from resolving the Macedonian issue, but needed help from Greece to do so.[220] In 1885, the son of the inventor of "Great Serbia", Milutin Garašanin, who was now Serbian Prime Minister, submitted a plan to the Serbian King Milan

---

[213] Biljana Vučetić, *Naša stvar u Otomanskom carstvu* (Beograd: Istorijski Institut 2012); Cvijić, *Govori i članci.*

[214] Vladimir Karić, *Udžbenik Zemljopisa – Geografije* (Beograd: N.P., 1879 and 1881); Cvijić, *Promatranja o etnografiji makedonskih Slovena.*

[215] Vladimir Karić, *Srpska zemlja* (Beograd: N.P., 1882).

[216] Vladimir Karić, *Srbija: opis zemlje, naroda i države* (Beograd: N.P., 1887).

[217] Vladimir Karić, *Srpska Zemlja*, p. 31.

[218] Mihailo Vojvodić, *Stojan Novaković i Vladimir Karić* (Beograd: Clio, 2003), pp. 126–172.

[219] Ibid.

[220] Dalibor Jovanovski, *Friendly Competition – Greek–Serbian Relations and Ottoman Macedonia in the Eighties of the 19th Century* (Skopje: Godišen zbornik na Filozofskiot fakultet, 2019), p. 122.

suggesting a manner of organisation of the Serbian policy in Ottoman Macedonia, or as it was referred to by the Serbian intellectuals – Old Serbia and Macedonia.[221] The crisis in the Balkans caused by the unification of Bulgaria and Eastern Rumelia in September 1885 was an event that influenced the acceleration of the Greek–Serbian cooperation against the Ottoman Empire and Bulgaria.[222] Therefore, the Serbian state undertook measures in a more organised way to reduce the Bulgarian activities in the region and to spread Serbian national consciousness through the establishment of several networks. In this regard, Serbia firstly tried to promote Serbian "Macedonianism" as its first move toward eventually Serbianising the local population of Macedonia. For this purpose, the Association of Serbo–Macedonians (*Društvo Srbo–Makedonci*) was established by political entrepreneurs from the region of Macedonia in Istanbul in 1886. Its founders had all formerly been members of the organisation such as Secret Macedonian Committee established in Sofia in 1885. Four of its members left Bulgaria, switched their loyalties, and went to Belgrade to support the Serbian policy. The praxis of switching sides in the Ottoman Macedonian context was quite common. During one's lifetime, one could support several ideologies or national projections according to the situation and various personal, economic, tribal, or family interests, as will be seen in chapter Four. One such example were the personalities gathered around the Association of Serbo–Macedonians, who initiated their activities on 23 February 1885. In Belgrade, its members met with one of the Serbian politicians named Stojan Novaković, who pledged his support and institutionalised the Serbian networks in Ottoman Macedonia.[223] The decision to create such Association in Istanbul, it was taken at a meeting of the Serbian government's members in early August 1886. At the same meeting the decision was also reached to create the Saint Sava Society based on the "Serbian sacred ruler" with the purpose of "spreading Serbian propaganda in the region of Macedonia."[224] The latter

---

[221] A quote from Ksenija Šulović, *Stevan Vladislav Kaćanski (1828–1890)* (Novi Sad: Katalog izložbe, 2003).

[222] Almost simultaneously, Greek Minister for Foreign Affairs Kontostavlos gave instructions to the Greek envoy in Belgrade to start the talks about the delineation of a line of the sphere of interests in Macedonia.

[223] Ibid.

[224] Rohdewald, *Götter der Nationen.*, pp. 391–407.

society and its educational department (established in March 1887) would organise the majority part of the religious and educational work in Ottoman Macedonia, while Stojan Novaković would be appointed Serbian Ambassador to Istanbul (1886–91), and organised the educational and cultural life through the consulates in Kosovo vilayet (Skopje and Priština in 1887), Solun vilayet (1887) and Bitola vilayet (1889). Their main aims were to educate and indoctrinate population on the ground by installing the national consciousness through education and religious (church) activities.[225] For this puropse, Novaković was appointed as diplomat to Istanbul and thus, played a significant role in the realisation of the 'Serbian cause' by establishing the Association of Serbo–Macedonians.[226] He was assisted by the two members of the Macedonian committee named K. Grupchev and N. Evrov.[227] These political entrepreneurs were partially successful in forging the Macedonian language, based on strong Serbian linguistic influence. This emergence of "Macedonism" in the region was seen as a stage of the gradual Serbianisation of the Macedonian Slavs.[228] One of the important personalities of this network was the above–mentioned Miloš Milojević, a cofounder of the Society of St. Sava in Ottoman Macedonia. He was also a prominent politician and writer, whose work was described as "on the border between history and literature." Interestingly, these political entrepreneurs, such as Milojević, were often active at the local, regional, or global levels. They could be teachers, state

---

[225] Slavenko Terzić, "Konzulat Kraljevine Srbije u Bitolju (1889–1897)," *Istorijski časopis* (57) 2008: 327–342, in pages 329–331.

[226] Ibid; The Society provided paid scholarships for individuals who identified themselves as Serbo–Macedonians, and also established specialised schools in Serbia for children from Macedonia and Stara Serbia. The organization carried out propaganda campaigns among Macedonians working in Serbia, which were so successful that within three years, its executive body became part of the Serbian Ministry of Foreign Affairs. As a result of this propaganda, a group of 34 students from the Bulgarian Men's High School of Thessaloniki were convinced to accept an offer to study in Belgrade. However, they soon realised the true intentions behind the program when they were forbidden from possessing Bulgarian literature. Consequently, most of them left Belgrade to continue their education in Bulgaria, including notable figures such as Dame Gruev, Petar Pop Arsov, Krste Misirkov, Kosta Shahov, and others.

[227] Klara Volarić, "Carigradski Glasnik: A Forgotten Istanbul–based Paper in the Service of Ottoman Serbs (1895–1909)" (MA Thesis, Central European University, 2014).

[228] Mihailo Vojvodić, "Stojan Novaković et la politique étrangère de la Serbie," *Balcanica* 45 (2014): 229–266.

agents, politicians, or diplomats in their lifetimes. In this regard, Milojević, along with his friend Kosta Šumenković, published several books and a map: the "historical and ethno–geographical map of Serbs and Serbian/Yugoslavian lands in Turkey and Austria (*istorijsko–etnografska geografska mapa Srba i srpskih/jugoslovenskih zemalja u Turskoj i Austriji*)."[229] Miloš Milojević also travelled to Ottoman Macedonia, where he recorded his travels in a book "*Putopisi dela prave – Stare Srbije.*"[230] During his travellings between 1871 and 1877, he released three volumes of data and maps, where he tried to prove that the "Serbs [were] the majority and Albanians the minority population."[231] In similar ways, Milojko Veselinović opposed the Bulgarian presence in Ottoman Macedonia. Accordingly, he wrote several books regarding those topics, such as "*Pogled kroz Kosovo*" (1895),[232] "*Srbi u Maćedoniji i u Južnoj Staroj Srbiji*" (1888),[233] and "*Granični dijalekt među Srbima i Bugarima*" (1890).[234] In this regard, the Serbian state and its intellectuals tried to influence the local population of Ottoman Macedonia by travelling to these lands and publishing books about its history and geography. In this sense, one should also note the work of Spiridon Gopčević,[235] "*Makedonien und Alt Serbien*" (1889). Gopčević's was a famous Serbian nationalist book about "Old Serbia" and Macedonia, arranged for German–speaking

---

[229] Miloš Milojević, *Istorijsko etnografsko geografska mapa Srba i srpskih (jugoslavenskih) zemalja u Turskoj i Austriji* (Beogradu: Kosta Atanaskov – Šumenković, 1873).

[230] Mirčeta Vemić, *Etnička karta dela Stare Srbije: Prema putopisu Miloša S. Milojevića 1871–1877. godine* (Beograd: Geografski institut 'Jovan Cvijić' SANU, 2005).

[231] Ibid.

[232] Milojko Veselinović, *Pogled kroz Kosovo* (Beograd: N.P., 1895).

[233] Milojko Veselinović, *Srbi u Maćedoniji i u Južnoj Staroj Srbiji* (Beograd: N.P., 1888).

[234] Milojko Veselinović, *Granični dijalekt među Srbima i Bugarima* (Beograd: N.P., 1890).

[235] Spiridon Gopčević, a prominent shipowner from Trieste, which was part of the Austrian Littoral (now in Italy), hailed from the village of Podi near Herceg Novi in Boka Kotorska, which was then under the Austrian Empire's control (now in Montenegro). After working as a shipowner, Gopčević entered Serbian foreign service and served as a diplomatic attaché in Berlin (1886–1887) and Vienna (1887–1890). Later, he returned to his family estate in Trieste in 1891, where he worked as a journalist for several German–language newspapers. In his writings, Gopčević expressed his opinions on the Serbian and Albanian populations in Kosovo, as well as the issue of the *Arnautaš theory*, or the belief that Albanians had Serbian ancestry. His book is considered to have paved the way for Serbia's unprecedented territorial claims in the region.

readers. As an appendix to this book a pro–Serbian ethnographic map on Macedonia was also published.[236] Other important works of this period were the records of the Bitola consul Mihailo L. Ristić (P. Balkanski), laid out in the book *"Kroz Groblje – opažanja i beleške prilikom putovanja kroz Srpsku zemlju pod Turskom 1892. godine"*[237]; Branislav Nušić's *"Sa obala Ohridskog jezera"*[238] (1892) and *"S Kosova na sinje more"*[239] (1894); and Ivan Ivanić *"Maćedonija i Maćedonci – putopisne beleške"*[240] (1906). Also in these works, one can find plenty of contested politics between the Serbian intellectuals and their difficulties to deal with local compatriots who often opposed their projections. Furthermore, these Balkan states and their mobile intellectuals promoted various national ideas and tried to use the dissatisfaction of the locals for the installation of a national feeling on the ground, but the locals did not work along the lines of of "nationalist" affiliation. Oftentimes it appeared that locals manipulated the pseudo–nationalist fears expressed by their "protectors" from Belgrade. In this regard, as the frequent shifts in the focus of these local efforts will suggest, the activities of the local communities should not be exclusively interpreted as "nationalist" in nature.[241] In Isa Blumi's opinion, these schools proved incapable of inculcating the loyalty Istanbul-–based officials had envisioned; rather locals often used these "colonising" institutions to dictate the terms of state penetration in their lives and thus maintain a balance of power between themselves and the outside world.[242] The importance of including the local level lies in the fact that the reformers in Istanbul or in other cities (Belgrade, Sofia, or Athens)

---

[236] Spiridon Gopčević, *Makedonija i Stara Srbija* (Beograd: Sazvežđe, 2016). First published in 1890.

[237] Mihailo L. Ristić, *Kroz Groblje – opažanja i beleške prilikom putovanja kroz srpsku zemlju pod Turskom 1892 godine* (Beograd: N.P., 1892).

[238] Branislav Nušić, *Sa obala Ohridskog jezera* (Beograd: N.P., 1892).

[239] Branislav Nušić, *S Kosova na sinje more* (Beograd: N.P., 1894).

[240] Ivan Ivanić, *Maćedonija i Maćedonci – putopisne beleške* (Beograd: N.P., 1906).

[241] See the raports of the Serbian Consulars to Thessaloniki and Sevres: Aleksej Timofejev, *Istorija srpske Diplomatije Dokumenta: Generalni konzulat Kraljevine Srbije u Solunu (1887–1902)* (Beograd: Arhiv Srbije, 2016), and Aleksej Timofejev, *Istorija srpske Diplomatije Dokumenta: Generalni konzulat Kraljevine Srbije u Serezu (1897–1900)* (Beograd: Arhiv Srbije, 2016).

[242] Isa Blumi, *Foundations of Modernity*, p. 15.

frequently had difficulties in sustaining their goal to create uniformity in how the Empire's citizens traded, communicated, or acted.

3.4. Conclusion

Here I highlighted the Balkan states' policies and the Ottoman consolidation during the period from 1878 to 1903, that is, after the Congress of Berlin and up to the Ilinden Uprising. I demonstrated how the Ottoman state, especially the Hamidian regime, tried to keep its remaining territories in Rumelia by enforcing a special policy towards the Albanian–speaking locals who were considered by Ottoman state officials as "an Ottoman fortress in Rumelia." In this regard, the Hamidian regime tried to integrate and recruit them on the basis of Unity of Islam (*İttihadi İslam*). This ideological and political attempt, I argued, can be analysed within the framework of the Ottoman counter–colonialist strategy known as "borrowed colonialism." Influenced by European ideas of that time, this strategy aimed to build a "civilised centre" (Istanbul) that directed a *mission civilisatrice* towards Ottoman Macedonia. Despite the reluctance of a few Ottoman scholars to recognise this parallel to European colonialism, this study tries to demonstrate that the same notions of superiority and civilisation found among the Great Powers also informed Ottoman reforms. By using Ottoman and Albanian sources, I demonstrated that the 'Albanian element,' especially Albanian intellectuals played a very important role in keeping the three vilayets close to its centre – Istanbul. One of their policies was the support of Ottoman (and Albanian) schools by the Albanian intellectuals that aimed to counter Balkan "small–state imperialism." In contrast to this, I showed also how the Serbian, Bulgarian, and Greek sides formulated policies in Macedonia, often by opening their own "national" and "religious" schools in order to indoctrinate the local members of Macedonian societies. Much like their colonial counterparts elsewhere, Serbian, Greek, and Bulgarian state schools were created to monitor and supervise the national consciousness of the local population in Ottoman Macedonia. In this attempt, they founded a spate of organisations and schools (*Društvo Sveti Sava, Društvo Srbo–Makedonci, Vtreshna revolucionna organizatsia, Ethniki Etaireia* etc.) in order to inject a national consciousness and feelings about ancient Hellenism or the mediaeval Bulgarian and Serbian empires. What is demonstrated here by studying the various cases to indoctrinate these people through churches or education activities are contradictory results on the ground. In this respect, I do not conclude that these Balkan policies of the souls" were successful, but rather that these policies were often opposed by local practices. What is more, it was often the case that these promoters of such national meta–narratives clashed over the "indoctrination" of certain national programmes or ideologies and were not able to realise them on the ground according to their previous plans. What I here argue, it is rather that locals had also agency and the processes been happening through negotiations – outside the vacuum.

Networks on the Ground: A Perspective From Below in Ottoman Macedonia (1903–1908)

If we accept a definition of borderlands as inhabited territories located on the margins of a certain state and subject to contestation by the imaginations of various power centres, then the case of Macedonia represents a borderland *par excellence*. As we have seen above, Bulgaria, Greece, and Serbia were the main claimants to the Ottoman province of Macedonia. In anticipation of the Ottoman collapse in Europe, these Balkan rivals sought the national and religious allegiance of the inhabitants of the province, employing both propaganda and guerrilla tactics. Thus, from the 19th century to the present, Macedonia has also been "continually in flux," having its borders altered with each attempt of a (neighbouring/regional) nation–state to claim it as part of its imagined territories. [1] Furthermore, complicating matters were the several interventions by the Great Powers into this territory at the turn of the 20th century, alongside the (existing) involvements of the Ottoman and Balkan states. In this regard, as I showed in previous chapters by taking into consideration international, regional, and (less) local complexities based on top–down approaches, this chapter will rather deploy a bottom–up approach. On the one hand, the chapter aims to open up a discussion on the extraordinary imperial(ist) administration in Ottoman Macedonia of the late Hamidian Period (1878–1909) from a top–down perspective, and on the responses to this policy by different actors from a bottom–up perspective. While the international and Ottoman state perspectives have been elaborated in several works,[2] the current literature on the Macedonian Questions has so far dealt only partly with bottom–up perspective(s), leaving a room for the posing of various (relevant) questions. Thus, most of this literature[3] take socio–political actors such as IMARO, Chetnik Guerrilla Organisation, Committee of the Union and Progress, etc. as ethno–nationally primordial and does/do not analyse them as constructed entities that emerged through various complexities of negotiation and

---

[1] Yosmaoğlu, *Constructing National Identity*, pp. 160–188.
[2] See aforementioned works by: Nadine Lange–Akhund, Gül Tokay, Mehmet Hacısalihoğlu, Fikret Adanır etc. mentioned in Introduction.
[3] See aforementioned works by: Nikola Pandevski, Kyril Drezov, Tome Boshevski, Aristotel Tentov etc.

interaction. In contrast, my research moves beyond reductive national–historic and Eurocentric perspectives, while "giving a voice" to less researched communities that established entanglements and transfers of a multidirectional character as their response to the Ottoman administration. In line with the latter, Isa Blumi suggests that Ottoman Macedonians (and other Balkan nations) did not have a quintessential "fixed identity" prior to the trauma of the Balkan Wars of 1912 and 1913; and he warns against a teleological emphasis of their national belonging.[4] Moreover, Isa Blumi, Selim Deringil, Ussama Makdisi, and others draw attention to the possibilities rather than restrictions of identities during the late Ottoman Empire. In this chapter, I (try to) analyse the processes that took place on the ground, the ways in which the imagination of Macedonia was contested among different groups, gangs, and organisations, and their respective responses. However, I maintain the awareness that sometimes the states and revolutionaries on the ground had (mutually) differing responses as well, participated in different programs, and lobbied for diverse and sometimes contradictory strategies. Hence, it should not be assumed that inside the states' politics and these communities or gangs there was a unified, proto–, or supra–national sensibility. Rather their ambitions were varied and contested, and the discussions on Ottoman Macedonia too often resulted in clashes and contradictory tendencies. In this regard, the aim of this chapter is to analyse their contested political agendas and detached strategies, to trace their networks comparatively, and to investigate their entanglements, cooperation and interconnectivity through various historical examples in order to deconstruct statist Balkan historiographies and Eurocentric points of view.

4.1. International Intervention(s) and Local Organisations in Ottoman Macedonia

At the turn of the 20th century a general Eurocentric point of view continued to be present in the media, which presented the Muslim population of the Ottoman Empire as "barbaric" in nature, and the Christian population as tortured under their yoke. For this purpose, there

---

[4] Isa Blumi, *Foundations of Modernity: Human Agency and the Imperial State* (New York: Routledge, 2011); Isa Blumi, *Reinstating the Ottomans – Alternative Balkan Modernities (1800–1912)* (London: Palgrave Macmillan, 2011), p. 115.

were several interventions in the Ottoman Empire organised by Great Powers such as Great Britain, France, Germany, Austro–Hungary, and Russia. The intervention in Ottoman Macedonia warrants consideration in the context of the European powers' imperial rivalries in the Ottoman space, and of the European powers' relations with the Ottoman Empire in the aftermath of the Congress of Berlin (1878).

During this period, the Ottoman Empire served as a testing ground for humanitarian intervention, where in fact many European powers were interested in the Armenian, Cretan, and Macedonian cases in the Empire.[5] In order to further attract the European public, the Macedonian and Armenian revolutionaries led various uprisings for the implementation of their local or regional agendas. Bulgarian nationalists in particular made Macedonia the focal point of their expansionist projects, where their imagination clashed with that of Greek and Serbian nationalists. Towards the end of the century, Albanian nationalist propaganda, favouring its population, came to play a further destabilising role. Such events on the ground also clashed with the Ottoman state centralisation policy, often reinterpreted in European media as a struggle of the local Christian population against "Ottoman barbarity." [6] Thus, the *"principes d'humanite"* of the intervention in Ottoman Macedonia were evoked in diplomatic and governmental correspondence, as well as in the press and pamphlets. For instance, the French liberal and socialist politicians, as well as journalists and intellectuals, expressed interest in the Macedonian Questions in various newspapers like *"Le Temps"* and *"L'Aurore"* or French international law reviews like *"Revue Générale de Droit International Public."*[7] They were searching for a legitimate power for interventions into the Ottoman Empire, because the "[Ottomans] were a presence of this offensive return of barbarism (*en presence de ce retour*

---

[5] Ibid.

[6] David Rodogno, "The 'Principles of Humanity' and the European Powers' Intervention in Ottoman Lebanon and Syria in 1860–1861," in *Humanitarian Intervention: A History*, eds. Brendan Simms and David J. B. Trim (Cambridge: Cambridge University Press 2011), p. 183.

[7] Among the supporters of Macedonian issue were journalists such as: Victor Bérard in the *Revue de Paris*, René Henry in the *Correspondant*, and Raymond Recouly in the *Revue Politique et Parlementaire*.

offensif de la barbarie)."[8] Furthermore, the Ottoman centralisation project that clashed with the local population was rather reinterpreted in the light of Bulgarian and Greek or Christian atrocities, than a conflict for revenues as part of the aim of the Ottoman centralisation to retrieve its peripheries (Macedonia). In one such example, written by philo–Macedonians in France, it was emphasised that "[a]s of the present, the Christians of Armenia and Macedonia are the most massacred subjects of the Sultan, there is a patrimonial glory of France to protect these Christians of the Orient." [9] This protection of the Christians of the Orient was often represented as an obligation since the Crusade times (*Cette protection date du jour même des Croisades*). As a part of this obligation, there was also the façade of "a grand moral idea that had enveloped all European nations in the unity of one religious' belief. This force had risen against the unity of the invader who came from Asia."[10]

Numerous authors in Great Britain who had animated the debate on the Armenian Question now participated in the related issue of the Macedonian Questions. Especially active was the centre of philo–Macedonian agitation, known as the London Balkan Committee, which aimed to promote discussions and form an opinion about "justice and humanity."[11] Despite this expertise, the Balkan Committee began with many preconceived ideas and was not promoting "justice and humanity" in a proper manner. Noel Buxton's 1907 book named *"Europe and the Turks"* stated that atrophies like those in Congo were deplorable because they were carried out by Europeans, but that those of the Ottoman Empire were the "greatest atrocity on the surface of the world, because the sufferers themselves [were] civilised beings."[12] Thus, he stressed that his

---

[8] Victor Berard, Pierre Quillard and Francis de Pressense, *Pour l'Arménie et la Macédoine* (Paris: Societe Nouvelle de librairie & D'edition, 1904), p. 38.

[9] Ibid., p. 48; in original: *"Mais puisqu'aujourd'hui les chrétiens d'Arménie et de la Macédoine sont les plus massacres des sujets du Sultan, permettez–moi de vous rappeler que la protection des chretiens d'Orient est dans le patrimoine glorieux de notre France."*

[10] Ibid., p. 48; in original: *"En ces temps–là, dans la chrétienté, la force matérielle s'était mise au service d'une grande idée morale qui avait enveloppé toutes les nations européennes dans l'unite d'une seule croyance religieuse. Cette force s'était levée contre l'unité d'une seule l'envahisseur qui venait de l'Asie."*

[11] Rodogno, *Against Massacre*, p. 235.

[12] Noel Buxton, *Europe and the Turks* (London: Routledge, 2020), p. 130. The book was first published in 1912; David Rodogno, "The European Powers' Intervention in

book was supposed to enlighten the British public about Macedonia or "the field of the great battle between the East and West – between barbarism and civilisation."[13]

This Pro–Macedonian agitation against the "Ottoman barbarity" rapidly became transnational, probably because of the previous experience of the Armenian movements who were supressed by the 'Ottoman barbarians.' News and reports were published everywhere, describing the Christian atrocities as dreadful in order to awaken readers' interest.[14] By lobbying for diplomatic intervention in the name of "humanity" and "civilisation," the intervening states acted collectively, politically, and militarily united on behalf of the Christians in the Ottoman Empire. On 23 September 1902, when the Bulgarian speaking men crossed the Ottoman frontier during the uprisings in Djumaja, it attracted a great deal of interest among the Great Powers and incited them to get more involved into these events. Although the crisis was not provoked by the local civilian population, but from the neighbouring countries, it was popularised by the Great Powers and European media. The Ottoman forces easily suppressed the uprising induced by neighbouring Bulgaria, but this action was denounced by Europeans as "the barbaric actions" of Ottoman soldiers.[15]

The locals organised informational campaigns that suited their political purpose. For instance, a member of a Macedonian organisation in Bulgaria (the Supreme Macedonian Committee) sent Stojan Mihajlovski (a local intellectual) on a tour of the European capitals to report that regular Ottoman troops massacred women and children. Neighbouring countries and local agents were aware that those massacres and atrocities would increase the possibility of intervention from the Great Powers. These actors also knew that evidence of the Ottoman authorities' unwillingness or incapacity to put an end to the massacres would further increase the likelihood of a humanitarian intervention.[16] According to Biliotti, "the

---

Macedonia, 1903–1908: an Instance of Humanitarian Intervention?," in *Humanitarian Intervention: A History,* eds. Brendan Simms and David J. B. Trim (Cambridge: Cambridge University Press, 2011), p. 215.

[13] Ibid., p. 215.

[14] Rodogno, *Against Massacre*, p. 236.

[15] Ibid.

[16] Rodogno, "The European Powers' Intervention in Macedonia," p. 208. See also: Gustav Hubka, "Bandenkämpfe: Erfahrungen der makedonischen Reformgendarmerie

publication of accounts of atrocities alleged to have taken place in Macedonia in 1902 and 1903, was purely a strategy designed to rouse Europe to intervene on behalf of the Bulgarians."[17]

4.1.1. The Great Powers and the Ottoman Administration in the Three Vilayets

In Constantinople, British ambassador Sir O'Conor personally relayed to Sultan Abdulhamid the necessity of implementing "meaningful reforms" in Macedonia. The British reported the situation in Macedonia as "worrisome and grave." Along these lines, the French ambassador to St. Petersburg warned that "the Great Powers had to act in order to forestall the unrest to come in Macedonia."[18] On 30 November, therefore, Ottoman Sultan Abdulhamid issued an *irade* or decree for reforms in the three vilayets of Macedonia titled *Rumeli Vilayetleri Hakkında Bir Talimat* (Instructions for the Rumelian Provinces) and established the *Umumi Rumeli Müfettişliği* (Rumelian Inspectorate for Reforms). The decree consisted of 18 articles, divided into four chapters. Sultan Abdulhamid decreed that "the administration, instruction, public works, and the judiciary in Macedonia were to remain under Ottoman control."[19]

Additionally, on 8 December 1902 the Sultan appointed Hüseyin Hilmi Pasha as inspector–general for the European provinces of the Ottoman Empire in order to prevent interference by the European powers in Ottoman Macedonia.[20] Nevertheless, the Ottoman overtures were not sufficient to avoid the Great Powers' interference in Macedonia. Two Great Powers (Russia and Austria–Hungary) had a particular and direct interest in those territories and observed the events on the ground. They were not satisfied with the Ottoman reinforcement of its peripheries and observed the reforms introduced by the Sultan with extreme skepticism. The Austro–Hungarian and Imperial Russian emissars to Istanbul, Heinrich Chalice and M.I. Zinoviev, accepted the duty to formulate the

---

Offiziere," *Streffleurs militärische Zeitschrift: Organ der militärwissenschaftlichen Vereiene* 90/2 (1909): 1501–1526.

[17] Perry, *The Politics of Terror.*

[18] Yosmaoğlu, *Blood Ties.*

[19] Ibid.

[20] BOA. Y. PRK. HR. 33/63.

joint plan for reforms in Ottoman Macedonia. This plan of reforms contained six points that became known as the Vienna Plan. On 21 February 1903, the Russian foreign minister, Count Wladimir Lamsdorff, and his counterpart from Dual Monarchy, Count Agenor Goluchowski, presented this plan to the Ottoman leadership. According to this plan, the Ottoman inspector–general was to serve for a preordained time period in Macedonia with the assistance of the Great Powers, in order to achieve his obligations according to the planned reforms. Furthermore, the gendarmerie was to be reorganised by foreign officers (as in Crete) recruited from the ranks of the Muslims and Christians. Furthermore, the government "had to take the necessary measures to suppress the crimes and offences committed during the revolt and to grant amnesty to all political prisoners."[21] Additionally, fiscal reforms were also required, together with reorganisation of the budget, because all the expenses were to be covered by the Ottoman state.[22] This interference of the Great Powers in Ottoman domestic affairs, brought about deep dissatisfaction in Istanbul and paralysed the Ottoman administration in the practice in Ottoman Macedonia. Moreover, the announcement of these new reforms resounded negatively throughout the region as well the discontent of Istanbul caused a wave of negative reactions in the (Ottoman Macedonian) region as well. Bulgaria questioned the moderation of the Austro–Russian requirements, while the Serbian government criticised the lack of guarantees for the manner in which they were to be applied. Furthermore, many actors on the ground opposed these interventions and reforms enforced by the Great Powers and their acceptance by the Ottoman Empire. As an expression of their dissatisfation, they organised several protests and an uprising during 1903, and the most important event, known as the Ilinden Uprising, ensued in August. With quick suppression of the uprising by the Ottoman state, the Vienna Plan lay dead. The gravity of the situation caused a second set of interventions by the Great Powers. Thus, in September, Tsar Nicholas II of Russia visited Emperor Francis Joseph of Dual Monarchy in Mürzsteg (today Austria), where they signed a new memorandum. In content the memorandum was identical to the Vienna Programme, and called for the

---

[21] Rodogno, "The European Powers' Intervention in Macedonia," p. 211.
[22] Ibid.

appointment of Austro–Hungarian and Russian civil agent to supervise the reforms of the administration, judiciary, and local gendarmerie in the three vilayets. The participation of the local Christian in these institutions was to be managed by an Ottoman statesman known as Hüseyin Hilmi Pasha, the Inspector–General of Macedonia. [23] According to the Mürzsteg programme, each Great Power appointed an advisory official to the Ottoman official in charge of reforming the gendarmerie in each province.[24] Dual Monarchy (Austro–Hungary) appointed personnel to the

---

[23] BOA.Y.PRK.MK.12/43. 28 Kanun-ı Sani 1318

[24] Nadine, *The Macedonian Question*, pp. 142–144; Hacısalihoğlu, *Die Jungtürken und die Mazedonische Frage*; See: Mürzsteg programme of nine articles:

1. In order to establish control of the activity of local Ottoman authorities concerning the application of reforms, Civil Special Agents from Austria–Hungary and Russia are appointed to the office of Hilmi Pasha, and obligated to accompany the General Inspector everywhere, to call his attention to the needs of the Christian population, signal him the abuses of local authorities, transmit their recommendations to the Ambassadors in Constantinople, and inform their Governments of all that happens in the country. As aides to the Agents, Secretaries and Drogmans could be appointed and charged with the execution of their orders and are authorised to tour the districts in order to question the inhabitants of Christian villages, supervise local authorities, etc.

The mission of the Civil Agents is to watch over the introduction of reforms and the appeasement of the populations; their commission will expire in two years starting from the day of their nomination. The Sublime Porte will prescribe to the local authorities to grant these Agents all the assistance so that they can fulfill their mission.

2. Since the reorganisation of the gendarmerie and the Turkish police constitutes the most essential measure for the pacification of the country, it is urgent to ask the Sublime Porte for the introduction of this reform.

Taking in consideration, however, that the Swedish officers and other people employed until presently, who do not know the language or the local conditions, and did not render themselves useful, it would be desirable to introduce modifications and supplements in the initial project as follows:

a) The reorganisation of the gendarmerie in the three vilayets will be entrusted to a general of foreign nationality, in the service of the Imperial Ottoman Government, to whom could be added Deputies, among the military personnel of Great Powers, who would share the circumscriptions between them and who would act as supervisors, instructors and promoters. In this way they would also oversee the behavior of troops towards the population.

b) These officers will ask, if it appears necessary to them, for the addition of a certain number of officers and under–officers of foreign nationality.

3. As soon as an appeasement of the country will be noted, the Ottoman Government will be asked for a modification in the administrative di- vision of the territory in view of a more reGülar grouping of different nationalities.

4. Require simultaneously the reorganisation of administrative and judicial institutions, and it would be desirable to open their access to

sanjak of Üsküp (Skopje), while Imperial Russia to the sanjak of Thessaloniki, France to the sanjak of Siroz, and Great Britain to the sanjak of Drama. In accordance with this, the Inspectorate underwent a fundamental transformation in the years 1903–1909 in line with the reform schemes for Ottoman Macedonia drawn up by the European powers. The interventions entailed protracted and comprehensive interference in Ottoman internal affairs, which the Great Powers considered a necessity and viewed the Ottoman administrative capacity as "barbarous" and "half civilised." In the following years, these "civilisation measures" exacerbated the situation on the ground and brought about complications by not only further weakening the Ottoman administration, but also by encouraging the communities involved to take advantage of it and to express their political or national aspirations. Thus, David Rodogno stressed that "nineteenth–century international law established a discriminatory hierarchy among European and non–European states, based on the principle of the alleged superiority of European civilisation,"[25] and in practice this "superiority" greatly intensified the gang conflict following 1903 and brought about the failure of the Ottoman government in 1908.

---

indigenous Christians, and to encourage local autonomy.

5. Establish immediately in the principal centers of vilayets Mixed Commissions formed of an equal number of Christian and Moslems Delegates for the examination of political and other crimes perpetrated during the troubles. The consular representatives of Austria–Hungary and Russia should participate in these Commissions.

6. Require the Turkish Government to allocate special funds for:
a) reinstatement, in the localities of their origin, the Christian
families which took refuge in Bulgaria or elsewhere.
b) help the Christians who lost their wealth and homes.
c) restore houses, churches and schools, destroyed by Turks during the insurrection.
Such commissions will decide the distribution of these funds with the participation of notable Christians. Austro–Hungarian and Russian consuls will supervise their use.

7. In the Christian villages burned by Turkish troops and Bashi–Bazouks, the reinstated Christian inhabitants will be free of payment of all taxes during the year.

8. The Ottoman Government will reintroduce with no further delay the reforms mentioned in the project formulated in February of the current year as well as those which become subsequently necessary.

9. As most of the excesses and cruelties were perpetrated by ilaves (Redifs of II class) and Bashi–Bazouks, it is urgent that the first are laid off, and that the formation of gangs of Bashi–Bazouks be absolutely prevented.

[25] Rodogno, "The 'Principles of Humanity'," p. 160.

4.1.2. The Ottoman Administration and the Local Actors in Macedonia

After the Berlin Treaty (1878) Ottomans believed the survival of the Empire depended upon the preservation of their remaining territories in the Balkans. This included strengthening of central power and preventing Bulgarian, Greek, and Serbian activisms in Macedonia, which had serious aspirations towards these territories, which they viewed as an issue to be exploited when the time was ripe. Therefore, the Macedonian Question became the core cause of tension not only among these states but prior to the Balkan Wars, amongst the Great Powers too. One of the major Ottoman concerns was undoubtedly the establishment of the new Bulgarian state, with its many unsettled questions. The decisive factor was the fundamental ambition of all Bulgarians to regain the Macedonian provinces they had lost at the Congress of Berlin. Soon after the Treaty, the Bulgarians increased their activities in the Macedonian provinces through the influence of the Exarchate by establishing cultural ties and sending clergy and teachers from the Principality to awaken the national aspirations of the populace, while at the same time there were those revolutionary activists who believed the only way to regain the lost territories was to take arms.[26] In order to manage this chaos, the Ottoman state took measures to integrate its peripheries and to extend its influence to the local population. The Hamidian regime tried to apply a strategy in the peripheries known as "avoiding the source of trouble (*çıban başı koparmamak*)" or "no discontents (*sızıltı çıkarmamak*)."[27] The common core of this strategy among the leaders of the Ottoman Empire was to create a hegemonic presence – a single authoritative rule – even in the far corners of society. The goal was to penetrate society deeply enough to shape how individuals throughout the society identified themselves, while the role of the state

---

[26] Tokay, *The Macedonian Question,* pp. 2–7; Janet Klein, "Çevreyi İdar Etmek: Osmanlı Devleti Ve Hamidiye Alayları." in *Türkiye'de ordu, devlet ve güvenlik siyaseti*, eds. Evren Balta Paker and İsmet Akça (Istanbul: İstanbul Bilgi Üniversitesi Yayınları, 2010), pp. 105–124.

[27] Kemal H. Karpat, *The Politicisation of Islam: Reconstructing Identity, State, Faith, and Community in the Late Ottoman State* (Oxford: Oxford University Press 2001), p. 237; Gökhan Çetinsaya, "II. Abdülhamid'in iç politikası: Bir dönemlendirme denemesi," *Osmanlı araştırmaları/The Journal of Ottoman Studies* 47 (2016), p. 383; Gökhan Çetinsaya, "'Çıban başı koparmamak': II. Abdülhamid rejimine yeniden Bakış," *Türkiye Günlüğü* 58 (Kasım–Aralık 1999): 54–64.

apparatus was to provide such far–reaching domination. It included vertically connected agencies to promote the "state's system of meaning and legitimacy; to make universal rules (legislative bodies); to execute those rules (bureaucracies); to adjudicate (courts), and to coerce (armies and police)."[28] However, it is worth noting that the states did not succeed in establishing their own domination by default without negotiating with local actors. It often happened that state apparatus ended up with disengagement or a lack of engagement in the local arena. Thus, failures to engage in arena struggles in even the most remote parts of the country affected the state in the capital city.[29] In this context, the lack of capacity of the Ottoman Empire to penetrate into the (deep layers of the) society in the European/Rumeli provinces, transformed Ottoman Macedonia into a cradle of revolutionary and guerrilla organisations. Hence, the Ottoman state found itself increasingly facing a new sort of challenge to establish a public order that ended up without successful results. Besides, neighbouring states and locals formed revolutionary and guerrilla organisations in an attempt to transfer the fight onto an international platform. For instance, in the 1880s, many of these organisations started to appear in Belgrade, Sofia, and in Athens with the aim of fomenting agitation in Macedonia. Two groups existed among the Serbs, one (the Society of Saint Sava) representing the convictions that any and all Serbian activities should be directed from Belgrade, the other, founded by the Metropolitan of Üsküp (the Serbian Chetnik Organisation), favouring independent action. In similar ways, organisations appeared in Sofia, Athens, and Thesaloniki, which were founded to provide Greek or Bulgarian state agendas, or working independently for the "Macedonian

---

[28] Ibid. pp. 24; Joel S. Migdal, "The State in Society: Struggles and Accommodations in Multiple Arenas," *States and Social Structures Newsletter* 13 (1990): 2–3; According to Joel S. Migdal, there are four ideal types of conflict between state and social forces. Firstly, the state can completely transform society. Secondly, the state can partially transform society and allow social forces to have a symbolic presence. Thirdly, existing social forces can incorporate the state. Lastly, the state may fail in its attempt to penetrate society.

[29] Joel S. Migdal, Atul Kohli and Vivienne Shue (eds.), *State Power and Social Forces: Domination and Transformation in the Third World* (Cambridge: Cambridge University Press, 1994). p. 26; Andreas Kosmas Lyberatos, "Introduction: Through Nation and State: Reform and Nationalism 'from Below' in the Late Ottoman Balkans," *Turkish Historical Review* 7/2 (2016): 121–133, here in 123.

cause." Not only among the Christian population, but also among the Muslim communities in Macedonia, the Albanian intellectuals demanded autonomy with a reorganisation of their provinces under an Albanian governor. In order to calm down discontent among the local population in Macedonia, the Grand Vizier, Said Pasha came up with a series of reforms in legal, financial, educational, and agricultural areas and reorganised the police and gendarmerie. As has been mentioned in previous chapter, Said Pasha proposed reforms for the Albanian–populated areas.[30] However, the Ottoman initiatives did not satisfy the local Christian communities, which maintained their activities with the expectation of attracting European attention and a possible intervention. The turning point in the Macedonian developments, however, was the Ilinden Uprising, which had always been a part of the IMARO (Internal Macedonian–Adrianople Revolutionary Organisation) agenda, and which began at Saint Iliya's Day (*Ilinden*) on 2 August in the Manastir vilayet.[31] Hence, neither did the Ottoman reforms nor the European intervention in the form of the Vienna Plan and Murszteg programme satisfy the local and regional actors. The Bulgarian intellectuals and politicians were disappointed because they hoped for at least an autonomous Macedonia with a Christian governor–general. The Greek and Serb representatives might have expressed their satisfaction with the reforms but this did not prevent them from intensifying their activities on the ground. It soon became obvious that conflicts on the ground were not just between the "barbarous Ottomans" and "civilised Christians," but also among the Christian population itself. In this regard, the Greek government insisted that many of these "Greek bands" in Macedonia did not feel any hostility against the Ottomans, rather they openly stated that the hostilities were directed "against the Bulgarian bands."[32] Accordingly, neither the "Ottoman barbarity" nor the Great

---

[30] Gül Tokay, "Macedonian Question, 1878–1908," in *War and Diplomacy, The Russo–Turkish War of 1877–1878 and the Treaty of Berlin,* eds. Hakan Yavuz and Peter Sluglett (Salt Lake City: Utah University Press, 2011). pp. 15–17.

[31] Ibid. p. 17.

[32] Ibid., p. 20; BBA, HRSYS 1772/30, Rifat to Tevfik, Athens, 19 November 1904; It was not until 1905 that Hilmi Pasha and other local authorities became aware that the Greek movement had become uncontrollable, and that measures needed to be taken to stop their rebellious actions and the assistance they received from mainland Greeks, including their government; See: Robert Shannan Peckham, "Internal Colonialism: Nation and Region

Powers' "civilised measures" could bring peace in the provinces, rather both communities, the Christian and the Muslim, once again stepped up their activities in plain view of the Great Powers and Ottoman officials.

4.2. The Networks of Local Organisations in Ottoman Macedonia

The failure of the Vienna and Mürszteg Reforms led to a continuing increase in the power of the Macedonian revolutionaries and their engagements against the Ottoman state or other organisations on the ground. Such groups attacked the Ottoman railway's telegraph post in January 1903; detonated a bomb on the Salonika–Constantinople railroad line at the Perai Station; in May 1903 a group of anarchists in Thessaloniki attacked the Ottoman Bank, while the major uprising was staged on 2 August of the same year. As I elaborated above, neither the Great Powers nor the Ottoman state could bring order into Ottoman Macedonia. The reforms were not implemented according to the plans of the powerful states, rather they often needed to be negotiated with the local population. Also, the "civilised measures" introduced by the Great Powers in the form of reforms failed on the ground. Even the "Ottoman barbarity" could not suppress local gangs anymore. Commenting on these developments, Joel Samuel Migdal points out that patterns of domination on the ground are determined by key struggles in society's "multiple arenas of domination and opposition."[33] Officials at different levels of the international arena or state levels can be the key figures in these struggles – interacting or conflicting – with an entire constellation of social forces in disparate arenas. From the one side, the various struggles can move societies towards integrated domination where the state enforces broad power, while from the other side the conflicts and violence developes in the "multiple arenas of domination and opposition" that leads to dispersed

---

in Nineteenth–Century Greece" in *Balkan Identities: Nation and Memory*, ed. Maria Todorova (London: Hurst & Company, 2004), pp. 41–59; Spiros Tsoutsoumpis, "Land of the Kapedani: Brigandage, Paramilitarism and Nation–building in 20th Century Greece," *Balkan Studies* 51 (2016): 35–67; Theodora Dragostinova, "Continuity vs. Radical Break: National Homogenization Campaigns in the Greek–Bulgarian Borderlands before and after the Balkan Wars," *Journal of Genocide Research* 18/4 (2016): 405–426; Dmitar Tasić, *Paramilitarism in the Balkans: Yugoslavia, Bulgaria, and Albania, 1917–1924* (Oxford: Oxford University Press, 2020).
[33] Migdal, *State Power*, p. 9.

domination. This dispersed domination means that neither the state, nor any other social force manages to achieve countrywide domination.[34] In the Ottoman Macedonian context, there were various local organisations that struggled to achieve this countrywide domination and opposed the central power and the reforms introduced by the Great Powers. From their inception, these organisations, whether pro–Macedonian, pro–Bulgarian, pro–Greek, pro–Albanian, or pro–Serb, who had already witnessed the failure of the Armenians, made it clear that they did not believe in the efficiency of the Vienna or Mürzsteg programs.[35] In what follows, this chapter will analyse the relations between these organisations on the ground, by placing the actors in a trans–regional context from a "bottom–up" perspective and analysing their activities from "inside" the organisations.

4.2.1. Internal Macedonian–Adrianople Revolutionary Organisation (IMARO): National or Supra–National?

After the Gorna Cuma uprising in 1902, the Dual Monarchy and Imperial Russia took the initiative for introducing reforms in Macedonia. Abdulhamid II was aware of the imminent imposition of radical reforms and pre–empted them by introducing his own programme in December 1902. However, this programme was not directed only at "three vilayets," but rather to Rumelia as a whole. In this respect, Sultan introduced a new administrative unit known as the *Rumeli Umum Müfettisligi* (General Inspectorate of Rumeli). At its head of the Inspectorate was appointed Hüseyin Hilmi Pasha, a veteran of the Ottoman administration who had held, among other posts, the governorship of Adana and Yemen.[36] On the other hand, the Vienna Plan was presented by Dual Monarchy and Imperial Russia to the Ottoman government in February 1903 and was immediately accepted by Sultan Abdulhamid II, but in the practice, it remained a dead letter. The consensus among the Great Powers was in favour of keeping the *status quo* in Ottoman Macedonia rather than supporting any ideas of autonomy. As we have already seen, at the turn of the 20th century various state actors were involved in Ottoman Macedonia that were analysed by

---

[34] Ibid., p. 9.
[35] Rodogno, *Against Massacre,* p. 230.
[36] Yosmaoğlu, *Blood Ties*, p. 33. Adanır, *Die makedonische Frage*, p. 99.

several scholars. To the contrary, the organisations on the ground were analysed less and have not been covered in detail yet, thus, I undertake here the "bottom–up" approach and try to highlight the multiple decisions taken by the local population. In this regard, I argue that the situation at the local level was much more complex than what has been represented by nationalist historiographies. These "specialists in violence" on the ground, as Charles Tilly has termed them,[37] often included military personnel, guards, jailers, gang leaders, bandits or executioners. They were often cooperating with states or political entrepreneurs such as teachers, priests, and intellectuals, but also worked outside of government. Guerrilla warriors, fighters, armed guards, paramilitary forces, bandits or any members of fighting bands, sometimes enjoyed governmental protection, but it was also the case that they operated outside of government that enabled them to take multiple decisions. Such examples one can find among the Internal Macedonian–Adrianople Revolutionary Organisation (IMARO, often referred as IMRO)[38] members, who were a miscellaneous group of people that often–supported various strategies and cooperated with different states (or local leaders) for achieving distinct and blended aims. From one side, this organisation had been often marked by an ethnic "Bulgarian" since its establishment, while from other side, it is represented as multi–ethnical organisation that was supposed to include various people

---

[37] Tilly, *The Politics*, p. 40; Radomir Milašinović and Nenad Putnik, "Gerila kao specifičan vid društvenog konflikta," in *Guerrilla in the Balkans: Freedom Fighters, Rebels or Bandits – Researching the Guerrilla and Paramilitary Forces in the Balkans*, eds. Momčilo Pavlović, Tetsuya Sahara and Predgrad J. Marković (Tokyo/Beograd: University Meiji, Institute for Disarmament and Peace Studies, Tokyo – Institute of Contemporary History, Beograd/ Faculty for Security Studies, Beograd, 2007), pp. 337–338; Alf Lüdtke, "Akteure: Täter, Opfer, Zuschauer," in *Gewalt: Ein Intedisziplinäres Handbuch*, eds. Christian Gudehus and Michaela Christ (Stuttgart/Weimar: Verlag J. B. Metzler, 2013), pp. 177–183; Alf Lüdtke, "Introduction: What Is the History of Everyday Life and Who Are Its Practitioners?" in *The History of Everyday Life: Reconstructing Historical Experiences and Ways of Life*, ed. Alf Lüdtke (Princeton, NJ: Princeton University Press, 1995), pp. 3–40.

[38] In its initial years, this group was referred to by various names including "Macedonian Revolutionary Organisation/Committee" or "Bulgarian Macedonian–Adrianople Revolutionary Committees" between 1896–1902, "Secret Macedonian–Adrianople Revolutionary Organisation" from 1902–1905, and finally "Internal Macedonian–Adrianople Revolutionary Organisation" since 1905. Since the 1920s also known as IMRO (VMRO). See: Lange–Akhund, *The Macedonian*; Adanır, *Die makedonische Frage.*

living in Macedonia. However, in order to understand the IMARO and profiles of its members, one should take a closer look at the genesis of the movement. At the beginning, this movement was organised in Thessaloniki on 23 October 1893 by six local young men from Macedonia – Andon Dimitrov, Damyan Gruev, Hristo Tatarchev, Hristo Batandzhiev, Ivan Hadzhinikolov, and Petar Pop Arsov. Furthermore, most of their members attended or were closely related to the Bulgarian School in Solun that was mentioned in Chapter Three. Out of the six founding members, four were teachers who studied abroad. Dame Gruev, Petar Pop Arsov, and Ivan Hadzinikolov lived in Bulgaria, where they were influenced by nationalist and socialist ideas that were popular in Europe. In Sofia in 1891–1892, all three of them participated in "the Young Macedonian Literary Association,"[39] whose members created a magazine called *Loza* (*Grapevine*) in 1892–1894 under the leadership of Pop Arsov.[40] In the beginning this group of intellectuals insisted firstly on the implementation of Article 23; secondly, at this early stage the idea encompassed not only Macedonia, but also Adrianople; and thirdly, there were two basic opinions in the discussions of the goal – autonomy or direct annexation with Bulgaria. It appears likely that at the early stages of the struggle, a desired outcome of the autonomy for the regions of Macedonia and Adrianople was terminal unification with Bulgaria.[41] In this regard, in 1901, one of its leaders Gotse Delchev, emphasised the political aims against the Ottomans:

---

[39] The Young Macedonian Literary Society was established in Bulgaria in 1891 with the aim of protecting the various Macedonian regional dialects. However, the official newspaper of the People's Liberal Party, 'Liberty (*Svoboda*),' accused the society of promoting separatism from the Bulgarian national cause. In response to these accusations, the members of the society stated that they did not support separatist ideas, and emphasised that their ideal was to promote unity within the entire Bulgarian nation. See: Dimitar Kosev, Hristo Hristov, Nikolay Todorov and Valentin Stankov, *Makedonia – Sbornik ot dokumenti i materiali* (Sofia, Izdatelstvo na Bŭlgarskata Akademia Naukite, 1978).

[40] See also State Archives of North Macedonia (DARSM) in Skopje,v IV.102/1894, 94, inv.br. 280/76, discussed also in Novini, No. 94, Istanbul/Tsarigrad–Örtaköy, 26 August 1894.

[41] Jonathan Bousfield and Dan Richardson, *Bulgaria* (London: Rough Guides, 2002.), p. 450; Daskalov, *Bulgarian Historical Review;* Stepanov, *The Bulgars*; Miller, *Bulgaria During the Second World War*; Mazower, *The Balkans*.

"...We have to fight for the autonomy of the regions of Macedonia and Adrianople as a stage for their future unification with our common fatherland, Bulgaria."[42]

Furthermore, its primary name Bulgarian Macedonian–Adrianople Revolutionary Committees emphasised a Bulgarian element that was also evident in its first Constitution (*Ustav*). In the first chapter of the Constitution, the Organisation outlined its goals in Art. 1. "to secure full political autonomy for the regions of Macedonia and Adrianople;" and in Art. 2. "to achieve this goal they (the committees) shall raise the awareness of self–defence in the Bulgarian population (*bulgarskoto naselenie*) in the regions" and "to prepare and carry on a general uprising (*edno povsemvstvo vostanne*)."[43] In this respect, one of its members Hristo Tatarchev, emphasised the importance of the 'Bulgarian element' within the words:

"We discussed the aims of this organisation at length and later we settled on the autonomy of Macedonia, with the predominance of the Bulgarian element. We could not accept the principle of the 'direct unification of Macedonia with Bulgaria' because we could see that this would be opposed by the Great Powers and by the aspirations of the small neighbouring states and Turkey. It came to our minds that an autonomous Macedonia could later be more easily united with Bulgaria, or, if this could not be achieved,

---

[42] Kosev et al., *Makedoniya*, about Gotse Delchev's statment in 1901: "*...Treba da se borime za avtonomnosta na Makedania i Odrinsko, za da gi zachuvame vo nivnata tselost, kako eden etap za idnoto im prisoedinuvanye kon opshtata Bŭlgarska Tatkovina.*" See also State Archives of North Macedonia (DARSM) in Skopje, v IV.101/1943 edin broj, 21.04.1903 – 21–5–1943, inv.dr. 278/76, discussed also in "Gotse Delchev List", 21.iv. 1903, and 2.v.1943 g. on 25.06.1902, Sofia. About Gotse Delchev's short biographical description see: Adanır, *Die makedonische Frage*, p. 119.: Quote: "*Es war der makedonische Revolutionär Gotse Delchev (1872—1903), der sich diese Auffassung zu eigen machte und versuchte, sie in die Praxis umzusetzen. Delechev war im Jahre 1891, nach Abschluß der sechsten Klasse des bulgarischen Gymnasiums in Saloniki, in die Offiziersschule von Sofia aufgenommen worden. In Sofia machte er von der Möglichkeit Gebrauch, die sozialistische Literatur der Zeit kennenzulernen. Bald geriet er unter den Einfluß bekannter makedonisch–bulgarischer Sozialisten, wie D. Blagoev, D. Hadzi Dimov und V. Glavinov. An den Aktivitäten verschiedener makedonischer Gruppierungen in Bulgarien nahm er regelmäßig teil.*"

[43] Ibid; Illustratsia Ilinden (Godina 8), Sofia, 1936; See also:DARSM,v IV.60/1902,24, v.br. 203/76, Skopje, discussed also in Delo,No. 24, Sofia, 25. June 1902.

211

it could be the uniting link of a federation of the Balkan peoples. The district of Odrin (Adrianople), as far as I remembered, did not enter into our programme at the beginning, and I think that later we thought of including the area as a part of an autonomous Macedonia."[44]

Similarly, another member of the organisation, Ivan Hadzhinikolov, in his memoirs lists the basic principles of the foundation of the Bulgarian Macedonian–Adrianople Revolutionary Committees including the moral and material help for the struggle of the Macedonian revolutionaries provided by the Bulgarian society. [45] In this respect, Tatarchev and Hadzinikolov admitted that the "Bulgarian element" and "Bulgarian society" generally played an important role in the Macedonian society and revolutionaries on the ground. Oftentimes, an autonomous status among its founding members was seen as a transitional step towards a possible unification with Bulgaria. Such were one part of these members who joined also the revolutionary organisation, known as the Supreme Macedonian Committee (SMC) or *Virhovists*.[46] This outcome was based on the example of short–lived Eastern Rumelia that was annexed by the

---

[44] Illustratsia Ilinden (Godina 8), Sofia, 1936 in Document No. 142. and 94: *"Deklaratsija ot TMORK sastavena ot Hr. Matov, dr. Tatarchev i Simeon Radev do predstavitelite na Velikite sili za prichinite dovely do izbuhvaneto na vastanieto v Makedonia i Odrinsko.";* Hristo Tatarchev, *Spomeni, dokumenti, materiali* (Sofia: Nauka i izkustvo, 1989); Memoari na Vatrashnata Organizatsia, Makedonia i Odrinsko (1893–1903), 1904; Lyubomir Miletich, *Materiali za Istoriata na makedonskoto osvoboditelno dvizhenie, kniga IX* (Sofia: Pechatnitsa P. Gluskov, 1928), p. 102. See in original: *"Raziskva se na dalgo varhu tselta na taya organizatsia i posetne se sprahme varhu avtonomiata na Makedonia sa predimstvo na bŭlgarskia elementa. Ne mozhehme da vzpriemem gledisheto – 'pryamo prisedinenie na Makedonia s Bŭlgaria,' zashoto vizhdahme, che tuy she sreshne golmi machnotii poradi protivodeystvieto na velikit sili i aspiraciit na susednit malki drzhavi i na Turcia. Minavashe ni prez uma, che edna avtonomna Makedonia setne bi mogla polesno da se sŭedini s Bŭlgaria, a v kraeni sluchay, ako tova ne se postigne, che she mozhe da posluzhi za obedinitelno zveno na edna federatsia na balkanskita narodi. Odrinsko, do kolkoto si pripomnyamŭ, prvonachalno ne vlizashe v nashata programa, i mislya che posetne se zamisli da se vklyuchi i taya oblast km avtonomna Makedonia."*
[45] Ibid. Illustratsia Ilinden (Godina 8), Sofia, 1936, b. I, p. 4–5; Lyubomir Miletich listed basic principles in his book: *Lyubomir Miletich, La Macédoine bulgare* (Sofia: La Cour royal, 1918).
[46] Yosmaoğlu, Blood Ties, p. 30; Adanır, *Die makedonische Frage*, pp. 111–116; Hacısalihoğlu, *Die Jungtürken und die Mazedonische Frage*, p. 113.

Principality of Bulgaria in 1885.[47] However, by that time the ideas among its other members had become contested from within and often oppositional to each other. Their understanding of autonomy for Macedonia was a multidimensional concept giving rise to various interpretations: some moved from the idea of unification with Bulgaria towards advocation of harmony among different communities in one Macedonian federation. Thus, few members belonged to a strong leftist and anarchistic wing(s) who opposed unification with Bulgaria. In this respect, some of its members moved away from an ethno–national concept of the Organisation and distanced themselves from the "Bulgarian element." In this spirit, Dame Gruev in his memoirs insists that the goal of the first Committee was "only a demand for the implementation of the Berlin Treaty" and that their motto was "implementation of the provisions of the Berlin Treaty."[48] Accordingly, the aims of the Organisation and its members were "continually in flux" and changed dramatically fast, especially inside the socialist circle, which supported a transformation of the Balkans into a federal state, in which Macedonia and Thrace would enter as equal members. In an article published in June, 1902, the IMARO revolutionaries promoted the idea of autonomy and the slogans

---

[47] At the beginning of XX century, they realised how useful a role the media played in their activism, therefore they started to publish newspapers, such as *Avtonomija: Zagranichen list na Vatreshnata Makedono–Odrinska organizatsia (1903), Revolutsyonen list: Vatreshna Makedono–Odrinska revolutsiyona organizatsia (1904–1906), Ilinden (1907–1908), Konstitutsionna zorya: Organ na Makedono–Odrinskata revolutsiona organizatsia (1908–1909)*; Apart from the newspaper, there were published also many anonymous books and documents: *Makedonia i Odrinsko 1893–1903, s dve karti: Memoar na Vatreshnata Organizatsia* (Sofia, 1904); or with authors such as: Hristo Matov, *Osnovi na vatreshnata revolyutsionna organizatsia* (Sofia: N.P., 1904); Hristo Matov, *Shto byahme – shto sme* (Plovdiv: N.P., 1905); Hristo Matov, *Za upravlenieto na Vatreshnata revolutsionna organizatsia* (Sofia: N.P., 1905); Hristo Matov, *Vastanishki deystvya* (Sofia: N.P., 1906); Angel Tomov and Georgi Bazhdarov, *Revolutsionnata borba v Makedonia* (Sofiia: N.P.,1917); Or books that recorded the memoirs of the events before the Balkan Wars: Lyubomir Miletich, *Materiali za istoriata na makedonskoto osvobitelno dvizhenie; kniga I–IX (*Sofia: N.P., 1925–1928); Stane Avramov, *Materiali za istoryata na makedonskoto osvobitelno dvizhenie; kniga X* (Sofia: 1929); Bojan Mirchev, *Materiali za istoryata na makedonskoto osvobitelno dvizhenie; knjiga XI* (Sofia: N.P., 1931).
[48] Kosev et al., *Makedonia,* Document No. 101: *"Dame Gruev on the Creation of Revoutionary Organisation in Macedonia."*

"Macedonia for the Macedonians".[49] In this year, one part of the members of the Organisation changed its exclusively "Bulgarian element," and opened it to all Macedonians and Thracians regardless of nationality, who wished to participate in the anti–Ottoman movement. These members actually imagined an autonomous Macedonia as a multinational polity. Thus, if one traces back the origins of the demand for autonomy among the Macedonian intellectuals in the Bulgarian Principality and traces the imagination of Macedonia among a group that opposed the Bulgarian intervention, then one can more easily understand the complexities on the ground. By regarding it as a trans–regional example, one can achieve the understandings of the differentiations of these groups and organisations at the local level. In this respect, I will analyse how these two (or more) groups viewed autonomy and perceived Macedonia. Furthermore, I argue that there were contested and disputed standing points and led to an inconsistent policy during the Ilinden Uprising of 1903. I will follow Joel Samuel Migdal's argument that the study of domination and change requires an examination of multiple sites of political struggle promoted by different groupings.[50] Partly undermining Max Weber's definition of state capacity, I will try to show that the practices at the periphery of the state can also play a far more important role than previously theorised. Here I will try to bring a point of view from the periphery in the form of a "bottom–up" perspective by analysing different imaginations and views of the "specialists in violence" on the ground.[51] The Macedonian and

---

[49] Tchavdar Marinov, "We, the Macedonians, The Paths of Macedonian Supra–Nationalism (1878–1912)," in *We, the People: Politics of National Peculiarity in Southeastern Europe*, ed. Mishkova Diana (Budapest/New York: Central European University Press, 2009), pp. 117–120; Tetsuya Sahara, "Paramilitaries in the Balkan Wars: The Case of Macedonian Adrianople Volunteers," in *War and Nationalism: The Balkan Wars, 1912–1913, and Their Sociopolitical Implications*, eds. M. Hakan Yavuz and Isa Blumi (Salt Lake City: The University of Utah Press, 2013), pp. 399–401.

[50] Migdal, *State in Society*; Elçın Kürsat–Ahlers, "Die Brutalisierung von Gesellschaft und Kriegsführung im Osmanischen Reich während der Balkankriege (1903–1914)," in *Gewalt im Krieg: Ausübung, Erfahrung und Verweigerung von Gewalt in Kriegen des 20. Jahrhunderts*, ed. Andreas Gestrich (Münster: LIT Verlag, 1996), pp. 51–74.
[51] On the similar topic, see also: Wolfgang Knöbl and Gunnar Schmidt, *Die Gegenwart des Krieges: staatliche Gewalt in der Moderne* (Frankfurt am Main: S. Fischer, 2000); Wilhelm Heitmeyer, *Gewalt: Entwicklungen, Strukturen, Analyseprobleme* (Frankfurt am Main: Suhrkamp, 2004); Jan Köhler and Sonja Heyer, *Anthropologie der Gewalt*

Bulgarian historiography analysed these revolutionaries through the lens of ethno–national vacuum giving them a fixed identity that fits into Macedonian or Bulgarian nation building narratives. My aim is here to deconstruct these narratives and to show they contained such complexities that indicated that this group of people was more diverse than represented in the national historiographies.

4.2.2. IMARO – Its "Left" and "Right" Wings: An Organisation of Contradictions?

In this sub–chapter I will highlight the common profile of this group of important IMARO members (including both the leading members of the right and left wings). One should bear in mind that there are many differences among its members, their projects, imaginations, and their discourses. In many instances, there was also a vehement opposition between the leaders' imaginations and existing social realities. Some of the leaders of IMARO formed a kind of "intellectuals" which adopted discourses and strategies to influence the local population by applying "national" consciousness, while others supported "supranational" projections, while others yet opposed both. Thus, the responses were various and should not be analysed through the lenses of national historiographies that situate these mobile actors and IMARO members in a national vacuum. Hence, trans–imperial history has the potential to open up new questions and to contribute to a more global context by understanding these actors in a multidimensional space of "multiple arenas of domination and opposition."[52] Here I concentrate on several events that

---

(Berlin: Verlag für Wissenschaft und Forschung, 1998); Markus Koller, *Bosnien an der Schwelle zur Neuzeit: eine Kulturgeschichte der Gewalt (1747–1798)* (Munich: R. Oldenbourg, 2004); Helga Breuninger and Rolf Sieferle, *Kulturen der Gewalt: Ritualisierung und Symbolisierung von Gewalt in der Geschichte* (Frankfurt am Main: Campus–Verlag, 1998); Furthermore see also: Hannes Grandits, *Herrschaft und Loyalität in der spätosmanischen Gesellschaft: Das Beispiel der multikonfessionellen Herzegowina* (Vienna/Cologne/Weimar: Böhlau, 2008); Eva Anne Frantz, "Violence and its Impact on Loyalty and Identity Formation in Late Ottoman Kosovo: Muslims and Christians in a Period of Reform and Transformation," *Journal of Muslim Minority Affairs* 29/4 (2009): 459; Wolfgang Höpken and Michael Riekenberg, *Politische und ethnische Gewalt in Südosteuropa und Lateinamerika* (Vienna/Cologne/Weimar: Böhlau, 2001).
[52] Ibid.

reveal the complexities of the actors and multiple projections of the IMARO members. As has already been explained, the secret meeting in Thessaloniki in 1893 led to the formation of the BMARC (forerunner of the IMARO). Its founders were young men mostly originating from small towns in Ottoman Macedonia. Many of their members were educated in the newly Bulgarian autonomous state, which they saw, at the very least, as a more legitimate patron of the Slav Orthodox Christians of Ottoman Macedonia.[53] Other members were also educated in European colleges, especially in Geneva, where they came under the influence of socialist and anarchist ideas. This group, prevalently (but not exclusively) would go on to establish the "left" wing of the IMARO. From another side, the neighbouring states and its political entrepreneurs offered paid scholarships to these locals, trying to construct a "Bulgarian," "Serbian" or "Greek" national identity in Ottoman Macedonia. In one of the examples with the greater Serbian state imagination, it consequently led to a few student protests in the Bulgarian Men's High School based in Selanik, where a group of dozen students accepted a Serbian offer to continue their studies in Belgrade. After some time, this group of students became aware of the ulterior motives of Serbian state, as they were not allowed to possess Bulgarian literature.[54] Subsequently, majority of this group left Belgrade and continued its education in Bulgaria. Among that group were the IMARO's founding members such as Dame Gruev and

---

[53] Perry, *The Politics of Terror*; Niklas Luhmann, *Funktion Der Religion* (Frankfurt am Main: Suhrkamp, 1982); Niklas Luhmann, "The Nation in the Balkan Village: National Politicization in Mid–Nineteenth–Century Ottoman Thrace" *Turkish Historical Review* 7/2 (2016): 167–193.

[54] Uroš Šešum, "Društvo protiv Srba 1897–1902," *Srpske Studije/Serbian Studies* 4 (2013): 73–103; Momčilo Pavlović and Predrag J. Marković, "Guerrilla in the Balkans: Historical Conditions and Developments," in *Guerrilla in the Balkans: Freedom Fighters, Rebels or Bandits – Researching the Guerrilla and Paramilitary Forces in the Balkans*, eds. Momčilo Pavlović, Tetsuya Sahara and Predgrad J. Marković (Tokyo/Beograd: University Meiji, Institute for Disarmament and Peace Studies, Tokyo – Institute of Contemporary History, Beograd/ Faculty for Security Studies, Beograd, 2007), pp. 21–30; Georg Elwert, Stephan Feuchtwang and Dieter Neubert, "The Dynamics of Collective Violence: An Introduction," in *Dynamics of Violence: Processes of Escalation and De–Escalation in Violent Group Conflicts*, eds. Georg Elwert, Stephan Feuchtwang and Dieter Neubert (Berlin: Duncker & Humblot, 1999), pp. 9–11.

Petar Pop Arsov, as well as prominent Macedonian personalities such as Krste Misirkov,[55] Kosta Shahov,[56] etc. As individuals with strong ties to the Bulgarian culture and Bulgarian Exarchate Church, the IMARO leaders unanimously agreed that this proselytisation of Greek projects and Serb nationalism could not be tolerated in the three vilayets.[57] As a reaction against them a Society Against Serbs (1897) was established in Thessaloniki by Dame Gruev, a member of the IMARO.

The opening of Serbian schools in Ottoman Macedonia and the agitation of political entrepreneurs in Belgrade was met with protest demonstrations, fights, and riots organised by the Society Against Serbs. In this respect, the organisation openly called for violence against Serbs and thus, in the Bulgarian magazine in Thessaloniki named *Narodno Pravo*, promoted anti–Serb sentiments. Hence, in the article on the Bulgarian educational cause in Macedonia (*bŭlgarskoto uchebnoto delo v Makedonia*), it was stated that "the Serbs [would], with fire and sword, be annihilated from Macedonia (*Srbe treba ognyem i machem istrebiti iz Makedonia*)."[58] The first victim, found in a street in Thessaloniki with a cross in Thessaloniki, was the professor of the Serbian gymnasium with the name Ilija Pejčinović. Few of these IMARO members also established guerrilla groups known as chetas (*cheti*) against the armed groups who allegedly supported the Serbian and Greek states. These personalities were

---

[55] Misirkov, *Za makedonskite raboti.*

[56] Kosta Shahov championed a Macedonian national identity that went beyond national borders. He established the newspaper Macedonia on October 21st, 1888, with the first issue emphasising the need for Macedonians to remember their homeland. The newspaper's objective was to advocate for the cultural and spiritual advancement of Macedonians. Shahov contributed to the newspaper, which was published from 1888 to 1912, and also wrote for other publications such as *Glas Makedonski* (1893–1898) and *Strannik*. Additional sources, including *Borba za svobodata na Makedonia i Odrinsko*, *Borba* (1905), and various newspapers, provide further insight into his work. See: Kosta Shahov, *Edno osvetlenie po nashite raboti, in Ot Sofia do Kostur: Spomeni* (Sofia: IK Sineva, 2003), pp. 38–68.

[57] Šešum, *Društvo protiv Srba*; Milić J. Milićević, "Četnička akcija neposredno pre objave i tokom prvih dana srpsko–turskog rata 1912. godine," in *Prvi balkanski rat 1912/13. godine: Društveni i civilizacijski smisao (međunarodni tematski Zbornik)*, ed. Aleksandar Rastović (Niš: Univerzitet u Nišu Filozofski fakultet, 2013), pp. 229–234.

[58] Ibid., from Narodno Prava, 1897.

known as the centralist faction or the "right" wing of IMARO.[59] This organisation was challenged by two other societies known as the Macedonian Supreme Committee in Sofia (*Virhovni makedonsko–odrinski komitet*) [60] and the Bulgarian Secret Revolutionary Brotherhood (*Bŭlgarsko Tayno Revolyutsionno Bratstvo), which was a smaller group based in Solun. [61] Actually, the Bulgarian Secret Revolutionary Brotherhood became later part of IMARO by 1902 but some of its

---

[59] Christo Matov, Christo Tatarchev, Boris Sarafov, and Ivan Garvanov (assassinated by the leftist faction) were among the leaders of the revolutionary organisation. While declaring their support for the liberation of Macedonia, the delegates also acknowledged that Bulgaria had a natural obligation to assist its non–liberated compatriots in Turkey. The group frequently collaborated with the Supreme Macedonian Committee (SMC), a revolutionary organisation established in 1895 in Sofia. See: Kosev et al., *Makedonia, Document No. 269: "Rezolyutsia na Kyustendilskia obsht kongres na VMORO,"*; as well in: Martin Valkov, *The Internal Macedonian–Adrianople Revolutionary Organization and the Idea for Autonomy for Macedonia and Adrianople Thrace (1893–1912)* (MA Thesis, Central European University, 2010).

[60] The Varhovists, members of the Supreme Macedonian–Adrianople Committee from 1895 to 1903, included leaders such as Trayko Kitanchev, who served as the first chairman and was under the control of the Bulgarian Democratic Party and P. Karavelov between 1896–1899, Boris Sarafov, who served as the leader after 1899–1901, and Ivan Tsonchev, who was the leader from 1901–1903. See: Adanır, *Die makedonische Frage*, p. 149; See also: Eduard Boyl, *Srbia i Makedonia*; Klaus Almendinger *Makedonski vŭpros*. Those two articles were published in Hristo Stanishev, *Sayuz na makedonskite emigrantski organizacii v Bŭlgaria – 'Dve statii po makedonskia vŭpros: I. Sirbia i makedontsite II. Makedonskiat vŭpros'* (Sofia: Pechatnitsa P. Glushkov, 1927).

[61] The Secret Revolutionary Brotherhood was founded in 1897, led by Ivan Garvanov who was a teacher at the Bulgarian Men's High School of Thessaloniki. This organisation established friendly relations with the Macedonian Supreme Committee and began creating branches throughout Macedonia and Southern Thrace. However, conflicts arose with the Bulgarian Macedonian–Adrianople Revolutionary Committees (IMARO), leading to mutual assassination attempts, although no one was killed. Boris Sarafov's election as leader of the Macedonian Supreme Committee and the Bulgarian Exarchate's help facilitated a reconciliation, leading to the dissolution of the Brotherhood in 1900, and its members joined the IMARO. Notably, members such as Ivan Garvanov had significant influence on the Internal Organisation and pushed for the Ilinden–Preobrazhenie Uprising, later becoming the core of IMARO's right–wing faction. Members of the Secret Revolutionary Brotherhood included Ivan Garvanov, Georgi Bazhdarov, Tirpen Markov, Andrei Kazepov, Georgi Hristov, Georgi Todorov, Hristo Tenchev, Hristo Ganov, and Hristo Karamandzukov. See: Boris Nikolov, Mario Tsvetkov and Vasil Stanchev, *Ivan Garvanov: Vencha se za Makedonia* (Sofia: Stara Zagora, 1995); Georgi Bazhdarov, *Moite spomeni* (Sofia: Sastavitel Angel Dzonev, 1929); Hristo Karamandzukov, *Rodopa prez Ilindensko–Preobrazenskoto vostanie, Spomeni i dokumenti* (Sofia: Izdatelstvo na Otechestvenia front 1986).

members, like Ivan Garvanov, were to exert significant influence on the organisation. The assassination of Ivan Gavranov and Boris Sarafov by the "left" wing member Todor Panitsa in 1907 deepened the differences inside IMARO. As a consequence, the congress in Kyustendil of the right faction of the IMARO in 1908 sentenced Sandanski to death, which led to a final disintegration of the Organisation resulted through a fight between its "right: and "left" wings. At the beginning of the 20th century were obvious the differences between these two fractions. The "right" wing, as well as those of the other revolutionary organisation – the Macedonian Supreme Committee – also known as the *Varhovisti*, also aimed at autonomy, but followed by annexation with Bulgaria. The members of the left wing of the IMARO were rather advocating for a supranational option that opposed the irredentists' projects (as in the case of the right/centralist wing). The leaders of this "left" group were firstly Gotse Delchev and Vasil Glavinov, who edited several Socialist newspapers. Gotse Delchev was born in Kilkis (in the Selanik vilayeti) and was inspired by the first generation of Bulgarian revolutionaries such as Hristo Botev and Vasil Levski.[62] As many prominent figures born in Ottoman Macedonia, he originated from an area with ethnically and religiously mixed population. Coming from this background, he rather imagined Macedonia as a "multi–ethnic region" and promoted the slogan "Macedonia for the Macedonians."[63] The same idea was shared by Vasil Glavinov. Although he lived in Sofia, he rather focused on the political activism that imagined the establishment of state Macedonia as a republic inside the Balkan Federation. Together with Dimitar Blagoev, he established the first Social–Democratic group in Ottoman Macedonia in 1894. Two years later, Glavinov established the Macedonian–Adrianople Revolutionary Social–Democratic Union of the Bulgarian Workers' Social–Democrat Party. Furthermore, the first Conference of Macedonian Socialists was held near Krushevo on 3 June 1900, during which the activities of Vasil Glavinov's political group defined the basic aspects of the creation of a Republic of Macedonia as a

---

[62] Maria N. Todorova, *Bones of Contention: The Living Archive of Vasil Levski and the Making of Bulgaria's National Hero* (Budapest/New York: Central European University Press, 2009).
[63] Klaus Roth and Ulf Brunnbauer, *Region, Regional Identity and Regionalism in Southeastern Europe* (Münster: LIT Verlag, 2009).

part of a Balkan Socialist Federation, that is, a "Switzerland on the Balkans" of sorts.[64] Within this framework, the IMARO left wing also moved forward in 1906 by proclaiming a new Statute/Constitution (*Ustav*) pointing out new supranational goals. Its first chapters identified two goals that aimed "to unite any and all dissatisfied elements in Macedonia and the Adrianople Vilayet without regard to their nationality" and " to oppose any other country's intentions to divide and conquer these two regions."[65] Furthermore, in the second chapter, the leaders of the IMARO emphasised that they aimed also "to abolish chauvinist propaganda and nationalistic disputes."[66] To achieve this aim, Vasil Glavinov together with Yane Sandanski gravitated towards the People's Federative Party after the Young Turk Revolution in 1908.

Yane Sandanski was a prominent leader of the IMARO, inspired by socialist ideas and federal political systems, imagining Macedonia as an autonomous region within the Ottoman Empire.[67] Thus, he struggled primarily against the Bulgarian nationalists and right–wing members of the IMARO. In this respect, he also wanted to stop the activities of the political entrepreneurs who promoted state nationalisms, which is the reason that brough him to cooperate with the members of the Young Turk Movement. Sandanski gained a support from the leftist intellectuals such as Dimo Hadzidimov and Pavel Deliradev to contact the Young Turks' Committee. Furthermore, since the beginning of the 1908, the socialists from Adrianople supported Yane Sandanski against the "right wing" and began to propagate the idea of a "constitutional Turkey" in their newspaper *Odrinski Glas*.[68] On the first day after the Young Turk Revolution, he joined the Young Turks leader of Nevrokop in Gaytaninovo, and travelled with him to Thessaloniki, to the centre of the Young Turks' Committee. He was received by Enver Bey – a hero of Young Turk Revolution. In the

---

[64] Diana Mishkova, *We the People: Politics of National Peculiarity in Southeastern Europe* (Budapest/New York: Central European University Press 2009), p. 122.

[65] Dimitar Gotsev, *Ideyata za avtonomia kato taktika v programite na natsionalno–osvoboditelnoto dvizhenie v Makedonia i Odrinsko* (1893–1941) (Sofia: Izdatelstvo na Bŭlgarska Akademia na Naukite, 1983), p. 34.

[66] Ibid.

[67] Mehmet Hacısalihoğlu, "Yane Sandanski as a Political Leader in Macedonia in the Era of the Young Turks," *Cahiers Balkaniques* 40 (2012).

[68] Ibid.

Ottoman public, Sandanski was also named "King of the Mountains" and "Sandan Pasha."[69] After the Revolution, Sandanski together with Hristo Chernopeev, worked on a creation of the leftist political party in the Ottoman Empire, known later as People's Federative Party,[70] whose headquarters were in Thessaloniki. Their friend, Dimo Hadzidimov, advocated for a Balkan federation with the "other 'nationalities' of Macedonia" outside Bulgaria too. For him the answer lay not in the dissolution of the Ottoman Empire but in "regional self–government within the empire" as well as "self–government for districts within regions; and for local communities within districts."[71] Other important members were Hristo Chernopev, Todor Panitsa, and Dimitar Vlahov.[72]

---

[69] Ibid; See also: DARSM, v. IV. 67/1412, 567. Skopje, 11. August, 1908.

[70] Ibid; The Bulgarian section of the People's Federative Party outlines in Article 1 of its statute that any Bulgarian, Ottoman citizen who is at least 20 years old and agrees with the party's agenda and actively participates in one of its local organisations can become a member. See also: Uğur Ümit Üngör, "Paramilitary Violence in the Collapsing Ottoman Empire, " in *War in Peace: Paramilitary Violence in Europe after the Great War*, ed. Robert Gewarth and John Horne (Oxford: Oxford University Press, 2012), pp. 164–83; Erik Jan Zürcher, "Macedonians in Anatolia: The Importance of the Macedonian Roots of the Unionist for their Policies in Anatolia after 1914, " *Middle Eastern Studies* 50/6 (2014): 960–975; Emre Erol, "'Macedonian Question' in Western Anatolia: The Ousting of the Ottoman Greeks before World War I," in *World War I and the End of the Ottomans: From the Balkan Wars to the Armenian Genocide*, eds. Kerem Öktem, Maurus Reinkowski and Hans–Lukas Kieser (London/New York: I. B. Tauris, 2015), pp. 103–107; Uğur Ümit Üngör, "Mass Violence Against Civilians during the Balkan Wars," in *The Wars before the Great War: Conflict and International Politics before the Outbreak of the First World War*, eds. Andreas Rose, Dominik Geppert and William Mulligan (Cambridge: Cambridge University Press, 2015), pp. 76–81; Benjamin C. Fortna, *The Circassian: A Life of Eşref Bey, Late Ottoman Insurgent and Special Agent* (Oxford: Oxford University Press, 2016); Ali Güneş, *Gayrinizamı Harp: Balkan Harbi'nde Komita, Çete, Jandarma ve Milisler (1912–1913)* (Istanbul: Kronik, 2020).

[71] Houri Berberian, *Roving Revolutionaries: Armenians and the Connected Revolutions in the Russian, Iranian and Ottoman Worlds* (Berkley: University of California Press, 2019), p. 132; See the sources: Dimo Hadzidimov, *Nazad kim avtonomiata: Deklaratsia po razreshenieto na makedonskia vŭpros* (Sofia: N.P., 1919); Dimo Hadzidimov, *Makedonskoto osvoboditelno delo* (Lom: Pechatnitsa na A.M. Dimitrov, 1900).

[72] Dimitar Vlahov, *Memoari* (Skopje: Nova Makedonija, 1970), p. 356.

4.2.3. Transnational Anarchists, Regional Networks: The Art of Not Being Governed

As has been demonstrated above, these groups were far from univocal in their view or compatible in their activities to the point that they often remained in opposition to the political aspirations of the Bulgarian, Serbian, or Greek states.[73]However, the networks of organisations they established can also be seen as early examples of the trans–border communities engaged in the imaginary processes of building a homeland. One such organisation was The Macedonian Secret Revolutionary Committee (MSRC), [74] established in Plovdiv in 1895 by Michail Gerdzikov, [75] Petar Mandzukov, [76] Petar Sokolov, [77] Slavi Merdzanov,

---

[73] Bernard Lory, "Schools for the destruction of society: school propaganda in Bitola 1860–1912," in *Conflicting Loyalties in the Balkans: The Great Powers, the Ottoman Empire and Nation–Building*, eds. Hannes Grandits, Nathalie Clayer and Robert Pichler (London: I.B. Tauris, 2011).

[74] Program of the Organisation was published as *"Programa na Makedonskia Taen Revolutsionen Komitet"* in Politicheska Svoboda, No. 11, Sofia, 1898. In original:
"I. Palna nezavisimost i nayshiroka svoboda za Makedonskia narod, za da si naredi toj sam kakvoto obicha upravlenie.
II. Ponezhe Makedonia se naselyava ot razni narodnosti, Komitetet zayavyava, che nma da protezhira nikoya ot tih otdalno v vrada na drugit; toy nama da pooshrgva natsionalniat im antagonizmi, a she se trudi da gi organizira v edno selo, za sisipvaneto na turskata vlast v Makedonia; i vednizh tova postignato, toyi pridostavia na samiti tihi razrshenieto na vŭprositi; da se prisedinyat li kimi nikoya ot sisidniti drzhavi, ili da si obrazuvat svoja nezavisima oblast.
III. Pri razrshavanieto na tozi vŭprosa, Komitetiti ne dopuska nikakva chuzhda namisa; toyi iska naselenieto samo da se proiznese bez nikakavi vanshnen natisk.
IV. Za nepriateli Komiteta schita ne samo turskit vlasti, no i vsichki onia litsa, koito po nikakavi nachin prichat na rabotiti mu i primo ili kosveno nanesat vrida na naroditi i negovoto osvoboditelno delo.
V. Mirnoto tursko naselenie, ne samo, che ne se schita za nepriatel, no naprotiv – she zavisi ot Komitetat da prieme, ili ne, pomoshta mu v sluchay, che i to bi zayavilo zhelanie da deistvuva zaedno s nas za sasipvaneto na sultanovata neogranichena vlast. Nuzhdna zabileshka. Lishen ot vsekakvi shovinisticheski pretencii i patrioticheski zamisli, Komitetat obavtava tsye: 'na vsichki shovinisticheski destvia v Makedonia, bile t ot bŭlgare, gartsi, sarbi ili koito i da se drugi, nashit komitetski rabotnitsi s dllyazhni da protivodeistvuvati, a samit dyatsi v tuy napravlenie she se presledvata, kato nai–golemi narodni vragove."

[75] Mihail Gerdzikov, *V Makedonia i Odrinsko* (Sofia: Pechatnitsa P. Glushkov, 1928).

[76] Petar Mandzukov, *Predvestnitsi na buriata Spomeni* (Sofia: Federatsiata na anarhistite v Bulgaria, 2013).

[77] Description of Petar Sokolov by Pavle Shatev in: Pavle Šatev, *Makedonija pod ropstvo* (Skopje: Makedonika, 2013).

Varban Kilifarski,[78] Dimitar Ganchev, Pavel Shatev,[79] and Konstantin Antonov (a member of the Supreme Macedonian–Adrianople Committee, IMARO, and the Bulgarian Communist Party). In the same city, Plovdiv (Filibe), this group of people established their first contacts with Armenian Hunchak and later with the members of the Armenian Revolutionary Federation (ARF).[80] According to some members of the ARF, the Armenian organisations were inspired by those movements in Ottoman Macedonia and the case was also reversed, where various local organisations in Macedonia were inspired by the Armenian groups.[81] Few members of these organisations in Macedonia also made close connections with the revolutionary expatriots and established the so–called Geneva Group, an extension of the MSRC.[82] Their first meetings occurred in Geneva in 1896–97, where some of the leading Armenian Revolutionary Federation officers lived and were in close contact with Simeon Radev, a well–known Bulgarian nationalist.[83] It should be also noted that some members of anarchist organisations also supported the Bulgarian state, as was case with Radev. On the other hand, other members rather supported a supra–national state or independent Macedonia. Gerdzhikov became a member of the IMARO along with a close friend of Gotse Delchev. Some other members of MSRC became involved in IMARO, but also switched sides in favour of the Supreme Macedonian Committee. Thus, as mentioned above, I argue that these groups were not always univocal, although sometimes cooperated or undertook the same actions. Few

---

[78] Varban Kilifarski together with Mihail Gerdzikov founded the first periodic anarchistic newspaper in Bulgaria (*Svobodno Obshevstvo and Bezvlastye*).

[79] Shatev, *Makedonija pod ropstvo.*

[80] BOA, Rumeli Mufettişliği Tasnıfi, Manastır Evraki (TFR.İ.MN) (1322–23, 1904–5, Cıld II), 2222–46–126 (1889), in original: *"Petrof günlerinde hudud tecavuz etmek üzere Kostendilde Makedonya Cemiyyeti fesadiye tarafından açılan deftere bazı kişilerin kaydedilmeleri."*

[81] Garabet K. Moumdjian, "Rebels with a Cause: Armenian–Macedonian Relations and their Bulgarian Connection, 1895–1913," in *War and Nationalism: The Balkan Wars, 1912–1913, and the Sociopolitical Implications*, eds. Hakan M. Yavuz and Isa Blumi (Salt Lake City: University of Utah Press, 2013). p. 136.

[82] See: Gerdzikov, *V Makedonia.*

[83] Simeon Radev, *Ranni Spomeni, Novo korigiran i dopolneno izdanie pod redakciata na Trayan Radev* (Sofia: Izd. Kusha Strelets, 1994); Simeon Radev, *Tova, koeto vidia hot Balkanskata voinam Narodna kultura* (Sofia: Zabravenit bŭlgari, 2012); Simeon Radev, *Stroitelite na Svremenna Bŭlgaria, Tom 1,2,3* (Sofia: Bŭlgarski pisatel, 1910–1911).

actions between the Geneva Group, the Gemici and Armenian "specialists in violence" are worthy of mentioning such as the attempt at assassination of the Sultan (1899), the attack of the Ottoman Bank in Istanbul (1900), the attack of the Orient Express in Adrianople (1901) and of boats in Thessaloniki (1903).

Emboldened by various trans–regional contacts and clearly learning from various organisations, a small group of Macedonians and Bulgarians established an organisation in Geneva in 1898, which extended an offshoot in Thessaloniki in 1899, and was launched by the anarchist Slavi Merdzhanov. They were influenced by anarcho–nationalism, which emerged in Europe following the French Revolution and at least as far back as the time of Mikhail Bakunin and his involvement with the Pan–Slavic movement. Together with the Armenian revolutionaries, the group organised weaponry smuggling and trafficking, set up a modest bomb factory, and traded cannabis across the region, as recounted in the memoirs of Petar Mandzukov, one of the members of this group. [84] Their collaboration strengthened when these "specialists in violence" planned to assassinate the sultan and bomb the Ottoman Central Bank in Istanbul as well as its branch in Salonika. The group of Macedonian anarchists together with Armenian speaking personalities under the leadership of Slavi Merdzanov planned the assassination of the Sultan. However, in September 1900 the Ottoman authorities found the members of this organisation and arrested them because they were carrying the explosives. After the unsuccessful event for this transregional group, Merdzanov did not stop a plan to weaken Ottoman authorities. He focused on new solutions such as to hold up the Orient Express near Adrianople, and to gain possession of the telegraph. This group managed to place a large

---

[84] DARSM, v IV.67/570, Skopje, 1912; Mandzukov, *Predvestnici na buriata*, p. 85; Quote: *"Hashishit se dobia ot tsvetnite lyuspi na edno konopeno rastenie – Cannabis Indica, koeto se kultivira za taya tsel v Mala Azia. Mezhdu dvete gole– mi voiini tova rastenie e bilo kultivirano po kontrabanden nachin ot nyakoi armentsi–bezhantsi i v Bŭlgaria, imenno v Pazardzishko. Tova rastenie vansh– no ne se razlichava po nisho ot obiknovenia konop (Cannabis Sativa), osven po tova, che ne stava tolkova visoko. Kogato, smesen v tyutyuna, se pushi, hashishit izdava edna specifichna silna, oshtra i nepriatna mirizma; pri pusheneto negovoto deiistvie e po–birzo, po–meko i po–kratkotraiino; upotreben vav vid na sladko, toiy deiistvuva po–bavno, no mnogo po–silno i dŭlgotraiino, a i po– razheniata varhu organizma v takav sluchai sa mnogo po–golemi. Zaharta, vzeta sled hashishovo sladko, usilva mnogo negovoto deiistvie."*

quantity of dynamite on the railway line, but the railway passed undamaged. Ottoman authorities captured Merdzanov alive, together two Armenians and one Bulgarian from Lozengrad. These captives were taken to Adrianople and were condemned to death by the Ottoman authorities. Slavi Merdzanov and his Macedonian and Armenian comrades were publicly hanged in November 1901. As a revenge to these Ottoman actions, few members of this group decided to launch a campaign of terror bombing the Ottoman Bank in Thessaloniki. This group known as Gemici aimed to attract the attention of the Great Powers to Ottoman oppression in Macedonia. These revolutionaries, guerrilla warriors, terrorists, paramilitary forces or gang fighters were a diverse group of people who supported each other, but also they often advocated for different ideas and had various visions regarding Ottoman Macedonia. From one side, Mihail Gerdzikov put hope to "liberate Macedonia (*se osvobodi Makedonia*),"[85] from other side Slavi Merdzanov wanted to destroyed Ottoman institutions and supported terrorism. His collaboration with Armenian speaking anarchists and their entangled contacts with European anarchists in Geneve, provides a fascinating case study for trans–regional analysis from multiple disciplines, including history, political science and sociology. By examining the historical and sociopolitical context of anarcho–nationalism, the role of political violence, and the importance of cross–border collaboration, we can better understand the dynamics of social and political movements in Ottoman Macedonia as well. One should mention that inside the leftist wing of IMARO were also members who did not support such actions and broke down with anarchism. On the contrary, some locals such as Sandanski, supported Ottoman empire and cooperated with Young Turks, while Tatarchev and Radev wanted unification with Bulgaria. Also, during their lifetime, a same personality could support several ideological views, and also participate in different activities that were opposite to his primary views. Often, some of the fighters and revolutionaries gave more importance to localities, neighbours and relatives than to broader "greater state" projects. Sometimes, the members developed their own strategies that opposed the state projections. During

---

[85] Gerdzikov, *V Makedonia*, p. 87; Üngör, *Paramilitary Violence*; Zürcher, *Macedonians in Anatolia*; Erol, *'Macedonian Question.'* pp. 108–112.

the certain period of their activities, a member of a group could be a specialist in violence, while later enter the state hierarchy and become teacher or intellectual in the form of political entrepreneur. Furthermore, one could be at the same time political entrepreneur and specialist in violence, as will be seen also in other cases that will be covered in following sub–chapters. We can talk here about multiple trajectories and activities of the actors who were intersecting with their comrades and opponents on local, region, trans–regional or global levels.

4.3. Greek Organisations: "Conquering the Souls" in Ottoman Macedonia

Within less than one century, the Greek intellectuals built their modern national state, defined their national interest found in the *Megali Idea*, and deployed bandits over several regions to influence the national consciousness of the locals.[86] This was often carried out with support of the state for the irredentist upheavals, [87] especially implementing heroification of warriors (*agonistai*) and encouraging bands to "conquer the souls."[88] The chief of the band was the captain (*capitanos*) or bouloukshi (*boulouksis*), who was at the same time the head brigand (*listarchos* or *archilistis*) and, in the eyes of population, the brain that moved and kept the band together.[89] Furthermore, they established a foster–brotherhood (*stavradelphoi, adelphopoitoi, vlamides, bratimoi*) in order to strengthen existing bonds, uniting bandsmen with each other within the concept of a nation. These former Greek acardites created bonds that transcended the kinship logic and gave them a "higher" ideal of fighting for the nation and conquering other souls.[90] Oftentimes these bands were recruited by the

---

[86] Basil Gounaris, "Preachers of God And Martyrs of Nation – The politics of Murder in Otto man Macedonia in the Early 20th Century," *Balkanologie* 9/1–2 (December 2005): 33.

[87] Johns. Koliopoulos, *Brigands with a Cause: Brigandage and Irredentism in Modern Greece 1821–1912* (Oxford: Oxford University Press, 1987), p. 239.

[88] Dimitris Livanios, "'Conquering the souls': nationalism and Greek guerrilla warfare in Ottoman Macedonia, 1904–1908," *Byzantine and Modern Greek Studies* 23 (1999):195–196.

[89] Koliopoulos, *Brigands with a Cause*, p. 260.

[90] Vemund Aarbakke, "Die Region Makedonien," in *Das Südosteuropa der Regionen*, eds. Oliver Jens Schmitt und Michael Metzeltin (Vienna: Verlag der Österreichischen

Greek foreign ministry with the help of the Epirote Society, a state–sponsored irredentist society.[91] They were actually Greek "specialists in violence" or guerrilla bands, who did not always originally come from Macedonia, but fought for Greece in order to conquer this region, mostly led by regular army officers.[92] One such example was Pavlos Melas, who was a Greek officer that entered Macedonia with his band and attacked Bulgarian–speaking villages in order to conquer their souls. This narrative of the struggle for Macedonia (1904–1908) and "conquering the souls" of the locals was a product of an older conflict between the Patriarchist and Exarchist churches that had started in the 1870s. As a reaction of the already established "Bulgarian" bands in the region of Ottoman Macedonia, the Greek side reflected its Panhellenic ideas by including many armed volunteer gangs, priests, and other personalities from the Greek political and intellectual life. The perception of the *Megali Idea* became more active among those policymakers and intellectuals who increasingly looked for inspiration to British and French imperialism. The Greek "political entrepreneurs" viewed themselves as an imperial ancient nation whose mission in the Balkan peninsula was similar to those of France and Britain in East Asia and North Africa, bringing "civilisation" and Christianity to populations that were seen as backward, savage and, despite their European origins, essentially Asiatic. In fact, for a long time the state had distributed the function to paramilitary bands and brigand groups that acted as its unofficial representatives who should bring "civilisation." [93] Irredentist ideas were fused with Social Darwinist arguments to produce an ideology that, according to Mark Mazower, "verged on a sort of political messianism." [94] Indeed, "political entrepreneurs" such as Ion Dragoumis (1878–1920), the promoter of

---

Akademie der Wissenschaften, 2015), pp. 603–609; See also: Historical Archive of Macedonia (IAM) in Thessaloniki, ABE: 284.

[91] Karakasidou, *Fields of Whet;* See: IAM, AEE: biork/ 148–57. Thessaloniki, 1882.

[92] Spyros Tsoutsoumpis, "Land of the Kapedani: Brigandage, Paramilitarism and Nation–building in 20th Century Greece," *Balkan Studies* 51 (2016): 44.

[93] Spyros Tsoutsoumpis, "Morale, ideology and the barbarization of warfare among Greek soldiers," in *The Wars of Yesterday the Balkan Wars and the Emergence of Modern Military Conflict, 1912–13*, eds. Sabine Rutar and Katrin Boeckh (New York: Berghahn Books, 2018), p. 209.

[94] Ibid; Uğur Z. Peçe, "The Conscription of Greek Ottomans into the Sultan's Army, 1908–1912," *International Journal of Middle East Studies* 52/3 (2020): 433–448.

Greek nationalism, and Neoklis Kazazis (1849–1936), the rector of Athens University and founder of the irredentist society *Ellinismos*, turned the *Megali Idea* into a *mission civilisatrice*. In this respect, several Greek bands in Macedonia fought for Helen heritage of Alexander the Great and Greek civilisation. One of such organisations was the *Ethniki Etaireia* or "National Society," which was a secret Greek nationalistic organisation created by young nationalist officers in November 1894 in Athens, with the purpose to "rejuvenate the national sensibility."[95] Soon, the politicians and distinguished citizens of Greece joined this society and advocated the *Megali Idea* among the Greek–speaking Orthodox population living in Ottoman Macedonia. Its aim was to revive the morale of the country and prepare the liberation of the Greek people still under the Ottoman Empire. It was established immediately after IMARO, but it came to dissolution of organisation in 1897, after the Ottoman–Greek war. The second such organisation was the Hellenic Macedonian Committee, founded in 1903 to strengthen the Greek position in Macedonia that was led by a Greek publisher Dimitrios Kalapothakis. The members of this organisation were the abovementioned Ion Dragoumis and Pavlos Melas.

These "specialists in violence" were actually known as Macedonian fighters or in Greek language as "*Makedonomachoi*." They were portrayed in the books as "the Secrets of the Swamp" (*Ta Mystiká tou Váltou*) of the Greek nation. Some of these fighters, who fought on the Macedonian front, as Spiros Tsoutsoumpis emphasises, were "obsessed with locating the birthplace of Alexander the Great and discovering parallels between the modern inhabitants and their ancestors. These associations reinforced the Greek territorial claims, as well as the view of the war as a clash between East and West, civilisation and barbarity."[96] While the state and its elite tried to produce such Orientalist discourses and meta–narratives in order to influence the locals in the Salonika and Manastir vilayets, the situation on the ground was a turning point for the Greek band activities in Macedonia after the Ilinden Uprising in 1903. During this uprising, there were such cases in Ohrid, Manastir, Florina, and Kostaria where Ottoman

---

[95] See the raports in Historical Archive of Macedonia (IAM) in Thessaloniki, one of them is an Annual Series, No 2730, by Diplomatic and Consular Reports (Trade of Consular District of Salonica).
[96] Ibid.

troops, accompanied by the Greek bishop, forced the population to surrender their arms and to recognise the Patriarchate Church over the Exarchate.[97] The "Greek" bands were assisted by the supervision and even silent cooperation of the Ottoman authorities, who viewed them as a counterweight against IMARO.[98] The inquiry into the ethnic composition of the "Greek" bands in Macedonia raises questions about the extent to which these groups were "exclusively Greek."

Photo 1 Greek guérillas with Ottoman captain Şerafettin[99]

The Photo 1 illustrates cooperation between the Young Turk officer Şerafettin Bey and the two *capitanos*, members of *Ethniki Etaireia* and the Macedonian Committee, Prodromos Skotidas (on the left of Şerafettin) and Yanis Simanikas (on the right of Şerafettin). Standing together "Turks" and "Greeks" in the photograph suggests a willingness to overcome religious, ethno-national and political differences in pursuit of a

---

[97] Christopher Psilos, "The Young Turk Revolution and the Macedonian Question" (PhD diss., University of Leeds, 2000).
[98] Mazarakis–Ainian, Konstantinos Ioannu, *O Makedonikos Agon – Anamneseis* (Salonica: 1963). See in: Basil Gounaris, "Reassessing Ninety Years of Greek Historiography on the Struggle for Macedonia 1904–1908," *Journal of Modern Greek Studies* 14/2 (1996).
[99] İBB Atatürk Kitaplığı: N. G. Vicopoulos (ed.), *Portre Rum/Rum çeteleri*, Krt_009365, Selanique

shared goal inside the Ottoman Macedonia. Moreover, the fact that these individuals were able to work together and establish alliance, it indicates that their ethno-national programs and understandings were in flux, and that they were not defined solely by their ethnic or religious backgrounds. In this regard, there are several examples were local Muslims also actively joined the bands and sometimes sided with the Christians – be they Greek, Serbian, or Bulgarian. Cooperation between these different ethno–national and religious communities may shed light on the fluidity in the region during this period of history. The above shown photograph highlights the potential for cooperation across various ethnic, religious, and political boundaries, and suggests that these divisions may be more permeable than initially perceived.

Contrary to the practices on the ground, between 1903 and 1913, the national elites of the Balkan states shared in their documents and books the "spirit of fighting patriotism," classifying the Christians in Macedonia into two categories, as "heroes and traitors, Greeks and Bulgarians, victims and assassins."[100] In this line, battles and sacrifices were represented in the media within historical rights of Greece over Macedonia. The return to the past was necessary because of the need of a meta–national narrative for immortality. Thus, according to Basil Gounaris, the arguments in Athens were running as follows: "Ancient Macedonians were ethnic Greeks; Medieval Slavs and Bulgars were culturally converted to Byzantine Hellenism and were ethnically assimilated; and Slav–speaking Macedonians were not necessarily Bulgars or Slavs. Considering their loyalty to the Patriarch and their active contribution to Greek 19th–century irredentism, it is evident that they were ethnically Greek beyond doubt."[101] The discrepancy between the national elites' rhetoric and the reality on the ground raises several questions, including: Did the local actors spark conflict or rather was it a state initiative (or intellectual) that produced meta–narratives and the claims of the *Megali Idea*? Was there a significant difference between the rhetoric of national elites and the actions of local actors on the ground, or were they largely aligned in their goals and methods? To what extent did external factors, such as the influence of

---

[100] Ibid., p. 27.
[101] Gounaris, *Social cleavages and national 'awakening'*, p. 412.

neighbouring states or the interests of imperial powers, shape the development of nationalistic narratives in the Balkans during this period? The cases like Naoum Spanos, who firstly fought together with Pavlos Melas against the Ottomans in 1897, but in 1903 recruited fighters for the Bulgarian chetas, suggest that many members of the bands were not rigidly bound to a specific ethnic or national identity. Instead, they were motivated by various factors such as personal interests, alliances, and the desire for autonomy. The fluidity of identity and shifting loyalties among members of these guerilla bands highlights the complexity of the social and political landscape in Macedonia during this time period.[102] A similar shift was true for a certain Stefos from Manastir who became vojvoda.[103] From other side, few Greek band leaders such as Katehakis and Karavangelis succussed in recruiting former IMARO members for their lines, which were later reinforced with soldiers sent from Greece. These examples illustrate the complex nature of identity and allegiance among the local population in Macedonia during the period under study. Rather than adhering to a fixed, immutable sense of ethno–national identity, many individuals adopted multiple identities over the course of their lives, and were willing to switch sides based on personal or familial interests. The imposition of a "Greek identity" in Macedonia was thus largely a result of the efforts of political and military elites, rather than a reflection of the "organic" identity of the local population.[104] As a result of these dynamics, priests and educators were often targeted for violence, due to their perceived role in shaping and reinforcing particular identities. For instance, IMARO's right wing carried out attacks on Serbian and Greek priests and intellectuals, who had resisted Bulgarian efforts to exert

---

[102] Basil Gounaris, "Social Gathering and Macedonian Lobbying: Symbols of Irredentism and Living Legends in Early Twentieth Century Athens," in *Greek Society in the Making, 1863–1913: Realities, Symbols and Vissions,* ed. Philip Carabott (Aldershot: Ashgate Publishing Ltd, 1997), p. 102.

[103] Ibid.

[104] Ibid. p. 103; Such statemen and intellectuals were: Stefanos Dragoumis, former Minister of Foreign Afairs and veteran sponsor of Greek irrendentism in Ottoman Macedonia; the brothers Yeroyiannis, founders of the Central Macedonian Association; Dimitrios Kalapothakis, editor of the newspaper Embros; an Ecumenical patriarchist who did not accept the Bulgarian Exarchic Church; and former fellows of the Ethniki Etaireia.

[104] Mehmet Hacısalihoğlu, "The Young Turk Revolution and the Negotiations," *Turcica* 36 (2004): 184.

influence in the region. These attacks often targeted places of religious or cultural significance, such as sites affiliated with the Ecumenical Patriarchate, considered "sacred" for Greek or Serbian clerics (priests) and intellectuals, because of their "special rights of the Ecumenical Patriarchate and the Rum millet (as these [had] always been acknowledged and protected by the state up to [that moment])."[105] In this respect, some of the clerics and educational personnel behaved as the "political entrepreneurs" who tried to install "national pride" among the political committees and local population. Ottoman sources too confirm several acts of terror in Macedonia, performed either by the "exarchist" or the "patriarchist."[106] The complex interplay of religious, ethnic, and political factors thus contributed to a highly volatile and contested environment in Macedonia.[107]

This emergence of the Exarchate and Bulgarian bands (not only the IMARO) into the southern parts of Ottoman Macedonia reinforced the positions of patriarchist and Greek "political entrepreneurs" to undertake measures against these "Bulgarians." Even on the ground, joining the "schismatic" Church was not an easy decision for locals notorious for their attachment to tradition. Furthermore, in terms of dogma and worship practices, locals could hardly see any difference in practicing the faith. The overwhelming majority of them could not even understand the services at all, either in Old Church Slavonic or in Hellenic Greek.[108] In this respect, this entire "struggle for Macedonia" resembled an arena of "conquering [of] the souls,"[109] but the locals were not aware of the "rigid" division

---

[105] Mehmet Hacısalihoğlu, "The Young Turk Revolution and the Negotiations," *Turcica* 36 (2004): 184.

[106] See the archival documents collected in: Arşiv Belgelerine Göre Balkanlar'da ve Anadolu'da Yunan Mezalimi: III Gayr–ı Müslimlere yapılan Yunan Mezalimi (Ankara: TC BOA Yayınları No, 31, 1996), p. 241; In original: *"Dihova karyesindeki kilise ve mekteb ve kabristan ve akarat–i sa'ire Rum taraftarların yedinde kalmasi taht–i karara alındığı mahallinden Eksarhaneye vurud eden..."*

[107] Ibid., 187; Document: Manastır Vilayeti, Mektubi Kalemi, Aded. 373, 18. June 1907; In original: *"...altmış kişilik bir Rum çetesinin, Kesriye'ye bağlı Osteme köyüne saldırarak Bulgar Eksarhhanesine mensup dört kişiyi öldürüp üç kişiyi de yaralamaları üzerine sevkolunan mufrezenin eşkiyadan üç kişi ölü olarak ele geçirdiği, diğer eşkiyanın ise olay yerinden kaçtığı"*

[108] Gounaris, *Preachers of God*, p. 36.

[109] Livanios, *'Conquering the souls.'*

between "Greek" or "Bulgarian", rather they identified themselves as Christians.[110] There were also cases when priests served in the Exarchic Church, but were supporters of the Patriarchists, like in the instance of the Triandafilia (Lazen) village, where, in late August (of year 1904), a priest confessed:

> "Even myself, I pretend to be a Bulgarian. During the service I loudly honour the Exarch but whispering in my prayers I praise the Patriarch. Only God knows what's in my soul."[111]

The case of the priest from Triandafilia (Lazen) village highlights the complex nature of religious and national identity in Macedonia during the early 20th century. The fact that this priest was serving in the Exarchic Church but secretly held loyalty to the Patriarchists demonstrates that individuals often held multiple and conflicting loyalties. This case is not unique and is representative of broader trends in the region during this time period. Furthermore, it underscores the idea that national and religious identities are not always clear-cut or mutually exclusive, and suggest that we should take into consideration familial ties, regional affiliations, and personal beliefs as well. Many individuals thus did not necessarily view themselves or their communities through a national lens, but instead prioritised other social and cultural factors, such as family ties, village identity, or affiliation with a particular church as Christians. In this respect, in 1903, the British journalist Noel Brailsford interviewed a group of Slavic–speaking young villagers and asked if they knew who built the city. Their response "the freemen, our ancestors" and "they were Christians" demonstrated that they did not think in terms of national identities but rather saw their ancestors as freemen who were Christians.[112] Similarly, Muslim residents in the region likely had their own complex sets of social

---

[110] Brailsford, *Macedonia*; See also: Gounaris, *Preachers of God*, pp. 36–37; Quote: "There is evidence that priests had even killed with their own hands their predecessors or their competitors. This was the case of the Exarchic priest pop Nikola in the village of Perikopi (Prekopana) on Mt Vitsi, who killed his predecessor, papa–Christo, in July 1903."
[111] Ibid; Basil Gounaris ed., *The Autumn of 1904 in Macedonia: The Unpublished Diary of Euthymios Kaoudis [in Greek]* (Thessaloniki: Mouseio Makedonikou Agona, 1992), p. 30.
[112] Brailsford, *Macedonia*.

and cultural values that guided their actions and beliefs. The existence of these diverse and overlapping identities and loyalties underscores the complexity of the conflict on the ground. These personalities often lived together in the streets, also known as *mahale*, which were not only an administrative entity, but also places for building social networks. Their members could be Christian and Muslim, Greek–, Slavic, Turkish– or Albanian–speaking, connected into solidarity that was sometimes stronger than religious affiliation. An example worth mentioning is the Modis family, a Greek-speaking Christian family that resided in a Muslim neighbourhood. Even though they were surrounded by Muslims, the Modis family provided shelter and protection to Greek brigands who were wounded. The locals of the neighbourhood also participated in this act of kindness and helped conceal the brigands. This was done in order to prevent their friends from being embarrassed, arrested, or punished.[113]

It is clear that the promotion of nationalist propaganda and the use of armed conflicts aimed to create and solidify ethnic groups. However, this goal was not achievable before 1912, and it could not be accomplished within a single generation. It is important to note that aligning oneself with a particular guerrilla group did not necessarily imply subscribing to different cultures or genealogical and historical myths. These groups were not yet closed social units, but rather flexible options that individuals could choose from. Furthermore, violence and terror were frequently instigated by non-local actors, such as those in Sofia, Athens, or Belgrade, and sometimes their decisions influenced local participation in the conflicts. However, it is important to acknowledge that brutalities in Ottoman Macedonia were also often the result of local vendettas, rather than being inspired solely by national wars and ethnic cleansing.[114]

---

[113] Basil Gounaris, "From Peasants into Urbanites, from Village into Nation: Ottoman Monastir in the Early Twentieth Century," *European History Quarterly* 31/1 (2001): 53; Alf Lüdtke, "Introduction: What Is the History of Everyday Life and Who Are Its Practitioners?" in *The History of Everyday Life: Reconstructing Historical Experiences and Ways of Life*, ed. Alf Lüdtke (Princeton, NJ: Princeton University Press, 1995), pp. 3–40.

[114] Basil Gounaris, *Social cleavages*, p. 421.

4.4. The Chetnik Movement
The topic about the Serbian bands in Ottoman Macedonia is neither recent nor neglected in Serbian historiography. Still, there are also other approaches that could contribute to the studies of these organisations that were established in the period of "struggle for Macedonia." While, most of the studies[115] approached the topic from the state–centred perspectives, I aim to contribute from a "bottom–up" approach, emphasising the lives of the local population that were ethnically and religiously diverse. Hence, this sub–chapter will be focused on the activities of the Serbian Revolutionary Organisation known as "Chetniks," and formally as Serbian Defence (*Srpska Odbrana*) and their cooperation with locals in Ottoman Macedonia. I will also not undermine the state initiatives, since these bands later became part of the Serbian state policies directed at influencing the Slavic inhabitants of the Ottoman Empire. As the previous chapter elaborated, the Serbian state first tried to influence this population by introducing cultural programmes, mostly through church activities and schools that emerged in the three vilayets. The first Serbian organisation, Sveti Sava, was organising educational and religious activities, while the second one was a military organisation known as the Chetnik Organisation. For this state policy, the primary responsibility was in the hands of political entrepreneurs such as teachers, priests, and intellectuals.

---

[115] Miloš Jagodić, *Srpsko albanski odnosi u kosovskom vilajetu (1878–1912)* (Beograd: Zavod za udžbenike, 2009); Uroš Šešum, "Srpska četnička organizacija u Staroj Srbiji 1903–1908: Terenska organizacija," *Srpske Studije/Serbian Studies* 2 (2011): 239–258; Gligor Todorovski, *Srpskata četnička organizacija i nejzinata aktivnost vo Makedonija*, Glasnik na institutot za nacionalna Istorija 1 (1968): 181–204; Mihailo Apostolski, *Istorija na makedonskiot narod II: Od početokot na XIX vek do krajot na Prvata svetska vojna* (Skopje: Institut za Nacionalna Istorija, 1969); Manol Pandevski, *Nacionalnoto prašanje vo makedonskoto osloboditelnoto dviženje (1893–1903)* (Skopje: Kultura, 1974); Gligor Todorovski, *Srbija i reformite vo Makedonija: sredinata na XIX vek do Mladoturskata revolucija 1908* (Skopje: Institut za nacionalna istorija, 1987); Vladimir Ilić, *Srpska četnička akcija 1903– 1912* (Beograd: Ecolibri 2006); Biljana Vučetić, "Srpska revolucionarna organizacija u Osmanskom carstvu na početku 20. veka," *Istorijski časopis* 53 (2006): 359–374; Miloš Jagodić, "Srpske čete u Makedoniji 1897–1901 godine," in *Zbornik radova sa naučnog skupa Ustanci i pobune Srba u Turskoj u XIX veku (povodom 170. godina od izbijanja Niške bune)* ed. Miloš Jagodić (Niš: 2012), pp. 111–130; Uroš Šešum, "Društvo protiv Srba 1897–1902," *Srpske Studije/Serbian Studies* 4 (2013): 73–103; Šešum, "Četnička organizacija u Skopskoj Crnoj Gori 1903–1908, godine."

Second in line were the supposed assistants to the first, who later became "specialists in violence." Their programme was to awaken the national consciousness of the local population and to teach them about the importance of Macedonia for Serbian history. In these efforts, the political entrepreneurs tried to ingrain their imagination of Macedonia and teach about the glorious history of the time of Tsar Dušan, who ruled the Serbian Empire from Prizren and Skopje.[116] However, this imagination could not be imprinted easily on the local population, because Bulgarian bands had already organised a network through which to influence the Slav–Macedonian population for their "Bulgarian cause." Thus, teachers were often the first targets for enemy bands who were perceived as individuals that were "fighting a corrupted battle."[117] The next most frequent target were the priests as representatives of the church, "without whom a school activity could not progress."[118] In this respect, the situation on the ground turned into a struggle of "multiple arenas of domination and opposition." In other words, different actors and different agendas could clash, but could also lead to negotiations between different sides. In claiming this, I do not present an argument that different groups had determined their primordial ethno–national identities, but rather that those groups or personalities within a group interacted, negotiated, and struggled in multiple arenas. To understand how local, national, regional, and probably international practices of "struggle for Macedonia" related to one another, the focus will be on the multiple arenas in which, local, national, and regional actors got involved and interacted, built up alliances, but also incited violence and bloodshed.

---

[116] DAS/Beograd, ŠVK–PO 1912/13, B–2388; See also: DAS/Beograd, MID–PO 1913, R399, F12, D8, XII/828, 1366, 30.01.1913, Prizren.

[117] Ibid., Document: Pravilnik "Organizacija Bugar – Komitet Rada" red 208, knjiga II, sveska 1/2; p. 750; Danilo Šarenac, *Top, vojnik i sećanje: Prvi svetski rat i Srbija 1914–2009* (Beograd: Institut za savremenu istoriju, 2014); Iva Lučić, *Im Namen der Nation: Der politische Aufwertungsprozess der Muslime im sozialistischen Jugoslawien (1956–1971)* (Wiesbaden: Harrassowitz Verlag, 2018).

[118] AC, MIDS, PPO, 1906, II – red 626, knjiga II, sveska 1/2; p. 751. In original: *"Kao što je poznato Ministarstvu Srpska škola je otvorena u Debru prošle godine. Ni škola ni uopšte naš rad u jednom mestu ne može napredovati bez crkve. Zato je potrebno da se u Debru otvori paraklis."*

4.4.1. Private Initiative: Interaction of Individuals with the State

From the outset, the Serbian bands, contrary to the Greek ones, were private initiatives of individuals – the non–state project that could be analysed from the "bottom–up" approach. The Chetnik action was in fact at first a private initiative of "political entrepreneurs" that with time received support from the Serbian state and included guerrilla activities organised by "specialists in violence". At the very beginning, these bands were not under central command of their respective Serbian government. The Serbian teachers (*prosvetni radnici*) in Skopje and Manastir, as well as in other places of Ottoman Macedonia, insisted to organise armed action against other ethnicities, especially against the Bulgarians. However, the Serbian government was not supportive of this initiative from its very beginning, especially not until 1905, when the Serbian state decided to support cheats on the ground in order to defend the "Serbian population" (*srpsko stanovništvo*) in Old Serbia and Macedonia by establishing an organisation named Serbian Defence (*Srpska Odbrana*).[119]

Thus, *Srpska Odbrana*[120] started its activities in 1902, firstly under the name Macedonian Committee (*Makedonski komitet*), initiated by a group of private persons (*privatnih lica*), such as Milorad Gođevac – the engine of this private initiative (*glavni pokretač private inicjative*), who was joined by a merchant, Luka Ćelović, and General Jovan Atanacković. It started by collecting material help for the local population in the three vilayets, which was threatened by the Muslim population, especially by Albanians (*naročito Arbanasa),* and the Principality of Bulgaria, which conducted its actions through one part of the IMARO.[121] The Serbian Consul Mihailo Ristić, however, opposed the actions led by the private initiators, and hence sent a report to the Ministry of Foreign Affairs, demanding that the Serbian government, and not "patriot organisations"

---

[119] Vučetić, *Srpska revolucionarna organizacija.*
[120] Dokumenti o spoljnoj politici Kraljevine Srbije 1903–1914, Knjiga II, supplement 1, p. 748; About official army see: Milić J. Milićević, "Imena Srpskih Pukova," *Glasnik Istorijskog arhiva Valjevo* 33 (1999): 115–121; Milić J. Milićević, *Reforma Vojske Srbije 1897–1900* (Beograd: Vojnoizdavački zavod Beograd, 2002); Milić J. Milićević, "Regrutni Sastav vojske Srbije 1883–1912. Sistem poziva i neki njegovi društveni aspekti," *Vojno–istorijski glasnik* 66/1 (2016): 9–25.
[121] Dokumenti o spoljnoj politici Kraljevine Srbije 1903–1914, Knjiga II, supplement 3, p. 627.

(*patriotska udruženja*), should take control in Macedonia.[122] In the very first stage, most of these "political entrepreneurs" only wanted financial and material support by the Serbian government. However, by 21 June 1905, these private initiators institutionalised this action by founding the Main Board (*glavni odbor*) based in Belgrade. In the same year, its Supreme or Managing Board (*upravni ili vrhovni odbor*) became part of the Ministry of Foreign Affairs of the Kingdom of Serbia, while their Main Executive Board (*Izvršni odbor*) was situated in Vranj and executed operative tasks (*operativno nadležan*) via the General Consulate in Skopje (since 1907).[123] Furthermore, this Chetnik Organisation developed from different centres and was not unified in the beginning. For example, several sources indicated different places for the "first action of the Chetniks." Its member Živojin Rafajlović stated that the first action was organised in the city of Vranj, where in the summer of 1903, he deployed this band headed by Arsa Gavrilović.[124] According to Vasilije Tbić, he was the first initiator and founder of the first cheta in the villages Jablanica and Starca, supported by Živojin Rafajlović from Vranj.[125] Additionally, Aleksa Jovanović–Koča reported that the first action of the Chetniks started in April 1904, on behalf of vojvoda Mićko Krstić in Poreč.[126] Jovan Hadži Vasiljević pointed out that the first cheta was actually organised by Anđelko Aleksić,[127] who was sent by the Central Board (*centralni odbor*)

---

[122] Dokumenti o spoljnoj politici Kraljevine Srbije 1903–1914, Knjiga I, sveska 1, dok. No 212; Dmitar Tasić, "Vojni Odgovor Kraljevine SHS na komitske, kačačke i druge gerilske akcije na prostoru Južne i Stare Srbije 1919–20," in *Guerrilla in the Balkans: Freedom Fighters, Rebels or Bandits – Researching the Guerrilla and Paramilitary Forces in the Balkans*, eds. Momčilo Pavlović, Tetsuya Sahara and Predgrad J. Marković, (Tokyo/Beograd: University Meiji, Institute for Disarmament and Peace Studies, Tokyo – Institute of Contemporary History, Beograd/ Faculty for Security Studies, Beograd, 2007), pp. 137–152.

[123] Ibid; DAS/Beograd, MUD–P 1913, F15/R41, #2041, 18.05.1913.

[124] Vučetić, *Srpska revolucionarna organizacija*; See also: Živojin Rafajlović, "Naša prva četa," *Južni pregled* 6–7 (1930): 263–272.

[125] Ibid. Vasilije Trbić, *Memoari* (Beograd: Kultura, 1996), p. 34; Momčilo Zlatanović, "Četnički (komitski) pokret (1904–1912) (Vranje i Preševska kaza)," *Leskovački zbornik* 32 (1992): 85.

[126] Aleksa Jovanović Kodža, "Vojvoda Savatije. Početak srpske četničke akcije u Maćedoniji," *Letopis Matice srpske* 326 (1930): 128.

[127] Jovan Hadži Vasiljević, *Četnička akcija u Staroj Srbiji i Maćedoniji* (Beograd: N.P., 1928).

from Belgrade in May 1904 and died during this action in Cetirca near Kumanovo. For his death, Stevan Simić – a teacher at the Serbian schools in Manastir, Skopje, and Thessaloniki – accused the local "Serbs" from Kumanovo, who did not help this action, because they "did not have a national organisation (*nisu imali narodnu organizaciju*)."[128] The shape that this "Serbian" action took on the ground was also explained by Antonije Todorović, a "national worker" who dedicated his life "to the idea of the unity of Serbdom."[129] In his memoirs, Antonije Todorović wrote:

"Opening primary and secondary schools allowed Serbian peoples to establish themselves as a national educational organisation in Turkey. This paved the way for pushing back Bulgarians south of Kačanik, where they had already begun to take root. In the beginning, this work occurred only in the area of education and the church. Feeling they would not be able to endure this fight on a purely cultural level, the Bulgarians took to other means to suppress us. They tried to take leadership of the Christian state in the Balkans for the liberation of Christians in the Balkans. The Macedonian Odrin Revolutionary Organisation, which promoted liberation from the Turks with armed illegal units, was established in Sofia in 1893. Naturally, the Christian population was delighted with this idea and acceded to the organisation irrespective of its ethnic traits (*sasvim prirodno, hrišćanski se živalj oduševljava tom idejom i pristupa organizaciji bez obzira na nacionalno obeležje*)."[130]

In light of the above, it seems that at the beginning of the 1900s, many of the local inhabitants of Ottoman Macedonia did not have a "national organisation" (read: consciousness) and regardless of ethnicity, they joined the chetas, who they might have thought could protect their families, kin, or villages. In order to change this situation on the ground, the Serbian "political entrepreneurs" organised "specialists in violence" to influence the local population regarding the construction of their national identities.

---

[128] Stevan Simić, *Srpska revolucionarna organizacija, komitsko četovanje u Staroj Srbiji i Makedoniji 1903–1912* (Beograd: N.P., 1998), p. 140.

[129] Biljana Vučetić, "Prilog za biografiju Antonija Todorovica (1880–1971)," *Istorijski Institut* 55 (2007): 265–277.

[130] Biljana Vučetić, "Sećanja Antonija Todorovića," *Istorijski Časopis* 55 (2007): 265–307; Vučetić, *Srpska revolucionarna organizacija*, p. 360, and p. 364.

The "specialists" were mostly members of Serbian border troops, volunteers from the Austro–Hungarian Empire (the Bosnian provinces) and Montenegro, or Macedonian refugees who were educated in Serbia.[131] The most prominent leaders, such as Captain Blažarić, Božin Simić, Vojislav Tankosić, Vasilije Trbić, Sreten Vukosavljević, or Major Vojin Popović (known as Vojvoda Vuk) recruited local Macedonian population into the guerrilla boards (*gorski štabovi*) operating on the left and right sides of the Vardar River. Their actions were multifaceted. While some of them, like Sreten Vukosavljević, tried to save lives of civilians, others, like Tankosić, became infamous for brutality and had a terrifying reputation.[132]

4.4.2. Organisation of Chetas on the Ground

During the period of "struggle for Macedonia," the Serbian chetas kept up correspondence with Serbian government bodies, such as the Ministry of Foreign Affairs and the consulates in Skopje, Bitola, and Thessaloniki, and had strong support from the secret society Unification or Death (*Ujedinjenje ili smrt*) that was also known as the Black Hand (*Crna ruka*). This secret organisation exerted a strong influence on the military circle of National Defence (*Narodna odbrana*), which was also responsible for the Serbian *coup d'etat* in 1903. The members of those organisations provided important support to the chetas and participated in the battles during the Balkan Wars (Kumanovo).[133] Their main task was to perform a reconnaissance mission or to create diversions in the enemy rear,[134] but also to try to attract various strata of the population including foreigners[135] and Muslim volunteers, possibly Turks and Albanians with previous

---

[131] Dmitar Tasić, *Paramilitarism in the Balkans: Yugoslavia, Bulgaria and Albania 1917–1924* (Oxford: Oxford University Press, 2020), p. 14.

[132] Ibid; Dmitar Tasić "The Institutionalization of Paramilitarism in Yugoslav Macedonia: The Case of the Organization against the Bulgarian Bandits, 1923–1933," *The Journal of Slavic Military Studies* 32/3 (2019): 388–413; Sreten Vukosavljević, *Istorija seljačkog društva: sociologija seljačkih radova* (Beograd: Srpska akademija nauka i umetnosti, 1953), pp. 380–386.

[133] Vladimir Ilić, "Učešće srpskih komita u Kumanovskoj operaciji 1912 godine," *Vojnoistorijski glasnik – Organ Vojnoistorijskog Instituta* 1–3 (1992): 200.

[134] Dmitar Tasić, "Repeating Phenomenon: Balkan Wars and Irregulars," in *Les guerres balkaniques (1912–1913): Conflits, enjeux, mémoires,* ed. Catherine Horel (Bruxelles: P.I.E. Peter Lang, 2014), p. 29.

[135] Foreign Chetnik vojvoda: Bogdan Hajnc (Jugović).

military experience.[136] However, the result of this was that some Muslims from Bosnia (and the Kosovo vilayet) joined these chetnik detachments as in the case of the Labski detachment led by Captain Vojo Tankosić.[137] Of Captain Tankosić plenty has already been written,[138] therefore I will only briefly list his activities between 1903 and 1912. At the very beginning of the Chetnik action in Macedonia, he joined the Chetnik group to influence locals' expression of their national consciousness. At the same time, he participated in a conspiracy against the Serbian king Aleksandar Obrenović, who was dethroned in the May Coup of the same year, in 1903. He was also active in Bosnia and Herzegovina, which was under the rule of the Dual Monarchy and became a member of Young Bosnia, one of the founders of the Unification or Death (Black Hand), the organisation whose constitution he wrote, with the aim of the unification of Serbdom.[139]

Photo 2 Chetnik action in Ottoman Macedonia[140]

---

[136] Dmitar Tasić, *Repeating Phenomenon*, p. 30.
[137] Jovana D. Šaljić–Ratković, "Muslimani u oslobođenu Srbije 1912/13: od mita do stvarnosti," *Prvi balkanski rat 1912/13 godine: društveni i civilizacijski smisao* 1 (2016): 325–339.
[138] See: Silvija Đurić, *Dnevnik pobeda, Srbija u balkanskim ratovima 1912–13* (Beograd: Filip Višnjić, 1990); Jovan M. Jovanović, *Borba za narodno ujedinjenje 1914–1918* (Beograd: Geca Kon, 1935).
[139] Belić, *Komitski Vojvoda*.
[140] Ibid., p. 88.

As can be seen in Photo 2, Muslims (and Albanian–speaking individuals) were present and actively took places in Chetnik movement. Also, one of its members (Milan Milošević) is wearing a *plis,* a hat that became a symbol of Albanian national identity. According to his name and surname, he was ethnically Serb and Orthodox. Therefore, it is worth questioning why a member of a "Serbian" cheta would don an Albanian hat, a symbol of the supposed enemies of the Serbian nation. One possible explanation is that national identity is not inherent and is instead a social construct. Additionally, the *plis* hat had not yet become an exclusively Albanian national symbol at the time, and individuals may have placed stronger importance on local, family and tribal ties rather than national identity. Next–door neighbours that belonged to different communities and churches (or religions) could wear the same "ethnical" clothes too. Rather, a better way to think of their clothing in this photograph is that they signalled to others from which valley, region or village came. [141] According to Isa Blumi, "in many of the regions from which these men came (we know this by learning to 'read' the subtle differences in design), the closest neighbour, and thus someone who would share to an extent the same clothing patterns, may have been someone of a 'different' faith and ethnicity."[142] Thus, thinking in terms of "national" at a time when locals were still not "national" could be misleading. An illustration of this was one of the active participants of the cheta led by Tankosić, who was a young Muslim from Herzegovina (Stolac) named Mustafa Golubić and was trained in a chetnik school in Prokuplje. He was also a member of the Young Bosnia organisation and guerrilla fighter in Ottoman Macedonia, especially during the Balkan Wars. [143] Known as "man of conspiracy" (*čovjek konspiracije*), [144] Golubić was also accepted into the Black Hand

---

[141] Mary Ellen Roach–Higgins, *Dress and Identity* (New York: Fairchild Boos, 1995); Bogdan Trifunović, "Memory of Old Serbia," p. 252; Miloš *Jagodić, Srbija i Stara Srbija (1839–1868): Nasleđe na jugu* (Beograd: Evoluta, 2016); and Atanasovski, *Mapiranje Stare Srbije.*

[142] Blumi, *Reinstating*, p. 17.

[143] Marko Attila Hoare, *Genocide and Resistance in Hitler's Bosnia: The Partisans and the Chetniks, 1941–1943* (Oxford: Oxford University Press, 2006).

[144] Sead Trhulj, *Mustafa Golubić, čovjek konspiracije* (Sarajevo: Zalihica, 2007); Uroš Vujošević, "Prilozi za biografiju Mustafe Golubića," *Istorija XX veka 1–2* (1993): 217–230.

Organisation that was led at that time by another famous Serbian general Dragutin Dimitrijević Apis. In 1914, he was an active member of the action of the assassination of Archeduke Franz Ferdinand in Sarajevo.[145]

Similar to Golubić's was the life path of Smajo Ferović – an Albanian speaking Muslim – who originated from the castle guard (*dizdar*) family Omeragić from Plav (nowadays Montenegro). His grandfather, Jakup Ferri, and his uncle Hasan have in present–day Albanian historiography been honoured as "heroes of the nation" (*hero i kombit*) who fought against Montenegro in 1878 for the "Albanian cause."[146] However, Smajo (on the Photo 2 sitting above Milan Milošević) personally took part in the Chetnik Organisation together with his comrade Mustafa Golubić. Hence, he was also trained in a chetnik school in Prokuplje that prepared him for the chetnik action and Serbian Border troops, who were responsible for the infiltration of Serbian chetniks in Ottoman territories and building networks with local notables (*krerë*) of the Albanian families in the Kosovo vilayet.[147] As a person who was fluent in Albanian, (*dobro govorio arnautski*) he played an important role with the Albanian notables in the Kosovo vilayet,[148] especially with Isa Boletini –considered a hero in Albanian historiography – whose uncle, Hasan Ferri (Ferović), was a very close friend of Isa. In addition to their friendship, they had family connections, as two sisters of Smajo Ferović were married to Isa Boletini's sons. During the time of the Kingdom of the Serbs, Croats, and Slovenians, one of Isa's sons, named Bajazit, wrote to the Ministry of the Interior as follows:

> "I, as a Serb and as a son of the great patriot and Serb, the late Isa Boljetinac, regret that in these parts [in the Mitrovica area] we have such authorities that work according to their whim and spite, and not at all for the good of our fatherland."[149]

---

[145] Tasić, *Paramilitarism in the Balkans*, p. 176.

[146] Aleks Buda, *Fjalor enciklopedik shqiptar* (Tiranë: Akademia e Shkencave e RPSSH, 1985), p. 261. Quote: *"Ferri Hasan (1860–1946) – luftëtar dhe udhëheqës i shquar popullor nga Plava. Mori pjesë aktive përkrah të atit, Jakup Ferrit, në betejat e zhvilluara për mbrojtjen e Plavës e të Gucisë më 1879–1880."*

[147] Politika, Beograd, 15. Februar, 1928, p. 4.

[148] Ibid.

[149] Jovo Miladinović, "Shifting State Loyalty: The Case of an Officer Serefeddin or Milan Milovanović," *Glasnik Etnografskog instituta* 68/3, (2020), p. 716; In the document:

Although his father Isa was not known as a Serb, the examples of Bajazit Boletini and Smajo Ferović represent the complexities of the actors on the ground who could have multiple identities or switch sides, accept new national constructs and shift to other ideologies according to their economic, social, or other profits. The situation on the ground was often more complex than how national historiographies represent it through meta–narrative stories. Along with the fact that members of chetas could switch sides, they were sometimes also connected with their "enemies" via families, kinship, or friendships. When we try to integrate the "bottom–up" approach, we realise that this "struggle for Macedonia" was actually a "multiple arena of domination and opposition" that always included negotiation among diverse sides. Thus, we should not neglect the agency of the participants, but rather integrate their points of view and try to understand the situation via their complexities. Smajo Ferović was definitely one such personalities, as he was often appointed to negotiate with locals in the Kosovo Vilayeti and to undertake initiatives on behalf of the Serbian government. In this respect, he negotiated with two famous Kosovo notables such as Hasan Husejin from Budakova and Redžep Hadži Abdul,[150] who moved to Leskovac (Serbia) during the Young Turk military expedition in Kosovo in 1910. They staged an uprising against the Young Turks between 23 April and 12 May 1910 on the Caraleve Mountain and were forced to ask for help. Smajo Ferović offered them a possibility to move to Leskovac, and stayed in contact with a member of the Main Board of the "Serbian Brothers" (*glavna uprava – "srpske braće" – Beograd)* and the secretary of the General Consulate in Skopje, J.J. Studić.[151] Furthermore, Ferović once wrote to the Foreign Minister of Serbia, Dr. Milovan Đ. Milovanović, with the words, "upon my return from Skoplje and Veleš to Leskovac, I met up with Husein Budakova and Aljuš Barjaktar from Ostrozuba, who wanted me to forward a message to you." Budakova and Bajraktar's message demanded more intensive activities in the Kosovo vilayet on behalf of Serbia, "hoping and believing

---

AJ/Belgrade, 14–181–670–45, Statement by Bajazit Ise Boljetinca made on August 11, 1922 in the Ministery of the Interior.

[150] Generalni konzulat Kraljevine Srbije Skoplje, Jovan M. Jovanović, 27.03.1911 g. AC, MIDS, PO, 1911, F–IX, D–8.

[151] Ibid.

that Serbia trusted their loyalty and would support their actions, because they had given themselves over to the King of Serbia."[152] Although, they had given themselves over to the king and showed their loyalty to Serbia in 1910 and 1911, when the Balkan Wars broke out, Hasan Husein Budakova fought against Serbia with other 400 Kosovars (*me Hasan Hyseinin e Budakoves ne krye*).[153]

Another Muslim member that joined the Serbian actions and supported the Serbian policies in Macedonia, was the Turkish Gandarmerie Captain (*turski žandarmerijski kapetan*) Redžep Abdurahman Adrović. He was born in Đakovica (Kosovo vilayet) as the son of Abduraman Adrović, who moved to the Ottoman Empire from the city of Niš that became part of Serbia in 1878. As a child from a *muhadžir* family from Serbia, he was given the opportunity to enter the Ottoman army and become a gendarmerie captain for five years. However, due to political reasons during the Albanian uprisings in the Kosovo vilayet, he was imprisoned by the Ottoman government and released after a few months. This became his main reason to migrate to Serbia, because he considered "Niš as his fatherland" (*Niš smatram za moju otadžbinu*). Upon his arrival, he joined the Serbian action and was engaged in the Kosovo vilayet as a Serbian

---

[152] AC, MIDS, SPA, 1911, F–IV, D–6. P. 652; Secretary J.J. Studić to Minister of Foreign Affairs, in original: *"Vraćajući se iz Skoplja i Velesa svratio sam u Leskovac, probavio jedan dan i sastao se sa Huseinom Budakovcem i Aljuš Barjaktarom iz Ostrozuba, koji su me molili da Vam ovim putem podnesem njihove molbe i želje. Događaji, koji su se počeli odigrati na jugozapadnom kraju Crne Gore I upadi Arnauta I Malisora u Tursku, veoma su uzbudili Hasana i Barjaktara. Oni smatraju da oni ne treba više da sede ovako skrštenih ruku, pa se u toj želji obraćaju Vama, sa molbom, da im se dozvoli da i oni sa svojim drugovima odu u svoje krajeve i pokrenu akciju protiv današnjeg režima u Turskoj. Na ime te akcije, oni mole, da im se, za prvi maj, da po jedna brzometna puška, nekoliko bombi, dinamita i potrebna municija, i oni bi se odmah krenuli za Tursku. Pojmljivo je, da se ove njihove molbe i želje osnivaju na nepokolebljivoj nadi I veri, da će ih Vlada Kraljevine Srbije verujući u njihovu odanost, štititi i pomagati u njihovoj akciji i da će im, na slučaj neuspeha i buduće ukazivati gostoljubivo utočište, ne samo njima lično no svakome ko se bude pridružio njihovoj akciji. (...) Oni su, kažu, sebe i svoje predali Kralju Srbije i oni su u njegovim rukama. "*

[153] Tafil Boletini, *Kujtime: Prane Isa Boletinit dhe përballë sfidave të kohes* (Tiranë: Ndërmarrja Gazetare–Botuese Album, 1996), p. 154; Quote: *"në Diber u bashkuem me se 400 kosovarë dhe për këte arsye, e pranuem propozimin dhe u bame gati me çue nji fuqi me Hasan Hyseinin e Budakoves në krye, Isuf Bardhoshin e Isniqit dhe ten ji djali te axhes Isa."*

agent.[154] During his stay in Serbia, he gave a "word of honor that [would] protect Serbian interests and return a thousand times more to Serbia for all good things that this state did."[155] In this respect, I try to give voices to these actors, who (can) lead us to rethink and question our knowledge constructed mostly by meta–narrative historiographies. I aim to prevent these stories from falling into oblivion and to highlight new cases that show multiple interactions and complexities at the ground levels. Another notable instance is found in the man known as "Turk," named Ahmet Musa or Miloš Srbinović, who served the Serbian Defence Organisation, while he worked as tipstaff (Serbian *gavaz*, Turkish *kavas*) in the Ottoman Consulate in Vranj. In one of his reports, he wrote of himself that he "[came] originally from Kumanovo in Old Serbia" and that he was "ethnically a Turk."[156] During one of the first Chetnik actions, he was contacted by Živojin Rafajlović – one of the founders of the Chetniks and organiser of the bands. In the years of the "struggle for Macedonia," Musa Ahmet was transferring to Rafajlović the entire consular post of the Ottoman Consulate in Vranj (*svu konzulatsku poštu predao na kopiranje i upotrebu*), as well as all the documents that the Ottoman Consul in Vranj was sending to the Ottoman Embassy in Belgrade or the Ottoman government in Istanbul (*svu poštu koju je g. Konsul slao u Beograd, Carigrad*).[157] In one of the important documents, he listed: "1. The

---

[154] Document: Načelstvu okruga Niškog, Komesar policije Man. M. Mrvić, 25.03.1901, p. 668.

[155] Ibid; In original: *"Turski žandarmerijski kapetan Redžep Abdurahman Adrović. "Ja sam se rodio u Đakovici. Sin sam Abduramana Adrovića, koji je se odavde, iz Niša, iselio onda kada je Srbija zauzela Niš. Još za doba vladavine Sultana Abdul–Hamida, usljed izvesnih nemira u mome plemenu, koje se zove "Sač", ja sam, kao viđen član ovog plemena, bio pozvat u Solun. (...) kao žandarmerijski oficir proveo sam pet godina – računajući i ovo vreme koje sam u zatvoru proveo (zbog albanskog pokreta). Posle podužeg razmišljanja našao sam da mi je najbolje da emigriram u Srbiju tim pre, što Niš smatram za moju otadžbinu. (...) Izgledi su da će se prilike u Arbaniji uskoro promeniti te ću se vratiti svojoj kuci. Dajem časnu reč da ću voditi računa o interesima Srbije a uveren sam da ću imati toliko moći da ću za svaku učinjenu mi dobrotu od strane Srbije, njoj – Srbiji – to hiljado–struko vratiti."*

[156] Document: AS. MIDS, SPA, 16.12.1907, F–III, D–3, knjiga II, supplement 3, p. 490.

[157] Ibid.: Quote: *"Ja sam rodom iz Kumanova u St. Srbiji i po narodnosti sam Turčin po imenu Musa Ahmet i duže vremena bio sam gavaz u turskom Konsulatu u Vranju. U 1903 godine stupio sam u vezu sa g. Živojin Rafajlovićem tadašnjim pešadijskim kapetanom i predsednikom komiteta, te sam mu svu konzulatsku poštu predao na kopiranje i upotrebu. Svu poštu koja bi dolazila u Konzulat a koju sam ja trebao predavati g. Konzulu ja sam*

Ottoman Consulate in Vranj; 2. The Ottoman Embassy in Belgrade; 3. Kosovo Vilayet; 4. Manastir/Bitola Vilayet; 5. The Ottoman Foreign Ministry in Istanbul." [158] However, the moment that he raised the suspicion of the Ottoman authorities, he left the Consulate and was converted to Orthodox Christianity, married to a Serbian woman from Vranj, and baptised with the new name of Miloš Srbinović. His godfather was no other than Rafajlović himself, who was actively organising Serbian bands in Ottoman Macedonia. Rafajlović enabled him to participate in a Serbian action in Skopje and "other towns in Old Serbia in order to bring back detailed information from the ground."[159] In this respect, he admitted that he worked only for "the interest of our chetniks" (*sve to svršio u korist naših četnika*).[160] For this service, he was paid 300 dinar by the Minister of Foreign Affairs. [161] In a similar way, Jovo Miladinović argues the case of the Ottoman officer Şerefeddin who

---

prvo predao g. Rafailoviću te je on kopirao, ponova je kovertirao i pečatio pa mi je vraćao da je predam g. Konsulu. Tako isto i na isti način predavao sam g. Rafailoviću i svu poštu koju je g. Konsul slao u Beograd, Carigrad itd. Sva ta pisma – neka u kopiji, neka u originalu – g. Rafailović je predao ministru spoljnih poslova, naročito g. Sveti Simiću, a prevodio ih je sa turskog jezika g. Trajan Živković činovnik. Taj sam posao produžio raditi 4–5 mjeseci, dok nisu u Konsulatu posumnjali u moju vernost. Kad sam to osetio ja sam se morao odmah skloniti, a posle nekoliko dana i pokrstiti. Kumovao mi je g. Rafailović i dobio sam srpsko ime Miloš Srbinović. U Vranju sam se oženio Srpkinjom i imam dvoje dece. Otvorio sam berbersku radnju kojoj sam bio vičan ali bez ikakvog kapitala. Od odbora sam dobio svega 200 dinara."

[158] AS. MIDS, SPA, 16.12.1907, F–III, D–3, knjiga II, supplement 3, p. 491, 11.12.1907; see in original: *"1. Vranjskog turskog konzulata 2. Beogradskog turskog poslanstva 3. Kosovskog vilajeta 4. Bitoljskog vilajeta 5. Turskog ministra inostranih dela u Carigradu."*

[159] AS. MIDS, SPA, 16.12.1907, F–III, D–3, knjiga II, supplement 3, 11.12. 1907, p. 492; See in original: *"u konzulatu radio sam razne stvari u korist Srbije i uvek sam izveštavao tadanji odbor (u Vranju). Nekoliko puta sam bio u Skoplju i drugim varošima u Staroj Srbiji u cilju da donesem što tačnije podatke odboru."*

[160] AS. MIDS, SPA, 16.12.1907, F–III, D–3, knjiga II, supplement 3, 11.12. 1907, p. 492; See in original: *"docnije smo uspeli, a po mojoj pretpostavci turskom konzulu, da se zatvore nekoliko bugaraša, među kojima je čuveni Petar Karamanov, učitelj u Kumanovskoj kazi, koji je osuđen na 15 godina robije. Češće me je zvao turski konzul, napominjući mi, da je saznao da će i te noći preći granicu srpski četnici, i tražio je od mene da ja potvrdim tu vest, naravno ja sam sve to svršio u korist naših četnika, izveštavajući o svemu čika Lazu biv. Magacionera komiteta odbora, koji mi je bio najbliži."*

[161] AS. MIDS, SPA, 16.12.1907, F–III, D–3, knjiga II, supplement 3, 18.12.1907, p. 492; See in original: *"Rešavam da se iz vanrednog kredita odobrenog zakonodavnim rešenjem od 23. 10. 1906 g. izda Milošu Srbinoviću (Musi Ahmetu, Turčinu) iz Kumanova za usluge koje je učinio Srbiji kao kavaz u turskom Konzulatu i Vranju suma od tri stotine dinara."*

changed his name to Milovan Milovanović. He points out that loyalties were not built only around national or religious affiliation, but they were impacted by a myriad motives such as love, momentary war settings, economic situation etc., which would influence individuals to switch their loyalties in order to survive in a new context produced by war and violence – as in the case of the Ottoman officer Şerefeddin.[162] During the Balkan Wars, when the Ottoman army was losing its positions in the three vilayets, Şerefeddin voluntarily joined the army of the Kingdom of Serbia.[163] As in the case of Ahmet Musa (Miloš Srbinović), Şerefeddin (Milan Milanović) also learned the Serbian language and married a Serb woman from Pljevlja, with whom he lived in the Kingdom of the Serbs, Croats, and Slovenians.[164] Furthermore, such examples are not "unique" and "exceptional;" to the contrary, one can trace similar cases in other settings worldwide as well. This diverse image of actors shows that these individuals who were Ottoman personnel, but also belonged to the chetnik or other Serbian organisations, were an active and dynamic group, influencing the locals, as well as influenced by the locals and often coming from the ranks of the locals. Accordingly, their networks with the locals or with other ethnicities cannot be considered in a vacuum as a static structure, but rather as processual constructs of multi-layered identities and historical intersectionality. Similar to the above was the engagement of chetnik Savatija Milošević, who cooperated and established friendships with local Muslims (Albanians) like Mula Zeka and Isa Boletini.[165] In the early 1900s, the Serbian state proclaimed him a robber and hajduk, and therefore he spent a long time hiding in the house of Mula Zeka, the founder of the Peja League, in the Kosovo vilayet. In 1905, Milošević died in battle as a Chetnik, fighting for "our thing" (*našu stvar*). Another notable example is found in vojvoda Tankosić's search for an "Albanian" who broke his *besa* (word of honor) during the battle in Velike Hodže. This "Albanian" betrayed the cheta of vojvoda Lazar Kujundžija, in a group with nine other comrades who were killed in the battle. However,

---

[162] Miladinović, *Shifting State Loyalty.*
[163] Ibid.
[164] Ibid; See also: Vojislav Šikoparija, *Sećanja srpskog oficira (1900–1918)* (Beograd: Zavod za udžbenike i nastavna sredstva, 2016), pp. 237–238.
[165] Vučetić, *Srpska revolucionarna organizacija*, p. 364.

interestingly, this "Albanian" (his name has not been registered), was hiding alongside two other "Albanians" into the house of one Serbian woman (*pronašli su skrivenog kod neke Srpkinje*) who tried to save their lives.[166]

One should also be aware that sometimes members within the Serbian organisations had different responses as well, participating in different programs and lobbying for diverse and sometimes contradictory strategies. Thus, it should not be assumed that the interior of their own organisations had a unified, proto–, or supra–national sensibility. Rather the ambitions of Serbian organisations were varied and contested, and also often resulted in clashes and contradictory tendencies. In this respect, one should also emphasise that there was no unified policy among those organisations and gangs. For example, the Serbian Defence boards in Belgrade and in Macedonia (i.e. in Bitola) did not always cooperate and share the same aims. Thus, Aleksa Jovanović–Kodža, a Serbian teacher in Manastir at that time, stressed the differences between the Bitola board which "executed a meticulous organisation of the movement on its terrain," while the organisers from Belgrade "did not even bother to visit the field as inquisitive travellers in order to meet the popular representatives, and most importantly, to direct their movement to the urgent popular need."[167] Another prominent personality, Pavle Blažarić, also known as vojvoda Bistrički, described the situation of the chetniks on the ground as one of "no law and order," rather led by many conflicts, especially between vojvoda Nikola Janković–Kosovski and Panta Radosavljević–Dunavski.[168] Furthermore, in 1907, the rift and conflict

---

[166] Belić, *Komitski Vojvoda,* p. 41.

[167] Biljana Vučetić, "Some considerations on the emergence of the Serbian Chetnik Movement in Macedonia during the last period of Ottoman rule," *Zapisi, Istorijski Institut Univerziteta Crne Gore* 3/4 (2015): 117; Jovanović Kodža, *Vojvoda Savatije,* p. 128; Aleksa Jovanović Kodža, "Početak srpskog četničkog pokreta u Južnoj Srbiji i Makedoniji," *Književni Jug* 1 (1929): 14–19; Aleksa Jovanović Kodža, *Četnički spomenik: Vojvoda Micko, život i rad* (Skoplje: Krajničanac, 1930); Milutin Lazarević, *Naši ratovi za oslobođenje i ujedinjenje, srpsko–turski rat 1912* (Beograd: Porta Libris, 2019), first time published in 1928; Vladimir Dedijer, *Sarajevo 1914* (Beograd: Agencija Obradović, 2014); Stanoje Stanojević, *Srpsko–turski rat 1912* (Beograd: Svet knjige, 2021) first publication was in 1928.

[168] DAS, Izvršni odbor Vranja, f. VII, Izvestaj Bistričkog, Pov. Br. 169, Beograd, 9/22, Januar, 1907; Pavle Blažarić, *Memoari* (Leposavić: Centar za kuturu Sava Dečanac,

between the various Serbian organisations was escalated as well. A report from 11 December 1907 states that the "executive board of the Serbian Defence" already had difficulties in its cooperation the "with Society of Serbian Brotherhood."[169] The representatives of the Serbian Defence urged that the Society of the Serbian Brotherhood (*Društvo Srpska braća*) should cooperate, otherwise it "[could] lead to a discord within the Organisation" (*svojim radom stvori rascep u Organizaciji*) and from there to "far–reaching consequences, as in the Bulgarian cases – the formation of many different committees" (*a za tim dođe do onih posledica, kao Bugarskoj*).[170] Comparably, one can find conflicts between the Circle of Serbian Sisters (*Kolo Srpskih sestara*),[171] a women's charitable society established to help the Serbian Chetnik Organisation and the Society of Serbian Brotherhood.[172] Moreover, in 1907 a clash between the "consulate" and "church" sides occurred, which was led by metropolitan Vićentije and the director of the Gymnasium in Skopje, Luka Lazarević. A similar conflict first arose in October 1906 between Milan Rakić, who was the then Consul in Priština, and the Prizren metropolitan Nićifor.[173] To mediate their reconciliation was appointed Bogdan Radenković, who

---

2006). See also about the conflicts: Miloš Škarić, *Četnici i dobrovoljci u ratovima za oslobođenje i ujedinjenje* (Novi sad: Savez dobrovoljaca za Srem, Bačku i Baranju, 1925); Vojvoda Kosta Pećanac, *Četnicka akcija 1903–1912* (Beograd: Dom, 1933); Jaša Tomić, *Rat na Kosovu i Staroj Srbiji* (Novi Sad: Portalibris, 1913); Milorad Belić, *Komitski vojvoda Vojislav Tankosić* (Valjevo: Međuopštinski istorijski arhiv, 2005).

[169] AC, MIDS, Izvršni odbor S.O. u Vranju, F–H, 1907, knjiga II, supplement 3, p. 500; See in original: *"...(izvršni odbor Srpske odbrane u Vranju) smatra, da se sa ovakvim radom (na svoju ruku prelaze granicu) Društvo Srpske Braće, udaljuje od svog prvog poziva, jer se sa ovakvim radom može kompromitovati, pa s toga i još mnogih drugih razloga ne bi trebalo da se bez odobrenja i sporazuma meša u posao koji je ovome Odboru poveren. Na ovaj način lako se može stvoriti rascep u Organizaciji, a to društvo Srpska braća treba da ima na umu, ako ne želi da svojim radom stvori rascep u Organizaciji a za tim dođe do onih posledica, kao što je to u Bugarskoj, te i kod nas da se stvore nekoliko komiteta, koji mogu biti samo od štete a nikako od neke uobražene koristi."*

[170] AC, MIDS, Izvršni odbor S.O. u Vranju, F–H, 1907, knjiga II, supplement 3, p. 500.

[171] Ibid. 752; Founders of Kolo Srpskih Sestara: Nadežda Petrović, Dafne (Delfa) Ivanić (the wife of Ivan Ivanić and she met her husband Ivan in Skopje, where she was a teacher between 1900 and 1903), Savka Subotić, Milica Luković, Mila Dobrić.

[172] Ibid. 753; See in original: *"Društvo Srpska Braća – rodoljubi udruženja izbeglica iz Turske, osnovano početkom 1905. Predsednik Golub Janjić, Josif Studić."*

[173] Biljana Vučetić, "Bogdan Radenković i Milan Rakić," *Istorijski časopis* 57 (2008): 415.

was one of the founders of the secret society Black Hand and assumed to have written the first rulebook of the Serbian Defence. In Serbian historiography he is known as a "national worker" (*nacionalni radnik*) who graduated from Galatasaray Lisesi and worked in Skopje as a teacher. To the public he was a "loyal citizen of the Ottoman Empire," but away from the public eye he was an agent of the Consulate of the Kingdom of Serbia and an organiser of Serbian chetas, appointed also to reconcile and mediate between discordant sides.[174] He also cooperated closely with the Serbian vice–consul in Thessaloniki, Milan Rakić (October 1907 – October 1908), who was always "informed about the course of our affairs" (*mi ćemo Vas redovno izveštavati o toku naše stvari*).[175] Along with Dragutin Dimitrijević Apis, he was meeting with Isa Boljetini and providing him with arms and weapons.[176] Therefore, he was not only a "loyal citizen of the Ottoman Empire" who taught children at school, but also a conciliator between Serbian sides, and a co–operator with the local Albanians in the Kosovo vilayet and organiser of Serbian chetas.[177] Together with Stevan Simić, he argued that Serbia should use all capacities to penetrate Ottoman Macedonia, because "the anarchy [would] last until the moment when the Macedonian, in other words the Turkish or Near East Question, [was] resolved" (*a anarhije će biti uvek do god se ne reši maćedonsko odnosno tursko ili bližeg istoka pitanje*).[178] Indeed, many Serbian "political entrepreneurs," considered the Macedonian Question crucial for the survival of Serbdom and that it should be resolved by the Serbian state.

---

[174] Biljana Vučetić, "Izveštajji obaveštajca diplomati, pisma Bogdana Radenkovića Milanu Rakiću (1907–1912)," *Miscellanea* 29 (2008): 159–160.
[175] Ibid., p. 156.
[176] Ibid., p. 168.
[177] Ibid., pp. 153–169.
[178] Stevan Simić, Kratovo, Ministarstvu inostranih dela Kraljevine Srbije – Beograd, 11/24.12 1904, AC, MIDS, PPO, 1904, K – red 28; Ljiljana Aleksić–Pejković, Knjiga II, supplement 1, p.746; see: *"Bugari su bili u stanju da naoružaju celu Maćedoniju, (Južnu) St. Srbiju i Jedrenski vilajet, a Srbija se ustručava da prebaci nekoliko hiljada komada i to onih pušaka, koje stoje po starim magacinima i koje se neće nikada upotrebiti! Zar nije to greh da hrđaju tolike puške, a preko granice padaju glave kao bundeve? (...) a anarhije će biti uvek do god se ne reši maćedonsko odnosno tursko ili bližeg istoka pitanje."*

4.5. Trajectories of *Toskë Kaçak*: A Micro-Historical Experience and Everyday Empire

As has been seen, the final decades of the Ottoman rule were marked by various bands who took to the hills to fight for the end of the Ottoman rule or to protect their villages and regions from others' bands. Among these members of bands, the most renowned in Albanian historiography are such intellectuals and guerrilla fighters as the two brothers Bajo and Çerçiz Topulli, the cousins Fehim and Menduh Zavallani, and the two Orthodox Christian Albanians Gjergj Qiriazi and Mihail Grameno, who was also a writer. Namely, Bajo Topulli and Gjergj Qiriazi, in collaboration with the cousins Fehim and Menduh Zavalani, founded the Secret Committee for the Liberation of Albania (*Komitet i shqipëtarëve për lirin e Shqipërisë*) in Manastir in November 1905.[179] In their Statute they proclaimed the aims of the organisation, which prioritised "enlivening Albania through brotherhood, love, unity and the spread of civilisation" (*të ngjallurit e Shqipërisë, duke mbjellë vëllazërimin, dashurinë, bashkimin, duke përhapur udhën e qytetërimit*). As part of these values, this organisation also focused on "progress of the nation that [was] at the moment in a very dark stage" (*për mbrothësinë kombit dhe të shpëtuarin nga zgjedha dhe errësira në të cilën gjendet sot*).[180] As previous chapters have made clear, at the *fin de siecle* various intellectuals shared a common rhetoric that emphasised (the opposites of) "progress" and "darkness," "civilisation" and "barbarity." Its ideological father was Bajo Topulli, who was director of the Ottoman Secondary School (*idadiye*). In the construction of a "colonialist" ideology toward the Turks, Topulli was greatly supported by his brother, Çerçiz, who in the newspaper *Drita* ("Light") wrote: "We [Albanians] should not shed our blood for the Turks, because they are Tatars, Mongols that came from Asia, and we are Europeans."[181] In the

---

[179] Gawrych *The Crescent,* p. 147; The Secret Committee for Liberation of Albania was joined by Jashar Bidineka, Nuçi Naçi, Riza be Viliçishti, Grigor Cilka, Qani be Ypi; See: Mihal Grameno, *Kryengritja shqiptare* (Korçë: Direttore, 1925) First Publication; Mihail Grameno, *Kryengritja shqipetare* (Tirane: N.SH. Naim Frashëri, 1959).

[180] Zaho Golemi, "Çerçiz Topulli dhe çeta flamur lirie: Me rastin e 110 vjetorit të krijimit të çetës së Çerçiz Topullit," *Mbrojtja* (2016): 49.

[181] Drita, No. 17, Sofia, August, 1903, p. 1; Quote: *"E drejta pra është, se neve pashketajdhi nukë duhete të derdhme as një pike gjaku per Tyrqite, se ata jane Tartare, Mongolie e kanë ardhure prej Asie, e neve jemi Evropjane e nje nga më të mbaruarate degë të farës Kafkasiane."*

Age of Empire, being European meant being "superior" and "progressive," in contrast to the "Tatars" and "Mongols." Some of these "political entrepreneurs" also referred to the Turks as "Anadolian" and "stuborn/rude (*halldupë*)."[182] This "colonist" attitude was regularly iterated in almost racist tones, where "progress" of the nation entailed "civilisation." Its aim was to implement "development" or "expansion," which would again mirror the patronising, often racist discourses associated with western European colonialism of the time. There is no doubt that members of the Secret Committee for the Liberation of Albania perceived the Ottoman government as "barbaric" and not legitimate to rule over Albanians, who were "Europeans." The above mentioned personalities tried to construct a narrative of Albanians as the legitimate nation that should inherit "the lands of Alexander the Great."[183] In their imagination, there was a clear narrative that Albanians are his descendants whose sole condition implied "the liberation and resurrection of Albania" (*liria ishte sharti dhe kushti dhe ilaçi për tu ringjallur Shqipëria*).[184] Accordingly, the Albanian nation had the difficult task of fighting on two fronts: both against the "barbaric" Turkish rulers, and against the "fake" Greeks who also claimed right to the heritage of Alexander the Great in Macedonia. [185] These "political entrepreneurs" tried to construct an Albanian ethnogenesis and national identity framed by the "Illyrian" theory of Albanian ethnical and cultural origin and the main political consequences that were likely to arise from the implementation of this theory in the Macedonian case, since these lands were "under Illyria." [186] Furthermore, this dispute about the ancient heritage also spread penetrated the daily life of intellectuals and

---

[182] Clayer, *Aux origines du nationalism albanais*, p. 412.

[183] Arkivi Qendror Shtetëror: AQSH/Tiranë, F.102.D.82.f. 1–2.

[184] Golemi, *Çerçiz Topulli*, p. 50. See in original: "*Me anën e kësaj letre dua të lajmëroj të gjithë vëllezërit patriotë, shqiptarë, miqtë tanë, si dhe gjithë të tjerët që interesohen për Çështjen e Shqipërisë, se unë me gjithë shokët e mij (duke lënë shtëpijat, familjet e gjithë pasurinë), kemi dalë ndër male si kry– engritës, kundër qeverisë barbare tiranike, për Lirinë e Shqipërisë... qeveria kërkon e i merr me pahir pagesat e ndryshme të rënda, jo vetëm, por edhe duke na grabitur, plaçkitur sa s'durohet dot më... Liria ishte sharti/kushti dhe ilaçi për tu ringjallur Shqipëria...*"

[185] Helen Abazi, "Historical Greek–Albanian Relations: Some Mysteries and Riddles?," *Mediterranean Quarterly* 22/1 (2011): 41–60, here in 52.

[186] Vladislav B. Sotorović, "Who are Albanians?," *Serbian Studies Journal of the North American Society for Serbian Studies* 26/1–2 (2012): 45–79, here in 77.

clergymen. Indeed, the Albanian teacher and parish priest, Papa Kristo Negovani refused to hold the Orthodox Divine Liturgy in Greek, and initiated use of the Albanian language during prayers.[187] For this activity, he was murdered on 12 February 1905 by a Greek guerrilla band by order of Bishop Karavangelis from Kastoria. He was killed in the village of Negovan, in the Manastir vilayet (Ottoman Macedonia). As a response, some of these Albanian "political entrepreneurs" decided to establish the first cheta in the Manastir vilayet.[188] Its founders were the brothers Topulli, Bajo and Çerçiz,[189] who decided to engage in guerrilla warfare after leaving the comforts of their town life in Manastir. Thus, they established the "First Albanian Cheta" in March 1906, at the Bektashi tekke of Melçan, near Korça (Manastir vilayet). The Bektashi clergy was very active in the creation and operation of this cheta, whose members took to the mountains to liberate the country. In this respect, in January 1907, Çerçiz Topulli published an article in the newspaper *Shpresa e Shqypnisë* ("Hope of Albania"):

> "With this letter I want to inform all our brothers patriots/compatriots, Albanians, our friends, and all others who are interested in the Albanian Question, that I, with my friends, left the houses, families, and our wealth, and went to the mountains as rebels, to fight for the liberty of Albania against the barbaric and tiranic government."[190]

The establishment of the First Albanian Cheta should not be analysed in isolation from the broader Ottoman dynamics. This cheta–building was not a unique case for Macedonia, but rather resonated in important ways throughout the larger Eastern Mediterranean world in Anatolia (in six vilayets, where Armenians established several bands), Libia, and elsewhere. In order to understand their emergence, activism, and

---

[187] Jashar Rexhepagiqi, *Zhvillimi i arësimit dhe i sistemit shkollor të kombësisë shqiptare në teritorin e Jugosllavisë së sotme deri në vitin 1918* (Prishtinë: Enti i teksteve dhe i mjeteve mësimore i Krahinës Socialiste Autonome të Kosovës, 1970). p. 87.

[188] BOA, Rumeli Müfettişliği Makamât Evrakı (TFR.I.MKM), 28/2742, H. 29.03.1326 (1 Mayıs 1908).

[189] Bajo Topulli, *Topullarët e Gjirokastrës, Bajo e Çerçizi: Pararendësit dhe pasardhësit* (Tiranë: Albin, 2008).

[190] Ibid. Golemi, *Çerçiz Topulli.*

instigation of violence in a (trans)regional context,[191] one should also take into consideration their local custom, moral values or geographic position by situating them in a wider time span. In other words, their purpose, violence, coexistence, and cooperation with the governing elites cannot be properly comprehended without considering the locally rooted values, perceptions, norms, and structures.[192] These are not separate but rather mutually empowering and influencing areas of life.[193] To place them in the local context, the establishment of an Albanian cheta was made possible by the bleak situation in Ottoman Macedonia, influenced by factors that have already been detailed. One of the members of the First Cheta, Mihail Grameno, known in Albanian historiography as a writer and freedom fighter, emphasised that the "Ottoman troops and policies of Sultan Abdul Hamid II," together with the "Greek *andartes*, organised in Greece by the Greek government, [created] a climate of terror among the Albanians by

---

[191] Albanian cheta received letters of support from Egypt. See: Mihail Grameno, *Kryengritja shqipëtare* (Tiranë: N.SH.Naim Frashëri, 1959), p. 201; In original: *"Jani Vruhoi cili me fjalë patriotike na jepte kurajo, edhe na shkruante që për shpejti, do ten a dergonin ndihma. (...) muarme edhe nga Bukureshti një leter prej Vasil Irakli Zografit, i cili na jepte kurajo edhe na dërgonte 25 napoleona nga ana e Komitetit te Romanise me qënder ne Bukuresht."*

[192] Hannes Grandits and Siegfried Gruber, "The Dissolution of the Large Complex Households in the Balkans: Was the Ultimate Reason Structural or Cultural?," in *Household and Family in the Balkans: Two Decades of Historical Family Research at University of Graz*, ed. Karl Kaser (Berlin: LIT Verlag, 2012), pp. 387–406; Peter Waldmann, "Rache ohne Regeln. Wiederaufleben eines archaischen Gewaltmotivs in Albanien und in Boyacá (Kolumbien)," in *Politische und ethnische Gewalt in Südosteuropa und Lateinamerika*, eds. Wolfgang Höpken and Michael Riekenberg (Vienna/Cologne/Weimar: Böhlau, 2001), pp. 173–194; Stephanie Schwandner–Sievers, "Humiliation and Reconciliation in Northern Albania: The Logics of Feuding in Symbolic and Diachronic Perspectives," in *Dynamics of Violence: Processes of Escalation and De–Escalation in Violent Group Conflicts*, eds. Georg Elwert, Stephan Feuchtwang and Dieter Neubert (Berlin: Dunckler & Humblot, 1999), pp. 133–152.

[193] Jovan Miladinović, "Heroes, Traitors, and Survivors in the Borderlands of Empires Military Mobilizations and Local Communities in the Sandžak (1900s–1920s)" (PhD diss., Humboldt University, 2021). p. 6; Nikolaus Buschmann and Horst Carl, "Zugänge zur Erfahrungsgeschichte des Krieges: Forschung, Theorie, Fragestellung," in *Die Erfahrung des Krieges: Erfahrungsgeschichtliche Perspektiven von der Französischen Revolution bis zum Zweiten Weltkrieg,* eds. Nikolaus Buschmann and Horst Carl (Paderborn: Ferdinand Schöningh, 2001), pp. 11–26; Reinhart Koselleck, "Der Einfluß der beiden Weltkriege auf das soziale Bewußtsein, in *Der Krieg des kleinen Mannes: Eine Militärgeschichte von unten,* ed. Wolfram Wette (Munich: Piper, 1992), pp. 324–343.

persecuting and killing people every day."[194] As a result of this fear from the Ottoman authorities and Greek bands, Albanian "political entrepreneurs" decided to become also "specialists in violence."[195] These personalities, such as Bajo and Çerçiz Topulli and Mihail Grameno had generous support from the Bektashi tekke, which was possible as the fighters were mostly situated in the countryside and in isolated regions, far from the Ottoman authorities. Thus, the Bektashi tekke of Melçan played an important role as it served as the virtual headquarters of this cheta and the essential centre for spreading information on the activities between the çeta's leaders and the supporting population on the ground.[196] Selim Pojani, a member of the cheta, remembers the day when the patriots gathered at the tekke of Melçan:

> "The meeting was opened by Baba Hysejn who held an impassioned speech abouth love for the fatherland. He was followed by Bajo (Topulli) who said that the Ottoman Empire was a vestige of the past and called on us to assemble and take to arms to fight for the freedom of our country. The çeta was created. (…) The main task of our çeta was to spread information and agitate among the peasant masses. We also distributed the books and spellers sent to us by Grigor Cilka. The çeta agitated in the villages of Kolonja, Gora and the Plain of Korça."[197]

---

[194] Grameno, *Kryengritja shqipëtare*, p. 143; In original: *"antaret greke, të organizuar në Greqi prej qeverisë greke, u kishin shtënë tmerrin popullit shqiptar në ndjekjet edhe vrasjet që vepronin per dita kundra tyre."*

[195] Ibid., p. 202; Mihail Grameno described this process within the words: *"Nga këto frika (kryengritje e përgjithshme), turqit kishin lënë menjëane e në qetesi te plote komitat bullgare edhe antaret greke edhe gjithë fuqine e perkujdesjen e kishin hedhur kundra shqipëtareve."*

[196] Robert Elsie, *The Albanian Bektashi, History and Cluture of a Dervish Order in the Balkans* (London: I.B. Tauris, 2019), p. 147.

[197] See: Selim Pojani, "Çeta e parë nacionaliste," in *Kujtime nga levizja për çlirimin kombëtar në vitet 1878 – 1912*, ed. Petraq Pepo (Tiranë: Universiteti Shtetëror i Tiranës, Instituti i Historisë e Gjuhësisë, 1962). p. 112. Quote: *"Shkuam në Teqene e Melçanit ku gjetem aty Baba Hysejnin me shtatë a tetë Dervishë, Bajo Topullin, Riza Velçishtin, Mehmet Panaritin dhe Seferin nga Panariti. Atë ditë në Teqë 'Mejdan' (Vend lutje) u zhvillua mbledhja ku moren pjesë të gjithë Dervishet që kishin te skalitur ndjenjen kombetarë në terë qenien e tyre. Mbledhjen e hapi Baba Hysejn patrioti i cili foli me një elekuence dhe ndjenjë të thellë patriotike plot zjarre për dashurinë ndaj Atdheut. Pas tij foli Baju e të tjerë me radhe. Çeta u formua. Për këtë mbledhje kanë pasur dijeni edhe plotë patriotë të tjerë të Korçes si: Orhan Pojani, Vani Cico, Thimi Marko, Grigor Cilka të cilet nuk moren pjesë për motive sigurie të kesaj mbledhje. Çeta e parë me kapedan*

Although the cheta tried to agitate for the "liberty of Albania" (*per lirinë e Shqipërisë*), the peasant masses were not aware of national and ethnical differences. Mihail Grameno describes an event in Kolivicë, at the fortress of Abidin Shaho, where Çerçiz Topulli talked to some peasants in Greek (*Çerçiz u thërret ca fshatarëve, në gjuhën greqishte*) and asked about their relations with their Muslim neigbours (*qysh shkojnë me fqinjët e tyre muhamedanë*). An old man replied to him that "the problem [was] in the Turks [meaning the Muslims] who are on the throne" (*janë gjith ata turqe që kanë qenë kurdohere*). Çerçiz replied: "Right! The greatest fault lies with the Turkish government in Istanbul, which brings about problems for our brothers here, dividing the Christians and Mohammedans."[198] The çeta leader Çerçiz spoke to the peasants in Greek, the old man who replied to him demonstrated only an awareness of a distinction between Christians and Muslims. Furthermore, their everyday life contained rather a mixture of peaceful coexistence and cooperation, than of conflicts and violence. Closer contacts between these religiously divided groups also developed at the markets in the town or the agricultural estates between mostly Muslim land owners and Christian peasants, but also Christian merchants and Muslim peasants.[199] While the conflict and violence were an important

---

Bajon ka qënë e përbere prej 7 veta dhe kanë qendruar në Teqene e Baba Hysejnit afersisht një javë, e cila mbasi mori udhezimet e duhura është nisur për në Kolonjë ku janë takuar me patriotin Sali Butka. Shumë njerez u bashkuan dhe kam nderin te përmend në këtë shkrim edhe Dervish Kozelin. Baba Hyseni ndihmoi ngritjen e deges së komitetit ,Për lirinë e Shqipërise' në Korçë dhe në Kolonjë."

[198] Grameno, *Kryengritja shqipëtare*, pp. 163–164; In original: *"Kini të drejtë! Fajin më të math i ngarkohet qeverisë turke të Stambollit, e cila dëshëron që të mos ketë kurrë qetësi edhe vëllezeri në vendin tënë, midis të krishterëvet edhe muhamedanëvet."*

[199] Eva Anne Frantz, "Zwischen Gewalt und friedlicher Koexistenz – Muslime und Christen im spätosmanischen Kosovo, 1870–1913" (PhD diss., University of Vienna, 2014); Apart from coexistens, the local population was also involved into conflicts that were rather tribal than national. Here are some sources about local custom and laws: John H. Hutton, "Introduction," in *The Unwritten Law in Albania*, ed. John H. Hutton (Cambridge: Cambridge University Press, 1954), pp. 76; Michael Schmidt–Neke, "Der Kanun der albanischen Berge: Hintergrund der Nordalbanischen Lebensweise," in *Der Kanun: Das albanische Gewohnheitsrecht nach dem sogenannten Kanun des Lekë Dukadjini kodifiziert von Shtjefën Gjeçovi*, ed. Robert Elsie (Pejë: Dukadjini Publishing House, 2001), pp. 18; Robert Elsie, "Vorwort," in *Der Kanun: Das albanische Gewohnheitsrecht nach dem sogenannten Kanun des Lekë Dukadjini kodifiziert von Shtjefën Gjeçevi*, ed. Robert Elsie (Pejë: Dukadjini Publishing House, 2001); Halit Trnavci, "Predgovor," in *Kanon Leke Dukađinija*, ed. sakupio i kodificirao (posthumno

component of social interactions at that time, some sources show that at the turn to the century, the lines of violence could not be limited to national categories or an Albanian–Greek or Serbian–Albanian antagonism. Additionally, Mihail Grameno admitted that the "Greek people were innocent and without knowledge, but rather the politicians, the knowledgeable, and the journalists were the sources of danger."[200] In fact, on the ground and at the local level in late Ottoman Macedonia was seen rather a variety of pre–national or religious identities, than ethno–national monolith ones. Also, the members of the chetas did not always originate from the same ethnical and religious background. For instance, Mihailo Grameno was an Orthodox Christian, while Bash Çaush was Turkish–speaking (*Bash Çaushi, një turk*).[201] There was also often cooperation between bands, like in the Albanian and Bulgarian cases, observed also by Ahmet Niyazi, an Albanian who became symbol of the Young Turk Revolution. He emphasised that "in Resne, Prespe and Ohrid, the Bulgarian chetas were gathered around the Albanian Toska commander Çerçiz."[202] One should also note that Çerçiz's cheta played one of the leading roles in the Young Turk Revolution in July 1908. It was actually a

---

djelo) Štjefen Konstantin Dečovi (Zagreb: Stvarnost, 1986), p. 16; Ema Pašić and Dina Pašić, "Zakonik Leke Dukađinija: Pitanje kodifikacije Štjefena Konstantina Đečovića," *KSIO: Humanities Journal for Postgraduates and Early Career Researchers* 1 (2018): 28–40; Haris Hadžić, "Refleksije Kanona Leke Dukađinija na običaje i kulturu Bošnjaka u Rožajama," *Islamska misao: Godišnjak Fakulteta za islamske studije Novi Pazar* 6 (2012): 279–300; Shtjefën Gjeçovi, *Kanuni i Lekë Dukagjinit* (Shkodër: Libri, 1933); Özer Özbozdağlı, "Osmanlı Hükmetinin Kosova Arnavutları arasındaki Kan Davalarına Çözüm Bulma Çabaları 1908–1912," *Belleten* 82/271 (2010): 979–1011.

[200] Grameno, *Kryengritja shqipëtare*, p. 229; Quote: *"...të ketilla bisedime (rreth kombit, shqiptarët ortodoks a janë grek) patme edhe ne vapor kur qendruam ne Pater edhe në Pire, edhe nga këto kuptova që populli grek është i pafajshem meqenë i paditur, edhe kur udhehiqet prej njerës politikane, të ditur edhe gazetarë, të cilet nuk janë gjesendi përveç tabako prej historie."*

[201] Ibid; In original: *"Bash Çaush, një Turk (...) kishte ikur prej ushterisë në Gjirokaster, edhe duke kërkuar, andej–këtej, nga shqiptarët atdhetare, mundi të benje të njojture edhe t'u lutet që ta bashkonin me neve.(...) pas zakonit shqiptar e donim, nderonim edhe e ruani më teper se veten tënë. Mjerisht dolli i pa besë ose më mirë mbushi detyrën e tij, se ndofta për këtë qëllim u bashkua me neve, me dijen e kumandantit të tij!"*

[202] Ahmed Niyazi Bey, *Hatırat–i yahut tarihçe–i inkilab–i kebir–i Osmani'den bir sahife* (Istanbul: Sabah Matbaası, 1326 [1910]), p. 174; In original: *"Hususiyetle Resne'de, Prespe'de, Ohri'de Bulgarların mahallî ve seferî çeteleri, Arnavutların Toska komitalarının başı Çerçis ile birleşmiş, geniş bir çalışma yoluna koyulmuşlardı."*

Baba Hysejn initiative since he persuaded Çeriçiz and Mihail Grameno to join Nijazi Beu, the leader of the Young Turks in the Manastir vilayet. In his memoirs, Nijazi Beu described his cooperation with Çerçiz as "a need to get united and work together in order to save our fatherland."[203] For this purpose, Baba Hysejn behaved as mediator between those two leaders. Mihail Grameno reminisces: "We had a long discussion with Baba Hysejn on nationalist affairs and in particular about a meeting with Nijazi Beu (Niyazi Bey) whose intentions were unclear to us. Baba Hysejn told us that Nijazi had the same objectives as we did and that we ought to support him. (…) We kissed the hand of Baba Hysejn and departed."[204] After a meeting with Baba Hysejn, Mihailo and Grameno went to Pogradec to meet up with Nijazi Beu[205] who was already "anguished and tired from the Young Turks, thus, he wanted to work as an Albanian for Albania."[206] To the contrary, Nijazi Beu wrote that the meeting was more about "the Constitution in Rumelia and all the Ottoman motherland."[207] However,

---

[203] Ibid. pp. 231–232; A letter from Ahmet Niyazi to Çerçiz Topulli:*"Aziz Çercis! Vatanımın uğradığı felâketi nazarı itibara alarak düştüğü taksim edilme istikametinden kurtarmak için hayatımız bahasına silâhlanarak iki yüz erimle istibdat idaresine karşı bayrak kaldırarak balkana çıktım. Takip ettiğimiz istikamet vatanın felâketine sebep olacağından seninle en çok mücadele eden bendim. Fakat şimdi sana elimi uzatıyorum. Bundan böyle birleşip beraber çalışmanın zamanı geldi. Arzu ettiğin şartlar içinde nerede dilersen görüşelim, elele vererek vatanın kurtuluşuna beraber çalışalım. Çünkü sürüden ayrılanı kurt kapar.'Resne Millî Taburu Kumandanı Kolağası Ahmet Niyazi"*
[204] Grameno, *Kryengritja shqipëtare*, p. 219.
[205] Ibid., p. 221; In original: *"Niaz be na priste në Poradec. Rame në bisedime edhe një nga oficeret i qojtur Remzi be, hapi programin për tën a e shtruar neve. Thote që programi qëndron në Konstitucion të lirë një jesine (baraza) për gjith kombet e mbretërisë, dituria në gjuhë amtare të çdo kombi, drejtësia edhe shumë gjëra për të përmirësuar rrojtjen e popujve."*
[206] Ibid., p. 223; In original: *"Niaz beu ishte deshpëruar edhe mërzitur me në fund nga Xhon Turqit, meqeneqe nuk e kishin gjurmuar, prandaj vendosi të punonte si shqiptar për Shqipërine. Me këtë program po fitonte simpathine e shqipetarëve, të cilet besonin edhe e gjurmonin. Mbi këtë program, pra, na shkrojti edhe neve ae të vinim të hasemi, për nji bashkepunim në një fushe me të gjërë."*
[207] Niyazi Bey, *Hatırat-i yahut*, p. 326; Resneli Niyaz wrote about this meeting:*"Kendileriyle Ittihat ve Terakki'nin Rumeli'de ve bütün Osmanlı memleketinde yapmak istediği Kanun-ı Esasi teşebbüsünü ve Meşrutî idarenin kurulmasından temin edilecek faydaları münakaşa ettik. Netice olarak Çerçis'in zaman geçirmeden yanındakilerle beraber bana iltihak etmesi için karar verdik."* Furthermore, he states: *"Arnavut komitası taraftarı olan bu ileri gelenler, bana diyorlardı ki: Türklerin şimdiye kadar Osmanlılık adına çalışmakta gösterdikleri umursamazlık, Toskaların yalnız başlarına bir şeyler yapmak hevesine kapılmalarına sebep oldu. Istibdat idaresinin*

this cheta helped Nijazi Beu to stage an uprising and turned the situation in favour of the secret Ottoman organisation named *Committee and Union* (CUP), which succeeded in bringing the Revolution in July 1908. The Albanian leaders supported CUP for the sake of liberation, but this alliance with the Young Turks did not last long after the 1908 revolution. Mihail Grameno reported that Çerçiz Topulli immediately started to sing a song: "Albania, my Albania, Albania of five vilayets, why did you not fight for yourself, but for all nations?"[208] For Çerçiz the imagination of Albania was an Albania of five vilayets that included all three vilayets of Macedonia. Aligned with this, Mihailo wrote that Çerçiz was a leader of our nation, a hope for Albania (*u bë pishtari i Lirisë Kombëtare, u bë Shpresa e Shqypnisë*). He also named him as a "dragon of the war" (*dragua ne lufte*).[209] However, I would rather argue that this cheta action was more focused only on the region of nowadays south Albania, northern Greece and south-western parts of North Macedonia known as *Toskëri*, than on purely "Albanian" territories of five vilayets. The Ottoman documents suggest that the individuals in question were known as "*Toska fedaileri*,"

---

tesiriyle sarsılan koca memleket, şu son senelerde ecnebi devletlerin ve vatandaşları olan azınlıkların hırs ve tamahına hedef olduklarından büsbütün ellerinden çıkmak– tehlikesiyle karşı karşıya geldi." See also: *"Akşam yemeğini güneş batmadan bir saat önce yiyerek 17 Temmuzda yola çıktık. Buğradiç'ten gelen idare heyetiyle görüştükten sonra bundan böyle Istarova'da dolaşmaya, Çerçis ile beraberlik tesis etmek için kalmayı uzatmaya lüzum olmadığı kararını vermiştik. Ittihat ve Terakki Manastır merkezinden aldığım emirde bugünlerde iki mühim şahsiyetin Kışrani merkezi vasıtasıyla bana iltihak edeceği tebliğ edilmiş olduğundan o istikamete doğru gitmek mecburiye–tindeydim."*
[208] Grameno, *Kryengritja shqipëtare*, p. 224; In original: *"(...) ishte 10 korrik, në Ohrid (...) ku u shpall një Koshitite e lirë në Hyqumet. Nuk e di edhe as qe munda ta kuptoja shkakun e asaj ftohtesire, me të cilen u prit fermani Konshtutes, jo vetem nga ana tone, po pergjitherish nga gjithë gjindja, e përbere nga hume kombe e fe. (...) Çerçizi ngrihet edhe na mbleth të gjithë në valle duke kenduar këte kënge: ,Shqiperi, moj Shqiperi, Shqiperi pes Vilajete, Pse s'u përpoqe për vete, por për shumë milete!'"*
[209] Ibid. p. 38; Furthermore, Mihailo also registered the role of women in their activities, emphasising, "women were part of our movement." On one occasion he stated that he had absolute support from his mother who used to say that she "married Mihailo to Albania" (*kam dasme se Mihalin e martova me Shqipërine!*)." in page 200. See also: pages: 227 and 228; Quote: *"Shum here gratë, delnin përpara që qeronin udhen me pushkat në dore, kur shkonim neve nga shtëpia. Në shum gjendje kritike, kur nuk munt të vepronin burrat, e mbushnin këto këtë barrë të rëndë burrerrisht e plotërisht. Me një fjalë, ishin pjesëtaret të levizjes sonë."*

260

and were also referred to in French as "*la comite Tosca*."[210] In addition, Mihail Grameno admits that members of this band were "gathered as representatives of Toskëria" (*u mbloth parësia e Toskerisë*).[211] Ahmet Niyazi Bey further describes Çerçiz as "leader of band of the Toska Albanians" (*Arnavutların Toska komitası başı Çerçis*).[212] Many members of this so–called "First Albanian Cheta," were actually located only in the region of the Toska Albanian population, inhabited, as we have seen, by other ethnical members and groups as well. The nationalist meta–narrative tried to prove this cheta as a well–organised Albanian group, unified by common causes and misrepresented in narrow ethnonational terms. Rather than thinking of these groups' activities as an inevitable nationalist, nevertheless, I highlight that there were more complicated factors on the ground in such events that require multiple approach of possibilities at play. Labelling all these personalities into a "pure national" group, would be a misleading note for further researches, thus, I suggest that we should undertake a path "beyond (national) identities." One of the ways of demonstrating this is through an analysis of the members of the bands how they wore clothes. Although some of its members insisted on nationalist indoctrination, one can plausibly argue that we cannot identify larger population along generic "national" lines on account of what is assumed to be ethnic–specific styles.[213] A better way, suggested Isa Blumi, is "to think about their ways of clothing is that they did not possess national clothes. Rather the photographs indicate from which region, valley, and even extended family someone came."[214]

---

[210] İBB Atatürk Kitaplığı: Attar A. Faik (ed.), *Manastır: Hürriyet fatihi ve Tasko fedaileri = La comite Tosca a Monastir*, No: 0173, Krt_009551, Monastir.

[211] Ibid., p. 175.

[212] Niyazi Bey, *Hatırat–i yahut*, p. 230.

[213] See also: Hannes Grandits and Siegfried Gruber, "The Dissolution of the Large Complex Households in the Balkans: Was the Ultimate Reason Structural or Cultural?," in *Household and Family in the Balkans: Two Decades of Historical Family Research at University of Graz*, ed. Karl Kaser (Berlin: LIT Verlag, 2012), pp. 387–406.

[214] Blumi, *Reinstating the Ottomans*, p. 16.

Photo 3 Toskë Kachak band in Ottoman Macedonia[215]

On this photograph 3, we see that only one member is wearing the hat called *plis* (in some regions *qelesheja*), which became a symbol of Albanian national identity. What is more, this photograph demonstrates that the clothes of other cheta members corresponded more to the region of Epirus and to regional Macedonian clothing (and not national). It would be a mistake to assume that these personalities from the photograph came from the same ethno–national background, because the image rather suggests that the men originated from the same region that combined different ethnic and religious groups. Thus, they could be Albanian-speaking Muslims or Christians, but also Greek–, Slavic–, or Turkish-speaking locals. It is not possible to identify these men so definitively as "Albanian" kachaks, since these men wore also distinct caps, suggesting that the only "Albanian" (first from the right, lying down) is the person who is wearing the *plis*. As for the others, they were wearing various caps, concluding that this group of people (cheta) was composed of men with a number of possible cultural, social or religious affiliations ranging from Greek, Albanian or Macedonian, but also Orthodox Christian to Muslim

---

[215] "Nga dëshmitë e Mihal Gramenos për Çerçizin," *Gazeta Konica* 15. July, 2022; See also the State Central Archive of Albania: AQSH, Jeta politike 1900–1912; A–II–3, No. 30, 1908 named "*Fotografi të çetës së Çerçiz Topullit dhe Mihal Gramenos.*"

or Bektashi dervishes.[216] This image, thus, reveals that a complicated social and political dynamic was at play in the Ottoman Macedonia. In this respect, these clothes could challenge the idea that this cheta was only affiliated with the nationalist indoctrination projects who wanted to fight for "Albanian cause." Also, from the examples given by Mihail Grameno (in the Photo 3, standing on the right side), this cheta comprised Turkish- and Greek–speaking personalities along with Albanian ones. Furthermore, Ahmet Nijazi Beu defined the cheta within a regional rather than any other context, emphasising that it was rather a *Toskë kaçak* than a wholly "Albanian" project.[217] Its members mostly (but not always) self–identified with the family, village, and region Toskëria, rather than with an abstract concept of "nation" that for many (but not all) did not exist yet.[218] Therefore, the analysis of these events should be seen from local point of view, especially if we realise that such dynamic was animated by local codes and not defined by ethnic difference. According to Hannes Grandits, a basic differentiation between the peaceful and conflict times (war, revolt, and organised violence) must be made, because during the conflict times, people tended to be compelled by the warring parties to clearly "take sides."[219] In this context, only after the Young Turk Revolution, we can

---

[216] Ibid; AQSH/Tiranë, F.99D.18 f.1.

[217] Niyazi Bey, *Hatırat–i yahut,* p. 166.

[218] Rather, the social structure of Albanian speaking population was divided into tribes, especially in the parts of today's Northern Albania, Kosovo and Montenegro. See: Michael Schmidt–Neke, "Der Kanun der albanischen Berge: Hintergrund der Nordalbanischen Lebensweise," in *Der Kanun: Das albanische Gewohnheitsrecht nach dem sogenannten Kanun des Lekë Dukadjini kodifiziert von Shtjefën Gjeçevi,* ed. Robert Elsie (Pejë: Dukadjini Publishing House, 2001); Elsie, "Vorwort," in *Der Kanun,* pp. 9– 10; Scholars on tribes see also: Reşat Kasaba, "Do States Always Favor Stasis? The Changing Status of Tribes in the Ottoman Empire, " in *Boundaries and Belonging: States and Societies in the Struggle to Shape Identities and Local Practices,* ed. Joel S. Migdal (Cambridge: Cambridge University Press, 2009), pp. 27–48; Reşat Kasaba, *A Moveable Empire: Ottoman Nomads, Migrants, and Refugees* (Seattle and London: University of Wanshington Press, 2009); About the local life in the Ottoman and post– Ottoman world see: Cengiz Orhonlu, *Osmanlı İmparatorluğunda aşiretleri iskan teşebbüsü* (Istanbul: Edebiyat Fakültesi Basımevi, 1963); Lisa Anderson, *The State and Social Transformation in Tunisia and Libya, 1830–1980* (Princeton, NJ: Princeton University Press, 1986); Köksal, "Coercion and Mediation: Centralization and Sedentarization of Tribes in the Ottoman Empire," *Middle Eastern Studies* 42/3 (2006): 469–491.

[219] Grandits, *Conflicting Loyalties in the Balkans,* p. 6.

argue that the Albanian "political entrepreneurs" and "specialists in violence" from the regions of Toskëria and Gegeria (the northern parts) started to cooperate closely and their cooperation took a fairly "pan–Albanian" dimension. In order to understand these processes, one should take a closer look at regional and local dynamics. Namely, in July 1908, immediately after the Young Turk Revolution, Enver Pasha, who became the hero of the revolution, held a speech in Thessaloniki and finished it within the famous words: *"Vive la Nation Ottomane!"* ("Long live the Ottoman Nation!").[220] As an outcome of the Revolution, the Young Turks or more specifically the CUP, made some crucial changes in the mode of leading the government. After the attempted counter–Revolution of 31 March 1909, CUP started to suppress all groups that were against centralisation. In this regard, its main politicians brought many new laws such as regulation of labour affairs, law on vagabonds and suspicious persons, law on public meetings, prohibition of political parties established on a national basis, etc. These laws were adopted in order to suppress any organised protests or activities of the committees and ethno–national organisations that could open up questions of autonomy and decentralisations.[221] Thus, the CUP introduced a law on bands on 27 September 1909, and sanctioned every kind of armed movement and sought help from the locals in order to catch the band leaders and punish them with death. Those who did not collaborate with the state would also be punished as "helpers and shelterers" (*muin ve yatak*) of the bands.[222] This interference of the Ottoman state in the local level and the centralisation attempt, for example, provoked revolts among the Albanians in the south and the north. The breakdown of the legislative measures and a new campaign of state violence opened up a new space for the Albanian revolts and new "terrorist" activities in Macedonia. The government went even further to even greater lengths in disarming the Albanian population. According to local custom, this action was understood as provocation and

---

[220] Mehmet Hacısalihoğlu, "The Young Turk Policy in Macedonia, Cause of the Balkan Wars?" in *War and Nationalism*, eds. M. Hakan Yavuz and Isa Blumi (Salt Lake City: University of Utah Press. 2013), p. 108.
[221] Ibid.
[222] Ibid., p. 117.

disrespect towards their local tradition.[223] Hence, the disarming process of early 1910 in particular provoked a much more severe reaction, preparing the ground for an eventual alliance between Albanian local notables and the countries of Montenegro and Serbia. Ismail Kemal Bey, an Albanian–speaking deputy in the Ottoman Parliament at that time, described these actions of the CUP government as "criminal attacks" against the Albanians.[224] Furthermore, Çerçiz Topulli, a supporter of the CUP and Niyazi Bey during the Revolution, immediately changed his position and called upon Albanians "not to shed a single drop of blood for the Turks anymore."[225] With this purpose, on 29 May 1909 he founded in Gjirokastër a secret society called the Candle (*Kandilja*).

A former member of the Albanian Committee for Liberation, Menduh Zavallani joined the new secret organisation known as the Black Society for Salvation (*Shoqëria e zezë për shpëtim*) and would soon be a member of its leadership. The society established in 1909 and founded its branches throughout the Toskëria region in Korçë, Yannina, Gjirokastër, Vlorë, Filat, Delvinë, Përmet, Elbasan, Tiranë, Ohër/Ohrid, Strugë/Struga, Dibër/Debar, but also Gegeria in the Kosovo vilayet (Shkup/Skopje) and Shkodër. Its headquarters were situated in Manastir and it used a seal with the letter "*Q*" to mean "centre" (*Qendra*). Initially, the organisation was intended to be named The Black Hand (*Dora e Zezë*), in line with other various secret societies of that time. The main task of the Black Hand was to organise uprisings in Albania and Macedonia, both seen as Albanian territories. The aim was to struggle for establishment of one single Ottoman Albanian vilayet consisted from Shkoder, Kosovo, Manastir and Janina.[226] One of its main contributors was Nikollë beu Ivanaj, a Geg Albanian from the territories of Montenegro, who became a link between Tosk and Geg notables. He was born in Montenegro and studied and worked in Trieste and Belgrade. There he was inspired by "Serb, Greek,

---

[223] Ibid; Süleyman Külçe, *Osmanlı Tarihinde Arnavutluk* (İzmir: Ticaret Matbaası, 1944).
[224] Ibid., p. 118; Kemal Bey, *The Memoirs*, 367.
[225] Ryan Gingeras, *Fall of the Sultanate: The Great War and the End of the Ottoman Empire 1908–1922* (Oxford: Oxford University Press. 2016), p. 67.
[226] Nikollë Ivanaj, *Historija e Shqipëniës së re: Vuejtjet e veprimet e mija* (Tiranë: Shtypëshkronja e shtetit 'Atdheu', 1943/45), p. 4.

and Bulgarian gang revolutionary activities in Kosovo and Macedonia."[227] In the period between 1905 and 1908 he published the newspaper *Shpnesa e Shqypnisë* in Albanian, Croatian, and Italian in Dubrovnik, Trieste, and Rome.[228] The aim of the newspaper was to broadcast "a call to Albanian liberty and self– determination."[229] The most important stress was placed onto the "liberation of our homeland, [as] otherwise there [would] not be peace in the Balkans."[230] Similarly to (the work of) Pashko Vasa and Sami Frashëri, Nikollë beu Ivanaj glorified personalities like Alexander the Great and Scenderbeg Castrioti, who ruled the region and led uprisings against the Ottomans. In this context, he had written that "it is time to restore our ancient greatness (…) and to break the chains – to liberate our homeland."[231] The terms "homeland" and "liberation" implied Macedonia as well, where he emphasised that "there is no such thing as a Macedonian Question, we can talk only about an Albanian Question."[232] Only in this way, he assumed, can Article 23 from the Congress of Berlin, which guaranteed autonomy for Macedonia [233] (i.e. Albania), be fulfilled. [234]

---

[227] Ibid., p. 7; In original: *"Tue pasë qënë inspirue (aty në Beligrad) me veprimet çetnore rivolucjonare të Serbve, Grekve dhe Bullgarve nëpër Kosove, Maqedoinii etj."*

[228] Ibid. p. 10; Quote: *"5 Shtator 1905 botimi i gazetes Shpnesa e Shcypniis, ni her në jav për 4 vjet në Ragus, Triest dhe Rom (gjithsehit 44 numra)."*

[229] See a newspaaper: Shpnesa e Shcypeniis (translation: The Hope of Albania), Ragusa (Dubrovnik), 10. September, 1905, p. 1; This newspaper published some articles in Albanian, but also Serbo–Croatian. In orginal: *"e sidha e ka te shkurten e te kjar programin, deshirin e te thirmjen: Lirimi e veturdhnimi i Shcypniis."*

[230] Ibid; See: *"të këpusim vargojt – të e lirojm Atëdhen (...) të sidhat deri sa mos të na jepen – paqe në Ballkan ska me kjen."*

[231] Shpnesa e Shcypeniis, Ragusa, 10. September, 1905, p. 3; In original: *"Në këtë mënyr edhe me marrue e poshtnue ata të paart të mëdhejt ëe padekunit ton, sikurse: mretin Aleksandrin e Madh, baben e tij Filipin, Pirrin e Madh, Kastriotin etj. (...) se koha ka ardh, për me na u kthye prap, ka pak e pak, mirësija, madhnija e lumenija e hershme (...) koha ësht: të kepusim vargojt – të e lirojm Atedhen."*

[232] Ibid. p. 2; In original: *"bile, sadhte në këtë mënyr kisht me u marue shcim shum e njemna – bevetja (pyetja) e Shcypniis e jo e Makedonijes, se të saj të bevetme, vetmas ska."*

[233] Shpnesa e Shcypeniis, Ragusa, 1. Jul, 1906, p. 2; Also written and published in Serbo–Croatian: *"Zborovi po Albaniji na svim će se zborovima zatražiti pretres i privođenje u djelo 23. članka berlinskog kongresa, koji glasi: 'sve pokrajine evropske Turske imati će jednu polunezavisnu administraciju, s olakšicom i pravom da mogu imati po jednu opštu Narodnu Skupštinu."*

[234] Ibid; In original: *"Zborovi po Albaniji, takozvano makedonsko pitanje (premda ono zasebno i ne postoji, nego – skupa – albansko), koje se kroz toliko vremena ne može*

Nevertheless, when he spoke of autonomy, he assured that it should only be the first stage towards independence from the Ottoman Empire."[235] For this achievement, he was aware that he needed to bring under cooperation notables from Toskëria and Gegëria. Thus, he underlined that Albanian notable should "put in efforts towards a general Albanian Uprising that [would] unite Northern Albania (Gegeria) with Southern Albania (Toskëria)."[236] In this respect, he was in contact with Toska notables such as the borthers Topulli, Mihail Grameno and Themistokli Germenji,[237] who organised uprisings in Toskëria during the spring in 1911. On the other hand, Ivanaj went to Montenegro in 1911 to meet with Geg notables such as Isa Boletini, Sylejman Batusha, and Hasan Ferri in order to organise uprisings in the Shkodra and Kosovo vilayets in April 1911.[238] One can infer that a cooperation between south and north Albanians began only after the Young Turk Revolution and the CUP's attempts at a centralisation policy. During this period, new local actors such as Nikollë Ivanaj and Isa Boletini played very important roles and transformed the dynamics on the ground. While Ivanaj connected two Albanian regions and was in constant communication between the cheta leader Themistokli

---

nikako a nekmoli povoljno da riješi, zadalo je veliku brigu našem narodu..." In this case he further argues: *"da se našemu vilajetu dade ona Uprava, što je Imperatorsko Upraviteljstvo obećalo 23. čl. Berlinskog ugovora, i time se, jednom za svagda, i kod nas počne uvoditi toliko i davno željeni poredak, mir i blagostanje."*

[235] Ivanaj, *Historija e Shqipëniës*, p. 11; In original: *"Shqipëria me katër vilayetet e saj, vetem si një aleat i Turqis, çka, po të ishte qënë e mundun, përkohsisht, do tishte qen pun e mir dhe e levërtishme për shqiptart ende për Turqien."*

[236] Ibid. p. 39; In original: *"Nga Kryetart Kryesor të Kryengritjes Kosovare, Isa Boletini, Sulejman Batusha e Has Feri, me 300 luftar Kryengrites erdhne në Mal të Zi, ku ndejne deri në Marc 1911, kur plasi kryengritja e Maleve Shkodrës, që e kishe përgatite unë në kohën që pata shkue në Cetinje, në muej të Dhetorit, 1910, për t'u pjeke me Kryetart e Kryengritsve shqiptar e për t'ë organizur Kryengritjen e pergjithshme të Shqipnies së Siperme, si ende atë të Shqipnies së Jugut, që mandej, nga Korfuzi, me Temistokle Germenjin e shoket e pata organizue 'dhe që plasi me 14 Qershuer 1911. Por, pikë së pari, që lidhe besa me e fillue Kryengritjen vilajeti i Shkodrös e i Kosoves paërnjiher, për në muej të Prillit, 1911."*

[237] During the year 1911 (*në Pranverë*), Menduh established a cheta from around 50 people who went from Korca to a city of Permet. There he was joined by another cheta of Spiro Bellkameni and Qamil Panariti. They were arrested by the Ottoman government, among whom were also Mihal Grameno and Themistokli Gërmenji. About this event see: Mikel Zavalani, *Studime Historike 2* (Tiranë: Akademia e Shkencave e RPSSH – Instituti i Historisë, 1983).

[238] Ivanaj, *Historija e Shqipëniës*, pp. 18–19.

Germenji and the Geg notables, Isa Boletini was the man of action between the Kosovo notables and the states of Montenegro and Serbia. In cooperation with these states, he staged several uprisings against the Ottoman army between 1909 and 1912, whereby implementation of centralisation policies was attempted. The rebels started to control multiple roads in the mountains and between cities, intercepted the communication of the army, attacked official authorities, etc. This became the only method to fight against the centralisation policy of the CUP.

In 1910 Isa Boletini moved to Montenegro and stayed until March 1911, where an uprising was organised in Malësia in the Shkodra vilayet. [239] After his stay there, on 23 March 1911 Isa Boletini wrote a proclamation to the Albanians in the south and the Albanians from the Shkodra vilayet to join the Albanians from the Kosovo vilayet in their uprising.[240] He was one of the leading figures against the CUP policy regarding Ottoman Macedonia. Even the Serbian diplomat J.J. Studić wrote to Serbian Minister of Foreign Affairs regarding this conflict, stating that "we should take care of them [the Albanians] as our neighbours in Old Serbia. We should use this opportunity to keep them closer, because they are having a violent conflict with the Young Turks and will never unite again."[241] Nevertheless, Boletini, together with Qerim Mahmutbegollaj from Peja, was even developing a business with Serbia and Montenegro of smuggling and selling weapons in the Kosovo vilayet.[242] During this period of uprisings (1909–1912), Boletini's little corner of the world became the centre of Balkan state rivalries. He took advantage of these opportunities

---

[239] Clayer, *Aux origines du nationalism albanais*, p. 116.

[240] Gazmend Shpuza, *Shpërthimi i kryengritjes dhe veprimet luftarake (Mars – fillimi i Qershorit 1911)* (Prishtinë: Rilindja Kombëtare Shqiptare, 1984).

[241] AC, MIDS, SPA, 1911, F–IV, D–6. P. 652; knjiga IV, sveska 3/1; See in original: *"moramo voditi računa o njima (arnautima), kao susedima našeg življa u Staroj Srbiji, onda nebi nikada trebalo propustiti prilike da ih za sebe obvežemo, jer oni su sa Mladoturcima krvno zavadili Ii između njih i Mladoturaka postoji takva provalija koja nikada ne može sajediniti Arnaute i Mladoturke. Posle onih prošlogodišnjih terora i pustahiluka oni se samo mogu krviti a nikako izmiriti. Treba samo čuti kako žučno i bolno traže Arnauti osvetu za pretprljene sramote njihovih çeljadi i njih samo ih i onda viditi, da se oni nikad neće smiriti i pokloniti režimu, kojim upravljaju njihovi "dušmani i otpadnici vere."*

[242] Zekeria Cana, "Qëndrimi i Serbisë ndaj kryengritjes së përgjithshme shqiptare të vitit 1912," *Gjurmime Albanologjike – Seria e shkencave historike* 35 (2005): 237; AIH, Ref.I, 18. VIII.1912; No.81/sekret, Prizren, 13.VIII. 1912.

to promote the agenda that earned him a significant spot in regional politics. For this purpose, he negotiated with King Nikola of Montenegro, as well as with Serbian state representatives, whereby he hired arms and (arranged recruitment of) Serbian and Montenegrin population (together with Albanian speaking personalities) for new uprisings against the Ottoman government. One report (from the time) informed that "many Serbs [were] among the rebels" (*dosta veliki broj Srba je među ustanicina*), and "three Montenegrins joined them in Dečan" (*tri crnogorca u Dečanima*).[243] By building his local power base, Boletini formed stronger commercial, political, and human cross–border networks with Serbia and Montenegro. For this purpose, he met with Prince Aleksandar Karađorđević (the future king) and Prime Minister Nikola Pašić in Prokuplje and Kuršumlija in 1912.[244] In this regard, he reflected his established links not only with fellow Gegë, but also with Serbian and Montenegrin state representatives and local Slavs with whom he would do business. The Serbian consul to Priština, M. Đ. Milojević also stated that "Albanians [were] feeling that the Turkish Empire [was] falling apart and therefore they wanted to develop friendships with the neighbouring states of Serbia and Montenegro by protecting their fatherland against enemies."[245] As a final result, the local Serbs joined Albanian notables in these uprisings, which were also supported by the Serbian (organisations) National Defence and Black Hand, where Serbian and Albanian bands, vojvoda Tankosić, and Isa Boletini fought jointly this time against the Ottomans.[246]

---

[243] DASIP, MIDS, PPO, 1912, F–VI, D red, 96/III, Serbian Consul to Priština M.Đ. Milojević to Minister of Foreign Affairs Milovan Milovanović 21.5.1912.

[244] AIH, D–50, No.inv.955, Ref.I, No.74,5.VIII.1912; Beograd, 3.VIII.1912.

[245] Dr. M. Đ. Milojević to Jovan Jovanović (minister of Foreign Affairs), DASIP, MIDS, SPA, 23.VII.1912, F–5, D–3. Knjiga V, sveska 1, p. 1008; See in original: *"Na sastanku u Ugljaru, (Bajram) Dakljan (arnautski prvak iz đakovičke okoline) je izjavio g. (Ljubomiru) Nešiću da oni –Arnauti– osećaju kako se turska carevina postepeno ruši i tone i da žele za vremena vezati prijateljstvo sa svojim susedima Srbijom i Crnom Gorom, te da zajednički brane svoju otadžbinu od stranih neprijatelja."*

[246] Cana, "Qëndrimi i Serbisë."; DASIP, MIDS, PPO, 1912, F–VI, D red, 96/III, Serbian Consul to Priština M.Đ. Milojević to Minister of Foreign Affairs Milovan Milovanović 21.5.1912.

4.6. Conclusion

In this chapter I covered the period between the Ilinden Uprising (1903) and the Young Turk Revolution (1908) and I analysed the activities of various organisations and movements on the ground (i.e. IMARO, the Chetnik, Kachaks), which cooperated with the local population or often originated from the local regions of Ottoman Macedonia. Here I introduced a 'bottom–up' perspective and argued that the situation on the ground was far more complex than represented by nationalist promoters and the state elite, which have been defined by Charles Tilly as "political entrepreneurs." Next to this term, Tilly named political actors on the ground "specialists in violence." In this respect, those specialists showed that the organisations at local level were not 'purely' national, but consisted of members with different religious and ethnical backgrounds. This argument largely aimed to deconstruct state meta–narratives and nationalist claims that were produced by nation–states during the 'short' 20th century. In the previous chapter I already demonstrated that the governing elites worked to build "imagined communities" based on "invented traditions," which often failed on the ground. Thus, by moving beyond the debates on nationalism and rather adopting the approach of subaltern studies, I considered several local organisations and actors. In this chapter I highlighted that there were not only projects and actions initiated by states and intellectuals, but also projects and moves undertaken by the general population as well. I argued that one could not understand the complete situation of the Macedonian Questions, if one were not to take into account those local contexts. By deploying various local examples from Bulgarian, Macedonian, Serbian, Ottoman Turkish, and Albanian sources, it is shown that various reports, memoirs, and records from the archives deconstruct the nationalist projections made by the states. Rather, the 'bottom–up' perspective helps to understand actors on the ground who often cooperated. Without integrating this viewpoint in the research, we would not know that "eternal enemies," such as the parties to the Serbian–Albanian conflict today, and at that time 'Albanians' and 'Serbs,' were much more likely to interact with each other and share their daily life in the *mahale*. Next to them, 'Bulgarians,' 'Macedonians,' and 'Greeks' cooperated as well and often opposed the Balkan state policies from Sofia or Athens. Inside their own communities there were often various projections and contested discussions, as showed in the case of IMARO. I also demonstrated that the Chetnik organisation, as well as the 'Albanian' Kachaks, were also diverse and were not purely 'national' as presented in their national historiographies. Accordingly, in the Serbian–Albanian context, more specifically the Kosovo vilayet, I showed how these relations were much more complex and one could find Muslim Albanian–speaking members (e.g. Smajo Ferović) in Serbian chetas in Ottoman Macedonia. In this line [of argument], among the Albanian Kachaks one also traces Greek– or Turkish–speaking individuals who did not have Albanian origin.

Entangled Trajectories: From the Macedonian
Reforms to the Balkan Wars

In the *fin de siècle*, the political situation in the Ottoman Empire was a complicated "chessboard" where every Great Power together with the regional Balkan states took part in the game. As we have already seen, Ottoman Macedonia had become one of the active "chessboards" for political activism. On the one hand, Imperial Russia tried to have strong ties with its South–Slavic "brothers," especially by supporting Bulgarian nationalist attempts to Ottoman Macedonia. Serbian nationalist politicians assumed that their fate would have been sealed and hemmed in if parts of Ottoman Macedonia had been annexed to Bulgaria. The Greek government, together with some Serbian politicians, introduced various nationalist politics against the Bulgarian developments in the three vilayets (Kosovo, Salonika, and Manastir). Making matters even more complicated various movements were developed among the local population in Macedonia that did not support any of those states' projects. The movements on the ground reflected a different imagination of what Macedonia was and what it should be. On the other hand, the government of Austro–Hungary carried out an active policy among the Albanian intellectuals and population in order to win their trust and friendship. Countering their attempts, one part of the Albanian population supported the Ottoman government, especially Sultan Abdulhamid II, who developed a special policy towards the Albanians and behaved as their father figure (*baba*). The other part of the Albanian population – who mostly belonged to intellectual circles – supported the Ottoman presence in Rumelia, but were against Hamidian policy. These intellectuals accepted their role of collaborators with the Young Turks and even became a pivotal and active influence in this movement. In this regard, this chapter aims to show the complex ways in which societies in Macedonia were transformed from different regional centres (Istanbul, Athena, Sofia, Belgrade, Cetinje, Vienna, St. Petersburg, etc.) into a struggle over Macedonia. In order to understand both the internal and external dynamics of this process, I will focus on the interplay between Great–Power politics, regional states' influences, Ottoman state reforms, and social dynamics on the ground. In this case, I will consider how the Hamidian regime responded to the pressure of the Great Powers and how this in turn impacted the Macedonian Questions; as well as how several Ottoman intellectuals that established the Young Turk Movement understood the Eastern Question and Macedonian situation. Firstly, I will highlight how the Ottoman intellectuals' vision influenced the Ottoman state and adopted a Western–style education in order to counter pressures from the 'West,' and thereby safeguard the Empire's future in the three vilayets. Secondly, I will try to answer the question: what was the Ottoman intellectuals' impact on the society in Macedonia? What were the outputs and social dynamics on the ground? I am especially interested in the entanglements observable in the Ottoman administration, but also between Young Turks and Albanian population in Macedonia. What was the response of the Albanian intellectuals and population living in the rural areas? I will also highlight the role played by the 'Ottoman periphery' (i.e. Macedonia) in shaping state policies. What was the contribution of the peripheral actors in the central government and how did they influence Ottoman politics? As an outcome of the main questions, I will further develop a subset of questions that can contribute to a more nuanced understanding of Macedonian imaginaries, especially through the examples that mirror complexities on the ground.

5.1. Hamidian Reforms in Ottoman Macedonia: Center in the Periphery – Periphery in the Center

As has already been stated, the Great Powers, the regional states, and in part the local population expressed discontent with the Hamidian policy in Ottoman Rumelia, guaranteed by the Congress of Berlin (1878). To this end, the Inspectorate was established with an imperial order, as an outcome of "The Regulations regarding the Rumelian Provinces" (*Rumeli Umumi Müfettişliği*), issued on November 30, 1902. The main purpose of this regulation was to satisfy the Great Powers' demands for reforms in Ottoman Macedonia on the grounds of Article 23 of the Berlin Treaty (1878). Hence, the Great Powers' intervention and the Ottoman establishment of the Inspectorate further changed the situation on the ground. These bureaucratic and administrative reforms transformed the Macedonian society. However, it is worth noting these reforms were also the results of social changes. Both the state and society were closely interconnected and influenced each other. The administrative board of

Rumeli Umumi Müfettişliği[247] was stationed in Salonica and constantly conducted inspection tours. At the outset, its collocutor was the "Commission of Rumelian Provinces" at the Sublime Porte, which was presided by Avlonyalı Mehmet Ferid Pasha, who became Grand Vizier in January 1903. He was a descendant of Tepedelenli Ali, and his family later moved to Vlora (Avlonya), where he personally became a mobile actor of change, circulating throughout various provinces. Since many Albanians in Ottoman Macedonia were dissatisfied with the reforms introduced, as an Albanian, Ferid Pasha played an important role among the local Albanian population in the three vilayets. In this regard, in order to introduce reforms in the Ottoman periphery (i.e. Macedonia), Sultan Abdulhamid II also appointed a peripheral mobile actor in Istanbul to the position of Grand Vizier. Avlonyalı Mehmet Ferid Pasha belongs to the group of personages who played crucial roles in the enforcement of the 'centre–periphery' relations. Having served in many corners of the Ottoman Empire (Crete, Herzegovina, Bulgaria, and Konya) and in the centre (Istanbul), he understood the necessities of both the Empire and the local populations in the provinces. Brought to Istanbul in 1902, he was supported by German Ambassador Freiherr von Marschall, who counted on his abilities to calm down the Macedonian situation. He declared that "the energetic personality of Ferid Pasha [had] an upright stance against those above him and who, as a native Albanian, could allow himself things that would be dangerous if done by others."[248] However, he took the position of Grand Vizier in difficult times when armed conflicts between nationalist bands were occurring and gangs were contesting to influence

---

[247] The General Inspectorate of Rumelia was an Ottoman Institution founded in order to regulate Ottoman Macedonia and its conflicts. As a General Inspector was appointed Hüsein Hilmi Pasha, who had an administrative task to suppress bands and bring order to the provinces.

[248] Abdülhamit Kırmızı, "Experiencing the Ottoman Empire as a Life Course: Ferid Pasha, Governor and Grandvizier (1851–1914)," *Geschichte und Gesellschaft* 40 (2014): 47; See in original from the document Marschall an das Auswärtige Amt, Pera, den 3. Dezember 1902, No. 422, in: *Die Grosse Politik der Europäischen Kabinette 1871–1914. Sammlung der Diplomatischen Akten des Auswärtigen Amtes, vol. 18*, eds. Johannes Lepsius et al. (Berlin: 1924), p. 5484. Quote: "(…) *die energische Persönlichkeit Ferid Paschas, der nach oben hin einen sehr steifen Rücken hat und sich als Albanese Dinge erlauben kann, die für andere gefährlich wären.*"; See also: Abdülhamit Kırmızı, *Avlonyalı Ferid Paşa: Bir Ömür Devlet* (Istanbul: Klasik, 2014).

the Macedonian population and recruit them for the "national purpose." In May 1903 a terror(ist) attack in Salonica was mounted by an anarchist group known as Gemici.[249] In August of the same year, the Ilinden Uprsing broke out and in October the Dual Monarchy and Imperial Russia introduced the Mürzteg scheme. The Great Powers implemented reforms and divided Ottoman Macedonia into districts based on ethnic affiliations. This decision further intensified the rise of armed conflicts between religious and ethnic groups. Furthermore, a reorganisation of the Macedonian gendarmerie that was supposed to include the Christian population and the introduction of an international committee gave rise to additional violence organised in few regions (prevalently in Kosovo vilayeti) by one part of the Albanian population who refused to accept such decisions. The conflict escalated when Imperial Russia decided to open a Consulate in Mitrovica (Kosovo vilayeti). In March 1903, thousands of armed Albanians entered Mitrovica to attack the Russian Consul, Gregory Stepanovich Shcherbin,[250] clashing with the Ottoman army. During this month, an Ottoman soldier of Albanian origin shot the Russian Consul, who succumbed to his injuries ten days later. A few months later, on 8 August 1903, another Albanian Ottoman soldier assassinated Aleksandar Arkadievich Rostkovski, the Russian Consul in Manastir vilayet of

---

[249] See chapter 4; Gerdzikov, *V Makedonia*; Mandzukov, *Predvestnici*; Šatev, *Makedonija pod ropstvo*.

[250] Gregory Stepanovich Shcherbina was a Russian consul who was assigned to Kosovska Mitrovica in March 1903 with the purpose of gathering information about the Serbian population in the Kosovo vilayet. However, his presence was met with opposition from the local Muslim population, mainly Albanians, who did not welcome him and eventually attacked him. Shcherbina was shot at close range by an Albanian and died a few days later in March 1903. Despite his tragic death, Shcherbina became immortalised when he responded to Serbian requests to stay safe by saying, "You, Serbs, are not so lucky to see me die. My death would bring you freedom." This event was deeply felt by the Serbs of Kosovo and Metochia, who considered it a national tragedy. See: Zvezdana M. Elezovich, Ana M. Mumovich and Dalibor M. Elezovich, "Grigorii Stepanovich Sherbina (1868–1903) v Kulture Kosovskih Serbov," *Vestnik Tomskogo gosudarstvennogo universitetaa* No 420 (2017): 141–145; About the Russian involvement into the Balkans see: Pavel N. Miliukov, *Vospominaniia 1859-1917* (New York: Izdatelstvo im Chekhova, 1955). About the life of Miliukov see: Thomas M. Bohn, *Russische Geschichtswissenschaft von 1880 bis 1905: Pavel N. Miljukov und die Moskauer Schule* (Vienna/Cologne/Weimar: Böhlau Verlag: Beiträge zur Geschichte Osteuropas Band 25, 1998).

Ottoman Macedonia.[251] An Albanian protester wounded another Russian Consul in Skopje named M. Machkoff. The active role of Russia in the three vilayets was perceived by many Albanians as a potential Russian invasion of the Ottoman Empire and a Pan–Slavic victory over Albanian territories.[252] In order to calm down the Albanian population and to mollify their discontent, Sultan Abdulhamid II, who had adopted the role of their father (*baba*) appointed several Albanians to high positions of power in Istanbul and in the Ottoman provinces. This gave an opportunity to the peripheral mobile actors to gain more power and reinforce the central government, or to work in the periphery on behalf of the centre. Thus, Bajram Curri was appointed captain in Pristina's gendarmerie; Şemsi Pasha – commander of the 18th Division in Mitrovica; Yakovali Riza Bey –major of Halepo; Isa Boletini held rank in the palace guard (*tüfekçi*), while numerous other Malisors gained entry into the Sultan's palace guard; while Ferid Pasha became particularly notable as Grand Vizier. Sultan Abdulhamid II addressed him with the words: "You are a native of Avlonya. Moreover, you are an Albanian. Let not the good things that I feel about you be erased. Our sultanate and the state have seen good things from the Albanian people."[253] Even during his governorship in Konya, Ferid Pasha stated his fear of a revolution for an autonomous Macedonia staged by the Bulgarians and other Slav nations with Russian support. In his view, the only "instrument that could be counted on for the conservation of the Sultan's rights in the Balkans was the Albanian nation."[254] However, this should not be considered an "Albanian nationalist program," but rather activism of one peripheral population for

---

[251] Consul Rostkovskii began his professional journey in the Middle East, where he was stationed in Jerusalem and Beirut. During this time, he met and wedded a Bosnian lady known as 'Princess' Maria Dabitsa, according to official documents. Later, from 1884–85, he worked as the first secretary at the Russian embassy in Sofia. In 1893, he was appointed as the vice–consul in Brindisi before being relocated to Bitola in 1895. He later moved to Skopje in 1899, only to return to Bitola in 1901 as a consul. See: Hasip Saygılı, "1903 Makedonya'sında Reformlara Tepkiler: Manastır Rus Konsolosu Aleksandır Rostkovski'nin Katli", *Karadeniz Araştırmaları* No 39 (2013): 69–94.

[252] Hasip Saygılı, "Rumeli Müfettişliği Döneminde (1902–1908) Makedonya'da Yunan Komitecileri ve Osmanlı Devleti," *Güvenlik Stratejileri Dergisi* 21 (2015): 147–183.

[253] Gawrych. *The Crescent*, p. 132.

[254] BOA, Y.PRK.S,D 2/44, 1315 N 29, 21.2.1898; See also: Kırmızı, *Experiencing the Ottoman Empire*, p. 58.

the purpose of the penetration and centralisation of the state. With the aim of strengthening the Albanian element in the central government, the Grand Vizier favoured two other Albanian speaking Ottomans named Tefik Pasha, who was a Minister of Foreign Affairs; and Turhan Pasha, appointed as the Minister of Religious Estates. Grand Vizier seemed to have shared a common cause with those Albanian speaking Ottomans, especially regarding the future of Ottoman Macedonia, considered by many Albanian intellectuals and bureaucrats as a territory that belonged to the Albanians.[255] Those mobile peripheral actors who worked for the centre were supported by the Hamidian regime as an advantage granted to ameliorate the Albanians' exasperations against the egalitarian reforms in a peaceful way. By reaching this decision to appoint Ferid Pasha Grand Vizier in a time of Albanian uprisings against the Macedonian reform schemes, the Sultan certainly thought that he could take advantage of his Albanian ethnic origin.[256] Contrary to this, certain media in Europe circulated that many Albanian officers and bureaucrats were actually sympathetic towards the Young Turk Movement, opposing Hamidian rule. Therefore, Ferid Pasha was also subject to the suspicion of being complicit with the Young Turks and Albanian revolters.[257] On one occasion, the German ambassador Kiderlen wrote that "Ferid Pasha encouraged the Albanian movement" (*dass Ferid Pascha die Albanische Bewegung begünstige*).[258] Another report stated that "as a native Albanian, he was particularly susceptible to the suspicion of sympathising with the Albanian movement. There was even a rumour in the public that Ferid himself was the leader of this movement."[259] His brother Avlonyalı Süreyya bey noted in his memoirs that Ferid Pasha participated in several meetings of the oppositional committees in Istanbul, and was once assigned to negotiate

---

[255] BOA, HR.SYS. Dosya 1858, Gömlek 5, Tarih 28.07.1908; Kırmızı, *Avlonyalı Ferid Paşa,* pp. 82–86.

[256] Kırmızı, *Experiencing the Ottoman Empire*, p. 59.

[257] Macedonia. The Grand Vizier's Dismissal, in: The Times, 24.7.1908, p. 7. See: Hacısalihoğlu, *Die Jungtürken und die mazedonische Frage*, p. 190; Kırmızı, *Experiencing the Ottoman Empire*, p. 61.

[258] PA–AA, IA Türkei 159/2, Kiderlen to von Bülow, 22.7.1908.

[259] Ibid., Kiderlen to von Bülow, 2.8.1908; See in original: "*besonders wurde er als geborener Albanese verdächtigt, mit der albanischen Bewegung zu sympathisieren, ja es wurde ganz offen das Gerücht kolportiert, dass Ferid direkt der Leiter dieser Bewegung sei.*"

with two ambassadors about the conditions of the Ottoman Empire.[260] However, after the aggressive policies of the CUP against the Albanian population in the post–Hamidian period, he gave to the Albanian intellectuals solely moral support without participating actively in the (task of) building of the Albanian nation–state.[261] Hence, there is no doubt that he played an important role in the Ottoman administration and put in efforts to bring and draw the 'Ottoman peripheries' closer to its 'centre,' yet he also supported the periphery when the centre applied coercive policies.

In order to resolve the situation in the three vilayets, Hüseyin Hilmi Pasha was appointed general Inspector of Rumelia (*Vilayat–ı Selase Umum Müfettişliği*) in parallel with Ferid Pasha. In tandem they were the most successful governors of the time, appointed to inquire the general situation of the Rumelian provinces and the administration of improvements. As a result of their activities, the three provinces of Salonica, Manastir, and Kosovo were (officially) addressed in the documents as *vilayet–i selase*, and were under the direct supervision of general inspector (*müfettiş–i umumi*) Hüseyin Hilmi Pasha for six years from December 1902.[262] His position was directly connected to the administration of Ferid Pasha. As the two highest representatives of the Hamidian Regime in Rumelia, the Grand Vizier and General Inspector were instrumental in promoting peace and justice in the region. The British journalist H. Brailsford describes Inspector General, Hüseyin Hilmi Pasha as "the pivot of the new plan (…) who was supposed to be 'controlled,' wherever he might happen to be, by the local Austrian and Russian consuls. Hilmi Pasha is certainly a man of rather exceptional ability, with much more culture than is common among Ottoman officials. He has read a little, and speaks French well. (…) His manner is grave, courteous, and distinguished. He suggests the Arab rather

---

[260] Sureyya Bey Avlonyalı, *Osmanlı Sonrası Arnavutluk* (Istanbul: Klasik Yayınları, 2018), p. 354; See in original: *"cemiyet–i fâsidenin muhaliflerinden olan birader–i büzürgvârim Ferid Paşa merhum, cümlemizin re'y ü kararıyla süferâdan iki zatın mütalaasını istifsâr etmek üzere tavsît edilmiş ve lede'l–icab hukuk–i mengubemizin istirdadı ve bir idare–i muvakkate teşkili takdirinde müzaheretleri sureti temin edilmek istenilmiştir."*

[261] Kırmızı, *Experiencing the Ottoman Empire*, p. 66.

[262] Mustafa Birol Ülker et al., *Hüseyin Hilmi Paşa Evrakı Kataloğu*, p. 17; See in: Dosya No. 1. 1.05.1319.

than the Turk. One's first impression is that he is profoundly sincere and completely honest. His optimism is contagious, and one experiences in his presence that rarest of all emotions in the East — a thrill of hope."[263]

In the then daily newspaper of the time, *Asir*, the prominent Young Turk Fazlı Necip described his encounter with Hüseyin Hilmi Pasha as follows: "[O]ne day we received the news of Hüseyin Hilmi Pasha's appointment as Inspector General of the Rumelian Provinces. We asked each other, 'Who is this Hüseyin Pasha?' He was not a famed dignitary. He had never been to Rumelia. People talked about it everywhere for days in order to comprehend the characteristics of this inspector who was to rule the great territory of Rumelia as a semi–autonomous prince."[264]

This "man of exceptional ability" (Brailsford) and "semi–autonomous prince" (Fazlı Necip) served in the Empire's eastern regions in Adana, Ottoman Syria, and Yemen. Due to his skills in crisis management in Yemen, where he showed diplomatic adeptness at balancing between local communities and foreign powers that interfered in Ottoman internal affairs, Sultan Abdulhamid II decided to appoint him in Rumelia as well. He was without doubt a prominent Hamidian statesman who often shined a spotlight on the extent of Sultan Abdulhamid II's investments in centralisation policies. [265] However, when the situation in Ottoman Macedonia was no longer manageable due to armed conflicts between nationalist bands,[266] he sided with the Young Turk Movement. It appears

---

[263] Brailsford, *Macedonia.*

[264] Sena Hatip Dinçyürek, "Reading a Bureaucratic Career Backwards: How did Hüseyin Hilmi Pasha become the Inspector–General of Rumelia?," *in Middle Eastern Studies* 53/3 (2017): 386–405, in page 400 quote: "*işte bu sırada bir gün Rumeli Vilayetleri Umumi Mufettisliğine Hüseyin Hilmi Paşanın tayin olunduğunu haber aldık. "Bu Hüseyin Paşa kim?" birbirimizden soruyorduk. Kendisi meşhur ricalden değildi. Rumeli'de hiç bulunmamıştı. Simdi koskoca Rumeli'yi bir nevi prens gibi yarı istiklal ile idare edecek olan bu mufettişin halinin hususiyetini anlamak için her yerde günlerce bundan bahsedildi.*"; See also: Ciğdem Önal Emiroğlu and Kudret Emiroğlu, *Osmanlı Terakki ve İttihat Cemiyeti: Paris Merkezi Yazışmaları Kopya Defterleri (1906–1908)* (Istanbul: Tarih Vakfı Yurt Yayınları, 2017); Süleyman Kani İrtem, *Osmanlı Devleti'nin Makedonya meselesi* (Istanbul: Temel Yayınları, 1998); Fazlı Necip, "Makedonya'da son günlerimiz ve Umumi Müfettiş Hüseyin Hilmi Paşa," *Yakın Tarihimiz* 53/3 (1962): 362.

[265] Ibid., p. 399.

[266] See Christopher Psilos, "The Young Turk Revolution and the Macedonian Question (1908–1912)" (PhD diss., University of Leeds, 2000), p. 33; Starting in 1907, the Macedonian Inspector–General began to monitor the Greek Macedonian consular

that he supported the Second Constitutional Period and later was appointed Grand Vizier by the CUP. According to British sources, Hilmi Pasha was one of the most active members of CUP and that he was, indeed aware of the secret activities of Young Turk Movement and their political ideology.[267] Two days prior to the grant of constitution, on 21 July 1908, the Rumelia Inspector reported that large–scale rebellions were in the making in Salonica, Manastir, and Uskup, the capitals of the three Macedonian provinces (*vilayeti selase*), and increasing numbers of officers, soldiers, and gendarmes were leaving their posts to join the committee that would lead to the Young Turk Revolution. According to Mithat Şükrü Bleda, "if general inspector Hüseyin Hilmi Pasha wanted to suppress members of the CUP, he could do so. But with his clever mind and understanding of the situation, he seemed to be balancing between the palace and members of the CUP."[268]

It is worth noting that many Albanian intellectuals, bureaucrats, solders, and locals in the Kosovo vilayet were instrumental in bringing the Young Turks to power. This can also be analysed through a post–colonial lens and centre–periphery relations. Namely, not only did the Ottoman bureaucracy and imperial policy influence the peripheries, but it also impacted the lives of its local agitators (i.e. Albanians), shaping the core values of both the Ottoman peripheries and Istanbul. In this regard, the outbreak of the events in the Ottoman peripheries, that is in the three vilayets, such as the rebellion in Resne led by Ahmed Niyazi, known as a "hero of freedom" (*hürriyet kahramani*); the gathering of thousands of Albanians at the

---

institutions and the Patriarchist Metropolitan sees, while also ordering Albanian and Vlach bands to attack Greek partisans. By the end of that year, Hüseyin Hilmi Pasha managed to have the militant Greek diplomats Koromilas and Mavroudis removed from their positions in Salonica and Kavala.

[267] Ibid; Find in the document: British Parliamentary Papers. Accounts and Papers, P.P.A.P. CV 1909, p. 1007.

[268] Mithat Şükrü Bleda, *İmparatorluğun Çöküşü* (Istanbul: Destek Yayınları, 2010), p. 51; Quote: "*umumi Müfetti Hüseyin Hilmi Paşa istemiş olsaydı İttihat ve Terakki elemanlarına kötülük edebilirdi. Fakat zeki ve anlayışlı bir kimse olduğundan perşembenin gelişini çarşambadan anlamı ve davranışlarını ona göre ayarlamıştı. Bir yandan sarayın nabzını elinde tutarak, öteki yandan İttihat ve Terakki yöneticilerine güler yüz göstererek iki tarafı da mükemmelen idare etmişti.*"; See also: Süleyman Kani Irtem, *Osmanlı Devleti'nin Makedonya Meselesi* (Istanbul: Temel Yayınları, 1998); Tahsin Üzer, *Makedonya Eşkiyalık Tarihi ve Son Osmanlı Yönetimi* (Ankara: Türk Tarih Kurumu, 1999); Hacısalihoğlu, *Die Jungtürken und die Mazedonische Frage*, p. 72.

meeting in Firzovik; and the support given to the Young Turks by the Ottoman Third Army based in Salonika show the importance of the periphery in its influence on the centre.

These events represent striking examples of the agencies of peripheral actors who triggered the Revolution from the Ottoman provinces. To borrow Chakrabarty's famous term "provincialising,"[269] I hold that these events in 1908 should be interpreted as "provincialising Istanbul." Actually, provincialisation implies understandings of state–society relations and how they further "play out on and among different scales such as the local, national, regional, or international."[270] In this regard we need to theorise the complex interplay between different layers and link them to a deeper reflection of the "local." In order to bring perspectives from below or to analyse "the governance beyond the center" then, I will further keep deploying examples from the perspectives of the local actors and Ottoman peripheries. This enables me to imbue the analysis of core–periphery relations "with a better understanding of the role of agency, resistance, and multi–scalar power struggles, which link the many different cores with the quite variegated peripheries. "[271]

5.2. The Young Turks and Albanian Intellectuals in Ottoman Macedonia

The Young Turk Movement arose after that of the Young Ottomans (*Yeni Osmanlılar*) in the second half of the 19th century. It became a rallying point for diverse oppositional groups and devised alternative political trajectories against Abduulhamid II's oppressive rule, especially through their use of the printing press and their call to restore the constitution. The institutional kernel of the Movement was a secret organisation named the Ottoman Union and later Committee of Union and Progress (CUP). To gain a deeper understanding of the diverse legacy of this movement in the Ottoman Empire, one must take a closer look at the ethnic diversity of its members. This Committee was constituted of members of different

---

[269] Dipesh Chakrabarty, *Provincializing Europe: Postcolonial Thought and Historical Difference* (Princeton, NJ: Princeton University Press. 2000).
[270] See: Cilja Harders, "Provincializing and Localizing Core–Periphery Relations," *META Journal* 5 (2015): 36–45.
[271] Ibid.

backgrounds: Ibrahim Temo was an Albanian from Struga; Abdullah Cevdet had Kurdish origin; Mehmet Reshid hailed from a Circassian family born in the Russian Empire; Ahmed Riza was born into a Turkish family from Istanbul.[272] As is evident, three members were born in the Ottoman peripheries and just one belonged to an Istanbulite family. In aspiring to grow in diversity and include backgrounds other than the Muslim background of the Young Turks, the organisation included non–Muslim Ottoman subjects as well, like Orthodox Christians from Ottoman Macedonia (Nicolae Constantin Batzaria effendi) and Jews from Salonika (Emmanuel Karasu, Albert Fua, and Avram Galanti) and a Catholic Arab (Khalid Ghanem Effendi).[273] Hence, the Young Turks established contacts with like–minded critics of Abdulhamid's rule that included intellectuals and officials of the Ottoman empire, primary influenced by European political ideas. [274] These itinerant Ottomans comprised diverse personalities from Istanbul to the Ottoman provinces[275] and their activities spread between Istanbul and cities far afield such as Cairo, Alexandria, Thessaloniki, Manastir (Bitola), or Geneva and Paris.[276] By taking this trans–regional approach, my research moves beyond reductive national–historical and Eurocentric perspectives, while on the other hand it aims to give a voice to less researched communities who established entanglements and transfers of a multidirectional character.[277] Examples

---

[272] Şerif Mardin, *The Genesis of Young Ottoman Thought*; Ümit Kurt,'*Türk'ün büyük, biçare Irkı:' Türk yurdu'nda milliyetçiliğin esasları (1911–1916)* (Istanbul: İletişim, 2012); Ümit Kurt and Doğan Gulpınar, "The Young Turk Historical Imagination in the Pursuit of Mythical Turkishness and Its Lost Grandeur (1911–1914)" *British Journal of Middle Eastern Studies* 43/4 (2016): 560–564.

[273] On the Young Turks and their politics, see: Hasan Kayalı, *Arabs and Young Turks: Ottomanism, Arabism, and Islamism in the Ottoman Empire (1908–1918)* (Berkeley: University of California Press, 1997); Feroz Ahmad, *The Young Turks: The Committee of Union and Progress in Turkish Politics (1908–1914)* (New York: Columbia University Press, 2010).

[274] Bedross Der Matossian, *Shattered Dreams of Revolution: From Liberty to Violence in the Late Ottoman Empire* (Stanford: Stanford University Press, 2014).

[275] Blumi, *Reinstating the Ottomans*.

[276] Isa Blumi, *Ottoman Refugees, 1878–1939: Migration in a Post–Imperial World* (New York: Bloomsbury Academy, 2013).

[277] Benedict Binebai, "Voice Construction in the Postcolonial Text: Spivakian Subaltern Theory in Nigerian Drama," *African Research Review* 9/4 (2015): 206–220; Spivak, *Can the Subaltern Speak?*; Blumi, *Foundations of Modernity*.

of such "voices" are inter–personal conversations of the Young Turks and Ottoman Albanian intellectuals – with each other as well as the local population – that can be "heard" through their memoirs and diaries, personal letters and essays, and newspapers and journals. Such conversations were possible due to their still "hybrid identities."[278] Neither in the Albanian community, nor in the Young Turk Movement was there a "homogenous national society." Furthermore, Isa Blumi suggests that Ottoman Albanians (and other Balkan nations) did not have a quintessential "fixed identity" prior to the traumatic Balkan Wars of 1912 and 1913; and he warns about a teleological emphasis on migrants' national belonging.[279] On top of this, Isa Blumi, Selim Deringil, Ussama Makdisi, and others underline (the existence of) possibilities rather than restrictions of identities during the late Ottoman Empire. In this regard, one may argue that identities among the Young Turk and Albanian communities were in a state of evolution, which can be traced in archival documents and autobiographical writings, as well as in their political programmes and activism that challenged the state's attempts to impose homogenised policies. Thus, by focusing on the social and intellectual conversations of these mobile actors, this project firstly aims to return agency where it belongs. In this way, the project distances itself from imperialist and nationalist–essentialist historiographies that seek to create narratives based on Western knowledge without hearing local and trans–regional stories of entangled histories. In sum, then, this study wants to contribute to the provincialisation of Europe and to bring in questions from the 'peripheral' stories,[280] by elaborating examples of their multiple trajectories.[281] Within this context, various examples from within the Young Turk and Albanian movements pose a number of questions such as: what triggered these personalities to cooperate or clash? In other words, what were the "push" and "pull" factors motivating their communication? Did the Young Turks and Albanians have the same reasons for Ottoman

---

[278] Homi K. Bhabha, *The Location of Culture* (London/New York: Routledge, 1994).
[279] Blumi, *Foundations of Modernity*, p. 115.
[280] Chakrabarty, *Provincializing Europe.*
[281] Shmuel N. Eisenstadt, "Multiple Modernen im Zeitalter der Globalisierung, Die Vielfalt und Einheit der Moderne," in *Die Vielfalt und Einheit der Moderne*, ed. Thomas Schwinn (Wiesbaden: Springer VS Verlag für Sozialwissenschaft, 2006), pp. 37–39.

Macedonia? How did these mobile actors communicate and build networks in the trans–Ottoman space? What were their points of view regarding Sultan Abdulhamid II's autocracy and the Macedonian Question that became more burning since 1878? How much was their cooperation or were their clashes influenced by events in the Ottoman Balkans (i.e. the Macedonian Question)? Did Albanian community members perceive themselves as Ottomans and did the Young Turks include Albanians into their Ottomanism projects, and vice versa? Can we find actors who were active in both communities? What was their point of view and what did they write? How were categories of knowledge combined and how did they interact? In other words, how did thought translate into practice, words into action?

In order to answer these questions, the project attempts to set these cases in a broader context, acknowledging the relevance of knowledge circulations, interpersonal networks, and connections that shaped the lives and actions of mobile actors in Ottoman Macedonia. Hence, it will take into consideration the transfer of knowledge from Pan–Islamist and Pan–Turkist circles, anarchist and nationalist ideas that influenced both the Young Turk and Albanian communities in Ottoman Macedonia and their communication in daily life. Thus, an Ottoman trans–imperial history has the potential to contribute to the booming field of global history, going beyond hierarchical Euro–Centric points of view by trying rather to explain the history from an angle of interconnectedness. Here I concentrate on several events transpiring at the turn of the century, more specifically during the Young Turk Revolution of 1908. In relation to these events, I will also investigate the following questions: how are global waves (such as modernisation and ideologies) established on the ground, and how do various actors link their local upheavals to global waves ideologically and practically? [282] How was the periphery (i.e. Ottoman Macedonia) influenced by the centre , and how did the peripheral actors (i.e. Young Turks) have agency to influence the centre and profound changes in state politics?

---

[282] Nader Sohrabi, "Global Waves, Local Actors: What the Young Turks Knew about Other Revolutions and Why It Mattered," *Comparative Studies in Society and History* 44/1 (January, 2002): 46; Kurt,'*Türk'ün büyük, biçare Irkı.* '; Kurt, "The Young Turk Historical Imagination."

5.2.1. The Young Turks and Networks in Europe: From Ideology to Political Movement

In this subchapter, I will focus in part on the development of the Young Turk movement as an opposition that emerged against the Hamidian regime in the period between 1902 and 1908, with a particular focus on networks among various personalities and communities in the Macedonian context. Although the Young Turk Movement can be traced back to 1889,[283] its real political activity started in the period between 1902 and 1908. In this regard, Kazim Karabekir pointed out that the "first period of the foundation of the CUP happened in Istanbul in 1889, when the organisation was in the hands of the ranks of students of medicine who still had not expanded to the Ottoman army."[284] According to him, "its second period could be traced back to 1906, only this time far away from Istanbul, in Macedonia, among the civil population and army."[285] Kazim Karabekir was born in Istanbul (1882) and since 1906 served as a junior officer in the Third Army in the region around Bitola/Manastir (Ottoman Macedonia). In a joint effort with Enver Pasha he established a regional office of the CUP in Manastir. He acted (politically) on behalf of the Young Turk Movement.[286] Personally, as reflected in his memoirs, he could not imagine the Ottoman Empire without Macedonia.[287] In his imagination, he

---

[283] BOA, BEO, Dosya 3919, Gomlek 293860, Tarih: 25. B. 1329, p. 3.

[284] Kazim Karabekir, *İttihat ve Terakki Cemiyeti* (Istanbul: Yapı Kredi Yayınları, 2009), p 19; See in original: "*İttihat ve Terakki Cemiyeri kuruluşu bakımından iki devreye ayrılır. Birinci devre kuruluşuna 1889 (1305) tarihinde Istanbul'da henüz olgunlaşmayan bir muhitte ve yine henüz olgunlaşmayan beş tıbbiye talebesinin hürriyetseverlik heyecanları sebep olmuş ve teşkilatını hemen hemen Istanbul'a hasrettirmiş ve daha çok da mektep talebesini içine almıştır. Ordulara da el atamadığından sayıca çokluğuna rağmen kudretçe istibdadın merkezi olan Istanbul'da beceriksiz bir halde sözü ayağa düşürmüş ve ufak bir sarsıntıya karşı kayamayarak varlığını kaybetmiştir.*"

[285] Ibid, p. 19; Quote: "*ikinci devre kuruluşu ise 1906'da Istanbul'dan uzak olan Makedonya'da ihtilaller arasında olgunlaşan bir muhitte ve yine olgunlaşmış sivil ve asker başların zamanın kaplarını düşünerek ve daha uzun görüşmeler ve didişmelerle başlamış ve Selanik'te on kişilik bir merkezle faaliyete girişmiştir. Teşkilatını hemen ordulara hasretmiş, Manastır ınıntıkası gibi, istibdat mihrakından çok uzak bir yerde icra kudretini haiz bir kuvvet vücuda getirmiş*)."

[286] BOA, HR.SYS. Dosya 2105, Gomlek 55, T. 06.10.1915, p. 13.

[287] Ibid. See also: Karabekir, *İttihat ve Terakki Cemiyeti*, p. 55; In original: "*Ben bu tahlili yaptıktan sonra ortaya iki sual attım: Bu gidişle Makedonya bizde kalır mı? Makedonya bizden ayrılırken bütün Türkiye'yi de beraber uçuruma sürüklemez mi?*"

feared that "the fire over Macedonia could burn the whole motherland."[288] How, then, was it possible that one periphery could "burn the whole motherland"? What was the reason for the vital importance of Macedonia for the Ottoman Empire? Erik Jan Zürcher comments that "a group of people from the periphery" influenced "the course of events in these last years of empire" and "the direction of Ottoman and Turkish politics after the war." [289] Moreover, according to Şükrü Hanioğlu, the events in Macedonia and the Young Turk Revolution "made a profound impact on the shaping of the modern Middle East and the Balkans."[290] In order to find out the importance of Ottoman Macedonia for Turkish, Balkan, and Middle Eastern politics, I will trace back its activities and elucidate their inner networks. No organisation could be influential without solid networks that provided infrastructural power.

To begin with, the strong censorship of the Hamidian regime obliged many Young Turks to move to other countries and to lead intellectual and political discussions in various European capitals and in Egypt. Indeed, in those cities Young Turks were under the strong influence of global waves of ideas (European elitist theories, nationalism, modernisation, and westernisation) of the late 19th century. These itinerant Ottomans[291] tended to accept the ideas known in social science as the results of circulated knowledge. [292] Some of its members reflected a strong commitment to positivist approach and elitism, who promoted a vision of the ideal society based on the ideas of social darwinism. Others were rather proponents of accepting a multicultural empire and promoting decentralisation. In this respect, Prince Sabahaddin and Lutfullah Bey – nephews of Sultan Abdulhamid – and their father, Damad Mahmud Pasha, organised a congress to unite the various Young Turk factions, with respect

---

[288] Ibid., p. 64; *"Makedonya yangınının bütün memleketi uçuruma sürüklernesinden korkmalı ve buna göre hazırlıklı bulunmalıyız."*

[289] Jan Zürcher, "The Young Turks – Children of the Borderlands?," *International Journal of Turkish* Studies 9 (2003): 279–281; Kurt,'*Türk'ün Büyük, Biçare Irkı.'*; Kurt, "The Young Turk Historical Imagination."

[290] Şükrü Hanioğlu, *Preparation for a Revolution: The Young Turks, 1902–1908* (Oxford: Oxford University Press, 2001), p. 3. Kurt,'*Türk'ün Büyük, Biçare Irkı,'*; Kurt, "The Young Turk Historical Imagination."

[291] Blumi, *Ottoman Refugees.*

[292] Stefan Rohdewald et al. "Wissenszirkulation: Perspektiven und Forschungsstand," pp. 99–104.

to the various Ottoman ethnic groups. This congress was held in Paris in February 1902, and its' leaders debated substantial political issues for the first time.[293] However, the congress showed that the Young Turks in exile were more of an intellectual than a political organisation that had a clear strategy on the ground. Actually, they did not established networks with the local people or organisations within the territories of the Ottoman empire. Thus, the transformation of the Young Turk Movement from an intellectual endeavour into a political one gained momentum later in 1907, during the Second Young Turk Congress.[294] Its aim was based to unite all Ottoman elements in order to strength its political position, bring the revolution into practice and to bring back the constitution from 1876.[295] Furthermore, it should not be assumed that inside these communities there was a unified proto or supra–national sensibility. It is important to remember that in each organisation there were members who opposed the ideas and policies of the core. [296] This diverse picture of actors demonstrates that these personalities were an active and dynamic group, influencing each other and often being open to accepting ideas coming from the other communities. Accordingly, the formed networks thus, cannot be considered in a vacuum as a static structure, rather as processual constructs of multi–layered identities and historical intersectionalities. However, we should also be aware that at times the Young Turks also had divergent responses, participated in different programs, and lobbied for diverse and sometimes contradictory strategies. Rather the ambitions of the Young Turks were varied and contested, and the discussions often

---

[293] Hanioğlu, *Preparation for a Revolution*, p. 3.

[294] Dr. Bahaeddin Şakir successfully converted an intellectual movement into a well–organised activist body in the form of CUP; See: Mehmet Hacısalihoğlu, *Die Jungtürken und die Mazedonische Frage*.

[295] Ahmed Riza, *Ahmet Riza Bey'in anıları* (Istanbul: Dizgi Yayınları, 2001).

[296] The 1902 Congress of the Ottoman Opposition served to intensify the division within the Young Turk Movement, hastening the rift between the two groups that coexisted within the movement despite their different viewpoints. This division essentially created a split among the leaders of the movement. According to Şükrü Hanioğlu, there were two factions within the Young Turk Movement: the Majority led by Damad Mahmud Pasha and the Minority led by Ahmed Riza. Ahmed Riza, who had previously viewed the members of the old CUP organisation as a group of extortionists, made it clear that he had no respect even for Ishak Sukuti, who had passed away in San Remo during the Congress in February 1902. See: Hanioğlu, *Preparation for a Revolution*; Kurt,'*Türk'ün Büyük, Biçare Irkı.*'

287

resulted in clashes and contradictory tendencies. For example, as early as at their First Congress a rupture appeared between two groups: the decentralist (ones), led by Prince Sabahaddin by establishing the League for Private Initiative and Decentralisation (*Teşebbüs–i Şahsi ve Adem–i Merkeziyet Cemiyeti*), and the centralist, organised by Ahmed Riza who "insisted on the organisation of a central and centralising power at Constantinople in the interests of the purely Turkish element."[297] Prince Sabaheddin argued that the Young Turks should promote a European intervention, even military measures if needed, to end the autocratic rule of Sultan Abdulhamid II. On the contrary, Ahmet Riza Bey dismissed the idea of foreign interference. Thus, between 1902 and 1905, the Young Turk Movement displayed a polarised character and was undergoing a gradual disintegration.

An Albanian activist from Vlora (Avlonya), Ismail Bey[298] was among the most prominent members and supporters of the decentralised faction that supported decentralisation during the Congress which was held in Paris in 1902. He was in fact a cousin of the Ottoman Grand Vizier Avlonyalı Ferid Pasha and later became known as the first President of Independent Albania (1912) with the name Ismail Qemali. However, during the years 1902–1908, he cooperated with Prince Sabahudin to unite the various Young Turk factions. In his memoirs, he points out that "they [Sabahudin, Lutfullah, and Damat Mahmud Pasha] wanted [him] to take part in this [the Congress], and Prince Lutfullah came to Brussels to see [him] on the matter. [He] was willing to take part in the Congress on certain conditions — namely, that all the ethnical elements in Turkey should be represented, so that the desiderata of all the people of the Empire might be formulated."[299] Thus, the task of the Central Committee of the League (*Teşebbüs–i Şahsi ve Adem–i Merkeziyet Cemiyeti*) was to organise joint activities with the Albanian, Macedonian, and some members of the Armenian groups. Immediately after the 1902 Congress, Armenian organisations and the IMARO held negotiations for joint action against the Hamidian regime.[300] Ismail Qemali (Kemal) eminisces that, in those days,

---

[297] Kemal Bey, *The Memoirs*, p. 306.
[298] BOA. HR.SYS. 1805, 36, 27.07.1907. p. 2.
[299] Kemal Bey, *The Memoirs*. p. 306.
[300] Hanioğlu, *Preparation for a Revolution*, p. 14.

"subsequent meetings took place at the house of Prince Saba Eddine, in the Boulevard Malesherbes, where some forty delegates, representing all the races of the Turkish Empire, continued to sit for several days."[301] The role of mediator between these groups was assigned to Ismail Qemali. He still imagined a united Ottoman Empire including all its nationalities. In order to achieve this aim, he and Prince Sabahuddin decided to involve the British government as a foreign assistant to dethrone the Sultan and to get support from various Ottoman ethnic groups. Through their official medium *Osmanlî*[302] (and later *Terakki*), he first started to gather the numerous Albanians who published a new bilingual journal, *Ittihad–î Osmanî – La Fédération Ottomane*, in Geneva.[303] It was led by three members of Albanian origin, who were members of the old CUP (organisation): Ahmed Rîfat,[304] Dervish Hima,[305] and Halil Muvaffak.[306]

---

[301] Kemal Bey, *The Memoirs*, p. 307.

[302] On August 15th, 1903, the organisation in question was moved to Cairo. Edhem Ruhi and Abdullah Cevdet took over leadership of the group and promoted more anarchist ideas. The organisation in question is likely the Ottoman Freedom Society (OFS), also known as the Society for the Defense of Freedom and the Constitution, which was a secret society founded in 1908 by a group of young Ottoman exiles in Paris. The OFS aimed to overthrow the autocratic rule of Sultan Abdulhamid II and replace it with a constitutional government. The society's members, which included intellectuals, students, and military officers, believed in the principles of liberalism, democracy, and nationalism, and drew inspiration from European revolutionary movements. The OFS played a significant role in the Young Turk Revolution of 1908, which resulted in the restoration of the Ottoman constitution and the establishment of a constitutional government.

[303] Hanioğlu, *Preparation for a Revolution*, p. 52.

[304] Ibid., p. 173.

[305] Ibid; Dervish Hima, who represented Albania at the 1902 Congress, had his journal *Albania–Arnavutluk* shut down by the Italian government. However, he planned to restart publishing the journal in Geneva. Dervish Hima was an Albanian intellectual and activist who played an important role in the Albanian national movement. He attended the 1902 Congress of the Ottoman Opposition as a representative of the Albanian community, where he advocated for Albanian interests and demanded greater autonomy for Albanians within the Ottoman Empire.

[306] Ibid; Halil Muvaffak, who was the son of an Albanian notable from Larissa, had been entrusted with important responsibilities by the Committee of Union and Progress (CUP). Halil Muvaffak was a prominent figure in the CUP, a political organisation that aimed to modernise and reform the Ottoman Empire. He was born in Larissa, a city in Thessaly, which at the time was part of the Ottoman Empire. Muvaffak received a modern education and became a journalist and writer, contributing to various newspapers and journals. He joined the CUP and quickly rose through the ranks, becoming one of its leading members. Muvaffak was known for his strong personality and his commitment to the CUP's ideals,

They had the aim of "decentralisation" and transfer of power to the provinces, more precisely to Albania and Macedonia. In Ismail Bey's perception, Macedonia "[was] the country where 'Shkupetars' (Albanians) – the 'Men of the Eagle [had] lived for centuries. Dwelling in a sort of isolation, they were variously grouped under the generic name of Macedonians or Illyrians."[307] To him, there was no doubt that the three vilayets are Albanian provinces, which should be granted an autonomous status. He also admitted that "the last phase of the Macedonian affairs" made Albanians " feel acute anxiety" and "wonder what fate was in store for their country."[308] For this reason, they cooperated with various Young Turks in order to preserve Ottoman Macedonia and to save their country. According to Prince Sabaheddin, this could be possible only by the formation of an "organisational network from the west to the east of Asia Minor." [309] In the western parts of the Empire, Ismail Kemal was appointed, and as such, he recognised the need for a structured network of supporters and sympathisers. Therefore, he was in constant contact with Albanian intellectuals, such as Dervish Hima, Hamdi Ohri, Kadri Prishtina, Jashar Erebara, etc.[310] In the eastern parts of the Empire Prince Sabaheddin built networks with Armenians. Thanks to these personal connections, uprisings could be staged effectively in Eastern Anatolia (between 1905–1907) and Ottoman Macedonia in 1908. Furthermore, Ismail Kemal and Prince Sabaheddin started finding a way towards a reconciliation with Ahmed Riza. As a result, they came to an agreement to organise a Second Congress of Ottoman Opposition Parties, including the

---

which included constitutional government, nationalism, and modernization. He was also involved in various clandestine activities, including the planning of the Young Turk Revolution of 1908. After the revolution, Muvaffak held several high–level positions in the Ottoman government, including Minister of Education and Minister of Foreign Affairs. He continued to be active in politics until his death in 1914.

[307] Kemal Bey, *The Memoirs*, p. 356.

[308] Ibid., p. 365.

[309] Hanioğlu, *Preparation for a Revolution*, p. 91.

[310] Eqber Skendi, *Hoxhë Kadriu (Kadri Prishtina)* (Prishtinë: Rilindja, 1992), pp. 13–14: Quote:*"Kongresin që mbajtën xhonturqit në Paris më 20.02. 1902, ku nga krerët shqiptarë morën pjesë: Dervish Hima, i cili në atë kohë ndodhej në Romë, Ismail Qemail, mori pjesë nga Brukseli, Jashar Erebera, u dërgua nga studentët shqiptarë të Bukureshtit, Kadri Prishtina, shkoi nga Kajro, njëherësh ishte edhe nënkryetar i Partisë "Bashkim e Progres."*

Armenian Dashnaktsutiun Committee. They also hoped for IMARO participation in the congress. However, the IMARO, which was in total chaos due to the assassinations of its two important leaders such as Sarafov and Garvanov in November 1907, was not able to take part in the Congress. Following the agreement among the three organising committees (the decentralist, centralist, and Dashnaktsutsian committee), the Congress convened in three sessions between 27–29 December 1907 and agreed to cooperate on the Ottoman issues and to establish networks for the dethroning of the Sultan.[311]

5.2.2. Young Turks and Networks in Macedonia: From Political Movement to Revolution

As I have been delving into multiple regional entanglements, I propose further to view Ottoman Macedonia as a fluid space where social networks formed. Furthermore, these networks, whether recent or long–standing, were based on certain legacies that rendered them "legitimate." As a result

---

[311] Hanioğlu, *Preparation for a Revolution*, p. 205; See in original document: "Osmanlî Muhalifîn Fîrkalarî Tarafîndan Avrupa'da In'ikad Eden Kongre'nin Beyannâmesi," in *Şûra–yi Ümmet*, 128–29 (1908): 3; The declaration outlined three main objectives of the participating organisations: to compel Sultan Hamid to abdicate, to radically transform the current administration, and to establish a system of constitutional government with consultation. The declaration also provided a detailed plan of tactics to be employed by the revolutionaries. These tactics included armed and unarmed resistance against the government's actions and operations, strikes by policemen and government officials, refusal to pay taxes to the current administration, propaganda within the army to persuade soldiers not to move against the rebels, general rebellion, and other means of action to be determined based on the course of events. The declaration was a clear indication of the revolutionaries' determination to overthrow the existing Ottoman regime and replace it with a constitutional government. It reflected the growing discontent among various groups within the Ottoman Empire, who were frustrated with the Sultan's authoritarian rule and the government's failure to address the country's economic and social problems. The tactics proposed in the declaration reveal the revolutionaries' intention to use a combination of peaceful and violent means to achieve their goals. The strike and nonpayment of taxes were intended to cripple the government's operations and undermine its legitimacy, while the propaganda within the army was aimed at weakening the military's loyalty to the Sultan. The call for armed resistance and general rebellion demonstrated the revolutionaries' willingness to use force to achieve their objectives. Overall, the declaration represented a significant turning point in the history of the Ottoman Empire and set the stage for the Young Turk Revolution of 1908, which resulted in the establishment of a constitutional government.

of the networking, an "epistemic community"[312] was created, which can be viewed as a fluid social group, sweeping across borders in order to establish interconnections. The Young Turks in Europe and Macedonia were such an "epistemic community," which after the Second Congress of Ottoman Opposition Parties wanted to create connections with all Ottoman ethnicities. In this respect, this newly reconciled group of Young Turks employed a heavily Ottomanist rhetoric when it addressed non–Muslims, emphasising that it was "working toward the happiness of all Ottoman elements such as the Albanians, Turks, Kurds, Armenians, Bulgarians, [and] Greeks."[313]Şükrü Hanioğlu emphasises that, in written documents, they changed phrases from the ethnical and nationalist Turkish one, to invocations like "O Turkish sons! O Ottoman brothers!" to "O children of the Fatherland! O Ottoman brothers!" In addition, the words against the Christian members of the Ottoman empire were replaced by a passage reading: "You should understand that Bulgarians and Vlachs are not our enemies; on the contrary they are our confidants and our brothers."[314]

A prominent member of this reconciled Young Turk Movement was Ahmed Riza. In his memoirs he expressed the unity of all the different elements with the words:

> "I will work for the profit of all Ottomans. Therefore, I named this new organisation 'Union and Progress' (*ben bütün Osmanlıların çıkarları için çalışacağından dolayı Ittihad ve Terakki [Birlik ve Gelişme] adını daha uygun gördüm. Öyle kabul edildi)*."[315]

Since 1907, this united organisation was known as Ottoman Committee of Union and Progress (CUP), and Ahmed Riza represented the strong intellectual wing of the party. He played a very important role in organising the Young Turk Movement. Owing to it, he later became head of the Ottoman Chamber of Deputies as well as a senator. He was a man of thought and liberal personality rather than a professional activist. The

---

[312] About "epistemic community" see: Peter M. Haas, "Introduction: Epistemic Communities and International Policy Coordination," *International Organization: Cambridge Journals* 46/1 (1992): 1–35.

[313] Hanioğlu, *Preparation for a Revolution*, p. 175.

[314] Ibid., 186

[315] Riza, *Ahmet Riza Anıları*, p. 17.

professional activism on the ground was the responsibility of many personalities who worked in Ottoman Macedonia. One such prominent figure was Talat Bey (later Pasha). He was Ahmed Riza's man of connection in Macedonia[316] and a chief clerk of correspondence in the post office in Thessaloniki. He was founder of the Ottoman Freedom Society (*Osmanli Hürriyet Cemiyeti*), which helped to establish various networks throughout Macedonia. In September 1907, this society was united with Ahmed Riza's organisation Union and Progress. This was a merger of two committees pursuing the same goals and similar agendas. Regarding this, in his memoirs, Talat Pasha wrote that the "Young Turks, Arabs, Greeks, Albanians, Turks and others wanted to be united all together for the sake of the beloved fatherland and progress."[317] Furthermore, Talat Pasha, in concert with his friends from Macedonia (Ömer Naci, Mithat Şükrü Bleda, Evaronszade Rahmi, Dr. Nazim), was recruiting new members in order to expand CUP's activities in Macedonia. While they were all civilians, they realised that success in the struggle depended on military activity. Immediately afterwards, a Young Turk under the pseudonym of A. Raif travelled to Belgrade and the Ottoman–Serbian border in Kosovo vilayeti to start spreading propaganda among Ottoman officers and the Albanian population. His propaganda was especially successful among the Albanians.[318] However, the Young Turks spread very quickly their activities in various units of the Ottoman army in Macedonia, especially among the officer corps.[319] Thus, CUP started to establish branches headed by Ottoman officers, such as Enver Pasha and Kazim Karabekir in Bitola and Eyüb Sabri in Ohrid. These first cells also included members of the ordinary people, such as: Fethi [Okyar], Colonel Sadık, Aziz Ali al–

---

[316] Hanioğlu, *Preparation for a Revolution*, p. 73.

[317] Talat Paşa, *Hatıralarım ve Müdafaam* (Istanbul: Kaynak Yayınları, 2006), p. 14; In original: "*Jön Türkler, Araplar, Yunanlılar, Arnavutlar, Türkler vesaire gibi yurddaki bütün milletleri birleştirmeyi bu suretle de sevgili vatanın selâmet ve terakkisi için birlikte.*"

[318] Hanioğlu, *Preparation for a Revolution*, p. 214.

[319] Ahsene Gül Tokay, "Macedonian Reforms and Muslim Opposition during the Hamidian Era: 1878–1908," *Islam and Christan Muslim Relations* 14/1 (2010): 59.

Misri,[320] İsmet [İnönü], Ali [Çetinkaya], and Kâzım [Özalp].[321] They formed a separate subgroup within which they forged personal ties and friendships, often based on a shared history as classmates or fellow soldiers from military service. Talat Pasha's friend, Mithat Şükrü Bleda, who was a native of Thessaloniki, registered that "slowly we attracted many governors on our side. In this context, our first aim was the governor of Manastir, Hifzı Pasha, who was the husband of my aunt – my uncle. Therefore, it was much easier to separate him from the palace."[322] To the contrary, there was a rumour that governor of Manastir, Hıfzı Pasha, admitted to the Sultan Abdulhamid II that many became part of the CUP, but not him (*Manastır'da benden başka herkes İttihatçıdır*). [323] Furthermore, with the fast growth of various branches in the Kosovo, Manastir, and Salonika vilayets, for the first time the Young Turks succeeded in establishing a strong network maintained in a particular (their important operative) region of the Ottoman Empire, its periphery known as Macedonia. Thanks to these networks, the Young Turks could actively fight for the realisation of their goal: the re–establishment of parliamentary and constitutional government.[324] Members of the Young Turk Movement also opposed the European intervention and European favouritism towards Christians. There were constant demonstrations and an uneasy feeling

---

[320] Aziz Ali Al–Misri was an Egyptian diplomat (Egyptian ambassador to Moscow under Nasser) and writer who played a significant role in the Young Turk movement. As for his role in Macedonia, Al–Misri was a vocal advocate for the rights of the Ottoman Empire's non–Muslim minorities, particularly the Albanians. He believed that the Young Turk movement could only succeed if it addressed the grievances of these minority groups and implemented reforms to grant them greater political and cultural autonomy. Al–Misri's writings and speeches helped to raise awareness about the plight of Albanians in Macedonia and other parts of the empire, and he was seen as a leading figure among the Albanian intellectuals. However, his advocacy for Albanian rights put him at odds with some of the other Young Turk leaders who favored a more centralised and Turk–centric approach to governance. See: Hanioğlu, *Preparation for a Revolution*.

[321] Erik J. Zürcher, *The Young Turk Legacy and Nation Building: From the Ottoman Empire to Atatürk's Turkey* (London: Bloomsbury Publishing PLC, 2010), p. 100.

[322] Bleda, *İmparatorluğun Çöküşü*, p. 33; In original: *"yavaş yavaş valileri de kendi tarafımıza çekmeye başlamıştık. Bu konuda ilk hedef olarak Manastır Valisi Hıfzı Paşayı ele aldık. Hıfzı Paşa benim halamın kocası, yani eniştem oluyordu. Bu nedenle onu saraydan ayırmak daha kolay olacaktı. Kendisi o tarihlerde hayli yaşlanmıştı. Hassas bir kalbi vardı, onu inandırmak ve tarafımıza çekmek benim için zor olmayacaktı."*

[323] Ibid.

[324] Zürcher, *Young Turks*, p. 99.

among the Muslim population in Macedonia caused by the presence of the European reformers and Christian elements supported by many local bands. Many of the members of the Young Turks used the presence of the Europeans as "a propaganda tool to gain the support of the Muslim population and it easily attracted various groups, civilian and military, in the area."[325] The principal responsibility for this propaganda was in the hands of Bahaettin Şakir. He was one of the main architects of the transformation of the Young Turk Movement from an ideological into a political party. Şükrü Hanioğlu notes that he was deeply influenced by the IMARO and Dashnaktsutiun's programmes and regulations.[326] In this sense, the Young Turk Movement was not closed and did not develop inside a vacuum, rather was influenced by many other movements in the region and ideas that circulated among the West European intellectuals. As might be expected, those ideas reflected clearly the activist programme for the "Ottomanist" union among various Ottoman members, and they were open to all Ottoman subjects regardless of ethnicity and faith. Bahaeddin Şakir was deeply impressed by those ideals and accordingly he wrote a poem for unifying the various Ottoman elements together:

> "We will colour/paint our enemies with red blood
> We are called the brave sons of Turkistan
> We are renowned as glorious Ottomans
> We cry 'God!' and sacrifice our lives
> We become martyrs for God
> We should not be burned in this fire of oppression
> We cannot stand this vileness anymore."[327]

In one of the letters sent to a volunteer of the CUP, Bahaeddin Şakir also wrote: "We need young and brave children of the fatherland. This is the time to render to the fatherland an honorable and glorious service."[328] This conveyed clearly the message that members of the CUP were ready to take "action" and to recruit as many volunteers as possible for the purpose of unity and progress. Many officers and soldiers were invited "to join the

---

[325] Tokay, *Macedonian Reforms.*
[326] Hanioğlu, *Preparation for a Revolution*, p. 217.
[327] Ibid., pp. 187–188.
[328] Ibid. p. 219.

gaza for freedom," who were modelled on the guerilla bands in Macedonia. [329] It is beyond doubt that the presence of the various Macedonian chetas in general, and of the IMARO members in particular, made a deep impression upon the Ottoman officers and soldiers who served in Ottoman Macedonia during that time.

Some of the officers also admired these bands and were considering establishing a similar organisation that might stave off what they saw as the imminent collapse of the Empire. This influence on the Young Turks by different organisations and bands in Macedonia shows that the band members were an active and dynamic group, and sufficiently open–minded to accept ideas from other communities while also influencing other communities (i.e. Ottoman Albanians). Evidently, the networks thus formed cannot be considered in a vacuum and as a static structure, but rather as processual constructs of interactions and entanglements among various communities, that is in this particular case, between the Young Turks and Ottoman Albanians. Furthermore, Mithat Şükrü Bleda was aware that Young Turks they had major support in this matter from Muslim Albanian speaking personalities in Ottoman Macedonia. He described that "these networks of society (CUP) were spreading fast in all parts of Rumelia. In Bitola they were in the hands of Resneli Niyaz, in Skopje in the hands of Nexhip Draga, and in Ohrid in those of Ejup Sabri. All of them were working hard."[330] Many of these officers, such as Necip Draga in Uskup orAdjutant–Major Niyazi Bey in Resen, Captain Bekir Fikri in Grebená and Adjutant–Major Eyüb Sabri in Ohrid had a reputation and authority among the Ottoman Albanians of their respective regions. Since they could speak Albanian as well as Turkish, they found an easy task to correspond with the whole Muslim population in Ottoman Macedonia. Therefore, when they decided to go to the mountains they attracted many Albanian–speaking Muslim volunteers and secured their support. [331] In addition, the Young Turks devoted multiple efforts to include the Ottoman Albanians into their activism. This was possible due to the backgrounds of

---

[329] Ibid. p. 220.
[330] Bleda, *İmparatorluğun Çöküşü*, p. 33; Quote: "*cemiyetimiz kısa zamanda Rumeli'nin her tarafında yayılmış, dal budak salmış ve işlerimiz gelişmişti. Manastır'da Resneli Niyazi, Üsküp'te Necip Draga, Ohri'de Eyüp Sabri asker gibi çalışıyorlardı.*"
[331] Hanioğlu, *Preparation for a Revolution*, p. 228.

the Young Turk members. Namely, Erik Zücher noted that the Young Turks predominantly originated from the Ottoman borderlands, more precisely from Macedonia, and were closely linked to the Macedonian context and the Macedonian Question.[332] Thus, many Young Turks were born in the cities populated by many Albanians, where Albanianism could naturally find fertile ground.[333] Also, for many members of the Young Turk movement, the Ottoman Albanians were considered "the sons of Ottomans." For Tunali Hilmi, who wrote a pamphlet about Macedonia,[334] those Albanians were the brave people who were always prepared to defend Macedonia if the Ottoman government failed to do so. For him, the Ottoman Albanians are "sons of Ottomans" who guaranteed the continued existence of the Empire in the Balkans.[335] In a different vein, the support of the Albanian population for the Young Turk Movement could also be analysed as a function of "the simultaneity of multiple identities."[336] Various scholars of the late Habsburg Empire challanged the assumption of inherent opposition between national consciousness and imperial loyalty by positing "parallel realities."[337] In a similar way, Paul Gilroy defined these realities as "double consciousness," [338] which is a constitutive part of a more complex feeling of "two–ness," of disparate and competing "thoughts," "strivings," and "ideals." In the Ottoman context, one can find many instances of "two–ness," which stem from hybridisations of the individual persons who operated in a multicultural

---

[332] Zürcher. *Children of Borderlands.*

[333] Nathalie Clayer, *Aux origines du nationalism albanais.* p. 70.

[334] Hilmi Tunalî, *Makedonya: Mazi–Hâl–Istikbâl* (Kahire: 1898).

[335] Hacısalihoğlu, *Die Jungtürken und die Mazedonische Frage*, p. 81.

[336] Brunhilde Scheuringer, *Multiple Identities: A Theoretical and an Empirical Approach* (Cambridge: Cambridge University Press, 2016).

[337] Claudia Ulbrich, "Transkulturelle Perspektivenin Selbstzeugnisund Person," in *Selbstzeugnis und Person*, ed. Claudia Ulbrich (Cologne: Transkulturelle Perspektiven, 2012), p. 12; The writer suggests using terms such as Selbst–Verortung, Seitenwechsel, Ambivalenz, Rollenvielfalt, Personenspaltung, Hybridity, Entanglement, Entangled Histories, Überlagerungen, and Parallelwelten when discussing the concept of the "transcultural self."

[338] Paul Gilroy, *The Black Atlantic: Modernity and Double Consciousness* (New York: Verso Books, 1993); See also: Valentin Rauer, "Interobjektivität: Sicherheitskultur Aus Sicht Der Akteur–Netzwerk–Theorie," in *Sicherheitskultur: Soziale und politische Praktiken der Gefahrenabwehr*, eds. Christopher Daase, Philipp Offermann and Valentin Rauer (Frankfurt/New York: Campus Verlag, 2012), pp. 69–91.

milieu as transcultural selves. In this regard, Nathalie Clayer suggests that one should be aware that the Ottoman Albanians were not a monolithic "ethnic group" comprising a whole. Their way of interactions varied of course as much as their aims and interests. Therefore, some Albanian speaking personalities would describe themselves as Ottomans, without referring to a nationalist feeling, rather standing united to protect the Empire. By analysing the lives of these Ottoman Albanians who joined and actively supported the Young Turk Movement, one can find out their multiple trajectories and entanglements that overcame and surpassed the monolithic boundaries drawn by nationalistic historiographies.[339] In this line, Brunhilde Scheuringer posits that "the concept of symbolic interactionism between the groups plays a fundamental role here. Societies establish and form social roles by means of linked expectations."[340] These individuals expected a better future within their fatherland, which to them was the Ottoman Empire.[341] Therefore, many of them sided with other ethnicities to achieve the victory that would lead to unity and progress. Indeed, Mithat Şükrü Bleda notes that "no one had any doubt that the CUP would would record a victory."[342] It was the hope for the union of the various ethnicities in Macedonia that contributed to the growth of the Movement among its different subjects. Thus, in the Macedonian context, these "doubly conscious" or even ''multi conscious'' Albanians provided the chief source of support for the Young Turk Committee. In parallel with the above events, in June 1908 the situation in Ottoman Macedonia grew very tense due to the discussions held in Reval between King Edward VII and Tsar Nicholas II. Supposedly, the Great Powers would discuss yet another reform plan for Macedonia. Therefore, many members of the CUP

---

[339] See about Entangled Histories: Yuval Ben–Bassat, *Petitioning the Sultan: Protests and Justice in Late Ottoman Palestine* (London/New York: I.B. Tauris. 2013); Yuval Ben–Bassat and Eyal Ginio eds., *Late Ottoman Palestine: The Period of Young Turk Rule* (London/New York: I.B. Tauris. 2011); Zeynel Abidin Besneley, *The Circassian Diaspora in Turkey: A Political History* (London/New York: Routledge. 2014); Hans–Jürgen Bömelburg, Stefan Rohdewald and Dirk Uffelmann, "Polnisch–osmanische Verflechtungen in Kommunikation, materieller Kultur, Literatur und Wissenschaft," *Zeitschrift für Ostmitteleuropaforschung* 65/2 (2016): 159–166.

[340] Scheuringer, *Multiple Identities*, p. 1.

[341] BOA. HR.SYS. 155, 47, 11.11.1908. p. 2.

[342] Bleda, *İmparatorluğun Çöküşü*, p. 38; Quote: "*ittihat ve Terakki'nin atıldığı mücadeleden muzaffer çıkacağından artık kimsenin şüphesi kalmamıştı.*"

felt that they needed to act immediately or the Empire would be invaded by the Great Powers. This resulted in three events that triggered the Young Turk Revolution, and all of them occurred in Ottoman Macedonia.

The first event took place in June 1908, when Enver Pasha was sent on a mission to a Turkish–speaking village in the Tikvesh region by the Central Committee in Salonica (*Merkez–i Umumi, evvelce, Tikveş'e gelmem ihtimalini yazmış olduğundan*).[343] His mission was "to recruit villagers for the CUP's purposes" (*köylülerin örgütlenmesi*).[344] A close reading of Enver Pasha's memoirs indeed shows that he was establishing a band (*daimi çetenin oluşturulması*) and providing it with instructions, funds, and texts for proclamation of a constitution.[345] While he was in Tikvesh, two other important events occurred. First, Enver Pasha remembers that he got news in Tikvesh about the assassination of Shemsi Pasha (*Şemsi Paşa'nin vurulduğunu haber almıştım. Inanamiyordum, bunlar te'yid etdi*).[346] He was also still there when he got word about Ferzovik events in the Kosovo vilayet.[347] Later, when Enver Pasha received the information that in Ferzovik there were protests for the support of the constitution, he emphasised that "Northern Albania is also on our side" (*demek, asıl çekindiğimiz, Şimali Arnavudluk bizimle beraber olacak*).[348] In the second and third events, many "multi conscious" Albanians showed that they demonstrated their loyalty to Enver Pasha. One of his greatest supporters was an adjutant–major named Ahmet Niyazi Bey, who commanded a battalion in his native Resne in the Manastir vilayet. He was born into an Albanian–speaking and landowning family in Resne, and finished high military school in Manastir. He stated that at the Manastir military school he learned the meaning of one's fatherland and the love for it.[349] Thus, he

---

[343] Enver Paşa, *Enver Paşa'nin anıları* (Istanbul: İş Bankası Kültür Yayınları, 2018). p. 102.

[344] Ibid., p. 105.

[345] Ibid., p. 110.

[346] Ibid., p. 114.

[347] Ibid., p. 121; Quote: "*daha Tikveş kazasinda iken simalı Arnavudların Kaçanik'de toplandığını haber almış fakat maksadlarının ne olduğunu anlayamamıştım.*"

[348] Ibid., p. 121.

[349] Niyazi Bey, *Hatırat–i yahut*, p. 13; Quote: "*bu hislerimin tesiriyle askerliğe olan bağlılığım gittikçe artıyordu. Bundan böyle vatan sevgisi ufkumu güneş gibi aydınlatmış, gönlümü dünyalara açmıştı. Oraya ne yerleştirilirse yine bir boşluk, yine bir şeyler*"

hoped that one day he would fight for his fatherland's order and progress.[350] The opportunity for his (patriotic) fight presented itself on 3 July, when Niyazi Bey received permission from the Manastır headquarters of the CUP to spring into action to protect the Ottoman fatherland. He first headed into the mountains and formed the National Battalion of Resne from the ranks of Albanian Muslim villagers. There he was accompanied by Çerçiz Topulli, head of the Albanian Tosk çete.[351] As an Albanian–speaking adjutant–major, he had excellent connections with a number of Albanian–speaking villages. Relevant here is Erik J. Zürcher's emphasis that the religious aspect of these Albanian speaking people is very important, because Niyazi ordered the soldiers to gather locals[352] who were able to recite prayers while moving into action. Clearly the insurrection was primarily a Muslim movement of Albanian speaking personalities that highly pronounced religious motif.[353] Also, in Niyazi's imagination about the population of Macedonia, "Muslims did not arrive in Macedonia in the new period. History records that the Turks were here even before the Ottomans. In this sense, Macedonia has a relation with the Turks from the old times."[354] One can notice that he uses the terms "Muslims" and "Turks" as synonyms and that he does not make any distinction does not refer to different groups of Muslims, be they Turkish– or Albanian–speaking. Moreover, when Niyazi Bey arrived in the hills, he

---

koymak gerekiyordu. Orayı yalnız vatan sevgisinin doldurabileceğini bana gizli bir ses durmadan tekrarlıyordu."

[350] Ibid., p. 16; In original: *"ben de vatanımın intizam ve terakkisine faydalı kanunlara, lâzım gelen şekilde bağlanarak iyi bir zabit olmayı gaye edinmiştim."*

[351] According to Gawrych, the fundamental compatibility between the Turks and the Albanians and hence the need for them to work together was symbolised by the Enver–Niyazi couple, Niyazi representing the Albanians and Enver representing the Turks; Gawrych, *The Crescent*, p. 169.

[352] For Ahmet Niyazi Bey this was important due to his personal and family connections with those Albanian speaking villages. In this sense, one should not understand this selection as part of Niyazi Bey's nationalist feeling for Albanianism.

[353] Zürcher, *Young Turks*, p. 38; Fabio Bego, "Violence and State–Building after the Great War: Italian, Yugoslav and Endemic Challenges to Albanian Projections," *Qualestoria: Rivista di storia contemporanea* 48/1 (2020: 71–97.

[354] Niyazi Bey, *Hatırat–i yahut*, pp. 192–193; Quote: *"böylesine kötü ve böylesine az bilinen Müslümanlar, Makedonya'ya yeni gelmiş değillerdir. Tarih bize gösteriyi Türklerden meydana gelen birçok halk Makedonya'ya burasını Osmanlı sultanlarının ele geçirmesinden çok önce gelip yerleşmişlerdir. Bu bakımdan Makedonya'da Türklerin de çok eski bir tarihî alâkalan vardır."*

stated openly his true aim, that is, to force the government to restore the constitution.[355] For him, the reason of all problems in Macedonia and in other parts of the Empire was the absolutist Hamidian policy.[356] In order to overthrow this regime, all Ottoman elements were united against absolutism.[357] According to Niyazi Bey, "there is no one in Macedonia and other parts of the Empire who has not suffered because of this absolutist regime. Without any exception, we are oppressed by it."[358] Following these claims, he also comes to the conclusion that "the Macedonian problem (Questions) does not exist. If there is a problem, the Turks will solve it and provide with their children together."[359]

In response to the rebellion in Resne, General Şemsi Pasha, an experienced Albanian–speaking officer loyal to the Hamidian regime, together with other Northern (Geg) Albanians who supported the Sultan, ordered a garrison to head directly to the city of Manastir. He arrived to Manastir on 7 July and his next destination was (supposed) to be Resne, along with two battalions and an Albanian volunteer unit, gathered to suppress Niyazi Bey's action. But, upon his exit from the post office in Manastir, he was shot in broad daylight by the CUP volunteer, Atıf [Kamçıl].[360] This murder

---

[355] Zürcher, Young Turks, p. 32; See also: Niyazi Bey, *Hatırat–i yahut*, p. 199; Here: *"hükümeti Mesrutiyet idaresine döndürmek, müsavatı, adaleti temin etmek üzere milletçe umumî bir teşebbüse geçildiği."*

[356] Ibid., p. 191; In original: *"Yalnız Makedonya'nın değil, Osmanlı imparatorluğunun bütün vilâyetlerindeki kötülüklerin asıl mes'ulü bugün basta olan hükümetin istibdat idaresidir."*

[357] Ibid. p. 191; Quote: *"Türk, Arap, Arnavut, Çerkez, Kürt, Ermeni, Ulah, Yahudi, Sırp, Rum ve Bulgarlardan meydana gelen Osmanlı adıyla topladığımız ne kadar millet varsa hepsi de aynı istibdat idaresinin çilesini çekip boyunduruğunda inliyorlar."*

[358] Ibid. p. 191; Here: *"ne Makedonya ve ne de diğer Osmanlı memleketinde ayrıcalık ve zulüm görmüs iki çesit halk yoktur. Istisnasız hepimiz aynı istibdat tazyiki altında ezilmekteyiz."*

[359] Ibid. 192; Here: *"Sizin bildiğiniz gibi bir Makedonya problemi yoktur. Bugün ortalıkta görülen problem, Türklerin kendi aralarında hâl edecekleri ve bu toprağın çocuklarının beraber temin edecekleri ve er geç yapacakları bir tesekküldür."*

[360] Karabekir, *İttihat ve Terakki Cemiyeti*, p. 327; Kazim Karabekir described the assassination with the words: *"Millet Fedaisi Atıf Bey de vazifesine başladı. O kadar muhafızlar ve kalabalık arasında kendine yol açarak yaklaştı ve Şemsi Paşa üzerine bir Nagant tabancasıyla ateş etti, birinci kurşun boşa gitti, ikinci kurşun paşanın sağ omzundan içeriye girerek kalbi parçaladıktan sonra sol tarafa çıkmıştı. Paşanın muhafızları da Atıf'ın arkasından şiddetli bir ateş açtılar. Atıf ayağından yaralanmış ise de yoluna devam edebilmiş ve biraz sonra sağa sokağa saparak gözden kaybolmuş."*

is generally seen as the turning point in the revolution, for it eliminated a very dangerous opponent of the Young Turks, who could have mobilised *bashibozuk* Albanians against them. The murder demonstrated the power of the CUP in the towns, and demoralised the palace. Additionally, a band named the CPU or Ohrid National Regiment was organised by Ottoman adjutant–major Eyüb Sabri. Some kilometres away from this event, Captain Bekir Fikri gathered a large band in Grebená.[361] The local Muslims there regarded him as their protector against the Bulgarian and Greek bands.[362]

Independently of these developments in the Manastir and Selanik vilayeti, the gathering of Albanians at Ferizaj/Firzovik in the Kosovo vilayet started on 5 July (two days after Niyazi sprung to the hills). Additionally, it caused a sense of alarm to the *Yıldız*, which in the end contributed to the collapse of the resistance from the palace. This event happened in response to rumours spread throughout the Kosovo vilayet that Austro–Hungary[363] was planning to invade Kosovo. Initially, a train was intended to bring students of the Austrian–German railway training school from Skopje to Ferizaj/Firzovik, but its arrival was interpreted by the local population as the first step of an Austro–Hungarian invasion attempt. Therefore, a large population of Albanians gathered in Ferizaj/Firzovik to protest against this "invasion."[364] Although at the beginning there were some 5,000 armed gunmen, by 23 July the number of protesters grew to 30,000 local Albanians. In order to suppress this protest, the Ottoman Government dispatched the Kosovo Gendarmerie Commander–Colonel of the Ottoman troops in Skopje, Galip Bey. He received an order to disperse the Ottoman Albanians from Firzovik. The Ottoman Government was not informed that

---

[361] Fikri Bekir, *Balkanlarda Kuvve–i seyyare kumandanı yüzbaşı Bekir Fikri* (Istanbul: Belge Yayınları, 1985); Fikri Bekir, *Balkanlarda Tedhiş ve Gerilla* (Istanbul: TT Vakfi Yayınları, 2008).

[362] Hanioğlu, *Preparation for a Revolution*, p. 228.

[363] During the spring of 1908, the Dual Monarchy proposed a railway expansion plan to connect the Bosnian provinces to Novi Pazar, and eventually to Mitrovica in the Kosovo vilayet. At the same time, the Serbian government was also planning to build a railway that would pass through the Kosovo vilayet and connect directly to the Albanian coast. However, this plan was met with hostility from many Albanians.

[364] Although initially there were some 5000 armed men by 5 July, until 23 July gathered the number up to 30,000 people. See: Tokay, *Macedonian Reforms*, p. 61.

he was, in fact, a unionist (*ittihatçı*).[365] As a Young Turk, he was happy that he was assigned to this task. He managed to convince several notable Albanian Young Turk members, such as brothers Draga (Nexhip and Ferhat Draga), and Bajram Curri to attend a meeting in Firzovik (Kosovo Vilayet) and to use their capabilities for spreading fears of "foreign intervention" among this group and to gain their support in order to bring to the constitutional restoration.[366] Although initially they were in the minority, the configuration was soon to change in favour of the Young Turks. Allied with Albanian–speaking Young Turks, Galip Bey started to convince the gathered people at Firzovik to take an oath (*besa*) to the constitution.[367] He further explained that only a constitutional regime could avert the danger of foreign intervention and pointed out that the country was in danger, and that a foreign Christian invasion could mean the end for the Muslim "majority" in Macedonia.[368]

The rest of the Albanian–speaking Young Turks added that the corrupt government in Istanbul did nothing to avert this danger, and consequently the people had to put their trust in the CUP.[369] The constitution was thus presented as the solution to these very real and concrete concerns of the rural population. The members of the Young Turk Movement promised many more rights to the Albanians, including privileges they had enjoyed prior to the Hamidian regime. After receiving the support of the masses, the Young Turks sent a telegram to Istanbul asking the Sultan to reinstate the constitution.[370] At the same time, Sultan Abdulhamid II effected major changes to the central administration. The most important took place after the Albanian–speaking Grand Vizier Ferid Pasha refused to give any advice to Abdulhamid II on the Ferzovik/Ferizaj meeting. Rumours circulated that Ferid Pasha was secretly sympathetic towards the Young Turk and Albanian Movements in Macedonia.[371] Mithat Şükrü Bleda described this thusly:

---

[365] Süleyman Külçe, *Firzovik Toplantısı ve Meşrutiyet* (Istanbul: Kitabevi, 2013).
[366] Remzi Çavuş, "Firzovik Toplantılarının Meşrutiyetin İlanına Katkısı," *Humanitas* 3/5 (2015): 65–72.
[367] BOA, Y.PRK.ASK, 258/82/6.
[368] BOA, Y.PRK.ASK, 258/82/7
[369] Külçe, *Firzovik Toplantısı.*
[370] Tokay, *Macedonian Reforms.*
[371] Ibid, p. 62.

"The warning storm that began in Rumeli started to influence the palace and Abdulhamid II did not have any other option but to gather his officials to reach a new decision. He later learned that chaos had broken out."[372]

Thus, on 22 July Ferid Pasha was replaced and the new Grand Vizier Said Pasha advised the Sultan to agree to restore the Constitution from 1876. On the following day this was celebrated by unprecedented jubilation over the whole of Ottoman Macedonia, while a military parade was organised in Manastir. Mithat Şükrü Bleda remembers that "the celebration happened in all cities of Rumelia, except Istanbul, and the youth, elderly, children – all citizens together – celebrated this event."[373] on the same day, Ahmed Niyazi Bey, with his comrade, the Albanian Tosk guerilla leader Çerçiz Topulli, and the Macedonian band leader Apostol Mihajlovski, entered the city as a symbol of the Ottoman–Albanian–Macedonian cooperation in the revolution.[374] In the city of Thessaloniki, Enver Pasha returned from the Tikvesh region to declare triumph with the words: "We are all brothers."[375] All the population on the streets of Rumelia was celebrating by carrying portraits of Mithat Pasha, Enver and Niyaz, and Eyup Sabri (*Mithat Paşa'nın, Enver ve Niyazi'nin, Eyüp Sabri'nin resimleri kapısılıyordu*).[376] In conclusion, this Young Turk Revolution was undoubtedly the work of the military, yet augmented with the support of the Ottoman Muslim civilians in the Macedonian provinces. Gülay concludes that "the Young Turk Revolution could therefore also be called the revolution of the Macedonian Muslims, because it was the Macedonian situation that united the army and the Muslims."[377]

---

[372] Bleda, *İmparatorluğun Çöküşü*, pp. 49–50; In original: "*Rumeli'de kopan fırtınanın sarayın temellerini sarsmaya başladığını hisseden İkinci Abdülhamid artık başka çare kalmadığını anladığı için vükelâyı saraya toplamış durumu inceleterek kesin bir karara varmaları yolunda kendilerini zorlamaya başlamıstı. Saraya gelip gidenlerin hesabı yoktu. Bir keşmekeştir başlamıstı.*"
[373] Ibid, p. 50; Here: "*Bu mealdeki ilânın yayılmasından bir gün önce Istanbul hariç Rumeli'nin bütün sehirlerinde hürriyet ilân edilmis ve genç ihtiyar, çoluk, çocuk yüzbinlerce vatandas sokaklara dökülerek eylemlere başlamıs bulunuyordu.*"
[374] Tokay, *Macedonian Reforms*, p. 62.
[375] Ibid.
[376] Bleda, *İmparatorluğun Çöküşü*, p. 50.
[377] Tokay, *Macedonian Reforms*, p. 62.

5.3. The Young Turks and Albanian Speaking Population After the Revolution

The Young Turk Revolution of July 1908 marked the return to constitutionalism in the Ottoman Empire and the victory of the desire of the CUP members to modernise the central government with a vision of a multi–national state system. As we have seen, many diverse groups – including Ottoman Albanians – gave their support hoping to gain privileges or greater autonomy. However, of all the problems that the Young Turks inherited from the Hamidian regime after July 1908, the "nationalities question" proved to be the most difficult to resolve.[378] In this regard, the brother of the Grand Vezier Ferid Pasha, Sureyya Bey, has come to the conclusion that "the year 1908 was the worst and most threatening period for Albania (*1908 senesi Arnavutluk'un en mes'um, en hatarnâk bir devresi idi*)."[379] The Young Turk Revolution of 1908 caused change of power among the various Ottoman ethnic or religious groups that had been active as part of the political opposition organisations before these events. In its aftermath, organisations like Dashnaktsutiun, IMARO, some Albanian–speaking bands and their representatives, together with Ahmed Riza and Talat Bey became part of the Ottoman Chamber of Deputies such as Ismail Kemal, Necip Draga, Dukangjizade Basri, and made Jane Sandanski a respected participant in Ottoman politics.[380] On the other hand, following the Revolution, some Albanian intellectuals hoped that the CUP would grant them privileges and political rights to cultural activities. In the first days after the Revolution, the members of the CUP made certain concessions in the educational and cultural fields in accordance with the spirit of the constitutional monarchy.[381] In this regard they set up clubs and schools that supported the use of the Albanian language. The most active club was the Society for the Unity of the Albanian Language (Bashkimi) led in Manastir by Fehim Bey Zavalani, which emerged as the most widely recognised centre of Albanian political

---

[378] Ahmad, Feroz, *The Young Turks and the Ottoman Nationalities: Armenians, Greeks, Albanians, Jews, and Arabs, 1908–1918* (Salt Lake City: University of Utah Press, 2014), p. 1.
[379] Sureyya Bey, *Osmanlı Sonrası Arnavutluk*, p. 96.
[380] Hanioğlu, *Preparation for a Revolution*, pp. 6–7.
[381] Nuray Bozbora, "Albanian Perception of 1908 Revolution and its effects on Albanian Nationalism," *IBAC* 2 (2012), p. 631.

and cultural activism. Furthermore, the clubs that were established in the Manastir vilayeti did not have a "uniformed programme," but their common aim was to work for the Albanian cultural development.[382] Actually, the Bosnian annexation crisis in October 1908, and Bulgarian declaration of independence pushed the Albanian element to support Young Turks. In this respcet, many Albanian intellectuals feared that the new established Bulgaria can trigger the leaderships of Serbia, Montenegro, and Greece to seek territorial compensation in the three vilayets. The Albanian leadership had simoultanously laid claim to these areas too, considering them to be part of an imagined Albania. In the following months however, new developments were to create a rift between the CUP and the Albanian intellectuals, with events taking place in Ottoman Macedonia. Their contested policies started when a pan–Albanian Congress was organised by the Albanian intellectuals, who gathered to discuss the Albanian Alphabet scripts in Manastir between 14 and 22 November. This event is known in the Albanian historiography as the First Congress of Manastir. During the Congress, they agreed to use Latin scripts as a template for the Albanian alphabet. This decision was not welcomed by the Ottoman authorities, the Greek Orthodox Church (there was no Albanian Orthodox church at the time), and religious Muslim circles. Many Albanian–speaking *imams* opposed this decision and supported the Arabic scripts as a base for the Albanian alphabet. They had the absolute support of the CUP, and as a result, the Ottoman authorities organised another congress in July 1909, known as the Congress of Dibra (Manastir vilayeti). Nevertheless, this attempt was not successful due to the strong opossition of the Albanian delegates and it marked a start of future conflicts between the CUP and Albanian intellectuals. As a response, the Albanian intellectuals arranged another congress that was held in Elbasan (also in the Manastir vilayet) between 2 and 9 September 1909. It dealt primarily with the approach to the dissemination of Albanian education and cultural activities, considering the standard Latin script

---

[382] Nathalie Clayer, "Edhe një herë mbi kryengritjet shqiptare të pasvitit 1908," *Përpjekja* 30–31 (2013): 85–122, here in 98–99.

alphabet a closed chapter.[383] To this end, the Normal School of Elbasan was established and it became a milestone for Albanian education. Furthermore, more than sixty Albanian cultural and political clubs promoting the Albanian language and culture were formed throughout Ottoman Albania and Macedonia (the three vilayets). Apart from these Albanian intellectuals who opposed the CUP and Ottoman centralisation, the Albanian 'traditionalists' or 'reactionists' – supporters of Sultan Abdulhamid II and the *sharia* – organised a number of meetings to oppose CUP's centralisation policy. This Albanian reactionary movement was developing in parallel with the Istanbul events of 31 March 1909, which demanded the return of the Hamidian regime.[384]

In 1909, the situation in the Kosovo vilayeti was exacerbated when the Albanian speaking notable Isa Boletini, incited a protests in Mitrovica city, part of Kosovo vilayet. His success was in mobilising in a short period of time a lot of Albanian brigands who opposed the CUP policy.[385] As a reaction, the Ottoman forces suppressed these anti–Constitutional riots in Ottoman Macedonia. According to Christopher Psilos "until the counter-revolution of April 1909, the Albanian disturbances, predominantly in northern Macedonia, occurred on the instigation and with the active participation of local chieftains and band–leaders like Isa Boletini and his followers. Such was the case in the second half of March 1909, when three Ottoman battalions were sent to the Kosovo vilayet with a mission to suppress the irregulars of Isa Boletini and restore the Ottoman administrative and military control over the districts of lpek and Yakova."[386] During that time, Ottoman Macedonia kept the region where Albanian insurrections broke out in turmoil. In 1910, the CUP abolished all Albanian schools, Albanian cultural activities, societies and clubs, especially after the Kosovo Revolt of 1910. Between 1910 and 1912, the unionists applied centralisation policies in the region and used Ottomanism as an ideological instrument to translate the imperial identity to the Turkish

---

[383] Përse u zgjodhen dy alfabete, Materiale e Dokumente, Studime Filologjike No. 4. (author not mentioned) (Tiranë: Akademia e Shkencave e RPSSH Instituti i Gjuhësisë dhe i Letërsisë, 1988), pp. 149–159.

[384] Clayer, *Edhe një here*, p. 88.

[385] Stavro Skëndi, "Mendimi Politik Dhe Veprimtarija Kryengritese Shqiptare 1881–1912," *Përpjekja* 9 (1996): 133–157, here in 146.

[386] Ibid; Psilos, *The Young Turk Revolution,* pp. 164–165.

one. One can define this attempt as the CUP's aim of "nationalising (the) empire."[387] In this regard, Kazim Karabekir underlines that "in the case of Macedonia, the formula was the following: first, garnering the support of the non–Turkish elements for the revolution, and later controlling and restraining them by deploying the gendarmerie. However, Greeks, Armenians, Bulgarians, Serbs, as well as Arabs and Albanians who were mixed with the Turks, became provoked and started to bear arms."[388]

These developments made the Macedonian Question even more dangerous, whereby the Albanian intellectuals started to imagine their future independent Albanian state outside of the Ottoman Empire. Many of them imagined Macedonia too as part of their new nation–state, since it was the centre of their cultural activities.[389] For Sureyya Bey, the question of finding "the border between Albania and Macedonia" (*Makedonya ile Arnavutluk'un hadd–i fâsilini sual eyledim*) was still open.[390] Accordingly, the border started "from Mitrovica throughout Kacanink directly to Similina – where our border necessarily was to be. Furthermore, from Gora to the Adriatic Sea and straight to the Ambracian Gulf (in nowadays Greece) should definitely be a territory of Albania."[391] Not only Sureyya bey, but also other Albanian intellectuals, such as Ismail Kemali, Hasan

---

[387] Miller, *Nationalizing Empires*.

[388] Karabekir, *İttihat ve Terakki Cemiyeti*, p. 18; Quote: "*en çok Makedonya'da tecrübe sahasına koydukları bu formül şu idi: Türkten gayrı unsurlara ihtilaller yaptırmak, sonra da orayı nüfuz mıntıkalarına ayırarak jandarma ve idari kontrol koymak ve asayiş büsbütün bozulduktan sonra kati işgallere başlamak. Rumlar, Ermeniler, Bulgarlar, Sırplar... hatta dini camia içinde Türklerle kaynaşmış olan Araplar, Arnavutlar ... hep bu maksatla tahrik olunuyor ve silahlandırılıyordu.*"

[389] Clayer, *Edhe një herë*, pp. 101–108.

[390] Sureyya Bey, *Osmanlı Sonrası Arnavutluk*, p. 127.

[391] Ibid., p. 127; Together with Macedonia, he used the term "*vilayeti selase*" as well by emphasising "that three vilayets were under the command of the forigners (*ecnebi zabitlerin kumandası altında bulunan vilayet–i selase heyet–i zabitası bu keşmekeşe çaresa olamiyordu*). See: Avlonyalı, *Osmanlı Sonrası Arnavutlukç*, p. 96 in quote: "*Metroviçe'den Kaçanik Boğazina kadar mümted olan simendüfer hattının Makedonya kıtasından tefrîki ve Arnavutluk'a terkü ilhaki halinde (...) Her hale karşı Similina Boğazina ve silsile–i cibaline kadar hududumuzun çekilmesi zarurî olduğunu anlattı. Birçok mübâhasâttan sonra, gimalen Gora Dağlarından bed' ile Adriyatik Denizine munsab suların taksim–i miyahi boyunca ve cenuben Salahora Körfeziyle Adalar Denizi arasındaki taksim–i miyah hattını takib ederek Çamlik'ta vaki Fener Burunu'na müntehî kitanın Arnavutluk'a kalması şartıyla bir hududun vaz u tayinini ve bu suretle bir Arnavutluk'un teşkili.*"

Prishtina, Nexhip Draga, and others, shared a similar imagination about Ottoman Macedonia as an Albanian territory.[392] For example, the former supporter of the CUP and member of the Kosovo Vilayeti in the Ottoman Parliament, Hasan Prishtina, wrote in his memoirs: "I believe that the time has come to throw off this cruel yoke by means of a joint uprising with a view to creating an autonomous Albanian–Macedonian state."[393] This imagination of the Albanian–Macedonian state was even brought into even sharper relief when the neighbouring countries increased their irredentist activities in Ottoman Macedonia, and the repressive policies of the CUP towards the Albanians in Kosovo strengthened during the outbreak of the revolts in 1910, 1911, and 1912. When the Albanian insurgents realised that their salvation could not be achieved unless they combined their political activities with armed ones, many Albanian intellectuals demanded the unification of the Albanian vilayets with the Macedonian.[394] Since the Kosovo vilayeti was pacified in 1910, it was now the turn of *Malësi e Madhe* (Işkodra vilayeti) to be the centre of uprisings, which began in March 1911. During these revolts in Malësia, the Albanian intellectuals and locals signed an agreement called the Memorandum of Greca. In the twelve points of the Memorandum, the Albanian intellectuals requested the establishment of a civil and financial administration, legal structures, an Albanian gendarmerie and police force, and use of the Albanian along with Turkish language in administration.[395] The aim of these steps was to pave the way to the creation of an autonomous Albanian province. But they did not find significant support for their demands neither from the foreign powers nor from the Ottoman government until the Ottoman Sultan agreed to some of these demands in 1912.[396] During 1912, Albanians staged another uprising in the Kosovo Vilayeti, organised

---

[392] Clayer, *Penser, agir et vivredans l'Empire ottomanet.*

[393] Hasan bey Prishtina, *Nji shkurtim kujtimesh mbi kryengritjen shqiptare të vjetit 1912* (Shkodra: Shtypshkroja Franciskane, 1921), p. 24, in original: *"Pra, më duket se ka arrijtë koha me pështue prej kësaj zgjedhje mizore nderpermjet të nji kryengritje të përbashket per nji shtete autonom Shqiptaro–Maqedon."*

[394] Ibid.

[395] Bozobra, *Albanian Perception*, p. 631; Emine Bakalli, "Kryengritja e Malësisë së mbishkodrës e vitit 1911: Përkufizime dhe Refleksione," *Gjurmime Albanologjike – Seria E Shkencave Historike* 40 (2010): 187–202.

[396] Zekeria Cana, "Rreth Kryengritjes Së Vitit 1912," *Gjurmime Albanologjike – Seria E Shkencave Historike* 39 (2009): 9–23, here in 21.

by Hasan Prishtina and other local Albanians who argued for the implementation of fourteen points [397] and requests for Albanian autonomy. [398] Since the requests could not be granted due to the intervention of the neighbouring states, this anticipated the beginning of the Balkan Wars. As a result, more extreme violence and bloodshed were perpetrated in Ottoman Macedonia, and this time its territory was shared among the (neighbouring) Balkan states. Based on Sami Frashëri's vision of the future Ottoman Empire, Nuray Bozbora argues further that the Albanian and Turkish togetherness was a sort of long–lasting companionship, but there was an inevitable fragmentation of this cooperation that brought this companionship to an end for pragmatic

---

[397] Ibid; Hasan Bey, *Nji shkurtim kujtimesh*; The following were the demands made by Albanian leaders during an uprising against Ottoman rule:

1. Trained officials who know the language and customs of Albania should be employed.
2. Military service should only be carried out in Albania and Macedonia during peacetime, except during wartime.
3. Laws should be based on the 'law of the mountains' (djibal) in regions where judicial organs are not productive.
4. Albanians should be provided with enough modern arms, and arms depots should be constructed in sensitive regions.
5. Elementary schools should be founded and opened in all towns with a population of over 300,000 people in Kosovo, Monastir, Shkodra, and Janina, with a curriculum taught in the language of the country. Agricultural schools should also be opened.
6. Modern theological schools should be opened where needed.
7. Private schools should be allowed to be founded and opened.
8. The language of the country should be taught in elementary and secondary schools.
9. Particular attention should be paid to commerce, agriculture, and public works, with the construction of railroads.
10. Regional organisations should be established.
11. More attention should be paid to preserving national traditions and customs.
12. An amnesty should be declared without distinction of class or race, for all Ottomans who took part in the uprising.

These demands reflect the desire for greater autonomy and self–determination among the Albanian people. They sought to ensure that Albanians were better represented in government, that their language and culture were respected, and that they had access to education and economic opportunities. The demand for modern arms was also an assertion of their right to defend themselves and their communities. Overall, these demands were a call for greater recognition and inclusion of Albanians in Ottoman society.
[398] Kujtim Nuro and Nezir Bato, *Hasan Prishtina – permbledhje dokumentash (1908– 1934)* (Tiranë: Drejtoria e Përgjithshme e Arkivave të Shtetit, 1982), pp. 12–14.

reasons.[399] In similar ways, Hobsbawm emphasises that "any individual can sustain all sorts of multiple attachments, and not see them as incompatible, until some kind of conflict arises."[400] Hans Grandits, whose interest lies in such conflicts, reckons that multi–layered loyalty relations are always present in daily life during times of peace. However, during times of war, revolt, and organised violence, loyalties generally narrow down, and people tend to be compelled by the clashing parties to clearly take sides.[401] This was also present in the Young Turk–Albanian relations, where prior to the Young Turk Revolution cooperation and multiple attachments prevailed, but the period of revolts and uprisings brought this cooperation to an end. The reasons for this split and the causes for rebellions were many and varied, but Hasan Prishtina, in his memoirs "reduce[d] them to those which [were] the most important: the nationalism of the Young Turk committee; the incompatibility of Albanian, and particularly Geg, traditions, with the conditions of freedom under the Turks; the pan–Islamic intrigues of the government; the army's meddling in politics; the Turkish atrocities of 1910; the development of national consciousness in Albania; the terrible and illegal system implemented by the Young Turk government during the elections in 1912."[402]

---

[399] Bozobra, *Albanian Perception*, p. 638.

[400] Eric Hobsbawm, *Nations and Nationalism since 1780: Programme, Myth, Reality* (Cambridge: Cambridge University Press: 1990), p. 123; See the situation during the war: Stephan Rosiny, "Der Jihad: Historische und zeitgenössische Formen islamisch legitimierter Gewalt," in *Gerechter Krieg – gerechter Frieden: Religionen und friedensethische Legitimationen in aktuellen militärischen Konflikten*, eds. Ines–Jaqueline Werkner and Antonius Liedgehener (Wiesbaden: VS Verlag für Sozialwissenschaften, 2009), pp. 225–244; Erik–Jan Zürcher, "Introduction: The Ottoman Jihad, the Geman Jihad and the Sacralization of War," in *Jihad and Islam in World War I*, ed. Erik–Jan Zürcher (Leiden: Leiden University Press, 2016), pp. 13–28; M. Şükrü Hanioğlu, "Ottoman Jihad or Jihads: The Ottoman Shii Jihad, the Successful One," in *Jihad and Islam in World War I*, ed. Erik–Jan Zürcher (Leiden: Leiden University Press, 2016), pp. 117–34.

[401] Hannes Grandits et al., "Introduction: Social (Dis–)Integration and the National Turn in the Late– and Post–Ottoman Balkans: Towards an Analytical Framework," in *Conflicting Loyalties in the Balkans: the Great Powers, the Ottoman Empire and Nation–Building*, eds. Hannes Grandits, Nathalie Calyer and Robert Pichler (London: I.B. Tauris, 2011).

[402] Hasan Bey, *Nji shkurtim kujtimesh*, p. 7; Clayer, *Edhe një here*, pp. 101–108.

[402] Sureyya Bey, *Osmanlı Sonrası Arnavutluk*, p. 129.

Since 1908 the Young Turks agreed on Ottomanism, but were divided regarding its shape between a more "liberal Ottomanism" and "Turkist Ottomanism."[403] Ultimately, the "Turkist Ottomanism" ideology became oppressive towards non–Turkish subjects and broke down apart the Young Turk–Albanian cooperation and companionship. The CUP's *Weltanschauung* was committed to solving this issue, but was based on positivist principles and a centralisation policy. An attempt to realise these modernisation projects and nationalising the Empire increased the dominance of the Turkist elements over the multiple Ottoman identities.[404] This effort of the CUP of "nationalising empire" triggered multiple Albanian revolts and made room for the intervention of the Balkan states. As a reaction to the CUP policy, the neighbouring states attempted "imperialising (the) nation–state" and implementing their "small state imperialism."[405]

5.4. Entangled Imperialisms: The Great Powers and the Balkan States on the Road to the Balkan Wars (1912–1913)

As has been shown, the Balkans had been in a state of turmoil since the early 1900s, conditioned by the European imperialism, Balkan "small–state imperialisms," and the Ottoman "borrowed colonialism." These practices for realising the "greater state" projects clarified and energised in all the countries simultaneously the impulses towards joint action against the weakened Ottoman Empire after the Ottoman–Italian War in September 1911. In the autumn of 1911, Italy exhibited its imperialist aspirations of conquest towards an African province of the Ottoman Empire, triggering a chain of "small–state imperialism" policies towards Ottoman Macedonia across the Balkans. Eventually these rival Balkan states took joint action against the Ottoman Empire in 1912, which was

---

[403] Bozbora, *Albanian Perception,* p. 640; See also the statement of about Young Turk–Albanian cooperation: *"Die Jungtürken hätten das Leben des Reiches in Europa noch einige Jahre verlängern können, wenn sie Albanien und Mazedonien Autonomie gewährt hätten."* in: Ekrem Bey Vlora, *Lebenserinnerungen* (Berlin/Munich: De Gruyter Oldenbourg, 1973), pp. 193–194.

[404] Bozbora, *Albanian Perception,* p. 640; Clayer, *Edhe një here,* Avlonyalı, *Osmanlı Sonrası Arnavutluk.* Bey Vlora, *Lebenserinnerungen.*

[405] Marharyta Fabrykant and Renee Buhr, "Small state imperialism: the place of empire in contemporary nationalist discourse," *Nations and Nationalism* 22/1 (2015).

named the Balkan League. To the contrary, due to the establishment of the League, Dual Monarchy faced a new and threatening situation in its Balkan's "periphery", while "the retreat of Ottoman power raised strategic questions that Russian diplomats and policy–makers found impossible to ignore."[406] In this regard, the Macedonian Questions and the League of Balkans attracted the attention of the Great Powers as well. Nevertheless, during this "Macedonian crisis," the two continental alliance blocs were drawn even deeper into the antipathies of a region that was entering a period of conflict and violence that escalated into the Great War. It is conceivable that at this time, the Balkan states became closely intertwined with the geopolitics of the European system, but also the Great Powers were intermingled with the "Balkan system," creating a set of escalatory mechanisms that would lead the whole European continent into the "zone of violence" in 1912–1913 and 1914–1918.[407] In this regard, several questions warrant posing: how did the governments of the Balkan states came to the idea to join their forces and establish the League? How did they generate (their joint) foreign policy? Was this policy formulated according to the imperialist or nationalist logics, or both? How did the Balkans, a "peripheral region" of Europe's "centres," come to be the theatre of a Macedonian crisis and Great War of such magnitude? How did an international system that seemed to be entering an era of *détente* look on these events? How was it possible that a year later, in 1914, conflicts escalated into a world war? Was that due to the imperialist aspirations of the Great Powers? Why did such features of the pre–Balkan and World War I scene as the Macedonian Questions and the Albanian uprisings had such profound influence, and how were they combined and interpreted by the minds of those who had political power? When decision–makers discoursed on the international situation or on external threats, were they seeing something real, or projecting their own imaginations, or both? The aim so far has been to reconstruct as vividly as possible the highly dynamic 'decision positions' occupied by the key actors on various levels before the Balkan autumn of 1912 and European summer of 1914.

---

[406] Christopher Clark, *The Sleepwalkers: How Europe Went to War in 1914* (London: Penguin, 2013), p. 174.
[407] Ibid.

5.4.1. "Small–State Imperialism" – A Road Towards the Balkan Wars (1912–1913)

The greater portion of historical scholarship tends to view nationalism and imperialism as "two mutually exclusive phenomena," [408] but recent scholars John A. Hall and Siniša Malešević argue that "many forms of late imperialisms were fully compatible with nationalist projects and that empires and nation–states had more in common than is usually thought."[409] In contrast to the traditional accounts that posit nations and empires as mutually exclusive projects, in the Ottoman Macedonian case, I highlight that imperial and nationalist discourses can actually reinforce one another and that they are intertwined in a broader trans–regional perspective. In this regard, one should keep in mind that neither the empires nor the nation–states operated as fixed and mutually exclusive entities. Instead, they were characterised by sovereignty that was "shared out, layered, overlapping." [410] In practice a nation–state would often pretend and develop imperial(ist) aspirations and try to achieve them through national(ist) narratives. Such an interdependence of nationalism and imperialism was seen in the context of small Balkan polities (but also among the European powers) during the "Age of Empire." In contrast to the Young Turk practice that attempted to modernise the imperial state by means of nationalising the Empire, the new nation–states such as Serbia, Montenegro, Greece, and Bulgaria were built around the emerging nationalism and imperialism, and thus, made reverse attempts at imperialising the nation–state. Influenced by this *Zeitgeist* dominated by imperialism and nationalism, the Balkan nation–states were to foster an irredentist and imperialistic foreign policy that some historians have called "small–state imperialism."[411] Since all these Balkan nation–states self–consciously based their existence on either ancient primordial narratives or medieval dynastic statehoods, the borders of those ancient or medieval states became, quite consistently, the borders desired by the nationalist

---

[408] Siniša Malešević, "Nationalism and Imperialism as Enemies and Friends: Nation–State Formation and Imperial Projects in the Balkans," in *Nations and States, Power and Civility*, ed. Francesco Duina (Toronto: University of Toronto Press, 2018), p. 149.
[409] Ibid., p. 149.
[410] Ibid., p. 151.
[411] Fabrykant, *Small state imperialism;* Trifunović, "Memory of Old Serbia."; Jagodić, *Srbija i Stara Srbija*; Atanasovski, *Mapiranje Stare Srbije*.

leadership. As has been shown in previous chapters, the problem was that the borders of all of the ancient and medieval states fluctuated widely over the years and always overlapped in Ottoman Macedonia. At one time or another, the Ottoman Macedonia was ruled by Alexander the Great and the Byzantine Empire (Greece), the Illyrians (Albania), or the medieval empires of Tsar Dušan (Serbia) and Simeon the Great, as well as under several notable rulers such as Boris I and Ivan Assen II (Bulgaria). Since the Balkan intellectuals was inspired by the idea of reviving the glories of the medieval empire, they employed such slogans as "back to Simeon the Great,"[412] and "to the Kosovo battle," and "Dušan the Mighty,"[413] or fought over the ancient figure of Alexander the Great (in Greek and Albanian media).[414] In this attempt, they often imitated their European mentors and tried to achieve international recognition and garner support from the Great Powers. In this respect, similarly to the practices of the Great Powers applied in Africa and other parts of the world, the Balkan states too implemented imperial discourses and practices in order to increase domestic and international legitimacy. As if the problem of overlapping "historical" claims were not daunting enough, each of the nation–states claimed "historical rights" over imagined territories on the basis of imagined communities and threatened to thwart the plans and imperialist strategies of the neighbouring countries. In this regard, the General Consul of the Kingdom of Serbia to Thessaloniki, Živojin Balugdžić, in his address to the Serbian Foreign Minister Nikola Pašić maintained that, "according to certain ethnic forces, Europe [was] putting in efforts to enforce decentralisation in Turkey. Since many parts [were] governed by Arnaut [Albanian] lords [rulers], our aspirations towards Skoplje, Veles, and Prilep would risk being cast in an unfavourable light, because the Arnautluk [Albanian presence] suddenly emerged in the areas that [were] chiefly under our rule."[415] In a response, the then Minister of

---

[412] Daskalov, *Bulgarian Historical Review,* p. 230.

[413] Aleksandar Pavlović, "Rereading the Kosovo Epic," *Serbian Studies Journal* 23/1 (2009): 83–96, here in 88.

[414] Clayer, *Edhe një here.*

[415] DASIP, MIDS, PPO,4/17. IX 1912, F–VIII, D–red 125/II; In original: *"za nas je prebrojavanje u opšte nezgodno, a još nezgodnije danas, kada se Evropa trudi da na osnovu nekih etničkih snaga izvede u Turskoj izvesnu decentralizaciju. I kako će izbori svuda izvan krajeva, u kojima su Arnauti gospodari, biti relativno slobodni, naše*

Foreign Affairs, Nikola Pašić, wrote: "[I]t does not depend on our will if the situation in the Balkans will take such a shape that threatens the survival of the Serbs. If this (revolt and) agitation for a "greater Albania," which is directed against the life of the Serb element in Kosovo, will receive support."[416] He further added that "Austro–Hungary [was] laying the foundation for an autonomous Albania, which [would] consist of the whole of Old Serbia, the greater part of Macedonia, and the whole of Epirus; in other words, the vilayets of Kosovo, Manastir, Işkodra, and Yanina."[417] Such discussions about autonomous Albania were also led among the politicians and statesmen in Bulgaria. Namely, in the case that Ottoman government "[satisfied] the demands of the Albanians (*Porta ispuniti zahteve Arbanasa*)," [418] Bulgaria was to "force Turkey to implement reforms in Macedonia in accordance with the Treaty of Berlin" or even "declare war [to the Ottoman Empire]."[419] Also in the Bulgarian media was discussed this "Albanian Question" (*Albanskijat vŭpros*) as a "strategy of the Ottoman Empire to give power to the Albanians over Christian territories of (Turkey in) Europe."[420] In this vein, politicians from the neighbouring countries insisted on separation between Christians

---

pretenzije na Skoplje, Veleš i Prilep mogu se pojaviti u nezgodnoj svetlosti. (...) jer se je u krajevima u kojima je glavna snaga naša začario Arnautluk, koji je poslednjim uspesima svojim postao još osioniji, te je svako slobodno kretanje našem življu nemoguće."
[416] DASIP, MIDS, PO. 7.IX 1912, F–H, D–2; In original: *"od naše volje ne zavisi hoće li stvari na Balkanu primiti oblik, koji preti opstanku Srba ili ne. Hoće li se podržavati agitacija i bune za 'veliku Arbaniju,' koja je upravljena protiv života srpskog elementa na Kosovu."*
[417] DASIP, MIDS, PPO, 8.21. IX 1912, F–XVIII, D–red 619; Quote: *"u njemu je viđena samo priprema Austro–Ugarske za stvaranje jedne autonomne Arbanije, koja bi obuhvatila svu Staru Srbiju, veći dio Maćedonije i ceo Epir (vilajete: kosovski, bitoljski, skadarski i janinski)."*
[418] DASIP, MIDS, PO, 8.21. IX 1912, F–VIII, D–2.
[419] DASIP, MIDS, PO 8/21. IX 1912, F–XI, D–6. Raported by Simić; A Bulgarian Ambassador to St. Petersburg shared the view with Russian Minister of Foreign Affairs about situation in Macedonia that if Great Powers will not force Ottoman Empire to introduce reforms in Macedonia, then Bulgaria ist forced to start a war: See: *"ako sile u najkraćem vremenu ne prinude Tursku da izvede u Makedoniji reforme u smislu Berlinskog ugovora, Bugarska će biti prinuđena na rat."* See also: Trajanovski, *Ruski dokumenti za Makedonija i makedonskoto prašanje.* pp. 87–91.
[420] DARSM, v.VI,87/Xv; v.IV.104/1912, 1 inv.br.283/76, Skopje, 1909; See also in a Newspaper: "Albanskiat vŭpros," *Bŭlgaria,* Sofia, 2. November, 1912. See also a study: Nikola Rizov, *Albanskoto vazrazhdanie* (Sofia, Knizharnitsa Hr. Olchev, 1909).

and Muslims or more specifically between Bulgarians, Serbs, and Greeks on the one hand and the Turks (and Albanians) on the other. In other words, while the Ottomans were imposing legal measures and trying to reorganise Rumelia, rival Balkan states were ready to start collaborating among (even better: colluding with each other and the GPs) themselves and with the Great Powers against the Ottoman Empire.[421] The discursive medium by which Balkan states and its agents interfere into politics on the ground was the insistence on the "natural" dispositions of their imagined communities to struggle for ascendancy through violence in their ethno–religiously mixed societies. By the stroke of a diplomatic pen, the Balkan states declared themselves to be the "natural" defenders of "Christian" groups since "ancient" or "mediaeval" times, and thus expected from the locals to help the states to forge their imperialist policies in order to establish "greater states." For this purpose, in a report from 5 September 1912, Nikola Pašić pointed out that "all four Balkan Christian states (Serbia, Bulgaria, Greece, and Montenegro) should forge a quadruple alliance led by the motto 'Balkans for the Balkan people,' with the aim of defence and attack."[422] This cooperation of "the Balkan Christian states" was brought to fruition through a series of bilateral treaties known as the League of Balkans. With Russian assistance, Serbia and Bulgaria settled their differences and signed an alliance on 13 March 1912. However, an alliance among all parties was only created in September 1912, when it was already evident that Albania would be granted autonomy by the Ottoman government. The League of Balkans was supported by Imperial Russia, because it opposed the Austro–Hungarian policy that supported the Albanian national movement and the idea of autonomous Albania.[423] In the end, the Dual Monarchy 's objections to the expansion of Serbian,

---

[421] Isa Blumi, "Shifting Loyalties and Failed Empire: A New Look at the Social History of the Late Ottoman Yemen, 1872– 1918," in *Counter–Narratives: History, Contemporary Society, and Politics in Saudi Arabia and Yemen*, eds. Madawi Al–Rasheed and Robert Vitalis (New York: Palgrave Macmillan, 2004), pp. 103–105.

[422] DASIP, MIDS, PO, 5/18. IX 1912, F–Aneks, D–Ugovor između Srbije i Bugarske (Grčke?); *"da bi trebale sve četiri balkanske hrišćanske države Srbija, Bugarska, Grčka i Crna Gora da zaključe jedan četvorni sporazum na načelu 'Balkan Balkanskim Narodima' za odbranu i napad."*

[423] Teodora Toleva, *Vlianieto na Avstro–Ungarija za saŭzdavaneto na albanskata nacia: 1896–1908* (Sofia: Siela Norma AD, 2012), p. 78.

Bulgarian, and Montenegrin policies under Russian patronage in the Ottoman lands, amounted to enforcing counter measures by supporting the Albanian–speaking population.

As a consequence, the Dual Monarchy became very interested in the "Albanian element" in the Ottoman Empire, and through various imperialist policies, such as construction of railways,[424] the Albanian memorandum,[425] and the *Kultusprotektorat*,[426] tried to expand its power throughout the "Albanian lands" and all the way to Thessaloniki. For these reasons, the Austro–Hungarian authorities remained closely connected to local Albanian notables, with whom they often cooperated, and thought that "in the case that Turkey [i.e. the Ottoman Empire] were to decline, Albanians [would] yield to the Austro–Hungarian Army, because they [could not] mount resistance against the Slavs alone." The latter was stated in a report, in which the Austro–Hungarian consul to Skopje, Pözel claimed that the (Ottoman) government had become aware of the Slavic threat (*slavischen Gefahr*)" too.[427] In line with the latter, Austro–

---

[424] HHStA PA XIV/Kt. 41, f. 651r–654v; In original: *"(...) von diesem Gesichtspunkte aus betrachtet, ist es nie zu befürchten, dass die Arnauten dauernd dem slavischen Einflusse gewonnen werden. Wenn also die positiven Bestrebungen Serbiens und Montenegros nie grosse Erfolge in Albanien aufzuweisen hatten, ist die destruktive Wirkung des slavischen Intriguenspiels, namentlich in diesem Amtsbezirke, von nicht zu unterschätzendem, insbesondere für Österreich–Ungarn und die Türkei schädlichem Erfolge gekrönt. In diese Kategorie gehören: Verdächtigungen Österreich–Ungarns mit Gebietserwerbungsgelüsten und daran knüpfende Propaganda gegen die Sandjakbahn, mit der Gefährdung des Islams durch das Kultusprotektorat und zu befürchtende Proselytenmacherei, wie es in Bosnien geschehen soll, Provozierung fortwährender innerer Unruhen zur Schwächung der Türkei, Heraufbeschwörung von unaufhörlichen Grenzkonflikten, namentlich auf der montenegrinischen Grenze."*

[425] Teodora Toleva, *Vlijanieto na Avstro–Ungarija*, pp. 81–92.

[426] With the treaties of Karlowitz (1699) and Passarowitz (1718), the Austrians were able to have the Ottomans guarantee them a protectorate over the Catholics in the northern mountainous region of Albania. The Austrian protectorate had a positive influence on maintaining the national consciousness of the Albanians. Within the framework of this cult protectorate, numerous church buildings and renovations as well as clergy were financially supported. See: Engelbert Deusch, *Das k.(u.)k. Kultusprotektorat im albanischen Siedlungsgebiet in seinem kulturellen, politischen und wirtschaftlichen Umfeld* (Vienna: Böhlau Verlag, 2009).

[427] No. 157 Pözel an Berchtold HHStA PA XIV/Kt. 42, f. 171r–175v; Uskub, den 28. September 1912; In original: *"Verhandlungen der osmanischen Regierung mit albanischen Anführern. Umwerbung mit materiellen Zugeständnissen und Postenverleihungen sowie Warnung vor osmanischem Zusammenbruch auf dem Balkan.*

Hungarian authorities counted on the support of Albanian notables such as Hasan Bey and Nexhip Beu Draga to "turn against the Slavic enemies (*die Albaner sich insgesamt gegen den slavischen Feind kehren werden*)."[428] These local notables in fact played important roles at various levels (local, regional, and international) by negotiating with different sides. They were able to switch their loyalties according to the given situation and to adapt to new conditions. In other Austro–Hungarian reports, the Draga family

---

Erklärung Nexhip Beu Dragas an den Konsul zu Orientierung der Albaner an Österreich- –Ungarn im Falle eines Endes der osmanischen Herrschaft. Weitere Sympathisanten der Donaumonarchie. Beginn der Waffenausgabe an albanische Hochlandbewohner. Versuch der Umsetzung von Reformen. Teilweise Anwendung des Gewohnheitsrechts. Aktionen albanischer, bulgarischer und serbischer Banden. Reise der Konsuln Bulgariens, Großbritanniens, Frankreichs und Russlands in den Polog zur Überprüfung der Lage der christlichen Bevölkerung. Wie ich aus verlässlicher Quelle streng vertraulich erfahre, hat Ibrahim Pascha anlässlich der Verhandlungen den Albanesen– Führern vor Augen geführt, dass es den Albanesen zwar schliesslich gelingen könnte, das Osmanische Reich zu stürzen, dass sie hiebei aber selbst auch zu Grunde gehen müssen, weil sie einer fremden Macht zum Opfer fallen werden. Die Chefs sollen hierauf begeistert geschworen haben, treue Untertanen des Sultans zu bleiben. (...) Die Albanesen wollen mit der türkischen Regierung halten und dieselbe gegen jeden (besonders betont) äusseren Feind bewaffnet unterstützen. Deswegen hätten Nedžib und Hassan Bey auch diese Dummköpfe (imbéciles, sic) wie Riza Bey und Genossen hieher kommen lassen. Sollte jedoch die Türkei untergehen, so würden sich die Albanesen in die Arme Österreich–Ungarn[s] werfen, weil sie den numerisch überlegenen Slaven allein nicht widerstehen könnten und weil sie sehen, dass in ÖsterreichUngarn auch die Mohammedaner volle Religionsfreiheit geniessen. Dieselben Erklärungen wiederholte Nedžib Bey einige Tage später auch persönlich dem hieramtlichen Dragomane. Ich habe Herrn Mosel einfach geantwortet, dass es ein steter Wunsch Österreich–Ungarns ist, dass die Albanesen sich im Rahmen des türkischen Reiches kulturell und wirtschaftlich entwickeln. Aus derselben Quelle höre ich auch, dass Goracucchi (Luigj Gurakuqi) in der ersten Hälfte Septembers [sic] im strengsten Incognito hier geweilt und an der Annäherung der Nord– und Süd–Albanesen gearbeitet haben soll. (...) Auch sonst scheint die Regierung, um angesichts der „slavischen Gefahr" wenigstens von Seite der Arnauten Ruhe zu haben, in elfter Stunde einen energischen Anlauf zur Inangriffnahme der Reformen in Albanien nehmen zu wollen."
[428] Heimroth an Berchtold HHStA PA XII/Kt. 385, f. 22r–23v Bericht, Üsküb, den 8. Oktober 1912; Quote: *"Ich hatte in den letzten Tagen Gelegenheit, sowohl mit Hassan Bey als auch mit Nedžib Bey Draga zu sprechen. Diese beiden angesehenen Arnautenführer sagten mir spontan, dass die Albaner sich insgesamt gegen den slavischen Feind kehren werden. Es seien auch schon Vorkehrungen getroffen worden, um die frondierenden Malissoren auf den Weg der Pflicht zurückzuführen. Sowohl Nedžib als auch Hassan Bey erzählten es freimütig, dass die Albaner von den Serben Waffen bekommen haben. 'Mit eben denselben Waffen,' fügten sie hinzu, 'werden wir die Serben im Notfalle bekämpfen.'"*

were also described as Italophiles and opponents to the Dual Monarchy, while Hasan Bey was described as a supporter of the British Empire (Anglophile).[429] This process, it is important to note, also differed with the various developments on the ground and thus, local notables (like the abovementioned Hasan Bey and Draga) at one time supported the Kingdom of Italy or British Empire, and at another the Dual Monarchy[430] or any other regional state such as the Ottoman Empire, Montenegro, or Serbia, or were entirely against these claiming no allegiances whatsoever. Therefore, the local level was much more complex, led by multiple dynamics of various actors who took different trajectories according to the given situation. In line with this, I analyse the responses of the locals on the ground. As I have suggested in this thesis, attending to the local level is very important in understanding the complexities of the actors and their daily lives. Here I particularly highlight the local Albanian–speaking population who reacted towards these various policies and were actively involved in the policy–making. Numerous scholars who investigated the Macedonian Question have neglected this 'Albanian' factor as an important one for gaining a broader perspective of the developments on the ground. Oftentimes, these locals manipulated the Great Power interests in the region, winning in the process the financial and military support that they needed for regional stability and their daily survival. In this regard,

---

[429] HHStA PA XIV/Kt. 41, f. 651r–654v, Mitrovitza am 16. August 1912; See in original: *"Es ist nicht ausgeschlossen, dass er (Nedjib Bey Draga) zwischen den Aufständischen und der serbischen Regierung vermittelte. Die Familie Ali Draga Pascha ist italophil, gegen die Monarchie verhält sie sich feindlich. (...) Dagegen scheint Hassan Bey, dessen anglophile Gesinnung seit jeher bekannt ist, zumindest moralisch durch England unterstützt zu warden."*

[430] See about Involvements of Dual Monrachy: Ortner, "Erfahrungen einer westeuropäischen Armee auf dem Balkan," in *Am Rande Europas,* pp. 67–68; Heiko Brendel and Emmanuel Debruyne, "Resistance and Repression in Occupied Territories behind the Western and Balkan Fronts, 1914–1918," in *Frontwechsel: Österreich–Ungarns 'Großer Krieg' im Vergleich,* eds. Julia Walleczek–Fritz, Wolfram Dornik and Stefan Wedrac (Vienna/Cologne/Weimar: Böhlau, 2014), pp. 235–258; Also the Involvements of the Deutsche Bahn in the region see: Orientbahnen Ostrumelisches Netz or OR0610, Abtretung an Bulgarien Vol. 7, 1.1.1909 – 31.12.1911; OR1012 Macedonische (Saloniki–Monastir) Emission 30.6.1892 – 7.3.1893. In these activities see also the involvements of Deutsche Bank, Berlin Orientbüro: Orientbahnen Politische Situationsberichte Balkankrieg 1912/1913 (Proteste) Vol. 1, Müller an den Verwaltungsrat der Orientalischen Eisenbahnen, Wien v. 30.06.1910 betr. Aufstand in Albanien – Pazifizierung Albaniens.

the locals often cooperated and negotiated with many involved parties and shed new light onto the dynamics at play in the Balkans. To examine this more closely, we may look at how conversions worked in this process. However, on the ground some of the Albanian notables cooperated closely with the Serbian state and established agreements with Bulgaria as well (*o šurovanju naših političara s Arnautima i o našem sporazumu sa Bugarskom*).[431] The report from the office of the Foreign Affairs of Kingdom of Serbia at that time, particular notes the cooperation with Isa Boletini and that Serbia supplied the Albanians with large amounts of weapons (*iz Srbije šalje se velika količina oružja Arnautima i da se Isa Boljetinac otuda pomaže novcem i poklonima*).[432] Furthermore, those diplomatic reports depicted the local level as a place where "bandits (*seoski razbojnici*)" were not informed by national ideology, because they "attacked both Serbs and Albanians."[433] One could analyse the listed documents as sources that explicitly show that local conflicts and violence were not triggered by national consciousness as represented in regional media. On the contrary, the local Albanians supported the proliferation of weapons among the[ir] neighbours, the (local) Serbs, so that they (the Serbs) could defend themselves from the bandits that also posed a threat to the Albanian notables.[434] The Austro–Hungarian reports also support statements that Isa Boletini was provided with arms by the Serbian government,[435] which also equipped the locals with weapons, regardless of whether they were Albanian– or Serbian–speaking individuals and groups.[436] In fact Isa did not act alone, that is, he was organising the

---

[431] DASIP, MIDS, PO 10/23. IX 1912, F–III, D–7.

[432] Ibid.

[433] DASIP, MIDS, PO. 13/26. IX 1912, F–III, D–3. Dr. M. Đ. Milojević konzul kraljevine Srbije – Priština; Nikoli Pašiću; In original: *"žandarmerijske i vojne vlasti apsolutno ništa ne čine za održavanje poretka. S toga su sada pravi predstavnici vlasti i gospodari u ovim stranama seoski razbojnici. Naoružani i potpuno slobodni, oni krstare danju i noći po selima i uzimaju šta kome hoće. Napadaju kako Srbe tako i Arnaute."*

[434] Ibid; Quote: *"u ovoj opštoj zbunjenosti našem se življu jedino može pomoći davanjem oružja. Arnautski se prvaci tome neće protiviti. Mnogi i žele da se Srbi malo naoružaju, kako bi se mogli bar donekle braniti od mnogobrojnih pljačkaša, koji postaju opasni i za same arnautske poglavice."*

[435] HHStA PA XXXVIII/Kt. 405, n. f; See: *"Einzelheiten zu dem von Isa Boletini geleiteten Waffenschmuggel aus Serbien."*

[436] HHStA PA XIV/Kt. 41, f. 651r–654v, Mitrovitza am 16. August 1912; Quote: *"Schwierigkeit nachrichtendienstlicher Ermittlung serbischer Waffenlieferungen.*

smuggling together with his sons and other "Albanian bandits (*arnautischen Räuber*)" such as Mahmud, Bekir, and Rexhep.[437] This meant that conversion between regional states (i.e. Serbia) and local Albanian notables was taking place in all directions. These vast regions of the Kosovo vilayet were still not "ethnically" divided. Slavs and Albanians lived side by side in communities that had shared interests until the Balkan Wars. Interestingly, the local revolts which dominated the international and regional attention during those years were the joint village responses to Ottoman (Young Turk) reforms or raids by radical Serbian nationalists. To maintain that these revolts were exclusively of nationalist origin would be misleading and an instance of anachronistic analysis. The various documents on Serb and Albanian relations along the frontier zone suggest that these neighbours were cooperating and sharing their daily lives.[438] Furthermore, these locals were also often opposed to the state decisions of their "motherland." It is important to reiterate that many of their Serbian–speaking neighbours also joined in the defence of the local community (and Albanian–speaking population) against state outsiders from Belgrade or Istanbul Orthodox representatives.[439] It was often the case that these regional states, governed by "Serbian" citizens, were protected by Serbian consuls that created the tensions. Whether Serbian, Greek, or Bulgarian, foreign representatives on the whole were supportive of measures that created divided communities, whereby the construction of schools in

---

Beeinflussbarkeit der Albaner durch auswärtige Mächte und Wirkung gegen Österreich– Ungarn und das Osmanische Reich gerichteter Propaganda Serbiens und Montenegros. Serbische Einflusspolitik unter dem Schutz der französisch–russischbritischen Entente. Österreich–Ungarns Einstehen für friedliche Veränderungen und Kulturpolitik. Kompromittierung Isa Boletinis durch enge Kontakte zu Serbien. Analyse von Isa Boletinis politischer Laufbahn und der Tätigkeit seiner Verwandten. Politische Haltung der Familie Draga: Beziehungen zu Italien und Serbien. Orientierung Hasan Prishtinas an Großbritannien."
[437] HHStA PA XIV/Kt. 41, f. 651r–654v, Mitrovitza am 16. August 1912; In original: *"Sowohl Issa als seine Söhne, welche in Belgrad auf Kosten der serbischen Regierung geweilt haben, verfügen über bedeutende Barmittel, deren Herkunft unzweifelhaft zu sein scheint. (...) „Die arnautischen Räuber Mahmud, Bekir und Redjeb aus Selanca weilten des öfteren in Serbien, sie vermitteln übrigens schon seit Jahren den Waffenschmuggel."*
[438] HHStA PA XII/449.
[439] HHStA PA XXXVIII/Kt. 387, f. 10r–18v; Quote: *"Konflikt zwischen dem serbischen Metropoliten in Prishtina und dem serbischen Konsul sowie zwischen serbischen und einer neugebildeten griechischen orthodoxen Gemeinde in Ferizaj."*

particular was key for the nationalist indoctrination to take place (as seen in chapter Three). Even with this 'educational' program in force, Belgrade Serb efforts proved incapable of shifting the local Serb resistance to nationalist provocation emanating from pan–Slavist activities based in Belgrade and St. Petersburg.[440] There are plenty of cases in which these regional policies, combined with Russian support, tried to modify the local level by dividing the neighbours according to national or religious affiliations and categories. Often these political entrepreneurs clashed with their local "compatriots" and were obliged to modify their initial strategies because the (Serbian) state(s) often made faulty assumptions where the loyalties of the local Kosovar "Serbs" lay. In this regard, Nikola Pašić insisted on nationalisation of the local population by issuing the "First Serbian Project" (*i projekat srpski*) that was to fight "for a better fate of their compatriots in European Turkey" (*za bolju sudbu njihovih sunarodnika u evropskoj Turskoj*).[441] In this attempt, Pašić emphasised that his compatriots:

> "Live on a territory of the Ottoman Empire known as Old Serbia. This is where Serbs lived, developed, and saw their own glory and their own downfall. From this downfall to this day, they preserved their name, language and tradition. This territory nowadays consists of the whole Kosovo vilayet together with the Novi Pazar sancak, the north–western part of the İşkodra vilayet and the Adriatic Coast (Durres, Lesh, Medua etc.), as well as the northern and eastern parts of the Manastir vilayet (Drim, Debar, Porec, Prilep)."[442]

By mapping the people, he further also maps its borders by stating that the "[g]eographic border would extend from the triangle of the Serb–Bulgarian–Ottoman border from Patarice in the south, along a line between the rivers Zletovska and Bregalnica towards the Vardar, and thence to

---

[440] DASIP, MIDS, PO, 1912, F–IV, D–4; Quote from the document: *"Danas 7. Septembra 1912 došao je k meni ruski poslanik g. Gartvig i pročitao mi je depešu u koju je dobio da mi je pročita. Rusija ponašala se je vrlo 'sočustveno' k sporazumu i nije pravila nikakav pritisak (davnelnie) ostavljajući samima (Srbiji i Bugarskoj) da izrade sporazum. I gledala je na to 'soglasenie' kao na akt garancije njihovih opštih interesa i kao na sredstvo odbrane od napada."*
[441] DASIP, MIDS, PO, 5/18. IX 1912, F–Aneks, D–Ugovor između Srbije i Bugarske.
[442] Ibid.

Babun, Prilep, Kičevo, and Ohrid. From the Ohrid Lake it would continue to the Black Drim and the river Shkumbin." [443] This mapping was compatible with imperialist understandings and territorial nationalisation of the space that was considered as their "historic right." These rights were based on "invented traditions" that could facilitate the nationalisation of the local population in the mapped territory. Therefore, like the Bulgarian intellectuals, the Serbian political elite much more strongly emphasised the Christian Orthodox and Slavic roots of their imperial past regarding the Macedonian territories. In Siniša Malešević's view, thus, Serbia employed imperial and nationalist rhetoric, which was regularly deployed to sustain competing claims to rule by the process of imperialising nation states.[444] After becoming known the Italian declaration of war to the Ottoman state in October 1911, the Balkan states, specifically the Serbian and Bulgarian governments discussed a joint military venture against the "Asiatic Turks."[445] To this end, the first Serbian draft of about the alliance with

---

[443] DASIP, MIDS, PPO, 8.21. IX 1912, F–XVIII, D–red 619; In original document: *"territorija, na kojoj danas žive Srbi u Otomanskoj Carevini jeste Stara Srbija. U njoj su Srbi živeli, u njoj su se razvijali, u njoj su dočekali svoju slavu i svoju propast, u njoj su od propasti do danas čuvali, kako–tako svoje ime, jezik i tradicije. Ta oblast danas obuhvata ceo kosovski vilajet zajedno sa starim novopazarskim sandžakom, severo– zapadni deo skadarskog vilajeta s obalom jadranskom (Drač, Lješ, S. Đ. Medua itd.) severni i istočni deo bitoljskog vilajeta (Drimskog, Debar, Poreč, Prilep). Geografska granca te teritorije bila bi ovakva. Od tromeđe na srpsko–bugarsko–turskoj granici od Patarice na jug vodovelnicom između Zletovske (reke) i Bregalnice, a od utoka Zletovske reke Bregalnicom do utoka u Vardar, a odatle Babunom tako da Prilep i Kičevo s Ohridom i njihovom okolinom ulaze u sastav njen. Od ohridskog jezera donekle Crnim Drimom pa onda rekom Škumbom."*

[444] Malešević, *Nationalism and Imperialism*, p. 166; Jörn Leonhard and Ulrike von Hirschhausen, *Empires und Nationalstaaten* (Göttingen: Vamdenhoeck & Ruprecht, 2011).

[445] Ugron an Berchtold HHStA PA XII/Kt. 385, f. 300r–308r; Belgrad, am 19. Oktober 1912; "Amtsblatt "Srpske Novine", vom 6./19. Oktober 1912. In original document: *"An das serbische Volk! Die neuesten Ereignisse haben die Entscheidung des Schicksals der Balkanhalbinsel wieder an die Tagesordnung gestellt und mit ihr auch das Schicksal Altserbiens, der ruhmreichen, aber unglücklichen Mutter unseres Königreiches, wo der historische Mittelpunkt der Staaten unserer alten Könige und Kaiser ist, wo die berühmten Residenzen der Nemanjiče liegen: Novopazarski Ras, Priština, Skoplje, Prizren; wo unsere Brüder nach dem Blute, nach der Sprache, nach den Gebräuchen, nach dem nationalen Empfinden, nach ihren Wünschen und Tendenzen leben. Die gewalttätige und unduldsame ottomanische Regierung rottet schon seit Jahrhunderten diese unsere Brüder aus."*

Bulgaria was completed in November 1911. Furthermore, this "defensive Serbo–Bulgarian alliance" was signed in March 1912 and was followed by "an openly offensive one" in May, just as Italy was seizing the Dodecanese. Around this Serbo–Bulgarian alliance, a secret Balkan League now coalesced, whose purpose was "to expel the Turks from the peninsula."[446] Nikola Pašić commented that "European diplomacy was for keeping the peace, but unfortunately matters in the Balkans developed in different ways that conjured up ghosts (from the past) among the Balkan population."[447] According to him, "the first and most important reason [was] the Turkish administration," which allowed "Albanians to conquer the cities."[448] Furthermore, he thought that "autonomous Albania should not be allowed at all. These [the Albanian] tribes still live[d] primitively and without culture, (…) literature, and alphabet; as such, they [could not] achieve any independent development."[449] However, when it became obvious that Albania was likely to be an autonomous administrative unit inside the Ottoman Empire, the Serbian policy–makers, alongside their Bulgarian, Greek, and Montenegrin counterparts reacted and insisted on implementation of small–state imperialism. In this regard, Dr. J.M.

---

[446] Ibid.

[447] Predsednik Ministarskog saveta i ministar inostranih dela Kraljevine Srbije Nikola Pašić, Beograd, – Poslaniku kraljevine Srbije u Francuskoj i Belgiji, Vesniću; DASIP, MIDS, PO, 4.17. IX. 1912; F–VIII, D–2. Pov. Br. 3571; A Minister of Foreign Affairs of Kingdom of Serbia, Nikola Pašić in one raport wrote: *"Može se reći da cela diplomacija evropska želi da se mir održi. Ali nažalost tako su se stvari na Balkanu zatalasale, da je teško verovati da se mogu zadržati. Mnogi uzroci proizveli su takvo razdražrno stanje, da ga je sada teško umiriti. Sve što se desilo u poslednje vreme išlo je u prilog uzbuđenju duhova naroda balkanskih. (...) prvi i najglavniji uzrok taj je, što se u turskoj upravi dešavaju takve stvari, koje jasno pokazuju da je disciplina u otomanskoj vojsci isčezla i da se vlade smenjuju putem tajnih organizacija i pobuna u vojsci. (...) arnauti se bune, osvajaju varoši bez kapi krvi, negde vlasti beže, a negde se predaju i pridržavaju njima, a negde stoje i gledaju mirno. (...) Sve je to uplivisalo na duhove u Srbiji, i primoravaju srpsku vladu da preduzima blagovremeno mere da je događaji zateknu sasvim spremnu."*

[448] Clark, *The Sleepwalkers*.

[449] Dimitrije Tucović, *Srbija i Albanci* (Ljubljana: Časopis za kritiko znanosti, 1989), p. 94; See in text: *"Ton je davao predsednik vlade Nikola Pašič. U organu njegove Radikalne stranke, novinama 'Samouprava' objavljen je njegov intervju dopisniku francuskog lista 'Temps', u kome on objašnjava svetu: 'Oni koji misle da se mir može obezbediti stvaranjem autonomne Albanije, varaju se. Ta plemena i danas žive primitivnim životom i bez kulture, oni su u zavadi jedno s drugim, oni u istoriji nikad nisu imali kakav zajednički život. Ta su plemena podeljena na tri vere, oni nemaju svoje literature, pa čak ni bukvice; očigledno je da ona ne mogu imati samostalnoga razvitka.'"*

Nenadović, ambassador of Serbia to Istanbul, wrote to the Miniser of Foreign Affairs, Jovanović: "I hear that, from the four Rumelian vilayets, Kosovo, Manastir, Işkodra, and Yanina, they wish to create the geographic name of Albania and eventually autonomous Albania. They say (…) that England wants to help this idea of creating an autonomous Albania in order for it to be a wall of defence against the Austro–Hungarian penetration in the Balkans. In this sense, this Albania, would threaten the survival of Serbian and Bulgarian propaganda and the Macedonian Question would cease to exist because it would be subsumed under the Albanian (Question)."[450] Analysing this report, one can infer that the Great Powers were very active in "solving" the Albanian (and Macedonian) Questions, and their activity was often accompanied by the presence of the regional states. The potential ground for the establishment of autonomous Albania triggered the regional states to cooperate and declare war to the Ottomans. Moreover, Serbian diplomats found that Albanian autonomy would "threaten [their] survival" and transform "the Macedonian Question into an Albanian one." Thus, the Serbian policy–makers intensified their activities in Ottoman Macedonia, and through the Serbian media, such as the newspaper *Politika*, spread the propaganda that "war [was] what the Serbs wished for, war [was] their duty, and only by war [could] the Serbian tribe be liberated from foreign rule. That [was] the conviction of all Serbia, that [was] the wish of the people, that [was] the perennial dream of our soldiers."[451] Furthermore, this war against the Ottomans was also pictured as "a Balkan Christian alliance" against the inversion of Asians and a wish

---

[450] DASIP. MIDS, PO, 2.8. 1912, F–H, D–3, knjiga 5, sveska 1, p. 1115; In original: *"Čujem da od četiri rumelijska vilajeta: Kosovskog, Bitoljskog, Skadarskog i Janjinskog žele da stvore geografski pojam Arbanije i da se od ta četiri vilajeta ima eventualno izčauriti autonomna Arbanija. Kažu da je to zamisao Ćamil–paše i da će ga Engleska u tome potpomoći. Bilo da ovaj kabinet ostane ili da se odista uspe obrazovati Ćamil–pašina vlada, uticaj engleske politike u Turskoj biće presudan. Ako je odista Engleska voljna da pomogne misao o stvaranju autonomne Arbanije, i da ta oblas bude bedem protiv prodiranja Austro–Ugarske na Balkan, to držim da takva eventualnost – autonomija Arbanije u gore navedenom obliku – preti opstanku srpske i bugarske propaganda i mećedonsko pitanje prestaje postojati jer ga potpuno ekartira arbansko."*
[451] Politika, No. 3106, Beograd, 9. Septembar, 1912, p. 1; Quote from the text: *"Rat je želja Srbijanina, rat je njena dužnost, samo ratom i revolucijom može se osloboditi srpsko pleme od tuđinom. To je uverenje celog sveta u Srbiji, to je želja naroda, to je stalni san naše vojske."*

of "the whole civilised world and the Serbian people together with the Slavdom."[452] It is hence conceivable that these orientalist discourses of the "civilised" against the "Asians" were also present in the media during the Balkan Wars. They were significant in mobilising the population and in presenting the "fallen heroes" as "the dead soldiers of Alexander the Great." One of the local Metropolitans, Aksenije, depicted these "heroes" as "saviours of the Macedonian Christians" led by "our Alexander the Great (Prince of Serbia)."[453]

These media akin to *Politika* invoked "the legacies of the medieval Serbian empires." Hence the mass media and public sphere "glorified the early polities of the Serbs"[454] that were "stretching from the First Serbian Principality under the Vlastimirović dynasty in the 9th century to the Nemanjić dynasty established in 1217."[455] In this respect, the "dirty Belgrade newspapers" were praising the "colonial policy of conquest" (*kolonijalnu zavojevačku politiku*) that was represented as a liberated

---

[452] Politika No. 3124, Beograd, 26. Septembar, 1912, p. 2; In an entitled '*Balkanski rat*' Politika also reported: *"Crna Gora je objavila rat. (...) Crna Gora nije sama s njom su i balkanske hrišćanske kraljevine, sa kojima je Crna Gora u savezu. Kralj je uvek želeo taj savez, koji svi balkanski narodi očekuju od invazije Azijata. (...) Simpatije celog civilizovanog sveta prate Crnu Goru kao i one sveg srpskog naroda i sveg Slovenstva."[452]* This (Balkan) war was also represented in the media as "holy war." See in original: *"sveti rat balkanskih naroda je počeo. On ima da se završi oslobođenjem Balkana."* See also: Philip Jenkins, *The Great and Holy War: How World War I Became to Religious Crusade* (New York: Harper One, 2014), p. 78; Stefan Rohdewald, "Religious Wars? Southern Slavs' Orthodox Memory of the Balkan and World Wars," in *The Balkan Wars from Contemporary Perception to Historic Memory*, eds. Katrin Boeckh and Sabine Rutar (London: Palgrave Macmilian, 2016), pp. 249–273.

[453] Politika, No. 3170, Beograd, 12. Novembar, 1912, p. 2; Quote: *"U bitoljskoj egzarhijskoj crkvi održano je svečano blagodarenje... Činodejstvovao je mitropolit Aksentije sa mnogo sveštenika. Mitropolit je pozdravio 'dugim i dirljivim govorom Prestolonaslednika kao oslobodioca Macedonije i spasioca macedonskih potlacenih Hriscana' rijecima: 'U naknadu za vaše pale heroje i prolivenu srpsku krv mi Vama, našem Aleksandru Maćedonskom, predajemo sebe, a svoje molitve upućujemo Bogu za sreću Srbije i Njenog Aleksandra Velikog i srpske pobedne armije.'"*

[454] See: Dragoljub M. Dinić, *Prvi put kroz Albaniju sa Šumadijskim albanskim odredom 1912* (Beograd, Šumadija, 1922), pp. 3–4; In original: *"Potomci Srba, koji na Kosovu izgubiše bitku, sada kao da dolaze s neba... pa čak hoće i preko albanskih hrida i snežnih alpa, preko razbojničkih arnautskih gnezda na Jadransko more da pobodu viteški steg Srbije."*

[455] Ugron an Berchtold HHStA PA XII/Kt. 385, f. 300r–308r; Belgrad, am 19. Oktober 1912; "Amtsblatt „Srpska Novine", vom 6./19. Oktober 1912.

policy of "kulturtregers."[456] However, several politicians in the Kingdom of Serbia opposed these policies towards Ottoman Macedonia. In this line, Serbian socialist politician Kosta Novaković reported on the imperialist, Greater Serbian policy (*u dopisima iz Albanije raskrinkavao sam imperijalističku velikosrpsku politiku*). [457] In this respect, his most significant work was "Macedonia to the Macedonians, the Land to the Farmers" (*Makedonija Makedoncima, zemlja zemljoradnicima*),[458] and it opposed Serbian (and Yugoslav) policies towards its "peripheries." Furthermore, he pointed out that "rural Serbia already disappeared in 1912. An imperialist Serbia, pan–Serbia, was born in its stead, with a pan–Serbian dynasty and pan–Serbian militarism. This new imperialism [was] cruel, brutal, merciless, dream[ed] of a return of Dušan's empire and trie[d] to overtake as far as other imperialist powers in ten years."[459] Another socialist, Dimitrije Tucović, emphasised the Serbian imperialist aspirations and the invention of the mediaeval tradition. Tucović devoted his life to socialist ideals that opposed these imperialist practices. In doing so, he openly criticised the Serbian government and defined its policy as a "praxis of colonial extermination" (*praksa kolonijalnog istrebljenja*). [460] According to him, this praxis was the foundation on which to make "(Albanians) our sworn enemies," and compared these state practices against the local Albanian–speaking population with the European exterminations in overseas colonies.[461] This small–state imperialism was

---

[456] Tucović, *Srbija i Albanci*, p. 101.

[457] Ibid., p. 18; See also: Kosta Novaković, *Makedonija Makedoncima, zemlja zemljoradnicima* (Čačak: Čačanski glasnik, 1966).

[458] Ibid.

[459] Ibid. 32; Quote: "*Seljačka Srbija više ne postoji .... 1912. ona je potpuno nestala. Umesto nje, imperijalistička Srbija, pan–Srbija se pojavila, sa svojom pan–srpskom dinastijom i pan–srpskim militarizmom. Ovaj novi imperijalizam, surov, okrutan, nemilosrdan, sanja o povratku Dušanovog carstva i pokušava da dostigne u sledećih deset godina imperijalne sile koje postoje stotinama godina.*"

[460] Ibid. p. 39; Tucović, *Srbija i Albanci*. p. 51.

[461] Ibid. p. 23; In original: "*Srbija je htela i izlazak na more i jednu svoju koloniju, pa je ostala bez izlaska na more, a od zamišljene kolonije stvorila je krvnog neprijatelja. (...) Zavojevački pohod Srbije na Arbaniju (je) najgrublje odstupanje od načela zajednice balkanskih naroda. U njemu su do kostiju razgoličene netolerancija prema drugim narodima, zavojevačke težnje i gotovost buržoazije da ih sprovodi najbrutalnijim zločinstvima, kakva su do sada izvršivana samo u prekomorskim kolonijama.*" (...)

also reported in the Austro–Hungarian archives as "planned deportation and colonisation by Serbs" (*geplante Deportationen und Kolonisierung mit Serben*).[462] Not only the Great powers, but also the "small states" applied imperialist practices and defined the *Lebensraum* of their imagined greater state projects.[463] In this sense, as presented above, prior to the Balkan wars, it is observable that the local, regional, and international levels were not developed in isolation, rather were intermingling and influencing each other. As the "Albanian element" influenced the Balkan state policies, these regional states influenced the local population on the ground as well. These developments did not take place without the presence of the Great Powers, which intensified their policies and divided those countries further into what as of 1914 became known as the Triple Entente and Triple Alliance. Therefore, I highlight here how these levels were interacting and influencing each other in the framework of the Balkan small–state imperialism, yet without excluding the imperialist involvements of the Great Powers, especially the policies of the Dual Monarchy and Imperial Russia. The importation of nationalism and imperialism to the region during the Age of Empire created violent rivalries between various state– and nation–building projects. As the history of the Balkan Wars shows, these violent rivalries predated the European conflict of 1914–18.[464] Nowhere was this friction more apparent than in Macedonia, the last region to be "liberated" from the Ottomans. Here Serbian, Bulgarian, Greek, and Macedonian (together with Albanian) nationalists held competing territorial claims.

"sprovodi najbrutalnijim zločinstvima, kakva su do sada izvršivana samo u prekomorskim kolonijama."

[462] HHStA PA XXXVIII/Kt. 405, n. f; Prizren am 15. Oktober 1913.

[463] HHStA PA XXXVIII/Kt. 441, n. f; Üskub, den 24 Oktober 1913; In original: *"(...)eine ihren Zwecken entsprechende Kolonisierungspolitik durchzuführen. (...) Durch die geschilderten Methoden wird die Regierung jedenfalls sehr bald in den Besitz zahlreicher und ausgedehnter Grundkomplexe gelangen und, auf selben gestützt, alsbald eine rege Kolonisationstätigkeit entfalten."*

[464] John Paul Newman, "The Origins, Attributes, and Legacies of Paramilitary Violence in the Balkans," in *War in Peace: Paramilitary Violence in Europe after the Great War* eds. Robert Gerwarth and John Horne (Oxford: Oxford University Press, 2012), p. 145.

5.4.2. Montenegro and the Idea of a Greater State: Towards Ottoman Macedonia

The Montenegrin policy and its activities towards Ottoman Macedonia has thus far received scarce in the respective studies. Like the other Balkan states, Montenegro underwent the process of "colonisation of the mind" and played an important role in the Balkan League. According to Leften Stavros Stavrianos, "after obtaining its independence, Montenegro was in the forefront during the 19th century wars against the Ottoman Empire. The role of Montenegro in the South Slav and overall Balkan affairs was quite out of proportion to its ridiculously meagre material resources."[465] In a similar vein, John D. Treadway recorded that Montenegro's role in the Balkan affairs [had] been minimised by Western historical literature, and whose inquiries into the nature of Europe's powder keg frequently sidestepped Montenegro in order to tackle the seemingly more substantive and controversial case of Serbia.[466] Historically, the region of Zeta on the Adriatic Sea, which was later known as Montenegro (*Karadağ*), became part of the Ottoman Empire in 1496. Due to its geographic position and tribal social structure, this region was only nominally incorporated within the Ottoman administrative system subordinated to the *pashas* appointed by the Ottoman Imperial Council in Scutari (İşkodra/Shkodra/Skadar). Montenegro was actually a semi–independent principality under the Ottomans, and was initially represented by a bishop–prince (*vladika*). For most of Montenegrin history, *vladikas* conserved Montenegrin tradition, and maintained good relations with Imperial Russia via the Orthodox Church. As has been shown in the Chapter Two, Tsars often supported Montenegrin tribes in their efforts to strength their semi–independent status, as well as in anti–Ottoman movements.[467] Actually, during most of the nineteenth century, with the help of the traditional protector state of

---

[465] Leften S. Stavrianos, *The Balkans since 1453* (New York: Rienhart, 1958), p. 237.

[466] John D. Treadway, *The Falcon and Eagle, Montenegro and Austria–Hungary, 1908–1918* (West Lafayette: Purdue University Press, 1983).

[467] Armando Pitassio, "The Building of Nations in South–Eastern Europe, the Cases of Slovenia and Montenegro: A Comparative Approach," in *The Balkans: National Identities in a Historical Perspective* eds. Stefano Bianchini and Marco Dogo (Ravenna: Longo, 1998), p. 53; Pavel Apolonovič Rovinski, *Crna Gora u prošlosti i sadašnjosti, vol. II: Etnografija* (Beograd: Obod, 2004); Vasa Čubrilović, *Terminologija plemenskog društva u Crnoj Gori* (Beograd: Srpska akademija nauka, 1959).

Russia, Montenegrin rulers and intellectuals constructed national narratives of Montenegrins as the "chosen people,"[468] who should build a nation–state and carry out this final solution against "undeveloped barbaric Ottomans." Accordingly, Montenegrin rulers paid much attention regarding the Eastern Question and invented many traditions against the "Ottoman yoke." The invented traditions of the Montenegrins as a "chosen people" entrusted with the specific mission to "save the true faith and Serbdom," and to fight against the "Turkified Slavs" and "big Asiatic Mongols (Ottomans),"[469] were supported by Montenegrin newspapers at the *Fin de Siècle*. Furthermore, the *Montenegrin Voice* (*Glas Crnogorca*) newspaper remarked that Montenegrins "have the mission (*zadaću*) of being the interpreter of all Serbdom and the messenger (*vjestnik*) of their sorrow to the world, from those free high mountains of Montenegro" (*sa slobodnijeh visina crnogorskijeh*).[470] This small group of people must work for the liberation and unity of millions of Christians, who for many centuries had been in a state of shameful slavery (*u ropstvu najsramotnijem*) under the Mohammedan yoke (*u jarmu muhamedanstva*), the butchers of the faith of Christ (*zakletog krvinka vjere hristove*).[471] This concern for Christian "liberation" from the Muslim yoke emanated from the nationalistic meta–narratives that assumed conflict was inevitable among different ethnically constituted religions. In this light, the aim of this work is to present several examples that show the active Montenegrin role towards the Macedonian Questions. Thus, I do not to argue that Montenegro was the main actor in the Ottoman Macedonia and "solver" of the Eastern Question, but rather to present its important role in the Macedonian Questions and Balkan affairs in general. Nevertheless, it was the first state that declared war to the Ottoman Empire during the Balkan Wars and promoted actively the conquest of the Ottoman Macedonian

---

[468] According to Anthony D. Smith the notion of a "chosen people" can be applied only with the sanctification of national narratives as sacred communion. Furthermore, he points out that religious notions of the "sacred" and "profane" are integrated into the national culture that represents their nation as "chosen" and their policy as "sacred". See Anthony D. Smith, *Chosen Peoples: Sacred Sources of National Identity* (Oxford: Oxford University Press, 2004), 18.
[469] Petrović Njegoš, *Lažni car Šćepan Mali.*
[470] Glas Crnogorca, Cetinje, 21. April, 1873.
[471] Ibid.

territories. Moreover, Montenegrin authorities found legitimacy for this liberation and state–building in the Orientalism discourses popular throughout nineteenth century Europe—considered to be the "center of civilisation." In this regard, the more outside patrons insisted on using these discourses, the more local nationalist promoters insisted on exploiting various "barbarian" identities. The Montenegrin newspaper accordingly presented "the people of the East as being incapable of leading an independent life–style" (*istočni narodi nisu sposobni za samostalni život*), adding that "they do not know about the right of liberty" (*pravo na slobodu*). Because they are "incapable for civilisation" (*nesposobni za civilizaciju*) and "incapable of leading an independent life–style" (*nesposobni za samostalni život*) someone "should bring civilisation to them" (*nositi civilizaciju*).[472] Those who possess "progress" (*napredak*) are not just Montenegro and Serbia, but also other Christian populations of the Ottoman Empire that are "active, productive and smart" (*radni, proizvodni i umni*). Consequently, the condition for true progress was the complete liberation of the people from the Ottoman yoke (*potpuna narodna sloboda*).[473] Through this prism of imperialist projections, František Šistek analyses Montenegrin policy before the First World War. He situated Montenegrin identity and history narratives "within a wider Pan–Serb historical and national framework," combined with ideas of a greater imagined territory that should include all Serbs or South Slavs into one state.[474] This concept of the greater state is the culmination of the new type of European imperialism. The transformations that happened in the Balkans represent a microcosm or local manifestation of worldwide

---

[472] Ibid.

[473] Ibid.

[474] The aim of this work is not to argue that Montenegro was the main actor in the Balkan affairs and "solver" of the Eastern Question, but rather to present its highly important role in the Macedonian Question and Balkan affairs in general; Stefoska, *Fragments from the Medieval History*, p. 69; Glas Crnogorca (No 45), Cetinje, 25 October, 1903; Michael Palairet, *The Balkan Economies c. 1800–1914 – Evolution without Development* (Cambridge: Cambridge University Press, 2003), p. 342; František Šistek, "Pan–Serb Golden Age and Montenegrin Heroic Age: Reconstructing History and Identity Narratives in Montenegro, 1905–1914," in *New Imagined Communities*, eds. Libusa Vajdova and Robert Gafrik (Bratislava: Kalligram, 2010), p. 191.

impact."[475] As has been discussed, the relationship between the Balkans and Western Europe can be investigated as a substitution of an "imaginary" colonialism: accepting ideas of the West in order to define and create one's own colonial space. For Montenegro, the Macedonian lands were important in the legitimation of Montenegro's invented tradition of the "Montenegrins as the best or purest Serbs," who survived the decline of the Serbian Empire ("Dušanovo carstvo") and the battle of Kosovo. [476] This argumentation was based on the narrative that the Ottomans never truly conquered Montenegro and that the dynasty of Petrović played a historic part in safeguarding Serbdom ("Srpstvo"), especially after the Ottoman conquest of Prizren and Skopje.[477] The state ideology sought to affirm the "historical merit" of Montenegrin state aspirations for supremacy in the Serbian national liberation movement. This Montenegrin "primacy" was based on the invented tradition that Zeta was now the "cradle of Serbdom" and the historical core of Dušan's Serbian Empire, which was situated in Macedonia and Kosovo/Old Serbia. It posited that the Montenegro had a historic role as the centre of the Serbian nation and Serbian statehood. In one of his speeches, Prince Nikola's advisor, Jovan Popović Lipovac, declared that it was not by coincidence that Zeta [present–day Montenegro] was the political centre of the Serbian Empire, adding: "Zeta was to the Serbian nation as the Moscow principality was to Russia, Piedmont to Italy, and Prussia to Germany. It was precisely Zeta that gave rise and birth to the most important Serbian people, including the Nemanjić dynasty, which originated from Ribnica [a part of Podgorica, Montenegro]. After the Battle of Kosovo, when the Ottomans conquered the Serbian Empire, inhabitants of Zeta protected Serbdom until our present day."[478] In this regard, the cities of Prizren and Skopje, which were still part of the Ottoman Empire in the late 19th and early 20th centuries, had historical symbolism for Montenegro, as it aspired to liberate them from the

---

[475] Todorova, *Imagining*, p. 167; According to Maria Todorova, "the national was imposed as the hegemonic paradigm in Europe, as the gold standard of 'civilised' political organisation, the imperial or any other alternative could be viable."
[476] Andrijašević, *Srpstvo u Crnoj Gori.*
[477] Ibid.
[478] Ibid.

"uncivilised Ottomans." It is no coincidence that the popular anthem of Montenegro (which Prince Nikola referred to as a "military anthem"),[479] also known as the Serbian Marseillaise, was *Onamo, namo!*" or "There, over there." The use of the phrase "There, over there! "in the anthem demonstrated a clear rejection of Ottoman rule and represented the desire to liberate and reclaim the territories "there, over there" that were still under Ottoman control.

"Onamo, 'namo... da viđu Prizren!	There, over there... I see Prizren!
Tato je moje – domaću doć'!	It is all mine – home I shall come!
Starina mila tamo me zove,	Beloved antiquity beckons me there,
Tu moram jednom oružan poć'.	Armed I must come there one day.
(…)	
Onamo, 'namo... za brda ona	There, over there beyond those hills,
Kazuju da je zeleni gaj	Lies a green grove, they say,
Pod kim se dižu Dečani sveti:	Under which rises Holy Dečani:
molitva u njih prisvaja raj.	A prayer said within Paradise claims.
Onamo, 'namo... za brda ona,	There, over there beyond those hills,
Gde nebo plavo savija svod;	Where a sky of blue bends its arch;
Na srpska polja, na polja bojna	On to Serb fields, on to battle fields,
onamo, braćo, spremajmo hod!	There, brothers, prepare to march!
(…)	
Onamo, 'namo... za brda ona	There, over there beyond those hills,
Milošev, kažu, prebiva grob!	Lies there, they say, Miloš's grave!
Onamo pokoj dobiću duši,	There my soul eternal peace shall
Kad Srbin više nebude rob."	gain, When (the) Serb is no more slave.

The inclusion of these lyrics in the anthem reflected Montenegro's ambition to incorporate Ottoman Macedonia, specifically Kosovo vilayet, into its envisioned state. In this anthem, particular importance was given

---

[479] Kralj Nikola Petrović, *Memoari* (Cetinje: Obod, 1988); On the national coding of Montenegrins through the epic see: Aleksandar Pavlović, *Epika i politika: Nacionalizovanje crnogorske usmene tradicije u prvoj polovini XIX veka* (Beograd: Biblioteka XX vek, 2014).

to the cities in Kosovo vilayet such as Prizren, Dečani, and their "liberation from the Turks." This historical symbolism attached to Prizren and "holy Dečani" for Montenegro should not be understated, since the anthem and many other aforementioned documents represented the desire of Montenegrin state to free these territories from Ottoman rule and expand state boundaries. Nevertheless, the inclusion of lyrics in the national anthem referencing these cities reflects the aspirations and imagination of a new state seeking to assert its expansion toward "East," defining in this case a Montenegrin "Orient." This desire for territorial expansion was a testament to the fervent nationalism that prevailed during that era, common not only for Montenegro, but for the other Balkan states and Great Powers. As years later King Nikola would state, this anthem became the "dream" of his youth which "should come true."[480] Not only did the cities of Prizren and Dečani rose to prominence, but so did Miloš, alluded to in the phrase "Miloš's grave," who assassinated the Ottoman Sultan Murat. Accordingly, Montenegro should rise as the new "Miloš" and liberate all Serbs from the "Ottoman Yoke" in the form that "(the) Serb not to be a slave anymore." However, in order to realise this dream, King Nikola made multiple attempts at alliances with Balkan states and at liberating Ottoman Macedonia from the "big Asiatic Mongol." Another contributing factor in defining the Montenegrin *Lebensraum* was that Montenegro was blocked from expanding into Herzegovina and Sanjak by the Austrian army. Thus, Nikola's government was impelled towards continued imperialism towards the east, designing its own expansionist strategy of the *Drang–nach–Osten* type. He intended to carve a Greater Montenegrin or a united, South–Slavic state from the territories of Ottoman Albania and Ottoman Macedonia, with a seat in Prizren.[481] It is beyond doubt that the Montenegrin Prince was interested in the Scutari Vilayeti (which was not part of *vilayet–i selase*), considering Shkodra/Skadar the first capital of Duklja. However, Prince Nikola also considered the parts of Manastir and Kosova Vilayeti as the future Greater Montenegrin or united South–Slavic state. In a letter from 27 August 1896, Prince Nikola wrote to Prince Ferdinand of Bulgaria that the "Macedonians should leave the Sultan in

---

[480] Glas Crnogorca, No. 42, Cetinje, 26. September, 1912.
[481] Palairet, *The Balkan economies*, p. 214; DACG/Cetinje, OuPlj, 1912–1915/F16, #1, No. 403, 1912.

peace [*ostaviti na miru*], because the moment [would] come to leave these provinces [the three vilayets], inhabited by Slavs, to the three of us: Bulgarians, Serbians (*Srbijancima*), and Montenegrins."[482]

In December 1896, another 'solution' was presented by Prince Nikola to the Italian Ambassador to Cetinje, Mr. Bianchi, in the form of an expansionistic plan towards Ottoman Albania and parts of Ottoman Macedonia. Nikola Petrović claimed that the Montenegrin borders were under threat from the Austro–Hungarian Empire in the West, and therefore Montenegro should expand its territories in the south–east towards Iskodra and Vilayet–i Selase. According to this plan, Montenegro was to occupy almost all of the northern part of Albania and parts of the Manastir and Kosovo Vilayets, from the river Shkumbin/Işkomi river, through lake Ohrid and extending between Skopje and Prizren to Kaçanik, then upwards along the railway of Kosovska Mitrovica, where it would finish along the Ibar River to the Austrian border in the Sanjak of Novi Pazar. According to this plan, Italy would annex southern Albania, while some parts of the Janina Vilayet would belong to Greece. [483] This expansionist policy, inspired by European imperialist strategies, was based on the Montenegrin imagination of Macedonia as part of a Slavic mental map that was to be shared among the Slavic brothers (Bulgarians, Serbians, and Montenegrins) or to be included in a single state of South Slavs. Thus, in a letter from 1902, Prince Nikola wrote to the Serbian king Alexander Obrenović that "Austria [would] never arrive in Thessaloniki – not before us! Before us Serbs, and Bulgars, Austria [would] never take a position in Macedonia." He added that "thanks to Russia, the 'Macedonian pie' (*pogaču Makedonije*) [would] be shared among us and the Bulgarians so

---

[482] Kralj Nikola Petrović, *Pisma* (Podgorica: Cetinje Sveti Gora, 2009), p. 278; To the prince of Bulgaria Ferdinand on 27. Avgust 1896. from Cetinje: *"Reci, dakle, Makedoncima da ga ostave na miru, jer ko zna jednog dana da on ne bi mogao doći na pomisao da ustupi ovu provinciju (Makedoniju), naseljenu Slovenima, nama trojici: Bugarima, Srbijancima i Crnogorcima i da nam reče: podijelite je đeco moja, među vama kao braća i prijatelji."*; DACG/Cetinje, MID, 1896/F532, #4911, 26.06.1896.

[483] Gligor Stanojević, "Prilozi za diplomatsku istoriju Crne Gore od Berlinskog kongresa do kraja XIX vijeka," *Istorijski časopis* 11 (1961): 171–172; in a Rapport from Italian Ambassador to Montenegro on 8. December 1896: "I documenti diplomatic italiani, terzaserie vol. I," published in Roma, 1953, pp. 218–219.

that all [would] be satisfied." [484] This mental map, which imagined Macedonia as part of a Slavic state, was supported by the power of media in order to create a "new" mentality across the society, too. Therefore, during the Macedonian crisis of 1903, Macedonia was often presented as a "Macedonian–Serb Question" (*makedonsko–srpsko pitanje*).[485]

In one article, "The Macedonian and Old Serbian Problem" (*maćedonski i starosrbijanski problem*), *Glas Crnogorca* reported that the "population of the three vilayets [Macedonia and Old Serbia] [was] around three million and in all (three) vilayets the majority [were] Slavs (Serbs and Bulgarians)."[486] However, the border among these two Slavic tribes cannot be precisely drawn.[487] In order to legitimise the action that would liberate the Slavs in Macedonia, Nikola and his Petrović ancestors revealed the mediaeval events (the Battle of Kosovo) and mediaeval personalities (Marko Kraljević of Prilep/Macedonia, Miloš Obilić of Kosovo, etc.).[488] In general, Nikola Petrović wished to solve the Eastern and "Macedonian–Serb Questions", to lead a general uprising against the Ottomans in the Balkans and to rebuild the Greater Serb or broader South–Slavic state, led by the Petrović dynasty, which had "the longest tradition of independent government among the South Slavs."[489] Therefore, in one of his interviews for *Neue Freie Presse* (20 May 1883), he revealed: "I belong to a family that was in power when the Karađorđević and Obrenović were *rayahs* (Christian subjects of the Sultan) in the Ottoman Serbian vilayet!"[490] To achieve aspirations beyond the borders of old Montenegro/Crna Gora, Brda, and partly Herzegovina, king Nikola recognised the importance of employing rhetorical strategies rooted in romanticism and Pan-Slavism. He understood the significance of Njegoš's reputation and popularity among the South Slavs, as well as the construction of the national myth

---

[484] Nikola Petrović, *Pisma*, pp. 318–320; to the king of Serbia Aleksandar Obrenović in 1902: *"Rusija bi pogaču Makedonije lijepo među nama i Bugara podijelila na zadovoljstvo obojice."*

[485] Glas Crnogorca, No. 9, Cetinje, 22. February, 1903.

[486] Glas Crnogorca, No. 15, Cetinje, 4. April, 1903.

[487] Glas Crnogorca, No. 18, Cetinje, 26. April, 1903.

[488] Kilibarda, *Usmena književnost Crne Gore.*

[489] Boban Batričević, "Recepcija Petra II Petrovića u ideologijama crnogorskih vlasti," *Arhivski zapisi* 22/1 (2016): 84.

[490] Rotković, *Lažna Sablja kralja Milutina.*

depicting the "Montenegrins as the best/purest Serbs." By emphasising this narrative, he sought to establish the legitimacy required to unite all Serbian lands.[491] These strategies allowed him to assert his familial and historical connections, enhance his legitimacy, and mobilise support for their ambitions. In the arguments presented here, Jovan Plamenac, the Minister of Internal Affairs and Representative of the Minister of Education of Montenegro, during the crucial time of the Balkan Wars (1912–13), shared several ideas about Serbdom with the Ambassador of Serbia to Montenegro, Dr. Mihajlo Gavrilović, by putting forward the idea of "greater Serbia" with the aim of "establishing the greater Serbian Kingdom," because "we (Serbs and Montenegrins) are one people (…) striving towards a general Serb policy."[492] These Montenegrin narratives and imperialist ambitions attracted attention from the Ottoman media and authorities. Ottoman documents frequently highlighted the "Serb element" present in the three vilayets, as well as the closely monitored "Montenegrin request regarding these territories." [493] Among these requests was Montenegro's endorsement of Macedonian autonomy, along with Prince Nikola's desire to appoint his son Mirko as the General Governor (*d'introduire en Macédoine une administration autonome avec le Prince Mirko de Monténégro comme Gouverneur Général*).[494] The Ottoman

---

[491] Andrijašević, *Srpstvo u Crnoj Gori.*

[492] DASIP, MIDS, PO, 31.VIII/13.IX.1912, F–IV, D–2; Quote: *"Ovde Plamenac pada u vatru – on u opšte govori – i stade na dugačko govoriti o Karađorđu, Milošu, vladici Danilu itd., o velikoj Srbiji, o besmislici da Srbija i Crna Gora ovako životare; treba ići napred, hrabro, stvoriti jednu veliku srpsku kraljevinu i ne gledati kako se srpski živalj izvan granica Srbije i Crne Gore gubi i odrođava."* (...) *"kakve dinastije, kakve deobe sfera i interesa, nama treba jedna srpska država kao što smo jedan narod, narod je glavno, on će ostati, a kape može menjati! (...) Mi nećemo dinastičku i separatističku politiku, mi hoćemo opštu srpsku."*

[493] Rumeli Müfettişliği, Umum Evrâkı, TFR.1.UM 13/1212,11.03.1324; See in original: *"Sırp unsurunu çok göstermek maksadıyla Vilâyet-i Selâse dahilindeki Sırp mekteplerine Karadağ'dan bir takım talebelerin getirildiği istihbarat üzerine yapılan tahkikata dair."*

[494] Sinan Kuneralp and Gül Tokay, *Ottoman Diplomatic Documents of the Origins of World War One IV, The Macedonian Issue 1879–1912* (Istanbul: The Isis Press, 2011), p. 163; In a document: Ahmet Tevfik Pacha a Tevfik Pacha, Berlin, le 31 aout 1906. In original: *"Ayant lu d'une part dans les journaux d'hier que l'Angleterre avait proposé – âux Puissances d'introduire en Macédoine une administration autonome avec le Prince Mirko de Monténégro comme Gouverneur Général, que la France et l'aile auraient appuyé cette proposition et que l'Allemagne, l'Autriche– Hcrigrie et la Russie n'auraient*

media reported as well that Montenegro was very interested in the three vilayets, known as Macedonia, and had support from Imperial Russia and the British Empire. In the Ottoman newspaper *Balkan*, published in Plovdiv (Filibe), article entitled "Montenegro and Macedonian Principality" (*Karadağ ve Makedonya prensliği*) was published, which emphasised the Montenegrin interest in the three vilayets and the potential appointment of a Montenegrin prince (Mirko), which was already opposed by the Dual Monarchy.[495] In subsequent reports, the Ottoman newspaper *Balkan* stated that "Macedonia was an egg actively rolled around by political games (*desise–i siyasiye*)."[496] Accordingly, this "egg" was

---

pas encore exprimé à ce sujet leur opinion et de l'autre, que d'après le Neuer Wiener Tagblatt, le Prince de Bulgarie aurait fait sonder confidentiellement le Cabinet russe afin de savoir quelle attitude la Russie prendrait si la Bulgarie serait déclarée royaume – et que le Gouvernement russe aurait répondu qu'un tel changement lui serait indifférent, j'ai demandé au Ministre des Affaires Étrangères des renseignements sur ces deux points. Il m'a répondu qu'il n'en savait absolument rien mais qu'il se fera renseigner sur ces nouvelles. Vu l'état actuel des événements, j'ai cru pourtant utile de les signaler à l'attention de Votre Excellence."

[495] Newspaper: Balkan, No. 30, Filibe (Plovdiv), 4. September 1906; In a newspaper text: *"Karadağ ve Makedonya Prensliği Rumeli vilâyet–i şahânesinde mevkî'i tatbîke konan [...] ıslâhat programını gayr–i kafî add edüb vilâyet–i selâse–i mezkûreye muhtariyet–i idâre verilmesini iddi'â eden İngiltere, Rusya ve Avusturya kabinelerine Makedonya'ya ta'yin edilecek valinin Karadağ prensi intihâb edilmesini teklif etmişse de Avusturya hükümeti [..] ıslâhat programının Makedonya'da istalahat–ı idârîyeyi te'mine kâfî olduğu iddi'âsıyla bu teklifi şiddetle red etmekdedir. İngiltere'nin bu hesabca niyeti, bir 'Karadağ ve Makedonya Prensliği' teşkîl etmek olacak ki harita–i siyâsetde henüz böyle bir safha görülmüyordu. Bakalım mes'ele daha ne kalıblara girecek."*; See also: DACG/Cetinje, MUD, F6, 62, #1337 01.09.1906.

[496] Balkan, No. 31, Filibe, 5. September 1906; In original: *"Makedonya Yumurtasi Bakalim Ne Yumurtlayacak? Dünki Veçernepoşte'de görülen mizah resmi şâyân–ı dikkatdi. İngiltere kıralıyla fehâmetlü prens hazretlerini bu resimde konuşduruyor iken prens hazretlerini bir yumurta üzerinde oturdup diyor ki bakalım bu yumurtadan ne çıkacak? Ya'ni demek istiyor ki Makedonya bir yumurdadır. İngiltere'nin Karadağ prensini oraya vâli ta'yin itdirüb muhtâriyet–i idâre taleb itmesi bir desîse–i siyâsîyedir. Bu desîse–i siyâsîye şimdi yumurta içinde bir tohum gibidir. Bundan bir horos çıkacak ki o da fehâmetlü prens hazretlerinin an garîb tecellî idecek olan teşebbüsât–ı siyâsîyedir."* See also: Balkan, No. 33, Filibe, 7. September, 1906.: *"Makedonya'nin Muhtariyeti Hakkinda Atina'da müteşekkil Makedonya komitesinin reisi doktor Yerveyanis etdiği telgrafnâmeyi "Tan" gazetesine keşîde etmişdir. Avrupa matbû'âtının işâatına göre İngiltere'nin teklifi üzerine Karadağ prenslerinden Mirko Makedonya vâli–i umûmîliğine ta'yin olunacakmış. Biz, Makedonyalıların ahassı âmâlî Makedonya'yı mâder–i vatanımız olan Yunanistan'a ilhâk etmek olduğundan ecnebî bir prensin mukaddes toprağa ayak basmasına aslâ muvâfakat edemiyeceğimizi şedîden beyân eyleriz. Yıldız Sarayının*

involved in the playground among different actors, which I identified as the Great Powers and regional Balkan states. Several reports show that Montenegro was actively involved into diplomatic negotiations with various state actors, but also with the Macedonian local population on the ground.[497] During the years of frequent uprisings of Albanian speaking population (often joined by the local Slavic–speaking neighbours), especially in the Kosovo vilayet, Montenegro actively supported local Albanian notables with arms and weapons, and became a safe haven for Isa Boljetini, Hasan Ferri (Ferović), and a handful of other local personalities.[498]

As I have previously emphasized, it is essential to examine the intricacies between state and non–state actors across multiple layers in order to gain a comprehensive understanding of the dynamics at play. By analysing these complexities from local, regional, and global perspectives, we can gain valuable insights into the interactions and relationships between various actors involved. Through this multidimensional approach, we can uncover the nuanced dynamics that shaped the events and developments under consideration. It allows us to go beyond a simplistic analysis and delve into the deeper complexities of the interactions, influences, and power dynamics that unfolded at different levels. In this regard, the Montenegrin policy is just one of the instances that puzzles the broader picture of the Macedonian Questions and the Montenegrin "small–state

---

erkânı veliahd–ı saltanat Mehmed Reşad Efendi hazretlerinin vücüdunu mahva çalışıyorlarmış. Saray erkânı gelecek pâdişâhın kânûn–u esâsî tarafdârı olduğundan korkuyorlar! Erkânı arasında Burhâneddin Efendinin saltanata getirilmesinde en ziyâde ileri giden ve hap dâimâ bu gibi rolleri oynalan Hülü paşazade Şamî İzzet Paşadır. Almanya imparatorunun da bu mes'elede tarafdârlığı istişmam olunuyorsa da İngiltere ve Rusya buna kat'iyen muhâlefet etmekdedir. İngiltere kralı Yedinci Edvard ile Almanya imparatoru Vilhem hazretleri son mülâkâtlarında buna dâir arîz ve amîk konuşmuşlar."; DACG/Cetinje, MID, 1906/F133, #4161, 06.09.1906.

[497] HHStA PA XIV/Kt. 33, f. 25r–29r; Quote: *"Waffenschmuggel aus Montenegro. Albanisches Zweckbündnis mit Montenegro."*

[498] HHStA PA XIV/Kt. 40, f. 23r–24v; Mitrovitza am 1. Juli, 1912; In original: *"Rolle Isa Boletinis bei der Organisation des Aufstands. Albanerversammlung in Drenica unter den früheren Abgeordneten Hasan Prishtina und Zejnullah Bey. Versorgung der Aufständischen mit Waffen aus Serbien und Montenegro. Aktionen der Aufständischen gegen osmanische Steuerverwaltung und Gendarmerie. Weitgehender Boykott einer vom Vali einberufenen Versammlung der Dorfältesten aus Shala, Lab und Drenica. Vorgehen osmanischer Truppen gegen Isa Boletini."*

imperialism" is just an offshoot of the broader global imperialism. At this point, it is worthy to note that Montenegrin media also reported on the importance of Montenegro for the liberation of Slav–speaking Christians from the "Ottoman yoke" and supported the practices of imperialism. Thus, king Nikola's proclamation to the Montenegrins before the beginning of the First Balkan war, contained elements of an expansionist policy, combined with Montenegrin–Serb glory, and their duty to fight in Old Serbia and Macedonia. In a proclamation of Prince Nikola, Montenegro was described as a state whose "cries [were] coming from its oppressed brothers who live[d] in Old Serbia [and Macedonia]. There [was] merciless slaughtering of not only men, but also women and young Serb children, which [could] not be tolerated anymore. (…) Therefore, the duty of the Montenegrins was always to fight for the brothers of the Serb tribe and for Slavdom in general."[499] In this proclamation, Prince Nikola further asserted that, "in this battle we [would] fight with our brothers from Serbia" against the "cruel Turks (*turaka grdnih zulumćara*)." At the end of the proclamation, King Nikola Petrović stated that his "dream from his early youth [was] coming true. [He] predicted this day, and [his] anthem 'There, over there!' (*Onamo, namo*) instilled faith in Serbian hearts so that they would cross over those hills! Montenegrins lived! Long live the Balkan League!"[500] This dream escalated into the First Balkan War declared firstly by Montenegro, which soon turned into the Second Balkan War, and "bloodshed of brothers from Danube to Thessaloniki"[501] in order to "protect the Serbian heritage/achievement in Macedonia" (*srpske tekovine u Maćedoniji*).[502] In the Second Balkan War, the Montenegrin troops participated actively in Ottoman Macedonia, where Dečani division (*Dečanski odred*)[503] was established by king Nikola Petrović of Montenegro, which defeated the Bulgarian army near the Battle of Bregalnica.[504] Thus, the Balkan Wars were just one of the consequences of the global state imperialism, that was reflect among the Balkan states as

---

[499] Glas Crnogorca, No. 42, Cetinje, 26. September, 1912.
[500] Ibid.
[501] Glas Crnogorca, No. 28, Cetinje, 27. June, 1913
[502] Glas Crnogorca, No. 52, Cetinje, 9. November, 1913.
[503] Jevto A. Ružić, *Skadar i Bregalnica: Crna Gora u ratovima 1912–1918 godine* (Munich: Štamparija Iskra, 1964).
[504] Ibid.

the "small–state imperialism." The outbreak of war was the culmination of chains of decisions made by the Balkan states, who already have defined their space of expansion according to their invented traditions that overlapped in Ottoman Macedonia.

5.5. Conclusion

Here I traced the practices of the local and state agents during the period from the Young Turk Revolution (1908) to the First Balkan War (1912). In this chapter I adopted both a 'bottom–up' and 'top–down' perspective and I placed them within trans–regional dynamics by demonstrating how they influenced each other. To understand more comprehensively how these local, national, regional, and likely international practices of the "struggle for Macedonia" related to one another, I focused on the multiple arenas in which local, national, and regional actors engaged and interacted, built alliances but also perpetrated violence and bloodshed. As part of it, I showed how the locals were influential in changing the state strategies and projects, but also how the states transformed the region by applying "small state imperialism." As such, I presented several examples of Albanian– and Turkish–speaking locals (e.g. Ahmet Niyazi Bey, Enver Bey, Ohrili Eyüp Sabri) in the three vilayets and the importance of the Ferzovik meeting (Kosovo vilayet) in triggering the Young Turk Revolution from the ground inside the bottom up perspective. These events represent the significance of the 'periphery' and its influence on the 'centre' by changing the government in 1908 and dethroning Sultan Abdulhamid II in 1909. To borrow Chakrabarty's famous term "provincialising," I hold that these events of 1908 should be analysed as "provincialising Istanbul." In fact, I aimed here to show that the 'periphery' can be active too and its peripheral populations were not bereft of agency. In this regard, this chapter highlighted that Albanian–speaking population was playing a very important role and that the 'Albanian element' in the Macedonian Questions should be subject to closer inspection and important analysis. Especially, after the Macedonian–Albanian conflict in 2001 in North Macedonia, it was proved that the Albanian–speaking population play an important role in the region and their perspective(s) should be included. Apart from it, I also included the Montenegrin role in the Macedonian affairs. This actor was hitherto completely excluded from studies regarding the Macedonian Question. Through several examples, I emphasised that Montenegro and Albanian–speaking population played far more important roles than scholars have argued. In this respect, I took a closer look at the Kosovo vilayet, which was an integral part of *vilayeti selase*.

The uprisings throughout the region between 1909 and 1912 have shown that the potential for the creation of autonomous Albania, as promised by the Ottoman government in August 1912, triggered Montenegro (and other Balkan states) to declare war on the Ottomans. Thus, the 'Albanian element' on the ground, together with the state policies formulated by Montenegro and Balkan states during the year 1912 are very important in understanding complexities and dynamics from one side, and the causes and consequences of the Balkan Wars from other side.

Conclusion

The overall objective of this dissertation was to map and explore the role of contentious state policies and imaginations in and of Ottoman Macedonia during the period of the Age of Empire, and to situate my findings within the larger trans–regional space by arguing that there has not been one uniform Macedonian Question as a whole, but rather several questions conceived variously at the local, regional, trans–national, and international levels. Since various levels and many actors (Great powers, Balkan states, Ottoman Empire, and locals) were involved, I argued that one could not speak about one unified question, but rather more about the multifarious dimensions of the questions in all their interlocking complexity. On the one hand, if one were to follow the findings and realise (as has been shown) that Macedonia as a geographic space actually did not have clearly defined borders, and that various actors differently imagined this space, then this could be a reasonable argument to consider the Macedonian Question as a whole, since it was part of a spatial contestation. On the other, Macedonia as an imagined geography rather looked like a mass of multi–layered questions such as spatial, social, economic and material, and scholarly questions that proliferated during the 19th and early 20th centuries. In other words, this Macedonian Question was folded into 'larger' ones, like the Eastern Question, Pan–Slavic, nationality, and social questions, even as they competed for attention with countless 'smaller' ones, like the Albanian, Serbian, Bulgarian, Greek, or Vlach community questions. On the whole, however, these questions have been treated separately and not as a part of various complexities combining 'top–down' and 'bottom–up' approaches, integrating them in a larger trans–regional space and multiple perspectives. Inside one and the same community or even among the state politicians or intellectuals of the same national elite, could be a circulation of different views on these questions. It would be misleading if one would consider these actors as part of one unified national(ist) program who employed a uniform policy toward the Macedonian Questions. However, they all had something in common: they formulated these questions as the "definitive" or "final solution." This search for a "final solution" during the 19th century strove to "solve" these questions inside the nationalist projects and their various constructed imaginaries suggested by statesmen and intellectuals. These actors viewed problems as if they had been math equations, having only one possible solution, once and for all. It was mostly around conflicts and inflicted violence in social and political upheaval that these questions were most hotly debated, and then European intellectuals together with regional intellectuals hoped for expedient solutions. As Christopher Hitchens noted, "once one has defined a people or nation" as a "question" demanding a "solution," that people or nation has been turned into a problem. However, in the context of the Macedonian Question(s) these multi–faceted agents had often their own "final solution(s)" that differed from each other (international, regional, or local actors). Moreover, not everyone had the same "final solution," because each particular solution was proposed so as to serve a political purpose and often a personal gain that differed from that of another actor. In this respect, for some the Macedonian Question(s) was/were a problem of the Muslim presence in Europe, for others it was the Imperial Russian expansion, and for others still it was a regional problem in the form of "the Balkans for the Balkanians" or "Macedonia for the Macedonians," and thus implied another "final solution."

At other times, a question might seem to recede or even disappear during a certain period. In this regard, it is very important to follow its dynamics from different viewpoints and to consider the Macedonian as multi–layered questions that were not developed in a vacuum, but rather overlapped significantly with other questions of the time (social, national, agrarian, material and economic, or spatial etc.). What Holly Case called the "age of questions" began in the 1820s and 1830s as a result of the expansion and politicisation of press distribution, the enlargement of the voting franchise (in Britain), and a "tight series of international events." In this respect, Case posits that "these three developments gave rise to an international public sphere, the habitat in which questions thrived and proliferated." At that time, as has been seen in the second chapter, the European states began to explore the Ottoman territories, especially the Greek heritage, while European Philhellenes included these parts (Greece, Macedonia, other parts of the Balkans) as the source of their ancient civilisation. When the Greek Uprising in the Ottoman Empire (1821– 1832) broke out, the European public attention to the Macedonian Questions was already becoming apparent, especially by means of the calls of the European intellectuals to intervene in the Ottoman Empire on behalf of the Greeks. These calls were often based on political and personal interests as parts of the European colonial projects "to chase the Turks out of Europe once and for all." During the beginning of the 19th century, around Europe was developed an interest in classical antiquity, discovery, and imagination of "the ancient world through the lives of the contemporary inhabitants," which increased the awareness of the then Greeks and their "questions." This "ancient world," seen by the Great Powers as a "cradle of European civilisation," instigated the European actors to intervene on behalf of the "Greek cause." One of these Philhellenes, François–René de Chateaubriand, wrote about the "civilised" Christian Greeks that were under the yoke of "barbarity and Mahometanism." In his book *Note sur la Grece* (1825), he justified the intervention by arguing that the Greeks, a Christian people (*"comme les peoples chretiens"*), were usurped by the Turks, who did not observe the European laws (*"ne reconnoit point le droit politique de l'Europe"*), but were ruling according to their Asiatic customs (*"se gouverned' apres le code des peoples de l'Asie"*). In this respect, this small "civilised" group of people needed European assistance against "the fiery zeal and bigoted enthusiasm of the followers of Islam."

This delivery of "civilised" ideas – for Slavs, Catholics, Jews, Serbs, Bulgarians, and Greeks – transformed the Macedonian Questions into a European one or what Dostoevsky, writing in 1877, called a "world question." I showed that not only did the Macedonian Questions concern the East of Europe, or the Slavs, Russians, and the Turks, or, specifically, the Serbians, Bulgarians, Greeks, Macedonians or Albanians, but that it also concerned the whole of the West of Europe. I furthermore argued that by no means did it only concern the European intellectuals in relation to access to the seas and the Bosporus strait, but that rather it reached much deeper, was more fundamental: it was the "cradle of European civilisation." Furthermore, since these Ottoman parts were very important for European politics, the Macedonian Questions should also be studied as a globalised "problem." In this respect, in his "Pan–Europe," Coudenhove-–Kalergi argued along similar lines that "today the European Question signifies to the world what for more than a century the Balkan Question signified to Europe." With this claim, Coudenhove–Kalergi considered the

Balkan Question, or in other words the "Macedonian Question," as a European problem, and thus, "not merely of local but of international import." In fact, Macedonia was a "world problem" within globalised "question(s)" that included an active presence of international actors. In this small corner of the world, the international actors sometimes imagined "the Greeks a little too magnificent and the Turks a little too Tatar," yet at other times as a "majority Slavic speaking land." By the 1850s, the fickleness of public attention to the Greek Question was already disappearing and was soon extended to "the Slavs and other ethnic groups inhabiting the peninsula." Accordingly, Henri Thieres in his book *La Serbie: Son Passé et Son Avenir* (1862) pointed out that "Bosniaks and Bulgarians [were] of the same race (*sont de meme race*) as the Montenegrins and Serb" and that they "[would] form a Slavic empire that Europe [would] allow them to exist." Through the transfer of knowledge these ideas were circulating, were discussed among intellectuals, imagined, and projected into a "final solution." What is more, these actors often applied their strategies toward the Ottomans based on a "civilised" Europe versus a "barbarian" Orient.

This discourse and production of knowledge circulated around South–Eastern Europe, where the intellectuals accepted these ideas. Although "these are false dichotomies," this discourse founded a common frame in "the question idiom." As has been argued in the second chapter, the intellectuals in the Balkans also accepted these discourses due to the "colonisation of the mind," which was reflected in the form of "nesting Orientalism." This self–imagination among the Balkan intellectuals also constructed a "big Asiatic Mongol" that was an embodiment of the Ottoman Empire. This tendency to essentialise Self as "superior" and "civilised" had a political framework to construct the oriental Other as "backward" and "barbarian." For many intellectuals among the emerging Balkan nations, their *mission civilisatrice* at the turn of the 20th century was to apply these political programs into restoring the "European civilisation [back] to its roots." These political programs, developed in *Načertanije* and *Megali Idea* (or other programs elsewhere) envisioned Macedonia as 'liberated' from "the Ottoman/Turkish yoke" and imagined this space as part of their either ancient heritage (Hellen and Illyrian) or medieval empires (Serbian and Bulgarian).

These "emancipationist drives" in the Balkans were anti–imperial in order to create new empires by putting their "small–state imperialism" into practice. As I elaborated in the third chapter, these politicians and intellectuals or "political entrepreneurs" commonly viewed violence as a legitimate solution to the questions of this period. In fact, the Macedonian Questions offered a powerful example where the Balkan nations tried to "solve" the "Macedonian Question" by resorting to violence in order to liberate the people of Macedonia from the "Turkish yoke." In the third chapter, I demonstrated that, in the period of 1878–1903, education and the schools became the central battleground for competing the Balkan states' competitions in "small–state imperialism". Much like their counterparts elsewhere – the British, German, Italian, Austro–Hungarian, Russian, or even the Ottoman state – the Balkan countries applied imperialist strategies. Due to *millet system* of the Ottoman Empire, they were able to instrumentalise the foundation of the schools for imperialist purposes. From the very beginning, these schools in Ottoman Macedonia (together with the churches) were meant to monitor, supervise, and manipulate local populations in those ways that were best suited to support the Balkan "small–state" imperial ambitions long–term. These ambitions, however, were not new, because they were rather stemming from the *Zeitgeist* that was typical of the whole globalised world. As much as questions were globalised, the "final solution(s)" was/were also entangled in these "world" problems. Much like the Congress of Berlin (1878) that ended with the establishment of new Balkan states (Serbia, Montenegro, Romania, and semi–independent Bulgaria) and with the introduction of necessities for reforms in the Ottoman territories that became known as Macedonia, the Berlin Conference of 1884 and 1885 marked the climax of the European competition for territory in Africa, a process commonly known as the "scramble for Africa." Within a few years, Berlin became a cornerstone for the development of imperialist policies: during the first instance, in 1878, it became a base for the "small–state imperialism" of the Balkan states, while during the second instance, in 1884 and 1885, it became a core for the European global imperialism. At the Berlin Conference, the European states negotiated and formalised their claims to territories in Africa that included several invasions, occupations, divisions, and colonisation of most of its territories, a set of processes known to historians as the "New Imperialism." Throughout this "Age of Empire," the Western schooling during the colonisation of Africa was initiated by variety of European missionary organisations which had entered Africa to proselytise the natives and "envisioned themselves as bringing a higher view of life to benighted savages." At the very beginning, these missionaries did not hope to educate the local population, but rather to convert them. In ways similar to the Western educational institutions in Africa, especially with respect to the conversion and definition in school curricula of "what counts as valid knowledge," the Balkan states tried to police "valid knowledge" for the local population in Ottoman Macedonia in order to "convert" them into Serbs, Greeks, or Bulgarians. In fact, the whole history of colonial schooling is marked by the contestation between state and rival political groups with separate and conflicting vested interests, phenomenon that John Anderson calls "the struggle for the school." In the third chapter I highlighted how this "struggle for the school" was brought to the "scramble for Macedonia," which among the Balkan states was known as "the struggle for Macedonia." This was a battleground for the Balkan state authorities, their political entrepreneurs and specialists in violence over particular groups within the indigenous peoples in Ottoman Macedonia.

I argued that Bulgaria was especially important in creating a new range of possibilities for the indigenous population through the establishment of the Bulgarian Exarchate (1870) and the Bulgarian Men's High School of Thessaloniki (1880), which transformed the politics in Ottoman Macedonia as well as, ultimately, the way in which state personnel viewed education and schools as one of the instruments of state power. Juxtaposed to the long assumed "right" of the Patriarchate of Istanbul as Representative of the Orthodox Christians (*Rum*) in the Ottoman empire, a new set of tensions developed that created opportunities for political entrepreneurs on the ground that incited the Greek and Serbian states to provoked reactions from the Greek and Serbian states. All these Balkan states founded a spate of organisations and schools (*Društvo Sveti Sava, Društvo Srbo–Makedonci, Vtreshna revolucionna organizatsia, Ethniki Etaireia* etc.) in order to inject a national consciousness and feelings about ancient Hellenism or the medieval Bulgarian and Serbian empires. What emerged at the end was a rivalry between the Balkan states that mobilised the locals by providing them with education, school system and religious programs. At that time, the *Rum* church placed in Istanbul tried to utilise its networks to create a cultural monolith that would eliminate the particularistic loyalties of the various ethnic Orthodox communities such as Albanian Tosk and Bulgarian and/or Macedonian Orthodox members in the region. However, as demonstrated in the third chapter, the heavy emphasis on "Greek," "Bulgarian," or "Serbian" school construction highlighted the dynamics of local ambitions on the ground that contradicted previous scholarly assumptions about their significance to the "ethnoreligious" school and organisation. Ironically, the tactics of the political entrepreneurs of instrumentalising state assistance and their networks to "indoctrinate" the locals with meta–national narratives, often provided an instrument for resistance to the church or state hegemonies, and turned the indigenous population into "advocates of communal rights." What is more, it was often the case that these political entrepreneurs clashed over the "indoctrination" of certain national programs or ideologies. For example, in the second half of the 1890s, the "Bulgarian" organisations proliferated and separations inside their associations had already started occurring, joined by conflicts with the Bulgarian government and Exarchate. In the Greek and Serbian examples, the controversies between the ecclesiastical and educational parts, as well as between the state and brigandage, often resulted in clashes and support of various interests. In this regard, the third and fourth chapters challenged linear transformations towards a "nationalised" rationality. Nevertheless, I argued that the projects of these governing elites and political entrepreneurs were in fact often conflicting and contested. Their imaginations, projections, and discourses did not only conflict with one another, but they also diverged from the existing national or social realities. It has already been demonstrated that the governing elites worked to build "imagined communities" based on "invented traditions," which often failed on the ground. Thus, by moving beyond the debates on nationalism and rather adopting the approach of subaltern studies, I considered several local organisations and actors.

In the fourth chapter of the thesis, I highlighted that there were not only projects and actions initiated by states and intellectuals, but also projects and moves undertaken by the general population as well. One of such organisations was IMARO (but also Chetniks, Kachaks etc.). However, I intentionally did not want to focus only on IMARO members and their activities, because I believe that the Macedonian Questions were part of much bigger complexities, than trying to reduce this trans–national problematic (Macedonian Questions) as part of only one organisation that carries Macedonian name in the title: Internal Macedonian–Adrianople Revolutionary Organisation. Thus, this study did not pay attention only one IMARO due to two reasons: firstly, this topic has been already covered by dozen studies related to the Macedonian Question, and secondly, I believe that other actors have valuable importance –such as 'Albanian element' and Montenegro– to include them in this study. In this regard, I argued that only by taking into consideration various actors as relevant participants of "multiple arenas of domination and opposition," one can set them into the trans–regional dynamics and understand their complexities. Furthermore, I emphasised that one could not understand these divergences, if done were not to take into account those local contexts and issues that determined the way state projects and their networks were received, understood, transformed, and adapted at the local level. Thus, the inclusion of the "bottom–up" perspective and the local dynamics is crucial for an understanding of these complexities, named as the Macedonian Questions. Without integrating this viewpoint in the research, we would not know that "eternal enemies," as are considered those in one of the examples of the Serbian–Albanian conflict, were much more likely to cooperate with each other and share their daily life in the streets known as *mahale*. More often than not, this was not just an administrative entity, but also a place for social networks. Its members could be Christian and Muslim, speakers of Serbian or Albanian (or any other language), connected into solidarity that was sometimes more powerful than religious affiliation.

With regard to the Serbian–Albanian context, more specifically the Kosovo vilayet (one of three Macedonian vilayets), I showed how these relations were much more complex on the ground than represented by nationalist historiographies. Thus, thinking in terms of "national" for a time when locals were still not thinking through the lenses of "national" could mislead the analysis. Rather, we studied the example of one of the active participants in the Serbian cheta in Ottoman Macedonia led by

Vojislav Tankosić, Smajo Ferović, who was an Albanian–speaking (rather bilingual) Muslim who originated from the castle guard (*dizdar*) Omeragić family from Plav (present–day Montenegro). His grandfather, Jakup Ferri, and uncle Hasan, are celebrated in contemporary Albanian historiography "heroes of the nation" (*hero i kombit*) who fought against Montenegro in 1878 for the "Albanian cause." However, Ferović took part in the Chetnik Organisation. Considering that he spoke Albanian (*dobro govorio arnautski*), he played an important role among the Albanian notables in the Kosovo vilayet, especially in relation to Isa Boletini, another venerated hero in Albanian historiography. What is more, Ferović's uncle Hasan Ferri (Ferović) was a very close friend of Isa Boletini. As an outcome of this friendship, two sisters of Smajo Ferović were married to Isa Boletini's sons. Thus, as a Serbian chetnik, Ferović established family connections with Albanian national heroes, and in addition to that, they cooperated in daily life on different levels. In other words, there were circumstances at play whose analysis cannot rely on the *clichés* that leave an ethno–national imprint, but rather should take into consideration family, kinship, and tribal connections of the actors on the ground. The demonstrable family connections of the locals did not take place in a social, cultural, or political vacuum. They operated within a set of fluid social roles and had a strong agency to even force ascendant regional state administrations to adapt to conditions they created on the ground. Oftentimes when a certain situation did not fit their personal, family, or kinship interests, their agency could change state policies and break down state networks. The fact, however, that they took various paths and quite different (often contradictory) approaches to dealing with situations on the ground speaks volumes about the complexity of individual and group "agency" in late Ottoman Macedonia, and simultaneously about the poor analytical value of looking at these events through the lens of nation and nationalism. On the other hand, I also argued that the states had influence on the lives of locals, and centres such as Sofia, Athens, Belgrade, or Istanbul could propel the locals to participate in the raids and use of violence. By the late 1880s and into the 1900s, the "liberation" from the "Ottoman/Turkish yoke" simultaneously meant violence on a breath–taking scale, as political entrepreneurs together with "specialists in violence" operated on behalf of one or the other neighbouring state. By mobilising these regional and local perspectives, this dissertation conceptualised the Macedonian Questions as the space of "multiple arenas of domination and opposition." In other words, different actors on the ground clashed with various state agendas, but also often entered negotiations between state and non–state actors. In this regard, I did not argue that different groups were defined according to their primordial ethno–national identities, but rather that those groups or the individuals within them interacted, negotiated, and fought in multiple arenas.

To understand more comprehensively how local, national, regional, and likely international practices of the "struggle for Macedonia" related to one another, the fourth and fifth (final) chapters focused on the multiple arenas in which local, national, and regional actors engaged and interacted, built up alliances but also perpetrated violence and bloodshed. Thus, the present work has illustrated that the people on the ground cannot be investigated separately from the statesmen and politicians, intellectuals and priests, tribal chiefs and their families, with whom they negotiated or conflicted in everyday life. One should also emphasise that these conflicts were not always based on "ethno–national" hatred. Rather, the brutalities in the villages of Ottoman Macedonia were often also due to economic reasons or local vendettas. This "everyday violence" is also understood as "violence that is not motivated by politics and is not exerted by the state." Eva Anne Frantz emphasises that this form of violence was often motivated by economic hardships by triggering the practices of robbery. Furthermore, this practice was indeed independent from religion, confessional or ethnical factors and was rather a tribal component. Following the Eva Anne Frantz's statement, here especially I agree that the long–assumed role of 'tribal' violence within the Ottoman Balkans proved to have important, often neglected, implications. In this respect, it is also often neglected that, in these areas, the violence was incited by tribal motives and 'honor codes' much more often than religious or ethno–national differences. In the mountainous areas of this vilayet, extended family structures were dominant and the solidarity with and membership in a certain family or tribe was crucial. In late Ottoman Macedonia, especially in the Kosovo vilayet, the Ottoman state administration was virtually absent from the mountainous regions.

In order to integrate these parts into a broader centralisation apparatus, the Ottoman state firstly borrowed the ideas of the European state practices, and secondly tried to implement them by colonisation in the form of *mission civilisatrice*. This "borrowed colonialism," defined by Selim Deringil, led the Ottoman officials to depict the provincial subjects as living in "a state of nomadism and savagery." Influenced by the European discourses of the time, the Ottoman Empire also introduced the notions of "civilised" and "barbarian." In the Ottoman context, the latter term predominantly referred to the tribal groupings in the Kosovo vilayet and Debre (Manastir vilayet), depicted in Ottoman documents as *vahşi* (wild) and *cahiliyyet* (ignorant). These tribes (*asabiyet*), who inhabited the mountainous regions, governed themselves according to the Law of *Lek Dukagjini*. In order to establish control over them, the Ottoman "borrowed colonialism" was reflected through the notions of castigation (*tedbi*) and education/correction *(terbiye)* that aimed to bring them (locals) under discipline (*inzibat*). In other words, the Ottoman principles of civilising and disciplining were introduced as a process of "borrowed colonialism" in order to prevent the influence of the Great Powers or regional states on these populations in Ottoman Macedonia. The policy of integrating the "periphery" and including these "wild and ignorant" tribes within the bureaucratic apparatus can also be analysed in the broader context of the Ottoman counter–colonialist response to European imperialism. I have argued that this Ottoman colonial modernity was a "survival tactic" for ensuring the stability and protection of the state, which entailed an important quest for legitimacy. In this direction, the government administration was reorganised, a judiciary and executive councils were established, legislation and laws were enforced, technological developments in the form of roads, telegraphs, and railways were introduced, all in order to bring the provinces closer to the centre than ever before. With the goal of drawing the three vilayets (Macedonia) closer to the centre, Sultan Abdulhamid II, appointed a peripheral mobile actor in Istanbul to the position of the Grand Vizier. One such personality was Avlonyalı Mehmet Ferid Pasha, who belongs to the company of those who played a crucial role in the enforcement of the "centre–periphery" relations. Since many Albanian–speaking locals in Ottoman Macedonia were dissatisfied with the introduction of the reforms of 1903, as an

Albanian–speaking bureaucrat, Ferid Pasha played an important role among the local Albanian population in the three vilayets, trying to negotiate with notable locals. However, this influence was not one–sided, from the "centre" towards its "peripheries," but as I further argued, the practices at the periphery of the Empire proved far more influential (in state/governmental matters) than previously theorised.

Based on post–colonial theory and "centre–periphery" relations, in chapter fifth I highlighted that people living in the peripheries possessed agency and shaped the Ottoman bureaucracy and imperial policy as much as the Ottoman "borrowed colonialism" impacted the lives of its local agitators, shaping the core values of both the Ottoman peripheries (Macedonia) and Istanbul. I demonstrated that the outbreak of the events in Ottoman Macedonia in July 1908 such as the rebellion in Resne led by Ahmed Niyazi; the meeting of thousands of Albanian–speaking inhabitants in Ferizaj (Firzovik) whose local rebels sent telegraphs to Istanbul demanding the restoration of the 1876 Constitution, triggered the Young Turks and the Ottoman third army based in Thessaloniki to charge to Istanbul in the name of a Revolution. Indeed, reports suggest that the "revolt" in Kosova, as much as those surfacing throughout Macedonia, changed completely political constellation in the Ottoman Empire. Here I argued that the locals and the 'Albanian element' played a very important role in the Revolution. In this regard, I analysed detailed entangled relations between the Young Turks and Albanian–speaking members of this movement or Albanian notables, who cooperated with the Young Turks. In this chapter, I emphasised that without an understanding of these entanglements and the situation on the ground, we could not have a clear picture of the subsequent events in Ottoman Macedonia, such as the Albanian Uprisings and the Balkan Wars. Perhaps ironically, I suggested that these events represent also a good example of the agencies of 'peripheral actors' who triggered the revolution in the Ottoman provinces, respectively in Ottoman Macedonia and changed the regime in the 'centre.' To borrow Chakrabarty's famous term "provincialising," I hold that these events of 1908 should be analysed as "provincialising Istanbul." This enables us to imbue our analysis of "centre–periphery" relations with a better understanding of the role of agency, resistance, and multi–scalar power struggles which link the many different cores with the quite variegated peripheries. Furthermore, the research went beyond reductive national–historical and Eurocentric perspectives. On the other hand, it "gave a voice" to less researched communities who established entanglements and transfers with a multidirectional character. Such "voices" were exemplified in the fifth chapter by the personal conversations of the Young Turks and Ottoman Albanian intellectuals – with each other and the local population as well – which were "spoken" in their memoirs and diaries, personal letters and essays, newspapers and journals. Such conversations were possible due to their still 'hybridity.' Neither in the Albanian community, nor in the Young Turk Movement was there a 'homogenous national society.' However, Hanes Grandits points out that a basic differentiation must be made during the time of conflict (revolt and organised violence), because people tended to be compelled by the warring parties to clearly "take sides." In similar ways, Hobsbawm emphasises that "any individual can sustain all sorts of multiple attachments, and not see them as incompatible, until some kind of conflict arises." In connection to these analyses, the period between 1909–1912/13 were the years of increased violence in Ottoman Macedonia. After an attempt for a counter–revolution in the Ottoman Empire on 31 March 1909, the Young Turk regime started to suppress all groups that opposed the centralisation. I argued that this Young Turk attempt of centralisation was simultaneously a process of "nationalising empire." This was often applied by way of introduction of new laws that violated local traditions and codes and triggered many revolts in the peripheries. During the time, Ottoman Macedonia kept the region in turmoil, where Albanian insurrections broke out. Although, prior to the Revolution (1908), many Albanian–speaking notables were still guided by custom, tradition, and code of honour (*besa*) based on regional, tribal, or family codices that enabled multi–layered loyalty relations in daily life during times of peace. However, the years after 1908 became "the worst and most threatening period for Albania" guided by many conflicts and increased violence. In this respect, during times of conflict, revolt, and organised violence, loyalties generally narrowed down, and people tended to choose a side (with which they allied). These processes triggered many Albanian intellectuals to overcome regional divisions (*Toskë and Gegë*) or tribal differentiations and to stand for a "pan–Albanian" unity. It is therefore conceivable that a more intensive cooperation between south and north Albanians began only after the Young Turk Revolution and the CUP's attempts of centralisation (policy). During this period, new local actors, such as Nikollë Ivanaj and Isa Boletini, played very important roles and transformed the dynamics on the ground. While Ivanaj connected two Albanian regions and was in constant communication with the band *kaçak* leader Themistokli Germenji and the Geg notables, Isa Boletini was a man of action between the Kosovo notables and the states of Montenegro and Serbia. Because of the destructive military policies of the Young Turk regime, the once highly contested socio–political spaces such as Ottoman Macedonia were left vulnerable to external interests aimed at securing absolute power. That said, these centralisation policies introduced by the Young Turks did not always work out according to their plans. For example, border areas such as Kosovo vilayet in particular, became a place for new possibilities and ultimately cooperation with Serbian and Montenegrin states. In this respect, the Young Turk efforts of "nationalising empire" brought many local Albanian–speaking notables to cooperate with their "eternal enemies" – the "Serbs" – and the Serbian state. Moreover, the 'Albanian Uprisings' (1909–1912) triggered various policies of the Balkan states as well, which led the Balkan states to interfere into Ottoman affairs. The problem that I examined in chapter fifth was that the Balkan states feared the potential establishment of autonomous Albania, as promised by the Ottoman government in August 1912. In the documents also known as *Arnavutluk*, autonomous Albania was to consist of at least two vilayets of Macedonia, Kosovo and Manastir, but it also often included Selanik (the entire Ottoman Macedonia). As such, the Serbian diplomats and Minister of Foreign Affairs, Nikola Pašić, openly reported that the "Albanian presence" and "Greater Albania" posed a threat to "the survival of the Serbs." The same opinion was held by the Bulgarian and Montenegrin diplomats who insisted on implementation of reforms in Macedonia that would avoid the formation of the potential autonomous Albania. At the end, this 'Albanian presence' in fact led these, once rivalling states, towards cooperation and the establishment of the Balkan League, which Nikola Pašić called "four Balkan Christian states (Serbia, Greece, Bulgaria and Montenegro)." The Serbian consul in Prishtina, M. Ð. Milojević, asserted that "Albanians [were] sensing that the Turkish Empire [was] gradually falling apart and therefore they wished to build friendships with the neighboring states of Serbia and Montenegro so that they could jointly protect their fatherland(s) against foreign enemies." As a final result of this turmoil in Ottoman Macedonia, the local Serbs joined the Albanian notables in the uprisings. They were also supported by Serbian organisations of National Defense and the Black Hand, whereby Serbian and Albanian–speaking bands, vojvoda Tankosić, and Isa Boletini this time fought together and joined forces against the Ottomans. To this end, the Ministry of Foreign Affairs of the Kingdom of Serbia issued a Directive regarding the cooperation with the Albanians (*direktiva za rad sa arnautima*) on 11 July 1912, which clearly stated that Serbia "should support by all means the division between Turks and Albanians." It further declared that the Albanian struggle should be "encouraged and helped" by the Serbian state, but to the extent that supported "overall Serbian interests (*opšti srpski interes*)." In fact, the state interest was to "weaken the Albanians and Turks," because it was "inevitable to war with the Turks." Furthermore, Stevan Simić, a member of the Serbian Chetnik Organisation argued that Serbia should use all capacities to penetrate Ottoman Macedonia, because "the anarchy [would] last until the Macedonian, in other words Turkish or Near Eastern Question [was] solved" (*a anarhije će biti uvek do god se ne reši maćedonsko odnosno tursko ili bližeg istoka pitanje*). In order to implement a "final solution" to the Macedonian, that is Turkish, or Near Eastern Question, the Balkan states established the Balkan League (Montenegro, Serbia, Bulgaria, and Greece). In this attempt, the Balkan states declared war to the Ottomans known historical scholarship as the Balkan Wars (1912–13). The first country that declared war was Montenegro. On this topic I also highlighted the important role played by Montenegro, whose position has often been omitted by scholars when it comes to the Macedonian Questions. I examined the Montenegrin policy towards Macedonia, and showed that it was an active participant in the Kosovo vilayet by providing local notables with arms and offering them a safe haven, especially during the implementation of the Young Turk centralisation policy. As such, the Montenegrin policy needs a closer analysis and further detailed study with regard to the Macedonian Questions. Apart from it, Montenegrin rulers, in this case Prince Nikola, worked on the construction of the myth about

Montenegrins as the "purest Serbs," who had the right and legacy to rule over cities such as Dečani and Prizren – once important centers of the Serbian empire. In fact, Prince Nikola intended to carve out a Greater Montenegrin or a united, South–Slavic state of the territories of Ottoman Albania and Ottoman Macedonia, with a seat in Prizren. In this attempt, he also supported the idea that his son Mirko should be appointed General Governor of Ottoman Macedonia, a suggestion made by the Great Powers in 1906. The Ottoman media and various documents reporting of these attempts entitled them "Montenegro and the Macedonian Principality." In this regard, there is no doubt that Montenegro played an important role in Macedonia. Furthermore, in the fifth chapter, I argued also that the Balkan Wars were a by–product of the "small state imperialism" of the Balkan governments. These states also passed through the process of "imperialising the nation–state" as an inversed process of the Young Turk regime's attempt at "nationalising (the) empire." Already by the spring of 1912 these imperialist policies and their subsequent state apparatus were managed by the people who had little knowledge of the Macedonian region over which they expected to rule. These military regimes of Montenegro, Serbia, Greece, and Bulgaria, but also Ottoman military regimes, were no longer interested in understanding the locals, but tried to instrumentalise them for their imperialist purposes. As a result, their operating logic was to cooperate with the locals only if they contributed to the achievement of state–imperialism. In other words, in the peak of these imperialist policies, which erupted into the Balkan Wars, Ottoman Macedonia would become a zone of violence and conflicts. Focusing on the experience of the inhabitants of Ottoman Macedonia during the period of increased violence in the region (1903–1912/13), I illustrated how in fact solidarities and their interpersonal relationships broke down due to the imperialism and were forcefully replaced in the public by a sense of collective belonging to a certain nation (Bulgarian, Serbian, Greek, Albanian, or Turk). In order to lay the groundwork for the emergence of this violence, I argued that the wars and conflicts on the ground were not incited due to a "national awareness" and "primordial ethno–nationalism" of the locals, but were rather a by–product of the state–promoted nationalisms and their imperialist ambitions in the region that often influenced the locals to take sides in times of conflicts and violence. The opportunity of the states to envision imperialism allowed planners to abandon the practices of negotiation with the locals. Rather, the administrative goal was full–scale extradition of the people who "belonged" to other nationhood or religions. In this respect, Mark Mazower identifies the decade from the Balkan Wars (1912–1913) to 1922–1923 as "the catalyst for genocide, ethnic cleansing, and massive forced population movements for the first time in history." This process of violence, partition, and division of Ottoman Macedonia into smaller ethnically "homogeneous" entities was named "Balkanisation." The term was coined during the Balkan wars (1912–1913) and was widely used and accepted after the Great War (1914–1918), a time during which it referred to the fragmentation of Ottoman Macedonia. By that time, this term received a negative connotation of violent tensions that are usually accompanied with fragmentation of various entities. However, this fragmentation of Ottoman Macedonia (the Balkans) and the violence on the ground was not an isolated example in the geographic region of the Balkans and "unique" case for this part of the world. However, the use of the term 'Balkanisation' grew into 'abuse of language,' widely promoted in European media as a synonym for conflict, allegedly due to the Balkan geographical "zone of violence" that did not fit entirely within the "civilised" European ideals. In fact, incoming the Great War (1914–1918) and the Second World War (1939–1945) showed that neither the Ottoman Empire nor the Balkan states were completely "barbarian," nor were the European empires totally "civilised." At that time, the mentors of the Balkan states, known as the Great powers, enmeshed Africa and other parts of the world in the processes of Balkanisation and Imperialism, which resulted in slavery and exploitation, political alienation and racism, wars and violence, ethnic cleansings and genocide. The results of the Europeans' colonisation in Africa, the *Endlösung* of the Jews in Germany, the anti–Jewish *pogroms* in Imperial Russia, demonstrate that "the white man's burden" was to think through the lenses of "questions" and "final solutions." It seems that during this "Age of Empire" not only were the Macedonian Questions globalised, but also the Great Powers became balkanised. The primary lesson to be drawn from these stories is that (the picture of) the world was not divided between the "Occident" and the "Orient," the "civilised" and the "barbarian," the "progressive/advanced" and the "backward," but Europe, coupled with the

Balkans and the Ottomans, was more intricately connected and entangled into the "Balkanisation," a tool widely used to "solve" the Macedonian Questions.

Bibliography

Archival Records

Albania

- Arkivi Qendror Shtetëror (AQSH)

Fonde para Pavarësisë
FO 120: Sanxhaku i Korçës (Kaza)
FO 121: Vilajeti i Shkodrës
FO 122: Bashkia Shkodër

Fondet Personale
FO 65: Koleksion fondesh personale (Para vitit 1912)
FO 656: Letërkëmbimi personal i Italianëve në Shqipëri
FO 1010: Letërkëmbime të shtetasve të ish Jugosllavisë

Fondet e Shoqatave, Klubeve, Organizatave, etj.
FO 96: Koleksion i shoqërive shqiptare në Bullgari (1900–1935)
FO 97: Shoqëritë shqiptare në Egjipt (1908–1929)
FO 98: Koleksioni i shoqërive shqiptare e italo – shqiptare në Itali (1878–1944)
FO 99: Shoqëritë shqiptare në Rumani (1602–1960)
FO 100: Shoqëritë shqiptare në SHBA (1907–1967)
FO 101: Shoqëritë shqiptare në Turqi (1867–1924)
FO 102: Koleksioni i shoqërive dhe klubeve shqiptare (1893–1912)

Fonde të dhuruara nga Jashtë
FO 1500: Koleksion dokumentesh nga arkivat serbe
FO 1500/1: Ministria e Punëve të Brendshme e Serbisë
FO 1501/2: Arkivi i Ministrisë së Jashtme të Italisë
FO 1502: Koleksion dokumentesh nga arkivat e Austrisë
FO 1507/1: Arkivi i Kryeministrisë, Stamboll – Turqi
FO 1507/2: Arkivi i Perandorisë Osmane, Stamboll

- Biblioteka Kombëtare e Shqipërisë

Libra
Antikuarë
Dorëshkrime
Periodike

Harta

Austria

- Österreichisches Staatsarchiv (ÖStA Wien)
Allgemeines Verwaltungsarchiv – Finanz– und Hofkammerarchiv
FHKA SUS, Finanz– und Hofkammerarchiv, Sammlungen und Selekte, Fam.A.
Familienakten

Kriegsarchiv
KA NFA, Kriegsarchiv – Neue Feldakten, Armeeoberkommando

Haus–, Hof– und Staatsarchiv (HHStA Wien)
Gesandtschafts– und Konsulatsarchive (HHStA GKA)
Ministerium des Äußern – Politisches Archiv (HHStA MdÄ PA)
Ministerium des Äußern – Zeitungsarchiv (HHStA MdÄ Zeitungsarchiv)

Recherche in Mapire – Portal für historische Karten (Arcanum Maps)

Bulgaria

- Natsionalna biblioteka 'Sv. Sv. Kiril i Metodiyi'
Bŭlgarski istoricheski arhiv
Orientalski zbirki
Kartografski i grafichni izdania
Tselokupna Bŭlgaria

France

- Bibliothèque nationale de France Catalogue Général
Archives et manuscrits
Gallica

Germany

- Politisches Archiv des Auswärtigen Amts/Berlin

R 13385: Türkei 143, Albanien
R 14549: Orientalia Generalia 9, Der Muhamedanismus
R 14551: Orientalia Generalia 9, Der Muhamedanismus

- Deutsche Bank Berlin Orientbüro (OR)
OR0610 (Orientbahnen Ostrumelisches Netz)
OR1012 Macedonische (Saloniki–Monastir) Emission

- Staatsbibliothek in Berlin
StaBiKat classic

Greece

- Istoriko Arheio Makedonias (IAM)
Ottoman archives
Correspondence (foreign) files
Photograph collections
Maps and plans collections

Italy

- Biblioteca comunale dell'Archiginnasio
Historical catalogue 'Frati – Sorbelli'

Montenegro

- Državni arhiv Crne Gore/Cetinje (DACG)
Ministarstvo inostranih djela (MID)
Ministarstvo inostranih djela, Poslanstvo u Carigradu
Ministarstvo unutrašnjih djela (MUD)

North Macedonia

- Državen Arhiv na Republika Severna Makedonija (DARSM)

Centralen Del (CD)

CD 862: Zbirka Fermani

CD 863: Zbirka Berati

CD 864: Zbirka Vakufnami

CD 865: Bujuruldii

CD 866: Zbirka Biografii, Avtobiografii i Memoari

CD 867: Zbirka Hroniki

CD 868: Zbirka Poedinečni Dokumenti Varija

CD 870: Zbirka Fotografii

CD 871: Zbirka Karti

CD 1049: Poedinečni Dokumenti na turski jazik varija

CD 1109: Balkanski vojni

CD 1230: Diplomatska prepiska vo rumeliski vilaet

CD 1235: TFR –1M– Razna dokumentacija na rumeliskiot Inspektorat

CD 1241: Gruev Dame

CD 1242: Černopeev Dimo

CD 1249: Kolekcija – Makedonsko prašenje

CD 1260: VMRO – Obedinet

CD 1265: VMRO

CD 1266: Nacionalno–osloboditelni organizacii na makedoncite vo Bugarija po berlinskiot kongres

CD 1269: Ustav na ilindenskata organizacija

CD 1287: Jildz

CD 1292: Kolekcija nacionalno osloboditelno dviženje

Oddelenie Skopje

OS 238: matični knigi na rodeni, venčani i umreni

OS 240: Memoari i drugi materijali od istorijata na naprednoto rabotničko dviženje i narodnoosloboditelnata borba

Russia

- Sankt–Peterburgskoe gosudarstvennoe udrezhdenie 'Tsentralnhiyi gosudarstvenniyi istoricheskii arhiv Sankt–Peterburga' (TsGIA SPb)

Voennoe delo

Biografii i Memuari

Serbia

- Državni Arhiv Srbije/Beograd
Konzulat u Prištini
Konzulat u Skoplju
Konzulat u Serezu
Konzulat u Solunu
Ministarstvo inostranih dela
Ministarstvo unutrašnjih dela

- Matica Srpska
Zbornik radova „Kosovo i Metohija: juče, danas, sutra"
Kosovskometohijski odbor

Turkey

- Başbakanlık Osmanlı Arşivi/Istanbul (BOA)
Bâbıâli Evrak Odası Evrakı
Dahiliye Nezareti Eminiyet–i Umumiye Müdüriyeti Kısmı Adli
Nezareti İdare
Dahiliye Nezareti Siyasi Kısmı
Dahiliye Muhaberat–ı Umumiye İdaresi Evrakı
Hariciye Nezareti Siyasi Kalemi
Hariciye Nezareti Tercüme Odası
Rumeli Müfettişliği
Teftişat–ı Rumeli Kosova Evrakı
Teftişat–ı Rumeli Şikayet
Yıldız Askerî Maruzat Evrakı
Yıldız Mütenevvi Maruzat Belgeleri
Yıldız Esas Evrakı
Kosova Vilayeti Salnamesi
Manastır Vilayeti Salnamesi
Selanik Vilayeti Salnamesi

- İBB Atatürk Kitaplığı – Istanbul Büyükşehir Belediyesi

Dergi
Gazete
İstatistik
Takvim
Salname

Newspapers and Journals

- Albania, Brussel
- Bŭlgarin, Gjurgevo
- Bŭlgaria, Sofia
- Bŭlgarski Glas, Bolgrad
- Balkan, Filibe (Plovdiv)
- Bratstvo, Beograd
- Diturija, Selanik
- Drita, Bukuresh
- Fiamuri Arberit/La Bandiera dell'Albania, Corigliano Calabro
- Glas Crnogorca, Cetinje
- Istok, Beograd
- Kalendari Kombiar, Sofia
- Makedonia, Istanbul
- Makedonski pregled, Sofia
- Maritsa, Plovdiv
- Messager de Vienne, Vienna
- Narodno Prava, Beograd
- Nezavisimost, Bukurest
- Nova Bŭlgaria, Bukurest
- Politika, Beograd
- Shpnesa e Shcypeniis, Ragusa (Dubrovnik)
- Tercüman–ı Şark, Istanbul
- The Times, London
- Tselokupna Bŭlgaria, Tarnovo
- Vreme, Beograd
- XIX vek, Tsarigrad
- Yugozapadna Bŭlgaria, Sofia

Other Printed Sources

Aarbakke, Vemund. "Die Region Makedonien." In *Das Südosteuropa der Regionen*, edited by Oliver Jens Schmitt and Michael Metzeltin, 603–639. Vienna: Verlag der Österreichischen Akademie der Wissenschaften, 2015.

Abadzi, Helen. "Historical Greek–Albanian Relations: Some Mysteries and Riddles?" *Mediterranean Quarterly* 22/1 (2011): 41–60.

Abrahamsen, Rita. "Postcolonialism." In *International Relations Theory for Twenty–First Century*, edited by Martin Griffiths, 111–123. London/New York: Routledge, 2007.

Adanır, Fikret. *Die makedonische Frage: Ihre Entstehung und Entwicklung bis 1908*. Wiesbaden: Franz Steiner Verlag, 1979.

Adanır, Fikret. "Semi–autonomous provincial forces in the Balkans and Anatolia in Cambridge History of Turkey." In *The Later Ottoman Empire, 1603–1839*, edited by Suraiya Faroqhi, 157–185. Cambridge: Cambridge University Press, 2006.

Adanır, Fikret. *Balkans: History and Historiography*. Istanbul: Eren Yayıncılık, 2014.

Adanır, Fikret. "Ethnonationalism, Irredentism and Empire." In *The Balkan Wars from Contemporary Perception to Historic Memory*, edited by Katrin Boeck and Sabine Rutar, 13–55. London: Palgrave Macmillian, 2016.

Agoston, Gabor. "Military Transformation in the Ottoman Empire and Russia, 1500–1800." *Kritika Explorations in Russian and Eurasian History* 12/2, (2011): 281–319.

Ahmad, Feroz. *The Young Turks: The Committee of Union and Progress in Turkish Politics (1908–1914)*. New York: Columbia University Press, 2010.

Ahmad, Feroz. *The Young Turks and the Ottoman Nationalities: Armenians, Greeks, Albanians, Jews, and Arabs, 1908–1918*. Salt Lake City: University of Utah Press, 2014.

Aleksov, Bojan. "Nationalism in Construction, The Memorial Church of St. Sava on Vračar Hill in Belgrade." *Balkanologie Revue d'etudes pluridisciplinaries* 7/2 (2013): 47–72.

Aleksov, Bojan. "The Serbian Orthodox Church." In *Orthodox Christianity and Nationalism in Nineteenth–Century Southeastern Europe*, edited by Lucian N. Leustean, 65–100. New York: Fordham University Press, 2014.

Almendinger, Klaus. *Makedonski vŭpros*. Sofia: Pechatnitsa P. Glushkov, 1927.

Almond, Ian. *History of Islam in German Thought from Leibniz to Nietzsche*. London: Routledge Studies in Cultural History, 2009.

Almond, Ian. "Anti–Capitalist Objections to the Postcolonial on Žižek and History." *Ariel: A Review of International English Literature* 43/1 (2012): 1–21.

Anastasopulos, Antonis. "Introduction." In *Provincial Elites in the Ottoman Empire*, edited by Antonis Anastasopulo, xi–xxvi. Rethymno: Crete University Press, 2005.

Anderson, Benedict. *Imagined Communities: Reflections on the Origin and Spread of Nationalism*. London: Verso, 1983.

Anderson, James and Liam O'Dowd. "Borders, Border Regions and Territoriality: Contradictory Meanings, Changing Significance." *Regional Studies* 33 (1999): 583–604.

Anderson, John. *The Struggle for the School: the Interaction of Missionary, Colonial Government and Nationalist Enterprise in the Development of formal Education in Kenya*. Nairobi: Longman, 1970.

Anderson, Matthew. *Peter the Great (Profiles in Power)*. Harlow, UK: Pearson Education Limited, 1995.

Anderson, Lisa. *The State and Social Transformation in Tunisia and Libya, 1830–1980*. Princeton, NJ: Princeton University Press, 1986.

Apostolski, Mihailo. *Istorija na makedonskiot narod II, od početokot na XIX vek do krajot na Prvata svetska vojna*. Skopje: Institut za Nacionalna Istorija, 1969.

Appadurai, Arjun. *Modernity at Large: Cultural Dimensions of Globalisation*. Minneapolis: University of Minnesota Press, 1996.

Appendix to a report by Austro–Hungarian consul Jelinek of Prizren, to Consul Lippich in Shkodra, 13 July 1878. In *Aktetë Rilindjes Kombëtare Shqiptare, 1878–1912* edited by Stefanaq Pollo and Selami Pulaha. 46–49. Tiranë: Instituti i Historisë, 1978.

Atanasovski, Srđan. *Mapiranje stare Srbije: Stopama putopisaca, tragom narodne pesme*. Beograd: Biblioteka XX vek, 2017.

Athanassoglou–Kallmyer, M. Nina. *French Images from the Greek War of Independence (1821–1830): Art and Politics under the Restoration*. New Haven: Yale University Press, 1989.

Avramov, Stane. *Materiali za istoryata na makedonskoto osvobitelno dvizhenie; knjiga X*. Sofia: 1929.

Avramovski, Živko. *Britanci u Kraljevini Jugoslaviji: Godišnji izveštaji Britanskog poslanstva u Beogradu 1921–1938*, vol. I *(1921–1930)*. Beograd/ Zagreb: Arhiv Jugoslavije – Globus, 1986.

Baár, Monika. *Historians and Nationalism: East–Central Europe in the Nineteenth Century*. Oxford: Oxford University Press, 2010.

Bacık, Gökhan. "Turkey and Russia: Whither Modernization?" *Journal of Economic and Social Research* 3/2 (2001): 51–72.

Bakalli, Emine. "Kryengritja e Malësisë së mbi Shkodrës e vitit 1911: Përkufizime dhe Refleksione," *Gjurmime Albanologjike – Seria e shkencave historike* 40 (2010): 187–202.

Bakić–Hayden, Milica. "Nesting Orientalisms: The Case of Former Yugoslavia." *Slavic Review* 54/4 (1995): 917–931.

Barkey, Karen and George Gavrils. "The Ottoman Millet System: Non–Territorial Autonomy and its Contemporary Legacy." *Ethnopolitics* 15/1 (2015): 24–42.

Bastea, Eleni. "Nineteenth–century Travellers in Greek Lands: Politics, Prejudice and Poetry in Arcadia." *Dialogos: Hellenic Studies Review* 4 (1997): 47–69.

Bataković, Dušan. "A Balkan–Style French Revolution? The 1804 Serbian Uprising in European perspective." *Balcanica* 36 (2005): 113–129.

Batrićević, Boban. *Recepcija Petra II Petrovića u ideologijama crnogorskih vlasti.* Cetinje: Arhivski zapisi 2016.

Bauman, Zygmund. *Liquid Modernity.* Cambridge: Cambridge University Press, 2000.

Bayly, Christopher. "Rammohan Roy and the Advent of Constitutional Liberalism in India, 1800–30." *Modern Intellectual History* 4/1 (2007): 25–41.

Bayly, Christopher. *The Birth of the Modern World, 1780–1914: Global Connections and Comparisons.* Malden, MA: Blackwell Publishers, 2004.

Bazhdarov, Georgi. *Moite spomeni.* Sofia: Sŭstavitel Angel Dzonev, 1929.

Beckert, Sven. *Empire of Cotton: A Global History.* New York: Alfred A. Knopf, 2014.

Beidelman, O. Thomas. "Contradictions Between the Sacred and the Secular Life: The Church Missionary Society in Ukaguru, Tanzania, East Africa 1876–1914." *Comparative Studies in Society and History* 23 (1981): 73–95.

Belić, Milorad. *Komitski vojvoda Vojislav Tankosić.* Valjevo: Međuopštinski istorijski arhiv, 2005.

Ben–Bassat, Yuval and Eyal Ginio. eds. *Late Ottoman Palestine: The Period of Young Turk Rule.* London/New York: I.B. Tauris. 2011.

Ben–Bassat, Yuval. *Petitioning the Sultan: Protests and Justice in Late Ottoman Palestine.* London/New York: I.B. Tauris. 2013.

Berard, Victor, Pierre Quillard and Francis de Pressense. *Pour l'Arménie et la Macédoine.* Paris: Societe Nouvelle de librairie & D'edition, 1904.

Berberian, Houri. *Roving Revolutionaries: Armenians and the Connected Revolutions in the Russian, Iranian and Ottoman worlds*. Berkley: University of California Press, 2019.

Berger, Peter and Thomas Luckmann. *Die gesellschaftliche Konstruktion der Wirklichkeit: Eine Theorie der Wissenssoziologie*. Frankfurt am Main: Fischer, 2003.

Berktay, Halil and Suraiya Faroqhi. *New Approaches to State and Peasant in Ottoman History*. London/New York: Routledge, 2016.

Besneley, Zeynel Abidin. *The Circassian Diaspora in Turkey: A Political History*. London/New York: Routledge. 2014.

Bhabha, K. Homi. *The Location of Culture*. London/New York: Routledge, 1994.

Bilmez, Bülent. "Shemseddin Sami Frashëri. (1850–1904): Contributing to the Construction of Albanian and Turkish Identities." In *We, the People: Politics of National Peculiarity in Southeastern Europe,* edited by Diana Mishkova, 341–372. Budapest: Central European University Press, 2009.

Black, Cyril. "Russia and the Modernization of the Balkans." In *The Balkans in Transition,* edited by Charles and Barbara Jelavich, 145–183. Berkeley/Los Angeles: University of California Press, 1963.

Black, Jeremy. *Maps and History*. New Haven: Yale University Press, 2000.

Blanqui, Louis Auguste. *Considérations sur l'état social de la Turquie d'Europe*. Paris: W. Coquebert, 1842.

Blaquière, Edward. *Report on the Present State of the Greek Confederation, and on Its Claims to the Support of the Christian World*. London: G.B. Whittaker, 1823.

Blaquière, Edward. *Greece and Her Claims*. London: G.B. Whittaker, 1826.

Blažarić, Pavle. *Memoari*. Leposavić: Centar za kuturu 'Sava Dečanac', 2006.

Bleda, Mithat Şükrü. *İmparatorluğun Çöküşü*. Istanbul: Destek Yayınları, 2010.

Bloch, Ernst. *Das Prinzip Hoffnung*. Frankfurt am Main: Suhrkamp Verlag, 1959.

Blumi, Isa. "Teaching Loyalty in the Late Ottoman Balkans: Educational Reform in the Vilayets of Manastir and Yanya, 1878–1912." *Comparative Studies of South Asia, Africa and the Middle East* 21/1–2 (2001): 15–23.

Blumi, Isa. "Publishers, Hitmen, Diplomats, and Dreamers: Switzerland's Ottoman–Albanian Diaspora, 1899–1920." *Schweizerische Zeitschrift für Geschichte* 52 (2002): 309–320.

Blumi, Isa. *Foundations of Modernity: Human Agency and the Imperial State.* New York: Routledge, 2011.

Blumi, Isa. *Reinstating the Ottomans – Alternative Balkan Modernities (1800–1912).* London: Palgrave Macmillan, 2011.

Blumi. Isa. *Ottoman Refugees, 1878–1939: Migration in a Post–Imperial World.* New York: Bloomsbury Academy, 2013.

Blumi, Isa. "Reorientating European Imperialism: How Ottomanism Went Global." *Die Welt des Islams* 56 (2016): 290–316.

Blumi, Isa. "Shifting Loyalties and Failed Empire: A New Look at the Social History of the Late Ottoman Yemen, 1872– 1918." In *Counter– Narratives: History, Contemporary Society, and Politics in Saudi Arabia and Yemen*, edited by Madawi Al– Rasheed and Robert Vitalis, 103–119. New York: Palgrave Macmillan, 2004.

Bohn, M. Thomas. *Russische Geschichtswissenschaft von 1880 bis 1905: Pavel N. Miljukov und die Moskauer Schule.* Vienna: Böhlau Verlag: Beiträge zur Geschichte Osteuropas, 25, (1998).

Boletini, Tafil. *Kujtime: Prane Isa Boletinit dhe përballe sfidave të kohës.* Tiranë: Ndërmarrja Gazetare–Botuese Album, 1996.

Bolloten, Burnett. *The Spanish Revolution: The Left and the Struggle for Power during the Civil War.* Chapel Hill: University of North Carolina Press, 1979.

Boué, Ami. *La Turquie d'Europe ou observations sur la ge'ographie, la geologie, l'histoire naturelle, la statistique, les moeurs, les coutumes, l'archeeologie, l'agriculture, l'industrie, le commerce, les gouvernements divers, le clerge, l'histoire et l'etat politique de cet empire.* Paris: Arthus Bartrand, 1840.

Boue, Ami. *Beiträge zur Geographie Serbiens.* Vienna: K.–K. Hof–und Staatsdruckerei in Commission bei Karl Gerold's Sohn, 1856.

Bourdieu, Pierre. "Les conditions sociales de la circulation internationaldes idées." *Actes de la recherche en sciences sociales* 145/1 (2002): 3–8.

Bousfield, Jonathan and Dan Richardson. *Bulgaria.* London: Rough Guides, 2002.

Boyar, Ebru. *Ottomans, Turks and the Balkans: Empire Lost, Relations Altered.* London and New York: IB Tauris, 2007.

Bozbora, Nuray. *Osmanlı yönetiminde Arnavutluk ve Arnavut ulusçuluğu'nun gelişimi.* Istanbul: Boyut Kitaplari, 1997.

Bozbora, Nuray. "The Policy of Abdulhamid II Regarding the Prizren League." *Turkish Review of Balkan* Studies 11 (2006): 45–67.

Bozbora, Nuray. "Albanian Perception of 1908 Revolution and Its Effects on Albanian Nationalism." *IBAC 2* (2012): 623–644.

Bozbora, Nuray. "Failures and Achievements of Albanian Nationalism in the Era of Nationalism". *Balkan Araştırma Enstitüsü Dergisi–Trakya Üniversitesi* (2012): 3–22.

Bozhilova, Ruzha. "Srbia i Bŭlgarskoto nacionalnoosvoboditelno dvizhenie v Makedoniya v nachaloto na XX v." *Izsledvania po Bŭlgarska Istoria* 8 (1986): 17–34.

Bömelburg, Hans–Jürgen, Stefan Rohdewald and Dirk Uffelmann. "Polnisch–osmanische Verflechtungen in Kommunikation, materieller Kultur, Litcratur und Wissenschaft." *Zeitschrift für Ostmitteleuropaforschung* 65/2 (2016): 159–166.

Bradaška, Franz (Franjo). "Die Slaven in der Turkei." *Mitteilungen aus Junius Peters' geographischer Anstalt* 15 (1869): 441–458.

Brailsford, Henry N. *Macedonia – Its Races and Their Future*. London: Methuen & Co.,1906.

Braudel, Fernand. *Preface to The Mediterranean and the Mediterranean World in the Age of Phillip II*, trans. Siân Reynolds. Berkeley: University of California Press, 1995. Originally published as *La Méditerranée et le monde méditerranéen à l'époque de Philippe II*. Paris: Armand Colin, 1949.

Braudel, Fernand. "History and the Social Sciences: The Longue Durée." *On History*. trans. Sarah Matthews. Chicago: University of Chicago Press, 1980. Originally published as "Histoire et sciences sociales. La longue durée." Annales ESC 13/4 (1958): 725–753.

Braudel, Fernand. *La Méditerranée et le monde méditerranéen à l'époque de Philippe II.* Paris: Armand Colin, 1949.

Braodel, Fernan. *Mediteran – prostor i Istorija*. Beograd: Centar za Geopoetiku, 1995.

Brendel, Heiko and Emmanuel Debruyne. "Resistance and Repression in Occupied Territories behind the Western and Balkan Fronts, 1914–1918." In *Frontwechsel: Österreich–Ungarns 'Großer Krieg' im Vergleich*, edited by Julia Walleczek–Fritz, Wolfram Dornik and Stefan Wedrac, 235–258. Vienna: Böhlau, 2014.

Breuninger, Helga, and Rolf Sieferle. *Kulturen der Gewalt: Ritualisierung und Symbolisierung von Gewalt in der Geschichte*. Frankfurt am Main: Campus–Verlag, 1998.

Brewer, David. *The Greek War of Independence: The Struggle for Freedom from Ottoman Oppression and the Birth of the Modern Greek Nation.* New York: Woodstock, 2003.

Brooks, Julian. "Managing Macedonia: British Statecraft, Intervention, and 'Proto–Peacekeeping' in Ottoman Macedonia, 1902–1905." PhD diss., Simon Fraser University, 2014.

Brooks, Julian. "Education Race for Macedonia, 1878–1903*." The Journal of Modern Hellenism* 31 (2015): 23–58.

Bruendel, Steffen. "Negativer Kulturtransfer. Die 'Ideen von 1914' als Aufhebung der 'Ideen von 1789'." In *Kulturtransfer im 19. Jahrhundert*, edited by Marc Schalenberg, 153–169. Berlin: Centre Marc Bloch, 1998. and Marc Schalenberg.

Brunnbauer, Ulf and Robert Pichler. "Mountains as 'lieux de mémoire': Highland Values and Nation–Building in the Balkans." *Balkanologie: Revue d'études pluridisciplinaires* 6/1–2 (2002): 77–100.

Buda, Aleks. *Fjalor enciklopedik shqiptar.* Tiranë: Akademia e Shkencave e RPSSH, 1985.

Burbank, Jane. "Paul W. Werth, The Tsar's Foreign Faiths, Toleration and the Fate of Religious Freedom in Imperial Russia." *Cahiers du monde russe* 56/4 (2015): 817–820.

Burke, Peter. *History and Social Theory.* New York: Cornell University Press, 2005.

Buschmann, Nikolaus, and Horst Carl. "Zugänge zur Erfahrungsgeschichte des Krieges: Forschung, Theorie, Fragestellung." In *Die Erfahrung des Krieges: Erfahrungsgeschichtliche Perspektiven von der Französischen Revolution bis zum Zweiten Weltkrieg*, edited by Nikolaus Buschmann and Horst Carl, 11–27. Padaborn: Ferdinand Schöningh, 2001.

Buxton, Noel. *Europe and the Turks.* London: Routledge, 2020.

Cana, Zekeria. "Qëndrimi i Serbisë ndaj kryengritjes së përgjithshme shqiptare të vitit 1912," *Gjurmime Albanologjike – Seria e shkencave historike* 35 (2005): 215–265.

Cana, Zekeria. "Rreth Kryengritjes Së Vitit 1912." *Gjurmime Albanologjike – Seria E Shkencave Historike* 39 (2009): 9–23.

Case, Holly. *Between States: The Transylvanian Question and the European Idea during World War II.* Stanford: Stanford University Press, 2009.

Case, Holly. *The Age of Questions: Or, A First Attempt at an Aggregate History of the Eastern, Social, Woman, American, Jewish, Polish, Bullion, Tuberculosis, and Many Other Questions over the Nineteenth Century, and Beyond.* Princeton, NJ: Princeton University Press, 2018.

Cevdet Paşa, Ahmet. *Tezakir.* Ankara: Türk Tarih Kurumu Basımevi, 1953.

Cevdet Paşa, Ahmet. *Osmanlı İmperatorluğu Tarihi.* Istanbul: Bilgi Kültür Sanat Yayınlarıcılık, 2008.

Chakrabarty, Dipesh. *Provincializing Europe: Postcolonial Thought and Historical Difference.* Princeton, NJ: Princeton University Press, 2000.

Clark, Christopher. *The Sleepwalkers: How Europe Went to War in 1914.* London: Penguin, 2013.

Clayer, Nathalie. "The Albanian Students of the Mektebi–i Mülkiye: Social Networks and Trends of Thought." In *Late Ottoman Society: The Intellectual Legacy*, edited by Elisabeth Özdalga, 291–311. London/New York: Routladge Taylor and Francis Group, 2010.

Clayer, Nathalie. "The Dimension of Confessionalisation in the Ottoman Balkans at the Time of Nationalisms." In *Conflicting Loyalties in the Balkans: The Great Powers, the Ottoman Empire and Nation–Building*, edited by Hannes Grandits, Nathalie Clayer and Robert Pichler, 89–109. London/New York: I. B. Tauris, 2011.

Clayer, Nathalie. *Ne fillimet e nacionalizmit shqiptar: Lindja e nje kombit me shumice mysliman ne Evrope, botime.* Tiranë: Perpjekja, 2012. in original Nathalie Clayer. *Aux origines du nationalism albanais: la naissance d'une nation majoritairement musulmane on Europe.* Paris: Karthala, 2007.

Clayer, Nathalie. "Edhe një herë mbi kryengritjet shqiptare të pasvitit 1908." *Përpjekja* 30–31 (2013): 85–122.

Clayer, Nathalie. "The Young Turks and the Albanians or Young Turkism and Albanianism." In *Penser, agir et vivre dans l'Empireottoman et en Turquie,* edited by Nathalie Clayer and Erdal Kaynar, 67–83. Paris/Louvain/ Walpole: Peters – Collection Turcica, 2013.

Clayer, Nathalie. "Kosova: The Building Process of a Territory from the Nineteenth to the Twenty–First Century." In *Ottoman Legacies in the Contemporary Mediterranean: the Balkans and the Middle East Compared*, edited by Ginio Eyal and Karl Kaser, 79–92. Jerusalem: The European Forum at the Hebrew University, 2013.

Cocks, Geoffrey. *The State of the Novel: Britain and Beyond.* Chichester, UK: Wiley–Blackwell, 2008.

Connell, Raewyn. *Southern Theory: The Global Dynamics of Knowledge in Social Science.* London: Allen & Unwin, 2007.

Conrad, Sebastian, Shalini Randeria and Beate Sutterlüty. *Jenseits des Eurozentrismus: postkoloniale Perspektiven in den Geschichts– und Kulturwissenschaften.* Frankfurt am Main; New York: Campus, 2002.

Conrad, Sebastian. *What is Global History?*. Princeton, NJ: Princeton University Press, 2016.

Cooper, Frederick. *Colonialism in Question: Theory, Knowledge, History*. Berkley: University of California Press, 2005.

Coudenhove–Kalergi, Richard. *Pan–Europa*. Vienna: Paneuropa–Union Österreich, 1979.

Cousinéry, Esprit Marie, and Pierre Langlumé. *Voyage dans la Macédoine: contenant des recherché sur l'histoire la géographie et les antiquités de ce pays*. Paris: 1831.

Crampton, Robert. *Concise History of Bulgaria*. Cambridge: Cambridge University Press, 2005.

Crew, David. "Alltagsgeschichte: A New Social History 'From Below'?" *Central European History* 22/3–4 (1989): 394–407.

Crna Gora i Njemački rajh: Dokumenti iz Političkog arhiva Službe inostranih poslova u Berlinu 1906–1914, vol. II (1910–1914). Podgorica/Regensburg: Univerzitet Crne Gore Istorijski institut Crne Gore, Leibniz–Institut für Ost– und Südosteuropaforschung, 2019.

Cvijić, Jovan. *Osnove za geografiju i geologiju Makedonije i Stare Srbije. knjiga I*. Beograd, Štamparija kraljevine Srbije, 1906.

Cvijić, Jovan. *Promatranja o etnografiji makedonskih Slovena*. Beograd: G. Kon, 1906.

Cvijić, Jovan. *La Péninsule balkanique: géographie humaine*. Paris: Librairie Armand Colin, 1918.

Cvijić, Jovan. *Govori i članci (drugo izdanje), Sabrana dela. knjiga 3*. Beograd: SANU, 1991.

Czernichowski, Konrad, Dominik Kopiński and Andrzej Polus. "Polish African Studies at a Crossroads: Past, Present and Future" *Africa Spectrum* 47/2–3 (2012): 167–185.

Čolović, Ivan. *Smrt na Kosovu polju: Istorija kosovskoj mita*. Beograd: Biblioteka XX veka, 2017.

Čubrilović, Vasa. *Terminologija plemenskog društva u Crnoj Gori*. Beograd: Srpska akademija nauka, 1959.

Ćirković, M. Sima."Kosovska bitka kao istorijski problem." In *Kosovska bitka u istoriografiji (okrugli sto)*, edited by Sima Ćirković, 109–118. Beograd: Istorijski institu, 1990.

Çavuş, Remzi. "Firzovik toplantılarının Meşrutiyetin ilanına katkısı." *Humanitas* 3/5 (2015): 65–72.

Çetinsaya, Gökhan. "'Çıban başı koparmamak': II. Abdülhamid Rejimine Yeniden Bakış." *Türkiye Günlüğü* 58 (Kasım–Aralık, 1999): 54–64.

Çetinsaya, Gökhan. "II. Abdülhamid'in İç Politikası: Bir Dönemlendirme Denemesi, Osmanlı Araştırmaları." *The Journal of Ottoman Studies* 47 (2016): 353–409.

Dakin, Douglas. *The Greek struggle in Macedona 1897–1913.* Thessaloniki: Institute for Balkan Studies, 1966.

Daskalov, Roumen. *Bulgarian Historical Review: Special Issue on Bulgaria in the Twentieth Century.* Sofia: Bulgarian Academy of Sciences Press, 2005.

Davison, H. Roderic. *Reform in the Ottoman Empire 1856–1876.* Princeton, NJ: Princeton University Press, 1963.

De Chateaubriand, François–René. *Note sur la Grece.* Paris, 1825.

De Lamartine, Alphonse–Marie–Louis. *Souvenirs, Impressions, Pensées et Paysages Pendant un Voyage en Orient.* Paris, 1835.

De Sommieres, Vialla. *Voyage Historique et Politique au Montenegro.* Paris: Alexis Eymery Libraire, 1820.

Dedijer, Vladimir. *Sarajevo 1914.* Beograd: Agencija Obradović, 2014.

Demeter, Gábor and Krisztián Csaplár–Degovics. "Social Conflicts: Changing Identities and Everyday Strategies of Survival in Macedonia on the Eve of the Collapse of Ottoman Central Power (1903–1912)," *The Hungarian Historical Review* 3/3 (2014): 609–649.

Der Matossian, Bedross. *Shattered Dreams of Revolution: From Liberty to Violence in the Late Ottoman Empire.* Stanford: Stanford University Press, 2014.

Derek, Gregory. *The Colonial Present.* New Jersey: Blackwell, 2004.

Deringil, Selim. *The Well–Protected Domains: Ideology and the Legitimation of Power in the Ottoman Empire, 1876–1909.* London/New York: I. B. Tauris & Co Ltd, 1999.

Deringil, Selim. "They Live in a State of Nomadism and Savagery: The Late Ottoman Empire and the Post–Colonial Debate." *Comparative Studies in Society and History* 45/2 (April, 2003): 311–342.

Deschamps, Gaston. *La Grece d'aujourd'hui.* Paris: N.P., 1901. first published 1892.

Deusch, *Engelbert. Das k.(u.)k. Kultusprotektorat im albanischen Siedlungsgebiet in seinem kulturellen, politischen und wirtschaftlichen Umfeld.* Vienna: Böhlau, 2009.

Deutsches Reichsgesetzblatt Band. No. 31. Berlin: N.P., 1878.

Dimić, Ljubodrag and Đorđe Borozan. *Jugoslovenska država i Albanci, vol. 1–2.* Beograd: JP Službeni list SRJ/Arhiv Jugoslavije/Vojno–istorijski institut, 1998/99.

Dinçyürek, Sena Hatip. "Reading a Bureaucratic Career Backwards: How did Hüseyin Hilmi Pasha become the Inspector–General of Rumelia?" *Middle Eastern Studies* 53/3 (2017): 386–405.

Đorđević, Vladan. *Crna Gora i Austrija 1814–1894*. Begrad: Štamparija Rodoljub, 1924.

Đurđev, Branislav. "Osnovni problem srpske istorije u period turske vlasti nad nasim narodima." *Istoriski glasnik* 3/4 (1950): 102–124.

Đurić, Silvija. *Dnevnik pobeda, Srbija u balkanskim ratovima 1912–13*. Beograd: Filip Višnjić, 1990.

Dodani, Visar. *Memoriet e mija*. Constanza: Albania, 1930.

Dokumenti o spoljnoj politici Kraljevine Srbije 1903–1914. Knjiga I, sveska 1.

Dokumenti o spoljnoj politici Kraljevine Srbije 1903–1914. Knjiga II, supplement 1.

Dokumenti o spoljnoj politici Kraljevine Srbije 1903–1914. Knjiga II, supplement 3.

Dostoyevski, Fyodor. *A Writer's Diary*. Evanston: Northwestern University Press, 2009.

Dragostinova, Theodora. "Continuity vs. Radical Break: National Homogenization Campaigns in the Greek–Bulgarian Borderlands before and after the Balkan Wars." *Journal of Genocide Research* 18/4 (2016): 405–426.

Dragouni, Olimpia. "Macedonia in Greek Textbooks (19th–20th Century)." In *Macedonia: Land, Region, Borderland,* edited by Jolanta Sujecka, 415–432. Warsaw: University of Warsaw, 2013.

Dvorski, Viktor. *Crnogorsko–turska granica od ušća Bojane do Tare.* Podgorica: CID, 2000.

Edney, Matthew H. "Mapping Empires, Mapping Bodies: Reflections on the Use and Abuse of Cartography." *Treballs de la SCG* 63 (2007): 83–104.

Egro, Dritan. *Historia dhe ideologjia: Një qasje kritike studimeve osmane në historiografinë shqiptare (nga gjysma e dytë e shek. XIX deri më sot)*. Tiranë: Instituti i Historisë, 2007.

Eisenstadt, N. Shmuel. "Multiple Modernen im Zeitalter der Globalisierung." In *Die Vielfalt und Einheit der Moderne,* edited by Thomas Schwinn, 37–62. Wiesbaden: Springer VS Verlag für Sozialwissenschaft, 2006.

Eissenstat, Howard. "Modernization, Imperial Nationalism, and the Ethnicization of Confessional Identity." In *The Late Ottoman Empire. Nationalizing empires,* edited by Stefan Berger and Alexei Miller, 429–460. Budapest: Central European University Press, 2015.

Eldarov, Svetlozar. "Nachalo na Srbskata vaorazhena propaganda v Makedonia." *Veonnoistoricheski sbornik* 1 (1984): 96–112.

Eldarov, Svetlozar. "Srbskata vaorazhena propaganda i bŭlgarskoto nacionalnoosvoboditelno dvizhenie v Makedonia sled Ilindensko–Preobrazhenskoto vastanie (1903–1904)." *Voennoistoricheski sbornik* 3 (1984): 26–44.

Eldarov, Svetlozar. "Bŭlgarskoto pravitelstvo i VMORO v borba sreshu srbskata vaorazhena propaganda v Makedonia (1903–1908g.)." *Izvestiya na veonnoistoricheskoto nauchno druzhestvo* 44 (1987): 211–235.

Eldarov, Svetlozar. *Srbskata vaorazhena propaganda v Makedonia 1901–1912.* Sofia: Voennoizdatelski kompleks 'Sv. Georgi Pobedonosets', 1993.

Elezovich, M. Zvezdana, Ana M. Mumovich and Dalibor M. Elezovich, "Grigorii Stepanovich Sherbina (1868–1903) v Kulture Kosovskih Serbov," *Vestnik Tomskogo gosudarstvennogo universitetaa* 420 (2017): 141–145.

Ellis, Burcu Akan. *Shadow Genealogies: Memory and Identity among Urban Muslims in Macedonia.* New York: Columbia University Press, 2003.

Elsie, Robert. *The Albanian Bektashi, History and Cluture of a Dervish Order in the Balkans.* London: I.B. Tauris, 2019.

Elsie, Robert. "Vorwort." In *Der Kanun: Das albanische Gewohnheitsrecht nach dem sogenannten Kanun des Lekë Dukadjini kodifiziert von Shtjefën Gjeçevi*, edited Robert Elsie, 5–9. Pejë: Dukagjini Publishing House, 2001.

Elsie, Robert. *The Tribes of Albania: History, Society and Culture.* London/New York: I. B. Tauris, 2015.

Elwert, Georg, Stephan Feuchtwang, and Dieter Neubert. "The Dynamcis of Collective Violence: An Introduction." *Dynamics of Violence: Processes of Escalation and De–Escalation in Violent Group Conflicts*, edited by Georg Elwert, Stephan Feuchtwang and Dieter Neubert, 9–31. Berlin: Duncker & Humblot, 1999.

Engelbert, Deusch. *Das K. (U.) K. Kultusprotektorat Im Albanischen Siedlungsgebiet in Seinem Kulturellen, Politischen Und Wirtschaftlichen Umfeld.* Vienna/Cologne/Weimar: Böhlau Verlag, 2009.

Engell, James. *The Creative Imagination: Enlightenment to Romanticism.* Cambridge: Harvard University Press, 1981.

Enver, Paşa. *Enver Paşa'nin Anıları.* Istanbul: İş Bankası Kültür Yayınları, 2018.

Esmer, U. Tolga. "Economies of Violence, Banditry and Governance in the Ottoman Empire Around 1800." *Past & Present* 224/1 (2014): 163–199.

Etkind, Alexander. *Internal Colonization – Russia's Imperial Experience*. Cambridge: Polity Press, 2011.

Fabrykant, Marharyta and Renee Buhr. "Small State Imperialism: The Place of Empire in Contemporary Nationalist Discourse." *Nations and Nationalism* Volume 22/ 1 (2015): 103–122.

Fallmerayer, Jakob Phillip. *Geschichte der Halbinsel Morea während des Mittelalters.* Sttutgart: Cotta'sche Verlagsbuchhandlung, 1836.

Faludi, Andreas. "Multi–level (Territorial) Governance: Three Criticisms." *Planning Theory and Practice* 13 (2012): 197–211.

Faroqhi, Suraiya, Fikret Adanır. *The Ottomans and the Balkans – A Discussion on Historiography*. Leiden: Brill, 2002.

Fazlı Necip. "Makedonya'da son günlerimiz ve Umumi Müfettiş Hüseyin Hilmi Paşa." *Yakın Tarihimiz* 53/3 (1962): 362–399.

Fikri Bekir. *Balkanlarda Kuvve–i seyyare kumandanı yüzbaşı Bekir Fikri*. Istanbul: Belge yayınlarıları, 1985.

Fikri Bekir. *Balkanlarda Tedhiş ve Gerilla*. Istanbul: Türk Tarih Vakfi Yayınları, 2008.

Fink, Leon. (ed.) *Workers Across the Americas: The Transnational Turn in Labor History*. Oxford: Oxford Univiversity Press, 2011.

Fleming, E. Katherine. "Orientalism, the Balkans, and Balkan Historiography." *The American Historical Review* 105/4 (2000): 1218–1233.

Fortna, Benjamin. *The Circassian: A Life of Eşref Bey, Late Ottoman Insurgent and Special Agent*. Oxford: Oxford University Press, 2016.

Fortna, Benjamin. *Imperial Classroom: Islam, Education and the State in the Late Ottoman Empire.* Oxford: Oxford University Press, 2002.

Fortna, Benjamin. *Education for the Empire: Ottoman State Secondary Schools during the Reign of Sultan Abdulhamid II (1876–1909)*. Ph.D. Diss. University of Chicago, 1997.

Foucault, Michel. *The History of Sexuality Volume 1*. New York: Pantheon Books, 1976.

Foucault, Michel. *Power/Knowledge: Selected Interviews and Other Writings*. Edited by Colin Gordon. New York: Pantheon Books, 1980.

Frantz, Eva Anne. "Violence and its Impact on Loyalty and Identity Formation in Late Ottoman Kosovo: Muslims and Christians in a Period of Reform and Transformation." *Journal of Muslim Minority Affairs* 29/4 (2009): 57–75.

Frantz, Eva Anne. "Zwischen Gewalt und friedlicher Koexistenz – Muslime und Christen im spätosmanischen Kosovo, 1870–1913." PhD diss., University of Vienna, 2014.

Frantz, Eva Anne. "Kosovo." In *Das Südosteuropa der Regionen*, edited by Oliver Jens Schmitt and Michael Metzeltin, 201–275. Vienna: Verlag der Österreichischen Akademie der Wissenschaften, 2015.

Frashëri, Sami. *Shqipëria ç'ka qenë, ç'është e çdo të bëhet*. Tiranë: Mesonjëtorja e parë, 1999.

Frashëri, Sami Şemsettin. *İslâm Medeniyeti*. Istanbul: Mihran, 1879/1296.

Frashëri, Sami Şemsettin. "Medeniyet–i cedideninümem–i islamiyeye nakli." *Güneş* 1/4 (1883–1884): 179–184.

Frashëri, Sami–Bey. *Kamus al–alam I*. Istanbul: Mihran Matbaası,1306 [1889].

Frusetta, James Walter. *Bulgaria's Macedonia: Nation–Building and State–Building, Centralization and Autonomy in Pirin Macedonia, 1903–1952*. College Park, MD: University of Maryland, 2006.

Gade, Daniel. *Curiosity, Inquiry, and the Geographical Imagination*. New York: Peter Lang, 2011.

Gandhi, Leela. *Postcolonial Theor : A Critical Introduction*. Oxford : Oxford University Press, 2008.

Ganguly, Keya. "Temporality and Postcolonial Critique." In *The Cambridge Companion to Postcolonial Literary Studies*, edited by Neil Lazarus, 162–179. Cambridge: Cambridge University Press, 2004.

Ganev, I. Venelin. *Bulgaria: The Uneven Transition*. London: Routledge, 2003.

Gangloff, Sylvie. *La perception de l'héritage ottoman dans les Balkans/The Perception of the Ottoman Legacy in the Balkans*. Paris: L'Harmattan, 2005.

Garašanin, Ilija. *Načertanije*. Beograd: Ethos, 2016.

Garvanov, Ivan. *Vencha se za Makedonia*. Sofia: Stara Zagora, 1995.

Gawrych, George. *The Crescent and the Eagle: Ottoman Rule, Islam and the Albanians, 1874–1913*. New York: I.B. Tauris, 2006.

Gellner, Ernest. *Nations and Nationalism*. Oxford: Blackwell, 1983.

Georgiev, Velichko and Stayko Trifonov. *Istoria na Bŭlgarite (1878–1944) v Dokumenti (1878–1912)*. Sofia: Prosveta, 1994.

Georgiev, Velichko and Stayko Trifonov. *Grchkata i srbskata propagandi v Makedonia – Krayat na XIX–nachaloto na XX vek: Novi dokumenti*. Sofia: Prosveta 1995.

Gerd, Lora. *Russian Policy in the Orthodox East: The Patriarchate of Constantinople (1878–1914)*. Berlin: De Gruyter, 2014.

Gerdzikov, Mihail. *V Makedonia i Odrinsko Spomeni*. Sofia: Glusov, 1928.

Geyer, Dietrich. *Russian Imperialism. The Interaction of Domestic and Foreign Policy 1860–1914*. Hamburg/ New York: Leamington Spa, 1987.

Gilmartin, Mary. *Colonialism/Imperialism, Key Concepts in Political Geography*. London: Sage Publications Ltd., 2009.

Gilroy, Paul. *The Black Atlantic: Modernity and Double Consciousness*. New York: Verso Books, 1993.

Gingeras, Ryan. *Sorrowful Shores: Violence, Ethnicity, and the End of the Ottoman Empire, 1912–1923*. Oxford: Oxford University Press, 2009.

Gingeras, Ryan. *Fall of the Sultanate: The Great War and the End of the Ottoman Empire 1908–1922*. Oxford: Oxford University Press, 2016.

Gjorgiev, Dragi. *Makedonsko prašanjevo Osmanliski v parlament 1909*. Skopje: MANU, 2010.

Gotsev, Dimitar. *Ideyata za avtonomia kato taktika v programite na natsionalno–osvoboditelnoto dvizhenie v Makedonia i Odrinsko (1893–1941)*. Sofia: Izdatelstvo na Bŭlgarska Akademia na Naukite, 1983.

Goldsworthy, Vesna. *Inventing Ruritania: The Imperialism of the Imagination*. New Haven: Yale University Pres, 1998.

Golemi, Zaho. "Çerçiz Topulli dhe çeta flamur lirie: Me rastin e 110 vjetorit të krijimit të çetës së Çerçiz Topullit." *Gazeta Mbrojtja* (2016).

Gong, W. Gerrit. *The Standard of 'Civilization' in International Society*. New York: Clarendon Press, 1984.

Gopčević, Spiridon. *Makedonija i Stara Srbija*. Beograd: Sazvežđe, 2016. First published in 1890.

Gould, Eliga. "Entangled Histories, Entangled Worlds: The English–Speaking Atlantic as a Spanish Periphery." *The American Historical Review* 112 3 (2007): 764–786.

Gounaris, Basil. *The Autumn of 1904 in Macedonia. The Unpublished Diary of Euthymios Kaoudis* [g]. Thessaloniki: Mouseio Makedonikou Agona, 1992.

Gounaris, Basil. *Steam over Macedonia, 1870–1912: Socio–Economic Change and the Railway Factor*. New York: Columbia University Press, 1993.

Gounaris. Basil. "Social cleavages and national 'awakening' in Ottoman Macedonia." *East European Quarterly* 29/4 (1995): 409–426.

Gounaris, Basil. "Reassessing Ninety Years of Greek Historiography on the "Struggle for Macedonia 1904–1908." *Journal of Modern Greek Studies* 14/2 (1996): 237–251.

Gounaris, Basil. "Social Gathering and Macedonian Lobbying: Symbols of Irredentism and Living Legends in Early Twentieth Century Athens." In *Greek Society in the Making, 1863–1913, Symbols and Vissions*, edited by Philip Carabott. 99–114. Variorum: Ashgate Publishing Ltd., 1997.

Gounaris, Basil. "Ottoman Monastir in the Early Twentieth Century." *European History Quarterly* 31/1 (2001): 43–64.

Gounaris. Basil. "Preachers of God and martyrs of the Nation: The politics of murder in ottoman Macedonia in the early 20th century." *Balkanologie* 9/1–2 (2005): 31–43.

Gounaris, Basil. "IX. National Claims, Conflicts and Developments in Macedonia, 1870–1912." In *The History of Macedonia*, edited by Ioannis Koliopoulos. 508–528. Thessaloniki: Musesum of the Macedonian Struggle, 2007.

Gozzi, Gustavo. *Diritti e Civilta: Storia e filosofia del diritto internazionale*. Bologna: Il Mulino, 2010.

Gozzi, Gustavo. *Umano, non umano. Interventoumanitario, colonialismo, 'primavera arabe'*. Bologna: Il Mulino, 2015.

Göcek, Fatma Müge. "Parameters of Postcolonial Sociology of the Ottoman Empire, In *Decentering Social Theory*, edited by Julian Go. 73–104. Bingley: Emerald Group Publishing Limited, 2013.

Gradeva, Rossitsa. *Rumeli under the Ottomans 15th–18th Centuries: Institutions and Communities*. New Jersey: Gorgias Press, 2010.

Grameno, Mihail. *Kryengritja shqipëtare*. Korçë: Direttore, 1925. (First Published), Grameno, Mihail. *Kryengritja shqipëtare*. Tiranë: N.SH. Naim Frashëri, 1959.

Grandits, Hannes. *Herrschaft und Loyalität in der spätosmanischen Gesellschaft. Das Beispiel der multikonfessionellen Herzegowina*. Vienna/Cologne/Weimar: Böhlau, 2008.

Grandits, Hannes and Siegfried Gruber. "The Dissolution of the Large Complex Households in the Balkans: Was the Ultimate Reason Structural or Cultural?." In *Household and Family in the Balkans: Two Decades of Historical Family Research at University of Graz*, edited by Karl Kaser. 387–407. Berlin: LIT Verlag, 2012.

Grandits, Hannes, et al. "Introduction: Social (Dis–)Integration and the National Turn inthe Late– and Post–Ottoman Balkans. Towards an Analytical Framework." In *Conflicting Loyalties in the Balkans. The Great Powers, the Ottoman Empire and Nation–Building,* Hanne Grandits, Nathalie Calyer and Robert Pichler, 1–12. London: I.B. Tauris, 2011.

Gregory, Derek. *Geographical Imaginations*. New Jersey: Blackwell, 1994.

Gregory, Derek. *Violent Geographies: Fear, Terror, and Political Violence*. London: Routledge, 2006.

Griesebach, August. *Reise durch Rumelien und nach Brussa im Jahre 1839*. Göttingen: Vandenhoeck und Ruprecht, 1841.

Grothe, Hugo. *Auf turkisher Erde*. Berlin: N.P., 1903.

Grozdanova, Elena. "Bŭlgarskata osmanistika na granitsata mezhdu dve stoletia – priemstvenost i obnovlenie." *Istoricheski pregled* 1–2 (1998): 98–158.

Grozdanova, Elena. "Bulgarian Ottoman Studies at the Turn of Two Centuries: Continuity and Change." *Études balkaniques* (2005): 93–146.

Grubačić, Andrej. *Don't Mourn, Balkanize!: Essays After Yugoslavia*. San Francisco: PM Press, 2010.

Grunert, Heiner. *Glauben im Hinterland: Die Serbisch–Orthodoxen in der habsburgischen Herzegowina, 1878–1918*. Göttingen: Vandenhoeck & Ruprecht, 2016.

Guha, Ranajit. *Dominance without Hegemony: History and Power in Colonial India*. Cambridge: Harvard University Press, 1998.

Haas, Peter. "Introduction: Epistemic Communities and International Policy Coordination." *International Organization Cambridge Journals* 46 (1992): 1–35.

Haberland, Detlef. *Buch– und Wissenstransfer in Ostmittel– und Südosteuropain der Frühen Neuzeit*. Munich: Hamadeh Shirine, 2004.

Habermas, Jürgen. *The Theory of Communivative Action, vol. 2: Lifeworld and System: A Critique of Functionalist Reason*. Boston: Beacon Press, 1987.

Hacısalihoğlu, Mehmet. *Die Jungtürken und die Mazedonische Frage, 1890–1918*. Munich: R. Oldenbourg Verlag, 2003.

Hacisalihoğlu, Mehmet. "The Young Turk Revolution and the Negotiations." *Turcica* 36 (2004): 165–190.

Hacisalihoğlu, Mehmet. "Turkish Historiography on the Balkans during the Late Ottoman Period (1878–1914)." *Balkanistica* 22 (2009): 181–201.

Hacısalihoğlu, Mehmet. "Yane Sandanski as a Political Leader in Macedonia in the Era of the Young Turks." *Cahiers Balkaniques* 40 (2012): 1–28.

Hacısalihoğlu, Mehmet. "The Young Turk Policy in Macedonia, Cause of the Balkan Wars?" In *War and Nationalism*, edited by M. Hakan Yavuz and Isa Blumi. 100–131. Salt Lake City: University of Utah Press. 2013.

Hadži–Vasiljević, Jovan. *Prilep i njegova okolina*. Beograd: Nova Električna Štamparija Petra Jockovića, 1902.

Hadži–Vasiljević, Jovan. *Južna stara Srbija: istorijska, etnografska i politička istraživanja*. Beograd: Nova štamparija Davidović, 1913.

Hadži Vasiljević, Jovan. *Četnička akcija u Staroj Srbiji i Maćedoniji*. Beograd: N.P.,1928.

Hadžić, Haris. "Refleksije Kanona Leke Dukađinija na običaje i kulturu Bošnjaka u Rožajama." *Islamska misao: Godišnjak Fakulteta za islamske studije Novi Pazar* 6 (2012): 279–300.

Hadzidimov, Dimo. *Nazad kim avtonomiata: Deklaratsia po razreshenieto na makedonskia vŭpros*. Sofia: N.P., 1919.

Hadzidimov, Dimo. *Makedonskoto osvoboditelno delo*. Lom: Pechatnitsa na A.M. Dimitrov, 1900.

Hajdarpašić, Edin. *Whose Bosnia? Nationalism and Political Imagination in the Balkans, 1840–1914*. Ithaca: Cornell University Press, 2015.

Hamilton Daniel S. and Stefan Meister. *The Eastern Question: Russia, the West, and Europe's Grey Zone*. Washington, DC: Center for Transatlantic Relations, 2016.

Hanioğlu, Şükrü. *Preparation for a Revolution: The Young Turks, 1902–1908*. Oxford: Oxford University Press, 2001.

Hanioğlu, M. Şükrü. "Ottoman Jihad or Jihads: The Ottoman Shii Jihad, the Successful One." In *Jihad and Islam in World War I*, edited by Erik–Jan Zürcher, 117–134. Leiden: Leiden University Press: 2016.

Hanssen, Jens. "Practices of Integration: Center–Periphery Relations in the Ottoman Empire." In *The Empire in the City: Arab Provincial Capitals in the Late Ottoman Empire*, edited by Jens Hanssen, Thomas Philipp, and Stefan Weber. 49–74. Würzburg: Ergon, 2002.

Harley, Brian. "Deconstructing the Map." *Cartographica* 26/2 (1989): 1–21.

Hartmuth, Maximilian. *Centres and Peripheries in Ottoman Architecture. Rediscovering a Balkan Heritage*. Sarajevo: Cultural Heritage Without Borders, 2011.

Haslinger, Peter. *Nation und Territorium im tschechischen politischen Diskurs 1880–1938*. Munich: Oldenbourg, 2010.

Hechter, Michael. *Internal Colonialism: The Celtic Fringe in British National Development*. New Jeresey: Transaction Publishers, 1999.

Heitmeyer, Wilhelm. *Gewalt. Entwicklungen, Strukturen, Analyse probleme*. Frankfurt am Main: Suhrkamp, 2004.

Hemberger, Andreas. *Illustrierte Geschichte des Balkan Krieges 1912/13*, Vienna/Leipzig: Hartleben, 1914.

Heper, Metin. "Political Modernization as Reflected in Bureaucratic Change: The Turkish Bureaucracy and a 'Historical Bureaucratic Empire' Tradition." *International Journal of Middle East Studies* 7 (1976): 507–521.

Heper, Metin. "Center and Periphery in the Ottoman Empire: With Special Reference to the Nineteenth Century." *International Political Science Review* 1 (1980): 81–105.

Heraclides, Alexis. *The Macedonian Question and the Macedonians: A History*. London: Routledge Histories of Central and Eastern Europe, 2021.

Herzog, Christoph and Motika, Raoul. "Orientalism 'allaturca': Late 19th / Early 20th Century Ottoman Voyages into the Muslim 'Outback'." *Die Welt des Islams* 40/2 (2000): 139–195.

Herzog, Christoph. "Nineteenth–century Baghdad through Ottoman Eyes." In *The Empire in the City: Arab Provincial Capitals in the Late Ottoman Empire*, edited by Jens Hanssen, Thomas Philipp and Stefan Weber. 311–328. Würzburg, Ergon Verlag, 2002.

Hoare, Marko Attila. *Genocide and Resistance in Hitler's Bosnia: The Partisans and the Chetniks, 1941–1943*. Oxford: Oxford University Press, 2006.

Hobsbawm, Eric, and Terence Ranger. ed. *The Invention of Tradition*. Cambridge: Cambridge University Press, 1983.

Hobsbawm, Eric. *The Age of Empire, 1875–1914*. New York: Pantheon Books, 1987.

Hobsbawm, Eric. *Nations and Nationalism since 1780. Programme, Myth, Reality*. Cambridge: Cambridge University Press: 1990.

Hock, Klaus, and Gesa Mackenthun. *Entangled Knowledge: Scientific Discourses and Cultural Difference*. Münster: Waxmann. 2012.

Houben, Vincent. "New Areas Studies, Translation and Mid–Range Concepts." In *Areas Studies at the Crossroads: Knowledge Production after the Mobility Turn*, edited by Katja Mielke and Anna–Katharina Hornidge, 195–211. New York: Palgrave Macmillan, 2017.

Höbelt, Lothar. "Der Berliner Kongress als Prototyp internationaler Konfliktregelung." In *Am Rande Europas? Der Balkan – Raum und Bevölkerung als Wirkungsfelder militärischer Gewalt*, edited by Bernhard Chiari und Gerhard P. Groß. 27–53. Munich: R. Oldenbourg Verlag, 2009.

Hölscher, Lucian. *Die Entdeckung der Zukunft*. Göttingen: Wallstein Verlag, 1999.

Höpken, Wolfgang, and Michael Riekenberg. *Politische und ethnische Gewalt in Südosteuropa und Lateinamerika*. Vienna/Cologne/Weimar: Böhlau, 2001.

Hroch, Miroslav. "From National Movement to the Fully–formed Nation: The Nation–Building Process in Europe." In *Becoming National*, edited by Geoff Eley and Ronald Grigor Suny, 60–77. Oxford: Oxford University Press, 1996.

Hubka, Gustav. "Bandenkämpfe: Erfahrungen Der Makedonischen Reformgendarmerieoffiziere." *Streffleurs Militärische Zeitschrift: Organ der Militärwissenschaftlichen Vereiene* 90/2 (1909): 1501–1526.

Hutton, H. John. "Introduction." In *The Unwritten Law in Albania*, edited by John H. Hutton, xi–xv. Cambridge Cambridge University Press, 1954.

Hüseyin Hilmi Paşa Evrakı Kataloğu. Istanbul: ISAM Yayınları, 2006.

Iggers, Georg G.. *Historiography in the Twentieth Century: From Scientific Objectivity to the Postmodern Challenge*. Hannover and London: Wesleyan University Press, 1997.

Ignatiev, P. Nikolay. "Zapiskigrafa N. P. Ignatieva 1875–1877." *Istoricheskiivestnik* I (1914): 55–77.

Ilić, Vladimir. "Učešce srpskih komita u Kumanovskoj operaciji 1912 godine." *Vojnoistorijski glasnik: Organ Vojnoistorijskog Instituta* 1–3 (1992): 197–217.

Ilić, Vladimir. *Srpska četnička akcija 1903– 1912*. Beograd: Ecolibri, 2006.

Inaldžik, Halil. "Od Stefana Dušana do Osmanskog carstva." *Prilozi: Orijentalni Institut u Sarajevu* 3–4 (1953): 23–55.

Ippen, Theodor. *Skutari und die Nordalbanische Kuestenebene*. Sarajevo: Daniel A. Kajon, 1907.

Irtem, Süleyman Kani. *Osmanli Devleti'nin Makedonya meselesi*. Istanbul: Temel Yayınları, 1998.

İslamoğlu–Inan Huri. "Oriental Despotism in World–System Perspective." In *The Ottoman Empire and World–Economy*, edited by Huri İslamoğlu–Inan. 1–24. Cambridge: Cambridge University Press, 1987.

Ivanaj, Nikollë. *Historija e Shqipëniës së re: Vuejtjet e veprimet e mija*. Tiranë: Shtypëshkronja e shtetit 'Atdheu', 1943/45.

Ivanić, Ivan. *Maćedonija i Maćedonci – putopisne beleške*. Beograd: N.P., 1906.

Ivanov, Jordan. *Bŭlgarski starini iz Makedonia*. Sofia: Izvestiia na Instituta za arkheologiia, 1970. first published in 1931.

İleri, Celal Nuri. *İttihad–ı İslam ve Almanya*. Istanbul: Yeni Osmanlı Matbaa ve Kütüphanesi, 1333/1914.

Jagodić, Miloš. *Srbija i Stara Srbija (1839–1868): Nasleđe na jugu.* Beograd: Evoluta, 2016.

Jagodić, Miloš. *Srpsko–albanski odnosi u kosovskom vilajetu (1878–1912).* Beograd: Zavod za udžbenike i nastavna sredstva, 2009.

Jagodić, Miloš. *Srpske čete u Makedoniji 1897–1901 godine.* Niš: Zbornik radova sa naučnog skupa Ustanci i pobune Srba u Turskoj u XIX veku (povodom 170. godina od izbijanja Niške bune), 2012.

Jelačić, Aleksej. *Istorija Rusije.* Beograd: Romanov, 2000.

Jelavich, Barbara. *Russia's Balkan Entanglements (1806–1914).* Cambridge: Cambridge University Press, 1991.

Jelavich, Charles and Jelavich, Barbara. *The Establishment of the Balkan National States, 1804–1920.* Washington: University of Washington Press, 1986.

Jessop, Bob. *State Power: A Strategic–Relational Approach.* Cambridge: Polity Press, 2007.

Jezernik, Božidar. *Wild Europe: The Balkans in the Gaze of Western Travellers.* London: Saqi Books and the Bosnian Institute, 2004.

Jireček, Konstantin. *Geschichte der Bulgaren.* Prague: N.P., 1876.

Jovanović, Jovan. *Borba za narodno ujedinjenje 1914–1918.* Beograd: Geca Kon, 1935.

Jovanović Kodža, Aleksa. "Početak srpskog četničkog pokreta u Južnoj Srbiji i Makedoniji." *Književni Jug,* 1 (1929): 14–19.

Jovanović Kodža, Aleksa. "Vojvoda Savatije: Početak srpske četničke akcije u Maćedoniji." *Letopis Matice srpske* 326 (1930): 126–151.

Jovanović, Vladan. *Jugoslovenska Država i Južna Srbija 1918–1929: Makedonija, Sandžak, Kosovo i Metohija u lraljevini SHS.* Beograd: Institut za noviju istoriju Srbije, 2002.

Jovanovski, Dalibor. *Friendly Competition – Greek–Serbian Relations and Ottoman Macedonia in the Eighties of the 19th Century.* Skopje: Godišen zbornik na Filozofskiot fakultet, Ss. Cyril and Methodius, 2019.

Jubani, Zef. *Historia e popullit shqiptar: për shkollat e mesme.* Prishtinë: Libri Shkollor, 2002.

Kabashi, Vali. "Lidhja e Prizrenit – Organizata më e madhe politiko–ushtarake." *Koha Ditore* 09.06. 2018.

Kanchov, Vasil. *Orokhidrografia na Makedonia.* Sofia: Bŭlgarskoto knizhovno druzhestvo, 1911.

Karabekir, Kazìm. *İttihat ve Terakki Cemiyeti.* Istanbul: Yapı Kredi Yayınları, 2009.

Karadžić, Vuk. *Montenegro und die Montenegriner: Ein Beitrag zur Kenntniss der europäischen Türkei und des serbischen Volkes.* Stuttgart: Verlag der J. G. Cotta'schen Buchhandlung, 1837.

Karadžić, Vuk. *Crnogorci.* Beograd: Nolit, 1972.

Karadžić, Vuk. *Srbi svi i svuda – Kovčežić za istoriju, jezik i običaje Srba sva tri zakona.* Beč: N.P., 1849.

Karahasanoğlu, Selim. "Introduction." In *History from below: A Tribute in Memory of Donald Quataert*, edited by Selim Karahasanoğlu and Deniz Cenk Demir. 1–23. İstanbul: İstanbul Bilgi University Press, 2016.

Karakasidou, Anastasia. "Politicizing Culture: Negating Ethnic Identity in Greek Macedonia." *Journal of Modern Greek Studies* 11 (1993): 1–28.

Karakasidou, Anastasia. *Fields of Wheat, Hills of Blood: Passages to Nationhood in Greek Macedonia, 1870–1990.* Chicago: Chicago University Press, 1997.

Karaman, Kıvanç and Şevket Pamuk. "Ottoman State Finances in Comparative European Perspective, 1500–1914." *The Journal of Economic History* 70/3 (2010): 593–630.

Karamandzukov, Hristo. *Rodopa prez Ilindensko–Preobrazenskoto vostanie, Spomeni i dokumenti.* Sofia: Izdatelstvo na Otechestvenia front, 1986.

Karatay, Osman. "Osmanli hakimiyetinde Karadağ." In *Balkanlar el Kitabi'*, *cilt 1*, edited by Bilgehan A. Gokdag and Osman Karatay. 355–363. Ankara: Akçağ Yayınları, 2013.

Karić, Vladimir. *Srpska Zemlja.* Beograd: N.P., 1882.

Karić, Vladimir. *Srbija: opis zemlje, naroda i države.* Beograd: N.P., 1887.

Karić, Vladimir. *Udžbenik Zemljopisa – Geografije.* Beograd: N.P., 1879 and 1881.

Karpat, Kemal. *The Politicisation of Islam: Reconstructing Identity, State, Faith, and Community in the late Ottoman State.* Oxford University Press, 2001.

Karpat, Kemal. "The Social and Economic Transformation of Istanbul in the Nineteenth Century. " In *Selected Essays and Articles*, edited by Kemal Karpat. 243–290. Leiden: Brill, 2002.

Karpat, Kemal. "The Social and Political Foundations of Nationalism in South East Europe after 1878: A Reinterpretation, in Studies on Ottoman Social and Political History." In *Selected Essays and Articles*, edited by Kemal Karpat. 352–384. Leiden: Brill, 2002.

Karpat, Kemal. "Comments on Contributions and the Borderlands." In *Ottoman Borderlands: Issues, Personalities and Political Changes*, edited by

Kemal H. Karpat and Robert W. Zens. 1–15. Madison: The University of Wisconsin Press, 2003.

Kasaba, Reşat. "Do States Always Favor Stasis? The Changing Status of Tribes in the Ottoman Empire." In *Boundaries and Belonging: States and Societies in the Struggle to Shape Identities and Local Practices*, edited by Joel S. Migdal, 27–48. Cambridge: Cambridge University Press, 2009.

Kasaba, Reşat. *A Moveable Empire: Ottoman Nomads, Migrants, and Refugees.* Seattle/London: University of Wanshington Press, 2009.

Kaser, Karl. "Pastoral Economy and Family in the Dinaric and Pindus Mountain (14th–early 20th Centuries)." In *Household and Family in the Balkans: Two Decades of Historical Family Research at University of Graz*, edited by Karl Kaser. 289–305. Berlin: LIT Verlag, 2012.

Kaser, Karl. "Ahnenkult und Patriarchalismus auf dem Balkan." *Historische Anthropologie* 1/1 (1993): 93–123.

Kaser, Karl. *Hirten, Kämpfer, Stammeshelden: Ursprünge und Gegenwart des balkanischen Patriarchats*. Vienna/Cologne/Weimar: Böhlau Verlag, 1992.

Kastopoulos, Tasos. "'Land to the Tiller.' On the Neglected Agrarian Component of the Macedonian Revolutionary Movement, 1893–1912." *Turkish Historical Review* 7/2 (2016): 134–166.

Kašić, Lj. Dušan. "Koreni kosovke misli." In *Sveti Knez Lazar: Spomenica o šestoj stogodišnjici Kosovskog boja, 1389–1989*, edited by Episkop raško–prizrenski Pavle et al., 11–24. Beograd: Sveti arhijerejski sinod Srpska pravoslavna crkva, 1989.

Kayalı Hasan. *Arabs and Young Turks: Ottomanism, Arabism, and Islamism in the Ottoman Empire (1908–1918).* Berkeley: University of California Press, 1997.

Kechriotis, Vangelis. "Postcolonial Criticism Encounters late Ottoman Studies." *Historein: A Review of the Past and other Stories* 13 (2013): 39–46.

Keim, Wiebke. "Conceptualizing Circulation of Knowledge in the Social Sciences." In *Global Knowledge in the Social Sciences: Made in Circulation*, edited by Wiebke Keim, Ercüment Çelik, Christian Ersche and Veronika Wöhrer. 87–113. Farnham: Ashgate, 2014.

Kerchnawe, Hugo. "Die Militärverwaltung in Montenegro und Albanien." In *Die Militärverwaltung in den von den Österreichisch–Ungarischen Truppen Besetzten Gebieten*, edited by Hugo Kerchnawe et al. 270–304. New Haven: Wirtschafts– und Sozialgeschichte des Weltkrieges Hölder–Pichler–Tempsky A.G., 1928.

Keyserling, Hermann. *Europe*. London: George Allen & Unwin, 1928.

Kırmızı, Abdülhamit. "Experiencing the Ottoman Empire as a Life Course: Ferid Pasha, Governor and Grandvizier (1851–1914)." *Geschichte und Gesellschaft* 40 (2014): 42–66.

Kiminas, Demetrius. *The Ecumenical Patriarchate: A History of Its Metropolitanates with Annotated Hierarch Catalogs*. Cabin John: Wildside Press LLC., 2009.

Kiossev, Alexander and Daniela, Koleva. *Trudniat razkaz: Modeli na avtobiografichnoto razkazvane na sotzializma mezhdu ustnoto i pismenoto.* Sofia: Ciela, 2017.

Kiossev, Alexandar. *The End of Self–Colonization: Contemporary Bulgarian Literature and Its Global Condition*. Sofia: Bulgarian Literature as World Literature, 2020.

Kitromilides, Paschalis. "The Enlightenment East and West: a comparative perspective on the ideological origins of the Balkan political traditions." *Canadian Review of Studies in Nationalism* 10/1 (1983): 51–70.

Kitromilides, Paschalis. *The Enlightenment as Social Criticism: Iosipos Moisiodax and Greek Culture in the Eighteenth Century*. Princeton, NJ: Princeton University Press, 1992.

Kitromilides, Paschalis. "'Balkan Mentality': History, Legend, Imagination." *Nations and Nationalism* 2/2 (1996): 163–191.

Kitromilides, Paschalis. *An Orthodox Commonwealth: Symbolic Legacies and Cultural Encounters in Southeastern Europe*. Aldershot: Ashgate Press, 2007.

Kitromilides, Paschalis. *Enlightenment and Revolution: The Making of Modern Greece*. Cambridge: Harvard University Press, 2013.

Klein, Janet. "Çevreyi idar etmek: Osmanlı Devleti ve Hamidiye alayları." In *Türkiye'de Ordu, Devlet Ve Güvenlik Siyaseti*, edited by Evren Balta Paker and İsmet Akça, 105–124. Istanbul: Istanbul Bilgi Üniversitesi Yayınları, 2010.

Knöbl, Wolfgang, and Gunnar Schmidt. *Die Gegenwart des Krieges. Staatliche Gewalt in der Moderne*. Frankfurt am Main: S. Fischer, 2000.

Köhler, Jan and Heyer, Sonja. *Anthropologie der Gewalt*. Berlin: Verlag für Wissenschaft und Forschung, 1998.

Kofos, Evangelos. "Dilemmas and Orientations of Greek Policy in Macedonia: 1878–1886." In *Macedonia Past and Present,* edited by Evangelos Kofos as part of *Hidryma Meleton Chersonesou tou Haimou*. 135–152. Thessaloniki: Institute for Balkan Studies, 1992.

Kohn, Hans. *Pan–Slavism, its History and Ideology*. Indiana: University of Notre Dame Press, 1953.

Koliopoulos, S. John. *Brigands With A Cause: Brigandage and Irredentism in Modern Greece 1821–1912*. Oxford: Oxford University Press, 1987.

Koliopoulos, S. John and Thanos M. Veremis. *Greece: The Modern Sequel: From 1831 to the Present*. London: Hurst and Company, 2002.

Koller, Markus. *Bosnien an der Schwelle zur Neuzeit. Eine Kulturgeschichte der Gewalt (1747–1798)*. Munich: R. Oldenbourg, 2004.

Kołodziejczyk, Dariusz. "The 'Turkish Yoke' Revisited: the Ottoman Non–Muslim Subjects between Loyalty, Alienation, and Riot." *Acta Poloniae Historica* 93 (2006): 177–195.

Konstantinova, Yura. "Political Propaganda in Bulgaria during the Balkan Wars." *Institut za balkanistika s Tsentar po trakologia – Bŭlgarska akademia na naukite* 2–3 (2011): 79–116.

Korais, Adamantios. "Report On The Present State Of Civilization In Greece." In *Late Enlightenment – Emergence of the Modern 'National Idea'*, edited by Balazs Trencsenyi and Michal Kopecek. 144–147. Budapest/New York: Central European University Press, 2006.

Korsika, Bojan. *Srbija i Albanci: Pregled politike Srbije prema Albancima od 1878 do 1914. godine*. Ljubljana: Časopis "Kritiko znanosti", 1989.

Koselleck, Reinhart. "Der Einfluß der beiden Weltkriege auf das soziale Bewußtsein." In *Der Krieg des kleinen Mannes: Eine Militärgeschichte von unten,* edited by Wolfram Wette. 265–284. Munich: Piper, 1992.

Koselleck, Reinhart. *Vergangene Zukunft: Zur Semantik geschichtlicher Zeiten.* Frankfurt am Main: Suhrkamp Verlag, 1979.

Koselleck, Reinhart. *Futures Past: On the Semantics of Historical Time.* Columbia University Press, 2004.

Kosev, Dimitar, Hristo Hristov, Nikolay Todorov, Valentin Stankov. *Makedonia – Sbornik ot dokumenti i materiali*. Sofia, Izdatelstvo na Bŭlgarskata Akademia Naukite, 1978.

Kostić, Petar. *Crkveni život pravoslavnih Srba u Prizrenu i njegovoj okolini u XIX veku (sa uspomenama pisca).* Beograd: Grafički institut Narodna misao A. D., 1928.

Kovačević, Ljubomir. *Despot Stefan Lazarević za vreme turskih međusobica (1402 — 1413)*. Beograd: N.P., 1880.

Kovačević, Ljubomir. *Istorija srpskog naroda za srednje škole*. Beograd: Štamparija Kraljevine Srbije, 1893–94.

Kovačević, Ljubomir. *I opet kralj Vukašin nije ubio cara Uroša.* Beograd: N.P., 1884.

Kovačević, Ljubomir. *Vuk Branković*. Beograd: N.P., 1888.

Kovačević, Ljubomir. *Nekoliko pitanja o Stefanu Nemanji*. Beograd: N.P., 1891.

Kovačević, Ljubomir. *Žene i deca Stefana Prvovenčanog*. Beograd: N.P., 1901.

Koçunyan, Aylin. "The Millet System and the Challenge of Other Confessional Models, 1856–1865." *Ab Imperio* 1 (2017): 59–85.

Köksal, Osman. "Osmanlı Devletinde Sıkı Yönetim ile İlgili Mevzuat Üzerine bir Deneme." *AÜ Osmanlı Tarihi Araştırma ve Uygulama Merkezi Dergisi* 12 (2001): 157–172.

Köprülü, Fuad. *Bizans müesseselerinin Osmanlı müesseselerine tesiri hakkında: Türk hukuk ve iktisat tarihi mecmuası, I*. Istanbul: Evkaf Matbaası, 1931.

Krämer, Gudrun. "Der Reiz des Gesellschaftsvergleichs: Kategorien sozialer Ordnung im islamisch geprägten Vorderen Orient." In *Europa in der Welt des Mittelalters: Ein Colloquium für und mit Michael Borgolte*, edited by Tillmann Lohne and Benjamin Scheller, 101–118. Berlin/Boston: De Gruyter, 2014.

Krishna, Sankaran. *Globalization and Postcolonialism. Hegemony and Resistance in the Twenty–first Century*. Plymouth: Rowman & Littlefield Publishers, 2009.

Kruse, Jan, Kay Biesel, and Christian Schmieder. *Metaphernanalyse: Ein rekonstruktiver Ansatz*. Wiesbaden: VS Verlag für Sozialwissenschaften/ Springer, 2011.

Kuneralp, Sinan and Gül Tokay. *Ottoman Diplomatic Documents based on the Origins of World War I, the Macedonian Issue (1879–1912)*. Istanbul: ISIS Press, 2011.

Kurt, Ümit. *'Türk'ün Büyük, Biçare Irkı': Türk Yurdu'nda Milliyetçiliğin Esasları (1911–1916)*. Istanbul: İletişim, 2012.

Kurt, Ümit, and Doğan Gulpınar. "The Young Turk Historical Imagination in the Pursuit of Mythical Turkishness and Its Lost Grandeur (1911–1914)." *British Journal of Middle Eastern Studies* 43/4 (2016): 560–574.

Kurzman, Charles. *Modernist Islam, 1840–1940*. Oxford: Oxford University Press, 2002.

Kühn, Thomas. "Shaping and Reshaping Colonial Ottomanism: Contesting Boundaries of Difference and Integration in Ottoman Yemen, 1872–1919." *Comparative Studies of South Asia, Africa and the Middle East* 27/2 (2007): 315–331.

Külçe, Süleyman. *Firzovik Toplantısı ve Meşrutiyet.* Istanbul: Kitabevı, 2013.

Külçe, Süleyman. *Osmanlı Tarihinde Arnavutluk.* İzmir: Ticaret Matbaası, 1944.

Kürsat–Ahlers, Elçin. "Die Brutalisierung von Gesellschaft und Kriegsführung im Osmanischen Reich während der Balkankriege (1903–1914)." In *Gewalt im Krieg: Ausübung, Erfahrung und Verweigerung von Gewalt in Kriegen des 20. Jahrhunderts,* edited by Andreas Gestrich, 51–74. Münster: LIT Verlag, 1996.

Lampe, R. John and Constantin Iordachi. *Battling over the Balkans: Historiographical Questions and Controversies.* Budapest/New York: Central European University Press, 2020.

Landwehr, Achim. "Das Sichtbare sichtbar machen: Annäherungenan 'Wissen' als Kategorie historischer Forschung." In *Geschichte(n) der Wirklichkeit: Beiträge zur Sozial– und Kulturgeschichte des Wissens,* edited by Achim Landwehr. 61–93. Augsburg: Wißner Verlag, 2002.

Lange–Akhund, Nadine. *The Macedonian Question (1893–1908) from Western Sources, East European Monographs.* New York: Columbia University, 1998.

Langer, Benjamin. *Fremde, ferne Welt: Mazedonienimaginationen in der deutschsprachigen Literatur seit dem 19. Jahrhundert.* Bielefeld: Transcript Verlag, 2019.

Lazarević, Milutin. *Naši ratovi za oslobođenje i ujedinjenje, srpsko–turski rat 1912.* Beograd: Porta Libris, 2019.

Lejean, Guillaume. *Ethnographie de la Turquie d'Europe.* Gotha: Justus Perthes, 1861.

Leonhard, Jörn and Ulrike von Hirschhausen. *Empires and Nationalstaaten.* Göttingen: Vamdenhoeck & Ruprecht, 2011.

Leontis, Artemis. *Topographies of Hellenism: Mapping the Homeland.* Ithaca, NY: Cornell University Press, 1995.

Lilova, Desislava. "Barbarians, Civilized People and Bulgarians: Definition of Identity in Textbooks and the Press (1830–1878)." In *We the People: Politics of National Peculiarity in Southeastern Europe,* edited by Diana Mishkova, 181–207. Budapest/New York: Central European University Press, 2009.

Liotta, H. Patrick and Cindy R. Jebb. *Mapping Macedonia: Idea and Identity.* Santa Barbara: Greenwood Pub Group, 2004.

Livanios, Dimitris. "'Conquering the souls': nationalism and Greek guerrilla warfare in Ottoman Macedonia, 1904–1908," *BMGS* 23 (1999): 195–221.

Ljuljanović, Denis. "'Turkonegrins' between Montenegro and the Ottoman Empire: Brothers or Others?" In *Etnické komunity – Neviditelní, přehlížení, zapomenutí*, edited by Dana Bittnerová and Mirjam Moravcová, 35–57. Praha: Fakulta humanitních studií Univerzity Karlovy, 2019.

Longworth, Philip. *Making of Eastern Europe*. London: Palgrave Macmillan, 1997.

Loomba, Ania, Suvir Kaul, Bunzi Matti, Antoinette Burton, and Jed Esty. "Beyon What? An Introduction." In *Postcolonial Studies and Beyond*, edited by Ania Loomba, Suvir Kaul, Bunzi Matti, Antoinette Burton and Jed Esty, 1–38. Durham/London: Duke University Press, 2005.

Lory, Bernard. "Schools for the Destruction of Society: School Propaganda in Bitola 1860–1912." In *Conflicting Loyalties in the Balkans: The Great Powers, the Ottoman Empire and Nation–Building*, edited by Hannes Grandits, Nathalie Clayer and Robert Pichler, 46–63. London: I.B. Tauris, 2011.

Lučić, Iva. *Im Namen der Nation: Der politische Aufwertungsprozess der Muslime im sozialistischen Jugoslawien (1956–1971)*. Wiesbaden: Harrassowitz Verlag, 2018.

Luhmann, Niklas. *Funktion Der Religion*. Frankfurt am Main: Suhrkamp, 1982.

Luhmann, Niklas. "The Nation in the Balkan Village: National Politicization in Mid–Nineteenth–Century Ottoman Thrace." *Turkish Historical Review* 7/2 (2016): 167–193.

Lüdtke, Alf. "Akteure: Täter, Opfer, Zuschauer." In *Gewalt : Ein Intedisziplinäres Handbuch*, edited by Christian Gudehus and Michaela Christ, 177–83. Stuttgart/Weimar: Verlag J. B. Metzler, 2013.

Lüdtke, Alf. "Introduction: What Is the History of Everyday Life and Who Are Its Practitioners?" In *The History of Everyday Life: Reconstructing Historical Experiences and Ways of Life*, edited by Alf Lüdtke, 3–40. Princeton, NJ: Princeton University Press, 1995.

Lyberatos, Andreas Kosmas. "Introduction: Through Nation and State. Reform and Nationalism 'from Below' in the Late Ottoman Balkans." *Turkish Historical Review* 7/2 (2016): 121–133.

MacDermott, Mercia. *A History of Bulgaria: 1393–1885*. London: George Allen & Unwin, 1962.

Maggiolini, Paolo. "Understanding Life in the Ottoman–Montenegrin Borderlands of Northern Albania During the Tanzimat Era: Catholic Mirdite

Tribes, Missionaries and Ottoman Officials." *Middle Eastern Studies* 50/2 (2014): 203–232.

Majer, Hans Georg. "Herkunft und Volkszugehörigkeit muslimischer Amtsträger als historisches Problem in der Osmanistik." In *Ethnogenese und Staatsbildung in Südosteuropa*, edited by Klaus–Detlev Grothusen. 130–145. Göttingen: Vandenhoeck & Ruprecht, 1974.

Majer, Hans Georg. *Die Staaten Südosteuropas und die Osmanen.* Munich: Südosteuropa Gesellschaft, 1989.

Makdisi, Saree. *Romantic Imperialism – Universal Empire and the Culture of Moderny*. Cambridge: Cambridge University Press, 1998.

Makdisi, Ussama. "Ottoman Orientalism." *American Historical Review* 107/3 (Jun, 2002):768–796.

Makdisi, Ussama. "Rethinking Ottoman Imperialism: Modernity, Violence, and the Cultural Logic of Ottoman Reform." In *The Empire in the City: Arab Provincial Cities in the Ottoman Empire*, edited by Jens Hanssen and Thomas Philipp, 29–48. Würzburg: Ergon Verlag, 2002.

Malešević, Siniša. "Empires and Nation–States: Beyond the Dichotomy." *Thesis Eleven* 139/1 (2017): 1–9.

Malešević, Siniša. "The Foundations of Statehood: Empires and Nation–States in the Longue Durée." *Thesis Eleven* 139/1 (2017): 145–161.

Malešević, Siniša. "Nationalism and Imperialism as Enemies and Friends: Nation–State Formation and Imperial Projects in the Balkans." *Nations and States, Power and Civility*, edited by Francesco Duina, 149–172. Toronto: University of Toronto Press, 2018.

Malcolm, Noel. *Kosovo a short history*. New York: New York University Press, 1998.

Malcolm, Noel. "Myths of Albanian national identity: Some key elements." In *Albanian Identities: Myth and History* edited by Stephanie Schwanders–Sievers and Bernd J. Fischer, 1–28. Bloomington: Indiana University Press, 2002.

Mandzukov, Petar. *Predvestnici na buryata Spomeni.* Sofia: Federatsiata na anarkhistite v Bulgaria, 2013.

Mann, Michael. "The Autonomous Power of the State: Its Origins, Mechanisms and Results." *European Journal of Sociology*, 25/2 (1984): 185–213.

Manning, Patrick. *Navigating World History: Historians Create a Global Past.* New York: Palgrave Mcmillan. 2003.

Mano, A. Gaston. *Résumé géographique de la Grèce et de la Turquie d'Europe*. Paris: N.P., 1826.

Marchetti, Christian. "'Frontier Ethnography': Zur colonial situation der österreichischen Volkskunde auf dem Balkan im Ersten Weltkrieg." In *WechselWirkungen: Austria Hungary, Bosnia–Herzegovina, and the Western Balkans, 1878–1918*, edited by Clemens Ruthner et al., 363–381. New York: Peter Lang, 2015.

Mardin, Şerif. "Turkish Islamic Exceptionalism Yesterday and Today: Continuity, Rupture and Reconstruction in Operational Codes." *Turkish Studies* 6/2 (2005): 145–165.

Mardin, Şerif. "Center–Periphery Relations: A Key to Turkish Politics?" *Daedalus* 102/1 (1973): 37–54.

Marinov, Tchavdar. "We, the Macedonians, The Paths of Macedonian Supra–Nationalism (1878–1912)." In *We, the People: Politics of National Peculiarity in Southeastern Europe*, edited by Mishkova Diana, 107–137. Budapest/New York, Central European University Press, 2009.

Markovits, Claude, Jacques Pouchepadass and Sanjay Subrahmanyam (eds.). *Society and Circulation: Mobile People and Itinerant Cultures in South Asia, 1750–1950*. London: Anthem, 2006.

Materiali za Istoriata na makedonskoto osvoboditelno dvizhenie, kniga IX. Sofia: Pechatnitsa P. Gluskov, 1928.

Matov, Hristo. *Osnovi na vatreshnata revolyutsionna organizatsia.* Sofia: N.P., 1904.

Matov, Hristo. *Shto byahme – shto sme.* Plovdiv: N.P., 1905.

Matov, Milan. *Nai komitata raskazva, zhivot za Makedonia.* Sofia: Kulturno–blagotvoritelna fondatsia Bratia Miladinovi, 2002.

Matthews, Sally. "Colonised minds? Post–development theory and the desirability of development in Africa." *Third World Quarterly* 38/12 (2017): 1–18.

Mazower, Mark. "Violence and the State in the Twentieth Century." *American Historical Review* 107/4 (2002): 1158–1178.

Mazower, Mark. *The Balkans: A Short History*. New York: Modern Library, 2000.

Mazower, Mark. *Kratka povijest Balkana.* Zagreb: Srednja Europa, 2007.

Mbembe, Achille. "Necropolitics." trans. Libby Meintjes, *Public Culture* 15/1 (2003): 11–40.

Meininger, Thomas A. *Ignatiev and the Establishment of the Bulgarian Exarchate, 1864–1872.* Madison: State Historical Society of Wisconsin for the Dept. of History – University of Wisconsin, 1970.

Memoari na Vatrasnata Organizatsia. *Makedonia i Odrinsko (1893–1903).* Sofia: N.P., 1904.

Michalopoulos, Georgios. "Political Parties, Irredentism and the Foreign Ministry Greece and Macedonia: 1878–1910." PhD diss., University of Oxford, 2013.

Midell, Matthias and Katja Naumann. "Global History and the Spatial Turn: From the Impact of Area Studies to the Study of Critical Junctures of Globalization." *Journal of Global History* 5 (1) (2010): 149–170.

Migdal, Joel S. "The State in Society: Struggles and Accommodations in Multiple Arenas." *States and Social Structures Newsletter* 13 (1990): 1–5.

Migdal, Joel S., Atul Kohli, Vivienne Shue (eds.). *State Power and Social Forces: Domination and Transformation in the Third World.* Cambridge: Cambridge University Press, 1994.

Migdal, Joel S. *State in Society: Studying How States and Societies Transform and Constitute One Another*. Cambridge: Cambridge University Press, 2001.

Mignolo, Walter. *Local Histories/Global Designs: Coloniality, Subaltern Knowledge, And Border Thinking*. Princeton, NJ: Princeton University Press, 2000.

Mignolo, Walter. *The Darker Side of Western Modernity: Global Futures, Decolonial Options*. Druham, N.C.: Duke University Press, 2011.

Mihačević, Lovro. *Durch Albanien: Reise–Eindrücke.* Prague: Druck und Verlag des Bonifatius–Buchdruckerei, 1913.

Miladinović, Jovo. "Shifting State Loyalty: The Case of an Officer Serefeddin or Milan Milovanović." *Glasnik Etnografskog instituta* 68/3 (2020): 705–724.

Miladinović, Jovo. "Heroes, Traitors, and Survivors in the Borderlands of Empires Military Mobilizations and Local Communities in the Sandžak (1900s–1920s)." PhD diss., Humboldt University, 2021.

Miletich, Lyubomir. *Materiali za istoryata na makedonskoto osvoboditelno dvizhenie, knjiga IX.* Sofia: Pechatnitsa P. Glushkov, 1925–1928.

Miletitsch, Svetozar. *Die Orientfrage.* Neusatz: Serbish–Nationale Vereins–Buchdruckerei, 1877.

Milićević, Milić J. "Četnička Akcija Neposredno Pre Objave i Tokom Prvih Dana Srpsko–Turskog Rata 1912. Godine." In *Prvi Balkanski Rat 1912/13. Godine: Društveni i Civilizacijski Smisao (Međunarodni Tematski Zbornik)*, edited by Aleksandar Rastović, 221–234. Niš: Univerzitet u Nišu Filozofski fakultet, 2013.

Milićević, Milić J. "Imena Srpskih Pukova ." *Glasnik Istorijskog arhiva Valjevo* 33 (1999): 115–121.

Milićević, Milić J. *Reforma Vojske Srbije 1897–1900.* Beograd:

Vojnoizdavački zavod Beograd, 2002.

Milićević, Milić J. "Regrutni Sastav Vojske Srbije 1883–1912. Sistem Poziva I Neki Njegovi Društveni Aspekti." *Vojno–istorijski glasnik* 46/1 (2016): 9–25.

Miliukov, Pavel. *Vospominaniia (1859–1917)*. New York: Izdatelstvo im Chekhova, 1955.

Mill, S. John. "A Few Words On Non–Intervention, Foreign Policy Perspectives." *Fraser's Magazine 25* (August 1836): 214–221. This essay is also included in Mill's collected works, which were published as "Essays on Politics and Society." In *Collected Works of John Stuart Mill, Volume 18*. Toronto: University of Toronto Press, 1977.

Milašinović, Radomir, and Nenad Putnik. "Gerila Kao Specifičan Vid Društvenog Konflikta." In *Guerrilla in the Balkans: Freedom Fighters, Rebels or Bandits – Researching the Guerrilla and Paramilitary Forces in the Balkans*, edited by Momčilo Pavlović, Tetsuya Sahara and Predgrad J. Marković, 327–338. Tokyo/Beograd: University Meiji, Institute for Disarmament and Peace Studies, Tokyo/Institute of Contemporary History, Beograd/Faculty for Security Studies, Beograd, 2007.

Miller, Allexei and Berger, Stefan. *Nationalizing Empires*. New York: Central European University, 2014.

Miller, Allexei. *The Ukrainian Question: The Russian Empire and Nationalism in the 19th Century*. Budapest/New York: Central European University Press, 2003.

Miller, Marshall Lee. *Bulgaria During the Second World War*. Stanford: Stanford University Press, 1975.

Milojević, Miloš. *Odlomci istorije Srba i srpskih – jugoslavenskih – zemalja u Turskoj i Austriji*. Beograd: N.P., 1872.

Milojević, Miloš. *Istorisko etnografsko geografska mapa Srba i srpskih (jugoslavenskih) zemalja u Turskoj i Austriji.* Beogradu: Izdao Kosta Atanaskov – Šumenković, 1873.

Mintz, Sidney W. *Sweetness and Power: The Place of Sugar in Modern History*. New York: Penguin Books. 1986.

Mirchev, Boyan. *Materiali za istoryata na makedonskoto osvobitelno dvizhenie; knyiga XI.* Sofia, 1931.

Mishkova, Diana ed. *We the People: Politics of National Peculiarity in Southeastern Europe*. Budapest/New York: Central European University Press, 2009.

Misirkov, P. Krste, "Za makedonskite raboti," In *Krste P. Misirkov, Sobrani dela 1 – tekstovi na makedonski jazik (1900–1905)* edited by Blaže Ristovski and Biljana Ristovska–Josifovska, 125–162. Skopje: MANU, 2005.

Mitchell, Timothy. "Society, Economy, and the State Effect." In *State/Culture: State Formation after the Cultural Turn*, edited by George Steinmetz, 76–97. Ithaca, NY: Cornell University Press, 1999.

Mithat Paşa. *Hayatim Ibret Olsun.* Istanbul: Temel Yayınları, 1997.

Mithat Paşa. *Yıldız Mahkemesi ve Taif zindanı (Mirat–ı Hayret).* Istanbul: Temel Yayınları, 1997.

Mitrova, Makedonka. "The Kingdom of Serbia and Mursteg reforms in Ottoman Macedonia." *Journal of History* 1 (2015/2016).

Mitrović, Andrej. *Prodor na Balkan i Srbija, 1908–1918.* Beograd: Zavod za udžbenike, 2011.

Montemont, Albert. *Bulletin de la Société de géographie Société de géographie.* Paris: N.P., 1844.

Moumdjian, Garabet. "Rebels with a Cause: Armenian–Macedonian Relations and their Bulgarian Connection, 1895–1913." In *War and Nationalism: The Balkan Wars, 1912–1913, and the Sociopolitical Implications*, edited by Hakan M. Yavuz and Isa Blumi, 132–175. Salt Lake City: University of Utah Press, 2013.

Muir–Mackenzie, Georgina and Adeline Paulina Irby. *Travels in the Slavonic provinces of Turkey–in–Europe.* London: Daldy, Isbister and Company, 1877.

Munslow, Alun. *Deconstructing History.* London/New York: Routledge, 2006.

Müller, Joseph. *Albanien, Rumelien und die österreichisch–montenegrische Grenze. Nebst einer Karte von Albanien. Mit einer Vorrede von Dr. P. J. Šafarik.* Prague: N.P., 1844.

Nasser, Hussain. *The Jurisprudence of Emergency: Colonialism and the Rule of Law.* Ann Arbor: University of Michigan Press, 2003.

Nedeljković, Slaviša. "Delovanje Odbora za škole i učitelje u srpskim oblastima u Makedoniji od 1868. do 1876. godine." *Vardarski zbornik* 8 (2011): 283–306.

Nenadović, Mateja. *Memoari.* Beograd: Portalibris, 2017.

Newman, John Paul. "The Origins, Attributes, and Legacies of Paramilitary Violence in the Balkans." In *War in Peace: Paramilitary Violence in Europe after the Great War,* edited by Robert Gerwarth and John Horne, 145–163. Oxford: Oxford University Press, 2012.

Nicholas, Thomas. *Colonialism's Culture: Anthropology, Travel and Government*. Cambridge: Cambridge University Press, 1994.

Nietzsche, Friedrich. *Vom Nutzen und Nachteil der Historie für das Leben*. Leipzig: Verlag Panitzsch, 1874.

Niyazi Bey, Ahmed. *Hatırat–ı yahut tarihçe–i inkilab–ı kebir–i Osmanlı'dan bir sahife*. IIstanbul: Sabah Matbaası, 1326 [1910].

Nopcsa, Franz Baron. *Aus Šala und Klementi: Albanische Wanderungen*. Sarajevo: Druck und Verlag und Daniel A. Kajon, 1910.

Nora, Pierre. *The Realms of Memory: Rethinking the French Past*. New York: Columbia University Press, 1997.

Novaković, Kosta. *Makedonija Makedoncima, zemlja zemljoradnicima*. Čačak: Čačanski glas, 1924.

Novaković, Kosta. *Autobiografija Koste Novaković*. Čačak: Čačanski glasnik, 1966.

Nuro, Kujtim and Nezir Bato. *Hasan Prishtina – permbledhje dokumentash (1908–1934)*. Tiranë: Drejtoria e Pergjithshme e Arkivave të Shtetit, 1982.

Nušić, Branislav. *Sa obala Ohridskog jezera*. Beograd: N.P., 1892.

Nušić, Branislav. *S Kosova na sinje more*. Beograd: N.P., 1894.

O Tuathail, Gearoid. *Critical Geopolitcs: The Writing of Global Space*. London: Routledge, 1996.

Orhonlu, Cengiz. *Osmanlı İmparatorluğunda Aşiretleri İskan Teşebbüsü*. Istanbul: Edebiyat Fakültesi Basımevi, 1963.

Ortajli, Ilber. *Najduži vek imperije*. Beograd: Srpska književna zadruga, 2004.

Ortner, M. Christian. "Erfahrungen einer westeuropäischen Armee auf dem Balkan: Die militärische Durchsetzung österreichisch–ungarischer Interessen während der Interventionen von 1869, 1878 und 1881/82." In *Am Rande Europas? Der Balkan– Raum und Bevölkerung als Wirkungsfelder militärischer Gewalt*, edited by Bernhard Chiari und Gerhard P. Groß, 67–87. Munich: R. Oldenbourg Verlag, 2009.

Osmanlı Yönetiminde Makedonya. Istanbul: T.C. Başbakanlık Devlet Arşivleri Genel Müdürlüğü ve Makedonya Cumhuriyeti Devlet Arşivi, 2005.

Osterhammel, Jürgen. *Die Verwandlung der Welt. Eine Geschichte des 19. Jahrhunderts*. Munich: Beck, 2009.

Osterhammel, Jürgen. "'Colonialisme' et 'Empires coloniaux.'" *Labyrinthe* 35 (2010): 57–68.

Osterhammel, Jürgen. *Geschichtswissenschaft jenseits des Nationalstaats: Studien zu Beziehungsgeschichte und Zivilisationsvergleich.* Göttingen: Vandenhoeck & Ruprecht, 2011.

Önal–Emiroğlu, Çiğdem and Kudret Emiroğlu. *Osmanlı Terakki ve İttihat Cemiyeti: Paris Merkezi Yazışmaları Kopya Defterleri (1906–1908).* Istanbul: Tarih Vakfi Yurt Yayınları, 2017.

Özatalay, Fehmi. *Türk Silahlı Kuvvetleri Tarihi: Balkan Harbi, Garp Ordusu, Karadağ Cephesi, III. cilt / 3. Kısım, 20.* Ankara: Genelkurmay Başkanlığı, 1993.

Özbek, Nadir. "Policing the Countryside: Gendarmes of the Late 19th–Century Ottoman Empire (1876–1908)." *International Journal of Middle East Studies* 40/1 (2008): 47–67.

Özer, Özbozdağlı. "Osmanlı hükmetinin Kosova Arnavutları arasındaki kan davalarına çözüm Bulma çabaları 1908–1912." *Belleten* 82/2 (2010): 979–1011.

Özkan, Behlül. *From the Abode of Islam to the Turkish Vatan – The: The Making of a National Homeland in Turkey.* New Haven: Yale University Press, 2012.

Paasi, Anssi. "Constructing Territories, Boundaries and Regional Identities." In *Contested Territory: Border Disputes at the Edge of the Former Soviet Empire,* edited by Tuomas Forsberg. 42–61. Aldershot: Edward Elgar (1995).

Palairet, Michael. *The Balkan economies c. 1800–1914 – Evolution without development.* Cambridge: Cambridge University Press, 2003.

Pandevski, Manol. *Mladoturskata Revolucija i Makedonija.* Skopje: N.P., 1968.

Pandevski, Manol. *Nacionalnoto prašanje vo makedonskoto osloboditel–noto dviženje (1893–1903).* Skopje: Kultura, 1974.

Pandevski, Manol. "Razvitokot na političkiot život vo Evropska Turcija vo periodot na mladoturskoto upravuvanie 1908–1912" *Istorija* 15/2 (1979): 105–116.

Pandevski, Manol. "Yane Sandanski and the Macedonian Liberation Movement" In *Macédoine (Articles d'Histoire),* edited by Aleksandar Matkovski and Krste Bitoski. 243–264. Skopje: Institut d'histoire nationale, 1981.

Pandevski, Manol. *Vnatrešnata Makedonska Revolucionerna Organizacija i neovrhovizmot 1904–1908.* Skopje: Misla, 1983.

Pandevski, Manol. *Makedonskoto osloboditelno delo vo XIX i XX vek, vol. 4.* Skopje: Misla, 1987.

Papageorgiou, P. Stefanos. "Vasos Mavrovunotis (Vaso Brajović) – Crnogorac u grčkoj revoluciji." *Matica Crnogorska* 62 (2015): 45–80.

Pandey, Gyanendra. "Voices from the Edge: The Struggle to Write Subaltern Histories. " In *Mapping Subaltern Studies and the Postcolonial*, edited by Vinayak Chaturvedi, 281–99. London/New York: Verso, 2000.

Parker, J. Bradley. "Toward an Understanding of Borderland Processes."*American Antiquity* 71/1 (2006): 77–100.

Pashko Vasa. *Arnavutluk ve Arnavutlar*. Istanbul: N.P., 1287/1880.

Pashko Vasa. *The Truth on Albania and the Albanians: Historical and Critical*. London: Centre for Albanian Studies, 1999.

Pašić, Ema and Dina Pašić. "Zakonik Leke Dukađinija: Pitanje kodifikacije Štjefena Konstantina Đečovića." *KSIO: Humanities Journal for Postgraduates and Early Career Researchers* 1 (2018): 28–40.

Pavlović, Aleksandar. "Rereading the Kosovo Epic." *Serbian Studies Journal* 23/1 (2009): 83–96.

Pavlović, Aleksandar. "Naming/Taming the Enemy: Balkan Oral Tradition and formation of 'the Turk' as the Political Enemy." In *Us and Them Symbolic Divisions in Western Balkan Societies*, edited by Ivana Spasić and Predrag Cvetičanin. 19–36. Beograd: The Institute for Philosophy and Social Theory of the University of Beograd, 2013.

Pavlović, Aleksandar and Srđan Atanasovski. "From Myth to Territory: Vuk Karadžić, Kosovo Epics and the Role of Nineteenth–Century Intellectuals in Establishing National Narratives." *Hungarian Historical Review* 5/2 (2016): 357–376.

Pavlović, Aleksandar. *Epika i politika: Nacionalizovanje crnogorske usmene tradicije u prvoj polovini XIX veka*. Beograd: Biblioteka XX vek, 2014.

Pavlović, Momčilo and Predrag J. Marković. "Guerrilla in the Balkans: Historical Conditions and Developments." In *Guerrilla in the Balkans: Freedom Fighters, Rebels or Bandits – Researching the Guerrilla and Paramilitary Forces in the Balkans*, edited by Momčilo Pavlović, Tetsuya Sahara, and Predgrad J. Marković, 21–30. University Meiji, Institute for Disarmament and Peace Studies, Tokyo/Institute of Contemporary History, Beograd/Faculty for Security Studies, Beograd, 2007.

Peckham, Robert Shannan. "Internal Colonialism: Nation and Region in Nineteenth–Century Greece." In *Balkan Identities: Nation and Memory*, edited by Maria Todorova, 41–59. London: Hurst & Company, 2004.

Pećanac, Vojvoda Kosta. *Četnicka akcija 1903–1912*. Beograd: N.P., 1933.

Pejović, D. Đoko. *Politika Crne Gore u zatarju i Gornjem Polimlju*

1878–1912. Titograd: Istorijski institut u Titogradu, 1973.

Penchev, Boyko. "Tsarigrad/Istanbul and the Spatial Construction of Bulgarian National Identity in the Nineteenth Century." *Nexus* (2002–2003): 1–13.

Perry, Duncan. *The Politics of Terror: Macedonian Revolutionary Movements, 1893–1903.* Durham: Duke University Press, 1988.

Përse u zgjodhen dy alfabete: Materiale e Dokumente. Studime Filologjike. Tiranë: Akademia e Shkencave e RPSSH, Instituti i Gjuhësisë dhe i Letersisë, 1988.

Petrovich, Michael Boro. *The Emergence of Russian Panslavism.* New York: Columbia University Press, 1958.

Petrović, Milić F.. *Dokumenti o Raškoj oblasti, 1900–1912.* Beograd: Arhiv Srbije, 1995.

Petrović, Nikola. *Memoari.* Cetinje: Obod, 1988.

Petrović, Nikola. *Pisma.* Podgorica: Cetinje Sveti Gora, 2009.

Petrović Njegoš, Petar. *Gorski vijenac.* Beograd: Branko Dinović, 1963.

Petrović Njegoš, Petar. *Lažni car Šćepan mali.* Trieste: N.P., 1851.

Petrović, Tanja. "Understanding Southeastern Europe and the Former Yugoslavia (De)Colonising Socialist Experience." In *From the Highlands to Hollywood: Multidisciplinary Perspectives on Southeastern Europe Festschrift for Karl Kaser and SEEHA,* edited by Siegfried Gruber, Dominik Gutmeyr, Sabine Jesner, Elife Krasniqi, Robert Pichler, Christian Promitzer, 95–105. Vienna: LIT Verlag, 2020.

Pinson, Mark. "Ottoman Bulgaria in the First Tanzimat Period — The Revolts in Nish (1841) and Vidin (1850)." *Middle Eastern Studies* 11/2 (May, 1975): 103–146.

Pitassio, Armando. "The Building of Nations in South–Eastern Europe. The Cases of Slovenia and Montenegro: a Comparative Approach." In *The Balkans: national identities in a historical perspective,* edited by Stefano Bianchini and Marco Dogo, 33–60. Ravenna: Longo Editore, 1998.

Pllana, Emin. *Kosova dhe reformat ne Turqi.*Prishtinë: Rilindja, 1978.

Pojani, Selim. "Çeta e parë nacionaliste." In *Kujtime nga levizja për çlirimin kombëtar në vitet 1878 – 1912,* edited by Petraq Pepo, 111–127. Tiranë: Universiteti Shtetëror i Tiranës, Instituti i Historisë e Gjuhësisë, 1962.

Polith, Mihailo. *Die Orientalische Frage und ihre Organische Lösung.* Vienna: Franz Leo's Verlag, 1862.

Pollo, Stefanaq and Selami Pulaha. *La Ligue albanaise de Prizren, 1878–1881.* Tiranë: Institut d'Histoire, 1978.

Pollo, Stefanaq, Aleks Buda, Kristaq Prifti, Kristo Frashëri. *Historia e Shqipërisë (vitet 30 të shek. XIX–1912). vëllimi i dytë.* Tiranë: Akademia e shkencave e RPS te Shqipërisë – Instituti i Historisë, 1984.

Pomeranz, Kenneth. *The Great Divergence: China, Europe, and the Making of the Modern World Economy.* Princeton, NJ: Princeton University Press, 2001.

Pouqeville, Francois. *Travels in Epirus, Albania, Macedonia, and Thessaly.* London: Printed for Sir Richard Phillips and Co, 1820.

Prifti, Kristaq. *Botimi dhe përhapja në Evropë e vepres së Pashko Vases 'E vërteta për Shqipërinë dhe Shqipëtaret'.* Tiranë: Studime Historike, 2002.

Prifti, Kristaq. "Certain aspects des rapports de la Ligue albanaise de Prizren avec la Sublime Porte selon les documents ottomans (1878–1881*)*." *Studia Albanica* 1 (2012): 49–63.

Pringle, Robert. *Balkanization.* London: Encyclopaedia Britannica, 2006.

Prishtina, Hasan Bey. *Nji shkurtim kujtimesh mbi kryengritjen shqiptare të vjetit 1912. Shkrue prej Hassan Prishtinës.* Shkodra: Shtypshkroja Franciskane, 1921.

Protocols of Congress of the Representatives of Great Britain, Austria–Hungary, France, Germany, Italy, Russia, and Turkey; for the Settlement of Affairs in the East. Berlin: N.P., June/July, 1878.

Prousis, C. Theophilus. "British Embassy Reports on the Greek Uprising in 1821–1822: War of Independence or War of Religion?" *History Faculty Publications* 21 (2011): 171–222.

Psilos, Christopher. "The Young Turk Revolution and the Macedonian Question." PhD diss., University of Leeds, 2000.

Puto, Artan and Maurizio Isabella. "From Southern Italy to Istanbul: Trajectories of Albanian Nationalism in the Writings of Girolamo de Rada and Shemseddin Sami Frashëri ca. 1848–1903." In *Mediterranean Diasporas: Politics and Ideas in the Long 19th Century,* edited by Maurizio Isabella, Konstantina Zanou, 171–189. London: Bloomsbury Academic, 2015.

Qemali, Ismail. *The Memoirs of Ismail Kemal Bey.* London: Constable and Company LTB, 1921.)

Quataert, Donald. *The Ottoman Empire, 1700–1922.* Cambridge: Cambridge University Press, 2005.

Radenić, Andrija. *Dokumenta iz bečkih arhiva/Österreich–Ungarn und Serbien 1903–1918 – Dokumente aus Wiener Archiven.* Beograd: Istorijski institut, 1973.

Radev, Simeon. *Stroitelite na Sŭvremenna Bŭlgaria, Tom 1,2,3.* Sofia: Bŭlgarski pisatel, 1910–11.

Radev, Simeon. *Ranni Spomeni, Novo korigiran i dopolneno izdanie pod redaktsijyata na Trayan Radev*. Sofia: Izd. Kusha Strelets, 1994.

Radev, Simeon. *Tova, koeto vidya hot Balkanskata voinam Narodna kultura*. Sofia: Zabravenit Bŭlgari, 2012.

Radosavljević, Nedeljko. "Episkop, mirski sveštenik, monah: obeležja svakodnevnog života." In *Privatni život kod Srba u devetnaestom veku: od kraja XVIII veka do početka Prvog svetskog rata*, edited by Ana Stolić and Nenad Makuljević, 711–736. Beograd: Clio, 2006.

Randeria, Shalini. "Geteilte Geschichte und verwobene Moderne." In *Zukunftsentwürfe: Ideen für eine Kultur der Veränderung*, edited by Jörn Rüsen, Hanna Leitgeb and Norbert Jegelka, 87–96. Frankfurt; New York: Campus, 1999.

Rastović, Aleksandar. *Velika Britanija i Makedonsko pitanje 1903–1908*. Beograd: Istorijski Institut, 2011.

Raugh, Jr. E. Harold. "Introduction." In *Alliance Planning and Coalition Warfare: Historical and Contemporary Approaches*, edited by Jr. Harold E. Raugh, 7–16. Beograd: Institute for Strategic Research, 2019.

Rauer, Valentin. "Interobjektivität: Sicherheitskultur aus Sicht der Akteur–Netzwerk–Theorie." In *Sicherheitskultur: Soziale und politische Praktiken der Gefahrenabwehr*, edited by Christopher Daase, Philipp Offermann and Valentin Rauer, 69–91. Frankfurt/New York: Campus Verlag, 2012.

Readman, Paul, Cynthia Radding, and Chad Bryant. "Introduction: Borderlands in a Global Perspective." In *Borderlands in World History, 1700–1914*, edited by Paul Readman, Cynthia Radding and Chad Bryant, 1–23. London: Palgrave Macmillan, 2014.

Rexhepagiq, Jashar. *Zhvillimi i arësimit dhe i sistemit shkollor të kombësisë shqiptare në teritorin e Jugosllavisë së sotme deri në vitin 1918*. Prishtinë: Enti i teksteve dhe i mjeteve mësimore i Krahinës Socialiste Autonome të Kosovës, 1970.

Reinkowski, Maurus. "Double Struggle, No Income: Ottoman Borderlands in Northern Albania." *International Journal of Turkish Studies* 9/1 (2003): 239–253.

Reinkowski, Maurus. "The State's Security and the Subjects' Prosperity: Notions of Order in Ottoman Bureaucratic Correspondence (19th Century)." In *Legitimizing the Order: The Ottoman Rhetoric of State Power,* edited by Hakan Karateke and Maurus Reinkowski, 195–213. Leiden: Brill, 2005.

Reinkowski, Maurus. "The Ottoman Empire and South Eastern Europe from a Turkish perspective." In *Images of imperial legacy: modern discourses on the social and cultural impact of Ottoman and Habsburg rule in Southeast*

Europe, edited by Tea Sindbaek and Maximilian Hartmuth, 21–36. Berlin: LIT, 2011.

Reinkowski, Maurus. "Hapless Imperialists and Resentful Natioalists: Trajectories of Radicalization in the Late Ottoman Empire." In *Helpless Imperialists: Imperial Failure, Fear and Radicalization*, edited by Maurus Reinkowski and Gregor Thum, 47–66. Göttingen: Vandenhoeck & Ruprecht, 2012.

Renn, Jürgen. "From the History of Science to the History of Knowledge and Back." *Centaurus: An International Journal of the History of Science & its Cultural Aspects* 57 (2015): 37–53.

Rinke, Stefan, and Delia González de Reufels. *Expert Knowledge in Latin American History: Local, Transnational, and Global Perspectives.* Stuttgart: Heinz, 2014.

Ristić, Mihailo L. *Kroz Groblje – opažanja i beleške prilikom putovanja kroz srpsku zemlju pod Turskom 1892 g.* Beograd: N.P., *1892.*

Riza, Ahmet. *Ahmet Riza Bey'in Anıları*. Istanbul: Dizgi Yayınnları, 2001.

Rizov, Dimitar. *Bŭlgarite v tekhnite istoricheski, etnograficheski i politicheski granitsi 679–1917*. Berlin: Königliche Hoflithographie, Hof–Buch– und Steindruckere Wilhelm Greve, 1917.

Rizov, Nikola. *Albanskoto vazrazhdanie*. Sofia: Knizharnitsa Hr. Olchev, 1909.

Rodgers, Daniel. *Atlantic Crossings: Social Politics in a Progressive Age.* London: Belknap Press, 1998.

Rodogno, David. "The European Powers' Intervention in Macedonia, 1903–1908: An Instance of Humanitarian Intervention?" In *Humanitarian Intervention: A History,* edited by Brendan Simms and David J. B. Trim, 205–226. Cambridge: Cambridge University Press, 2011.

Rodogno, David. "The 'principles of humanity' and the European powers' intervention in Ottoman Lebanon and Syria in 1860–1861." In *Humanitarian Intervention: A History*, edited by Brendan Simms and David J. B. Trim, 159–183. Cambridge: Cambridge University Press, 2011.

Rodogno, David. *Against Massacre – Humanitarian Interventions in the Ottoman Empire (1815–1914)*. Princeton, NJ: Princeton University Press, 2012.

Roessel, David. *Byron's Shadow: Modern Greece in the English and American Imagination*. Oxford: Oxford University Press, 2002.

Rohdewald, Stefan. "Figures of (Trans–)National Religious Memory of the Orthodox Southern Slavs before 1945: An Outline on the Examples of Ss. Cyril and Methodius." *TRAMES* 12 (2008): 287–298.

Rohdewald, Stefan. *Götter der Nationen: Religiöse Erinnerungsfiguren in Serbien, Bulgarien und Makedonien bis 1944*. Vienna /Cologne/Weimar: Böhlau Verlag, 2014.

Rohdewald, Stefan, Albrecht Fuess, Florian Riedler, Stephan Conermann eds. *Wissenszirkulation: Perspektiven und Forschungsstand, in Transottomanica–Osteuropäisch–osmanisch–persische Mobilitätsdynamiken*. Göttingen:Vandenhoeck & Ruprecht Verlag, 2019.

Rohdewald, Stefan. *Sacralizing the Nation through Remembrance of Medieval Religious Figures in Serbia, Bulgaria and Macedonia*. Leiden: Brill, 2022.

Rohdewald, Stefan. "Religious Wars? Southern Slavs' Orthodox Memory of the Balkan and World Wars." In *The Balkan Wars from Contemporary Perception to Historic Memory*, edited Katrin Boeckh and Sabine Rutar, 249–273. London: Palgrave Macmilian, 2016.

Roth, Klaus and Ulf Brunnbauer. *Region, Regional Identity and Regionalism in Southeastern Europe*. Münster: LIT Verlag, 2009.

Rosiny, Stephan. "Der Jihad : Historische und zeitgenössische Formen islamisch legitimierter Gewalt." In *Gerechter Krieg – gerechter Frieden: Religionen und friedensethische Legitimationen in aktuellen militärischen Konflikten*, edited by Ines–Jaqueline Werkner and Antonius Liedgehener, 225–244. Wiesbaden: VS Verlag für Sozialwissenschaften, 2009.

Rossos, Andrew. *Russia and the Balkans: Inter–Balkan Rivalries and Russian Foreign Policy, 1908–1914*. Toronto: University of Toronto Press, 1981.

Roudometof, Victor. *Collective Memory, National Identity, and Ethnic Conflict: Greece, Bulgaria and the Macedonian Question*. New York: Praeger Publisher, 2002.

Rovinski, Pavel Apolonovič. *Crna Gora u prošlosti i sadašnjosti, vol. II*. Beograd: Obod, 2004.

Rumeli Vilayeti Kanunu Layiha. *Ahali–ı Vilayetin Hukuku Umumiyesi*. Istanbul: Matbaa–i Amire, 1296/1880.

Rustow, Dankwart and Ward, Robert. *Political Modernization in Japan and Turkey*. Princeton, NJ: Princeton University Press, 2015.

Ružić, A. Jevto. *Skadar i Bregalnica (Crna Gora u ratovima 1912–1918 godine)*. Munich: Štamparija Iskra, 1964.

Sahara, Tetsuya. "Paramilitaries in the Balkan Wars: The Case of Macedonian Adrianople Volunteers." In *War and Nationalism: The Balkan Wars, 1912–1913, and Their Sociopolitical Implications*, edited by M. Hakan Yavuz and Isa Blumi, 399–419. Salt Lake City: The University of Utah Press, 2013.

Said, Edward. *Orientalism*. New York: Pantheon, 1978.

Said, Edward. "Culture and Imperialism." Lecture held in Toronto at York University, February 10, 1993. See this lecture and collection of his essays in Edward Said, Culture and Imperialism (New York: Vintage Books, 1994)

Said, Edward. "Invention, Memory, and Place." *Critical Inquiry* 26/2 (2000): 175–192.

Said Paşa. *II Abdülhamid'in ilk mabeyn feriki Eğenli Said Paşa'nın hatıratı, I–II (1876–1880)*. Istanbul: Bengi Yayınları, 2011.

Sajkowski, Wojiciech. "From Vinko Pribojević to the French Encyclopaedia – The History of the South Slavs and the Historiography of the French Enlightenment." In *Macedonia: Land, Region, Borderland*, edited by Jolanta Sujecka, 331–348. Warsaw: Wydawnictwo DiG, 2013.

Šaljić–Ratković, D. Jovana. "Muslimani u oslobođenu Srbiju 1912/13: od mita do stvarnosti.*" Prvo balkanski rat 1912/13 godine: društveni i civilizacijski smisao (Povodom stogodišnjice oslobođenja Stare Srbije i Makedonije 1912)* 1 (2016): 325-339

Sarasin, Philipp. "Was ist Wissensgeschichte?" *Internationales Archiv für Sozialgeschichte der deutschen Literatur* 36 (2011): 159–172.

Šarenac, Danilo. "Remembering Victory: The Case of Serbia/Yugoslavia." *Südosteuropa-Jahrbuch* 42 (2018): 225–245.

Šarenac, Danilo. *Top, vojnik i sećanje: Prvi svetski rat i Srbija 1914–2009*. Beograd: Institut za savremenu istoriju, 2014.

Sarıca, Ragip. *Fransa'da ve Türkiye'de örfi idare rejimi*. Istanbul: Baro Macmuası, 1941.

Saygılı, Hasip. "1903 Makedonya'sında reformlara tepkiler: Manastır Rus konsolosu Aleksandır Rostkovski'nin katli." *Karadeniz Araştırmaları* 39 (2013): 69–94.

Saygılı, Hasip. "Rumeli Müfettişliği döneminde (1902–1908) Makedonya'da Yunan komitecileri ve Osmanlı devleti." *Güvenlik Stratejileri Dergisi* 11/21 (2015): 147–185.

Schama, Simon. *Landscape and Memory*. New York: Vintage, 1995.

Scheuringer, Brunhilde. *Multiple Identities: A Theoretical and an Empirical Approach*. Cambridge: Cambridge University Press, 2016.

Schiro, Giueseppe. *Gli Albanesi e la Questione Balkanica*. Napoli: A spese dell'editore Ferd. Bideri, 1904.

Schmieder, Falko. "Gleichzeitigkeit des Ungleichzeitigen: Zur Kritik und Aktualität einer Denkfigur." *Zeitschrift für kritische Sozialtheorie und Philosophie* 4/1–2 (2017): 325–363.

Schmidt–Neke, Michael. "Der Kanun der albanischen Berge:

Hintergrund der Nordalbanischen Lebensweise." In *Der Kanun: Das albanische Gewohnheitsrecht nach dem sogenannten Kanun des Lekë Dukadjini kodifiziert von Shtjefën Gjeçevi*, edited by Robert Elsie, 11–34. Pejë: Dukagjini Publishing House, 2001.

Schmitt, Oliver Jens. *Shqiptarët*. Tiranë: K&B, 2012.

Schmitt, Oliver Jens. *Südosteuropa im Spätmittelalter: Akkulturierung– Integration–Inkorporation?*. *Vorträge und Forschungen: Akkulturation im Mittelalter* 78 (2014): 81–137.

Schmitt, Oliver Jens and Eva Anne Frantz. *Politik und Gesellschaft im Vilayet Kosovo und im serbisch beherrschten Kosovo 1870–1914*. Vienna: VÖAW, 2020.

Schmitt, Oliver Jens. *Der Balkan Im 20. Jahrhundert: Eine Postimperiale Geschichte*. Stuttgart: Kohlhammer, 2019.

Schmitt, Oliver Jens. *Kosovo: Kurze Geschichte einer zentralbalkanischen Landschaft*. Vienna: Böhlau Verlag, 2008.

Schmitt, Oliver Jens, and Michael Metzeltin. "Das Südosteuropa der Regionen: Einleitung." In *Das Südosteuropa der Regionen*, edited by Oliver Jens Schmitt and Michael Metzeltin, 7–37. Vienna: Verlag der Österreichischen Akademie der Wissenschaften, 2015.

Schultz, Hans–Dietrich. "'Natürliche Grenzen' als politisches Programm." In *Grenzenlose Gesellschaft?*, edited by Claudia Honegger, Stefan Hradil, and Franz Traxler, 328–343. Oplande: Leske + Budrich, 1999.

Schneider, Ulrich Johannes. "Wissensgeschichte, nicht Wissenschafsgeschichte." In *Michel Foucault: Zwischenbilanz einer Rezeption,* edited by Axel Honneth and Martin Saar, 220–229. Frankfurt am Main: Suhrkamp, 2003.

Schulten, Susan. *The Geographical Imagination in America, 1880–1950*. Chicago: University of Chicago Press, 2001.

Schütz, Alfred and Luckmann, Thomas. *The Structures of the Life– World*, vol. 2. Evanston: Northwestern University Press, 1989.

Schwandner–Sievers, Stephanie. "Humiliation and Reconciliation in Northern Albania: The Logics of Feuding in Symbolic and Diachronic Perspectives." In *Dynamics of Violence: Processes of Escalation and De– Escalation in Violent Group Conflicts*, edited by Georg Elwert, Stephan Feuchtwang, and Dieter Neubert, 133–152. Berlin: Dunckler & Humblot, 1999.

Sciaky, Leon. *Farewell to Salonika – City at the Crossroads*. Sansom: Paul Dry Books, 2003.

Sediy, Miroslav. *Metternich, the Great Powers and the Eastern Question, Typos*. Pilsen, University of West Bohemia, 2013.

Sekulovski, Goran. "Le géographe Kiepert et les Balkans à Berlin (1878): les archives diplomatiques mises en perspective. Cartes & géomatique." *Cartographie et traités de paix (XVe–XXe siècle)* 228/6 (2016): 73–81.

Seliminski, Ivan. "Letter To Georgi Zolotovich." In *Late Enlightenment – Emergence of the Modern 'National Idea',* edited by Balazs Trencsenyi and Michal Kopecek. Budapest/New York: Central European University, 2006: 182–188.

Skendi, Eqber. *Hoxhë Kadriu(Kadri Prishtina)*. Prishtinë: Rilindja, 1992.

Šešum, Uroš. "Srpska četnička organizacija u Staroj Srbiji 1903–1908. Terenska organizacija." *Srpske Studije/Serbian Studies* 2 (2011): 239–259.

Šešum, Uroš. "Društvo protiv Srba 1897–1902." *Srpske Studije/Serbian Studies,* 4, (2013): 73–103.

Šešum, Uroš. "Četnička organizacija u Skopskoj Crnoj Gori 1903–1908, godine." *Zbornik Matice srpske za istoriju* 93 (2016): 55–70.

Shahov, Kost. *Edno osvetlenie po nashite raboti, in Ot Sofia do Kostur. Spomeni.* Sofia: IK Sineva, 2003.

Shapkarev, Kuzman. *Bŭlgarska Chitanka*. Istanbul, 1868.

Sharp, P. Joanne. *Geographies of Postcolonialism.* London: Sage Publications, 2011.

Sharpe, Jim. "History from Below." In *New Perspectives on Historical Writing,* edited by Peter Burke, 24–41. Pennsylvania: Pennsylvania State Universtity Press, 1991.

Shatev, Pavel. *Solunskiat attentat i zatochenitsitie v 'Fezan.* Sofia: Makedonski nauchen institut, 2015.

Shpuza, Gazmend. *Shpërthimi i kryengritjes dhe veprimet luftarake (Mars – Fillimi i Qershorit 1911).* Prishtinë: Rilindja Kombëtare Shqipëtare, 1984.

Šikoparija, Vojislav. *Sećanja srpskog oficira (1900–1918).* Beograd: Zavod za udžbenike i nastavna sredstva, 2016.

Silyanov, Hristo. *Osvoboditelnite Borbi na Makedonia.* Sofia: Darzhavna Pechatnia, 1983.

Simić, Predrag. "Balkans and Balkanisation: Western Perceptions of the Balkans in the Carnegie Commission's Reports on the Balkan Wars from 1914 to 1996." *Perceptions* 18/ 2 (2013): 113–135.

Simić, Stevan. *Srpska revolucionarna organizacija, komitsko četovanje u Staroj Srbiji i Makedoniji 1903–1912.* Beograd, N.P., 1998.

Simmel, Georg. *Soziologie: Untersuchungen über die Formen der Vergesellschaftung.* Berlin: Dunckler & Humblot, 2013.

Sindbaek, Tea und Maximilian Hartmuth. *Images of Imperial Legacy. Modern Dis–courses on the Social and Cultural Impact of Ottoman and Habsburg Rule in Southeast Europe*. Berlin: LIT, 2011.

Singleton, Fred. *A short history of the Yugoslav Peoples*. Cambridge: Cambridge University Press, 1985.

Šišić, Ferdo. *Jugoslovenska misao.* Beograd: Balkanski Institut, 1937.

Šistek, František. "Pan–Serb Golden Age and Montenegrin Heroic Age: Reconstructing History and Identity Narratives in Montenegro, 1905–1914." *New Imagined Communities*, edited by Libusa Vajdova and Robert Gafrik, 191–206. Bratislava: Kalligram, 2010.

Sivignon, Michel. "Le politique dans la géographie des Balkans: Reclus et ses successeurs, d'une Géographie universelle à l'autre." *Hérodote* 117/2 (2005): 153–182.

Skëndi, Stavro. "Mendimi Politik Dhe Veprimtarija Kryengritese Shqiptare 1881–1912." *Përpjekja* 09 (1996): 133–157.

Škarić, Miloš. *Četnici i dobrovoljci u ratovima za oslobodjenje i ujedinjenje.* Novi sad: Savez dobrovoljaca za Srem, Bačku i Baranju, 1925.

Skocpol, Theda. "Bringing the State Back In: Strategies of Analysis in Current Research." In *Bringing the State Back In,* edited by Peter B. Evans, 3–38. Cambridge: Cambridge University Press, 1985.

Slijepčević, Đoko. *The Macedonian Question: The Struggle for Southern Serbia.* Chicago: The American Institute for Balkan Affairs, 1958.

Slukan–Altić, Mirela. "Hrvatska kao zapadni Balkan – geografska stvarnost ili nametnuti identitet?" *Društvena Istraživanja Zagreb* 20 (2011): 401–413.

Slukan–Altić, Mirela. "German Contribution to the 19th Century Cartography of European Turkey – With Special Regard on the Map of Heinrich Kiepert." In *Joint Commission Seminar on Historical Maps, Atlases and Toponymy, International Cartographic Assotiation*, edited by Jana Moser, 79–89. Leipzig: Leibniz–Institut für Länderkunde, 2016.

Smith, Anthony. *The Ethnic Origins of Nations*. Oxford: Basil Blackwell, 1986.

Smith, Anthony. *Chosen Peoples: Sacred Sources of National Identity*. Oxford: Oxford University Press, 2004.

Smith, Steve and Patricia Owens. "Alternative Approaches to International Theory." In *The Globalization of World Politics: An Introduction to International Relations*, edited by John Baylis, Steve Smith, Patricia Owens, 174–191. Oxford: Oxford University Press, 2006.

Sohrabi, Nader. "Global Waves, Local Actors: What the Young Turks Knew about Other Revolutions and Why It Mattered." *Comparative Studies in Society and History* 44/1 (January, 2002): 45–79.

Soleimani, Kamal. "Modern Islamic Political Thought, "Islamism" and Nationalism," *Journal of Humanities and Cultural Studies* 2/1 (2017): 1–16.

Sonderegger, Ruth. *Hermann Keyserling: Eine Biographie*. Würzburg: Königshausen & Neumann, 2014.

Sotirović, Vladislav. "Who are Albanians?" *Serbian Studies Journal of the North American Society for Serbian Studies* 26/1–2 (2012): 45–76.

Sotirović, Vladislav. *Serbia, Montenegro and Albanian Question 1878–1912*. Saarbrücken: Lambert Academic Publishing, 2015.

Speich Chassé, Daniel and Gugerli, David. "Wissensgeschichte: Eine Standortbestimmung." *Traverse: Zeitschrift für Geschichte* 1 (2012): 85–100.

Speier, Hans. *Europe: A History of an Idea*. New York: Harper & Row, 1970.

Spencer, Edmund. *Travels in European Turkey, in 1850 through Bosnia, Servia, Bulgaria, Macedonia, Thrace, Albania, and Epirus – with a visit to Greece and the Ionian Isles: A Homeward Tour through Hungary and the Slavonian Provinces of Austria on the Lower Danube*. London: Colburn and Co., Publisher, 1851.

Spivak, Gayatri Chakravorty. *Can the Subaltern Speak? Postkolonialität und subalterne Artikulation*. Vienna/Berlin: Turia+Kant, Verlag, 2020.

Stachelbeck, Christian. "Lernen aus Imperialkriegen: Einführung." In *Imperialkriege von 1500 bis heute: Strukturen – Akteure – Lernprozesse*, edited by Tanja Bührer, Christian Stachelbeck, and Dierk Walter, 419–424. Paderborn/Munich/Zürich: Ferdinand Schöningh, 2011.

Stamatopoulos, Dimitris. *The Eastern Question or Balkan Nationalisms: Balkan History Reconsidered*. Vienna: Vienna University Press, 2018.

Stanishev, Hristo. *Dve statii po makedonskia vŭpros: I. Sirbia i makedontsite II. Makedonskiat vŭpros*. Sofia: Pechatnitsa P. Glushkov, 1927.

Stanojević, Gligor. *Prilozi za diplomatsku istoriju Crne Gore od Berlinskog kongresa do kraja XIX vijeka, Istorijski casopis*. Beograd, N.P., 1961.

Stanojević, Gligor. *Crna Gora pred stvaranje države 1773–1796*. Beograd: Istorijski Institut, 1962.

Stanojević, Ljubomir. *Stari srpski zapisi i natpisi*. Beograd: Srpska akademija nauka i umetnost, 1983.

Stanojević, Stanoje. *Srpsko–turski rat 1912*. Beograd: Svet knjige, 2021, first publication was in 1928.

Stanojević, Stanoje. *Narodna enciklopedija srpsko–hrvatsko–slovenačka*. Novi Sad: Izdavačka knjižarniza Zorana Stojanovića, 1929.

Stavrianos, S. Leften. *The Balkans since 1453*. New York: Rienhart, 1958.

Stavrianos, S. Leften. "The influence of the West on the Balkans." In *The Balkans in Transition,* edited by Charles and Barbara Jelavich, 184–226. Berkeley/Los Angeles: University of California Press, 1963.

Stedimlija, M. Savo. *The Foundation of Montenegrin Nationalism*. Zagreb, 1937.

Steedman, Carolyn. *Dust: The Archive and Cultural History*. New Brunswick, NJ: Rutgers University Press, 2001.

Stefoska, Irena. "Fragments from the Medieval History of Macedonia." In *Macedonia: Land, Region, Borderland,* edited by Jolanta Sujecka, 69–105. Warsaw: University of Warsaw, 2013.

Stepanov, Tsvetlin. *The Bulgars and the Steppe Empire in the Early Middle Ages: The Problem of the Origin of the Bulgars*. Leiden: Brill, 2010.

Stewart, Charles. *Colonizing the Greek Mind? The Reception of Western Psychotherapeutics in Greece*. Athens: DEREE–The American College of Greece, 2014.

Storey, David. *Territories: The Claiming of Space.* London: Routledge, 2012.

Strangford, Viscountess Emily Anne Beaufort Smythe. *The Eastern Shores of the Adriatic in 1863: With a Visit to Montenegro.* New York: Palala Press, 2015.

Sureyya Bey Avlonyalı. *Osmanlı Sonrası Arnavutluk (1912–1920).* Istanbul: Klasik Yayınları, 2018.

Subrahmanyam, Sanjay. "Connected Histories: Notes towards a Reconfiguration of Early Modern Eurasia." *Modern Asian Studies* 31/3 (1997): 735–762.

Sujecka, Jolanta. "The image of Macedonia and the Categories rod–narod–natsia in Literature from Macedonia in the 19th and first half of the 20th century." In *Macedonia: Land, Region, Borderland*, edited by Jolanta Sujecka, 137–228. Warsaw: University of Warsaw, 2013.

Sumiala, Johanna. "Circulation." *Keywords in Religion, Media, and Culture,* edited by David Morgan, 43–55. London: Routledge, 2008.

Sundhaussen, Holm. "Eliten, Bürgertum, politische Klasse? Anmerkungen zu den Oberschichten in den Balkanländern des 19. und 20. Jahrhunderts." In *Eliten in Südosteuropa: Rolle, Kontinuitäten, Brüche in Geschichte und Gegenwart*, edited by Wolfgang Höpken and Holm

Sundhaussen, 5–30. Munich: Südosteuropa–Gesellschaft, 1998.

Şensoy, Naci. "Osmanlı İmparatorluğunun sıkı yönetime müteallik mevzuatı üzerinde sentetik bir Deneme" *İÜHFM* 13/ 1 (1947): 95–114.

Tahsin Paşa. *Sultan Abdülhamid'in sırdaşı.* Istanbul: Yakın Plan Yayınları, 2000.

Taki, Viktor. "Orientalism on the Margins – The Ottoman Empire under Russian Eyes." *Slavica Publishers* 12/12 (2011): 321–352.

Taki, Viktor. *Tsar i Sultan – Osmanskaya imperia glazam i Rossian.* Moskva: Novoe literaturnoe obozrenie, 2017.

Talat Paşa. *Hatıralarım ve Müdafaam.* Istanbul: Kaynak Yayınları, 2006.

Tasić, Dmitar. "Repeating Phenomenon: Balkan Wars and Irregulars." In *Les guerres balkaniques (1912–1913): Conflits, enjeux, mémoires,* edited by Catherine Horel, 25–37. Bruxelles: Peter Lang, 2014.

Tasić, Dmitar. *Paramilitarism in the Balkans: Yugoslavia, Bulgaria and Albania 1917–1924.* Oxford: Oxford University Press, 2020.

Tasić, Dmitar. "The Institutionalization of Paramilitarism in Yugoslav Macedonia: The Case of the Organization against the Bulgarian Bandits, 1923–1933." *The Journal of Slavic Military Studies* 32/3 (2019): 388–413.

Tasić, Dmitar. *Rat posle rata: Vojska Kraljevine srba, hrvata i slovenaca na Kosovu i Metohiji i u Makedoniji 1918–1920.* Beograd: Službeni glasnik, 2012.

Tasić, Dmitar. "Vojni odgovor Kraljevine SHS na komitske, kačačke i druge gerilske akcije na prostoru južne i stare Srbije 1919–20. " In *Guerrilla in the Balkans: Freedom Fighters, Rebels or Bandits – Researching the Guerrilla and Paramilitary Forces in the Balkans*, edited by Momčilo Pavlović, Tetsuya Sahara and Predgrad J. Marković, 137–152. Tokyo/ Beograd University Meiji, Institute for Disarmament and Peace Studies, Tokyo/Institute of Contemporary History, Beograd/Faculty for Security Studies, Beograd, 2007.

Tatarchev, Hristo. *Spomeni, dokumenti, materiali.* Sofia: Nauka i iskustvo, 1904.

Temo, Ibrahim. *İttihat ve Terakki anılarım.* Istanbul: Alfa Yayınlarıcılık, 2013.

Terzić, Slavenko. "Konzulat kraljevine Srbije u Bitolju (1889–1897*).*" *Istorijski časopis* 57 (2008): 327–342.

Terzić, Slavenko. *Islam, Balkan i velike sile XIV–XX vek.* Beograd: Istorijski institut SANU, 1997.

Thiers, Henri. *La Serbie: son passé et son avenir.* Paris: Dramard–Baudry, 1862.

Thomas, Mohnike. *Imaginierte Geographien.* Würzburg: Ergon–Verlag, 2007.

Thompson, Ewa. *The Surrogate Hegemon in Polish Postcolonial Discourse.* Houston: Rice University, 2007.

Tilly, Charles. "War Making and State Making as Organized Crime." In *Bringing the State Back In,* edited by Peter Evans, 169–192. Cambridge: Cambridge University Press, 1985.

Tilly, Charles. *The Politics of Collective Violence.* Cambridge: Cambridge University Press, 2003.

Timofejev, Aleksej. *Istorija srpske Diplomatije dokumenta: Generalni konzulat Kraljevine Srbije u Solunu (1887–1902).* Beograd: Arhiv Srbije, 2016.

Timofejev, Aleksej. *Istorija srpske Diplomatije dokumenta: Generalni konzulat Kraljevine Srbije u Serezu (1897–1900).* Beograd: Arhiv Srbije, 2016.

Todorova, Maria. "Balkans: From Discovery to Invention." *Slavic Review* 53 Summer (1994): 453–482.

Todorova, Maria. *Imagining the Balkans.* New York: Oxford University Press, 1997.

Todorova, Maria. *Bones of Contention: The Living Archive of Vasil Levski and the Making of Bulgaria's National Hero.* Budapest/New York: Central European University Press, 2009.

Todorova, Maria. "The Ottoman Legacy in the Balkans." In *Imperial Legacy: The Ottoman Imprint on the Balkans and the Middle East*, edited by Carl Brow, 45–77. New York: Columbia University Press, 1996.

Todorova, Maria. "Introduction: Learning Memory, Remembering Identity." In *Balkan Identities: Nation and Memory*, edited by Maria Todorova, 1–24. London: Hurst & Company, 2004.

Todorova, Olga. "Drugiat hadzilŭk: kŭm istoriata na myusulmanskia hadz ot bŭlgarskite zemi prez XV–XVII vek." *Istorichesko bŭdeshte* 1–2 (2006): 220–277.

Todorovski, Gligor. "Srpskata četnička organizacija i nejzinata aktivnost vo Makedonija." *Glasnik na institutot za nacionalna Istorija* 1 (1968): 191–194.

Todorovski, Gligor. *Srbija i reformite vo Makedonija: sredinata na XIX vek do Mladoturskata revolucija 1908.* Skopje: Institut za nacionalna istorija, 1987.

Tokay, Gül. "The Macedonian Question and the Origins of the Young Turk Revolution, 1903–1908." PhD diss., University of London, 1994.

Tokay, Gül. "Macedonian Reforms and Muslim Opposition during the Hamidian Era: 1878–1908." *Islam and Christan Muslim Relations* 14/1 (2010): 51–65.

Tokay, Gül. "A Reassessment of the Macedonian Question, 1878–1908." In *War and Diplomacy, The Russo–Turkish War of 1877–1878 and the Treaty of Berlin,* edited by Hakan Yavuz with Peter Sluglett, 253–270. Salt Lake City: Utah University Press, 2011.

Toleva, Teodora. *Vlianieto na Avstro–Ungaria za saŭzdavaneto na albanskata natsia: 1896–1908.* Sofia: Siela Norma AD, 2012.

Toleva, Teodora. *Vanshnata politika na Dyula Andrashi i vaznikvaneto na Makedonskia vŭpros.* Sofia: Tsiela, 2013.

Tomić, Jovan. *Rat na Kosovu i Staroj Srbiji.* Novi Sad: N.P., 1913.

Tomov, Angel, and Georgi Bazhdarov. *Revolutsionnata borba v Makedonia.* Skopje : N.P., 1917.

Topulli, Bajo. *Topullarët e Gjirokastrës, Bajo e Çerçizi: Pararendësit dhe pasardhësit.* Tiranë: Albin, 2008.

Trajanovski, Aleksandar. *Ruski dokumenti za Makedonija i makedonskoto prašanje, 1859–1918.* Skopje: Državen arhiv na Republika Makedonija, 2004.

Trbić, Vasilije. *Memoari.* Beograd: Kultura, 1996.

Treadway, John D. *The Falcon & Eagle, Montenegro and Austria–Hungary, 1908–1918.* West Lafayette: Purdue University Press, 1983.

Trencsényi, Balázs, Ahmet Ersoy, Michal Kopeček, Maciej Górny and Vangelis Kechriotis eds. *Late Enlightenment: Emergence of modern national ides.* Budapest/New York: Central European University Press, 2006.

Tretiakov, N. Petr. *Istoriia Bolgarii.* Moscow: Akademiia nauk SSSR, 1954.

Trhulj, Sead. *Mustafa Golubić, čovjek konspiracije.* Sarajevo: Zalihica, 2007.

Trifunović, Bogdan. "Memory of Old Serbia and the Shaping of Serbian Identity," *Balcanica Posnaniensia: Acta et Studia* 24 (2015): 251–254.

Trnavci, Halit. "Predgovor." In *Kanon Leke Dukađinija*, edited by (posthumno djelo) Štjefen Konstantin Dečovi, i–xi. Zagreb: Stvarnost, 1986.

Troch, Pieter. *Nationalism and Yugoslavia: Education, Yugoslavism and the Balkans before World War II.* London/New York: I. B. Tauris, 2015.

Troebst, Stefan. "IMRO + 100 = FYROM? The politics of Macedonian historiography." In *The New Macedonian Question,* edited by James Pettifer, 60–78. London: Palgrave Macmillan, 2001.

Tsing, Anna Lowenhaupt. *Friction: An Ethnography of Global Connection.* Princeton, NJ: Princeton University Press, 2005.

Tsoutsoumpis, Spiros. "Land of the Kapedani: Brigandage, Paramilitarism and Nation–building in 20th Century Greece." *Balkan Studies* 51 (2016): 35–67.

Tsoutsoumpis, Spiros, "Morale, Ideology and the barbarization of warfare among Greek soldiers." In *The Wars of Yesterday The Balkan Wars and the Emergence of Modern Military Conflict, 1912–13*, edited by Sabine Rutar and Katrin Boeckh, 206–240. New York: Berghahn Books, 2018.

Tucović, Dimitrije. *Srbija i Albanci*. Ljubljana: Časopis za kritiko znanosti, 1989.

Tully, James. *Public Philosophy in a New Key, volume 2: Imperialism and Civic Freedom*. Cambridge: Cambridge University Press, 2008.

Tunalî, Hilmi. *Makedonya: Mazi–Hâl–Istikbâl*. Kahire, N.P., 1898.

Turesay, Özgür. "The Ottoman Empire seen through the lens of Postcolonial Studies: A Recent Historiographical Turn." *Revue d'histoire moderne et contemporaine* 60/2 (2013): 127–145.

Tziampiris, Aristotle. "Greek Historiography and Slav–Macedonian National Identity." *The Historical Review/La Revue Historique* 8 (2011):215–225.

Ubicini, Abdolonyme. *Letters on Turkey: an account of the religious, political, social and commercial conditions of the Ottoman Empire*. London: John Murray, 1856.

Uğur, Z. Peçe. "The Conscription of Greek Ottomans into the Sultan's Army, 1908–1912." *International Journal of Middle East Studies* 52/3 (2020): 433–448.

Ulbrich, Claudia. "Transkulturelle Perspektivenin Selbstzeugnisund Person." In *Selbstzeugnis und Person,* edited by Claudia Ulbrich, 419–426. Cologne: Böhlau, 2012.

Urquhart, David. *The Spirit of the East*. London: H. Colburn, 1838.

Usković, Vuk. "Identitet Crne Gore u prvoj polovini 18. vijeka." *O Identitetu*, edited by Dragan Vukčević, 465–519. Podgorica: CANU, 2015.

Üzer, Tahsin, Makedonya. *Eşkiyalık tarihi ve son Osmanlı yönetimi*. Ankara: Türk Tarih Kurumu, 1999.

Valaskivi, Katja and Johanna Sumiala. "Circulating Social Imaginaries: Teoretical and Methodological Refections." *European Journal of Cultural Studies* 17/3 (2014): 117–139.

Valdez, Damian. *German Philhellenism: The Pathos of the Historical Imagination from Winckelmann to Goethe*. London: Palgrave Macmillan, 2014.

Valkov, Martin. "The Internal Macedonian–Adrianople Revolutionary Organization and the Idea for Autonomy for Macedonia and Adrianople Thrace (1893–1912)." Master Thesis. Budapest: Central European University, 2010.

Van der Walt, Steven and Lucien Hirsch. *Anarchism and Syndicalism in the Colonial and Postcolonial World, 1870–1940.* Leiden: Brill, 2010.

Vangeli, Anastas. "Nation–building ancient Macedonian Style: The Origins and the Effects of the so–called Antiquization in Macedonia." *Nationalities Papers* 39/1 (2001): 13–32.

Vayrynen, Raimo. "Regionalism: Old and New." *International Studies Review* 5 (2003): 25–51.

Vemić, Mirčeta. *Etnička karta dela Stare Srbije: Prema putopisu Miloša S. Milojevića 1871–1877. god.* Beograd: Geografski institut Jovan Cvijić SANU, 2005.

Verli, Marenglen. *Shqipëria në dokumentet Austro–Hungareze (1912).* Tiranë: Qëndra e Studimeve Albanologjike Instituti i Historisë, 2012.

Veselinović, Milojko. *Srbi u Maćedoniji i u Južnoj Staroj Srbiji.* Beograd, N.P., 1888.

Veselinović, Milojko. *Granični dijalekt među Srbima i Bugarima.* Beograd, N.P., 1890.

Veselinović, Milojko. *Pogled kroz Kosovo.* Beograd, N.P., 1895.

Vlahov, Dimitri. *Memoari.* Skopje: Nova Makedonija, 1970.

Vlahov, Tushe. "Bŭlgaria i Mladoturskata Revolutsia." *Godishnik na Sofiskia Universitet Filosofski–Istoricheski Fakultet* 3 (1965): 3–77.

Vlahović, Vlajko. "Etnografija i folklor: Međuplemenski odnosi u Brdima (1)." *Zapisi* 22/2 (1939): 122–126.

Vlahović, Vlajko. "Etnografija i folklor: Međuplemenski odnosi u Brdima (2)." *Zapisi* 22/3 (1939): 184–189.

Vlora Bey, Ekrem. *Lebenserinnerungen.* Berlin/Munich: De Gruyter Oldenbourg, 1973.

Vogel, Jakob. "Von der Wissenschafts– zur Wissensgeschichte: Für eine Historisierung der 'Wissensgesellschaf'," *Geschichte und Gesellschaft* 30 (2004): 639–660.

Vojvodić, Mihailo and Milorad M. Radević. *Društvo Svetog Save: dokumenta 1886–1891.* Beograd: Arhiv Srbije, 1999.

Vojvodić, Mihailo. *Stojan Novaković i Vladimir Karić.* Beograd: Clio, 2003.

Vojvodić, Mihailo. "Stojan Novaković et la politique étrangère de la Serbie." *Balcanica* 45 (2014): 229–266.

Volarić, Klara. "Carigradski Glasnik: A Forgotten Istanbul–based Paper in the Service of Ottoman Serbs (1895–1909)." Master Thesis. Budapest: Central European University Press, 2014.

Von Hahn, Johann Georg. *Albanesische Studien*. Jena: F. Mauko, 1854.

Von Sax, Carl. *Geschichte des Machtverfalls der Türkei bis Ende des 19. Jahrhunderts und die Phasen der "orientalischen Frage" bis auf die Gegenwart*. Mainz /Vienna : N.P., 1913.

Vučetić, Biljana. "Srpska revolucionarna organizacija u Osmanskom carstvu na početku 20." *Istorijski časopis* 53 (2006): 359–374.

Vukosavljević, Sreten. *Istorija seljačkog društva: sociologija seljačkih radova*. Beograd: Srpska akademija nauka i umetnosti, 1953.

Vertovec, Steven, and Robin Cohen. *Conceiving Cosmopolitanism: Theory, Context, and Practice*. Oxford: Oxford University Press, 2002.

Vučetić, Biljana. "Prilog za biografiju Antonija Todorovića (1880–1971)." *Istorijski Institut* 55 (2007): 265–277.

Vučetić, Biljana. "Sećanja Antonija Todorovića." *Istorijski Časopis* 55 (2007): 256–305.

Vučetić, Biljana. "Bogdan Radenković i Milan Rakić." *Istorijski Časopis* 57 (2008): 413–426.

Vučetić, Biljana. "Izveštaji obaveštajca diplomati, pisma Bogdana Radenkovića Milanu Rakiću (1907–1912)." *Miscellanea* 29 (2008): 153–169.

Vučetić, Biljana. *Naša stvar u Otomanskom carstvu*. Beograd: Istorijski Institut, 2012.

Vučetić, Biljana. "Some considerations on the emergence of the Serbian Chetnik Movement in Macedonia during the last period of Ottoman rule." *Zapisi, Istorijski Institut Univerziteta Crne Gore* (2015): 113–128.

Vucinich, S. Wayne. "Some Aspects of The Ottoman Legacy." In *The Balkans in Transition*, edited by Charles and Barbara Jelavich, 81–114. Berkeley/Los Angeles: University of California Press, 1963.

Vujošević, Uroš. "Prilozi za biografiju Mustafe Golubića." *Istorija XX veka* 1/2 (1993): 217–230.

Waldmann, Peter. "Rache ohne Regeln: Wiederaufleben eines archaischen Gewaltmotivs in Albanien und in Boyacá (Kolumbien)." In *Politische und ethnische Gewalt in Südosteuropa und Lateinamerika*, edited by Wolfgang Höpken and Michael Riekenberg, 173–194. Vienna : Böhlau, 2001.

Wallerstein, Immanuel. *The Modern World–System I: Capitalist Agriculture and the Origins of the European World–Economy in the Sixteenth Century*. New York: Academic Press, 1974.

Walsh, Robert. *A Residence at Constantinople: During a Period Including the Greek and Turkish Revolution.* London: Westley & Davis, 1836.

Weber, Max. *Politics as a Vocation*, Published as *"Politik als Beruf,"* Munich: Gesammelte Politische Schriften, 1921.

Werner, Michael and Benedicte Zimmermann. "Vergleich, Transfer, Verflechtung: Der Ansatz der Histoire croisée und die Herausforderung des Transnationalen." *Geschichte und Gesellschaft* 28/4 (2002): 607–636.

Wiener, Leo. "America's share in the Regeneration of Bulgaria, 1840–1859." *Modern Language Notes* 13/2 (1898): 33–41.

Wilkinson, R. Henry. *Maps and Politics – A review of the Ethnographic Cartography of Macedonia.* Liverpool: Liverpool University Press, 1951.

Wolff, Larry. *Inventing Eastern Europe: The Map of Civilization in the Mind of the Enlightenment.* Redwood City: Stanford University Press, 1996.

Wright, K. John. "Terrae Incognitae: The Place of Imagination." *Geography Annals of the Association of American Geographers* 37 (1947): 1–15.

Yavorov, Peyo. *Gotse Delchev.* Sofia: Prosveta, 1992.

Yeşil, Fatih. *İhtilâller Çağında Osmanlı Ordusu: Osmanlı İmparatorluğu'nda Sosyoekonomik ve Sosyopolitik Değişim Üzerine Bir İnceleme (1793–1826).* Istanbul: Tarih Vakfı Yurt Yayınları, 2016.

Yıldız, Gültekin. *Neferin Adı Yok: Zorunlu Askerliğe Geçiş Sürecinde Osmanlı Devleti'nde Siyaset, Ordu ve Toplum, 1826–1839.* Istanbul: Çağaloğlu Kitabevi, 2009.

Yosmaoğlu, İpek. "Constructing National Identity in Ottoman Macedonia" In *Understanding Life in the Borderlands: Boundaries in Depth and in Motion,* edited by William Zartman, 160–188. Athens: The University of Georgia Press, 2009.

Yosmaoğlu, İpek. *Blood Ties: Religion, Violence and the Politics of Nationhood in Ottoman Macedonia, 1878–1908.* New York: Cornell University Press, 2014.

Yosmaoğlu, İpek. "Counting Bodies, Shaping Souls: The 1903 Census and National Identity in Ottoman Macedonia." *International Journal of Middle East Studies* 38/ 1 (2006): 55–77.

Young, J. C. Robert. *Postcolonialism: An Historical Introduction.* Oxford: Blackwell Publishing, 2001.

Young, Rovert. *While Mythologies: Writing History and the West.* London/New York: Routledge, 2004.

Yovanovich, Vladimir. *Les Serbes et la Mission de la Serbie dans l' Europe d' Orient.* Paris: A. Lacroix, Verboeckhoven et Cie Éditeurs, 1870.

Yovanovich, Vladimir. *The Emancipation and Unity of the Serbian Nation or the Regeneration of the Eastern Europe.* Geneva: H. Georg Corraterie, 1871.

Zavalani, Mikel. *Studime Historike.* Tiranë: Akademia e Shkencave e RPSSH, Instituti i Historisë, 1983.

Zeune, August. *Gea: Versuch einer wissenschaftlichen Erdbeschreibung, Blindenanstalt, Doct. der Weltweisheit, Mitglied der Jenaischen mineralogischen Gesellschaft. Nebst zwey Karten.* Berlin: Bey Wittich, 1808.

Zirojević, Olga. "Kosovo in the Collective Memory." In *The Road to War in Serbia: Trauma and Catharsis*, edited by Nebojša Popov, 189–211. Budapest: Central European University Press, 2000.

Zitara, Nicola. *L'unità d'Italia. Nascita di una colonia.* Milan: Jaca Book, 1971.

Zlatanović, Momčilo. "Četnički (komitski) pokret (1904–1912) (Vranje i Preševska kaza)." *Leskovački zbornik* 32 (1992): 82–97.

Zürcher, Erik–Jan. "Macedonians in Anatolia: The Importance of the Macedonian Roots of the Unionist for Their Policies in Anatolia after 1914." *Middle Eastern Studies* 50/6 (2014): 960–975.

Zürcher, Erik–Jan. "Teoride ve pratikte Osmanlı zorunlu askerlik sistemi (1844–1918)." In *Devletin Silâhlanması: Ortadoğu'da ve Orta Asya'da zorunlu askerlik (1775–1925)*, edited by Erik Jan Zürcher, 87–104. Istanbul: Istanbul Bilgi Üniversitesi Yayınları, 2003.

Zürcher, Erik–Jan. "Introduction: The Ottoman Jihad, the Geman Jihad and the Sacralization of War." In *Jihad and Islam in World War I*, edited by Erik–Jan Zürcher, 13–28. Leiden: Leiden University Press, 2016.

Zürcher, Erik–Jan. "The Young Turks – Children of the Borderlands?" *International Journal of Turkish Studies* 9 (2003): 275–286.

Zürcher, Erik–Jan. *The Young Turk Legacy and Nation Building: From the Ottoman Empire to Atatürk's Turkey.* London: Bloomsbury Publishing PLC, 2010.

Zundhausen, Holm. *Istorija Srbije od 19. do 21. veka.* Beograd: Clio, 2008.

Biography

Denis Š. Ljuljanović is a political scientist and historian specialised in southeastern Europe and the Ottoman Empire. During his studies at Marmara University (Turkey) and his working period at Justus–Liebig University (Germany), he wrote a PhD dissertation entitled "Imagining Macedonia in the Age of Empire: State Policies, Networks and Violence (1878–1912)." In 2016 he received a research fellowship in an exchange program at Alma Mater Studiorum – University of Bologna. Afterwards, he worked as a research and teaching Assistant in the department of Eastern European History, at the Justus–Liebig University in Giessen (Germany), where he was teaching following courses: Ottoman Rumelia from a Postcolonial Perspective; and Nationalism and Anarchism in the Ottoman Empire: South–East Europe in Focus.

Currently, his research explores social and cultural history in the Ottoman Empire, migrations, micropolitics and microhistory, transnational and entangled history. In his work, he applies a bottom–up perspective of ordinary life, in order to bring the greater visibility and understanding of the actors who have been overlooked and neglected in the past. Since 2021 Denis lives, works and writes in Berlin.

Studien zur Geschichte, Kultur und Gesellschaft Südosteuropas
hrsg. von Prof. Dr. Wolfgang Höpken (Universität Leipzig)

Cosmin Budeancă; Dalia Báthory (eds.)
Histories (Un)Spoken
Strategies of Survival and Social-Professional Integration in Political Prisoners'
Families in Communist Central and Eastern Europe in the '50s and '60s
Bd. 17, 2018, 394 S., 49,90 €, br., ISBN 978-3-643-90983-1

Jakob Konstantin Lanman Niese
Ungar, Jude, Amerikaner – Marcus Braun (1865-1921)
Eine Biographie aus der Epoche transatlantischer Migration
Bd. 16, 2018, 170 S., 29,90 €, br., ISBN 978-3-643-13723-4

Ulrike Schult
Zwischen Stechuhr und Selbstverwaltung
Eine Mikrogeschichte sozialer Konflikte in der jugoslawischen Fahrzeugindustrie
1965 – 1985
Bd. 15, 2017, 358 S., 59,90 €, br., ISBN 978-3-643-13690-9

Robert Kunkel
Visualisierung von Macht und Identität
Installation und Transformation von Erinnerungskulturen im jugoslawischen und
postjugoslawischen Kroatien am Beispiel der Stadt Osijek
Bd. 14, 2015, 152 S., 29,90 €, br., ISBN 978-3-643-12888-1

Stefanie Friedrich
Politische Partizipation und Repräsentation von Frauen in Serbien
Bd. 13, 2014, 392 S., 49,90 €, br., ISBN 978-3-643-12365-7

Carl Bethke
(K)eine gemeinsame Sprache?
Aspekte deutsch-jüdischer Beziehungsgeschichte in Slawonien, 1900 – 1945
Bd. 12, 2013, 464 S., 49,90 €, br., ISBN 978-3-643-11754-0

Sanela Hodžić; Christian Schölzel
Zwangsarbeit und der Unabhängige Staat Kroatien 1941 – 1945
Bd. 11, 2013, 232 S., 24,90 €, br., ISBN 978-3-643-11428-0

Tea Sindbaek; Maximilian Hartmuth (Eds.)
Images of Imperial Legacy
Modern discourses on the social and cultural impact of Ottoman and Habsburg
rule in Southeast Europe
vol. 10, 2011, 136 pp., 29,90 €, pb., ISBN 978-3-643-10850-0

Stephan Olaf Schüller
Für Glaube, Führer, Volk, Vater- oder Mutterland?
Die Kämpfe um die deutsche Jugend im rumänischen Banat (1918 – 1944)
Bd. 9, 2009, 560 S., 69,90 €, br., ISBN 978-3-8258-1910-1

LIT Verlag Berlin – Münster – Wien – Zürich – London
Auslieferung Deutschland / Österreich / Schweiz: siehe Impressumsseite

Studies on South East Europe
founded by Univ.-Prof. Dr. Karl Kaser (Graz) (†)

Anjeza Llubani; Gjergj Thomai; Karl Kaser; Anna Bruna Menghini;
Renato Rizzi; Spartak Bagllamaja
Kinematë dhe Teatrot. Cinemas and Theaters
Projekte Arkitektonike në Shqipërinë Komuniste (1945 – 1990). Architectural
Projects in Communist Albania (1945 – 1990)
Bd. 27, 2021, 496 S., 0,00 €, PDF, ISBN-CH 978-3-643-96205-8

Nikol Dziub; Greta Komur-Thilloy (Éd.)
Penser le multiculturalisme dans les marges de l'Europe
Bd. 26, 2020, 136 S., 34,90 €, br., ISBN-CH 978-3-643-91293-0

Siegfried Gruber; Dominik Gutmeyr; Sabine Jesner; Elife Krasniqi;
Robert Pichler; Christian Promitzer (Eds.)
From the Highlands to Hollywood
Multidisciplinary Perspectives on Southeastern Europe. Festschrift for Karl Kaser
and SEEHA
vol. 25, 2020, 448 pp., 44,90 €, pb., ISBN-CH 978-3-643-91194-0

Andra-Octavia Cioltan-Drăghiciu
„Gut gekämmt ist halb gestutzt"
Jugendliche im sozialistischen Rumänien
Bd. 24, 2019, 228 S., 34,90 €, br., ISBN 978-3-643-50907-9

Nikol Dziub
« Son arme était la harpe »
Pouvoirs de la femme et du barde chez Nizami et dans *Le Livre de Dede Korkut*
Bd. 23, 2018, 264 S., 39,90 €, br., ISBN-CH 978-3-643-91053-0

Dominik Gutmeyr; Karl Kaser (eds.)
Europe and the Black Sea Region
A History of Early Knowledge Exchange (1750 – 1850)
vol. 22, 2018, 416 pp., 34,90 €, pb., ISBN-CH 978-3-643-80286-6

Lena Mirošević; Gregory Zaro; Mario Katić; Danijela Birt (eds.)
Landscape in Southeastern Europe
vol. 21, 2018, 176 pp., 29,90 €, br., ISBN-CH 3-643-80283-5

Enriketa Pandelejmoni
Shkodra
Family and Urban Life (1918 – 1939)
vol. 20, 2019, 298 pp., 34,90 €, br., ISBN-CH 978-3-643-91017-2

Dominik Gutmeyr
Borderlands Orientalism or How the Savage Lost his Nobility
The Russian Perception of the Caucasus between 1817 and 1878
Bd. 19, 2017, 316 S., 34,90 €, pb., ISBN 3-643-50788-4

LIT Verlag Berlin – Münster – Wien – Zürich – London
Auslieferung Deutschland / Österreich / Schweiz: siehe Impressumsseite